The Society of the Screen

The Society of the Screen
Vilém Flusser's Radical Prescience

Martha Schwendener

THE MIT PRESS
Cambridge, Massachusetts . London, England

For Edith

Technocracy is imaginable, technoimagination is not.
Vilém Flusser, "Mutations in Human Relations" (1978)

Home Page

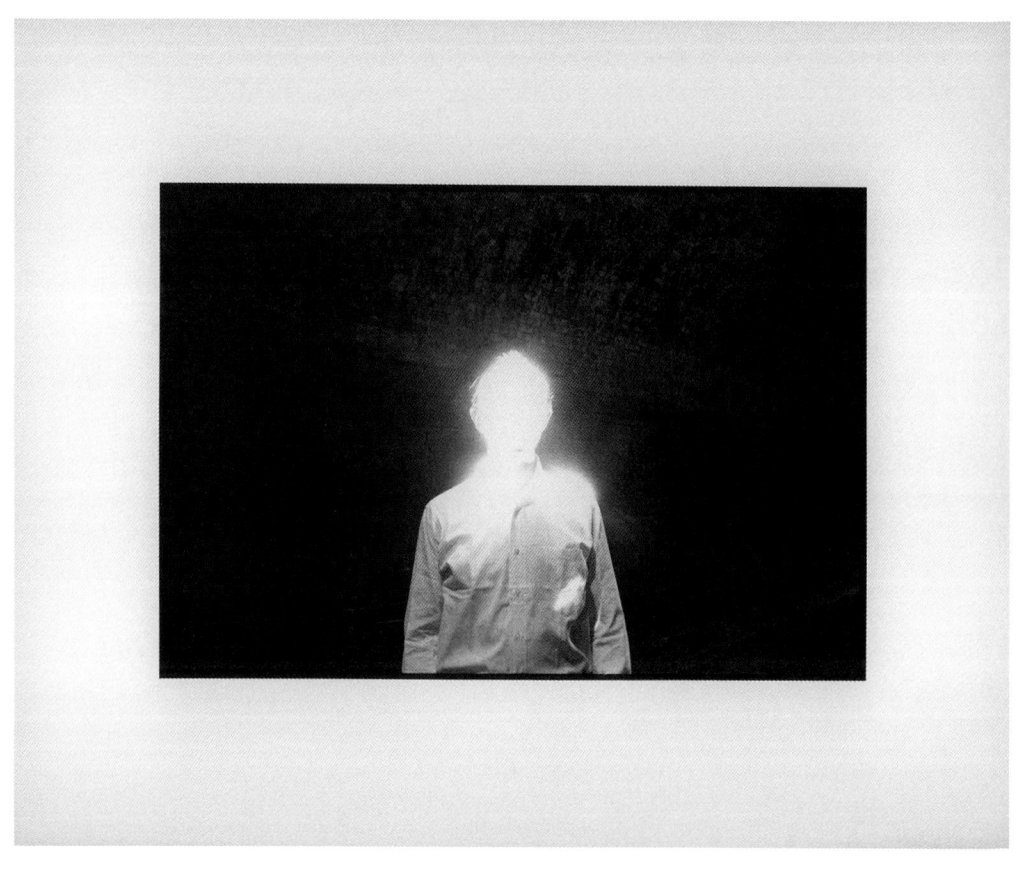

Figure 0.1
Duane Michals, *The Illuminated Man*, 1968. Silver gelatin print. © Duane Michals. Courtesy of DC Moore Gallery, New York. This photograph illustrated Flusser's "Curie's Children" column in *Artforum*, October 1987, 12.

This is how Vilém Flusser opened *Into the Universe of Technical Images* (1985), the second book in his technical image trilogy. Not with a gentle greeting or a salutary "*Hello!* I'm back with more thoughts on images generated by technological apparatuses, like photographs, television, fractals, or satellite images." Instead, he began with a warning: We are on the cusp of a radically different society. We are surrounded by bewitching images and screens. These could lead us toward a centrally programmed, totalitarian society, or another, better one characterized by open dialogue.[1] Flusser's "Warning" didn't offer any solutions, but it identified some of the challenges that lay ahead.

We are accustomed to warnings, though. The myth of Prometheus, Mary Shelley's *Frankenstein* (1818), and the *Jurassic Park* novel and films all serve as warnings of what could happen when humans tamper with nature. In the 1990s, the author Octavia Butler wrote about climate change, wildfires erupting in Los Angeles, and a politician running under the platform "Make America Great Again."[2] Her speculative visions have become realities. And information technology, with its global reach and increasing automation, presents a new cause for concern. Creators of the internet, social media, and artificial intelligence were given virtually free rein to develop their designs and unleash them on the planet—just as, in the nineteenth century, photography appeared and the few individuals who could afford this technology were given unlimited license to create images.

Now, developers of technology themselves are warning us. "I Worked on Google's AI. My Fears Are Coming True," read one headline.[3] Another, in the *New York Times*, pushed the panic button even harder: "A.I. Poses 'Risk of Extinction,' Industry Leaders Warn," with the subheading, "Leaders from OpenAI, Google DeepMind, Anthropic and other A.I. labs warn that future systems could be as deadly as pandemics and nuclear weapons."[4] Meanwhile, reports emerge on "The Internet's Final Frontier: Remote Amazon Tribes" and how satellite internet used by paramilitary forces, rebels, and emergency responders has turned indigenous life into yet another society of the screen.[5]

Technology is imprinted with the philosophy of its inventors. Now, however, these ideas are being stamped on the whole world.

And the regions where our platforms, interfaces, and devices were invented—that is, primarily Europe and the United States—were slow to focus on technology as a philosophical, social, and ethical issue (much less on its environmental impacts). A handful of thinkers, including Friedrich Nietzsche, Martin Heidegger, Bernard Stiegler, Donna Haraway, and Yuk Hui, have focused on what the Greeks called *techné*—art, skill, or craft—and its consequences. But how do we go forward now without crashing into the abyss created or exacerbated by technology?

Enter Vilém Flusser (1920–1991), as idiosyncratic and brilliant as any Silicon Valley technologist, hacker, or gonzo programmer. Born in Prague, he fled his native city for Brazil after the Nazi invasion in 1939. His entire family perished in the Holocaust, and he never earned a college degree. Nonetheless, he became one of the most prescient philosophers of emerging media and technology, including the screens on which we perform everything from earning a living to finding a mate. Partly because of his nontraditional background, Flusser thrived in the art world, which was becoming a global platform in the twentieth century. He collaborated with artists and served on advisory committees for the São Paulo Biennial. A military dictatorship arrived in Brazil (1964–1985), and Flusser migrated back to Europe in the early 1970s. In the 1980s, he found fame in an unexpected place: photography theory, which was thriving in the era of early digitization. Flusser expanded "photography" to the concept of "technical images," which meant still *and* moving images, art and popular culture, and new things like holograms, fractals, and satellite imagery. (And yes, video games—although Flusser died before the meteoric rise of that medium.)

Flusser argued that linear thinking—society based on writing, which produced linear "history," with one thing caused by another thing—was being disrupted. Surfaces and screens and a new form of consciousness were taking over: "We experience, know, and evaluate the world we live in through messages received through surface codes instead of written or printed texts," he wrote.[6] Television, computers, and now smartphones provide not just information but human connection (and, of course, *mis*information). Flusser wasn't the first to declare this. In the 1950s, Norbert Wiener, one of the founders of cybernetics—which laid the foundations for today's artificial intelligence (AI)—delivered a series of lectures on nonlinear physics, mathematics, electrical engineering, and physiology. He argued that communication wasn't linear—that

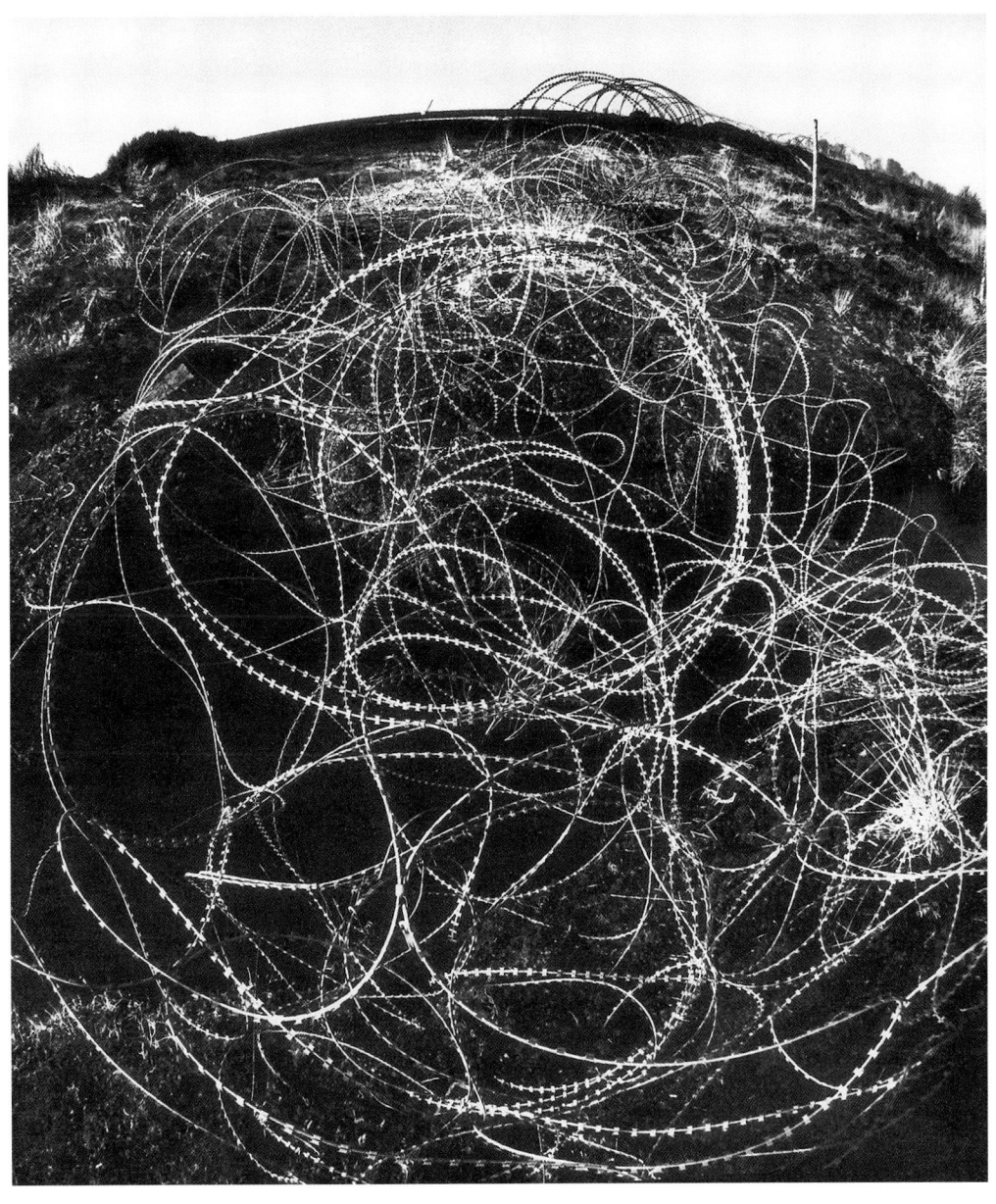

Figure 0.2
Robert Häusser, *Bedrohter Ort* (Threatened place), 1984. © Robert Häusser—Robert-Häusser-Archiv/Curt-Engelhorn-Stiftung, Mannheim. From Robert Häusser, *Photographische Bilder. Werkübersicht der Jahre 1941–1987* (Stuttgart: Württembergischer Kunstverein/Quensen, 1988) in the Vilém Flusser Archive, with an inscription by the artist to Flusser.

is, flowing seamlessly from sender to receiver—but functioned as a series of feedback loops.[7] Around the same time as Flusser, Gilles Deleuze and Félix Guattari, inspired by Franz Kafka's disjointed narrative structures, developed a theory of the *rhizome*: a nonlinear, nonhierarchical system in which social and political connections thrived. Flusser was interested in how nonlinear thinking was changing as our "codes" shifted from alphanumeric to digital ones. (For instance, I have written what appears to be a straightforward linear text, but I did it on a computer programmed with binary code.) "The basic structure of our thinking is about to experience a mutation," he wrote in the early 1980s. "What is involved here is not the classical problem of alienation, but an existential revolution for which we do not have any historical precedents."[8]

This is where technoimagination came in. (Sometimes translated as "technical imagination.") It would be a new way of deciphering technical images and interacting with the world, rather than being steamrolled by technology and unwittingly programmed by it. "Technoimagination is an inversion of the historical relation between symbol and meaning," Flusser wrote in 1978.[9] Photographs aren't innocent documents. (And neither are the internet or social media platforms.) A tourist photographing his wife in front of a cathedral, Flusser argued, is not merely making an image; he occupies a viewpoint shaped by science and politics. One solution, throughout history, has been to prohibit images because they lead to idolatry, madness, or what Flusser called "magical behavior."[10] (Now, we discuss banning social media platforms.) Another approach, however, is to acknowledge the difference between old images and new ones and the fact that the rules of linear writing don't work in the era of technical images. Similarly, if you design a building or an airplane on a computer, these images function very differently from cave paintings—and their models of thinking are vastly different. Humans will continue to "paint, write, and analyze," Flusser surmised. "Moreover, these gestures will continue to coexist in unpredictable tension and cross-fertilization. But what concerns us right now in an existential sense is the burdensome, but necessary, leap out of the linear into the zero-dimensional (into the realm of 'quanta') and into synthesizing (into computation). We have been challenged to leap into the new imagination."[11] That is what we will explore in this book, as well as how visual art, design, and new forms of writing—like Concrete poetry—were fundamental to Flusser's concept of a new imagination.

Flusser was adopted by the robust German media-theory scene in the 1980s, which included thinkers like his friend Friedrich Kittler, but his writings were largely ignored in the United States. Moreover, Flusser's involvement with the art world was often viewed by those familiar with his writing as a peripheral aspect of his philosophy rather than a central one. This book takes that involvement very seriously. Championing images and exploring how they were created and what they were *saying*, Flusser believed in art as a form of philosophy and argued that art, science, and other fields are interconnected. Art was, for him, an incubator of ideas—not merely decoration or a financial asset. For him, as for me and other people deeply engaged with visual culture, art provided a window into thinking about technology, which has been thrust on us as a universal, often standardized language—a colonial one (Flusser himself was a colonial European subject, since Germany had invaded his city and murdered all his close relatives).

Technology, as we know it, generally doesn't take individual cultures or specific localities into consideration, and direly needs to be examined as seriously as philosophy has examined ethics, morality, being, aesthetics, and other subjects in the past. When Martin Heidegger, a complicated figure who was nonetheless hugely influential for Flusser, argued that cybernetics signaled the end of Western metaphysics—we can no longer say, particularly in the age of AI, that humans and technology are separate entities—Flusser took note. The concept of *being* was changing. And although he started his career in philosophy examining language and how it shaped human reality, he ended it by focusing on art, technology, and design.

As you'll notice immediately, this book explores philosophy through images. Technology is not neutral, and neither are photographs or artworks. Art can hold both fiction and truth, and it is a *form* of thought, not merely a reflection of it. Additionally, in an age when technical images dominate, they are more available, readable, and relatable than most oral or written philosophy. French positivism literally informed the design of the Brazilian flag ("order and progress"), but in today's swift-moving world, memes and the messages they carry are more expedient and meaningful to most people. Similarly, our institutions are in flux and art exhibitions have become highly visible sites of protest, as Flusser experienced in his seminal work with biennials. However, like many of us, Flusser was both embraced by and excluded from institutions.

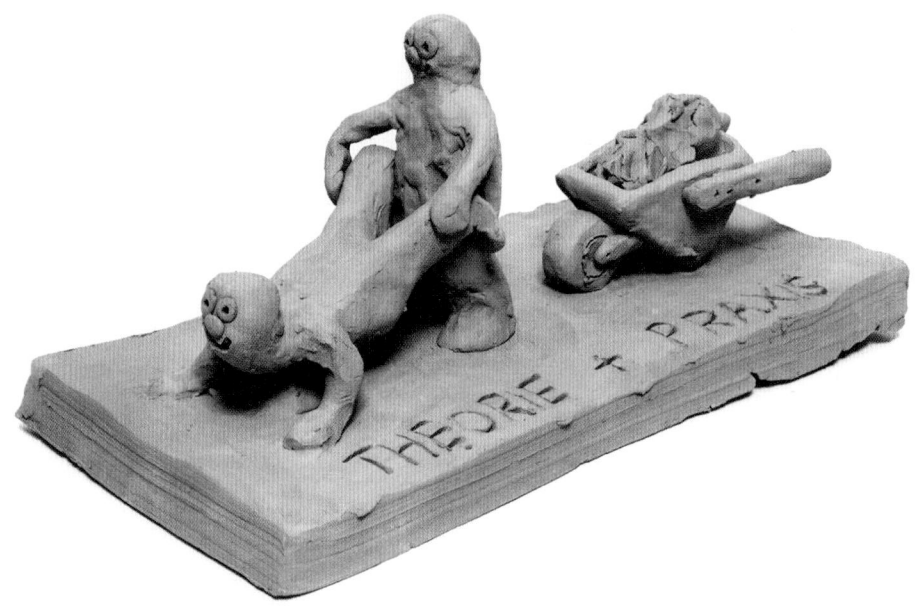

Figure 0.3
Peter Fischli and David Weiss, *Popular Opposites—Theory and Practice*, from *Suddenly This Overview*, 1980–2012. Series of approximately 600 sculptures; individual works undated, unfired clay, various dimensions, between 6 × 7 × 5 cm and 82 × 83 × 5 cm. © Peter Fischli and David Weiss, Courtesy Matthew Marks Gallery. Photo © 1981 Iwan Schumacher, Galerie Stähli. Flusser wrote about Fischli and Weiss in *European Photography* magazine in 1991, and in *Plötzlich diese Übersicht* (Suddenly This Overview, Galerie & Edition Stähl, 1981–1982) in the library of the Vilém Flusser Archive, Berlin.

This sharpened his sense of the apparatus of institutions and of being a functionary within one, but it also afforded him a sense of critical independence and clarity. And because of his unorthodox, autodidact education, he wrote in a manner that everyone could read, and he published in newspapers and other popular media, believing that philosophy could be discussed in the public sphere and that it was imperative to do so.

Can we get philosophy through a screen? Flusser felt it was being delivered through technical images, whether you knew it or not. This book's title reflects Guy Debord's idea of the "society of the spectacle," where post-World War II mass media and consumer society were turning people into passive observers of their own lives, as well as media theorist Lev Manovich's assertion—riffing on Debord and Jean Baudrillard's idea that life had become more like a "simulation" of reality than an authentic experience—that "we may debate whether our society is a society of the spectacle or simulation, but undoubtedly, it is a society of the screen."[12] Look around a subway car, an airport, or even a mountain in the so-called wilderness, and screens in the form of smartphones, laptops, and other devices are present. Flusser has been compared not just to Debord and Baudrillard but to other thinkers who considered technology, such as Marshall McLuhan, Hans Magnus Enzensberger, Roland Barthes, and Gilles Deleuze. However, this leaves out his three decades in Brazil, which impacted his philosophy as much as reading Heidegger and Wittgenstein did. This book explores Brazilian art histories like the rich connection between Concrete poetry and painting and the information aesthetics of Max Bense, in which Brazil played a large role, but also Flusser's interest in biophilosophers like Jakob von Uexküll, whose idea of the *Umwelt*, or surrounding worlds of animals, influenced Flusser's idea of the "universe of technical images," as well as his explorations of the natural world. Now these realms are merging. We are as likely to experience "nature" on a screen—or to insert ourselves into the forest via photography or let AI do it for us—as we are to walk in the woods. Flusser was fascinated with the impact of these gestures.

Screen 1 of this book starts with Flusser's childhood in cosmopolitan Prague, a design and architecture center that produced figures like Karel Čapek, the science fiction author who introduced the term "robot" with his 1920 play *R.U.R. (Rossum's Universal Robots)*. Franz Kafka informed Flusser's thinking about language and

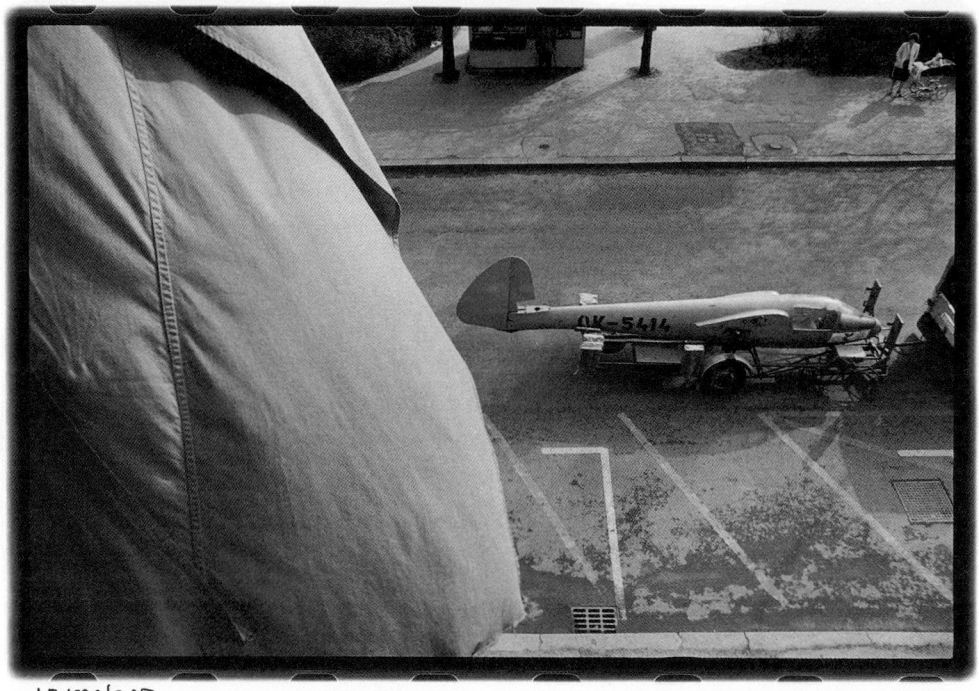

1.5.1986 | 9.05

Figure 0.4
Jiří Hanke, *Views from the Window of My Flat, 1.5.1986, 9:00*, 1986. Silver print. Courtesy of the artist. A bank clerk in Soviet-occupied Kladno, Czechoslovakia, Hanke took photographs of the street outside his window, which Flusser wrote about in *European Photography* 50 (Spring 1992): 42–43.

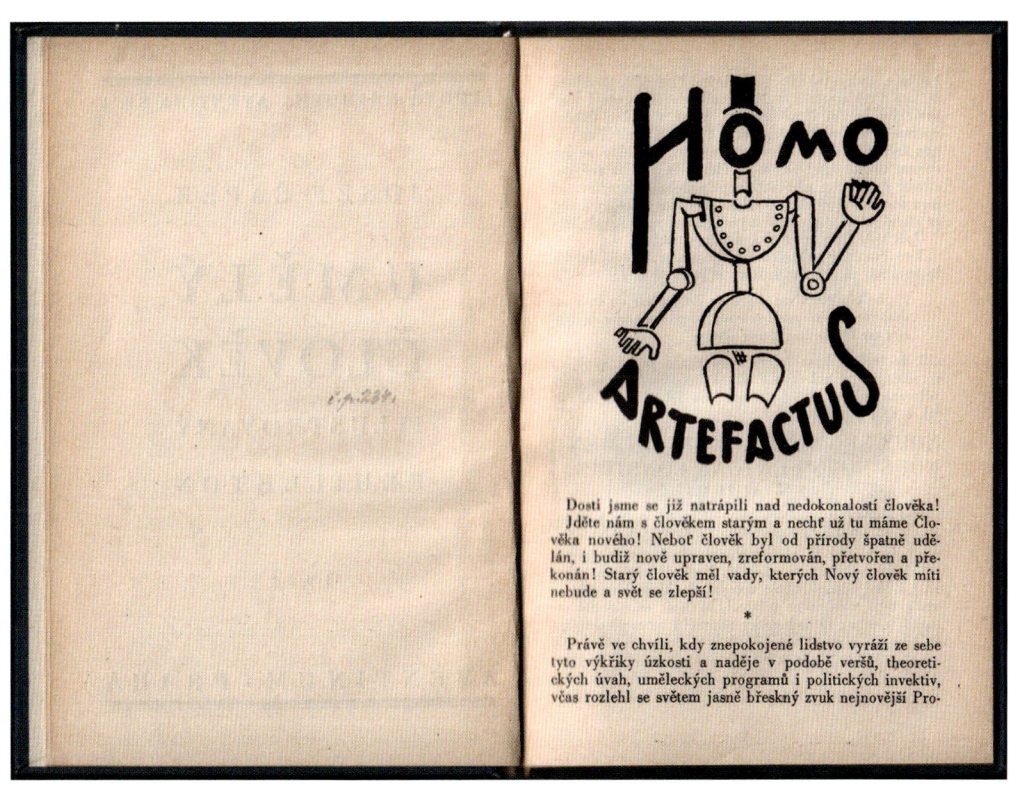

Dosti jsme se již natrápili nad nedokonalostí člověka! Jděte nám s člověkem starým a nechť už tu máme Člověka nového! Neboť člověk byl od přírody špatně udělán, i budiž nově upraven, zreformován, přetvořen a překonán! Starý člověk měl vady, kterých Nový člověk míti nebude a svět se zlepší!

*

Právě ve chvíli, kdy znepokojené lidstvo vyráží ze sebe tyto výkřiky úzkosti a naděje v podobě veršů, theoretických úvah, uměleckých programů i politických invektiv, včas rozlehl se světem jasně břeskný zvuk nejnovější Pro-

Figure 0.5
Flusser's copy of Prague author Karel Čapek's *Homo Artefactus* (1924) with Josef Čapek's illustrations. Vilém Flusser Archive, Berlin.

translation. Martin Buber, whom Flusser saw lecture in Prague as a teenager, served as a lifelong compass of ethical philosophy. Fleeing Prague, Flusser made his way with his future wife, Edith Barth, and her family to Brazil, where he was confronted with the legacy of Antropofagia, a literary movement that argued colonial influences could be devoured and combined with indigenous forms to create new aesthetic traditions. Abstract art and Concrete poetry were part of this landscape, but so was Max Bense, a German scientist and philosopher who viewed Brazil as a promising hotbed of intellectual and artistic development, following Europe's descent into barbarism and recurring wars. Flusser's friendships with artists Mira Schendel and Samson Flexor, who founded the first studio devoted to abstract painting, will also be explored.

Screen 2 begins with Flusser's role in the São Paulo Biennial, which facilitated his return to Europe. The Biennial had been founded in 1951 as part of a campaign to establish Brazil as a cultural and geopolitical force. Flusser wrote about the Biennial in Brazilian newspapers and later served as the "technical director" (a sort of proto-curator) for the 1973 Biennial, envisioning the position as an opportunity to translate theory into praxis. Flusser's 1972 presentation to the General Assembly of the Association of International Art Critics (AICA) in Paris was reported on by the French newspaper *Le Figaro*, which lauded his "revolutionary themes for the São Paulo Biennial in 1973" (September 19, 1972). However, in the late 1960s and early 1970s, there was an international boycott of the Biennial protesting Brazil's military dictatorship, organized in part by US-based artists such as Gordon Matta-Clark and Hans Haacke. Flusser returned to Paris in the 1970s to lecture at the experimental Institute of the Environment. He also participated in interdisciplinary roundtables there, including one on "Technologie et imaginaire" (Technology and the imaginary, 1973), which presaged the landmark exhibition *Les immatériaux* (The immaterials, 1985) at the Centre Pompidou in Paris, where art, computer hardware, and biotechnology sat alongside one another in the museum.

The 1970s also have been described as Flusser's "phenomenology" decade. In books and essays like *La force du quotidien* (The power of the everyday, 1973) and "Le monde codifié" (The codified world, 1974), he treated everyday objects from bottles to beds as "communications" devices—a perverse but rather canny response to media theorists who only studied television or the burgeoning

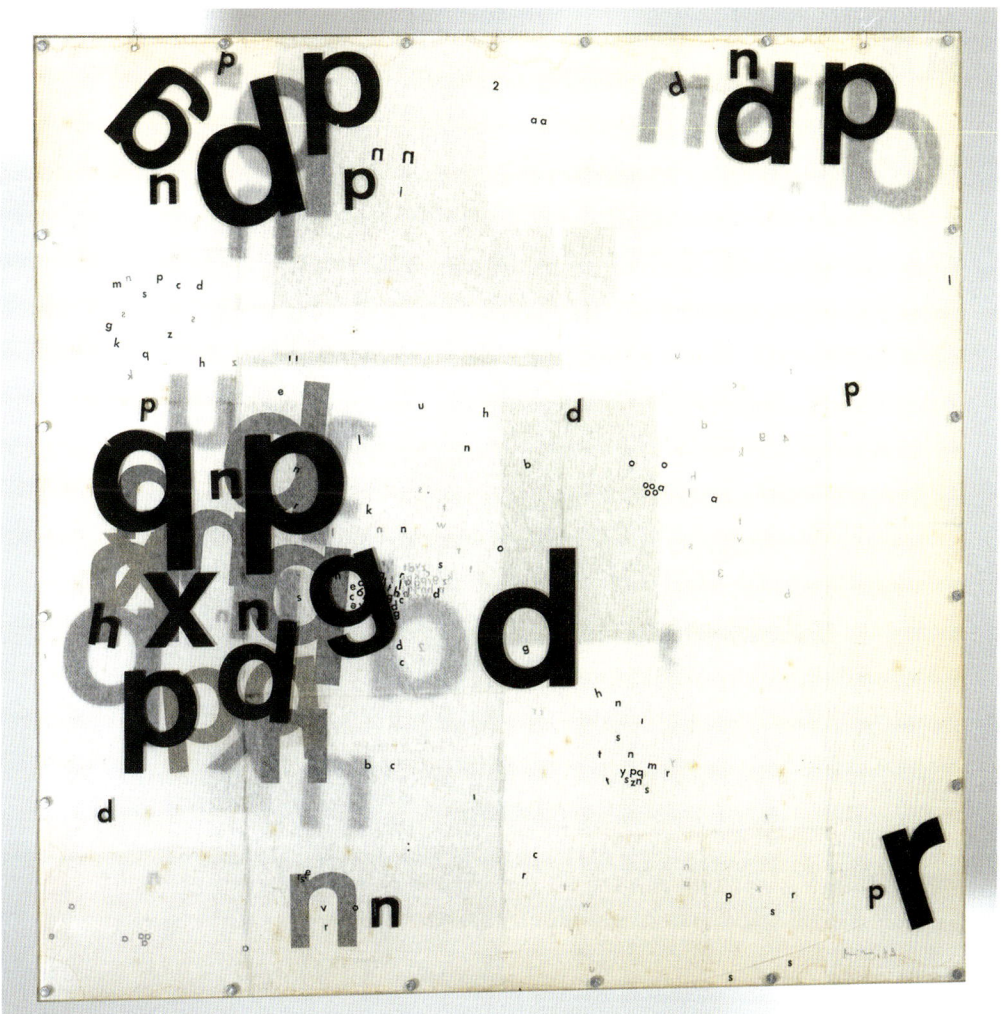

Figure 0.6
Mira Schendel, *Untitled*, from *Graphic Objects* (*Objetos gráficos*), 1973. Graphite, transfer type, and oil on paper between transparent acrylic sheets with transfer type, 55.9 × 55.9 × 1 cm (22 × 22 × ⅜ in.). Collection of Patricia Phelps de Cisneros. Photo: Gregg Stanger.

sphere of digital media.[13] How do we interface with the quotidian world? How do objects change our thought and gestures? Flusser collaborated with Fred Forest, an Algerian-born French video artist. Together they created *Gestures of the Professor* (1974), in which Flusser noted that being videotaped changed his thoughts and actions. (Fast-forward to everyone taking selfies or traveling around the globe to post a picture on Instagram.)

Flusser was also steeped in cybernetics, the study of feedback and control systems invented by computer scientists and mathematicians like Norbert Wiener, and he wrote about the artists Nicolas Schöffer and Wen-Ying Tsai, who created artworks based on cybernetics. (Tsai also remained a lifelong friend.) Flusser participated in the landmark conference "Open Circuits: The Future of Television" (1974) at the Museum of Modern Art in New York, which included an all-star roster of artists and thinkers: Joan Jonas, Vito Acconci, Shigeko Kubota, Stan VanDerBeek, Nam June Paik, Harald Szeemann, Richard Serra, Barbara London, Hollis Frampton, Hans Magnus Enzensberger, Gregory Battcock, John Baldessari, and Pierre Schaeffer. Impressed by artists working with video and television, he returned to Europe and continued to think about images, not in relation to philosophy but *as* philosophy.

Screen 3 focuses on Flusser's technical image theory. An amalgam of information aesthetics, technology activism informed by journals like *Radical Software*, and the vestiges of his language philosophy—except now words were being eclipsed by images—it remains his best-known body of work. Flusser began using the term "technical images" in the 1970s in manuscripts like "Mutations in Human Relations" (later published as *Communicology: Mutations in Human Relations?*) and the technical image trilogy from the 1980s—*Towards a Philosophy of Photography* (1983), *Into the Universe of Technical Images* (1985), and *Does Writing Have a Future?* (1987). These works highlight concepts like "apparatus," "program," "functionary," and even "magic," linking the latter to the bewitching capacity of technological images and devices. (Cue addictive smartphones and binge-watching streaming services.)

Flusser participated in numerous photography conferences such as "Reading the Image" in Paris in 1978 along with Jean Baudrillard, Gisèle Freund, and Yves Michaud and a 1981 symposium in Düsseldorf where he met Andreas Müller-Pohle of the magazine *European Photography*, who would publish Flusser's most important books in the 1980s. Flusser wrote for *European Photography*

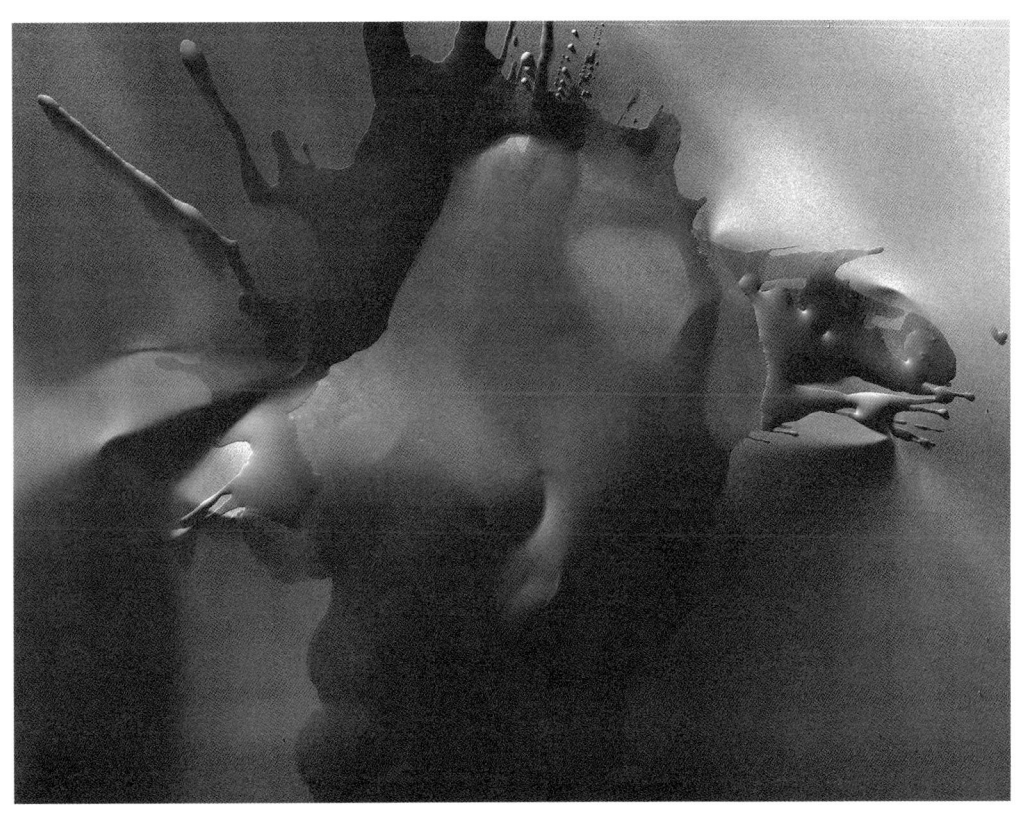

Figure 0.7
Gottfried Jäger, *Photogenic Landscape*, 1966. Gelatin silver print, 40 × 50 cm. © 2024 Artists
Rights Society (ARS), New York/VG Bild-Kunst, Bonn.

and *Camera Austria*, and corresponded and collaborated with artists like the generative photography pioneer Gottfried Jäger, the Spanish photographer Joan Fontcuberta, and Harun Farocki, the filmmaker and activist with whom he made the video *Schlagworte— Schlagbilder. Ein Gespräch mit Vilém Flusser* (Catch phrases—catch images: A conversation with Vilém Flusser, 1986). The 1989 Romanian revolution, which unfolded largely on state-controlled television, was a benchmark for both Flusser and Farocki and their understanding of technical images driving events, rather than merely documenting them.

One of the most exciting areas of Flusser's philosophy is his writing on nature and the environment, which will be discussed in Screen 4. Then, as now, the idea as well as the reality of nature was changing—and fast. Flusser's short text *Orthonature Paranature* (1978, based on a 1976 lecture) and collection of essays *Natural:Mind* (1979) attempt to collapse what he called the "nature-culture dialectic": how natural things are often cultural things, and many cultural products originated in the natural world (like animal paths that we adopted as roads). Predating the popular motif of treating animals as teachers more knowledgeable about survival and the phenomenological world than we are, Flusser's opus *Vampyroteuthis infernalis* (1987) gives a virtuosic reading of humanity through the mind of a giant squid. Flusser called it both a "fable" and "science fiction philosophy." Picking up that thread, his "Curie's Children" column for *Artforum* (1986–1992) tackled biological art and biotechnology and appeared alongside columns by Barbara Kruger, Max Kozloff, Carol Squiers, Greil Marcus, Glenn O'Brien, and other New York art world figures (although, by this time, Edith and Vilém Flusser were living in a sleepy village, Robion, in the south of France). Throughout this chapter, you can see parallels between Flusser and popular thinkers like N. Katherine Hayles, Rosi Braidotti, Jane Bennett, and Bruno Latour, among many others, in exploring what it means to be "posthuman" or to live in community with or proximity to other species.

Flusser's writings on design, color theory, and architecture are also fascinating and form the basis of Screen 5. One of the most significant ways people interface with technology is through design—the iPhone, for instance, famously copied a transistor radio created by mid-twentieth-century German designer Dieter Rams—and designers were among the first to embrace Flusser's writings. *The Shape of Things: A Philosophy of Design* (1999) is one of

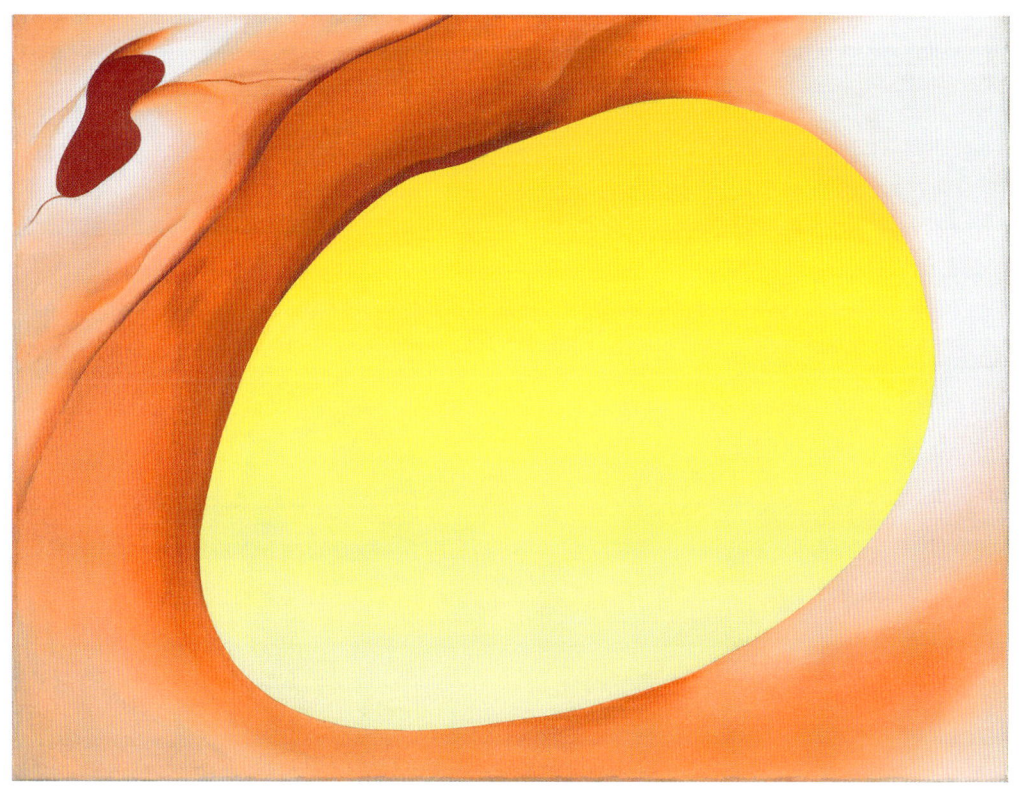

Figure 0.8
Georgia O'Keeffe, *Pelvis Series, Red with Yellow*, 1945. Oil on canvas, 36 × 48 in. Georgia O'Keeffe Museum. Extended Loan, Private Collection. © Georgia O'Keeffe Museum. [L.1997.3.4] © 2024 Georgia O'Keeffe Museum/Artists Rights Society (ARS), New York. This painting appeared alongside Flusser's "Curie's Children" column in *Artforum*, September 1987, 10.

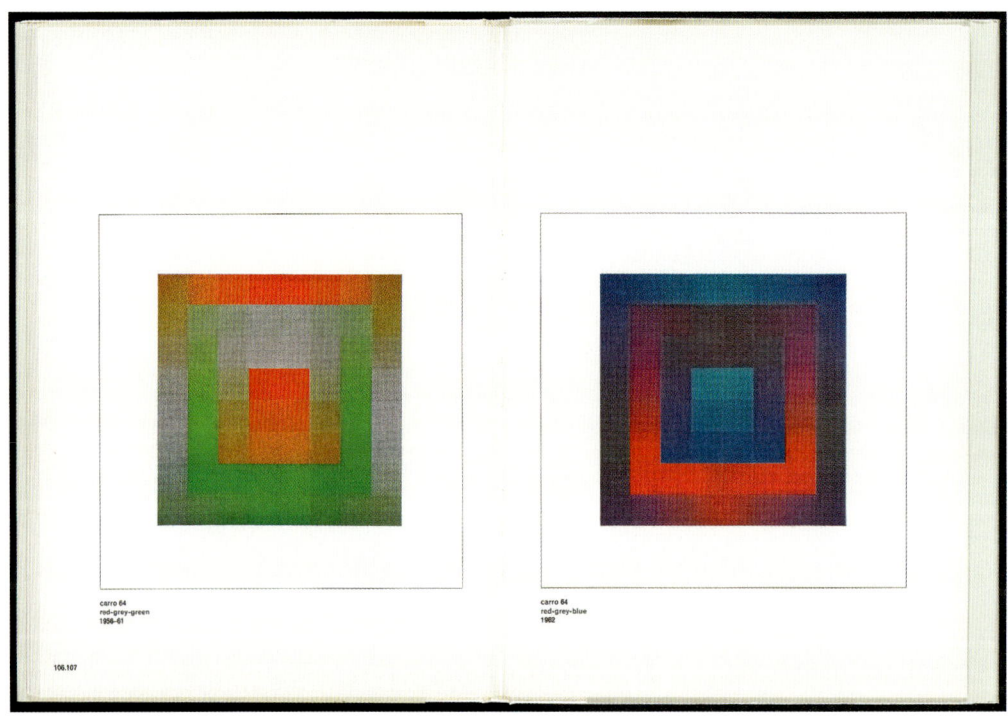

Figure 0.9
Karl Gerstner, *Carro 64* in *Designing Programs: Four Essays and an Introduction* (1964; Teufen, Switzerland: Niggli, 1968), 106 and 107. Swiss National Library, Prints and Drawings Department, Karl Gerstner Archive, and Muriel Gerstner.

Flusser's best-known books in English. Flusser also considered the ethics of design—what does making a "good" weapon mean? We often think of design as clever and innovative, but Flusser described design as "deceptive" (a lever, for instance, "tricks" gravity). Irony was Flusser's primary rhetorical weapon, and it shows up clearly in his design writings, as he simultaneously applauds and laments humans' technological ingenuity, and where it has landed us as a species.

In the late 1980s, Flusser also participated in a project devoted to color theory. A Casa da Cor (The house of color), a São Paulo–based project inspired in part by Goethe's color theories, imagined color as a new language, much like Esperanto, an international language created out of an amalgamation of preexisting languages. For Casa da Cor, Flusser collaborated with the Swiss artist and typographer Karl Gerstner, a towering figure in the world of graphic design, to write a new color theory informed by physics as well as art. Casa da Cor was also intended as a *house* of color, situated on a hill in São Paulo like the art deco *Cristo Redentor* statue in Rio de Janeiro. That never came to be, but the conferences and events surrounding it produced a body of writing that is fascinating in an age when color continues to be vital—not just in art, but in creating light-absorbent solar panels or reconsidering the bandwidth required by all those screens producing luminous liquid-crystal hues.

Flusser also wrote about architecture, imagining houses like Emmenthaler cheese (he was living in France, not far from Switzerland), perforated with cables and other communications devices. He considered what factories might look like in the future, describing them as "schools"—think of tech-company "campuses"—that would produce new humans and robots, both neurophysiological and biological ones. He considered landscape as a topology rather than a geography, with digital, oscillating wave troughs—not unlike the early electronic art of his friend, the science fiction author Herbert W. Franke—and which would replace traditional cartography. He also imagined metaphorical landscapes based on philosophical texts like Wittgenstein's *Tractatus*, similar to the Argentinian writer Jorge Luis Borges, whose short stories predicted the internet and "simulation," or a reality in which objects have copies but no original.

Finally, we end with Chamber Music. Again, not my invention but the title of the conclusion to *Into the Universe of Technical Images*.

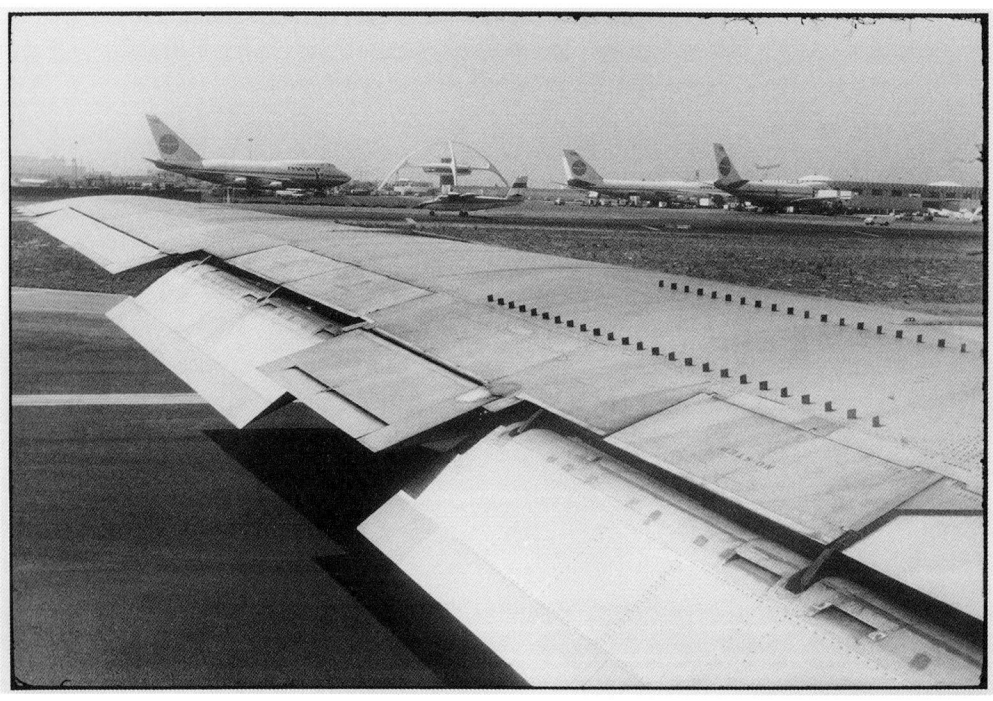

Figure 0.10
Garry Winogrand, *Los Angeles Airport*, no date. Silver gelatin print. From the collection of the Center for Creative Photography, The University of Arizona: Garry Winogrand Archive. © The Estate of Garry Winogrand, courtesy Fraenkel Gallery, San Francisco. This image appeared alongside Flusser's column in *Artforum*, April 1988, 15.

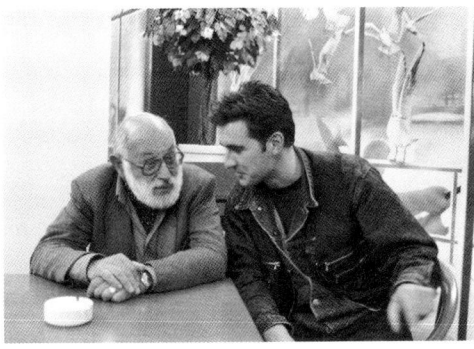

Figure 0.11
Vilém Flusser and Mischa
Kuball at 6:00 a.m. at the
Hotel Düsseldorf, 1991. ©
Archiv Mischa Kuball

Although he died before the internet reached critical mass and
the creation of social media, Flusser could see how images proliferating on a global scale would affect society and the planet, and
how artificial intelligences connected to humans, both electronically and physiologically, would create a new "universal spectacle." How could the new "telematic society" avoid catastrophe?
A great lover of music—particularly Mozart—Flusser attempted
to theorize here the future of technical images by suggesting a
poetic model: the small groups who gather to play chamber music.
Chamber music, which involves improvising, collaborating, and
harmonizing, was a cybernetic model for both dialogic and telematic communication. Chamber music—and jazz, which he saw as
a contemporary version of chamber music—might be the model
for a future society.

Technology and geopolitical events have been unfolding at
an accelerated rate in the decade and a half I have been writing
about Flusser. When I began my research, social media was still
seen as a somewhat positive force, instrumental in connecting
people and providing a new form of mass media entertainment.
Now, however, we have seen election interference, violence elicited
by social media campaigns, the rise of "bots" (short for "robots,"
the autonomous programs that mimic human behavior), and a
large-scale souring on the benefits of the platform. Flusser's own
optimism and pessimism vacillated (although his "optimism" was
often sharp Swiftian irony). The most important message in his
work is that it is imperative to think rigorously and profoundly
about technology—to test its limits and possibilities, as artists
have been doing for decades—not as an academic exercise but
for survival. Flusser eschewed "forecasting," but he nonetheless

predicted the end of linear history and the rise of post-history while being profoundly impacted by the events of his era. He predicted that art would become a forum for developing "technical imagination" and thinking about ethics and global power—and it has, in the form of everything from exhibition programming to museums as visible sites of protest. In our age of uncertainty, Flusser offers a vital model for engaging creatively with art, technology, politics, and the unknown. Waking early every morning to write, he was eager to dialogue with artists, students, scientists— anyone who wanted to discuss the catastrophes of our era and their possible solutions.

Screen 1   *Land of the Future*

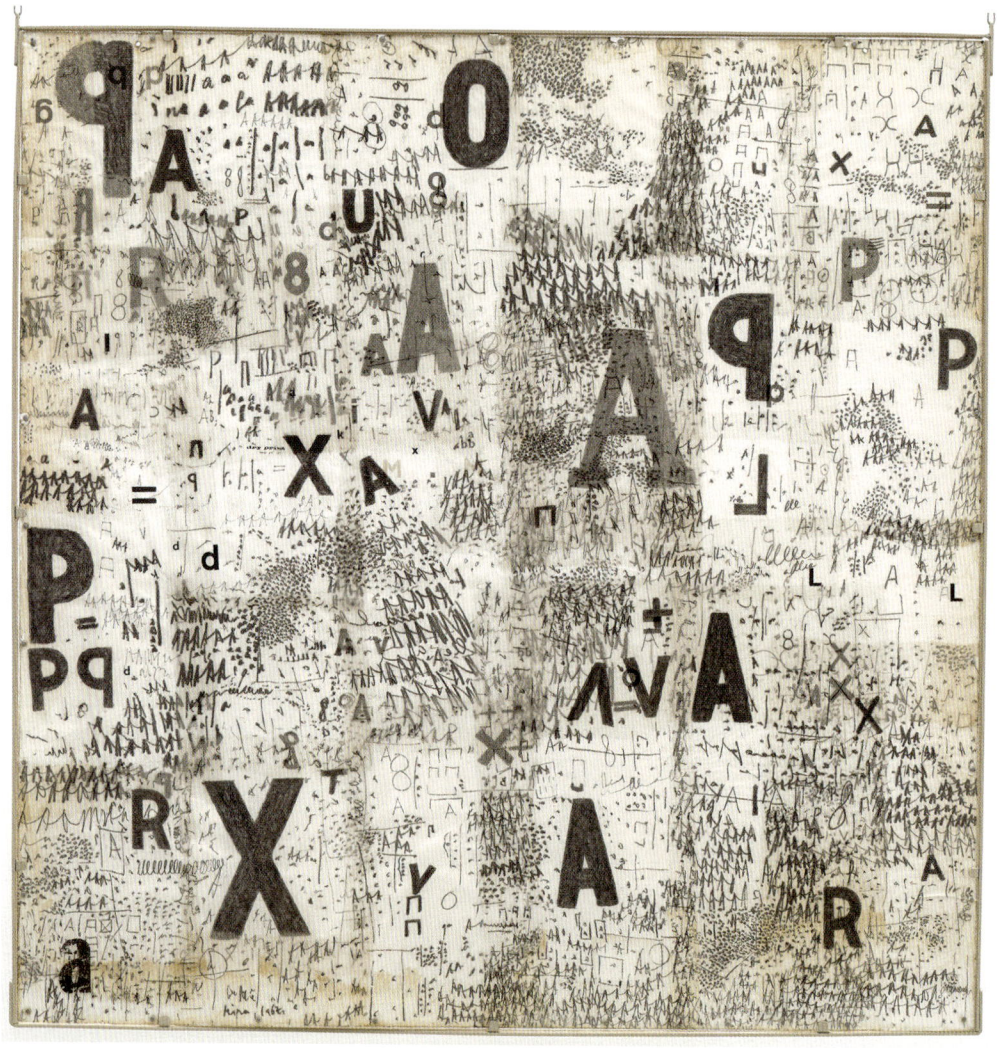

Figure 1.1
Mira Schendel, *Untitled*, from *Graphic Objects* (*Objetos gráficos*), 1967. Graphite, transfer type, and oil on paper between transparent acrylic sheets with transfer type, 39⁵⁄₁₆ × 39⁵⁄₁₆ × ⅜ in. (99.8 × 99.8 × 1 cm). Gift of Patricia Phelps de Cisneros through the Latin American and Caribbean Fund in honor of Luis Pérez-Oramas. © The Museum of Modern Art/Licensed by SCALA/Art Resource, NY.

Vilém Flusser was born in a magical city. It was the Prague of Franz Kafka and Josef and Karel Čapek, the brothers who invented the term "robot," and where, centuries before, the visionary painter Giuseppe Arcimboldo created wild portraits of people which, upon closer inspection, were composed entirely of fruits and vegetables. The city was known for its ties to alchemy and its mystical traditions. Bears lived in the moat of the local castle and, for good luck, people still rub the sculptures of saints lining the Charles Bridge crossing the Vltava River. It's no surprise, then, that the word "magic" would later appear in frequently in Flusser's writings on technology. Prague also functioned, for many, like a magical cultural melting pot. Flusser wrote, "The characteristic trait of Prague is that its essence overcomes all national, social, and religious differences: it does not matter if one is Czech, German, Jew, Christian, Protestant, Marxist, bourgeois, or proletarian. Before all else, one is Praguean. Prague is an existential climate, and every division, with its multiple tensions, happens in such a climate."[1]

Flusser was also born at a special time in Prague: right after the 1918 founding of the First Czechoslovak Republic, succeeding Austro-Hungarian rule and creating a historic union between the Czechs and Slovaks. Flusser grew up on the same street as his future wife, Edith Barth, in a new era of tolerance for Jews. Vilém's father, Gustav, who had studied with Albert Einstein in Vienna, would write a biography of the first president, Tomáš Masaryk. However, the results of recent ethnic cleansing were apparent: in the mid-1880s, the old Jewish quarter had been razed and new cultural monuments were built; Prague became a modern design and technology center. Flusser attended German-language schools, and one of his most memorable experiences was attending a 1937 lecture delivered by Martin Buber, the philosopher whose idea of the "I and you"—looking into the "face of the other" in dialogue—became central to Flusser's theories of media and communication. (Only, for Flusser, the face of the other appeared on a technological screen rather than through the medium of religion.) "To grow up in such a climate," Flusser wrote, "to sense these productive tensions in one's surroundings and within oneself, to participate in them actively since puberty, was entirely natural for the son of Jewish intellectuals. Only through the distance of time and space did this naturalness emerge as a privileged situation."[2] Then it all "shattered to bits," to cite a piece of verse attributed to the Persian astronomer and mathematician Omar Khayyam, which Flusser quoted frequently.

In 1938, Flusser matriculated in law at Charles University in Prague—and the Nazis invaded Czechoslovakia, annexing the Sudetenland that same year. Hitler declared war against Poland on September 1, 1939, and moved into Prague in March 1939. There was no armed resistance, and Prague's physical structures remained relatively untouched by the war—although the city was occupied longer than other regions: from six months before the outbreak of World War II through several months after the liberation in 1945. The young Czechoslovak Republic disintegrated immediately. Jews were instructed to register their apartments and deliver their radios to special locations. Later, they were not allowed to attend the cinema or theater performances, their identity documents had to be stamped with the letter *J*, and as of May 17, 1940, they were forbidden to linger in parks, gardens, or forests; to keep pigeons, use taxis, or sit in the front carriage of a tram. If a tram had only one carriage, they were to wait for the next one with two carriages.[3]

The situation was becoming urgent. Gustav Flusser, by then the director of the Commercial Academy in Prague, had received an invitation to teach at the university in Jerusalem, but he refused to make his *Aliyah* (literally, in Hebrew, "ascent" or "rise," but later

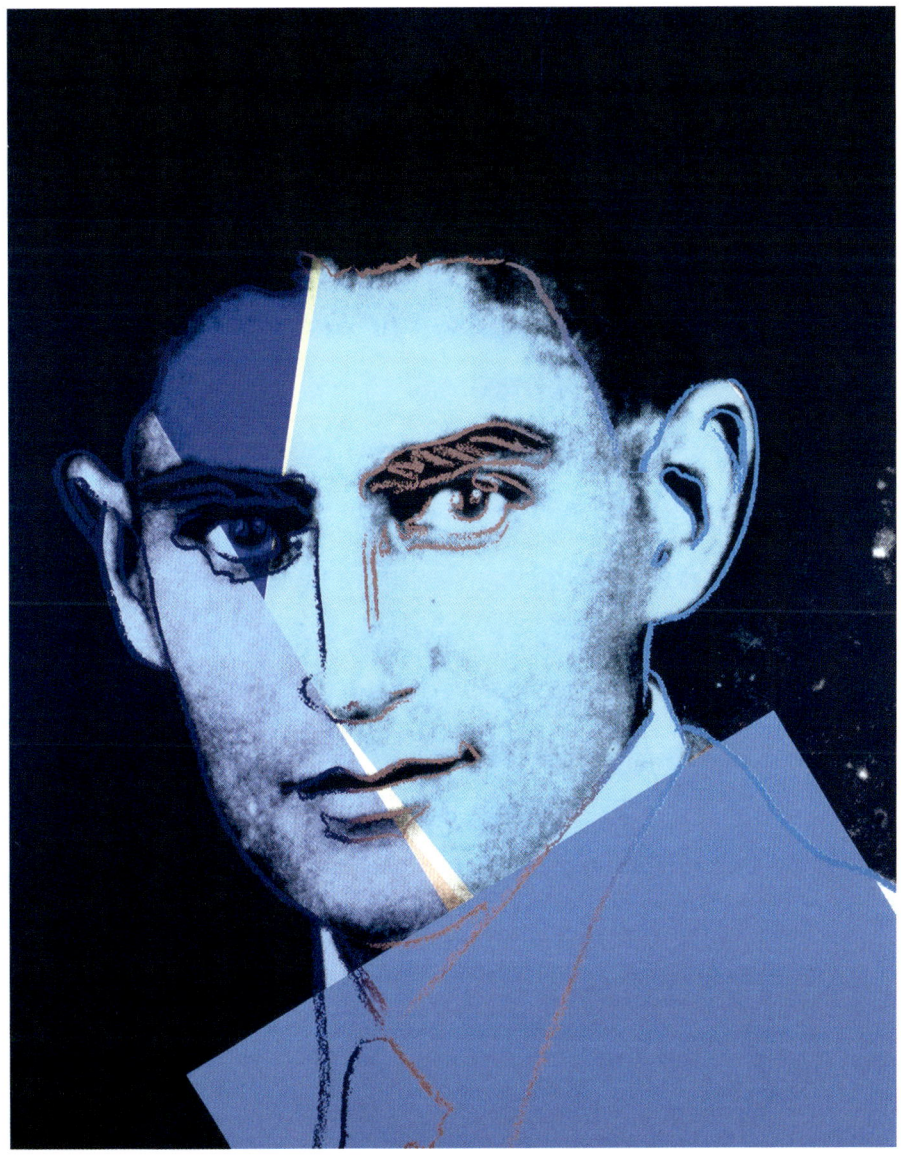

Figure 1.2
Andy Warhol, *Franz Kafka*, 1980. Screenprint on Lenox Museum Board, from the series *Ten Portraits of Jews of the Twentieth Century*. Courtesy of Ronald Feldman Gallery, New York. © 2024 The Andy Warhol Foundation for the Visual Arts, Inc./Licensed by Artists Rights Society (ARS), New York. This work appeared in Flusser's review of Warhol's exhibition *Ten Portraits of Jews of the Twentieth Century* at the Neue Galerie der Stadt Linz for *Camera Austria*, February 1980, 40.

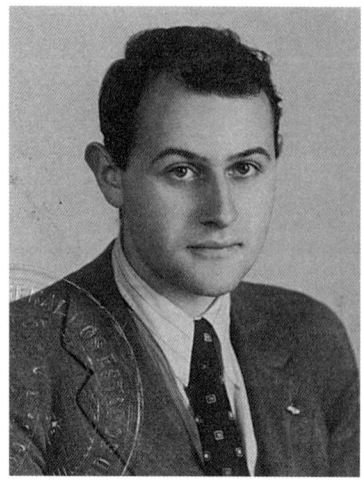

Figure 1.3
Flusser's passport photo, 1940.
Vilém Flusser Archive, Berlin.

meaning to immigrate to Israel). A verbal confrontation ensued between Edith's and Vilém's fathers, but Gustav Flusser refused to leave Prague. Vilém secured his papers. Edith later described a meeting in which a Nazi officer screamed insults at her and her mother while an assistant hastily stamped their passports.[4] In March 1939, Vilém, Edith, and her mother traveled by train to the Dutch border. Flusser carried two books with him: Goethe's *Faust* and a Jewish prayer book his mother had given him. They made it to England, but the bombardment of London started, making it unsafe to remain in the city. Gustav Barth rented a bus with other Prague families and instructed the driver to take them as far as the gas tank would allow.[5] They ended up in Cornwall, where they took up residence in an abandoned manor house. Unable to enroll at the university, Vilém cut hair and Edith apprenticed in the maternity ward of a local hospital. Opportunities for Jewish refugees to leave England were limited to Shanghai, Panama, and Brazil.[6] Moreover, the idea of Brazil as a tolerant haven for Jews was ultimately a myth: in an interview recorded two months before his death, Flusser admitted, "the Brazilian consul was corrupt, and he accepted relatively small bribes, and so he gave us a Brazilian visa."[7] Gustav Barth's money bought their safe passage to Brazil. After being baptized, as required, Flusser and the Barths left Southampton on the *Highland Patriot*, A.F., a British ocean liner accompanied by a cruiser to protect against German submarines.[8]

The monthlong voyage was made in darkness to avoid detection (passengers were even forbidden to light cigarettes).[9]

The trauma of war returned when they reached the port of Rio de Janeiro. Onboard ship in the harbor, Flusser learned that his father had been murdered at Buchenwald on June 18, 1940. In late 1943, his maternal grandparents, Julius and Olga Basch, were sent to Treblinka, where they were killed. In 1945, Flusser would learn the fate of his mother and his younger sister, Ludvíka, who were deported from the Theresienstadt ghetto in Terezín to the Auschwitz death camp on September 6, 1943, where they were eventually murdered.[10] Flusser later looked back on that period, musing, "I spent my youth in the spiritually and artistically inebriating atmosphere of the between-wars Prague," but then "I was vomited upon Brazil at a plastic and assimilable age, and I spent the last thirty years of my life in search of myself in Brazil, and in search of Brazil within myself."[11]

Flusser stayed with the Barths in a pension in Rio for a few months before moving to São Paulo, where he worked for Edith's uncle in an import-export company. Edith and Vilém were married on January 15, 1941. Despite his marriage and the birth of his children (Dinah, Miguel Gustavo, and Victor), it was a dark period, marked by grief and feelings of guilt for surviving the Holocaust. "The Nazis did not kill one's family," Flusser wrote; "one's own decision to escape did it. One killed them in order to save one's own shadow, this disgusting body. One could never again read Nietzsche's statement of the death of God without self-recognition."[12] Flusser recounted carrying a piece of paper with him, divided into two sections: one listing the reasons for suicide, the other, reasons against it.[13] Edith accompanied him to work daily because she was afraid he would kill himself.[14] Flusser found intellectual fellowship in Alex Bloch, another Jewish immigrant from Prague, who worked in a bookstore: in addition to their correspondence, the two met, sometimes daily, to discuss ideas and books such as Heidegger's *Being and Time*.[15] (Alex Bloch also assisted a Zen Buddhist monk and would introduce Flusser to Indian philosophy and yoga.) "One engaged in business during the day and philosophized at night," Flusser wrote. "One pursued both activities with detachment and both with disgust."[16]

Flusser felt he had been exiled to the periphery of intellectual culture and debate. And yet many people saw Europe as a civilization in decline after fascism and devastating wars. Brazil represented something different, as echoed in the title of Stefan Zweig's book *Brazil: Land of the Future* (1941): a territory filled with American-style skyscrapers and enchanting landscapes.[17] It was a young nation, attempting rapid industrialization while reckoning with a past rooted in colonialism and the enslavement of Africans and indigenous people. It was saturated by mass media and design, and the ruling classes were beginning to see how art and cultural institutions could serve as a form of "soft power," amplifying Brazil's presence on the global stage. (In the mid-1950s, Flusser founded a company that manufactured radios and transistors—in retrospect, appropriate work for a philosopher who would end up writing about technology and new media.)[18] Initially, Flusser read European authors and decided that language was going to be his "central problem."[19] Paradoxically, however, his early years in Brazil were also marked by a *lack* of language: he arrived in South America not knowing any Portuguese. He wrote in German and slowly transitioned to Portuguese. He also began to make contact with members of the Brazilian philosophical community. Milton Vargas, an engineer and lifelong friend, remembered the first time he met Flusser, at the home of Vicente and Dora Ferreira da Silva: "Vicente, who had introduced Heidegger's philosophy to Brazil, his wife Dora who was already a quite well-known poet, and I were deeply in conversation when someone knocked at the door," Vargas wrote. "It was a peculiar young man, bald already back then, with a sharp nose and impressive glasses. He was completely unknown to us. Confidently, he introduced himself and said that he was looking for people with whom he could exchange ideas. He added that São Paulo was a desert devoid of people and ideas."[20]

Through this circle, Flusser started lecturing on the "Philosophy and Evolution of Science" at Universidade de São Paulo (USP) and on the philosophy of language at the Instituto Brasileiro de Filosofia (Brazilian Institute of Philosophy), which was cofounded in 1949 by Miguel Reale. In 1960, Flusser published "De Língua Portuguesa" (On the Portuguese language), his first essay for the *Revista Brasileira de Filosofia*, beginning to lay the ground for his language philosophy.[21] His writing in newspapers was equally relevant to the project of becoming a language philosopher, however, since it allowed him to consider models outside traditional philosophy. In 1961, Flusser published "Prague, City of Kafka" in the literary supplement of the newspaper *O Estado de São Paulo*—largely due to the encouragement of his daughter Dinah and her classmates, who would gather on the patio of the Flussers' São Paulo home to engage in discussions around art, literature, science, and philosophy.[22]

Flusser published four books in Brazil: *Language and Reality* (1963), *The History of the Devil* (1965), *Philosophy of Language* (1966), and *Of Religiosity* (1966). In *Language and Reality*, as the title suggests, he posits that everything is linguistic: knowledge, truth, reality. Language gives form to reality and creates reality, but since there are different languages, and their structures vary, the realities created by them are different.[23] This argument would be echoed later in the idea that *images* structure reality. Following the publication of *Language and Reality*, Flusser received a telegram from the Brazilian author João Guimarães Rosa stating that Flusser's book had left him "amazed, excited, enthusiastic."[24] Guimarães Rosa was a medical doctor and diplomat based in São Paulo, but originally from the inland state of Minas Gerais in southeastern Brazil. During World War II, Guimarães Rosa was stationed in Hamburg and imprisoned in Baden-Baden for four months in 1942 for forging passports for Jews.[25] His 1956 opus, *Grande Sertão: Veredas* (*The Devil to Pay in the Backlands*)—which might be more literally translated as "The Great Wilderness: Pathways"—was notable for its experimentation with language and narrative, as well as its length: over 500 pages with no chapter divisions. Goethe's *Faust* was a prime inspiration for Guimarães Rosa, as it was for Flusser, who wrote the first version of *The History of the Devil* in German in 1958, shortly after reading *Grande Sertão*; later he rewrote the text in Portuguese.[26] A subversive book that looks at art and technology through the Christian structure of the Seven Deadly Sins, Flusser's *The History of the Devil* also considers Eastern philosophy and, particularly, Indian and Zen Buddhist teachings (or what Flusser loosely calls "yoga"), alongside European philosophy.[27] The book is notable, not just for its excursions into a philosophy of science, technology, and mass media, but for its attempts to explode the God-Devil dialectic, following the events of World War II, and to cast the reader into a state of existential questioning. It would be one of many dialectics Flusser tackled in his career, attempting to collapse or explode traditional and misleading—even harmful—binaries.

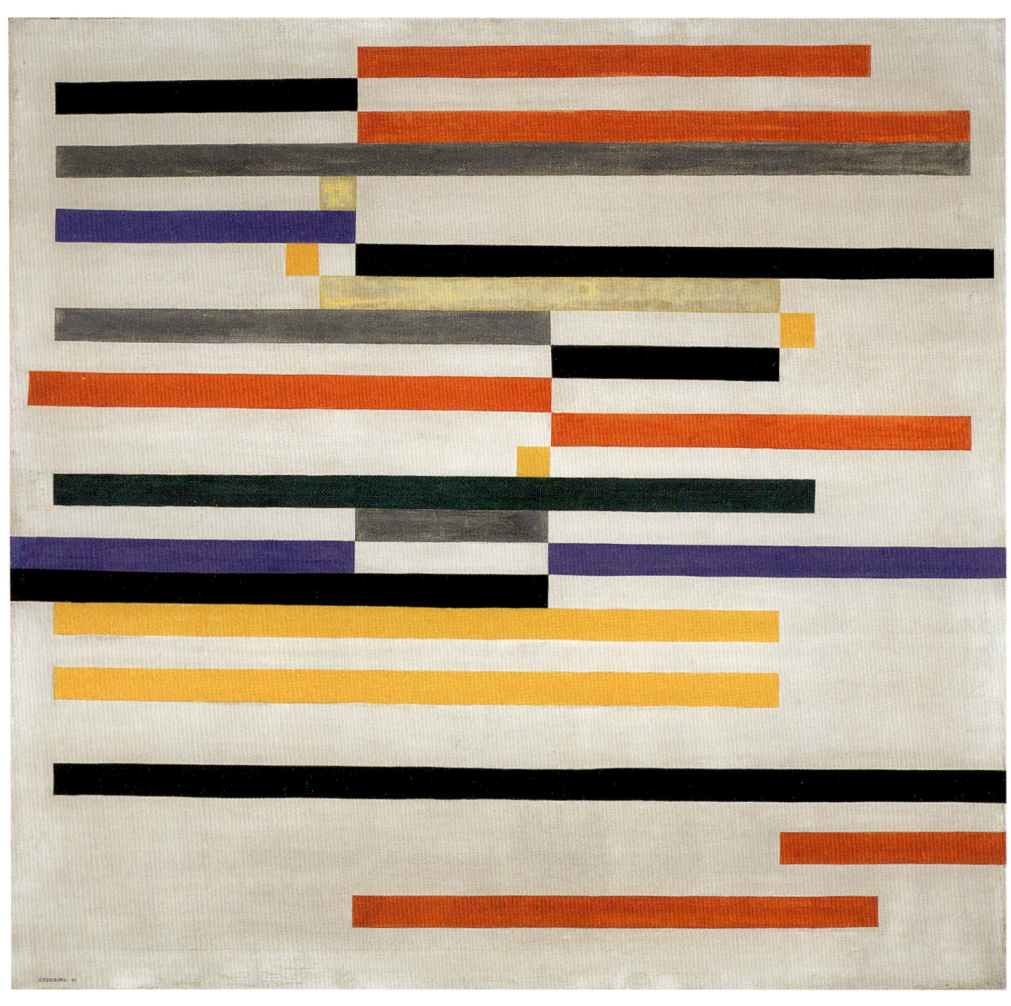

Figure 1.4
Waldemar Cordeiro, *Movimento*, 1951. Tempera on canvas, 90.1 × 95.3 cm. MAC USP
Collection [Museu de Arte Contemporânea da USP Collection, São Paulo, Brazil].

Art was increasingly eclipsing language, though, which Flusser could not ignore—and language and images themselves were changing. Concrete art and poetry flourished in Brazil in the 1950s, and Flusser, who had decided that his primary focus would be language, was introduced to these new forms. In particular, the formal layout of Concrete art and poetry, with their rigorous, abstract approaches to space, color, and typography, would impact Flusser. "The *Gestalt*," he wrote, and "the visual character of writing" in "Concretist experiments are rupturing discursive thought and endowing it with a second dimension of 'ideas' which discursive thought cannot supply."[28] These methods served as proto-interfaces or screens, predicting the digital revolution, and offering what Concrete poet Haroldo de Campos called a "new dialogical relationship" with "imperial" languages, since Concrete painting had become an international language in art and Concrete poetry took very little vocabulary to interpret and understand.[29] These phenomena would eventually inform Flusser's concept of "superficial" reading—the eye moving around the surface of an image—and nonlinear "post-historical" thinking, as well as the idea that philosophy itself could be practiced in images rather than text.

All of this happened because Brazil was not on the periphery at all: in fact, it was becoming a vital center for visual art. The Modern Art Week (Semana de Arte Moderna) in São Paulo in February 1922, with a flurry of exhibitions, lectures, poetry readings, and concerts, is often seen as a seminal moment for modern art in Brazil, analogous to the Armory Show in 1913, which introduced European modernism to New York. Also important is the emergence a few years later of the concept of Antropofagia, or Anthropophagy, in which European and colonial artistic influences could be "cannibalized" and digested. Oswald de Andrade's 1928 "Manifesto Antropófago" (Anthropophagic manifesto) argued that the European avant-garde would be critically absorbed—although, as Flusser's friend, the artist Mira Schendel, pointed out, "There are people out there saying that Brazilians import fashions, that Brazilians were colonized. I think Brazilians have done much that has been exported, but few have realized that. I think that there may be moments of greater give-and-take, but artists from different countries have always influenced each other."[30]

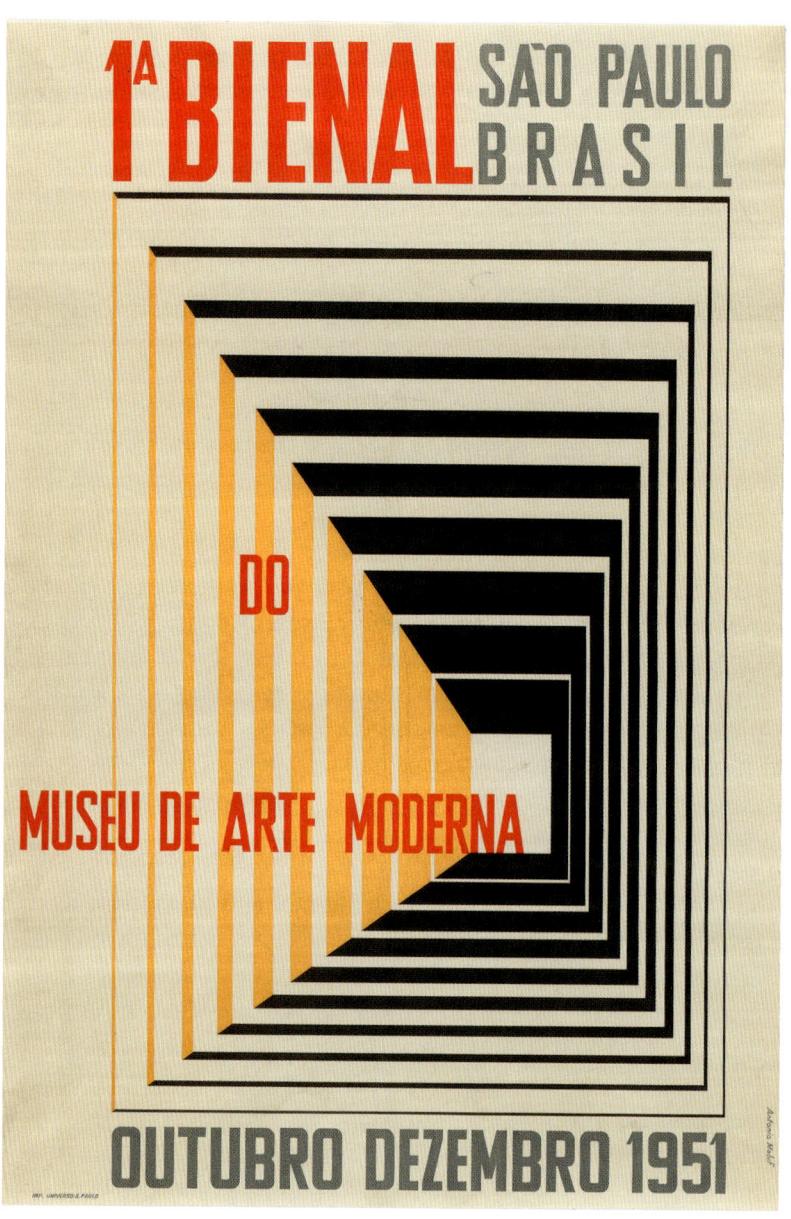

Figure 1.5
Antonio Maluf, *1ª Bienal do Museu de Arte Moderna, São Paulo, Brasil*, 1951. Lithograph,
25 × 37 in. (63.5 × 94 cm). Gift of Museu de Arte Moderna de São Paulo. © The Museum of
Modern Art/Licensed by SCALA/Art Resource, NY.

After World War II, Brazil witnessed a surge of visual arts activity: the opening of the Museu de Arte Moderna in São Paulo in 1948 and the Museu de Arte Moderna do Rio de Janeiro in 1949; the establishment of a commercial art market; and the 1951 inauguration of the São Paulo Biennial, modeled after the Venice Biennale. The Brazilian government saw the efficacy of using art as a platform for gaining visibility in geopolitics and embracing abstraction as a shorthand for the advanced modern state at a moment when Brazil was attempting to achieve warp-speed industrial development. Concrete art became an important component in this project. A form of geometric abstraction devoid of figurative elements and symbolic meaning and detached from observed reality, Concrete art was developed by the Dutch artist Theo van Doesburg. A founder of De Stijl, van Doesburg laid out this new form in a manifesto titled "The Basis of Concrete Art," published in the sole issue of *Art Concret* in April 1930.[31] The movement argued for painting constructed from pure plastic elements—planes and colors—and instructed artists to avoid nature, lyricism, and sentiment. After van Doesburg's death in 1931, Max Bill, a Swiss artist, designer, and architect who had studied at the Bauhaus and later became the founding director of the Hochschule für Gestaltung Ulm (HfG Ulm, or Ulm School of Design), served as Concrete art's primary proponent and cross-pollinator from Europe to Brazil.[32]

In fact, Bill found his most receptive audience in South America, where geometric abstraction was seen as a mode of cultural transformation, a unifying international style that could eradicate language differences and geopolitical borders. Swiss-derived Concrete art conveyed rigor and rationality, contradicting the stereotype of Latin American art devoted to protesting workers or peasants and tropical flora and fauna, and alleviating what one Brazilian writer described as "an anxiety about overcoming technological backwardness and the irrationalism caused by underdevelopment."[33] In 1951, a retrospective of Bill's work was held at the recently founded Museu de Arte de São Paulo (MASP), and he won the sculpture prize at the first São Paulo Biennial with his *Tripartite Unity* (1948–1949), an example of Concrete "good form" generated by mathematical operations.[34] Flusser took note of these developments. In *The History of the Devil*, he argued that "painters of concrete art are of a fundamental importance for an interpretation of current times. . . . They are, effectively, the advanced posts of the

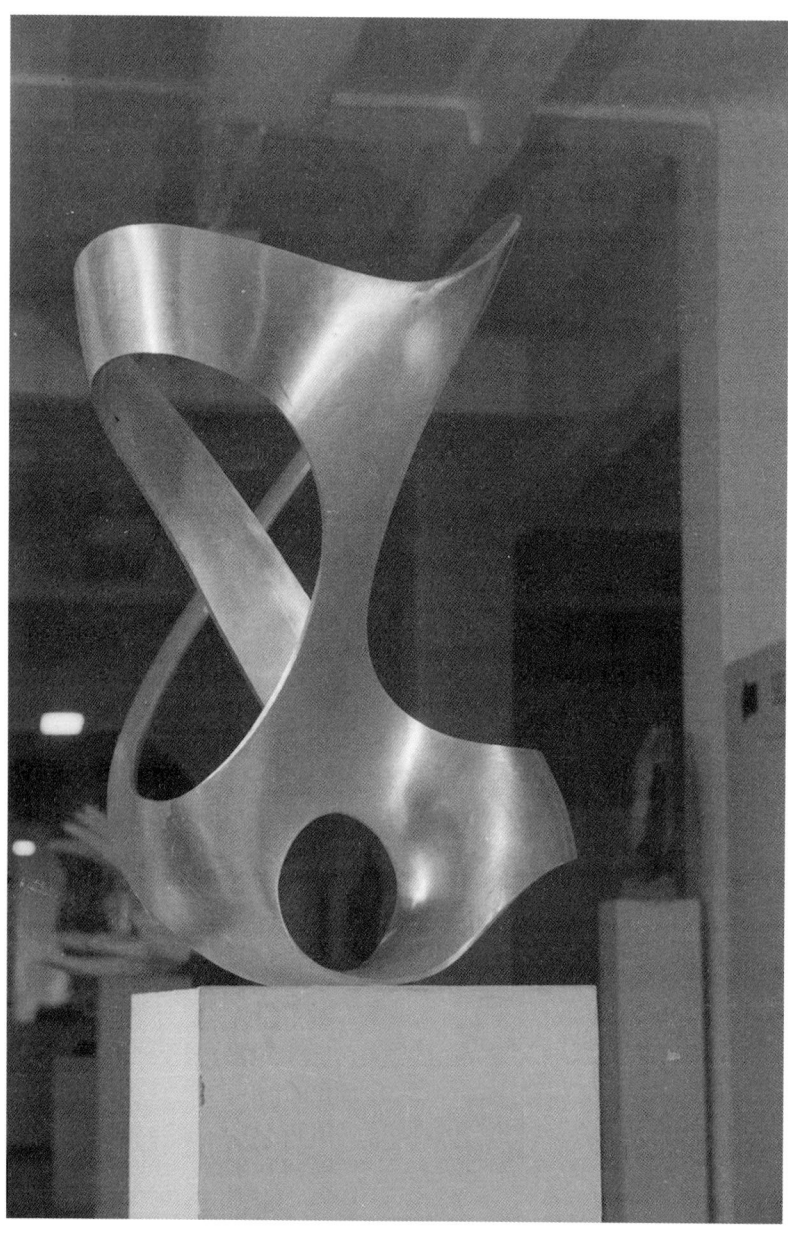

Figure 1.6
Max Bill, *Tripartite Unity*, 1948–1949. Stainless steel. Fundação Bienal de São Paulo.
© 2024 Artists Rights Society (ARS), New York/ProLitteris, Zurich.

natural sciences. Our scientists are still at the state of representational painting."[35]

And yet Brazil's diverse population of artists was significant for Flusser, too. Asian calligraphy, for instance, contributed to closing the gap between abstract painting and language. In his writing, Flusser mentioned Manabu Mabe (1924–1997), a Japanese immigrant who had worked on Brazilian coffee plantations and was largely self-taught. Following the Great Depression in the 1930s that affected coffee exportation, Mabe had sold painted ties on the streets of São Paulo but later rose to become one of the most prominent artists in Brazil: *Time* magazine declared 1959 "The Year of Manabu Mabe."[36] Mabe was also associated with the Seibi Group of Japanese-Brazilian artists that developed largely apart from the Bauhaus-derived constructivism that flourished in Brazil in the 1950s. The Seibi Group provided studios for its members and published its debates in the Japanese contemporary art magazine *Atelier*, but they never wrote a manifesto and didn't leave behind a trail of primary documents as the Concrete and Neo-Concrete artists and their supporters and detractors did.[37]

Mabe often used a vertically oriented canvas to simulate East Asian calligraphy, further fusing the link between modern abstraction and traditional writing. This interested Flusser, who wrote, "it is no accident that some of the most prominent names in Brazilian painting are Japanese, and I give Manabu Mabe as an example."[38] Flusser's fascination with Mabe is notable. In the United States, gestural abstraction was often treated as a mode of freedom that countered the socialist realism of the Soviet Union.[39] In Brazil, lyrical abstraction was seen as more romantic and less intellectual and rigorous than Concrete or Neo-Concrete art, somewhere in between the European *informel* and *tachisme*—and comprised overwhelmingly of art by Japanese immigrants. Most important, however—and something that Flusser picked up on—was the fact that calligraphic abstraction represented a rupture of writing from its meaning.[40] Mabe himself broke from traditional Japanese art's "language" by painting in oil or thinned lacquer rather than with ink. He was also in the same migrant-limbo Flusser himself had experienced: "no longer fully Japanese and not yet entirely Brazilian."[41] Mabe and lyrical abstraction reigned in 1959, but most post-World War II art histories are dominated by the Concrete art project in Brazil.[42] Flusser, looking at art through the lens of language philosophy, found value in both.

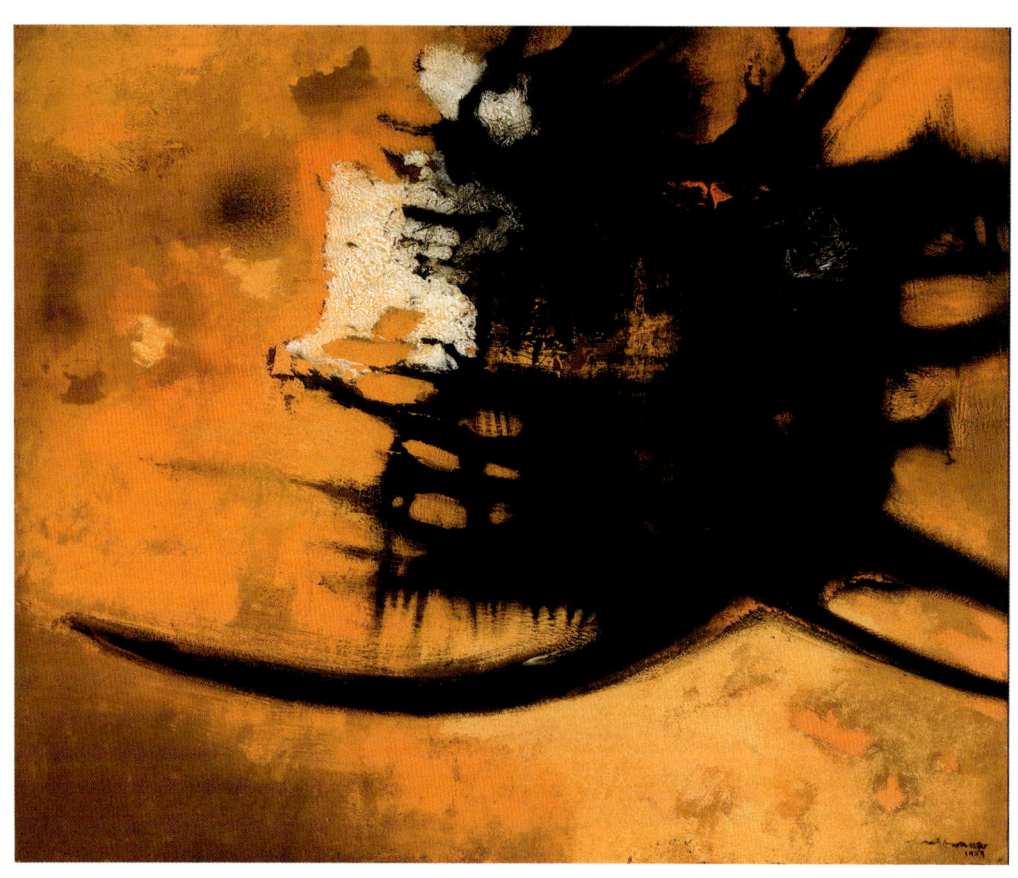

Figure 1.7
Manabu Mabe, *Estranho* (Strange), 1959. Oil on board, 105 × 122 cm. Museu Chácara do Céu,
Museus Castro Maya.

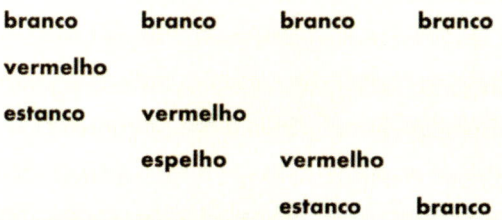

Figure 1.8
Haroldo de Campos, *branco* (white), 1958. Casa das Rosas, Centro de Referência Haroldo de Campos. A "transcreation" of Kazimir Malevich's painting *Suprematist Composition: White on White*, 1918.

Concrete art overlapped with Concrete poetry, which emerged in the early 1950s outside the European capitals afflicted by World War II, in Brazil, Sweden, Switzerland, and Austria.[43] Concrete poetry was concerned with the physical aspects of language—spatial syntax, typography, color, design, sound, translation, and the poem as an object. It drew from advertising, product logos, and street signage, as well as from Mondrian's constructivist paintings, Marshall McLuhan's media theories, John Cage's aleatory music, and the bold layout of Édition Gallimard's books. However, as Kenneth Goldsmith has pointed out, it also looks forward to the way text is presented on screens in the digital age; the universal nature of icons, emojis, and GIFs; and writing designed for shortened attention spans in the information age.[44]

Concrete poetry's literary roots were in many places: Stéphane Mallarmé's symbolist poetry; the syncopated concision of Emily Dickinson's verse; Walt Whitman's object lists; the *Dinggedicht* (thing-poem) of Rainer Maria Rilke; and the experimental modernism of William Carlos Williams, Gertrude Stein, and James Joyce.[45] Art provided several touchstones: Russian constructivist design; Mondrian's idea of a universal vision in the plastic arts; and optical art, which was reacting against the subjective expressionism of much US and European abstract art. The time-space experiments of composers like Anton Webern, Pierre Boulez, and Karlheinz Stockhausen, and other concrete and electronic music served as further sources.[46] Most important for Flusser was the Noigandres group, formed in São Paulo in 1952 by brothers Augusto and Haroldo de Campos, along with Décio Pignatari, and named after a line in Ezra Pound's Canto XX. For the Noigandres, the term "concrete" was inspired by modern architectural developments in Brazil, which attacked the colonial baroque architecture: their manifesto also nodded to Lúcio Costa's "Pilot Plan for Brasília" and the rhetoric of architects like Le Corbusier, who first visited Brazil in 1929, and Richard Neutra. They described the Concrete poem as a form of "metacommunication" that emphasized its structure rather than its message and functioned cybernetically, like a self-regulating "mechanism" that provides feedback and faster communication.[47]

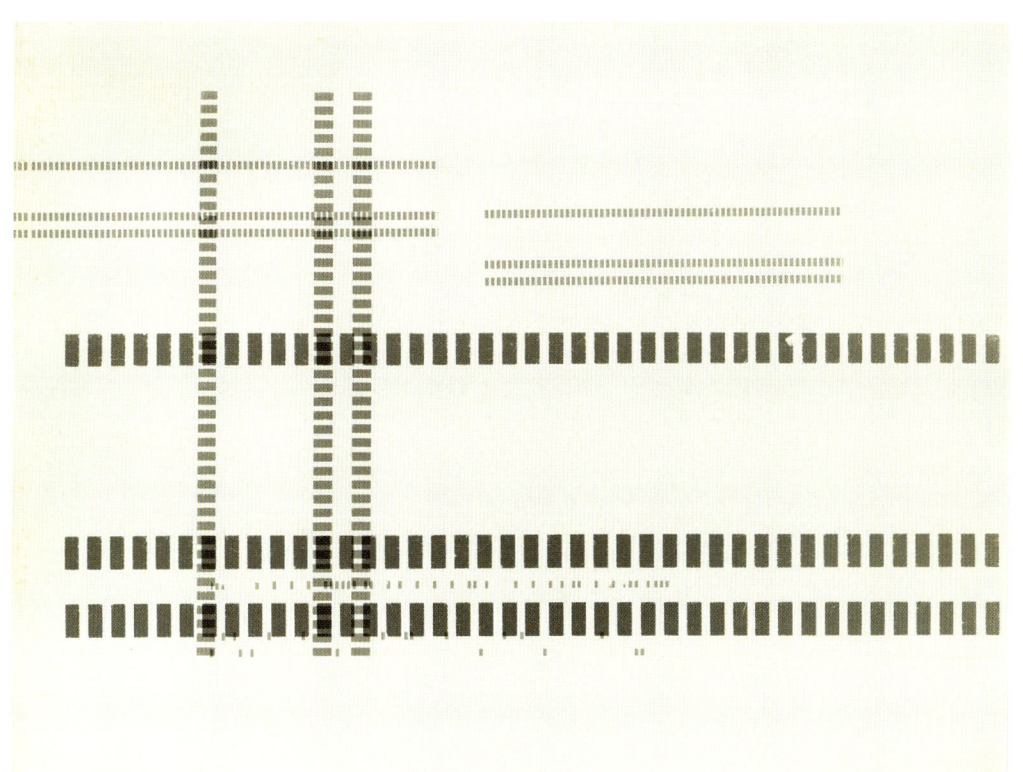

Figure 1.9
Geraldo de Barros, *Fotoforma*, 1952–1953. Gelatin silver print, 11¹³⁄₁₆ × 15⅛ in. (30 × 38.4 cm). Acquired through the generosity of John and Lisa Pritzker. The Museum of Modern Art/ New York, NY/U.S.A. © The Museum of Modern Art/Licensed by SCALA/Art Resource, NY.

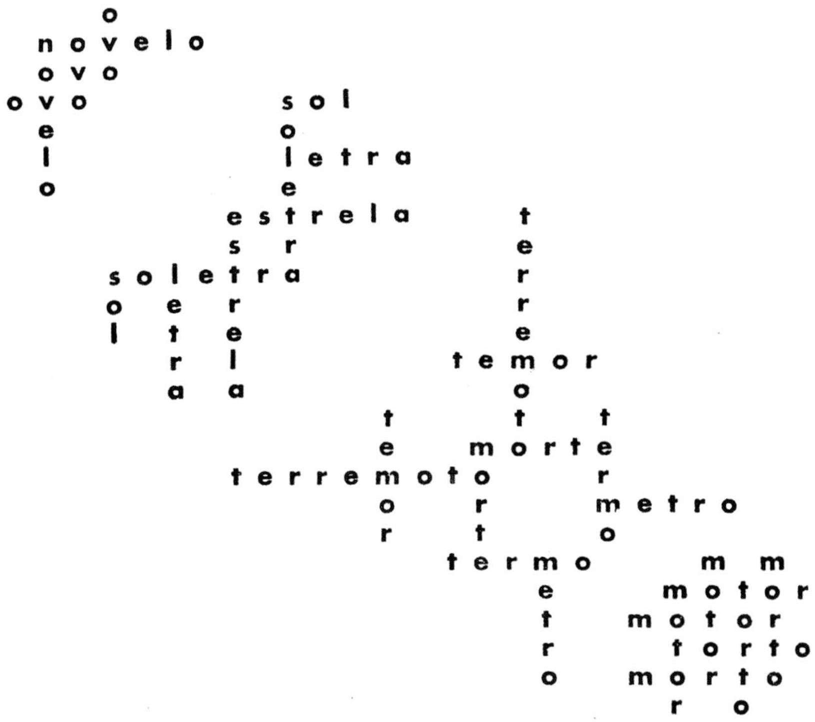

```
        o
    n o v e l o
    o v o
o v o                 s o l
    e                     o
    l                     l e t r a
    o                     e
            e s t r e l a              t
            s       r                  e
    s o l e t r a                      r
    o   e   r                          r
    l   t   e                          e
        r   l             t e m o r
        a   a                     o
                t                 t       t
                e         m o r t e
    t e r r e m o t o                     r
                o         r       m e t r o
                r         t               o
                t e r m o             m   m
                        e         m o t o r
                        t         m o t o r
                        r             t o r t o
                        o         m o r t o
                                  r   o
```

Figure 1.10
Augusto de Campos, *terremoto* (earthquake), 1956. Courtesy of the artist.

Flusser, absorbing the impact of Concrete poetry, saw a "crisis" in the literary novels of people like his friend Guimarães Rosa, since they presuppose "a universe where the author is omniscient and manipulates events—a universe that is unacceptable today."[48] Concrete poetry offered a gestalt that made it easier and faster to read, in a nonlinear fashion: it approached reading in a *perceptual* rather than *conceptual* way. Noigandres poet Haroldo de Campos's essay "The Open Work of Art" (1955), which preceded Umberto Eco's *The Open Work* (1962) by several years, describes a "circular organization" inspired in part by James Joyce, whose *Finnegans Wake* shifted linear reading to space-time reading: the text "is porous to the reader, accessible from any of the places one chooses to approach it."[49] Similarly, in *The History of the Devil*, Flusser wrote that Concrete poetry is "pictorial language" which refuses to be "dragged" into discourse, arresting language at its roots.[50]

Concrete poetry's relationship with technology is also notable. The Concrete poem's visual and spatial layout has been cited as a precursor to computer screens and interfaces, and several Concrete poets took their work into the digital realm, for instance the video poems created by Lenora de Barros and Augusto de Campos.[51] In much the same way that Jorge Luis Borges's short story "The Garden of the Forking Paths" has been seen as a fictional diagramming of the internet, *avant la lettre*, Goldsmith has stated that everything Décio Pignatari was saying in the 1950s "seemed to predict the mechanics of the internet . . . delivery, content, interface, distribution, multi-media, just to name a few."[52] Concrete poetry would go on to have variants like "dirty Concrete" poetry made on typewriters and mimeograph machines—often smudged or smeared—or the artworks Flusser's friend Mira Schendel made on a typewriter.

The affinities between Concrete art and poetry are often overlooked.[53] However, in their writings published in newspapers in the 1950s, the Noigandres poets referred to Kasimir Malevich, Piet Mondrian's *Boogie Woogie* series, Max Bill, and Josef Albers. An important moment came in 1955, when Pignatari traveled to Europe and visited Brazilian artists studying at the HfG Ulm. He met Eugen Gomringer, then serving as secretary for Max Bill, and they discovered they were both creating nonlinear poems.[54] The next year, the exhibition *1ª exposição nacional de arte concreta* (1956) opened, showcasing both visual artists and Concrete poets.[55] Later, the exhibition *Between Poetry and Painting* (1965) at the Institute of

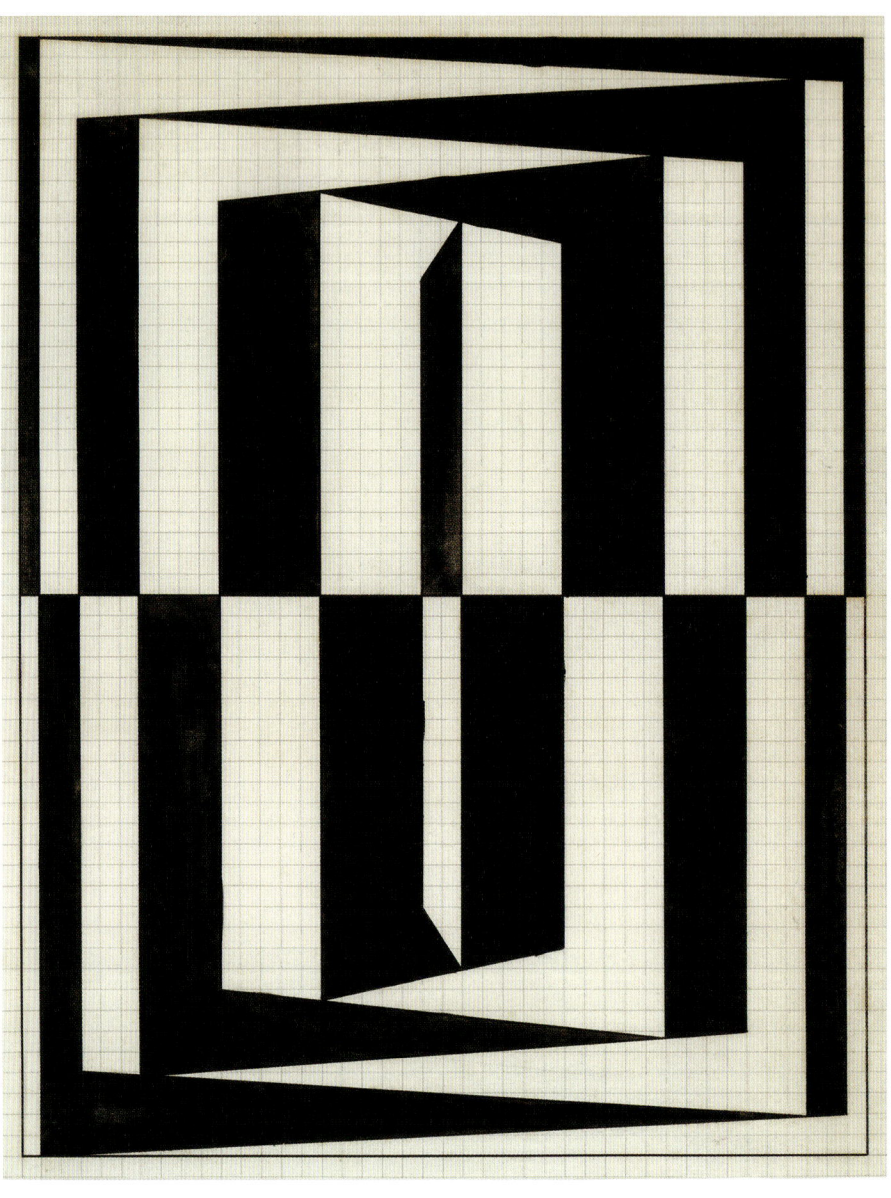

Figure 1.11
Willys de Castro, *Untitled*, c. 1958. Gouache on graph paper, 11 × 8¾ in. (27.9 × 22.2 cm). The
Museum of Modern Art/New York, NY/U.S.A. © The Museum of Modern Art/Licensed by
SCALA/Art Resource, NY. Courtesy the Estate of Willys de Castro. Artist, musician, and
graphic designer, Castro also published Concrete poetry.

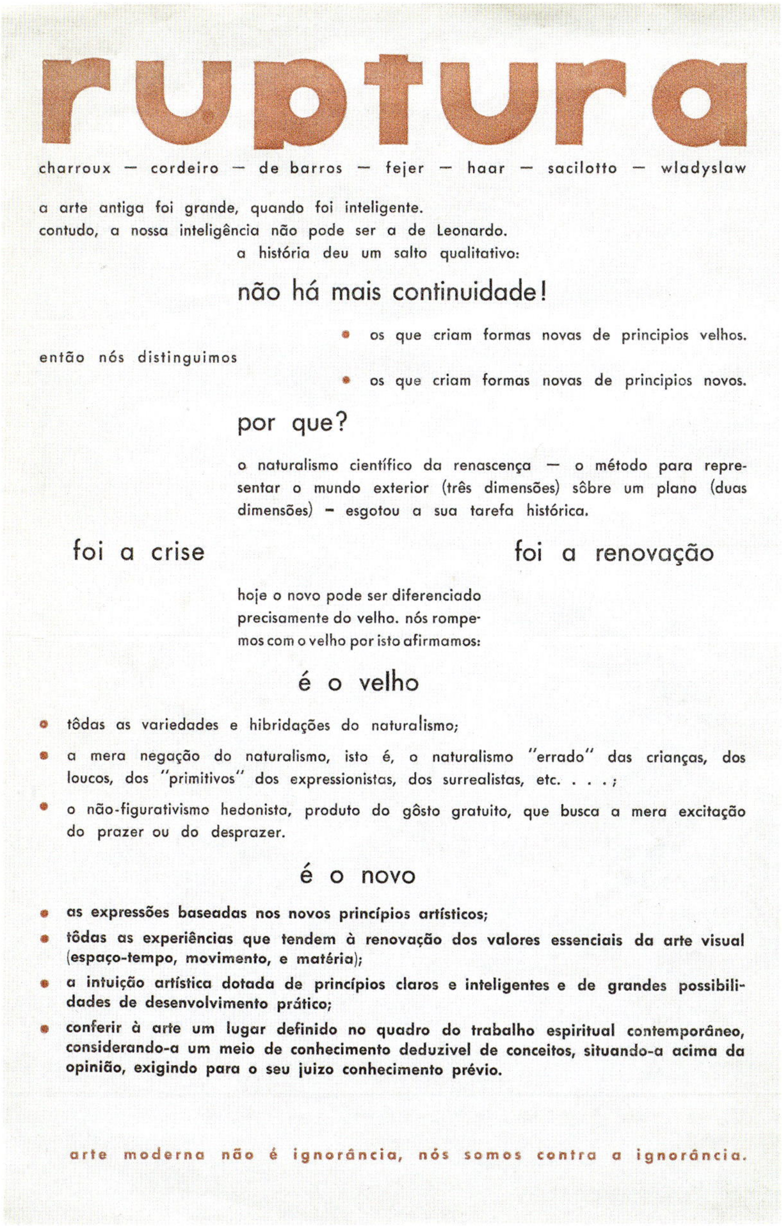

ruptura

charroux — cordeiro — de barros — fejer — haar — sacilotto — wladyslaw

a arte antiga foi grande, quando foi inteligente.
contudo, a nossa inteligência não pode ser a de Leonardo.

a história deu um salto qualitativo:

não há mais continuidade!

então nós distinguimos

- os que criam formas novas de principios velhos.
- os que criam formas novas de principios novos.

por que?

o naturalismo científico da renascença — o método para representar o mundo exterior (três dimensões) sôbre um plano (duas dimensões) — esgotou a sua tarefa histórica.

foi a crise   foi a renovação

hoje o novo pode ser diferenciado precisamente do velho. nós rompemos com o velho por isto afirmamos:

é o velho

- tôdas as variedades e hibridações do naturalismo;
- a mera negação do naturalismo, isto é, o naturalismo "errado" das crianças, dos loucos, dos "primitivos" dos expressionistas, dos surrealistas, etc. . . . ;
- o não-figurativismo hedonista, produto do gôsto gratuito, que busca a mera excitação do prazer ou do desprazer.

é o novo

- as expressões baseadas nos novos princípios artísticos;
- tôdas as experiências que tendem à renovação dos valores essenciais da arte visual (espaço-tempo, movimento, e matéria);
- a intuição artística dotada de princípios claros e inteligentes e de grandes possibilidades de desenvolvimento prático;
- conferir à arte um lugar definido no quadro do trabalho espiritual contemporâneo, considerando-a um meio de conhecimento deduzivel de conceitos, situando-a acima da opinião, exigindo para o seu juizo conhecimento prévio.

arte moderna não é ignorância, nós somos contra a ignorância.

Figure 1.12
Waldemar Cordeiro and Luís Sacilotto, *Ruptura Group Manifesto*, 1952. Letterpress in colors on wove paper, 12¹³⁄₁₆ × 8½ in. (32.5 × 21.6 cm). The Museum of Fine Arts, Houston, The Adolpho Leirner Collection of Brazilian Constructive Art, museum purchase funded by the Caroline Wiess Law Accessions Endowment Fund, 2007.16 © Família Cordeiro; © Valter Sacilotto. Photograph © The Museum of Fine Arts, Houston; Will Michels.

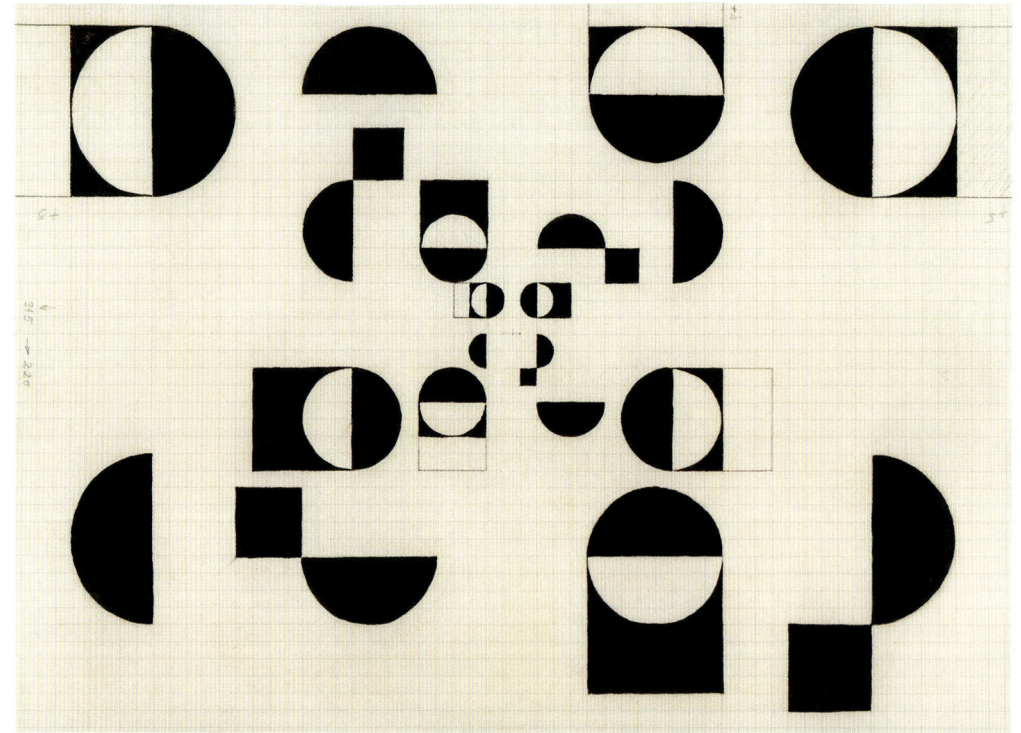

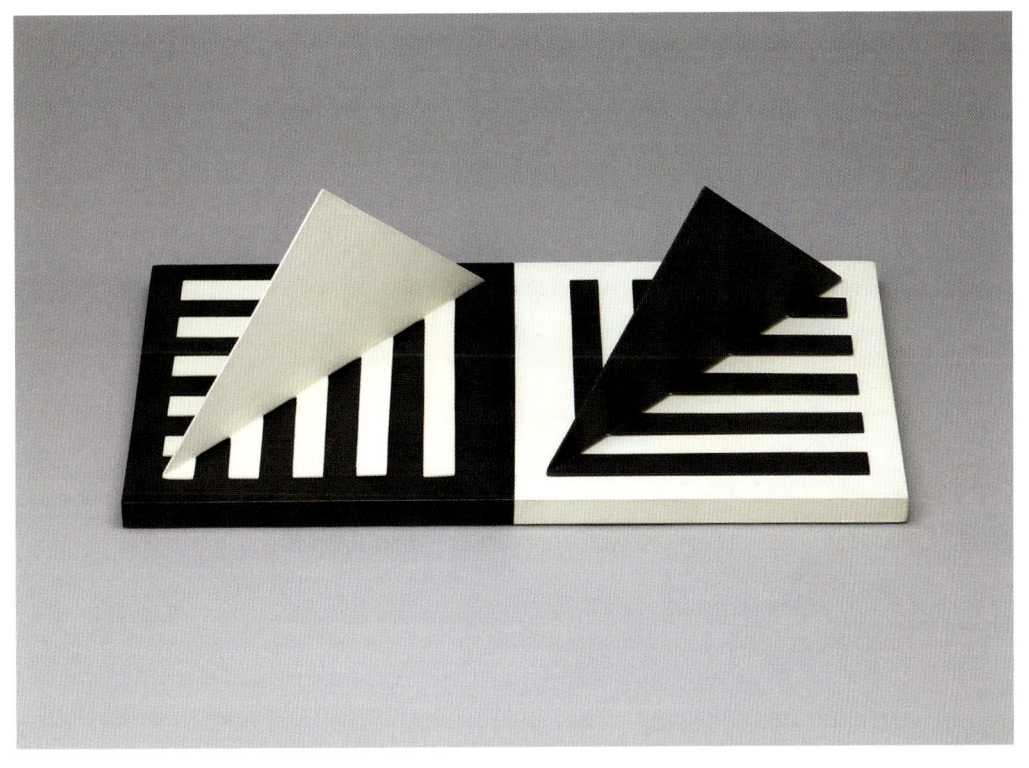

Figure 1.14
Luiz Sacilotto, *Concretion 58*, 1958. Alkyd on aluminum and wood, 7⅞ × 23⅝ × 12 in. (20 × 60 × 30.5 cm). Gift of Patricia Phelps de Cisneros through the Latin American and Caribbean Fund in honor of Rodrigo Cisneros-Santiago. The Museum of Modern Art/New York, NY/U.S.A. © The Museum of Modern Art/Licensed by SCALA/Art Resource, NY.

Contemporary Arts in London would include some of the same artists and poets, and make similar connections.

One can see in both poems and paintings the same interdependence of visual elements: disrupted grids, interlocking geometries, and nonlinear arrangements which force the eye to move in different trajectories. In both paintings and poems, straight lines, squares, and triangles, either of text or flat, solid color, traverse the surface, which needn't always be read from left to right. Concrete poets and artists both approached the grid—a traditional modernist structure and metaphor for progress and order—from a new angle, warping and bending its composition and meaning. The painter and designer Geraldo de Barros even encouraged Augusto de Campos to produce his multicolored *poetamenos* using typewritten copies with colored carbon paper, mimicking Concrete painting.

This worked across mediums: from painting to photography to objects that combine multiple forms, like Luiz Sacilotto's *Concretion 58* (1958). All of this would have an impact on Flusser, who argued that Concrete poetry cleared the "clogged up channels (from Gutenberg's galaxies) in order to transmit new types of messages."[56] Everything was changing. But as a writer and philosopher, how to analyze and describe this shift?

Information Aesthetics

A huge breakthrough occurred when Flusser discovered information aesthetics, a new approach to interpretation that drew from information theory, cybernetics, semiotics, mathematics, and communications, and which greatly informs the language of his technical image writings. Information aesthetics could be as dry as calculating syllables in a text or laying a grid over an image to determine a work's "aesthetic state," or it could be rich in generating new forms and methods: "programming" aesthetic situations and thinking of artworks not in terms of style but for their ability or failure to communicate information. Most important, it was a strategy for moving interpretation away from solely subjective speculation. The field was dominated by two figures: Max Bense and Abraham Moles. Flusser credits his friend Milton Vargas, a professor at the Escola Politécnica at the University of São Paulo, for bringing both Concrete poetry and Max Bense to his attention, and Bense would serve as an important model for Flusser, as a thinker who merged art and science and considered contemporary visual art and poetry as advanced realms for philosophy. (In the 1950s, Max Bill also recruited Bense to teach at the HfG Ulm.)

Concrete art and poetry caught the attention of Bense, a physicist, mathematician, and philosopher at the Technical University in Stuttgart who served as the inspiration for the landmark 1968 exhibition *Cybernetic Serendipity* in London, which set out to show "creative forms engendered by technology."[57] Important for both Bense and Jasia Reichardt, who curated *Cybernetic Serendipity*, was the fact that new technologies could also make artists out of nonartists. (Wen-Ying Tsai, an engineer-turned-cybernetic sculptor whose work Flusser wrote about, participated in *Cybernetic Serendipity*.) Bense himself began organizing exhibitions in seminar rooms at the University of Stuttgart in the late 1950s, and over the next twenty years he mounted more than ninety exhibitions. Several of these were devoted to Concrete poetry and Brazilian artists, such as Lygia Clark and Mira Schendel, and to computer-generated art.[58] Bense and Moles also influenced the New Tendencies movement, based in Zagreb: the first issue of their *bit international* journal in 1968 was dedicated to Bense and Moles and includes their essays on art, information, and programming—as well as computer-generated art by Frieder Nake and A. Michael Noll, and images of Nam June Paik's *Robot K-456* (1964) and John Billingsley's robot *Albert* (1967), both of which were exhibited at *Cybernetic Serendipity*.[59]

Bense met Haroldo de Campos in 1959 through the poets Pignatari and Gomringer, forging a fruitful—if fraught—connection between Brazil and Germany. Bense and his wife, the semiotician Elisabeth Walther, traveled to Brazil four times between 1959 and 1964, visiting Brasília and meeting architect Oscar Niemeyer, art critic Mario Pedrosa, and authors Clarice Lispector and João Guimarães Rosa, among others. Their visits culminated in Bense's book *Brasilianische Intelligenz. Eine cartesianische Reflexion* (Brazilian thought: A Cartesian reflection), published in 1965, which included images of sculpture by Lygia Clark and Bruno Giorgi, paintings by Alfredo Volpi, and the architecture of Brasília, as well as discussion of Concrete poetry and the Noigandres group. Bense concluded that Brazilian "intelligence" was rooted in progressive technology and design, in contrast to Europe, which had descended into barbarism.[60] The new poetry was important in that it functioned as a form of three-dimensional communication, not unlike the mass media proliferating in the 1950s, and exhibited an optimism that felt absent in postwar Germany.[61] It could also be seen as "negentropic" (stabilizing) rather than "entropic" (decaying), to use buzzwords that would be vital in visual art. However, like many using these terms in the 1960s, Bense himself shifted his position over time on the positive and negative aspects of entropy.

Concrete poetry, according to Bense, also required a new form of interpretation, and he became a figurehead of this new approach: information aesthetics, which was an attempt to create a more scientific, less subjective form of analysis. In a series of books written between 1956 and 1960 summarized in *Aesthetica: Introduction to the New Aesthetics* (1965), Bense drew heavily from the US mathematician George David Birkhoff's concept of aesthetic measure (a formula measuring a work's order and complexity), Charles Sanders Peirce's semiotics, Claude E. Shannon's information theory, Norbert Wiener's cybernetics, and Noam Chomsky's idea of generative grammar.[62] In *Aesthetische Information* (Aesthetic information) from 1956, Bense acknowledged Max Bill's modern approach to aesthetics and included a reproduction of Bill's *White Square* (1946), a paradigm of aesthetic rationality and order. Information aesthetics had a huge impact in Europe among young artists wanting to get away from what they saw as the subjective egoism of much abstract art, and to use the burgeoning information technologies for something other than industrial or military means. Borrowing from information and communications theory and semiotics, precision, objectivity, and *intersubjectivity* (a word Flusser loved) were stressed. The computer was treated as a generative tool rather than one used merely for analyzing data. Art was treated as "research."[63]

Flusser came later to Concrete poetry than Bense, but it would clearly inform his subsequent writings. In 1964, he wrote "Concreto—abstrato," published in *O Estado de São Paulo*, in which he considered the "radical" aspects of Concrete poetry and named Haroldo de Campos as one of its primary practitioners.[64] The same year, Flusser was included in a Spanish journal devoted to important thinkers in Brazil that included Augusto and Haroldo de Campos, as well as João Guimarães Rosa.[65] He also translated a fragment of Haroldo de Campos's epic *Galáxias* (1963–1976) for Bense and Elisabeth Walther's experimental journal *rot* (1966).[66] Flusser and de Campos clashed on the translation, though, and

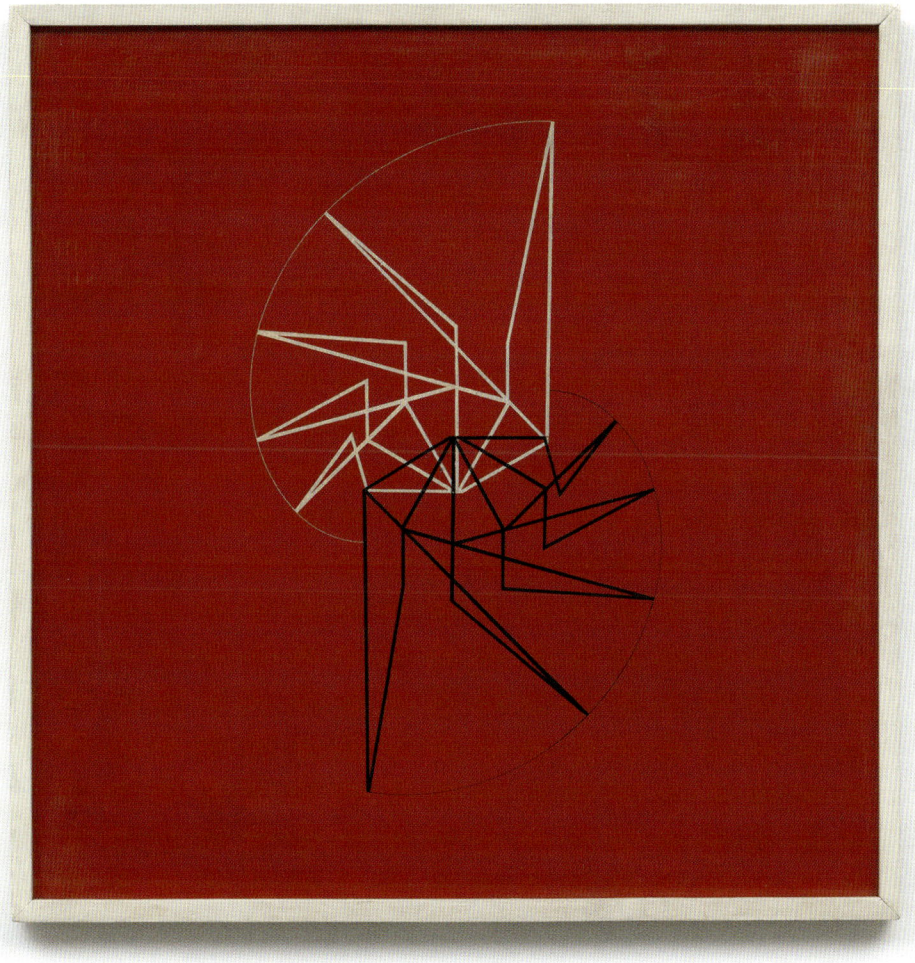

Figure 1.15
Waldemar Cordeiro, *Visible Idea*, 1956. Alkyd on board, 23⁹⁄₁₆ × 23⅝ in. (59.9 × 60 cm). Gift of Patricia Phelps de Cisneros through the Latin American and Caribbean Fund. © The Museum of Modern Art/Licensed by SCALA/Art Resource, NY. Courtesy the Estate of Waldemar Cordeiro.

Flusser used a section in his autobiographical essay "In Search of Meaning (Philosophical Self-portrait)" (1969) to jab back at de Campos's scientific approach to poetry: "I felt admiration," he wrote, "but also a deep divergence, for engineers in poetry such as Haroldo de Campos."[67] Instead, he was closer with poets like Theon Spanudis, a Greek immigrant, psychoanalyst, and art collector—particularly of Mira Schendel's work—with whom Flusser corresponded, in German. Flusser even provided a laudatory blurb on the back of Spanudis's collected volumes of Concrete poetry: "In all their rhythmic and thematic complexity," he wrote, "with all their Greek, German, and Brazilian layers, these verses are authentic poetry."[68]

Meanwhile, in Strasbourg, Abraham Moles's *Information Theory and Esthetic Perception* (1958) heavily informed Umberto Eco's *The Open Work* (1962), which was seen as a benchmark in treating art as interactive, with the viewer helping to complete the work. Moles leaned toward cybernetics and behavior systems, with computers modeling or simulating art and augmenting human intelligence. Aestheticians would provide "algorithms of thought" for artistic methods and art objects would be replaced by "artistic situations."[69] Moles was picking up on Birkhoff's ideas, which were grounded in nineteenth-century experimental psychology, but Bense and Moles were more interested in a calculable balance between redundancy and information, ideas central to Wiener's cybernetics and which would surface later in Flusser's writings.[70]

Information aesthetics was particularly influential in Germany, where the emerging technologies could be embraced for their generative aspects and programmed randomness, reaching beyond heroic gestures or the perceived egoism of *informe* or abstract expressionism. For Bense, the overlap with Concrete poetry and "generative" art was obvious: Concrete poetry functioned differently from existing writing systems—more like art and computer screens than like linear writing—and it generated meaning in an entirely different way. Rather than mechanically reproducing results, computers could also produce creative solutions (as chess and Go masters competing against computers would later report). Chance, randomness, and game theory also came into play: Claus Clüver writes about Concrete poetry, "There is nothing arbitrary here, and yet everything rests on chance.")[71]

Artists like Karl-Otto Götz, a painter and professor at the Kunstakademie Düsseldorf, created *Rasterbilder* (raster paintings)

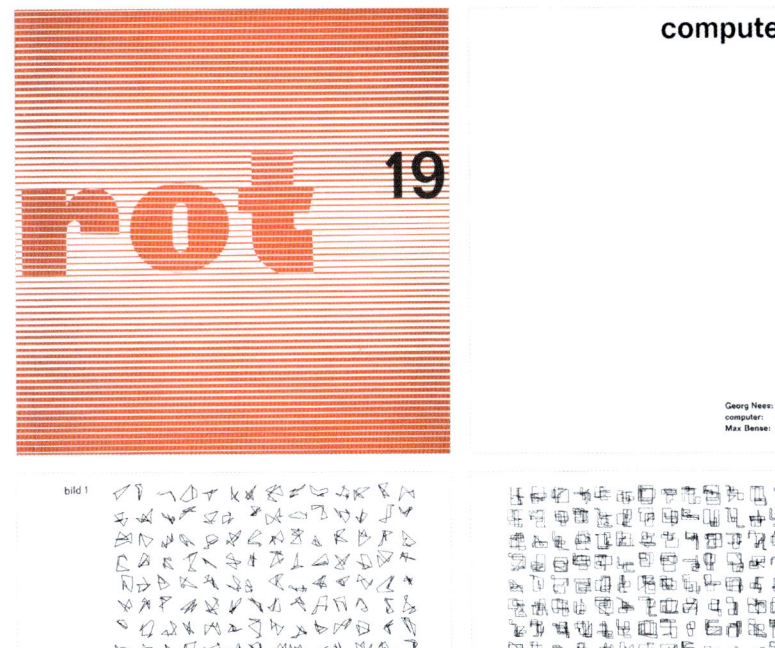

computer-grafik

rot 19

Georg Nees: programme
computer: stochastische grafik
Max Bense: projekte generativer ästhetik

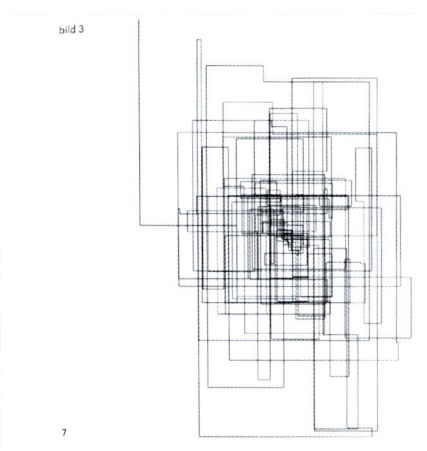

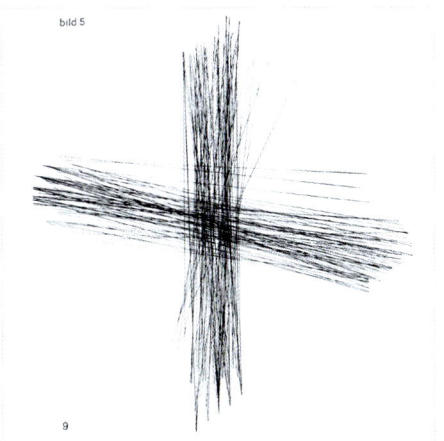

Figures 1.16–21

Georg Nees, "Computer-grafik," special issue, *rot* 19, 1965. ZKM | Center for Art and Media Karlsruhe and the Estates of Elisabeth Walther-Bense and Georg Nees. Commemorating the first known exhibition of computer art anywhere, held at the Studiengalerie in Stuttgart in February 1965.

in the late 1950s and early 1960s: programmed paintings, created with pencil and felt-tip pen, composed of squares arranged in a grid based on systematic permutations.[72] Inspired by Bense, Moles, and physicist Werner Meyer-Eppler, Götz designed tests to measure the speed and accuracy with which his students—among them Sigmar Polke, Gerhard Richter, Manfred Kuttner, and Konrad Lueg (aka Konrad Fischer)—were able to reproduce images.[73] Bense's new aesthetics of a "technical reality" was also picked up by mathematicians and engineers-turned-artists like A. Michael Noll, Konrad Zuse, Frieder Nake, and Georg Nees, a doctoral student of Bense.

Information aesthetics never gained currency in North America. Rudolf Arnheim wrote in a 1968 review of the English translation of Moles's *Information Theory and Esthetic Perception* that "information theory has been irresistible to philosophers, psychologists, and aestheticians who enjoy sporting the spacesuit of the latest terminology."[74] Arnheim, who leaned toward gestalt and perceptual psychology, felt that these techniques were too simple for understanding human behavior (or art). A 1970 panel discussion between Josef Beuys and Bense also served as fodder for art historians wary of technology and its impact on art and humanity. In the discussion, Beuys championed "human science," while Bense looked toward posthumans merging with machines into "technical being."[75] Bense had a huge impact in other quarters though: the Japanese philosopher Hiroshi Kawano was so inspired by Bense's writings that he learned how to program in order to implement information theory, becoming one of the first computer artists in the mid-1960s.[76] And the language of Bense's and Moles's information aesthetics permeates Flusser's writings, which describe technical images in terms of their programming and information value or redundancy; the artist's role as working against the limitations of the camera apparatus; and technology and algorithms serving as new models for creativity, with "elite" objects being replaced by more democratic forms of visual culture.

In April 1966, Flusser sent one of two letters to Bense, hoping to meet him when he traveled to Europe. "I am friends with Guimarães Rosa," Flusser wrote. "Maybe my name is not completely unknown to you. I have translated two poems of Haroldo de Campos into German."[77] Flusser sent another letter to Bense in June 1966, but he never heard back.[78]

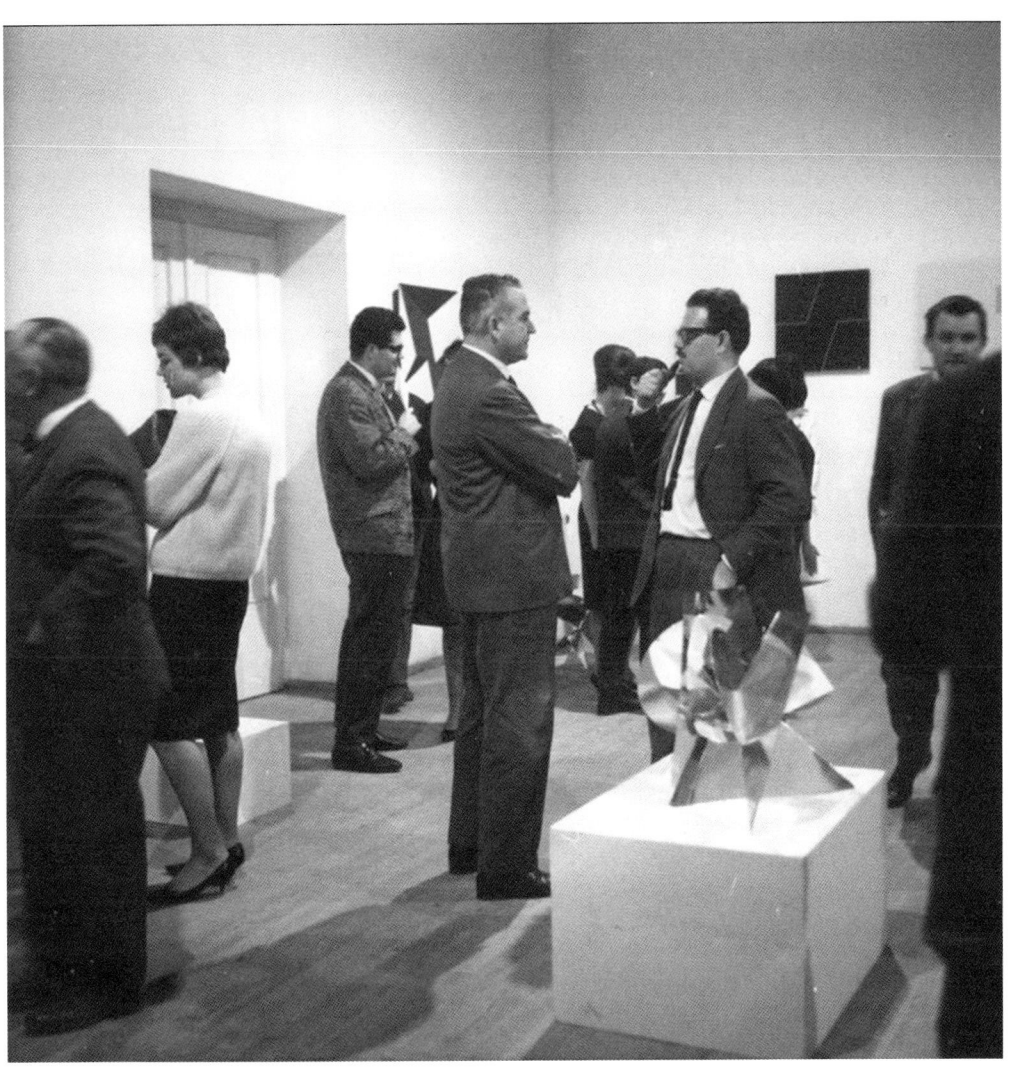

Figure 1.22
Max Bense (left) and Haroldo de Campos (right) at Lygia Clark's exhibition at the
Studiengalerie, Technical University of Stuttgart, 1964. Casa das Rosas, Centro de
Referência Haroldo de Campos, São Paulo.

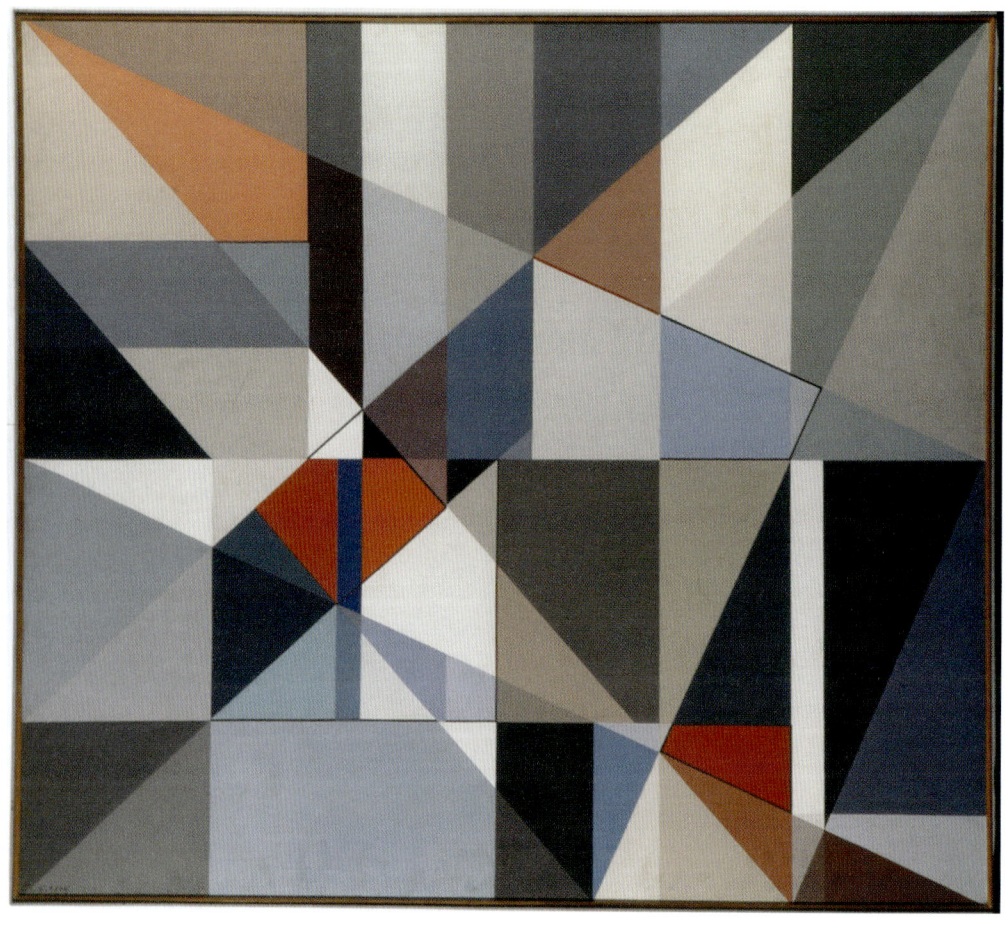

Figure 1.23
Samson Flexor, *Geométrico grande*, 1954. Oil on canvas, 160.5 × 179.5 cm. MAC USP Collection
[Museu de Arte Contemporânea da USP Collection, São Paulo, Brazil].

Mira Schendel and Samson Flexor

Ultimately, Flusser's closest affiliations in Brazil were with two artists who weren't aligned with any particular movements but had a huge impact on his thinking: Samson Flexor (1907–1971), the painter who started the first abstract painting workshop in Brazil; and Mira Schendel (1919–1988), a Swiss-born artist who created an idiosyncratic body of work that rigorously engaged both abstraction and language.[79] Flusser dedicated sections in his autobiography *Groundless* to each of these artists, and he wrote a memorial essay on the occasion of a retrospective of Flexor's work.[80]

Flexor was raised in Moldova and trained in Paris, absorbing theories and approaches of abstract painters like Wassily Kandinsky, Piet Mondrian, and Robert Delaunay. He participated in the French Resistance during World War II and moved to Brazil in 1948, committing himself to abstraction as a revolutionary and utopian form. His Atelier-Abstração, founded in 1951, exhibited the work of his peers and trained adults and children in the creation of abstract art with the idea of liberating people from old ideas and realizing new ones in pictorial form.

In addition to their conversations on the patio at Flusser's house in São Paulo, in the 1960s Flexor painted a cubist-style portrait of Flusser, as well as a series of "monsters" that resemble Rorschach blots. The "monsters" were made in response to Flusser's *The History of the Devil* (1965), a narrative of progress inspired by Goethe's *Faust* in which "the Devil is a criminal in order to be an artist, and is an artist in order to be a criminal."[81] (Small ink-and-watercolor versions of the large canvases of these works hang on the walls of the Flusser Archive in Berlin today.) Like Jean Dubuffet's figures, or Francis Bacon's painting, which crystallized philosophical existentialism for many viewers, Flexor's monsters had a huge impact on Flusser. He wrote, "the results were colossal monuments to Nothingness; monsters at the same time anthropomorphic, zoomorphic, and geomorphic, with holes dug out of their entrails, floating in subtle colors above a white background and casting plastic shadows when light was shed upon them. They remain terrifying and beautiful, like death and the human condition."[82]

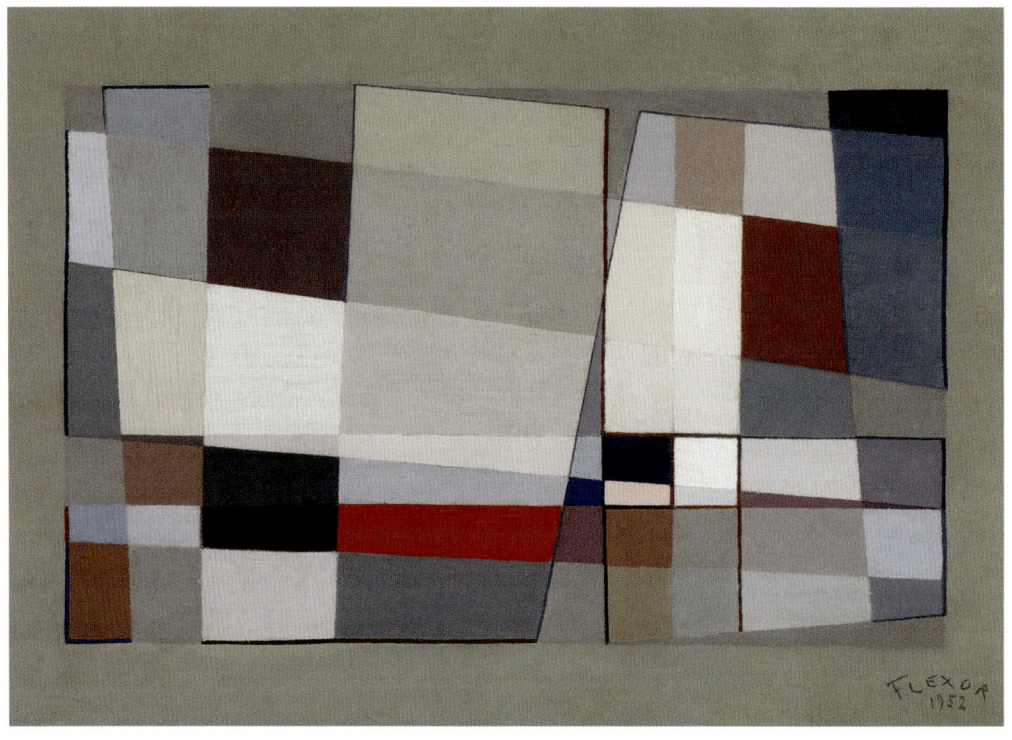

Figure 1.24
Samson Flexor, *Geométrico I*, 1952. Oil on canvas, 13⅛ × 18¼ in. (33.3 × 46.4 cm). The Museum of Fine Arts, Houston, The Adolpho Leirner Collection of Brazilian Constructive Art, museum purchase funded by the Caroline Wiess Law Foundation, 2005.1002 © André Victor Flexor. Photograph © The Museum of Fine Arts, Houston; Thomas R. DuBrock.

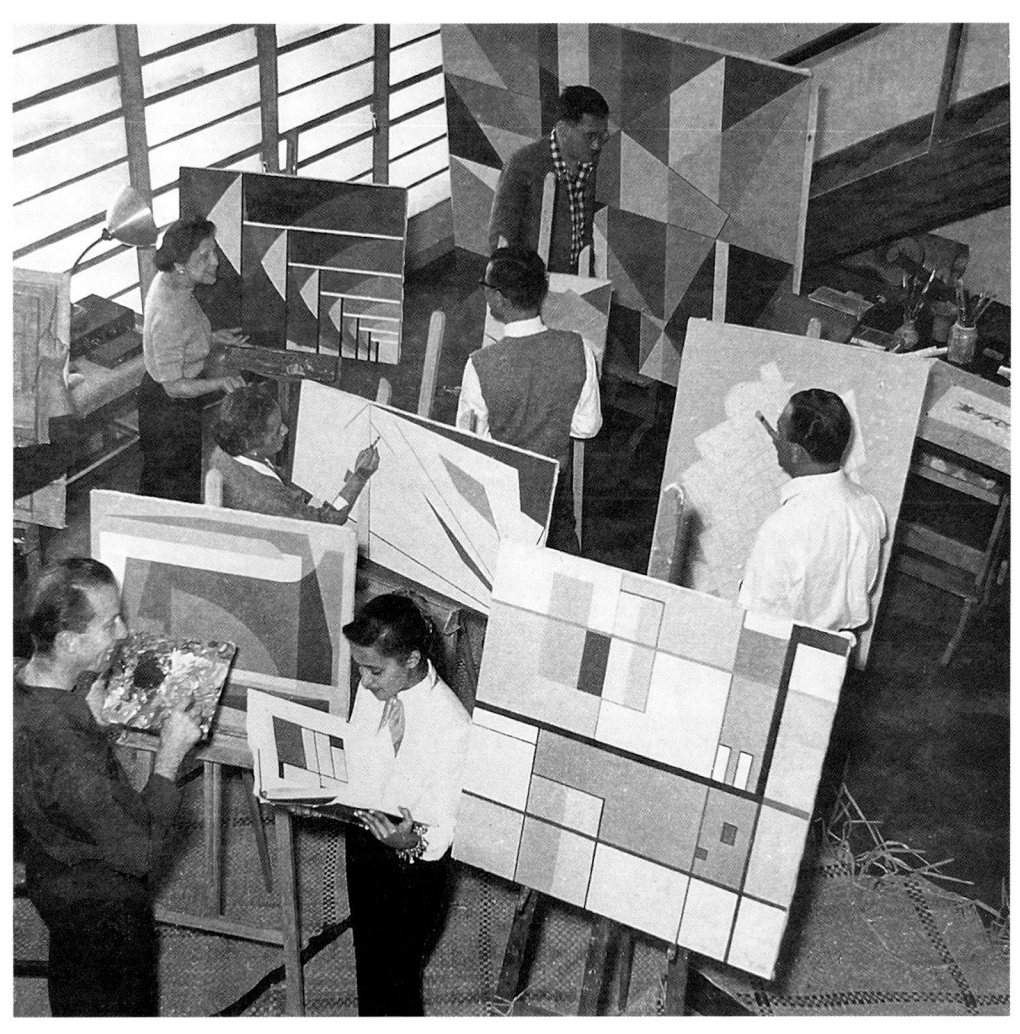

Figure 1.25
Samson Flexor's Atelier-Abstração, 1951. Archive of Jacques Douchez.
Photo: Jacques Douchez.

Flusser's dialogue with Schendel emerged in a different fashion. Born Myrrah Dagmar Dub in Zurich, Schendel spent her childhood in Italy with her mother and stepfather. She studied philosophy in Milan before being stripped of her Italian citizenship for being Jewish. After living in Bulgaria and Sarajevo during the war, Schendel migrated to Brazil, where she met Knut Schendel, a German bookseller, through whom she met Flusser and became part of that intellectual circle. Schendel began her artistic career painting dark still life canvases in the vein of Giorgio Morandi. By the early 1960s, she was making two-dimensional works in which letters, numbers, and symbols were arranged to resemble ancient hieroglyphs, math equations, or computer code. Although unaffiliated with major movements—for instance, as a signatory of the many manifestos produced in Brazil in the 1950s and 1960s—she was regularly included in the São Paulo Biennial, starting with the first edition in 1951. She was friendly with Haroldo de Campos, who wrote a poem for the catalogue of her exhibition at the Museu do Arte Moderna do Rio de Janeiro in May 1966 and introduced her to Max Bense, who exhibited her work in Stuttgart and dedicated an issue of *rot* to her graphic works.[83]

Bense's essay on Schendel includes some obvious kernels of Flusser's later thinking on writing, linearity, and gestures: "A letter performs as a point; a chain of letters, as a line; and several letter-lines define surfaces, outlining or unfurling them into planes," he wrote. Instead of linear text, Bense noted, Schendel's figures were scattered and "vehement, made by a hand featuring engagement and disengagement as it moves to and fro, guided only by the eye and by the impulse of what was perceived."[84] This approach also manifested in works like *Graphic Objects* (1967), exhibited in the Thirty-fourth Venice Biennale in 1968, where she represented Brazil along with Lygia Clark, Farnese de Andrade, and Letycia Quadros. The work includes a poem by Bense typed onto rice paper, so it can be read or viewed from both sides.

Schendel designed the cover for Flusser's first book, *Language and Reality* (1963); in many ways, the design leaps ahead of Flusser's own thinking about language by dissolving writing into jagged, gestural marks. She had discovered a method in which the artificiality of language is highlighted, transcending its own culturally imposed structures, essentially beating language philosophy at its own game. Flusser wrote about Schendel's work several times,

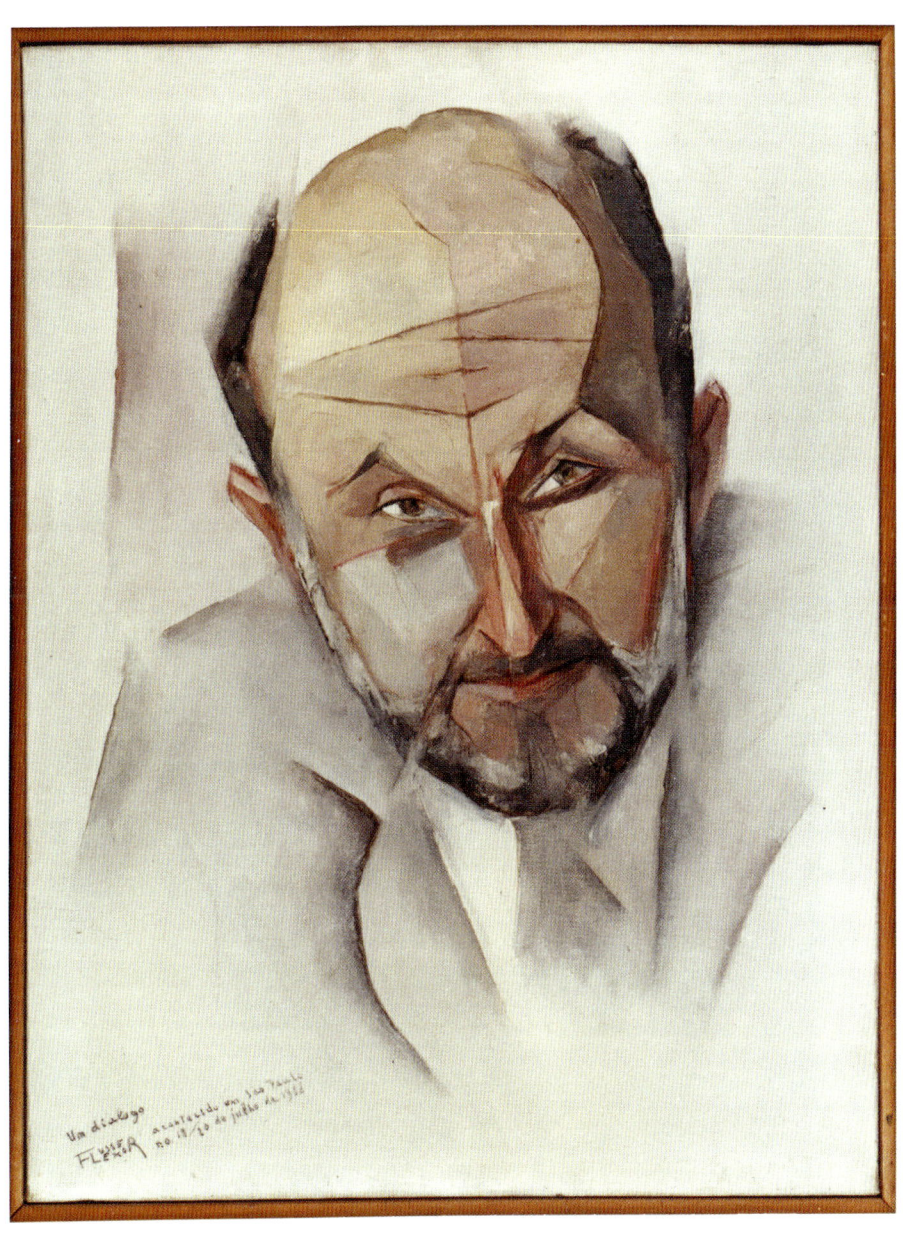

Figure 1.26
Samson Flexor, *Portrait of Vilém Flusser*, 1968. Watercolor. Vilém Flusser Archive, Berlin.
Inscribed, "um dialogo" (a dialogue).

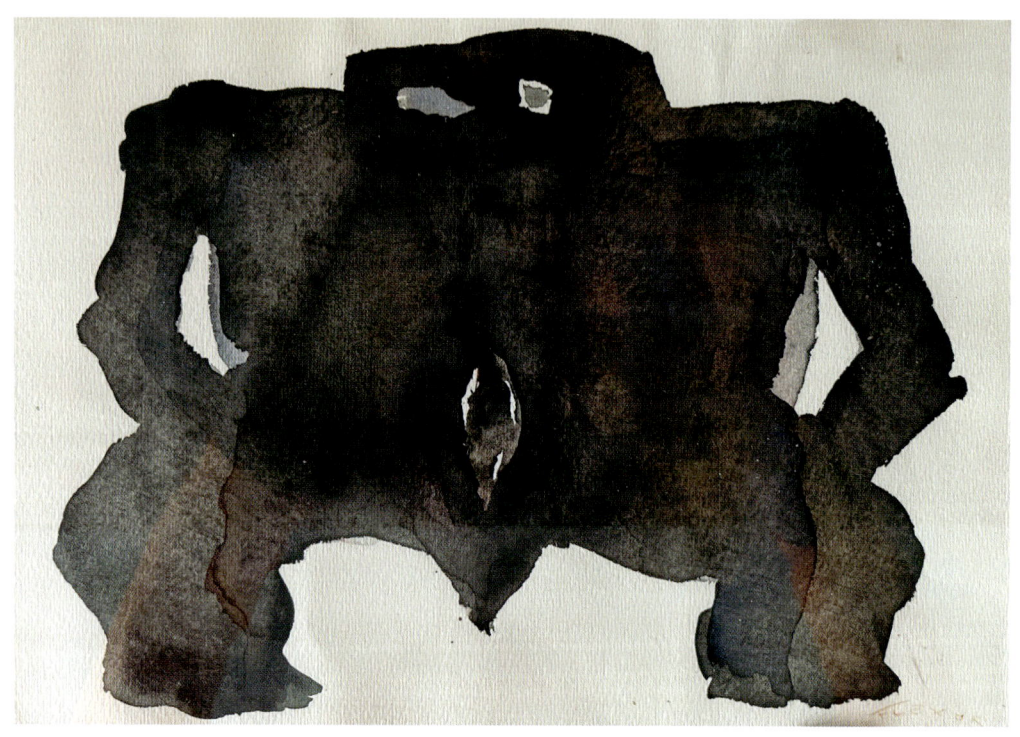

Figure 1.27
Samson Flexor, *Monster*, 1969. Ink and watercolor on paper with the inscription, "For my dear friends Vilhelm & Edith and children, this votive and, who knows, protective monster. With our best wishes for good and prosperity, Flexor assisted by his Margot." Vilém Flusser Archive, Berlin.

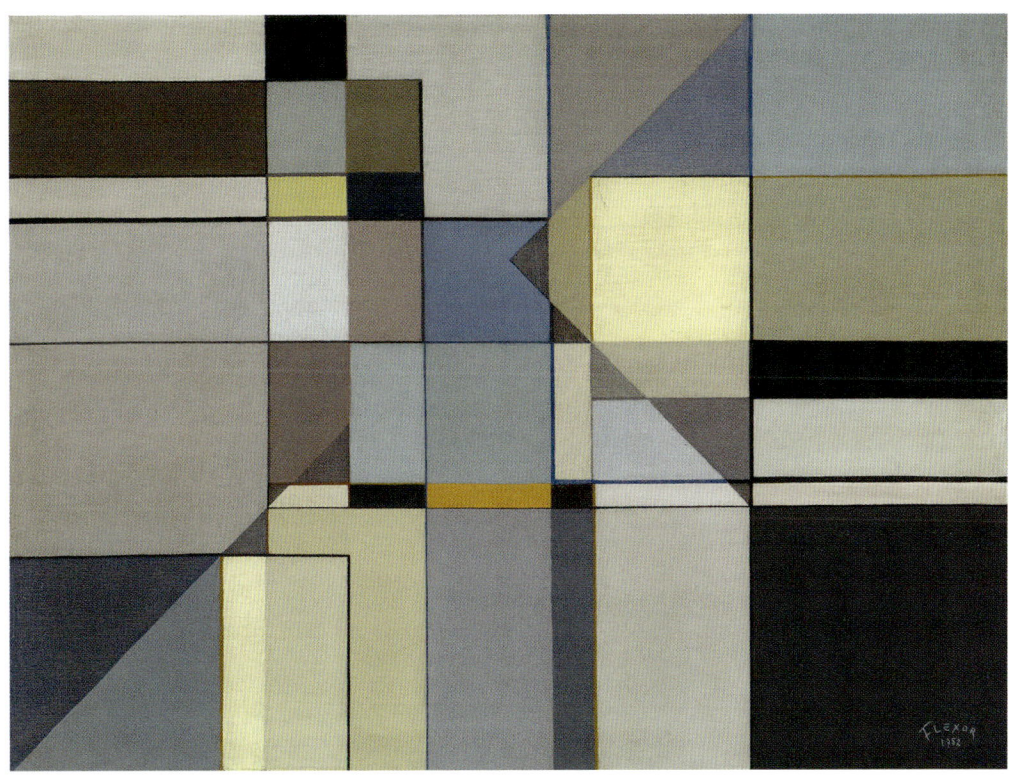

Figure 1.28
Samson Flexor, *Geométrico II*, 1952. Oil on canvas, 23⅝ × 32 in. (59.9 × 81.3 cm). The Museum of Fine Arts, Houston, The Adolpho Leirner Collection of Brazilian Constructive Art, museum purchase funded by the Caroline Wiess Law Foundation, 2005.1003 © André Victor Flexor. Photograph © The Museum of Fine Arts, Houston; Thomas R. DuBrock.

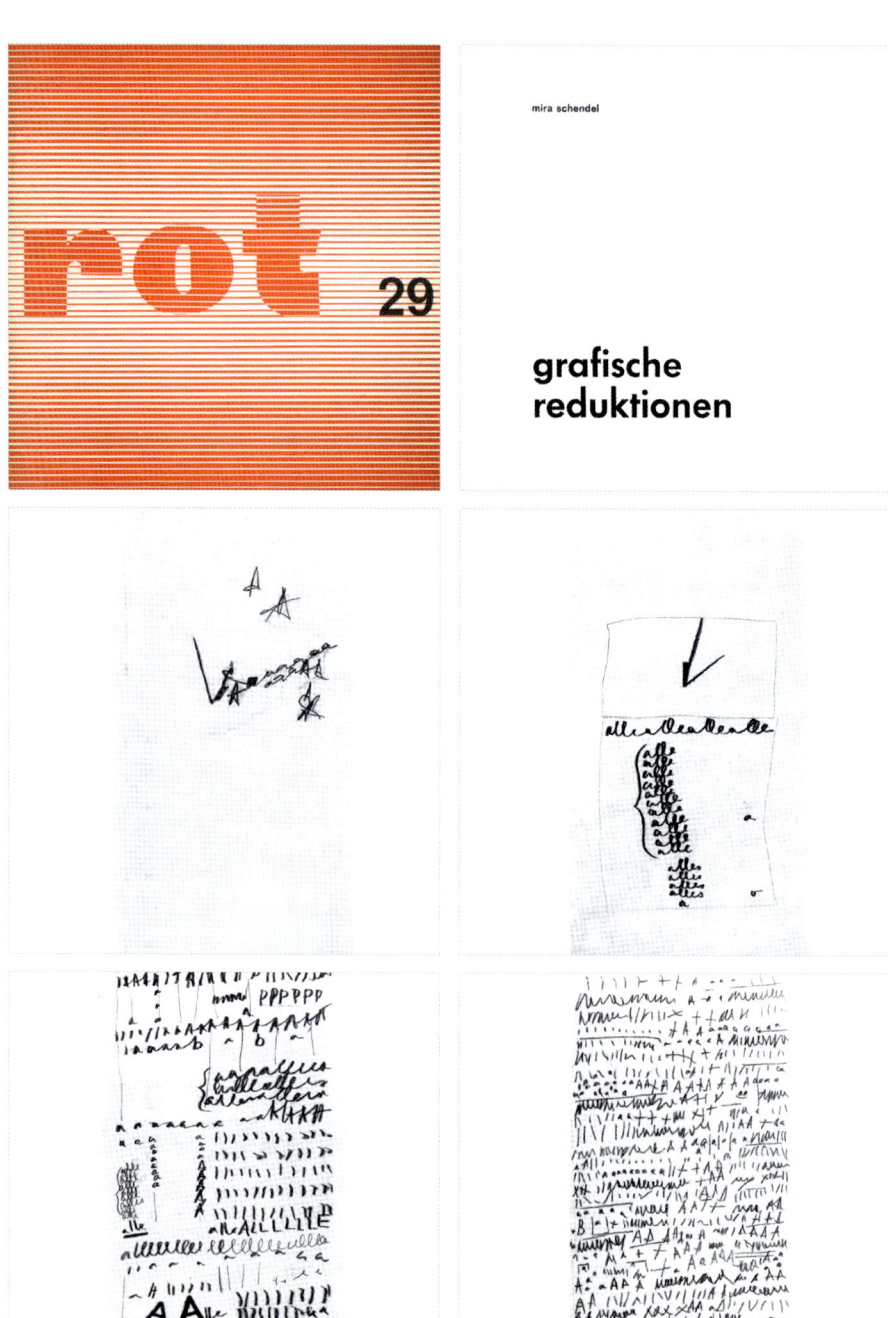

Figures 1.29–34
"Mira Schendel: Grafische Reduktionen" (Mira Schendel: Graphical reductions). *rot 29,*
special issue, published by Max Bense and Elisabeth Walther, 1967. Monotypes, with a
cover designed by Walter Faigle and a foreword by Haroldo de Campos. ZKM | Center for
Art and Media Karlsruhe and the Estates of Elisabeth Walther-Bense and Mira Schendel.

approaching it as a philosopher rather than a critic or an art historian.[85] In 1966, he wrote that Schendel's objects beg the following questions:

> What is language? What is information? What is meaning? How does a letter, or a line, or a word become meaningful? How does it arise from the void of the unutterable and how does it establish itself as a structure? Can it be transformed into new structures, two-dimensional, or three- dimensional, or even *n*-dimensional? And does such an amplification, if possible, give new meaning to the letter, the line, the word? Is it possible to learn to think, not in sentences, but in new structures of language? And what meaning have such thoughts, if any? Mira Schendel's creations are attempts to answer such questions.[86]

In a spectacular 1967 *O Estado de São Paulo* newspaper layout that sandwiches Flusser's text between two columns of Schendel's graphic marks, Flusser revisits these queries, formulating some answers around the "pious and blasphemous opacity" of her works and their approach to language: "Mira's writings are not texts. They don't say anything, which is why they cannot be read as representing anything. They are pre-texts. They are like a text before it is text. They talk among themselves. They do not quite represent anything—although they almost do."[87] The graphic marks altered reading and looking, writing and drawing. They upended language and perception.

Together, Flusser and Schendel studied the philosophy of Jean Gebser (1905–1973), a proto-New Age philosopher whose ideas would play an important role in Flusser's technical image writings.[88] Schendel was interested in Gebser's idea of *Diaphanität*— "transparency," or diaphanous consciousness—and her *Objetos gráficos* (Graphic objects), mounted in windows or suspended in the middle of rooms, reflected this, as well as new approaches to language. By encasing these works in clear acrylic, Schendel argued that it allowed for a "circular reading" but also highlighted the "false transparency of explained meanings, not the clear, flat transparency of glass, but the mysterious transparency of the clarification of problems."[89] Writing about Schendel's work, Flusser argued: "The world is becoming transparent—not in the sense that we can no longer see anything, but in the sense that now

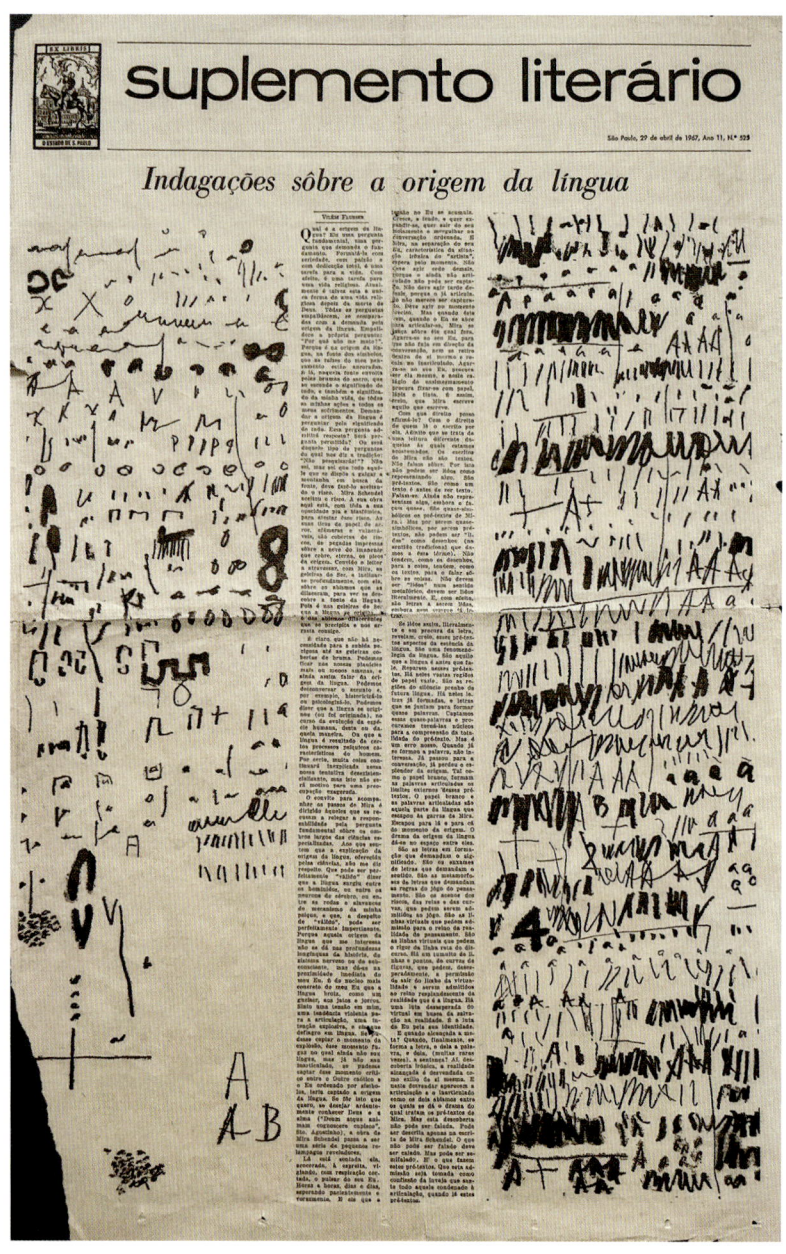

Figure 1.35
Vilém Flusser and Mira Schendel, "Indagações sobre a origem da língua" (Inquiries into the origin of language), with drawings by Schendel in *O Estado de São Paulo, Suplemento Literário*, April 29, 1967, 1. Courtesy O Estado de São Paulo, Estate of Mira Schendel, and Vilém Flusser Archive, Berlin.

we see transparent structures, which allow us to see other transparent structures, around us in all directions, including inside. We are becoming transparent to ourselves. Every object begins to dissolve"—which changes existence, since where there is no object, there is no subject.[90]

Transparency affected not just subject and object, but space and time. In a 1969 essay in *O Estado de São Paulo* about Schendel's work, Flusser wrote: "I suggest that transparency is a temporalization of space by which space evaporates and time seems to disappear, both giving way to an interpenetration of structures."[91] Schendel's art, for him, accomplished a "concrete presence of the abstract concepts, 'time' and 'space.'" However, for Flusser, the important concept in Gebser's writing that would make its way into his technical image texts was the idea of mutations in the structures of human consciousness over history: the way that knowing reality changes in different periods. Gebser's four *Bewußtseinsmutationen*, or mutations of consciousness, occupying five different dimensions (*Bewußtseinsstrukturen*), moving from zero to the fourth dimension, can be detected both in Flusser's phenomenological evolution of technology (hands, tools, machines, robots, as he laid out in his object and design writings in the 1970s and 1980s) and in *Into the Universe of Technical Images*, where codes evolve— but in typically Flusserian fashion, in reverse: from the fourth to zero dimensionality. The title of Flusser's 1970s communications-theory manuscript "Mutations in Human Relations," sections of which were published posthumously in *Kommunikologie* (and more recently as *Communicology*), obviously echoes Gebser, as well as Pjotr D. Ouspensky's *Tertium Organum*, which Flusser had read in the early 1950s.[92] ("However," Flusser wrote, "I capitulated that some systems function better than others: to go to the Moon, it is more intelligent to position ourselves according to Einstein's equations than to Anthroposophy.")[93] Flusser's use of the term "magic" in his technical image writings, which will be discussed later, can also be traced to Gebser, who pointed out the linguistic links between "magic" and "techné" in ancient thought.

Transparency takes on another hue, though: Flusser and Schendel were both working within the increasingly restricted sphere of Brazil under a military dictatorship. The Concrete artists and poets of the 1950s had approached constructivism and language in a progressive, even utopian manner, but these conditions were now contested.[94] Language was being used in new

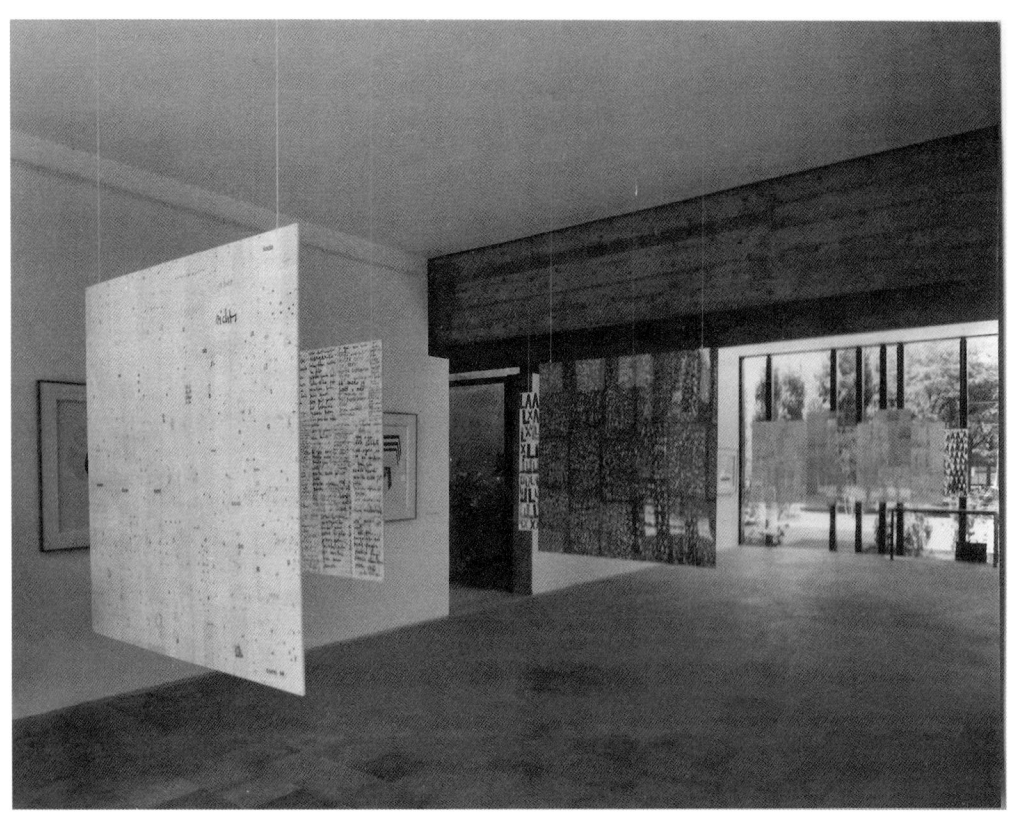

Figure 1.36
Mira Schendel, *Objetos gráficos* (Graphic objects), in the Brazilian Pavilion, Thirty-fourth
Venice Biennale, 1968. Estate of Mira Schendel.

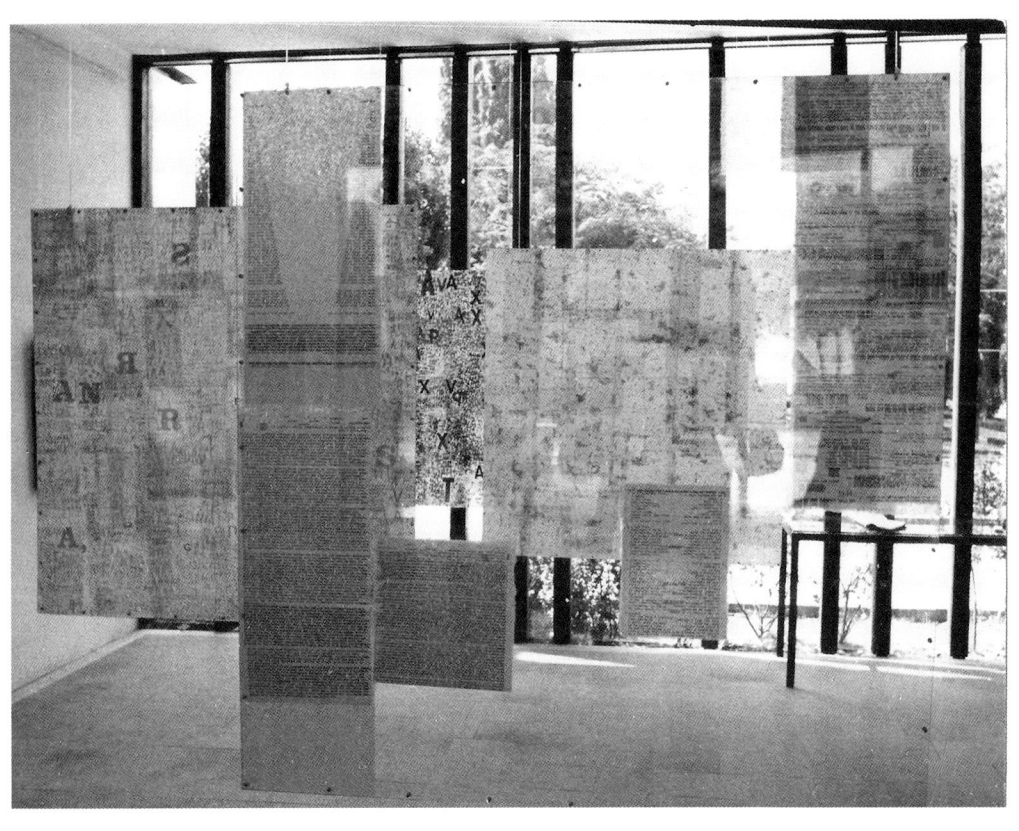

Figure 1.37
Mira Schendel, *Objetos gráficos* (Graphic objects), in the Brazilian Pavilion, Thirty-fourth
Venice Biennale, 1968. Estate of Mira Schendel.

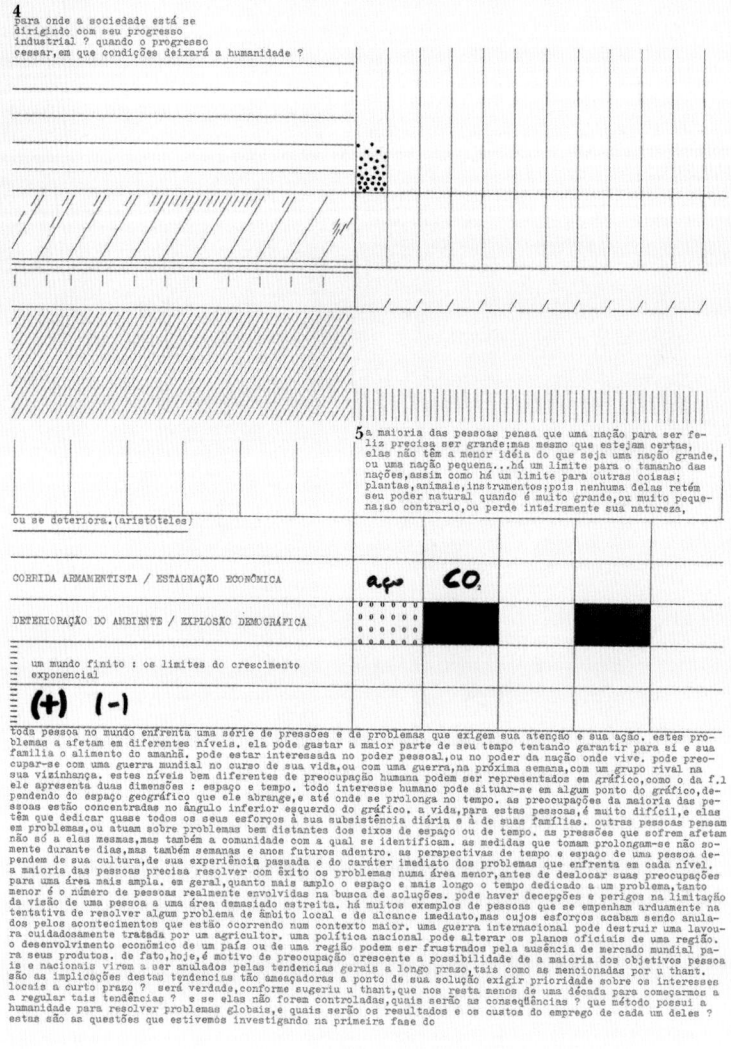

Figure 1.38
Mira Schendel, *Untitled*, from the *Datiloscritos* (Typed writing) series, 1974. Typewriting, ink, and transfer type on paper, 19¾ × 14¼ in. (50.2 × 36.2 cm). Committee on Drawings Funds.
© The Museum of Modern Art/Licensed by SCALA/Art Resource, NY.

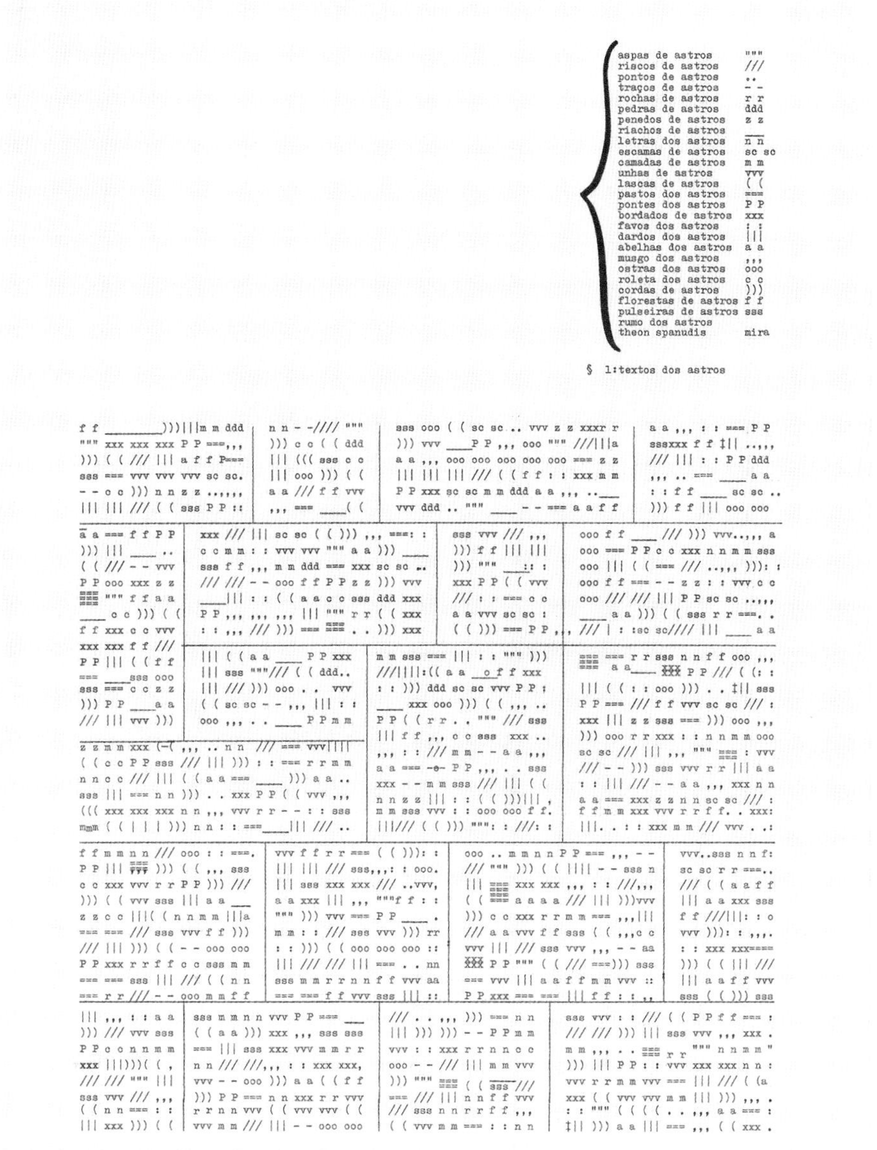

aspas de astros   """
riscos de astros   ///
pontos de astros   ..
traços de astros   - -
rochas de astros   r r
pedras de astros   ddd
penedos de astros   z z
riachos de astros
letras dos astros   n n
escamas de astros   sc sc
camadas de astros   m m
unhas de astros   vvv
lascas de astros   ((
pastos dos astros   ===
pontes dos astros   P P
bordados de astros   xxx
favos dos astros |¦|
dardos dos astros   ¦¦¦
abelhas dos astros   a a
musgo dos astros   ,,,
ostras dos astros   ooo
roleta dos astros   c c
cordas de astros   )))
florestas de astros   f f
pulseiras de astros   sss
rumo dos astros
theon spanudis   mira

§ 1:textos dos astros

Figure 1.39
Mira Schendel, *Untitled*, from the *Datiloscritos* (Typed writing) series, c. 1970s. Typewriting and ink on paper, 19¾ × 14¼ in. (50.2 × 36.2 cm). Committee on Drawings Funds. © The Museum of Modern Art/Licensed by SCALA/Art Resource, NY.

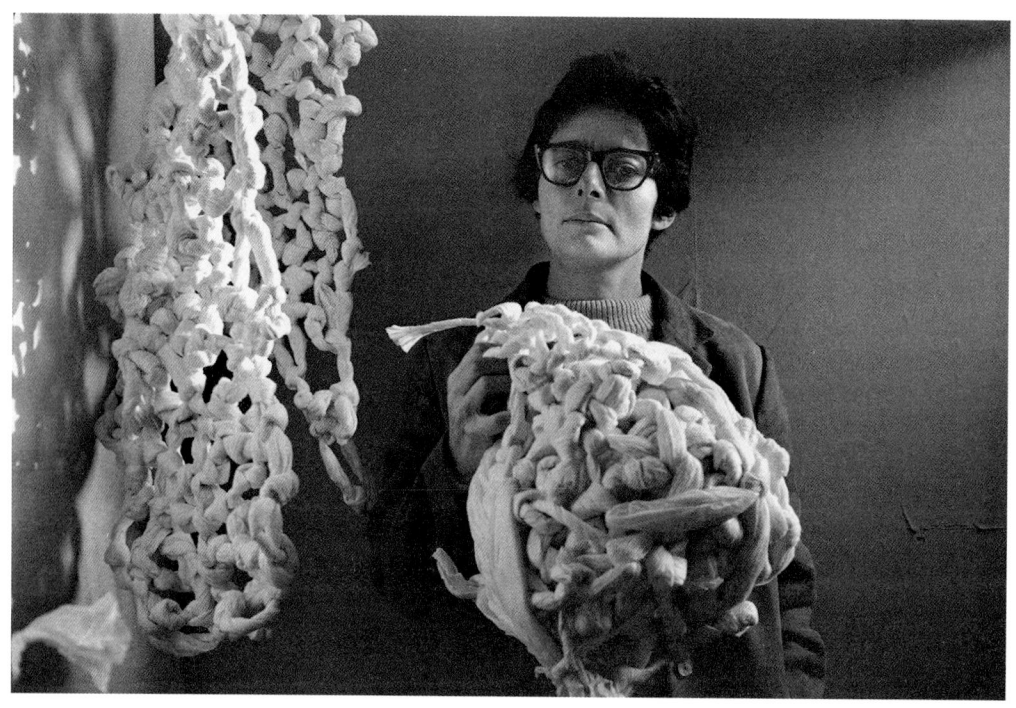

Figure 1.40
Mira Schendel with *Droguinhas*, at Signals, London, 1966. Photo: © Clay Perry, England
& Co., London. Made as ephemeral sculptures, the pieces have the title *Droguinhas* (little
drugs), from the Brazilian slang word meaning "little nothings" or something valueless.

ways—but also against its users. And where Concrete art often celebrated a nationalist progressive optimism and order, Schendel's works nakedly embraced—or exposed—uncertainty (Flusser's "doubt"), communicational "noise," and chaos. By the time Flusser moved back to Europe in the early 1970s, his relationship with Schendel was fraught—largely given his blunt and often tactless approach to describing his relationships with artists and thinkers in the "Dialogues" section in *Groundless*. In 1981, he attempted to reignite their conversation by writing to Schendel to describe a recent trip to Brazil and his impressions: "you in Brazil seem to live on an iceberg that is melting, and that is being dragged in the opposite direction of Europe by a current that no one is aware of . . . the artificial sky, yellowish like Louis Bec's sulfur [the sculptures of his new best friend], under which you are living, seems to me symptomatic of your situation: the exalted hell. The world turned upside down." For Flusser, it was no longer "*Umbruch* [radical transformation], but *Zusammenbruch* [collapse]. Or at least *Einbruch* [burglary/collapse] in the sense of 'assault,' with everyone individually against each other. What impressed me the most was that you are isolated from each other and yet you are all experiencing the same process of society disintegrating." Flusser longed to resume their lively exchange: "nothing would make me happier than the possibility of sharing my ideas and projects with you."[95] However, their period of intense dialogue was over, and Flusser by then had left Brazil.

Screen 2 *Cybernetic Feedback
and Television Screens*

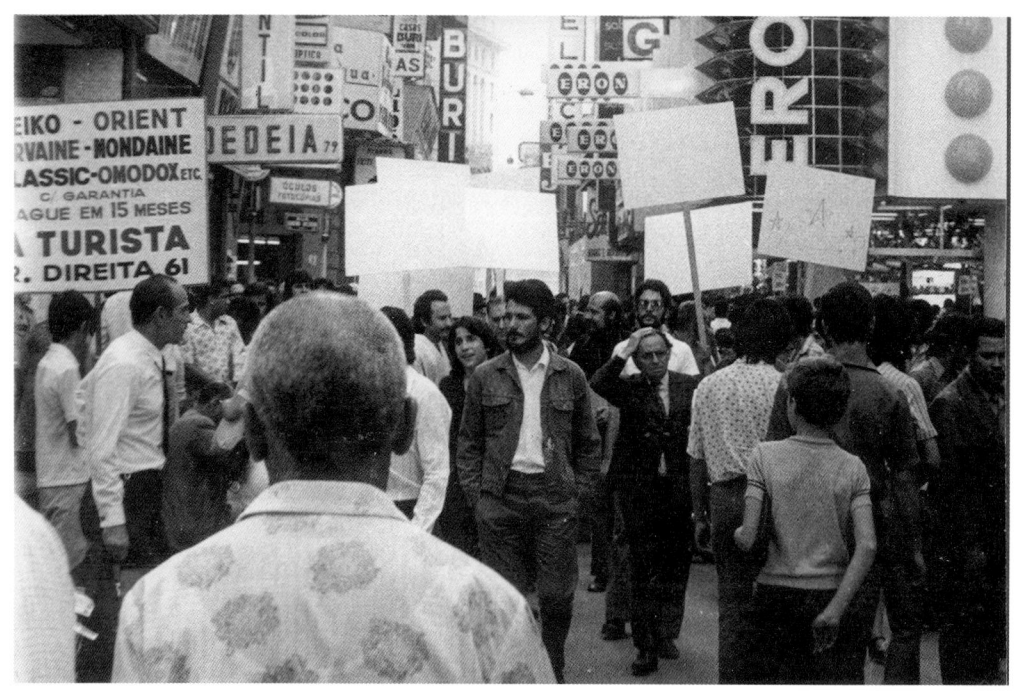

Figure 2.1
Fred Forest, *The City Invaded by Blank Space*, Twelfth São Paulo Biennial, 1973. © 2024 Artists
Rights Society (ARS), New York / ADAGP, Paris.

Flusser arrived in Brazil at a critical moment: during the reign of Getúlio Vargas, who rose to power after the Revolution of 1930 and created a new type of state that promoted industrialization and gave the military a central role.[1] Vargas remained in power for fifteen years. Reelected president by a popular vote in 1950, his term ended in 1954 when, on the verge of a second fall from power, he committed suicide. Juscelino Kubitschek's succeeding five-year administration was marked by the official motto "Fifty years in five," championing accelerated industrial and structural development. Brasília was built during this time, and an automotive industry was installed. Media and communications underwent a tectonic shift with more people owning televisions, due largely to extended personal credit. TV Globo became the national network, promoting "Brazil—a Great Power."

The nation was faltering, though. In 1961, the International Monetary Fund and Brazil's European and US creditors rescheduled its debt and the United States offered more aid to make sure the largest country in Latin America didn't fall into communism. Protest movements were on the rise, the result of instability caused by urban growth, increased migration, and discontent among rural populations.[2] After Fidel Castro came to power in Cuba, guerrilla warfare became a concern within the Brazilian military, which took control in April 1964. The notorious *Atos Institucionais*

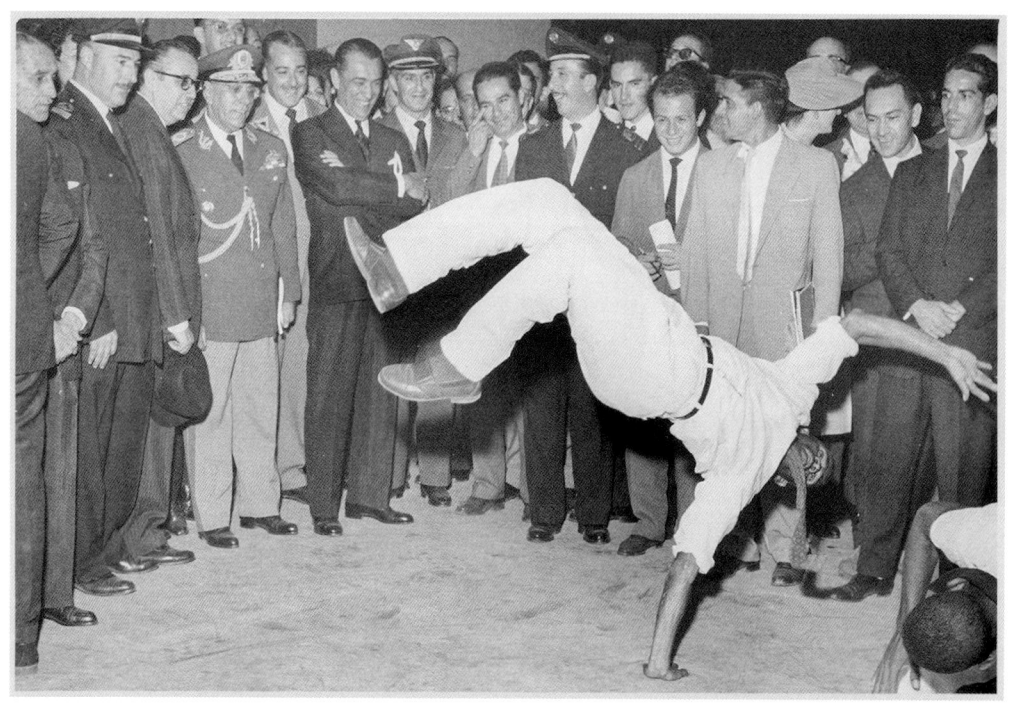

Figure 2.2
Capoeirista performs for President Juscelino Kubitschek and military personnel at the
Fifth São Paulo Biennial, 1959. Photograph: Athayde de Barros.

(Institutional Acts), or AIs, were instituted: citizens retained the right of habeas corpus and the press was left relatively untouched, but violent repression was carried out in the countryside and politically active students were targeted.

Flusser's affiliations were complicated. He eschewed both Marxism and Zionism, mostly because they seemed problematic during his early years in the melting pot of Prague. To embrace Zionism in this climate was to adopt the nationalist Nazi model—Jews as separate from other Europeans—which Prague (for Flusser, at least) had theoretically overcome in the early twentieth century. Marxism was also complicated. Flusser flirted with it when he was young, because he "believed that Marxism represented a system in which all religious problems (and especially the problem of existential engagement) were resolved," but later considered this "'Parlor Marxism'" that "the real Marxists derided."[3] São Paulo represented another melting pot—a very different one—and some of Flusser's associations were complicated. Miguel Reale, cofounder of the Brazilian Institute of Philosophy, was a fascist in the 1920s and a central figure in the Ação Itegralista Brasileira (Brazilian Integralists) who played a key role in the 1964 coup.[4] A legal scholar, Reale was involved in reviewing the Brazilian Constitution in the late 1960s and consolidating power under the military—but he had also been a key supporter of Flusser, who, remember, had no college degree and yet was published in Reale's philosophical journal. Flusser's early career as a philosopher was, in many ways, legitimized by Reale.

By the early 1960s, Vilém and Edith Flusser's house in São Paulo had become a gathering place for students, artists, scientists, and friends to think about new art and perceptions of the world. After the 1964 *coup d'etat*, Flusser would not have been wrong to think a renaissance might erupt in Brazil because, as other writers have noted, the new regime initially tolerated leftist subculture.[5] In 1970, the Viennese-born Brazilian literary critic Roberto Schwarz wrote: "Despite the existence of a right-wing dictatorship, the cultural hegemony of the left is virtually complete. This can be seen in the bookshops of São Paulo and Rio, which are full of Marxist literature; in incredibly festive and feverish theatrical premieres, threatened by the occasional police raid; in the activities of the student movement or the declarations of progressive priests. In other words, at the very altars of bourgeois culture, it is the left which dictates the tone."[6] Tropicalismo, a movement that started in São Paulo in popular music and branched out to film, theater, the visual arts, and literature, emblematized this. Led by Caetano Veloso and Gilberto Gil, two young musicians from Bahia, Tropicalismo merged Brazilian and African rhythm and street carnival aesthetics with British and American pop and psychedelic rock, breaking from bossa nova, which was associated with the middle class who frequented jazz clubs and had been exposed to music and movies from the United States. Technology was celebrated— Veloso and Gil used electric instruments—and song lyrics underscored the current historical contradictions: violence and poverty versus the national mythology of Brazil as a tropical paradise.[7] The album *Tropicália: ou Panis et Circencis* (1968) served as the movement's manifesto—a statement borrowing Oswald de Andrade's Antropofagia, but also resisting the military government.[8]

However, larger opposition to the military government began to assert itself. The death of Che Guevara in Bolivia on October 9, 1967, transformed the Argentine revolutionary into a hero for young people. In March 1968, demonstrations in Brazil were set off by the murder of a student by the Brazilian military police. In June 1968, the *Passeata dos 100,000* (Protest march of the hundred thousand) included students, clergy, and middle-class residents of Rio de Janeiro.[9] On December 13, 1968, AI-5 was passed, which closed congress. Unlike the earlier acts, AI-5 had no expiration date.[10] Government targets shifted to include middle- and upperclass citizens. Flusser's commentaries in his "Posto Zero" (Ground Zero) column—in Portuguese, "taking no position"—established in 1972 in the *Fôlha de São Paulo* newspaper, put him in a prominent and problematic position. How to speak in a dangerous climate of censorship? He had to write in code. One column served as a commentary on traffic problems in São Paulo, with Flusser offering a number of proposals, including opening the way to the "left," making a direct connection between the Paradise and Freedom districts, and erecting a Coca-Cola Viaduct—a reference, of course, to US interference in Brazilian politics that carried the echoes of Décio Pignatari's famous Concrete poem "Beba Coca Cola" (1957).[11] Another "Posto Zero" column analyzed the game of chess, with its light and dark squares—"the very image of the Enlightenment"— and rules which allow some pieces to move only laterally or diagonally.[12] Flusser concluded that, unless we understand the essence of such games, we function as mere pawns.

After AI-5 was passed on December 1968, there was a general crackdown on culture: most visibly, Gilberto Gil and Caetano Veloso

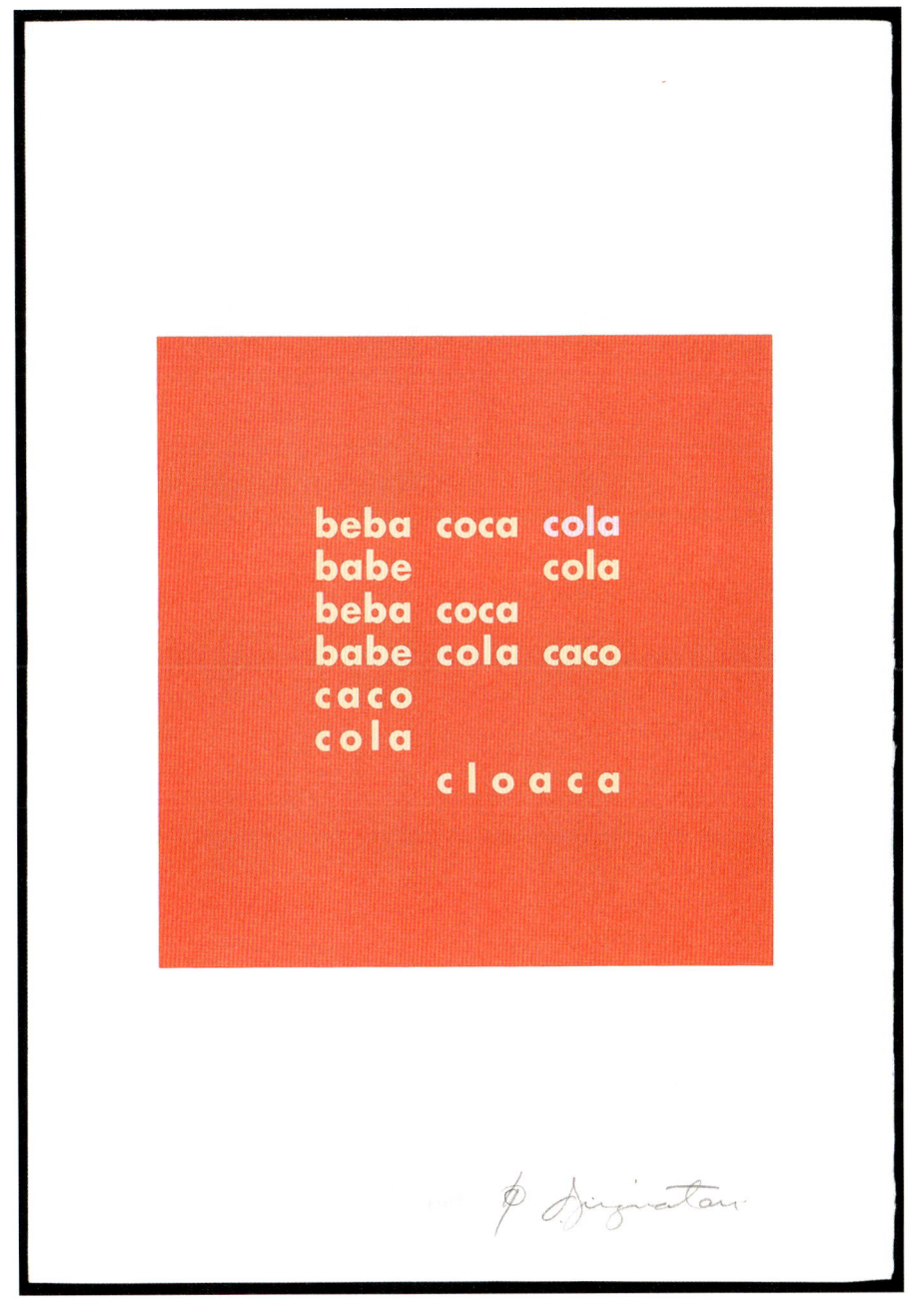

Figure 2.3
Décio Pignatari, *Beba Coca-Cola* (Drink Coca Cola), 1991. Silkscreen on paper. Courtesy of Getty Research Institute, Los Angeles, and the Estate of Décio Pignatari.

were arrested in São Paulo, held for fifty-seven days without explanation, and later exiled to London.[13] The governments of Artur da Costa e Silva (1967–1969) and Emílio Garrastazu Médici (1969–1974) brought an acceleration of censorship, arbitrary arrest, and torture. Visual artists like Lygia Clark and Hélio Oiticica had left the country, while Flusser's friend Mira Schendel remained. Flusser came to feel that Brazil was not a place where true freedom could be achieved because it is "subject to foreign manipulation."[14] He described this as a dark period, being a "teacher in a situation where one saw no way out. One knew it was necessary to guide the youth, but one did not know how."[15] Every day some of his students "disappeared."[16] Military personnel were entering the university to teach and Flusser described shaping his curriculum to avoid "snitches."[17]

Flusser managed to escape Brazil because of his involvement in the art world. Throughout the 1960s, he had written about the São Paulo Biennial, held in Ibirapuera Park, in a pavilion originally designed by a team of architects led by Oscar Niemeyer and Hélio Uchôa to showcase automobiles and farming equipment. In 1965, he described the exhibition as a populist, global phenomenon: "The governments of Ghana and Albania, or their equivalent, finance the transport of paintings, statues, artists, diplomats, and their respective wives, so that they can be admired in Ibirapuera," he wrote. "A dense network of correspondence is thrown over the globe to trap an impressive number of art critics, lecturers, and intellectuals in its meshes and dump them on São Paulo."[18] Flusser was prescient in seeing how biennials reflected a homogenization in globalized culture, with the same hotels, food, movies, paintings, and sculpture in Singapore as in Brazil. And yet he was optimistic that the Biennial might develop a set of new models, or as he wrote in his 1967 review of that year's Biennial, might serve as a productive and "amazing microcosm" of the world.[19] What is not said in the 1967 article—although hinted at—was the growing power of the authoritarian dictatorship: in the same Biennial, a box sculpture by Cybèle Varela that included a map of Brazil and an image of a military general was removed, as well as Quissak Junior's *Meditations on the National Flag*. Both artworks were destroyed, and Varela was questioned by the Division of Social and Political Police (DOPS).

By 1969, conditions in Brazil were impossible to ignore. Flusser used his space in *O Estado de São Paulo* to consider the Biennial through the etymology of words like "exposure" ("something previously hidden, placed in the open") and "exhibition," which he treated as if he were decrypting a cipher: "A quick analysis of the context reveals the following elements: (a) a public place, (b) an agent who places something, (c) an object placed, and (d) a client who encounters it," resulting in a structure that "is hierarchical and evaluative. The purpose of the place is the agent and the purpose of the agent is the client."[20] Flusser concluded that the Biennial was a "stubborn fact," orchestrated to demonstrate Brazil's competent modernism to an international clientele. What he did not mention in this article was the widely publicized international boycott of the Biennial occurring at that moment. The boycott was initiated in several quarters.[21] In Brazil, it was a response to repression: federal police had confiscated ten works of art at the Second Bienal da Bahia, a small exhibition in northeastern Brazil. Meanwhile, the French critic and curator Pierre Restany canceled an exhibition titled *Art and Technology* scheduled to run parallel to the 1969 São Paulo Biennial; it would have included works by César Baldaccini, Gyula Kosice, Piotr Kowalski, Julio Le Parc, Marta Minujin, Bernard Quentin, Martial Rayasse, Vassilakis Takis, and others. Eduard de Wilde, director of the Stedelijk Museum in Amsterdam, withdrew the Dutch delegation. Sweden, Greece, Belgium, Italy, Spain, and Mexico also withdrew, including seventy-three-year-old Mexican muralist David Alfaro Siqueiros, who had been invited to exhibit his mural *March of Humanity on Latin America*.[22] On June 16, 1969, a group of international artists and critics gathered at the Musée d'art moderne in Paris to listen to testimonies given by Brazilian artists describing violence, torture, and repression under the military dictatorship, and 321 artists and intellectuals signed a manifesto titled "Non à la Biennale" and voted to boycott the Biennial.[23]

The United States was another case. György Kepes, director of the Center for Advanced Visual Studies at MIT, was organizing a much-anticipated art and technology exhibition to be shown in São Paulo. Kepes was embroiled in protests at MIT about the complicity of that institution in the US "congressional-military-industrial-university complex," as one student organization called it. In April 1969, the German-born artist Hans Haacke wrote a strongly worded letter to Kepes outlining his concerns:

The American government is engaged in an immoral war in Vietnam and supports vigorously the fascist regimes in Brazil and other parts of the world. At this time, all exhibitions under the auspices of the American government are done to promote the image and the politics of this very government. It is a public relations operation no matter what the intentions of the organizers and participants are, and thanks to the tolerance of repressive governments, the energy of the artists is channeled to serve a policy that they rightfully despise. If they don't want to become involuntarily [sic] accomplices, they do not have another choice than to refuse to show their work in the national representations abroad.[24]

Haacke was not wrong. James Naylor Green writes that covert funding was channeled through the CIA to conservative Brazilian forces with an anti-left-wing agenda.[25] On July 14, in a joint press release with the Smithsonian, which had taken over sponsorship of the US delegation from the State Department, Kepes announced that nine of the twenty-three artists selected to participate in the exhibition had withdrawn.[26] Biennial organizers, assisted by Dr. Humbert Affonseca, a wealthy São Paulo businessman, and the Brazilian consul general in New York, tried to broker a last-minute deal with Leo Castelli to loan thirty-three engravings by Roy Lichtenstein and Jasper Johns and put these on view as the US exhibition. However, the United States was ultimately represented by only one artwork, by the sculptor Chryssa Vardea.

Not every Brazilian artist withdrew from the 1969 São Paulo Biennial. Flusser's friend Mira Schendel showed a work titled *Ondas paradas de probabilidade—Antigo Testamento, Livros dos Reis I, 19* (Still waves of probability—Old Testament, First Book of Kings 19), an installation of nylon threads hanging from the ceiling in the Biennial pavilion. 1 Kings 19 tells the story of the prophet Elijah on the run from the Israelites, who had killed all the other prophets: "I am the only one left," Elijah says in a conversation with God as he hides in a cave from King Ahab, "and now they are trying to kill me, too." God instructs Elijah to go back and enlist other warrior-prophets. Schendel's work might be read as an act of protest. She wrote to Jean Gebser about the Biennial boycott, "Perspectively, I agree with them. Aperspectively, however, I have to accept the invitation. Aperspectively, it has 'quantum value' that is also in the 'fore-ground.' Transparency."[27] In her journal, she called the work, with its delicate, transparent threads, the "whispering of the invisible."[28]

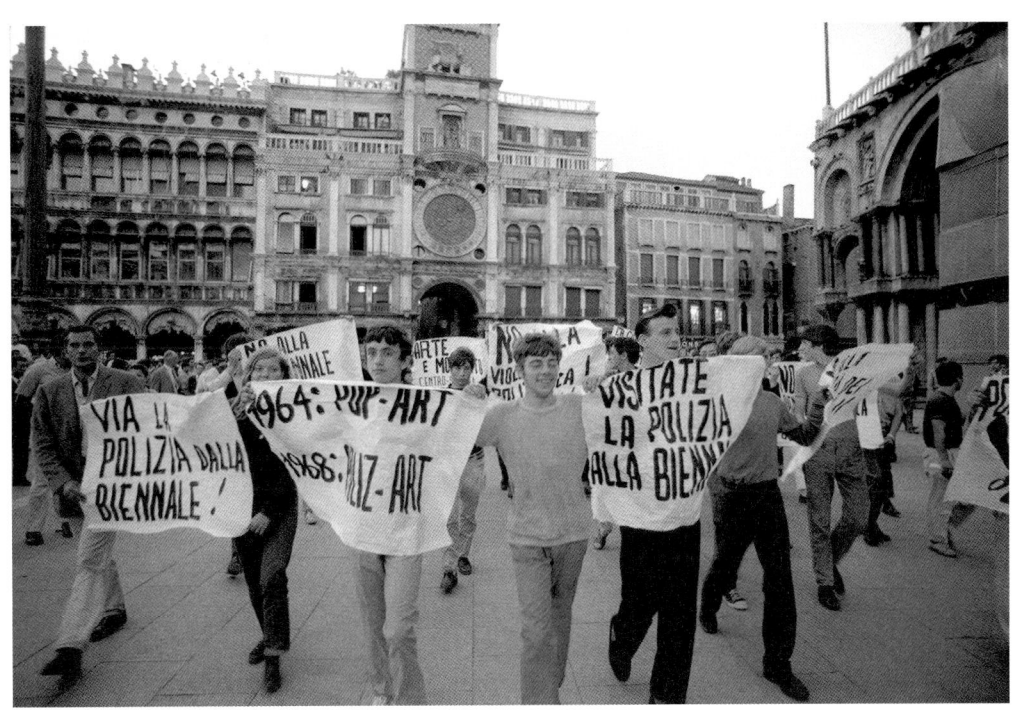

Figure 2.4
Ugo Mulas, *Student protests at the Venice Biennale*, 1968. Photo Ugo Mulas © Ugo Mulas Heirs.
All rights reserved.

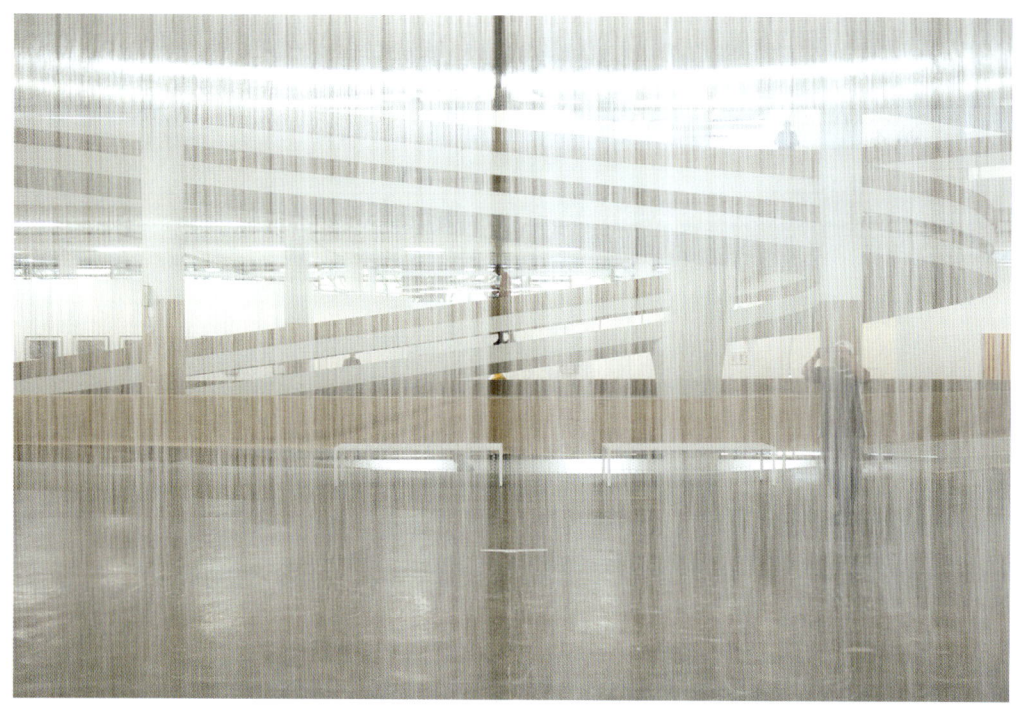

Figure 2.5
Mira Schendel, *Ondas paradas de probabilidade* (Still waves of probability) installation,
Thirtieth São Paulo Biennial, September 13, 2013. © Leo Eloy/Fundação Bienal de São
Paulo. There are no known photographs of the 1969 installation of this work.

Flusser entered the Biennial enterprise in a more prominent way at this moment. He had met Arnold Bode, curator of the first *documenta* in Kassel in 1955—an exhibition designed to put Germany "back in dialogue with the rest of the world after World War II."[29] Flusser corresponded with Bode in the mid-1960s about Brazilian culture and its relation to Europe.[30] By the late 1960s and early 1970s, however, exhibitions were presenting a host of new models, showcasing performance, video, and information technology. Examples include *Cybernetic Serendipity* (1968) at the Institute of Contemporary Arts in London; *Software* (1970) at the Jewish Museum in New York; *Information* (1970) at the Museum of Modern Art in New York; and Harald Szeemann's *documenta 5* of 1972 in Kassel, Germany; as well as experimental practices in São Paulo annual exhibitions like Salão de Arte Contemporânea (1966–1975) at the Museu de Arte Contemporânea Campinas, and JAC (Jovem Arte Contemporânea, 1963–1974) at the University of São Paulo Museum of Contemporary Art (MAC-USP), which occupied a space directly adjoining the third floor of the Biennial pavilion.[31] In 1971, Flusser presented an "Initial Proposal for the Organization of Future Biennials on a Scientific Basis" to the Biennial Foundation and participated in a roundtable of art critics during the Eleventh São Paulo Biennial in September 1971, which was written up in *O Estado de São Paulo*.[32] He was subsequently nominated to the role of "technical advisor" for the twelfth edition of the Biennial in 1973. He excitedly wrote to Abraham Moles, "like you, I want to translate theory into praxis. That is why I have accepted the invitation of the São Paulo Biennial to reorganize it in a communicological way. In short: dis-alienate senders and receivers, de-sacralize 'Art,' and abandon the *oeuvre* for something useful. Make art again part of everybody's daily life."[33] The Swiss curator René Berger, then president of the International Association of Art Critics (AICA), had invited Flusser to present his proposal to restructure the Biennial. Flusser's idea was to move away from national representation to a communications model, engaging local schools and factories and shifting from passive consumption to active participation, with the Biennial functioning as a "laboratory" for communication.[34] Art objects were one-way communicators, he argued, with viewers functioning as passive receivers, and he wanted to activate the possibilities of both the Biennial and art itself. René Berger even invited Flusser to Zaire to survey the art scene there, and Flusser proposed including African art, dancers, and other participants

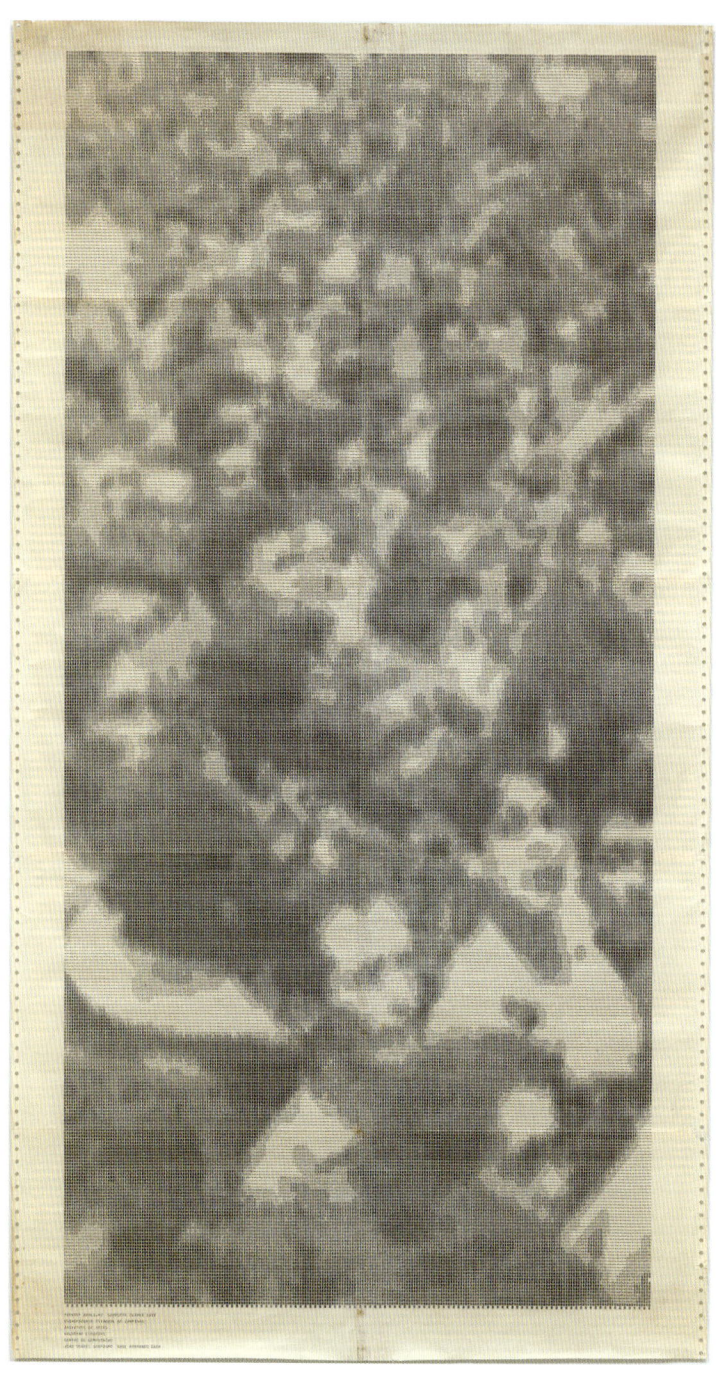

Figure 2.6
Waldemar Cordeiro, *Gente Ampli*2*, 1972. Computer output on paper, 52¹⁵⁄₁₆ × 28⁹⁄₁₆ in.
(134.5 × 72.5 cm). Courtesy the Estate of Waldemar Cordeiro. © The Museum of Modern Art/
Licensed by SCALA/Art Resource, NY.

in the Biennial.[35] (Zaire ultimately did not participate in the 1973 edition of the Biennial.)[36]

Flusser's proposal for São Paulo was met with resistance in Paris, mostly because Restany and others had already decided to systematically boycott the São Paulo Biennial. The French newspaper *Le Figaro* lauded Flusser, though, for attempting to revolutionize the exhibition and create less elite and alienating models: "Will Monsieur Flusser find enough followers to carry out his revolution?" the article asked.[37] Meanwhile, Flusser's relationship with the Biennial Foundation slowly deteriorated—more over financial than political issues—and Flusser departed as technical advisor in late 1972. Flusser's proposal for an "Art and Communication" section *was* installed on the third floor of the 1973 Biennial pavilion, though, alongside a room devoted to the work of Waldemar Cordeiro, a painter turned computer artist who published a treatise, *arteônica* (1971), on electronic art that presaged some of the ideas in Flusser's technical images writings.[38] Analívia Cordeiro, Waldemar's daughter, was in the Biennial with *M 3x3* (1973), a video that exhibits her computer-dance method, with performers' movements synched with the camera and appearing in a gridded matrix. Also included in the Biennial were two artists Flusser had recommended: the French video artist Fred Forest (to be discussed shortly) and Derrick de Kerckhove, Marshall McLuhan's assistant and collaborator, whose *Happening* (1973) involved a soundproof room where participants were blindfolded and led through the Biennial.[39] Echoes of Flusser's approach can also be seen in later exhibitions like those organized by Walter Zanini and Julio Plaza at the University of São Paulo's Museu de Arte Contemporânea in the 1970s and 1980s—*Prospectiva '74* (1974) and *Poéticas visuais* (1977)—that addressed communications and artistic networks and how these functioned under politically repressive regimes, as Forest had exposed earlier.

Back to Europe

Edith and Vilém Flusser moved back to Europe in the early 1970s, living in various locations like Merano in the South Tyrol region of northern Italy, a spa town where Kafka had gone in an attempt to cure his tuberculosis. (It was here, among the apple orchards grown to produce apple juice, that Flusser would write his greatest

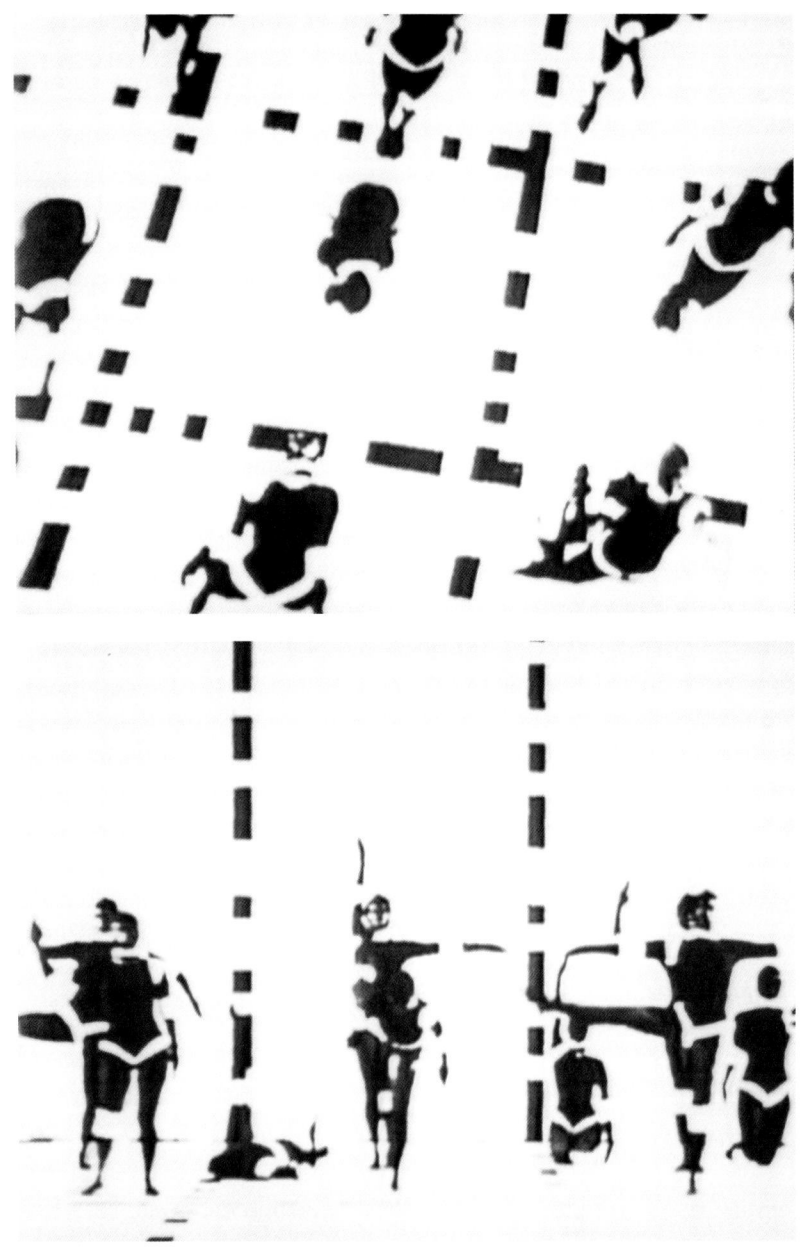

Figures 2.7–2.8
Analívia Cordeiro, *M 3x3*, 1973. Video, black-and-white, sound, 9:50 min.
Courtesy of the artist.

meditation on the environment in relation to human culture, *Natural:mente*, 1979.) Eventually they would settle in the south of France. Through his Biennial connections, particularly René Berger and Abraham Moles, Flusser began publishing in French-language publications, including *Communication et langages* and *Cause commune*. In a letter to Moles, Flusser voiced his interest in more imaginatively applying their shared interests in communications: "Did you ever use the new media of communication to articulate your thought (not to 'communicate it to others')?"[40]

Like Moles, Flusser would become involved with the Institute of the Environment (1969–1976) in Paris, an experimental school inspired by the Bauhaus and the HfG Ulm. The institute was interested in collapsing disciplinary categories and overhauling architectural education: the word "environment" was an attempt to move past stagnant architectural terms and encompassed a range of fields, including psychology, art, and agriculture.[41] One of the most interesting projects Flusser was involved in there was a roundtable about technology, culture, and the environment held on May 8, 1973, later published as a book, *Technologie et imaginaire* (Technology and the imaginary) in 1975.[42] The project clearly presaged future events like *Les immatériaux* (1985), the landmark exhibition at the Centre Pompidou organized by Jean-François Lyotard and Thierry Chaput that examined "new materials" in the digital and biotechnological ages.

The 1973 roundtable included nine people: Flusser; Klaus Blasquiz, singer and percussionist for the progressive rock group Magma; Alexandre Bonnier, an artist and organizer of the plastic arts curriculum at the institute; film director Enrico Fulchignoni, head of the audiovisual department at UNESCO; Jeanne Gatard, a painter and Bonnier's life partner; the sculptor Piotr Kowalski; information theorist Abraham Moles; Czech-born physicist and engineer Erich Spitz, director of the Thomson-CSF laboratory, which was devoted to electronics, aerospace, and defense technology and an innovator in the fields of radio communications, optical disks for information storage, and liquid crystal flat screens; and Jean Zeitoun, a mathematician concerned with architectural models. Bonnier initiated the discussion with this question: "In the future, what role will complex technologies play in artistic creation? Artists manipulating these technologies or inspired [by] them?"[43] He proposed discussing how advanced technology contained the kernels of a "new imagination." A lively conversation

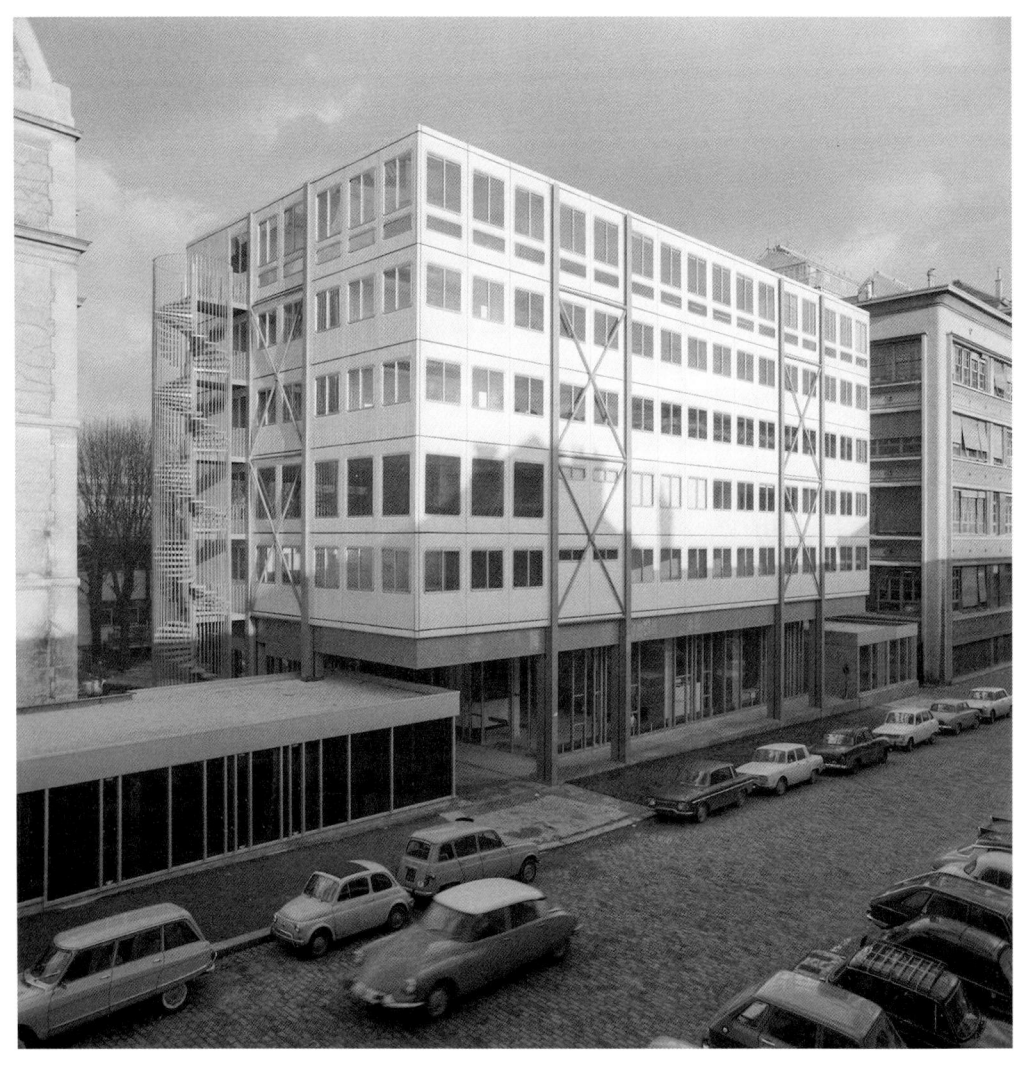

Figure 2.9
Robert Joly and Jean Prouvé, Institute of the Environment, 14–20, rue Erasme, Paris,
1968–1970, architecture by Robert Joly and facade panels by Jean Prouvé. © CNAC/MNAM,
Dist. RMN-Grand Palais/Art Resource, NY

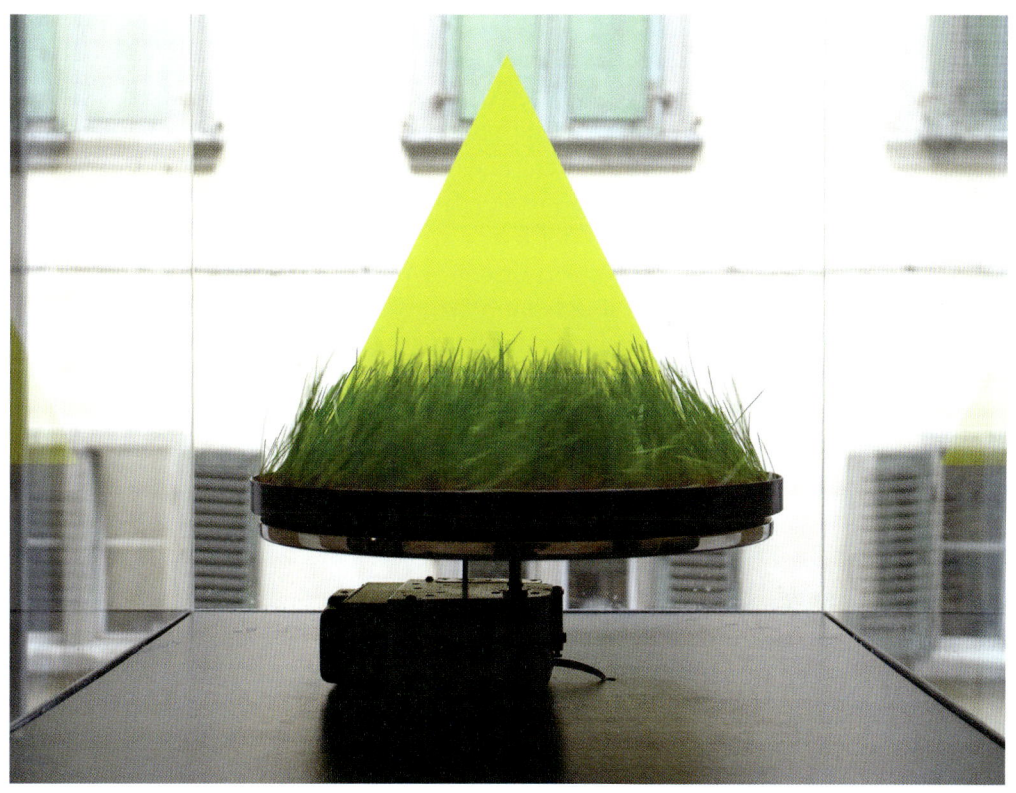

Figure 2.10
Piotr Kowalski, *Dressage d'un cone* (Cone dressage), 1967. Painted wood and folding metal table, four Plexiglas panels, five metal rotating trays, five motors, cotton, Italian ryegrass seeds. Exhibition view at Kunsthaus Centre d'art Pasquart, 2015. © 2024 Artists Rights Society (ARS), New York/ADAGP, Paris. Photo: Jean-Louis Boissier.

ensued, and the book includes images of everything from the cybernetic sculptures of Wen-Ying Tsai, which Flusser would write about in *Studio International*, to Yutaka Murata's pneumatic architecture; the solar furnace at Odeillo in France, a research center for studying materials at high temperatures; a still from Frederic Parke and Edwin Catmull's short 1972 film *A Computer Animated Hand* (Catmull would go on to cofound Pixar Animation Studios); and Kowalski's 1967 sculptural installation in which grass seeds planted on a spinning platform grew into geometric cone shapes. What stands out in *Technologie et imaginaire* is its cross-disciplinary method and the way nature and culture are shown to be increasingly, often technologically, intertwined. Flusser comments at one point that, whereas there used to be "nature" and "culture," now we are dominated largely by cultural objects and phenomena, and this is a new situation.[44] Moreover, from a philosophical standpoint, "natural things do not have a truly symbolic dimension," whereas "cultural things are entirely symbolic because they are manmade, and man is about 'symbolizing.' Man gives meaning to everything. Culture, including technology, is symbolic."[45]

Flusser's involvement with the institute shaped his first book published in France, *La force du quotidien* (The power of the everyday) in 1973, for which Moles wrote a foreword.[46] The book is made up of short philosophical essays exploring a phenomenology of everyday objects: canes, bottles, pens, glasses, carpets, walls, mirrors, books, beds, and automobiles. Flusser's interest in objects follows a long line of French writing on design, technology, and objects by Moles, Pierre Francastel, Gilbert Simondon, Jacques Ellul, André Hermant, Jean Baudrillard, and others—as well as the films of Jacques Tati, and the novels of Georges Perec and Alain Robbe-Grillet.[47]

In the introduction to *La force du quotidien*, Flusser cites Moles's 1972 book *Théorie des objets* (Theory of objects) as a touchstone.[48] Like Moles, Flusser viewed objects phenomenologically rather than through semiotics, structuralism, or reification, stressing that they serve as mediators between humans and the environment. He also stressed that he was approaching "media" through everyday objects like bottles, pens, and beds rather than technological media such as telephones, televisions, computers, and cinema.[49] This is, of course, a somewhat perverse approach to communications theory—although Gregory Bateson also used the idea of the cane, asking his students whether the blind man's cane was a part

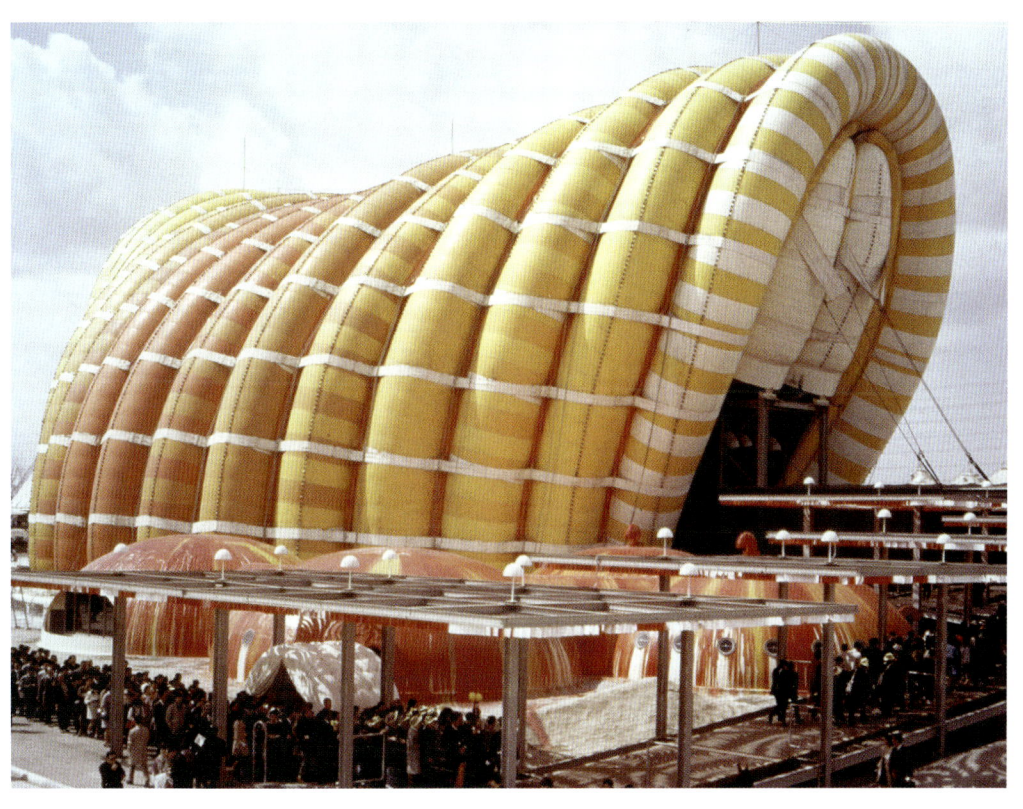

Figure 2.11
Yutaka Murata (architect) and Mamoru Kawaguchi (engineer), Expo'70 Fuji Group Pavilion,
Osaka, Japan, 1970. Diameter: 60 m, with 16 air-inflated arches. Courtesy of Kawaguchi
& Engineers. Images of this structure were included in the book *Technologie et imaginaire*
(1975), 15.

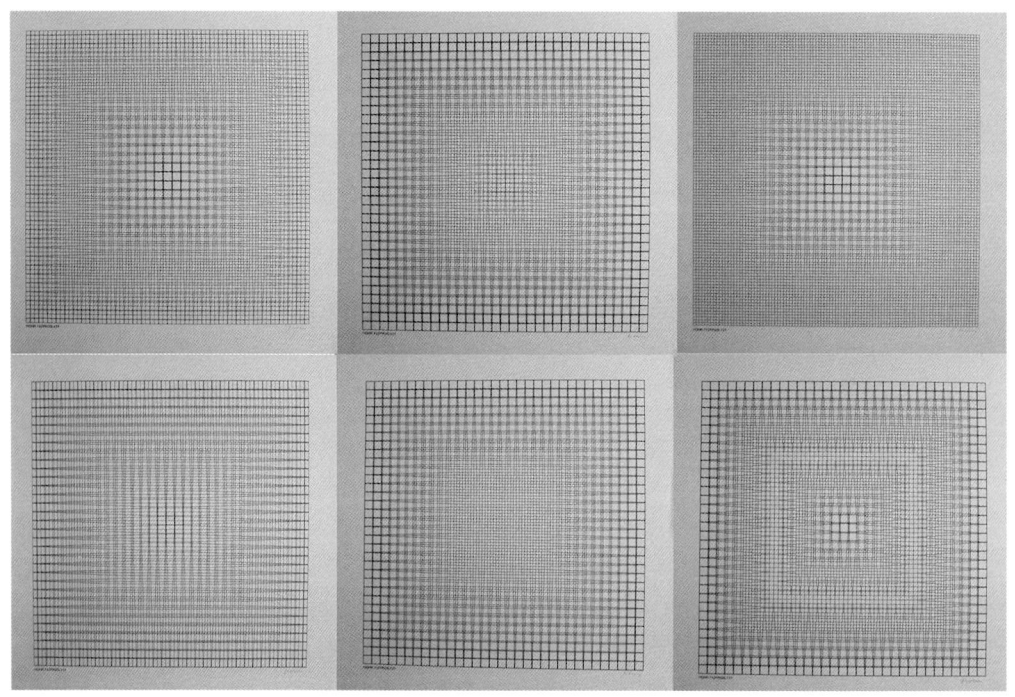

Figure 2.12
Manfred Mohr, *P-137*, 1973. Series of six plotter drawings, graph pattern. Computer drawings executed with a plotter, 28 × 28 cm each. These drawings were included in the book *Technologie et imaginaire*, 1975, no page.

of the blind man. (In cybernetic/systems theory, the cane becomes an information channel that enables the blind man to navigate his environment, becoming part of a larger sensory system.)[50] In his preface, Moles compares Flusser's text to Marshall McLuhan's *Understanding Media: The Extensions of Man* (1964).[51] However, where McLuhan argued that "the medium is the message," in which the medium itself generally overwhelms its content, for Flusser humans are not merely instruments of technology, controlled by the medium, but subjects motivated by, for instance, the *contents* of a telephone call. "The human being is moved *in his actions* by the contents of the phone call," Moles wrote, "he is moved *in its value* by the content of advertising, but it is the telephonic habitus that *inserts him into technical society*, with the possession of a small bright screen."[52] In other words, "The medium is not the message," Moles writes, but merely one of the components in the world of messages.[53] The McLuhan mention is crucial, though, since Flusser was often compared to the Canadian theorist, and both used similar terms like "medium," "message," "box," and "window onto the world." And yet McLuhan theorized the gradual disappearance of the human body (from knowledge production) in the electronic age, while Flusser was more interested in feedback loops between objects and the phenomenological information they provide.[54]

In 1973, the same year *La force du quotidien* was published, Flusser attended a conference at the Institute of the Environment which would serve as the impetus for the essay "Le monde codifié" (The codified world), published in French in 1974 as a forty-eight-page pamphlet—later rewritten in German and translated into English.[55] Here, Flusser shifts from thinking about objects to thinking about cultural codes and language, considering the "universe" of French language as a system of codes and gestures, and ending with a consideration of different types of communication: the discursive and the dialogic, which would appear in later texts.[56] Gestures, in particular, would play an important role in one of his most important collaborations with artists in the 1970s.

Video and Sociology: Fred Forest, Hervé Fischer, and the Gruppe Art Sociologique

Before he entered the world of photography and formulated his "universe of technical images," Flusser embarked on a tour through the emerging field of video art. He remained in contact with critic, curator, and art historian René Berger, whose commitment to video had a profound impact.[57] In 1973, Flusser wrote to Berger: "Maybe one day we can make (the two of us) a theory of communication against McLuhan (and also in some sense in conflict with Moles)? You from the point of view of the media, and I from the point of view of the (phenomenologically conscious) receiver?" It would be interesting, he noted, to work out a strategy for action; otherwise, they functioned as mere "clowns of the apparatus."[58]

Berger also provided introductions, putting Flusser in contact with Fred Forest, the artist about whom he wrote more at length than any other artist.[59] Forest, who grew up in Algiers, was one of the first artists in France to acquire a portable Sony Portapak, and he used it to approach art through a "sociological" lens. The Collectif d'Art Sociologique (1974–1980), a group formed by Forest with Paul Thenot, a practicing psychotherapist, and Hervé Fischer, who had degrees in philosophy and sociology, published a manifesto in *Le Monde* on October 10, 1974, calling for a move away from a focus on the individual and art grounded in communication and pedagogy.[60] The collective also founded the Interrogative Sociological School in Paris, in the basement of Fischer's house, where they hosted seminars, roundtables, and performances. Using documentary video, feedback from participants, publications, and collaborations with actual sociologists, they created an "aesthetic form of sociology," which might be seen as forerunner to relational aesthetics and social practice.[61]

Forest himself created a series of *Space-Media* collaborative works, where a square of blank space was printed on the front page of various newspapers. Readers were encouraged to fill in the rectangle in any manner they chose, cut out their handiwork, and mail it to Forest, who would exhibit the results. One of the most prominent versions appeared on the front page of the Parisian newspaper *Le Monde* in 1972.[62] Flusser wrote about this work, calling it a space for dialogue that transformed the reader from consumer into participant—although Flusser mused that "only" 800 people actually responded: a fraction of the readership, and many of these responses were puerile, pornographic, or of a caricature nature.[63] Nonetheless, even these responses were a subversion of the one-way "discursive" media of newspapers. Flusser imagined taking this approach to television, which Forest did in a work titled *Soixante secondes de blanc* (Sixty seconds of blank screen) in

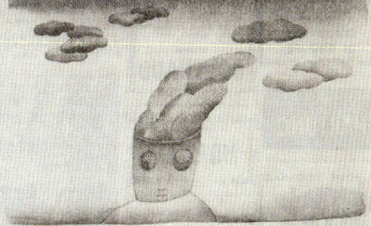
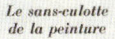
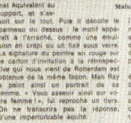
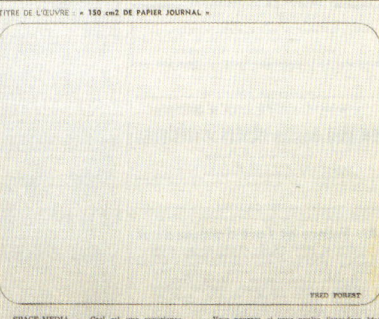

Figure 2.13
Fred Forest, *Space-Media*, front page of *Le Monde* newspaper, January 12, 1972. © 2024 Artists Rights Society (ARS), New York/ADAGP, Paris.

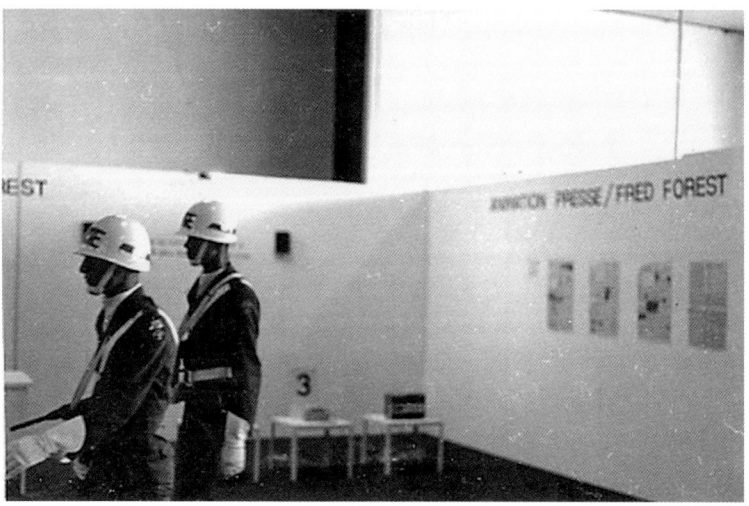

Figure 2.14
Military police arriving at the Twelfth São Paulo Biennial, 1973, to close Fred Forest's installation and arrest Forest, who was held briefly and released. © 2024 Artists Rights Society (ARS), New York/ADAGP, Paris.

1972, on French national television's second channel. Here, Flusser wrote, the mass media became the "material" of Forest's work, foregrounding the structure of the apparatus (*dispositif*) and the people running these networks.

Before parting from his role as technical director, Flusser recommended Forest for the "Art and Communication" section of the twelfth edition of the São Paulo Biennial in 1973. Forest lived in São Paulo for three months and created several works, including *Space-Media* published in newspapers in São Paulo and Rio de Janeiro and the incendiary work *The City Invaded by Blank Space* (1973), for which he hired people to walk through São Paulo carrying blank placards—a mock protest featuring a monochrome void placard—thus defying the military government's restrictions on free speech and public assembly. Inside the Biennial pavilion, Forest set up a bank of telephones where visitors could call in from all over Brazil and leave messages that would be broadcast by loudspeaker throughout the venue—another challenge to free speech in a tightly censored nation. Officers from the Department of Political and Social Order were sent to shut down Forest's exhibition, and he was held briefly before being released with the help of the French embassy and Biennial officials. However, by coaxing the "secret" police to

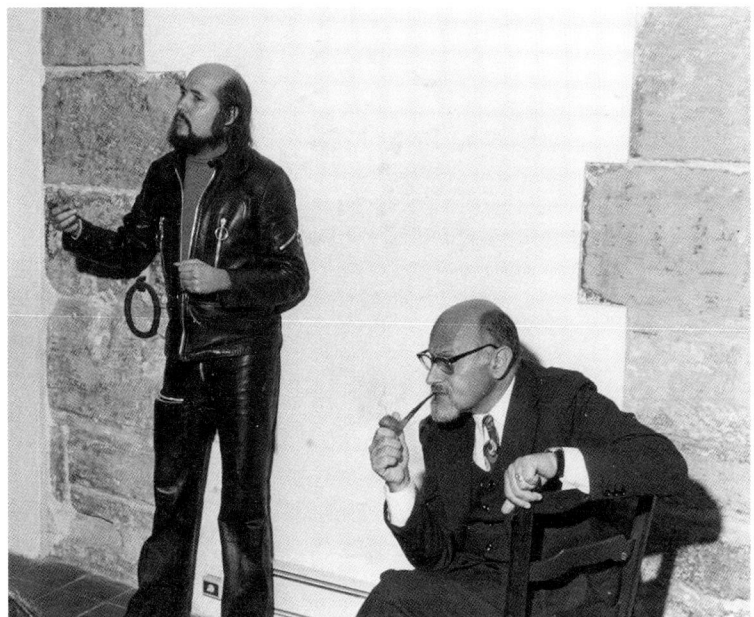

Figure 2.15
Fred Forest and Flusser at one of Forest's research and communication events in 1972. ©
2024 Artists Rights Society (ARS), New York/ADAGP, Paris.

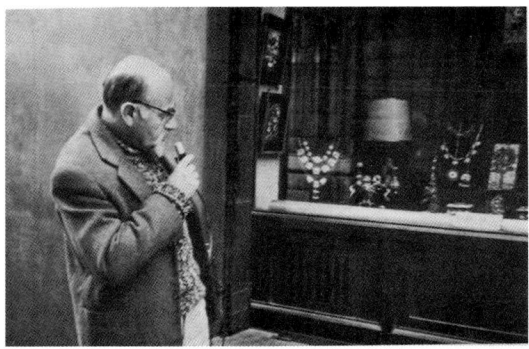

Figure 2.16
Fred Forest, *Archeology of the Present*, 1973. Closed-circuit television installation and video
installation. © 2024 Artists Rights Society (ARS), New York/ADAGP, Paris.

appear in public and arrest him, Forest showed how the Biennial
was only a facade for a repressive regime.

Back in France, Forest's interventions resulted in a verbal
altercation: Flusser, according to Forest, burst into the library at
the Institute of the Environment and bellowed, "You traitor!" He
berated Forest over his political naiveté in dealing with Brazilian

authorities. They quickly patched things up, though, and went on to collaborate on several video projects.[64] Flusser had already participated as a "critic observer" in Forest's *Video: Third Age* (1973), a series of on-camera interviews Forest made in a retirement home in Hyères, France, and in *Archeology of the Present* (1973) at the Galerie Germain in Paris. For this work, sometimes referred to as *Autopsy of Rue Guénégaud*, Flusser walked up one side of the street on the morning of April 18, 1973, talking into a microphone and describing the walls, shops, doors, and windows, while the critic Pierre Restany did the same on the other side of the street. The two recordings were played on a loop in the gallery, treating the street as a kind of found object.

Flusser played an even more central role in *Gestures of the Professor* (1972–1974), part of a larger series by Forest called *Gestures in the Professions and Social Life* (1972–1974) that highlighted how the presence of a video camera changed the behavior of both subject and videographer. Moreover, as Forest and Flusser sat down and viewed and discussed the video they had just made, another conversation—a "meta-dialogue"—emerged about gestures and the role of video. Flusser mused that video differs from the contemplation of philosophy or narrative film by becoming a real-time active technique. In the video, Flusser explains how he intends to write a theory of human gestures—which he ended up doing—but that traditional media, like books and essays, aren't in the same space-time as gesture itself. Video, on the other hand, allows the phenomenon to be commented on as it's happening. Flusser then reverses himself, claiming that he is not *entirely* free in gesturing, since he is adapting his movements to the technology. He flashes a small mirror at the camera, capturing Forest filming, thus drawing attention to the videographer and the apparatus. Flusser would later write that the dialogic video created a "set of mirrors," circular and virtually infinite, "a labyrinth of reflecting and reflexive reflections" that destroys established points of view and provides multiple viewpoints.[65]

Flusser's collection of essays *Gestures* (1991), which emerged from the collaboration with Forest, moves through a variety of activities: writing, speaking, painting, photographing, filming, shaving, listening to music, telephoning, making a video.[66] Flusser initially defines gestures as "movements of the body that express an intention," but he extends that into "a movement of the body or of a tool connected to the body for which there is no

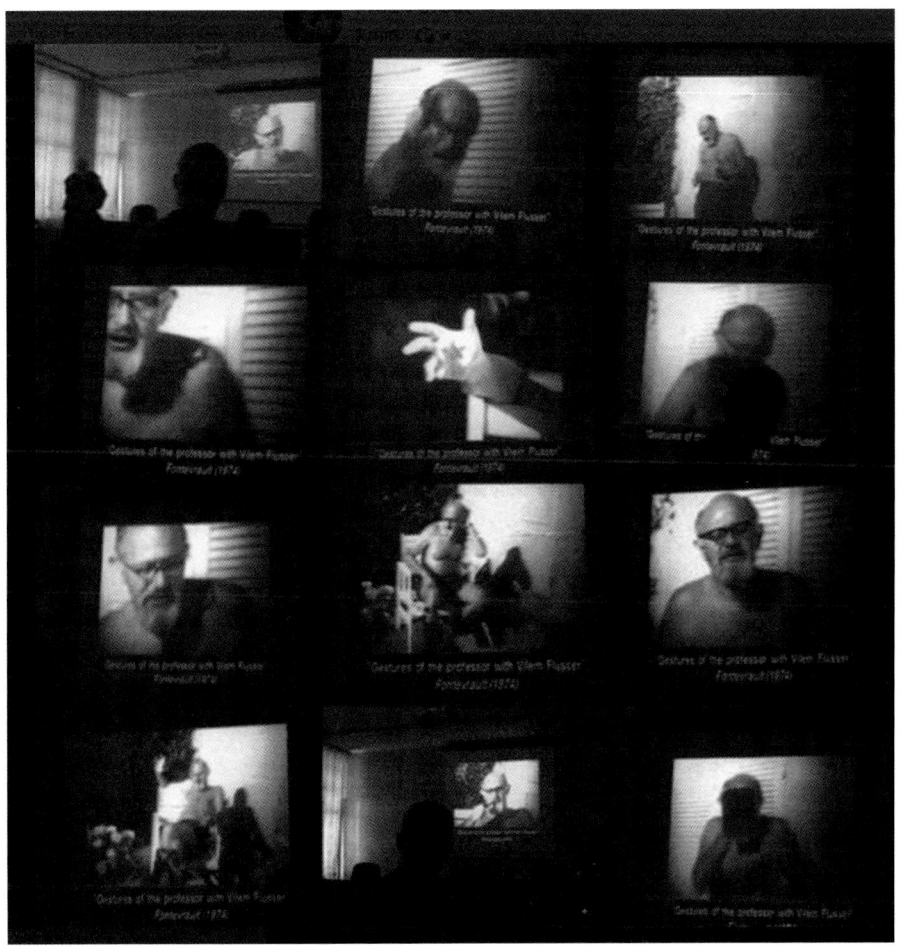

Figure 2.17
Fred Forest with Vilém Flusser, *Gestures of the Professor*, 1972–1974. Video stills. © 2024 Artists Rights Society (ARS), New York/ADAGP, Paris.

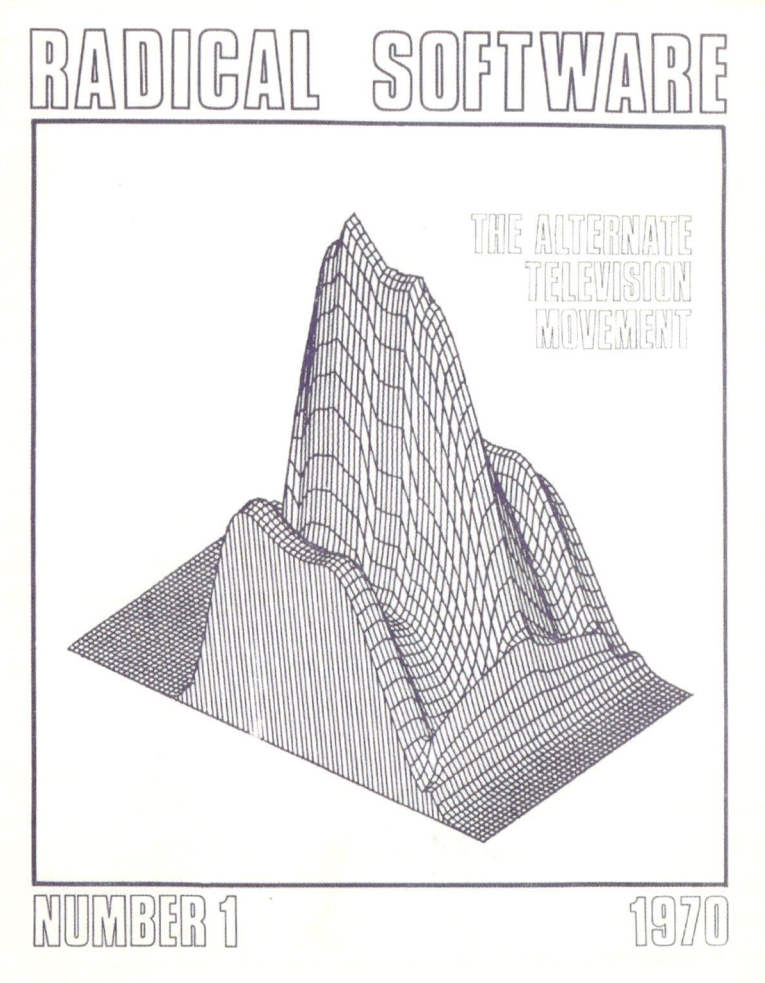

Figure 2.18
Radical Software 1, no. 1, "The Alternate Television Movement," Spring 1970. Magazine
cover. Courtesy Davidson Gigliotti and Daniel Langlois Foundation. This cover image
is a perspective view of the neutron distribution in a nuclear reactor produced at
Westinghouse Electric Corporation, West Mifflin, Pennsylvania. The same image appeared
in the exhibition catalogue for *Cybernetic Serendipity: The Computer and the Arts* (London:
Studio International, 1968), 98.

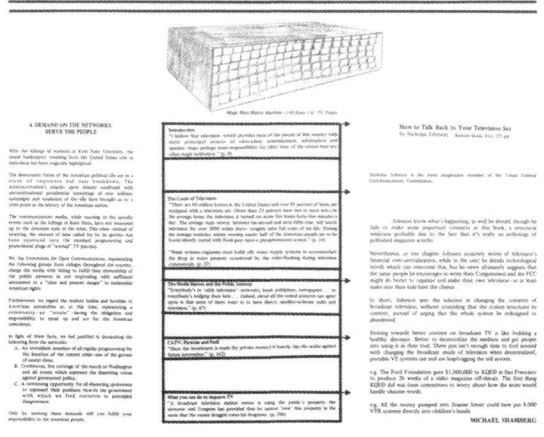

Figure 2.19
Radical Software 1, no. 1, "The Alternate Television Movement" (Spring 1970): 16. Courtesy Davidson Gigliotti and Daniel Langlois Foundation.

satisfactory causal explanation."[67] Flusser's motivation in study-ing gestures is to change communications theory from looking at artworks or cultural objects hermeneutically or semiologically to reading them phenomenologically. Hence, his essay "The Gesture of Writing" argues that linear thinking and occidental history arise from the physical movements of writing. "The Gesture of Paint-ing" describes that activity as self-analyzing—a Zen blurring of subject and object through material. The gesture of telephoning depends on whether you are the active caller or the recipient of the call. The gesture of photographing is one of seeing, but with the intent of "formalizing" that vision—hardly an "objective" gesture, but rather one that calls into question the concept of objectiv-ity itself. Likewise, in "The Gesture of Video," Flusser argues that video changes our relationship with time and serves as a "post-historical gesture," aiming not only to commemorate events but also composing "alternative" events.[68] We are our gestures: ges-tures are history—the *res gestae*, or events and circumstances of a legal case—as well as the physical movements shaped by new tech-nologies. "The Gesture of Planting" was new for hunter-gatherers in the Neolithic era, but in our era, gestures related, for instance, to smartphones—scrolling, texting, taking selfies—or sitting all day in front of a computer have shaped our existence. (Flusser's "The Gesture of Searching"—doing research in a world in which catego-ries like "subject" and "object" are eroding—takes on new meaning in the age of internet search engines.) We are in a revolution that requires reorienting ourselves in the world, and understanding gestures is a starting point for repositioning ourselves, since they offer concrete phenomena of our active "being-in-the-world," to use Heidegger's phrase.

Television: "Open Circuits" and a Theory of Communication

The "traveling library" (Edith Flusser's joke name for the col-lection of books Flusser hauled around with him) in the Vilém Flusser Archive in Berlin contains a copy of the first issue of *Rad-ical Software*, devoted to "The Alternate Television Movement" (1970).[69] Inspired by thinkers like Teilhard de Chardin—who would impact Flusser's *Vampyroteuthis infernalis* (1987)—as well as McLuhan, Bateson, Wiener, and others, this US journal from the era of the Vietnam War and Nixon considered strategies for turning television into something more than a medium of social control. It's not clear how *Radical Software* ended up in Flusser's library—or whether he even read it (although passages in the technical image trilogy from the 1980s around programming and liberating media sound suspiciously similar)—but in the 1970s he was clearly thinking about how television could exist as more than a technology for broadcasting to passive viewers. From Flusser's perspective—that is, the philosophical one—television was having a profound effect on human cognition and consciousness. In a pivotal essay from this period, "Line and Surface" (1973), he argued that surfaces are becoming more important than "lines" (linear text) in terms of how information is read and understood, since surfaces can be perceived more quickly, which changes our notion of time and understanding.[70] Film might be read as a series of images—that is, in a linear fashion—but television and videotape, which can be manipulated in real time, suggest a new structure of thought.

Based on this essay, Flusser was invited to participate in a landmark conference in media and communications theory: "Open Circuits: An International Conference on the Future of Television" (1974), held at the Museum of Modern Art in New York, co-organized by Douglas Davis, Fred Barzyk of WGBH-TV (a public broadcast station in Boston), and Gerald O'Grady, founder of the Center for Media Study at the University at Buffalo. The conference's title came from a 1966 statement by Nam June Paik ("we are in open circuits") and signaled the importance of art in thinking about communications technology.[71] Other conference participants included author and media theorist Hans Magnus Enzensberger; composer Pierre Schaeffer; artists John McHale, Nam June Paik, Joan Jonas, Stan VanDerBeek, Vito Acconci, Allan Kaprow, Shigeko Kubota, Richard Serra, Steina and Woody Vasulka, and Hollis Frampton; curators Harald Szeemann and Barbara J. London; and Flusser's curator friend René Berger. Enzensberger was riding the success of his influential essay "Constituents of a Theory of the Media" (1970), and Flusser hand-wrote on his conference program: "Enzensberger: Monolithic control, Simulation of lack, Censorship: Lack of Feedback."[72] Videotapes including Nam June Paik and John Godfrey's *Global Groove* (1973) were shown—although Flusser later expressed his preference for the videos by Steina and Woody Vasulka, founders of The Kitchen in New York in 1971 who had met in Prague in the early 1960s, and for Spanish

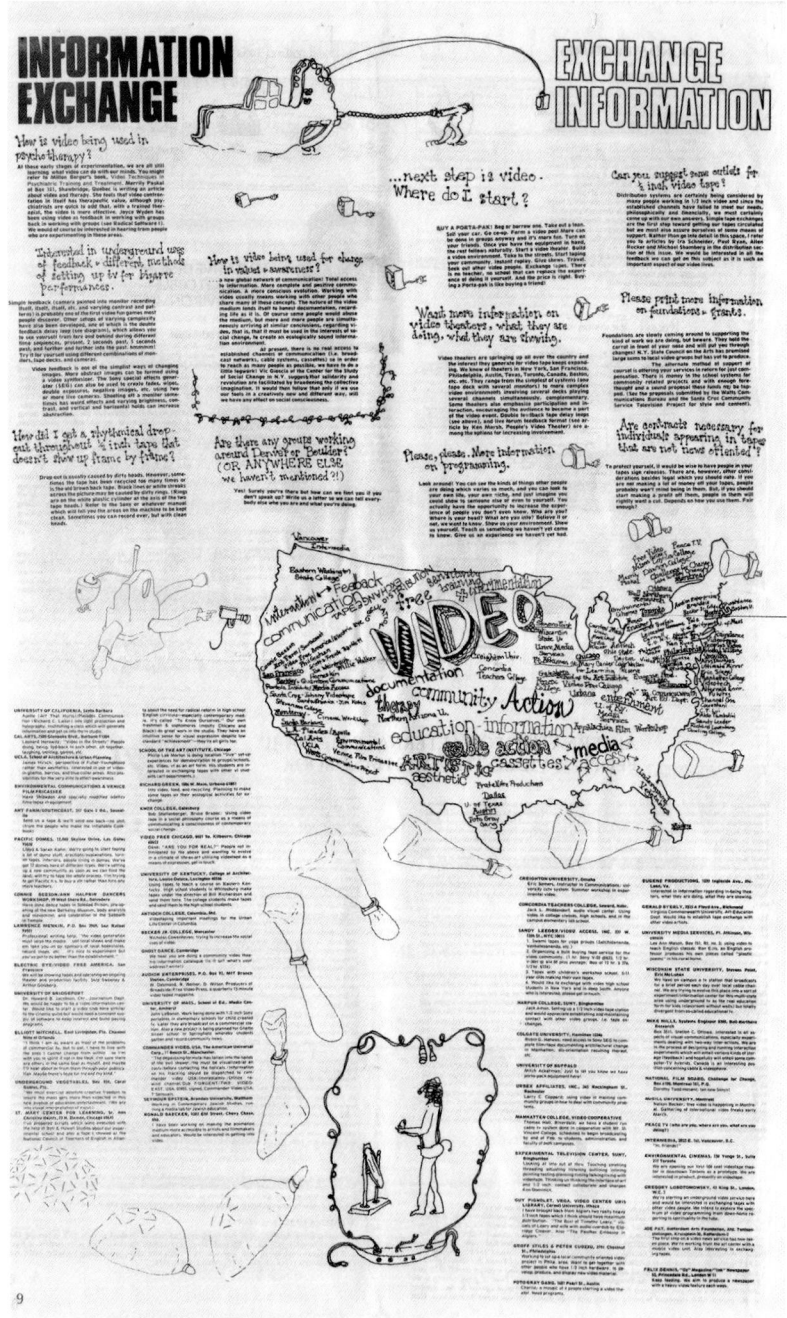

Figure 2.20
Radical Software 1, no. 3 (Spring 1971): 9. Courtesy Davidson Gigliotti and
Daniel Langlois Foundation.

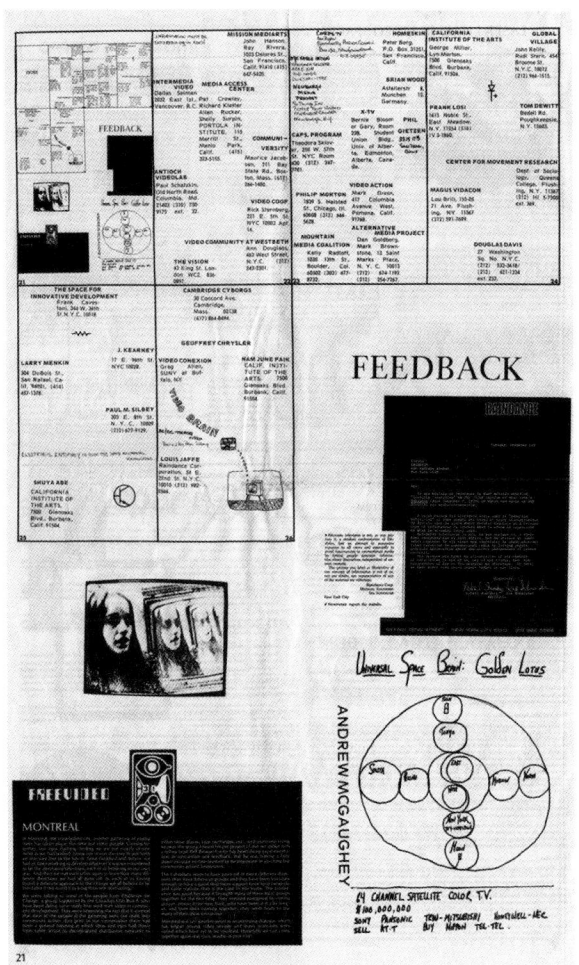

Figure 2.21
Radical Software 1, no. 3 (Spring 1971): 21. Courtesy Davidson Gigliotti and
Daniel Langlois Foundation.

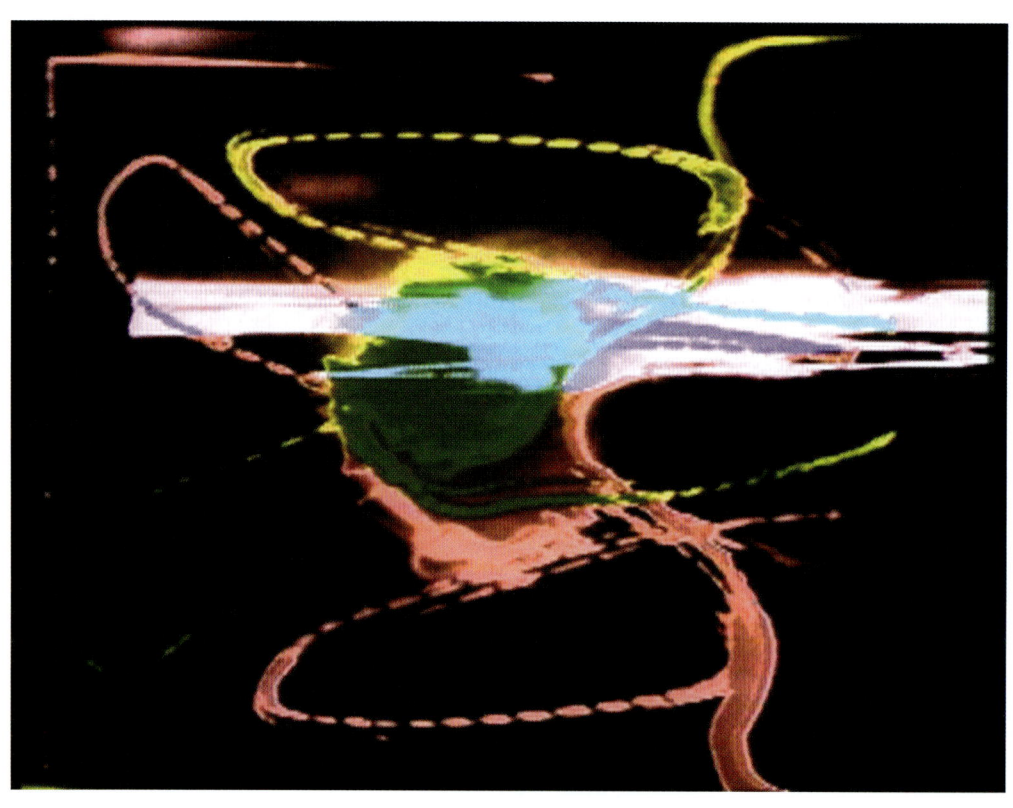

Figure 2.22
Nam June Paik and John Godfrey, *Global Groove*, 1973. Video, color, sound, 28:30 min.
Courtesy Electronic Arts Intermix and the Estate of Nam June Paik.

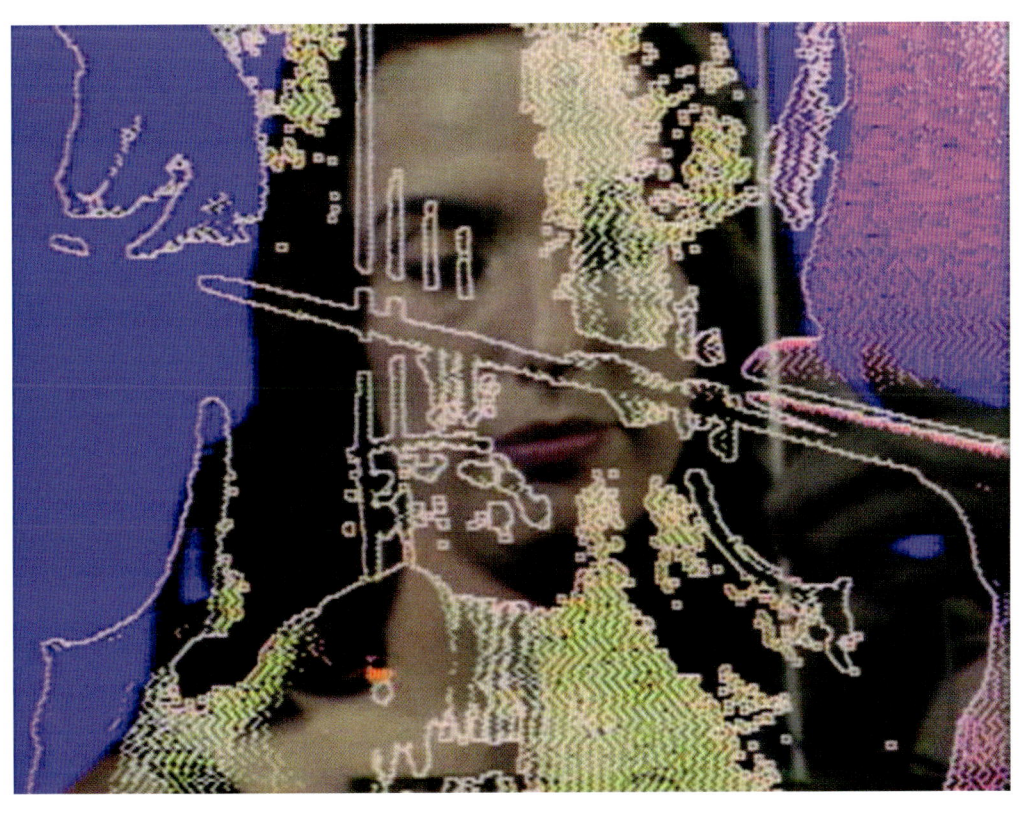

Figure 2.23
Nam June Paik and John Godfrey, *Global Groove*, 1973. Video, color, sound, 28:30 min.
Courtesy Electronic Arts Intermix and the Estate of Nam June Paik.

filmmaker José Montes-Baquer when he wrote about the potential of video art.[73]

Flusser's presentation for "Open Circuits," titled "Two Approaches to the Phenomenon, Television," considers television from a phenomenological perspective as a box in the living room around which people sit.[74] Borrowing an idea from Abraham Moles—and one he would apply to both chess and photography—Flusser described the television as structurally complex but functionally simple. People sit around the console receiving "messages" (à la McLuhan), although they only vaguely know where the images are being broadcast from. There are both "true" images (newsreels and political speeches) and "fictious" ones (TV plays and films). And yet these blur together, so that watching "the landing on the moon is like watching science fiction."[75] All images are manipulated, although viewers tend to forget this, which gives the box and messages magic and mythic qualities. What is key is that the box has buttons, and pressing these buttons gives viewers the illusion of freedom and control; meanwhile, the box emits messages but doesn't receive them. "The result is a passive attitude to the events of the world," Flusser writes, "accompanied by an illusionary impression of participation, which is due to the constant flow of messages from the box. In fact, this is one of the purposes of the messages: to create an illusion of participation while guaranteeing passive reception."[76] Moreover, television makes the distinction between fiction and reality uninteresting—an obvious precursor to our own moment of infotainment and "post-truth"—and yet television *could* exist as a new window onto the world, an updated version of ancient villages where people communicated with their neighbors but the private realm was separate from the public one. For television to become an "improved window," it needs to be treated as a new category of seeing, merging "imaginative" (immediate vision) and "conceptual" (textual) forms of thought, and viewers must change their attitude toward the television, treating the messages as raw material to manipulate. Flusser concluded by predicting exactly what smartphones and other digital gadgets would be accused of: "we live lonely in a lonely mass, because our tools tend to separate us from each other, and we have no good tools to unite us . . . the result of such a use of TV is a tendency toward a totalitarian society, in which man becomes a lonely tool manipulated by those who hold the powers of decision."[77] For him, the only hope was to reconfigure the way we approach such media.

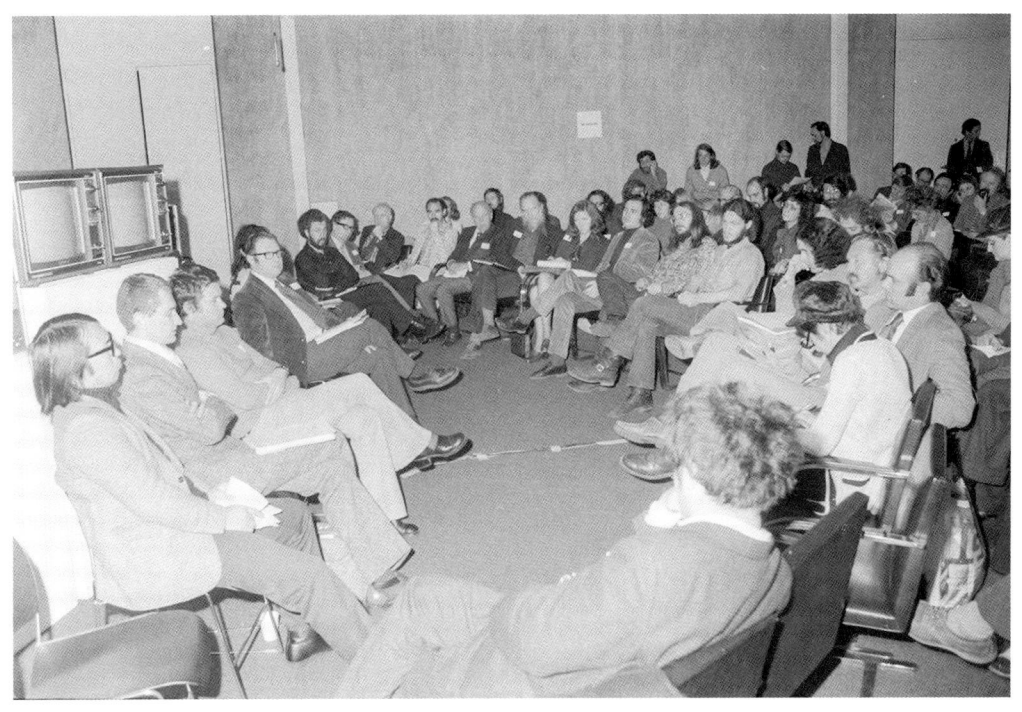

Figure 2.24
Session during the conference "Open Circuits: An International Conference on the Future
of Television" at the Museum of Modern Art, January 1974. Photographic Archive, MoMA
Activities. The Museum of Modern Art Archives, New York. © The Museum of Modern Art/
Licensed by SCALA/Art Resource, NY. Photo: Leonardo LeGrand.

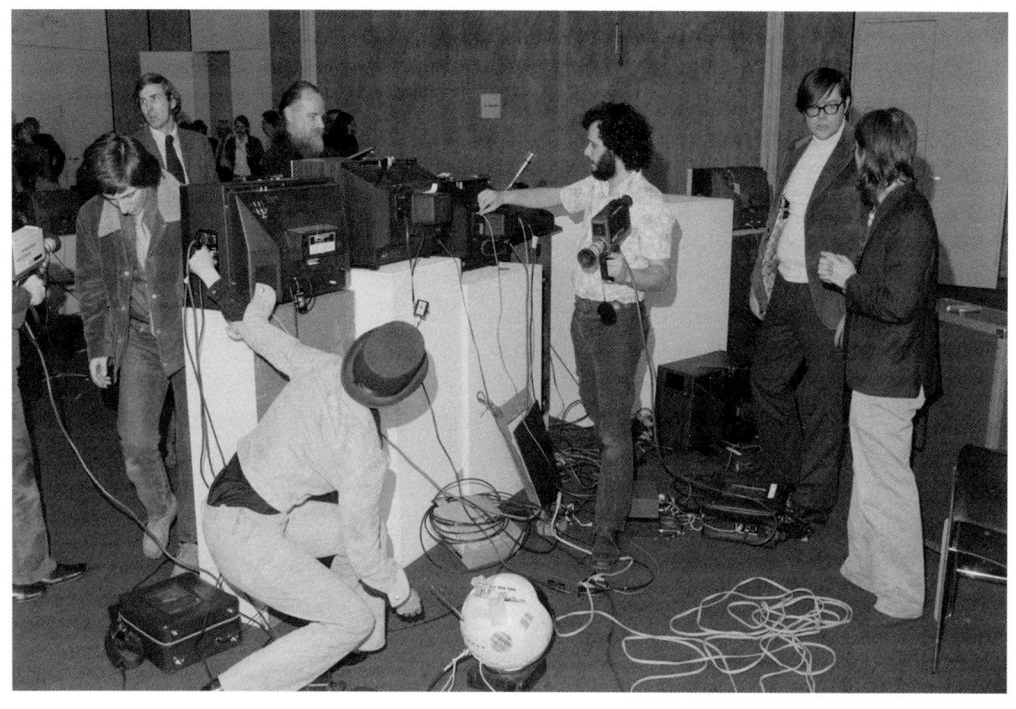

Figure 2.25
Session during the conference "Open Circuits: An International Conference on the Future of Television" at the Museum of Modern Art, January 1974. Photographic Archive, MoMA Activities. The Museum of Modern Art Archives, New York. © The Museum of Modern Art/ Licensed by SCALA/Art Resource, NY. Photo: Leonardo LeGrand.

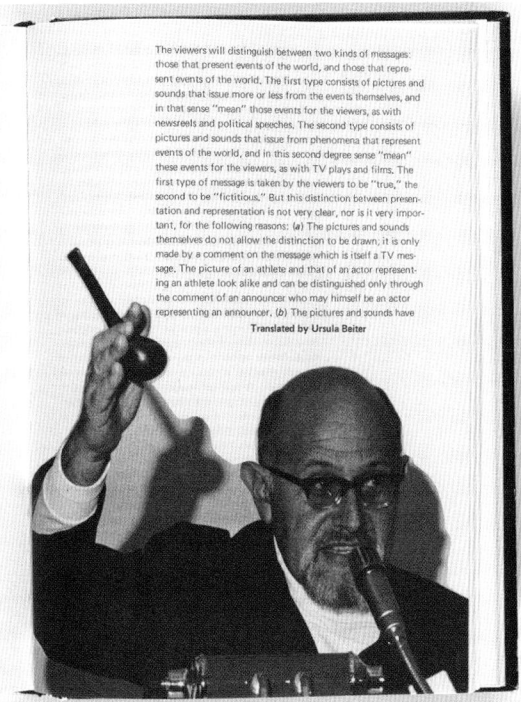

The most common form TV assumes at present is that of a box which stands among the furniture of a private dwelling. This box has a screen on which movie-like pictures appear, and a speaker from which radio-like sounds issue, if it is appropriately manipulated. The manipulation is simple, but the reasons for its effectiveness are complex. The box is, to speak with Moles, a structurally complex but functionally simple system. In order to see the pictures and hear the sounds, the dwellers of the room sit around the box in a semicircle. The pictures and sounds thus received have a meaning for those who receive them, and so has the box itself. The viewers recognize that these messages do not originate in the box, but their true origin is not clearly known. The viewers know vaguely that the box is somehow connected with a place where the messages are being manipulated and broadcast. They know vaguely that this is an expensive process, and that therefore those who finance it must have some sort of interest in it, an interest that must reflect itself in the messages the viewers are receiving. But this vague knowledge is suspended during the reception of the messages, and the viewer adopts the attitude that the pictures and sounds issuing from the box are messages from "his world." This is the meaning of the box for the viewers: it means communication of messages from the world in the direction of private dwellings.

Two Approaches to the Phenomenon, Television

Vilem Flusser

The viewers will distinguish between two kinds of messages: those that present events of the world, and those that represent events of the world. The first type consists of pictures and sounds that issue more or less from the events themselves, and in that sense "mean" those events for the viewers, as with newsreels and political speeches. The second type consists of pictures and sounds that issue from phenomena that represent events of the world, and in this second degree sense "mean" these events for the viewers, as with TV plays and films. The first type of message is taken by the viewers to be "true," the second to be "fictitious." But this distinction between presentation and representation is not very clear, nor is it very important, for the following reasons: (a) The pictures and sounds themselves do not allow the distinction to be drawn; it is only made by a comment on the message which is itself a TV message. The picture of an athlete and that of an actor representing an athlete look alike and can be distinguished only through the comment of an announcer who may himself be an actor representing an announcer. (b) The pictures and sounds have

Translated by Ursula Beiter

Figure 2.26
Flusser in *The New Television: A Public/Private Art* (MIT Press, 1977), 234–235. The Museum of Modern Art Library, New York. © The Museum of Modern Art/Licensed by SCALA/Art Resource, NY.

"Open Circuits: The Future of Television"

A Study Conference at The Museum of Modern Art, New York, January 23-25, 1974

Sponsored by Electronic Arts Intermix, Inc.

Supported by The New York State Council on the Arts, The National Endowment for the Arts, The Rockefeller Foundation, and The JDR 3rd Fund

CONFERENCE SCHEDULE

Wednesday, January 23

Theme: "The Structure of Television"

9:00 Viewing of Videotapes: International Artists

10:30 Panel: "Global Trends in Experimental Television," Chairman, Gerald O'Grady Panelists: Wolfgang Becker, Rene Berger, Jorge Glusberg, Bruce Kurtz, Shigeko Kubota, Edward Lucie-Smith, Toshio Matsumoto

12:00 Paper and Discussion: Vilem Flusser, "Two Approaches to the Phenomenon Television"

2:45 Viewing of Videotapes: Video Synthesis; Colorization; Computer Imagery

4:15 Special Panel: "The Rise of the Video Synthesizer," Nam June Paik and Stephen Beck; Chairman, Gerd Stern

5:30 Viewing of Videotapes: Work from the Experimental Television Centers, both U.S. and abroad

7:00 Evening Panel: "The Artist in the Experimental Television Center," Chairman, Fred Barzyk Panelists: Peter Campus, Paul Kaufman, David Loxton, Jose Montes-Baquer, Jean-Paul Pigeat, Nicolas Schoffer, Woody Vasulka

Figure 2.27
"Open Circuits" conference schedule, January 23, 1974. Electronic Arts Intermix Archives, New York.

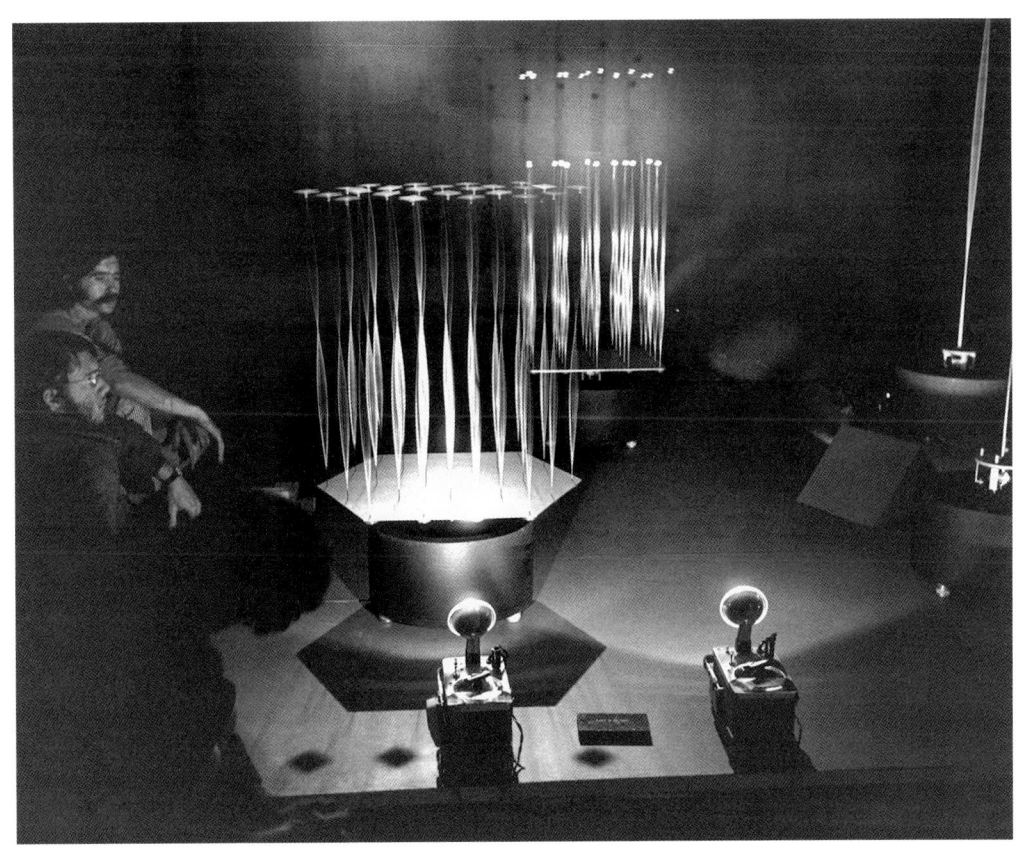

Figure 2.28
MIT students with Wen-Ying Tsai's cybernetic sculpture, 1970. © 2024 Tsai Art and Science
Foundation/Artists Rights Society (ARS), New York. Photo: Tsai Archives.

Artists were considering television in this "imaginative" way, obviously. Flusser mentions Gerald Minkoff, one of René Berger's former students, who was working with television in Geneva. Flusser had written about Minkoff's 1972 exhibition at the Musée des Beaux-Arts in Lausanne, describing it in terms of mirrors, since Minkoff used closed circuit television to interact with the video image.[78] (Nam June Paik, on the other hand, Flusser later described as "a totally insane illiterate idiot who is a brilliant video person"— and yet, as Peter Mahr argues, Paik, who was the central, celebrated figure at "Open Circuits," clearly impacted Flusser's approach to phenomenology and highlighted the possibilities of video art.)[79] From a theoretical standpoint, however, the aim would be to change television from a "discursive" or one-way form of transmission to a more "dialogical" one, allowing us to see and recognize other people. To achieve McLuhan's "cosmic village," Flusser writes, closed circuits must be opened; audiovisual dialogue must be produced.[80]

Nonetheless, Flusser was in foreign territory in the New York art world in 1974. (Later, he would be a columnist for the New York-based *Artforum*.) On the program for "Open Circuits," he wrote down the Chelsea Hotel address for Shirley Clarke, a fixture of downtown Manhattan experimental filmmaking. There is no record of Flusser making his way to this gathering. However, the idea of him bumping shoulders with Clarke, Warhol superstar Viva, Agnes Varda, or any members of Clarke's coterie at the Chelsea Hotel is amusing. He would stay in touch with O'Grady and continue to write isolated essays on television, although he increasingly considered it under the rubric of technical images and then *communicology*, his term for communications theory.[81]

Cybernetics: Nicolas Schöffer and Wen-Ying Tsai

Even more important than television was cybernetics, the science and study of how systems communicate and interact with their environment. The field was popularized in post–World War II circles where computers and information theory were being developed. One could cite many ancestors of cybernetics: eighteenth- and nineteenth-century scientists like André-Marie Ampère, who invented the galvanometer and worked with electromagnetics; Charles Babbage's mechanical computer; the telegraph, which changed communications, and British mathematician Alan Turing's *On Computable Numbers with Reference to the Entscheidungsproblem* (1937) and his 1936 Turing machine, a proto-computer that resulted from his work as a cryptologist decoding encrypted German messages during World War II.

Cybernetics burgeoned in the United States and Great Britain following the seminal Macy Conferences on Cybernetics from 1946 to 1953 and the work of Norbert Wiener, Ross Ashby, Gregory Bateson, and Margaret Mead. Wiener's work stemmed from his research during World War II and the development of an "anti-aircraft (AA) predictor"—a device that used electrical networks and data from previous pilot missions to predict the position of enemy aircraft—although later his thinking would include biological systems, just as Flusser would apply cybernetics in his para-biological fable *Vampyroteuthis infernalis*.[82] Wiener coined the term "cybernetics" in the summer of 1947, from the Greek word *kubernetes* for "steersman," but the word also appears in Plato's *Alcibiades*, meaning to self-govern. Cybernetics could be applied to everything from military weaponry to the human nervous system and became an amalgamation of engineering, computation, mathematics, and behavior psychology. Wiener's own theory was intermittently optimistic and nihilistic: cybernetics had the capability to save, enslave, or destroy humanity.[83] Flusser, too, would vacillate between techno-optimism and existential nihilism. His involvement with the Institute of the Environment put him in contact with artists and thinkers drawing from cybernetics—but particularly with Abraham Moles, who proposed the idea of generating high complexity from simple elements (Flusser's "structurally complex and functionally simple" reverses this formula) and simulation models in which machines could reproduce artistic creativity.[84]

Flusser's cybernetic thinking was also shaped by two particular artists: Nicolas Schöffer (1912–1992), the Hungarian-born French artist who was one of the primary innovators of cybernetic art, and Wen-Ying Tsai (1928–2013), a Chinese-born US sculptor who was one of the inaugural fellows at the Center for Advanced Visual Studies at the Massachusetts Institute of Technology (MIT). Adopting Norbert Wiener's ideas of cybernetic feedback, Schöffer created *CYSP 1* (1956), short for "CYbernetics SPaciodynamic," a kinetic or "spaciodynamic" sculpture on a wheeled base that included motors, photoelectric cells, and microphones. The

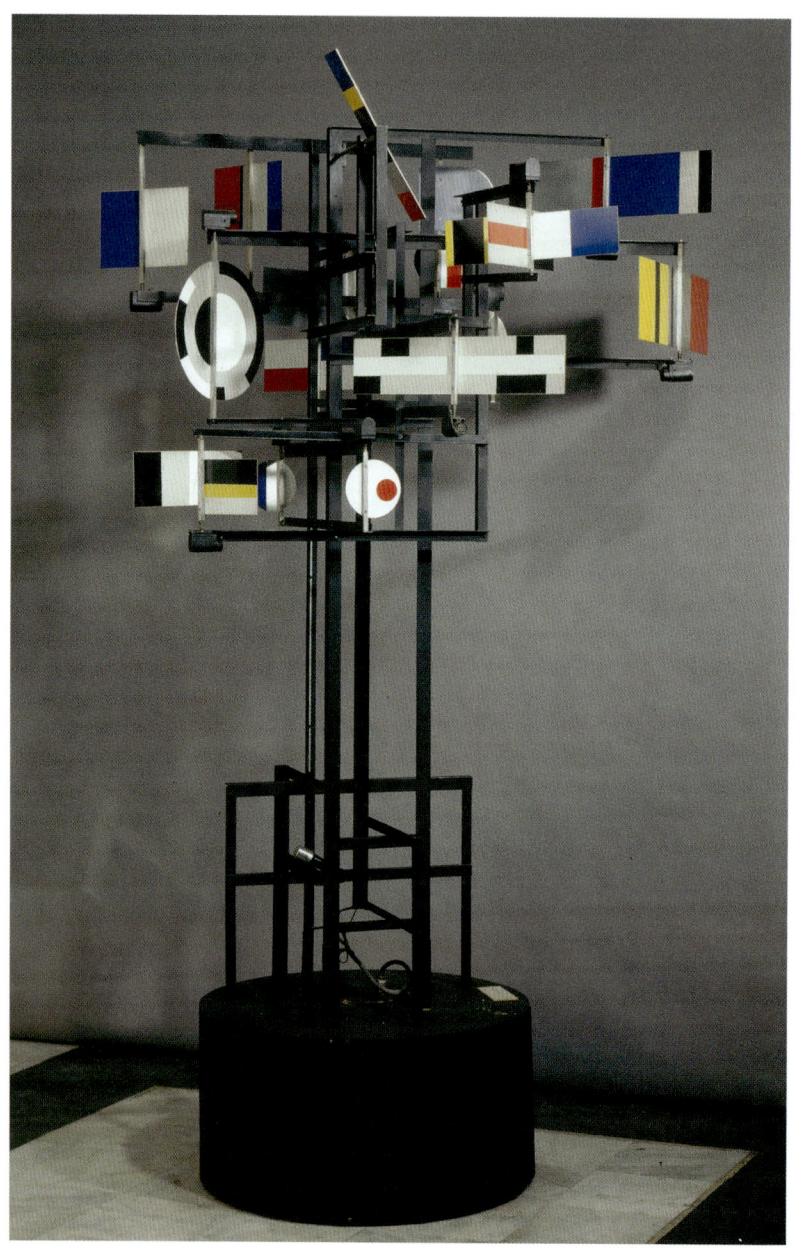

Figure 2.29
Nicolas Schöffer, *CYSP 1* (Cybernétique spatiodynamique) in the artist's studio (Villa des Arts no. 5), 1956. Private Collection. © 2024 Artists Rights Society (ARS), New York / ADAGP, Paris. Photo: Banque d'Images, ADAGP/Art Resource, NY.

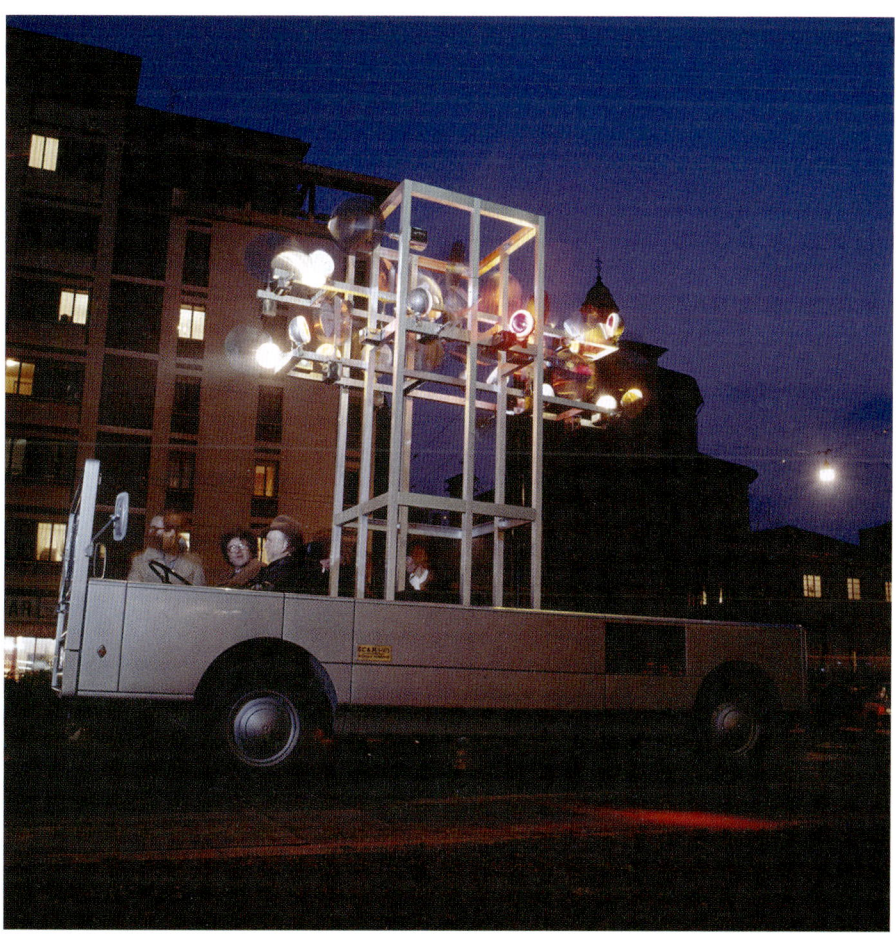

Figure 2.30
Nicolas Schöffer, *SCAM 1*, 1973. Sculpture automobile no. 1. First driven July 7, 1973, as a car
with the sculpture *Chronos 10* mounted on a platform. © 2024 Artists Rights Society (ARS),
New York / ADAGP, Paris. Photo: Banque d'Images, ADAGP/Art Resource, NY.

electronic feedback system, developed in collaboration with engineers at the Philips Company, caused the sculpture to respond to changes in light, color, and sound, activating sixteen polychromatic plates.[85] Schöffer became a celebrated figure, featured on the cover of *Paris Match* for his proposal for a cybernetic tower in Paris—a version of which would be erected in Liège, Belgium—and his visionary proposals for what might retrospectively be described as "smart" architecture that responded to its inhabitants.

In 1973, Schöffer drove a vehicle outfitted with his cybernetic system, consisting of moveable lights and disks, through the streets of Paris (and later Milan), passing monuments like the Arc de Triomphe and the Eiffel Tower and employing the idea of "perturbation," in which light, sound, and movement affect the perceptual environment of modern cities.[86] Flusser wrote an essay on Schöffer's book *La tour lumière cybernétique* (1973), devoted to the unrealized tower in Paris, approaching it from a phenomenological perspective and its being-in-the-world: the tower could be "either an important weapon in the fight for human dignity and freedom, or one more element in an ever more oppressing situation," much the way our own technologies vacillate between liberation and enslavement.[87] The tower functions for Flusser as an apparatus from which symbols are broadcast—but are they for the elite or for the masses? For propaganda or liberation? Flusser fears that the tower might become such a structure, controlled by the elite—and yet it could become a place where Parisians could enter into meaningful dialogue—maybe even an emblem of democracy, "if by 'democracy' we do not mean the rules of the 'majority,' but the right of every minority to articulate its message."[88] One thinks, obviously, of social media and its vacillating powers. Ultimately, Flusser rejects calling the tower "cybernetic" merely to validate its existence on scientific terms. Instead, he proposes a model that reflects the deep impact of Brazil on his thinking: "One has the impression that what Schöffer wants is a sort of church tower for the universal village. This would be a wrong model. He should try to build for us a drum, like they use in Africa and on the Brazilian hills, a drum that liberates by emitting messages, because these messages are deeply conventional, connotative, and have a dialogical structure."[89]

Other writers criticized Schöffer on different grounds. Jean Baudrillard read Schöffer's sculptures and writings in the context of Bauhaus functionalism and surrealist approaches to the city and

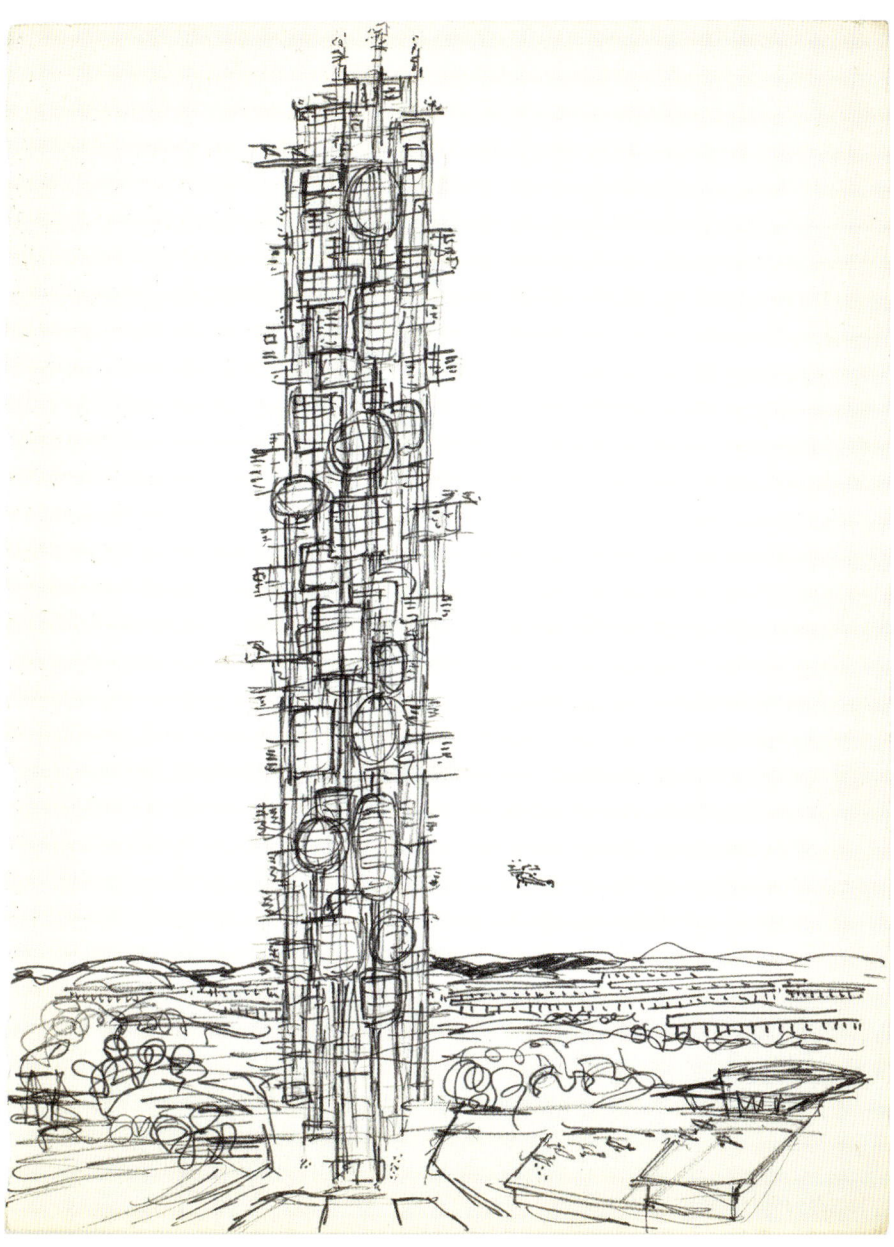

Figure 2.31
Nicolas Schöffer, *Elevation, Study*, part of the "Cybernetic City" ensemble, 1960. Felt-tip pen and paper, 32 × 24 cm. © 2024 Artists Rights Society (ARS), New York / ADAGP, Paris. Photo: © CNAC/MNAM, Dist. RMN-Grand Palais/Art Resource, NY. Photo: Janeth Rodriguez-Garcia.

found Schöffer's efforts lacking: "The hyper-reality of systems has absorbed the critical surreality of the phantasm. Art has become, or is on the way to becoming, total design, *metadesign*."[90] The US art historian Rosalind Krauss worried that the new brand of sculpture "theatricalizes" a space to the point where viewers become the focus, rather than the art objects.[91] More recent writers have seen Schöffer's towers as a version of Cold War modernism—but also as predicting the overstimulation of urban environments.[92] Schöffer's post-1968 urban projects clearly predicted the "smart city," in which infrastructure is affected by computational technology. Mostly, Flusser was captivated by Schöffer's embrace of cybernetic feedback that disrupted humans' customary space-time and Schöffer's argument, contrary to Krauss's formalism, that "aesthetic products" are more effective if "they are non-formalist, and immaterial in their essence, in which durations replace volumes, and temporal rhythms replace the configuration of surfaces."[93]

Wen-Ying Tsai was a very different sort of cybernetic artist. Born in Xiamen in southern China, across the strait from Taiwan, Tsai trained as a mechanical engineer and worked as an architectural consulting engineer for clients like Walter Gropius, Mies van der Rohe, Buckminster Fuller's Synergetics, and Skidmore, Owings and Merrill. However, he also studied painting at the Art Students League in New York and in Provincetown, Massachusetts, with Reginald Marsh and Hans Hofmann, and dance with Erick Hawkins, Martha Graham's husband and a choreographer and one-time dancer in her troupe. When he received the John Hay Whitney Opportunity Fellowship for Painting in 1963, the grant required him to become a full-time artist, and so he gave up his job as an engineer. Tsai's two-dimensional constructions made during this period with florescent paints and ultraviolet light were included in the landmark *Responsive Eye* (1965) exhibition at the Museum of Modern Art.

He had an epiphany during an artist's residency at the Mac-Dowell colony in New Hampshire in 1965: seeing the play of light in the trees, he realized he could create art that duplicated natural phenomena *and* utilized his scientific training. The results were sculptures made with vibrating steel rods, stroboscopic light, and electronic audio feedback systems, which were exhibited at the Howard Wise Gallery in New York in 1968. These works were also included in *Cybernetic Serendipity* (1968) at the ICA London, which featured art by Nicolas Schöffer, John Cage, Jean Tinguely,

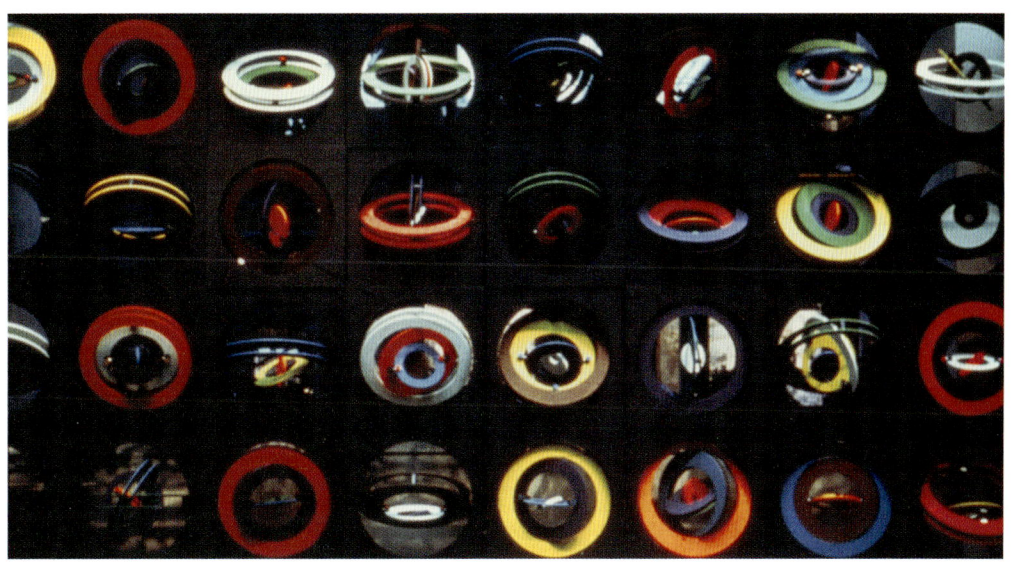

Figure 2.32
Wen-Ying Tsai, *Multi-kinetic Wall*, 1965. Detail of installation in *Art Turned On* at the Institute for Contemporary Art, Boston. © 2024 Tsai Art and Science Foundation/Artists Rights Society (ARS), New York.

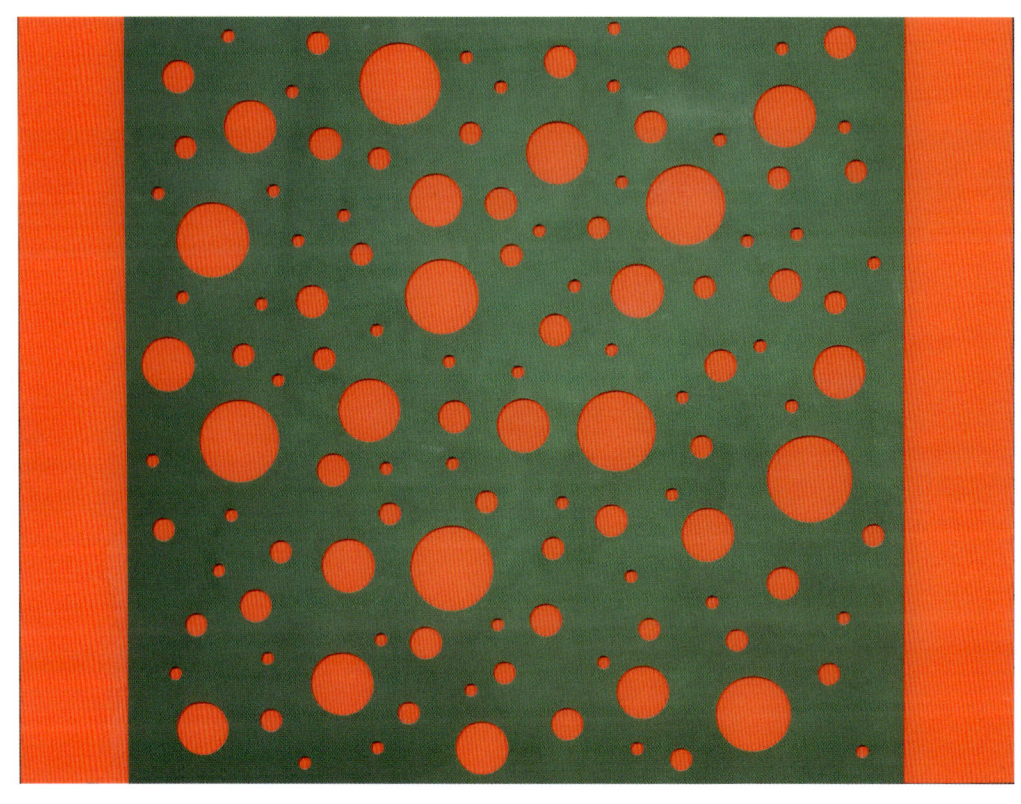

Figure 2.33
Wen-Ying Tsai, *Superimposed Painting: Random Field*, 1964. Fluorescent pigment, ultraviolet light. © 2024 Tsai Art and Science Foundation/Artists Rights Society (ARS), New York.

Iannis Xenakis, and the psychologist and cybernetician Gordon Pask. What might be noted about *Cybernetic Serendipity*, particularly in relation to Flusser's later theories, is that it emphasized digital computing over aleatory methods (that is, randomness or chance) and "software" (concepts and practices) over "hardware" (materials), since computers were largely out of reach to most people—including artists—in the 1960s.[94] (Tsai was also included in *Electra*, the 1983 exhibition at the Centre Pompidou in Paris organized by Frank Popper, and which Flusser mentioned in his technical image writings.)[95]

In 1969, György Kepes invited Tsai to the Center for Advanced Visual Studies at MIT (along with Jack Burnham, one of the main thinkers in systems art in the 1960s, Ted Kraynik, Otto Piene, Harold Tovish, Takis Vassilakis, and Stan VanDerBeek), where he met Harold Edgerton, who had developed the electronic stroboscope. Using a stroboscope and a feedback control system, Tsai created sculptures that interacted with viewers. In Tsai, Flusser saw the perfect marriage of art and science as well as nature and culture—but also a glimpse of the future, with art performing the groundwork for creating artificial life. In his essay "Aspects and Prospects of Tsai's Work" (1974), neither Tsai nor his works are mentioned until several paragraphs into the essay.[96] Instead, Flusser sets out a phenomenological analysis of our culture, in which objects "determine us" by forcing us into certain reactions and behaviors, and offers a brief description of the sculptures at the very *end* of the essay: "*Tsai's phenomena are wiry room-filling structures recalling botanical structures which respond to light, sound and touch in graceful lifelike movements that cannot be foreseen by those who play with them.*"[97] Tsai's cybernetic sculptures, Flusser concluded, provide a potential liberation. They present an initial stage in a revolution—playful ways of imagining a future populated with artificial objects and intelligence. They might be "diabolical artifices," but they reveal to us "the concrete experience of a future full of promise or abysmal danger," whether due to automation, artificial intelligence, or biotechnology.[98] They also feel, for Flusser, like phenomena culled from an Eastern tradition in which self and other—including the world of plants and animals—are not separated into categories like subject and object.[99]

Ultimately, Flusser was much closer to Tsai than to Schöffer, on both a personal and ideological level. Schöffer's proto-"smart city" structures demonstrate one approach to cybernetics, often

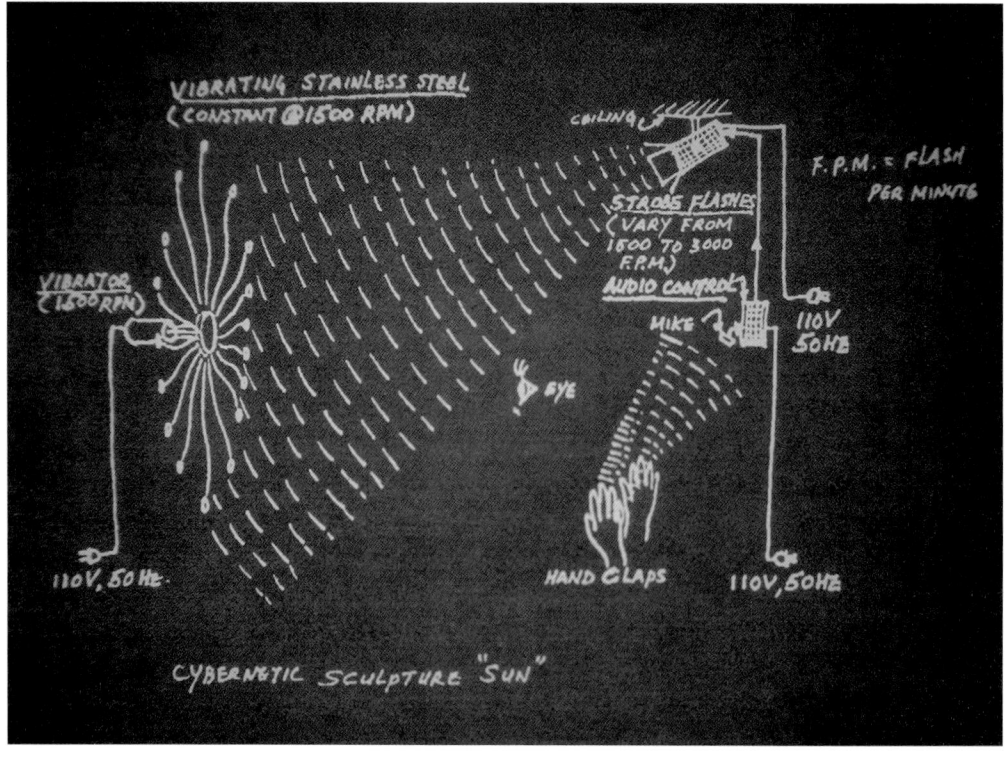

Figure 2.34
Wen-Ying Tsai, *Sketch Illustrating the Basic Ideas of His Cybernetic System Installations*, from *Tsai* (New York: Tsai Art and Science Foundation, 2018), 11. © 2024 Tsai Art and Science Foundation/Artists Rights Society (ARS), New York.

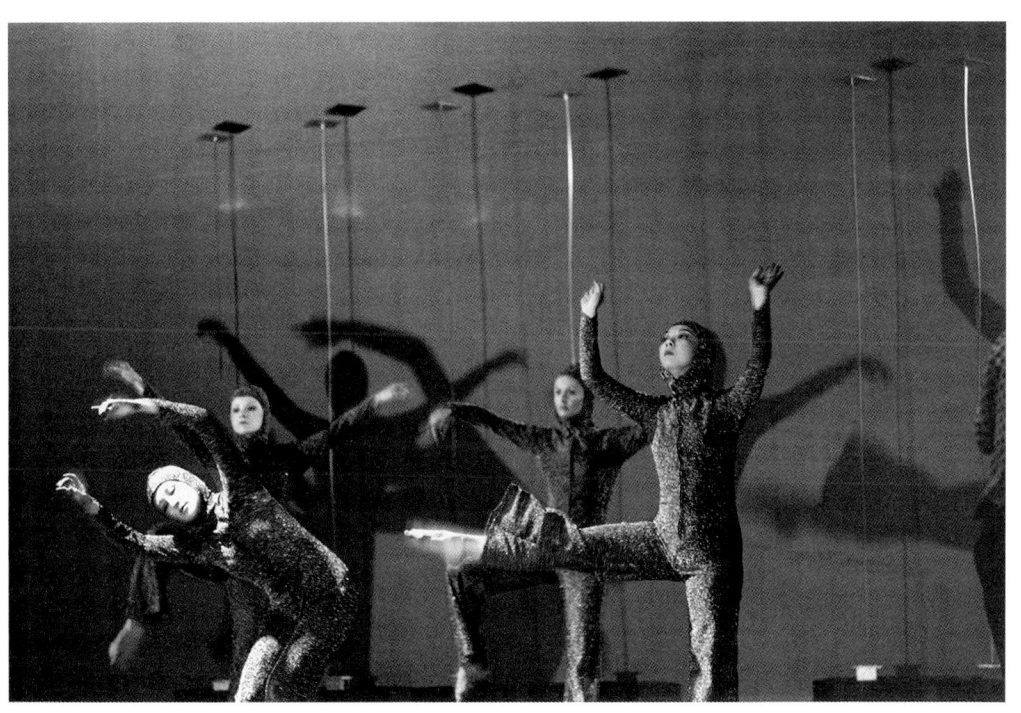

Figure 2.35
Chiang Ching Dance Company performing with Tsai's sculptures, 1979. © 2024 Tsai Art
and Science Foundation/Artists Rights Society (ARS), New York.

involving the apparatus and bureaucracy of cities and government. But Tsai, who was also an activist and a founding member of the Art Workers' Coalition (AWC) in New York in the late 1960s, engaged with technology and phenomenology in more intimate settings. Interacting with one of his cybernetic sculptures is similar to reading a Flusser essay and having one's sense of time, space, and consciousness subtly, or even profoundly, altered.

Mutations in Human Relations

Flusser remained in contact with several of the artists mentioned in this chapter. In the 1980s, Fred Forest made works like *How to Watch Television* (1984) and would form the Aesthetics of Communication Group (1983) with Italian theorist Mario Costa. In the 1990s, Forest would create another incendiary work around television, *Fred Forest président de la télévision bulgare* (Fred Forest for president of Bulgarian television, 1991), in which he briefly campaigned to become the head of state television for the Balkan nation, and he sued the Centre Georges Pompidou to reveal the price it paid for a Hans Haacke work, challenging French laws on transparency for public institutions.[100] Forest wrote that the last time he saw Flusser was in the summer of 1991 in Paris, in conjunction with Forest's project *The Electronic Bible and the Gulf War* (1991), an installation that included a single video monitor and LED messages emitting Bible passages and news dispatches from the war zone, in a pit filled with sand flown in from Kuwait.[101] Meanwhile, Flusser and Tsai remained close, and Miguel Flusser, Vilém's son, even went to Paris to apprentice with Tsai in his studio.

However, as the 1970s progressed, Flusser's ideas began to crystallize around communications theory and the burgeoning field of photography. In "Mutations in Human Relations" (1977–1978), posthumously published in its German version as *Kommunikologie* (Communicology) and part of the canon of German communications theory, Flusser argued that a communications revolution was under way which eclipsed any divide in politics (for instance, Marxist ideas about political-economic organization).[102] Flusser starts by describing human communication as an artifice, a device designed to cure loneliness and make us forget that we are going to die. And yet current communication is in crisis: we are not suitably programed for it, which is resulting in a rupture that Flusser describes

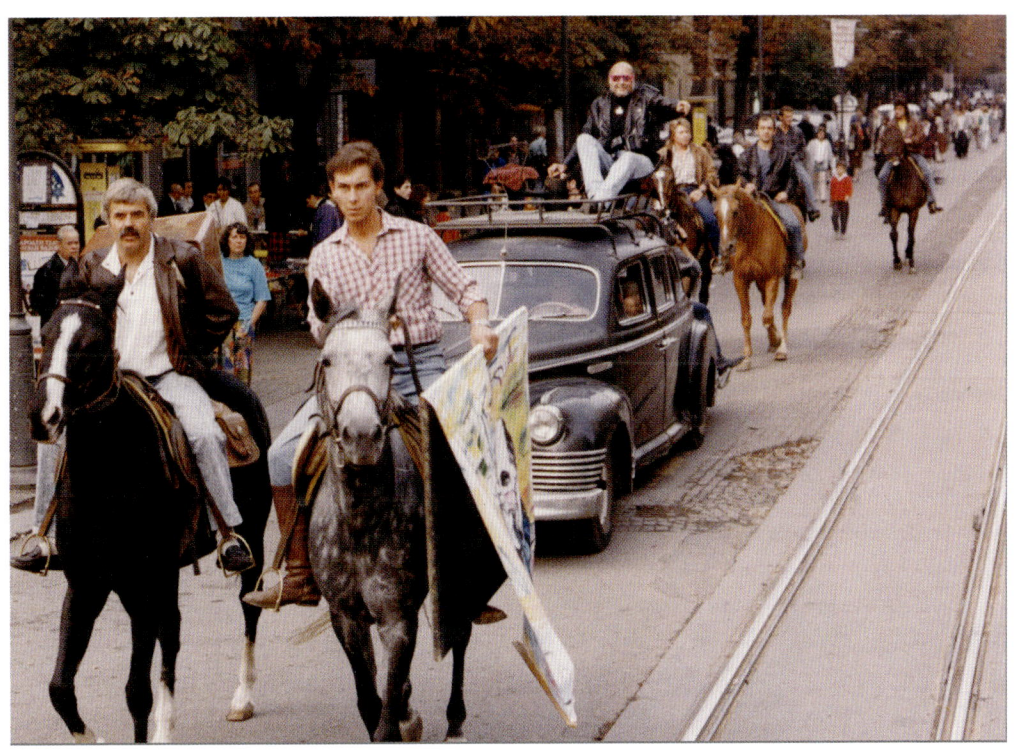

Figure 2.36
Fred Forest, *Fred Forest for President of Bulgarian Television*, 1991. Photograph of Forest
campaigning for president of Bulgarian national television, riding atop a Soviet-made
ZIL limousine formerly used by the Communist head of state in in Sofia, Bulgaria. © 2024
Artists Rights Society (ARS), New York/ADAGP, Paris.

as a "mutation of human relations."[103] (Remember, Flusser and Mira Schendel had read the work of Jean Gebser, whose idea of "mutations" in human consciousness informed Flusser's ideas.)

Briefly, Flusser argues that there are four models of discourse: theatrical (the theater, classroom, concert hall); pyramid (the church, political hierarchies like the Roman Republic); tree (science, technology, the arts, and some political and industrial institutions); and amphitheater (mass media, press, television—but also its prototype, the Roman Colosseum). Dialogue is broken down into circular (roundtable dialogues in parliaments, laboratories, committees, and symposia) and network ("open circuit" dialogue, including rumors, small talk, or the post office and telephone). And the epochs relating to various codes—Flusser admits these are radically simplified—include the era of printed books, the "manuscript situation" and the "techno-image situation," which seems like a return to the European medieval system and its "cosmic uniformity," except that feedback is limited between elite and mass levels. However, all forms of dialogue are in flux due to the revolution in codes. Dialogues are synchronized differently, and "history is being overcome by the transformation of events into pictures (be they still or moving)."[104]

Pictures, however, are of various types and categories—and this would become central to his technical image theory. Paintings in Lascaux are "projective images": they do not show a real situation (presumably) but serve as "hunting magic"—not to learn the anatomy of animals, but to hunt them. Meanwhile, we see the world differently when we look at Goya than when we look at Matisse. "The Goya and Matisse paintings are models of experiencing the world, and in this sense, both are road maps and blueprints. This is what makes 'art' of them."[105] Since the nineteenth century, Flusser argues, "techno-images" have taken over as codes, instigating an "ontological revolution" by replacing linear, textual thinking with images, starting with photographs—except that we have no foothold in this world. Causality, from Flusser's perspective, is in crisis. Technical progress has become meaningless. "We must, like the inventor of linear scripts, invent a new form of existence," he writes, "without being able to foresee what sort of existence that will be. We must, all the time, translate from line into techno-image, and invent this code while translating. In short: we know from experience the sort of situation which prevailed when History was invented."[106]

The danger in switching modes of consciousness without achieving a new one is that we may be unconsciously programmed (which, of course, we are, with many new technologies). Most people are *operators* of apparatuses, tools that produce techno-images, instigating a "radically new relation between tool and man, one for which classical analyses are useless."[107] Moreover, the apparatus operator is a *functionary*, or consumer. We believe that we are born with the capacity to understand images, which Flusser deems a "pernicious mistake" because even the *inventors* of techno-images are "illiterate."[108] "People were more aware of the meaning of films at the time of Lumière than they are at present," Flusser provocatively argues.[109] We need to learn "technoimagination" in order to think structurally rather than linearly, to change history *not* from within (by action) but from the outside (by recodification).[110] We need to build new models, drawn from fields like cybernetics. However, Flusser felt that even most video artists were unaware of (or not addressing) the potential of their materials. Instead, as long as "elite techno-images" are left to the specialists, one cannot begin to ask probing questions about the relationship between image and techno-image. "A 'theory of the technoimagination' is needed," but before such a theory exists, "we must be content with the tragicomical conflict between 'artists,' and with tragicomical events like film festivals and video-art exhibitions."[111] Flusser closes by considering the present mutation in human communication: we are in the midst of being "reprogrammed" by nonlinear media, and we participate and collaborate in the new ways in which we are manipulated. We are not in a classical master/slave relationship, but a new type of relation. We *know* the potentialities hidden in the new codes, and a new creative cosmic dialogue is possible, but we must develop new ways of thinking, with technoimagination.[112]

Post-History and Apparatus

Shortly after writing "Mutations in Human Relations," Flusser embarked on a series of essays that would be published as *Post-History* (1983), and which would serve as a springboard for the technical image writings that will be discussed in Screen 3.[113] *Post-History* is a profound, beautifully written book—one of my favorites of Flusser's essay collections conceived as a discrete book—although art is included less in the conversation than it is

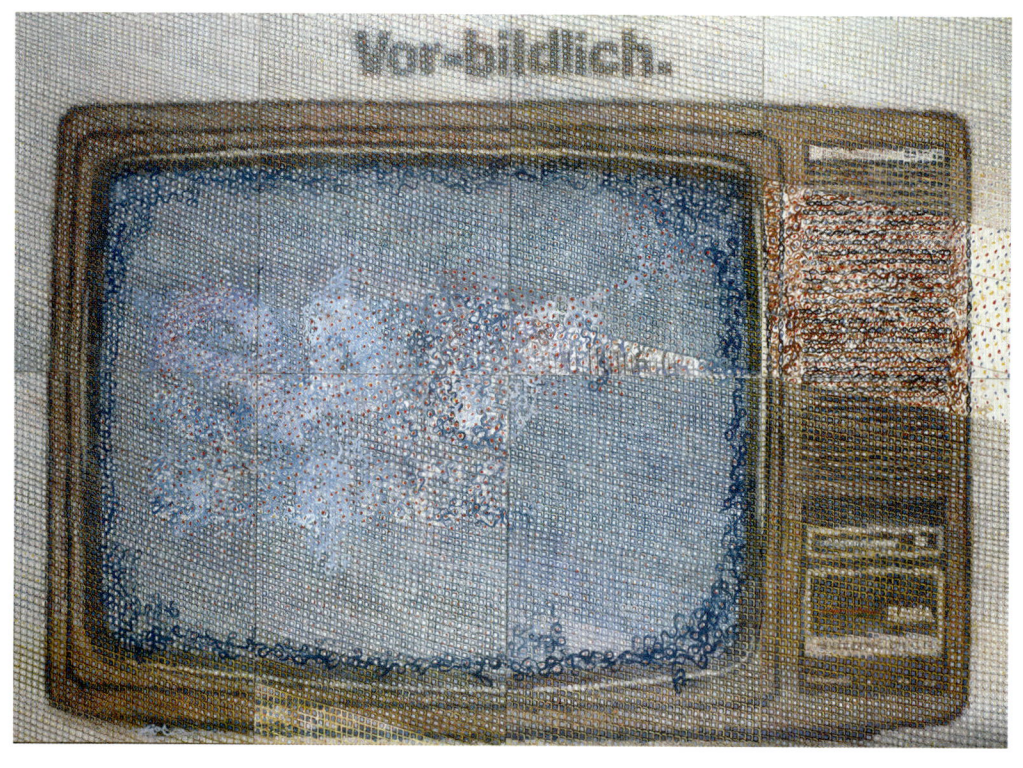

Figure 2.37
Thomas Bayrle, *TV Vor-bildich*, 1978. Oil on canvas. Courtesy the artist,
neugerriemschneider, Berlin, and Gladstone Gallery. Photo: Wolfgang Günzel. This
painting is reproduced in a book on Bayrle's work in the Vilém Flusser Archive in Berlin,
one of several Bayrle sent to the Flussers in the 1980s.

in many of his texts. Instead, he uses concepts derived from cybernetics, communications, information theory, and game theory to address science, religion, ideology, politics, progress, education, nature, and architecture. The book is formulated as a dialogue with individual thinkers—although the specific thinkers are not identified in the text. In a letter to Milton Vargas dated October 22, 1980, Flusser outlined who he was conducting a dialogue with in each essay: Hannah Arendt, Martin Buber, Rudolf Carnap, Karl Marx, Karl Popper, Ludwig Wittgenstein, Abraham Moles, José Ortega y Gasset, Jürgen Habermas, Theodor Adorno, Marshall McLuhan, A. Rappaport, Edmund Husserl, Ernst Bloch, the Hudson Institute (a conservative think tank founded in 1961 by Herman Kahn and colleagues from the RAND Corporation), Martin Heidegger, John Dewey, Jean-Paul Sartre, and Franz Kafka.[114] The list includes thinkers Flusser had grappled with during his teenage years in Prague (Marx, Kafka, Buber); his wartime and existential postwar years (Ortega y Gasset, Sartre, Heidegger, Arendt); his language philosophy years (Carnap, Wittgenstein); and his communications theory era (McLuhan).

The title of the brief opening section, "User's Manual," mimics the instruction manuals that come with consumer products, but also echoes the structure of experimental literature like Julio Cortázar's *Hopscotch* (1963) and Georges Perec's *Life, a User's Manual* (1978)—Perec being a member of the Parisian literary movement Oulipo, which used information theory to think about narrative structure.[115] Flusser writes that, although the sequencing of the essays is random and they can be read in any order—or "in leaps, like the movement of the knight on a chessboard"—there is still a discursive thread that "runs from despair toward hope, however tenuous."[116] In the first essay in *Post-History*, "The Ground We Tread," written as a dialogue with Hannah Arendt, Flusser introduces some of the elements causing ruptures: programs, apparatuses, and functionaries. Auschwitz, which informed both Flusser's and Arendt's philosophies—and where Flusser's mother and sister perished—serves as a pivot point. It was there that "the Western tendency toward objectification was finally realized and it was done so in the shape of an *apparatus*," Flusser wrote, and "once it started functioning, [it] developed in an automatic fashion, autonomous from the decisions of the initial programmers, even if it contributed to the defeat of the programmers, as it effectively did."[117] In "Our Program," addressed to the language philosopher

Rudolf Carnap, Flusser writes that the notion that the world and human existence are *programmed* is relatively new, replacing terms like "destiny" and "causality." However, this idea affects a range of phenomena: ideology, history, art, politics, and human freedom. This is because programs are actually games ("systems") based on chance—the disrupter of *causation*—and every virtuality, even the least probable, will eventually be realized if the game is played long enough.

In this programmed world, the worker described in "Our Work" becomes a functionary and society is transformed into a cybernetic system composed of functionaries and apparatuses, where the dominant "class" is the programmer (although programmers may, in fact, just be specialized functionaries). Moreover, knowledge ("Our Knowledge") and progress ("Our Health") are affected because science has become a game for programmers.[118] "Our Communication," written in dialogue with Moles, picks up arguments from "Mutations in Human Relations," analyzing the changing modes of discourse and dialogue, while "Our Inebriation," written in dialogue with Heidegger, looks at drugs, which come in many forms: poison (bad), medicine (good), or "narcotic media" (addictive). We are a culture of distraction rather than concentration—as he also points out in "Our Diversion" (dedicated to Husserl)—but every society has its preferred (and outlawed) drugs, from alcohol to hashish and magic mushrooms.

There is also "a specific drug called 'art'" in which the artist becomes "the inebriate who emigrates from culture in order to reinvade it."[119] However, art itself has changed, no longer functioning as a free or revolutionary romantic space, in the nineteenth-century sense. In "Our School," a response to John Dewey, Flusser argues that the industrial model of education produced fine art academies that crippled and amputated artists' "political and epistemological dimension."[120] Art can still serve as a model, though, because "creative inebriation" occurs in every discipline, turning private experience into a public declaration that can transform apparatuses. (This argument echoes those made by political theorists from Jacques Rancière to Michael Hardt and Antonio Negri, who posit art as a field where the political imaginary can flourish.) Flusser writes: "Notwithstanding: art is a kind of magic. As it publishes the private, as it 'turns conscious the unconscious,' it becomes a mediation of the immediate, a feat of *magic*. . . . And culture cannot forgo this magic: because without this source of new information, however ontologically suspect, culture would fall into entropy."[121]

Program and Apparatus

Two terms dominate *Post-History* that should be highlighted: *program* and *apparatus*. These serve as a springboard into the technical image writings, but obviously point back to Flusser's interest in cybernetics and Bense and Moles's information aesthetics. A great deal has been written about the term "apparatus" by theorists such as Bertolt Brecht, Louis Althusser, Michel Foucault, Gilles Deleuze and Félix Guattari, Giorgio Agamben, and more recent groups like Tiqqun.[122] It is also important to note that the term "apparatus" has different meanings and linguistic nuances, from Foucault's *dispositif* to the Portuguese *dispositivo*, which carries the original meaning of the Latin *dispositio*: in classical rhetoric, a system for organizing arguments.[123] Flusser translator Rodrigo Maltez Novaes notes that, when using the term in English, Flusser always used the Latin form of *apparatus* to connote both the singular and the plural.[124] However, from a historical perspective, if the French Revolution served as a benchmark for liberal Enlightenment, and a springboard for French apparatus theory, Auschwitz served as Flusser's Bastille. After Auschwitz, apparatuses sprang up "like mushrooms after a Nazi rain, from the ground that has become rotten."[125] For Flusser, there are smaller apparatuses—art, cinema, and the supermarket—but they are all synchronized by larger ones, such as transport, industry, entertainment, and governments. Some claim to be friends of mankind, like scientific, technical, and administrative apparatuses, but such labels are deceptive, serving only to cover up the essence of the apparatus, since "they are all just like Auschwitz, black boxes that function with complex inner workings in order to realize a program," which is "the annihilation of all their functionaries, including programmers," because "they objectify and dehumanize man."[126]

The term "black box" stands out here, too. For Norbert Wiener, black boxes were actual, physical objects: the black-speckled boxes used in MIT's Radiation Laboratory during World War II to house radar equipment.[127] For Flusser, a black box is a similarly opaque entity: something that is programmed and which its users barely understand (structurally complex but functionally simple).[128] The black box serves for him as an expanding metaphor: media are black boxes; the family can be a black box. In "Our Rhythm," dedicated to Marcuse, cinema is a black box that is both literal and metaphoric, but also an apparatus that produces "optical fraud" in the form of projected illusion, where receivers collaborate in their own "annihilation as subjects."[129]

What is important to note is not just the *existence* of apparatus, but their *effect*: they've produced an upheaval of history resulting in the migration of peoples and the reshuffling of space and time. Moreover, they've become increasingly automated—and we don't know how to operate them. We can *observe* the models of postindustrial society: "Eichmann as model functionary, Kissinger as model programmer, and Auschwitz as postindustrial society."[130] However, programmers are a new type of individual, and Flusser argues that we don't have theoretical structures to guide our thinking: "What is still missing for us is the equivalent of an Aristotle of the agrarian society and a Kant of the industrial society. What is urgent is to rethink the meaning of the term theory in this new context. . . . In the post-industrial society, 'theory' will very probably be a game strategy."[131] (As stated in the "Warning" at the beginning of this book, we're now at a moment when developers of social media and AI freely admit they didn't understand the power and nature of the programs they've assisted in advancing.) Flusser argues that, if we wish to emancipate ourselves from an apparatus, we need to treat it like an absurd form of game theory: "whether we continue to be 'men' or become robots depends on how fast we learn to play: we can become players of the game or pieces in it."[132]

Now we are ready to talk about Flusser's technical image theory. Program and apparatus serve as an important bridge. In "Our Images" in *Post-History*, written in dialogue with Marshall McLuhan, Flusser writes that traditional images are different from technical images in that the former are produced by humans and the latter by apparatuses. Furthermore, "apparatus are black boxes that are programmed to devour *symptoms* of scenes and to spew out these symptoms in the form of images," transcoding them in a fashion that makes decoding "even more arduous than that of traditional images: the message is even more 'masked.'"[133] This, of course, is a 180-degree turn from old adages and clichés like "photographs don't lie" and "a picture is worth a thousand words." In the final essay in the book, "Our Return," dedicated to Kafka, Flusser sums up the ramifications of these changes. While

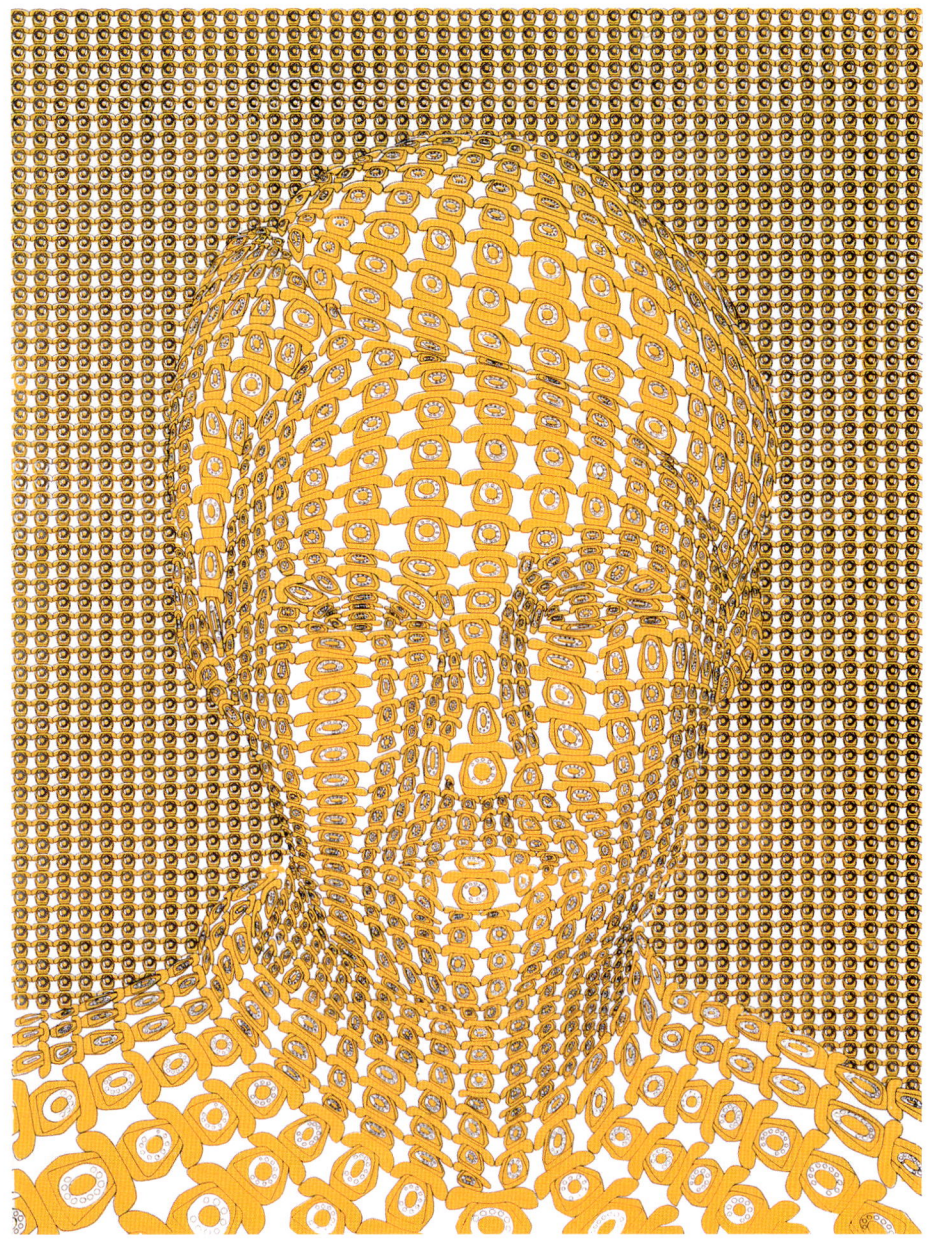

Figure 2.38
Thomas Bayrle, *Telefonbau-Normalzeit (gelbe Version)* [Telephone construction, Standard Time, yellow version], 1970. Silkscreen print on cardboard. Courtesy of the artist, neugerriemschneider, Berlin, and Gladstone Gallery. Photo credit: Wolfgang Günzel.

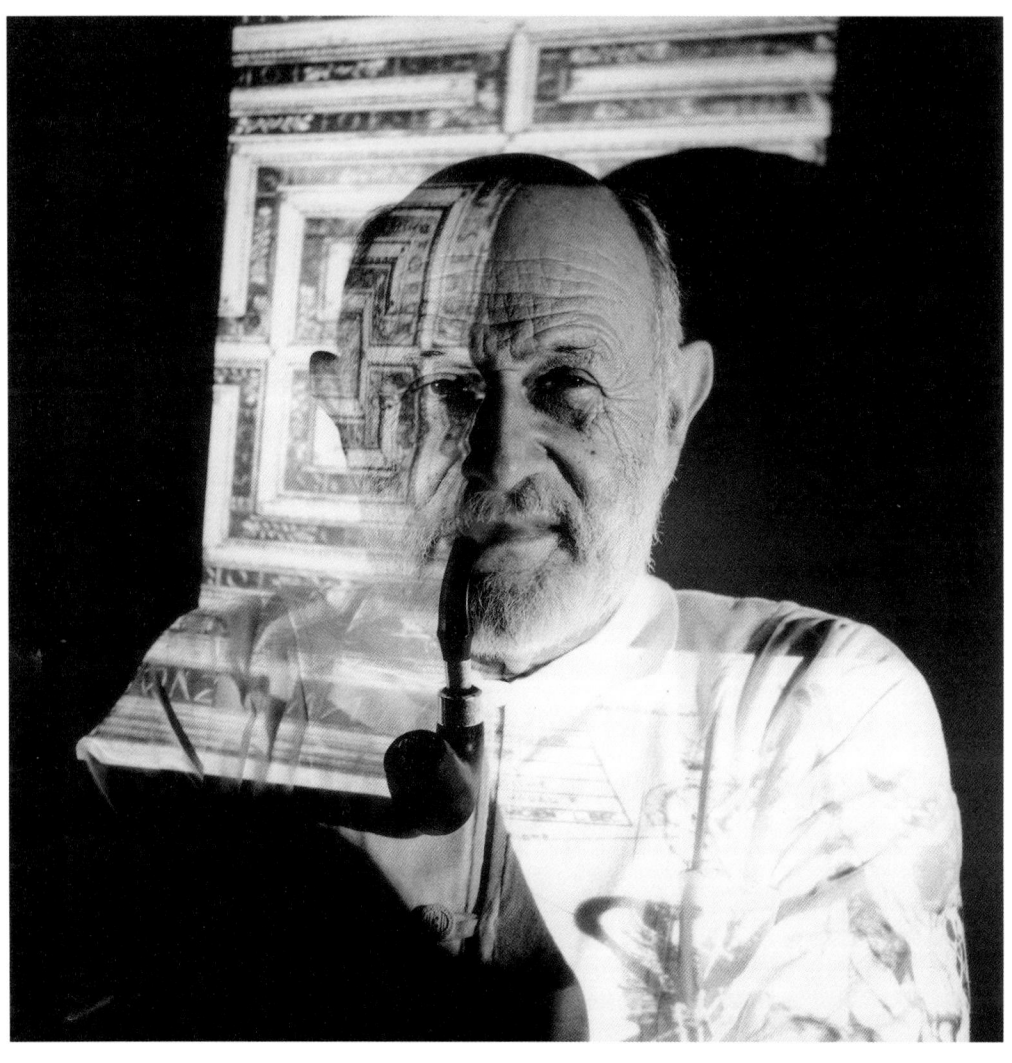

Figure 2.39
Ed Sommer, *Portrait of Vilém Flusser*, 1988–1989. Black-and-white photograph, 30 × 30 cm.
Private Collection. © Ed Sommer. A sculptor as well as a photographer, Sommer
participated in the New Tendencies movement, exhibiting in *nova tendencija 3* in Zagreb
in 1965.

industrial societies are transitioning into postindustrial societies, linear and historical thinking founded on texts is being challenged by the "post-textual codes" found in technical images. This creates a new type of consciousness that is difficult to characterize yet results in global structural change. The age of programs, apparatuses, and technical images propels us into post-history, where "technical imagination" will be needed. This *Einbildungskraft*—imagination or "visioning"—informed by informatics, cybernetics, and game theory rather than aesthetics, literary criticism, or other methodologies, would become Flusser's theory for deciphering technical images.

But we are getting ahead of ourselves. Flusser's ideas about technical images were largely in place in the late 1970s; they just weren't a "theory of photography." In that sense, one might say that Flusser's writings from this period comprise a constellation of ideas looking for a context. He would find one in European photography (literally: Andreas Müller-Pohle of *European Photography* magazine would become his biggest supporter) and the burgeoning field of media studies. "Post-history is rising," Flusser wrote.[134] As in earlier decades, the artistic and intellectual climate of the 1980s would profoundly inform his trajectory.

Screen 3 *Knots, Nodes, and Technical Images*

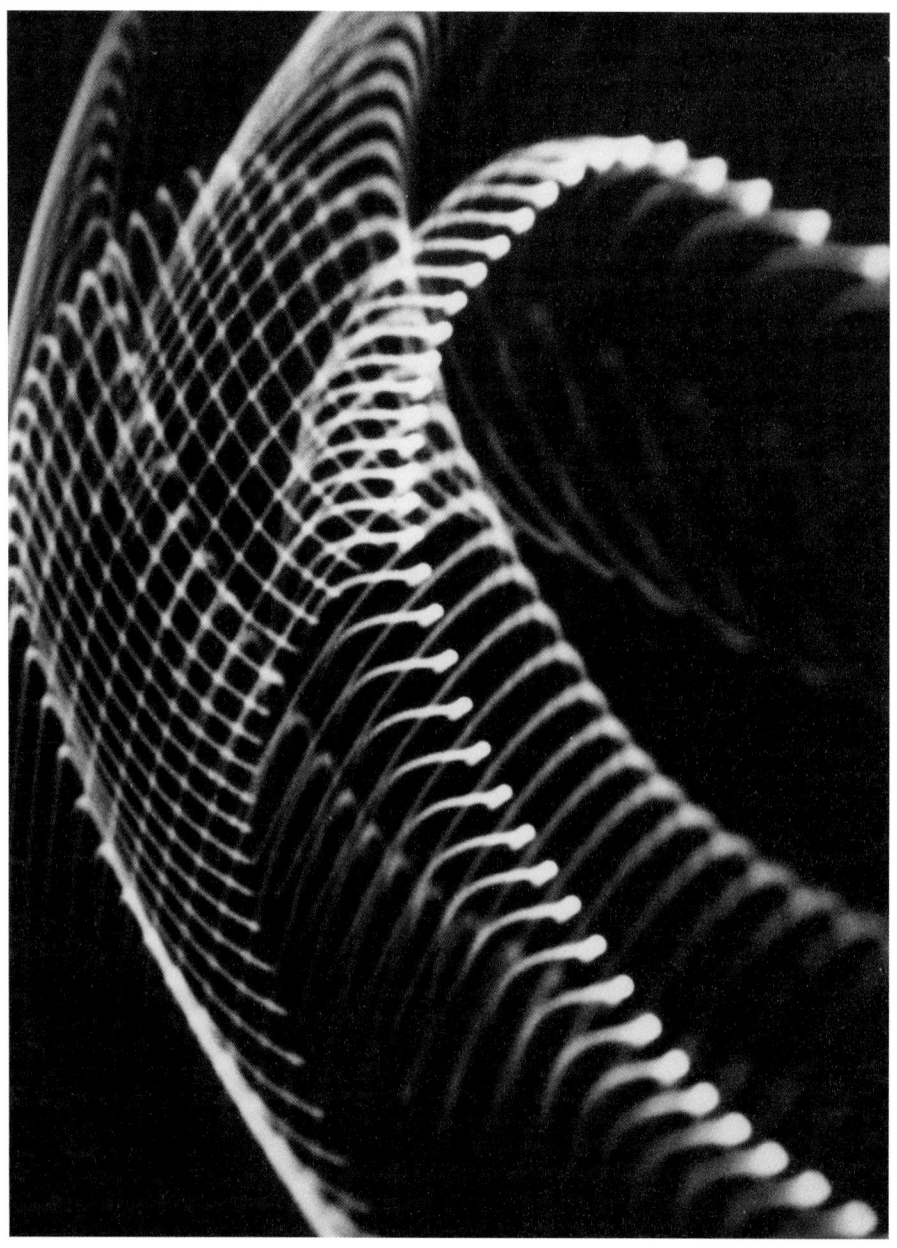

Figure 3.1
Herbert W. Franke, *Oscillogram*, 1954–1959. Analog computer and black-and-white photography. Estate of Herbert W. Franke and Susanne Päch.

Photography is not a tool like a machine; it is a game, like cards or chess. If we take photography as our model, we do not simply substitute one type of tool for another type of tool as model; we substitute one kind of model for another kind. . . . The basic structure of our thinking is about to experience a mutation. What is involved here is not the classical problem of alienation, but an existential revolution for which we do not have any historical precedents. To put it brutally: what is involved here is the challenge of reconsidering the problem of freedom in an entirely new context. This is what a philosophy of photography would really address. [1]

Flusser's entry into the field of photography coincided with an explosion of interest in that medium. Roland Barthes commented in an interview three days before his death in 1980, "There does seem to be a kind of 'theoretical boom' in photography. People who are not technicians, historians, or aestheticians are becoming interested in it." [2] In the United States and Europe, a canon of photography theory was being formed. Primary among these texts were Walter Benjamin's "A Little History of Photography" (1931) and "The Work of Art in the Age of Its Mechanical Reproducibility" (1936), which were translated and disseminated in English only in the late 1960s and 1970s. In 1968, A. D. Coleman's first column appeared in the *Village Voice*, signaling the perceived need for a dedicated photography critic. [3] (Flusser would correspond with Coleman and approach him for advice on publishing *Towards a Philosophy of Photography* in English.) In 1976, Coleman's writings were included in a special issue of *Artforum* devoted to photography, and *October*, a new US journal started by former *Artforum* editors and contributors, included photography as part of its focus. [4] In a special 1978 issue of *October* devoted to photography, editors Rosalind Krauss and Annette Michelson noted that the practice of photography was expanding and solidifying at the same moment that painting and sculpture were "in a state of low tension," and they called for a "radical sociology" of the medium

123

to counter the market-driven tendency of photography collecting and scholarship.[5]

Writing on photography from this period took different tacks. Susan Sontag's *On Photography* (1977) was marked by a post-Vietnam War malaise.[6] Laura Mulvey and Peter Wollen, writers for the British journal *Screen*, considered photography alongside film, and Victor Burgin and John Berger leaned toward post-1968 semiotics and Marxism.[7] In France, Pierre Bourdieu's *Photography: A Middle-Brow Art* was published in 1965.[8] Using a sociological approach, Bourdieu argued that photography offered a method for studying French society and its class divisions. The towering figure in photography theory, though—after Benjamin—has been Roland Barthes. In essays like "Photography and Electoral Appeal" and "Shock-Photos"—both included in *Mythologies* (1957)—and "The Photographic Message" (1961) and "Rhetoric of the Image" (1964), Barthes used structural linguistics, semiotics, and Brechtian Marxism to show how everyday images function like sign systems, loaded with ideological messages that aren't immediately apparent.

In 1980, Barthes published *Camera Lucida: Reflections on Photography*, his only book dedicated to photography.[9] Influenced by Proust, Sontag, and Benjamin, the book also reflects a late interest in Buddhism: the French edition of *Camera Lucida* even includes a quotation on its back cover taken from Chögyam Trungpa (it was removed in the English edition): "Marpa was very shaken when his son was killed, and one of his disciples said, 'You always say to us that all is illusion. Isn't the death of your son then an illusion?' And Marpa responded, 'Certainly, but the death of my son is a super-illusion.'"[10] Beyond this, however, *Camera Lucida* is a strongly autobiographical response to photography, focused on a snapshot of Barthes's mother when she was a child—which may or may not even exist—which serves as a marker for memory, death, and the power of photographs.

Critics have lamented that *Camera Lucida* is limited because Barthes focuses primarily on photographs of people (and the apocryphal photograph of his mother), creating a personal theory of photography with a mythical object at its center. Moreover, Barthes's fidelity to realism—"truth in photography"—is anachronistic at a moment when this very thing was being questioned, particularly by artists and audiences in the post-Vietnam era. Barthes's theory is also rather death-obsessed. This is the same author

Figure 3.2
Andreas Müller-Pohle, *Transformance 3590*, 1980. Black-and-white photograph. From a series of 10,000 photographs taken in motion without looking through the viewfinder, highlighting photography as an act of chance.

who wrote the landmark essay "The Death of the Author" in 1967, included a Tibetan death quotation in *Camera Lucida*, and a photograph from James Van Der Zee's *The Harlem Book of the Dead* in the same book.[11] In a 1977 interview, Barthes called every encounter with photography "a contact with death" and "a fascinating and funereal enigma."[12] Despite critiques, however, *Camera Lucida* remains "the most quoted book in the photographic canon."[13]

Enter Flusser. His position in the canon of German photography theory is secure: open a German anthology of photography and he is not just represented, but *amply* present.[14] His work has been translated into more than thirty languages, including nearly a dozen during his lifetime. He is still a marginal figure in the United States within the discourse of contemporary photography theory, though. And his entry into photography discourse was gradual but strategic, reflecting what Barthes said in 1980 about nonspecialists—people who are *not* photographers, technicians, historians, or aestheticians—becoming interested in photography. It began in the 1970s. At the 1975 Festival of Arles, Flusser spoke at a roundtable on art and photography, offering a phenomenological argument that overlapped with his theory of gestures. We are moving past the three-dimensional realm, he said, plunged into a world mediated by two-dimensional images, which changes our relationship with our surroundings. For instance, a presentation by the portrait photographer Yousuf Karsh—famous for photographing Winston Churchill, Nikita Khrushchev, and Dwight D. Eisenhower, among others—refined his opinion of how a photographer manipulates a situation; the camera affects the photograph in the same way a doctor holding a stethoscope interacts with a patient, but the element of "choice" is absent, because the camera is already programmed with Cartesian ideology.[15] At "Reading the Image," a 1978 conference in Paris that included Jean Baudrillard, Gisèle Freund, and Yves Michaud, Flusser presented "Iconoclasm," an essay arguing that history expressed in alphanumeric code (writing) served as a form of iconoclasm, an attempt to destroy images.[16]

Towards a Philosophy of Photography

A turning point came in early 1981 when Flusser met Andreas Müller-Pohle, a photographer and publisher of the bilingual journal *European Photography*, at a symposium organized by photographer Erika Kiffl in Düsseldorf.[17] Müller-Pohle recounts that shortly after they met, he asked Flusser to write a book on photography. Flusser responded enthusiastically: "We'll call it 'Towards a Philosophy of Photography.' We'll organize it in a focused way, let's say, in nine chapters. That makes sixty pages. Do you agree?"[18] Flusser wrote the book in nine months, although the ideas were largely in place already. In December 1982, he mailed a final version to Müller-Pohle. "I have tried to either incorporate or refute your objections to the first version," he wrote. "I think the enclosed version is ready for printing."[19] Müller-Pohle responded that it was still possible to make changes: "your book is just too important and meaningful" to rush it to print. "Incidentally," Müller-Pohle continued, "your book is already crying out for a sequel—a PHILOSOPHY OF THE COMPUTER. But we should talk about that as soon as we are done with the current topic."[20] The German edition appeared in 1983, and Flusser's practically unknown English translation—the one that will be quoted here—was published in a small edition in 1984. A Portuguese version, also translated by Flusser, appeared in 1985. Eventually the book was translated into over twenty languages.[21]

Towards a Philosophy of Photography explores the "photographic universe": the permanently shifting landscape of media, advertising, and other images so ubiquitous we are not even aware they exist. "To find oneself within the photographic universe," Flusser wrote in an oft-quoted passage, "is to experience, to know, and to evaluate the world as a function of photographs."[22] The book focuses on four terms already familiar to us: *image*, *apparatus*, *program*, and *information*. "Image" is defined in Flusser's enigmatic lexicon at the back of the book as "a meaningful surface within which the elements relate magically."[23] The first essay in the book, "The Image," defines images (not specifically photographs) as "significant surfaces" where meaning rests on the surface and may be "seized at a glance" by scanning, rather than reading in a linear fashion.[24] The discussion of images opens the way for thinking about how the photographic universe operates differently from the era of historical consciousness. Texts were created in the second millennium BCE as meta-codes of images, to explain images and transcode them into concepts. The second essay, "The Technical Image," defines these images as the "indirect products of scientific texts," since they are produced by technological apparatuses,

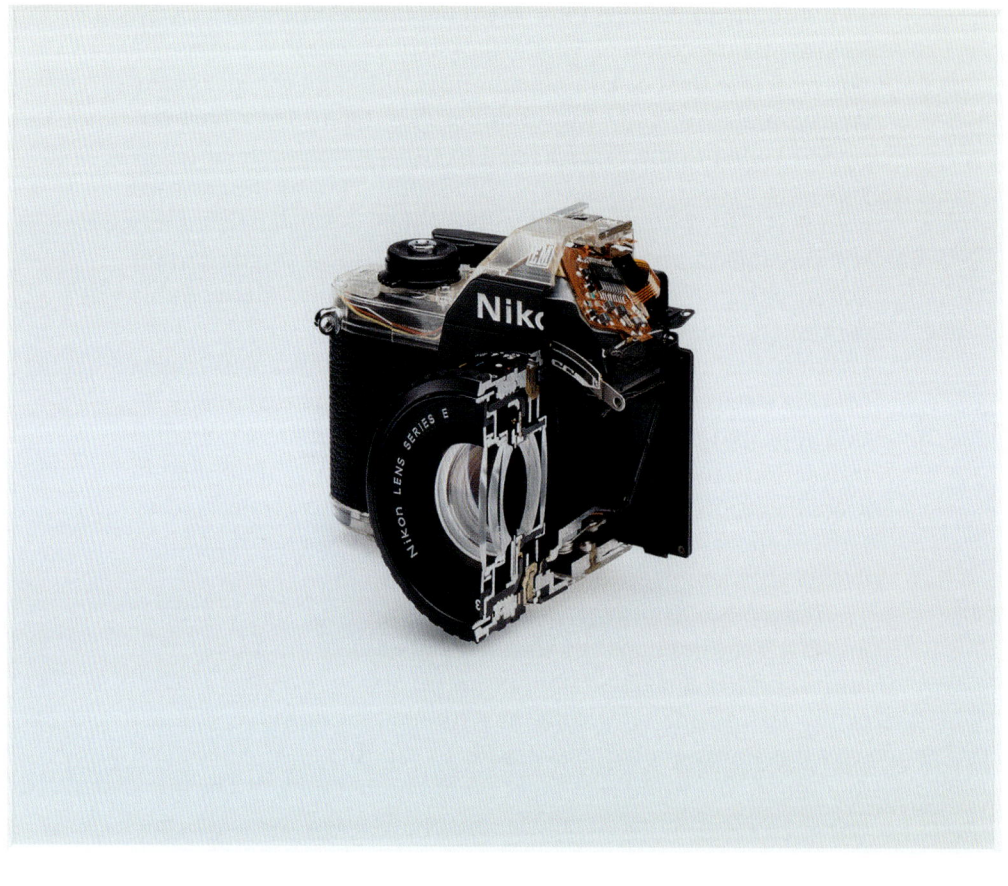

Figure 3.3

Christopher Williams, cutaway model Nikon EM. Shutter: Electronically governed Seiko metal blade shutter, vertical travel with speeds from 1/1000 to 1 second, with a manual speed of 1/90th. Meter: Center-weighted Silicon Photo Diode, ASA 25–1600 EV2–18 (with ASA film and 1.8 lens). Aperture Priority: automatic exposure. Lens Mount: Nikon F mount, AI coupling (and later) only. Flash: Synchronization at 1/90 via hot shoe. Flash automation with Nikon SB-E or SB-10 flash units. Focusing: K type focusing screen, not user interchangeable, with 3mm diagonal split image rangefinder. Batteries: Two PX-76 or equivalent. Dimensions: 5.3 × 3.38 × 2.13 in. (135 mm × 86 mm × 54 mm), 16.2 oz (460g). Photograph by the Douglas M. Parker Studio, Glendale, California, September 9, 2007–September 13, 2007, 2008, 20 × 24 in. (50.8 × 61 cm), chromogenic print. © Christopher Williams. Courtesy the artist, David Zwirner, and Galerie Gisela Capitain, Cologne.

which result from scientific texts.[25] And yet, despite their ties to science, technical images are magical: they seduce and bewitch viewers. Think of an infant in front of a television for the first time, or a crowd of adults, eyes glued to their smartphone screens.

Next comes apparatus. Here it is important to clarify how Flusser was inspired by Martin Heidegger—and particularly Heidegger's later writings: "The Age of the World Picture" (1938), "The Turning" (1949), and "The Question Concerning Technology" (1955).[26] For instance, in "The Question Concerning Technology," Heidegger performs a lengthy analysis of the word *technē* and its relationship to "technology," which clearly inspired Flusser.[27] One can see the same approach in Flusser's analysis of the word "apparatus" in the eponymous essay in *Towards a Philosophy of Photography*: "The Latinate term 'apparatus' stems from the verb 'apparare,' which is 'to prepare,'" Flusser begins, concluding that "in this sense, an apparatus would be an object which makes itself ready for something," and "the camera makes itself ready to take pictures, tries to ambush them, is on the lurk for them. This lying-in-wait for something, this predatory character of the apparatus, must be understood in our attempt to define 'apparatus' etymologically."[28] I have already outlined, briefly, some of the discourse around the term *apparatus*. However, in *Towards a Philosophy of Photography*, Flusser lands on a concrete example: "The camera," he writes, "constitutes a prototype for all the immense apparatus which threaten to become monolithic (such as the administrative apparatus) as well as those microscopic apparatus which threaten to slip from our grasp (such as the chips in electronic apparatus)—and which determine the present and immediate future to such a high degree. Analyzing the camera helps [us] to understand apparatus in general, in other words."[29] And yet photographers—at this point in history, you and me with our cameras inside our phones—are not complete slaves to their apparatuses. Photography runs on a program: fashion photographs, art photographs, war photographs—even snapshots and selfies—are all identifiable by certain markers, as well as by how they are disseminated and displayed. In the lexicon at the back of the book, Flusser defines an apparatus as "a toy which simulates thought"—an extremely curious definition, unless you consider his interest in game theory.[30] The camera is programmed with a series of virtualities, and playing *against* the program—as artists often do—offers the possibility to avoid becoming a mere functionary of the apparatus.

Searching for undiscovered virtualities in the camera program enables the photographer to produce new information (signal, in information theory, rather than infinite noise).[31] But photography is a serious game: "Such an activity is not dissimilar to playing chess," Flusser wrote. "A chess player plays with chess figures; a photographer plays with the camera. The camera is not a tool, but a toy, and the photographer is not a worker as such, but a player: not *homo faber*, but *homo ludens*." Flusser continued: "Except: the photographer does not play with, but against, his toy. He crawls into the camera in order to discover the tricks hidden there."[32] Using a camera *without* playing against its program resulted in becoming a mere functionary.

The term "functionary" carries distinct Kafkaesque overtones that tie Flusser to an older model of apparatuses and administrative control—and Flusser does refer to Kafka in *Towards a Philosophy of Photography*: "Functionnaires [Flusser's term for functionaries] are people who dominate a game [in] which they cannot be competent. Kafka."[33] However, in the universe of technical images, one is not merely a pawn—a de facto functionary—but a programmer: the question is not merely who controls the program, but how one can exist as both a programmer and a functionary of the program. "Photographs must be deciphered in order for the hidden interests of the controllers to be made visible," Flusser wrote. "For example, the interests of the holders of Kodak shares, the owners of advertising agencies, and so on, all of the people, in other words, who pull the wires behind the industrial establishment, and in the end, the interests of the entire industrial, military, and ideological complex. Should anyone succeed in evidencing this kind of interest-complex, each single photograph and the photographic universe as a whole might be considered to have been deciphered."[34] Here, in sum, is technoimagination—although in the lexicon of *Towards a Philosophy of Photography*, it is shortened to "*Imagination*: the capacity to produce and decipher images."[35]

Flusser doesn't cite specific photographs in *Towards a Philosophy of Photography*, but he does distinguish between *photography* and *technical images*. Technical images exist in the photographic universe of Technicolor images, while photography has its roots in black-and-white images. All are abstractions, or "theoretical" images—although color photography for Flusser is *more* abstract than black-and-white photography. For instance, the difference between the green of a lawn and how it is represented in a color

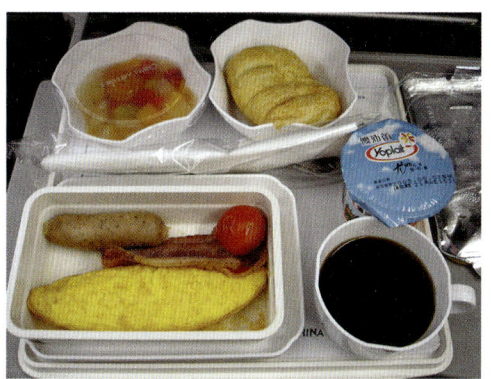
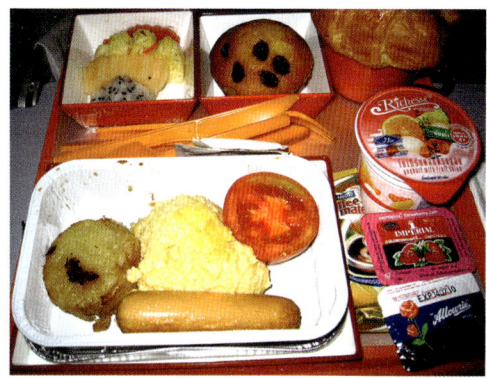
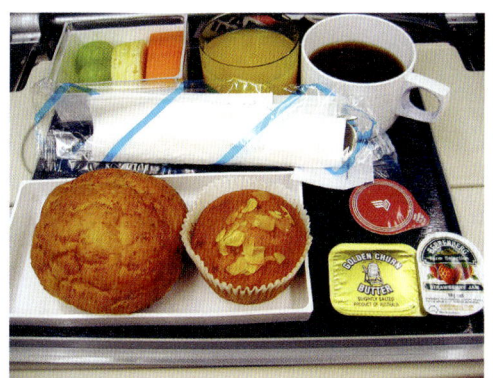
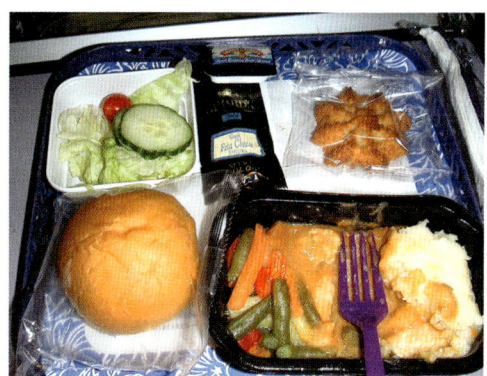

Figure 3.4
Joachim Schmid, *Airline Meals*, 2008–2011. Photograph from the 96-volume series *Other People's Photographs*. Courtesy of Joachim Schmid.

photograph is more complex than information coded in black-and-white photographs (and more difficult to regulate, as anyone who has color-corrected digital images can attest). Color would become one of Flusser's primary concerns in the late 1980s in relation to design and the Casa da Cor (House of color), as we will see in Screen 5. Here, however, we can see threads of an argument being debated in the 1980s: photography's historical reputation as a purveyor of the "real." Fidelity to realism haunted Barthes and other theorists, but it wasn't an issue for Flusser since, for him, photography transforms phenomena into codified information.[36] This is not to say that Flusser completely ignored the concept of the *index*, popularized by art historians like Rosalind Krauss.[37] In *Towards a Philosophy of Photography*, he wrote that technical images "are apparently in no need of being deciphered. Their meaning seems to impress itself automatically on their surfaces, as in fingerprints where the meaning (the finger) is the cause and the image (the print) is the effect."[38] However, for Flusser, the purported "objectivity" of technical images is an illusion; they are "meta-codes" of the scientific texts to which they are historically linked and abstractions rather than records of reality.[39] The history of photographic portraiture underscores this. From nineteenth-century daguerreotype studios in Paris to twentieth-century masters in Bamako and twenty-first-century social media influencers around the globe, photographers have been realizing virtualities in the camera's program, creating situations that exist solely to be photographed. It's not the world "out there" that's real in these photos or the concepts contained in the apparatus program, but the realization of the image itself.

Toward the end of the book, Flusser pulls back to examine the *universe* of technical images, a concept that might be traced back to thinkers like Henri Bergson and Deleuze, in his writings on cinema, but more pointedly to Heidegger.[40] In "The Age of the World Picture," originally delivered as a lecture in 1938, Heidegger argued that when we reflect on the modern age we see ourselves "in the picture"—not a "picture of the world but the world conceived and grasped as picture."[41] Moreover, for Heidegger, "the world picture does not change from an earlier medieval one into a modern one, but rather the fact that the world becomes picture at all is what distinguishes the essence of the modern age [*der Neuzeit*]."[42] For Flusser, "the photographic universe"—the subject of the penultimate essay in *Towards a Philosophy of Photography*—is the condition

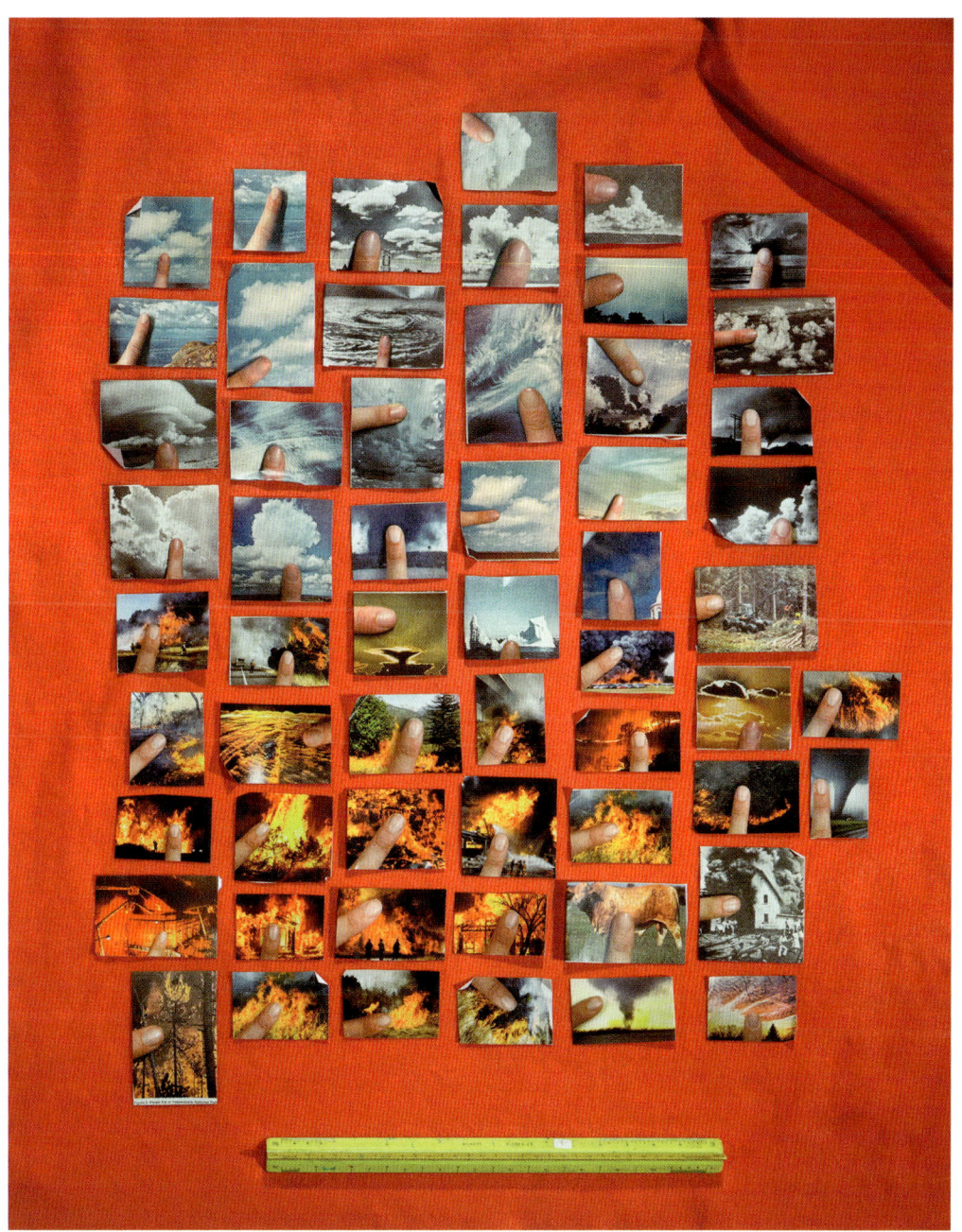

Figure 3.5
Sara Cwynar, *Encyclopedia Grid (Weather)*, 2024. UV print on Red Hot car paint mounted on Dibond in metal frame, 42¾ × 34¾ in. Courtesy the artist and Foxy Production, New York.

in which one is "to know and to evaluate the world as a function of photographs," and where the images in our world change so frequently they become redundant; to experience a static state would be extraordinary. Additionally, technical images and apparatuses are becoming increasingly automated, and the "automatic program" is "a game of combinations based on accident, on chance."[43] To exist in the photographic universe, surrounded by these chance realizations of program options, is to exist in flux with one redundant photograph replacing another. (One only need think of the urban environment, of city streets or subway systems, where advertisements and announcements change incessantly—and we have limited or no control over these changes.) There are photographers who can play against the photographic program, though, creating informative rather than redundant photographs to create situations not inscribed in the program. Here one thinks of the urban interventions of the Lettrist and Situationist International— particularly the practice of *détournement*, in which media images are disfigured or defaced, altered like collages or graffiti—or the culture jamming and memes of digital activists.

Photography criticism provides another venue for disrupting the program. The critic nowadays must dive into the darkness of the black box, and criticism therefore becomes a heroic battle. (It should be noted that Flusser's own writing, with its enigmas and neologisms, could itself be, at times, an inscrutable black box.) "The task of a photographic philosophy is to reveal this struggle between man and apparatus in the realm of photography, and thus to contribute to a possible solution to the conflict," Flusser writes; a task which, if it were to succeed, "would be of importance not only in the realm of photography but also for post-industrial society in general."[44] This is true because the photographic universe is only one among many universes of apparatuses—and not even the most dangerous one. In the final essay of *Towards a Philosophy of Photography*, "The Need for a Philosophy of Photography," Flusser stresses the fact that we are living in a new structure of reality, which is no longer historical and linear, and so we can no longer look for *causal* answers to our questions.[45] And here, Flusser flags a term that was essentially forbidden in photography discourse: *magic*, which disrupts the linear narrative dominated by causality.

I mentioned in the beginning of Screen 1 that Flusser was destined, perhaps, to revive the term "magic." Born in Prague, a city that has been described as a "heterotopia of the magical," he was drawn to texts by Giordano Bruno, Jakob Böhme, and Carlo Mongardini that examine magic in contrast to the European Enlightenment.[46] However, the term only begins to proliferate in Flusser's technical image writings. In *Towards a Philosophy of Photography,* he argues that the humans who invented writing in the second millennium BCE transcoded the circular time of magic into the linear time of history, but that the magic of photography is different because it conjures tricks with particles—originally the tiny grains of silver in chemical photography; now the pixels in our digital devices. In a famous section of the book, Flusser writes, "The world of magic is structurally different from the world of historical linearity, where nothing ever repeats itself, where everything is an effect of causes and will become a cause of further effects. For example, in the historical world, sunrise is the cause of the cock's crowing; in the magical world, sunrise means crowing and crowing means sunrise. Images have magical meaning."[47] In the book's lexicon, magic is defined as "existence in a world of eternal return," emphasizing its temporal and circular quality, the feedback loop of post-history.[48] And whereas prehistoric magic dealt with myths, post-historical magic relies on programs.

What is the result of this cataclysmic change? The photographic universe has programmed us to think functionally—linearly—but causality has been altered, throwing us into an existential crisis. Our screens, smartphones, algorithms, and AI are just another chapter in this crisis. Flusser approached the problem philosophically: "To put it brutally: what is involved here is the challenge of reconsidering the problem of freedom in an entirely new context. This is what a philosophy of photography would really address."[49] But how do we address the question of human freedom—particularly, as Flusser argues, if everything comes about by chance? The simple answer is within the *gesture* of photography, outwitting the stupidity of the apparatus and producing something unexpected and informative. Flusser stresses that photographers do not generally acknowledge their activities in this light. But that is the task. Freedom is playing against the apparatus. The book ends: "The task of a philosophy of photography is to analyze the possibility of freedom in a world dominated by apparatus; to think about how it is possible to give meaning to human life in the face of the accidental necessity of death. We need such a philosophy because it is the last form of revolution which is still accessible for us."[50] Like most of the medium's theorists,

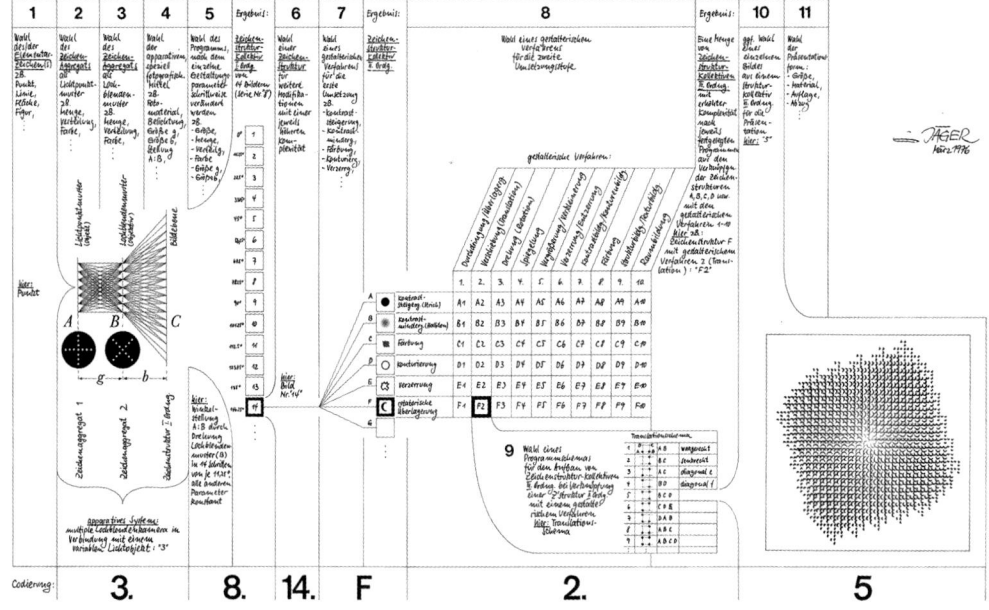

Figure 3.6
Gottfried Jäger, *Steps in the Creation of Modified Pinhole Structures of the Series 3.8.14*, 2015.
Archival print (Epson Digigraphy) from the original 1967 hand drawing. © 2024 Artists
Rights Society (ARS), New York/VG Bild-Kunst, Bonn.

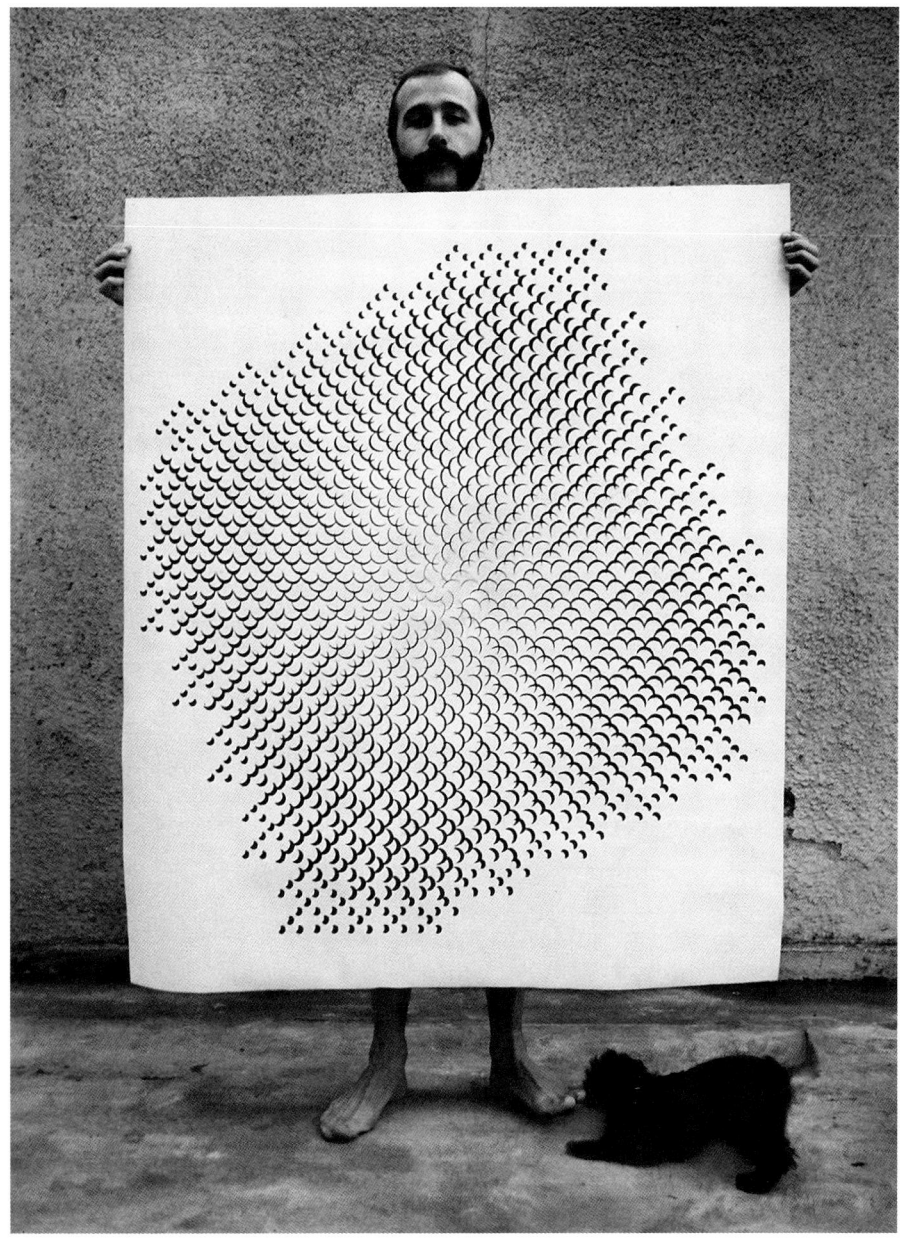

Figure 3.7
Gottfried Jäger presents his *Pinhole Structure 3.8.14, Modification F 2.6*, 1967. Photo: Ursel Jäger. © 2024 Artists Rights Society (ARS), New York/VG Bild-Kunst, Bonn.

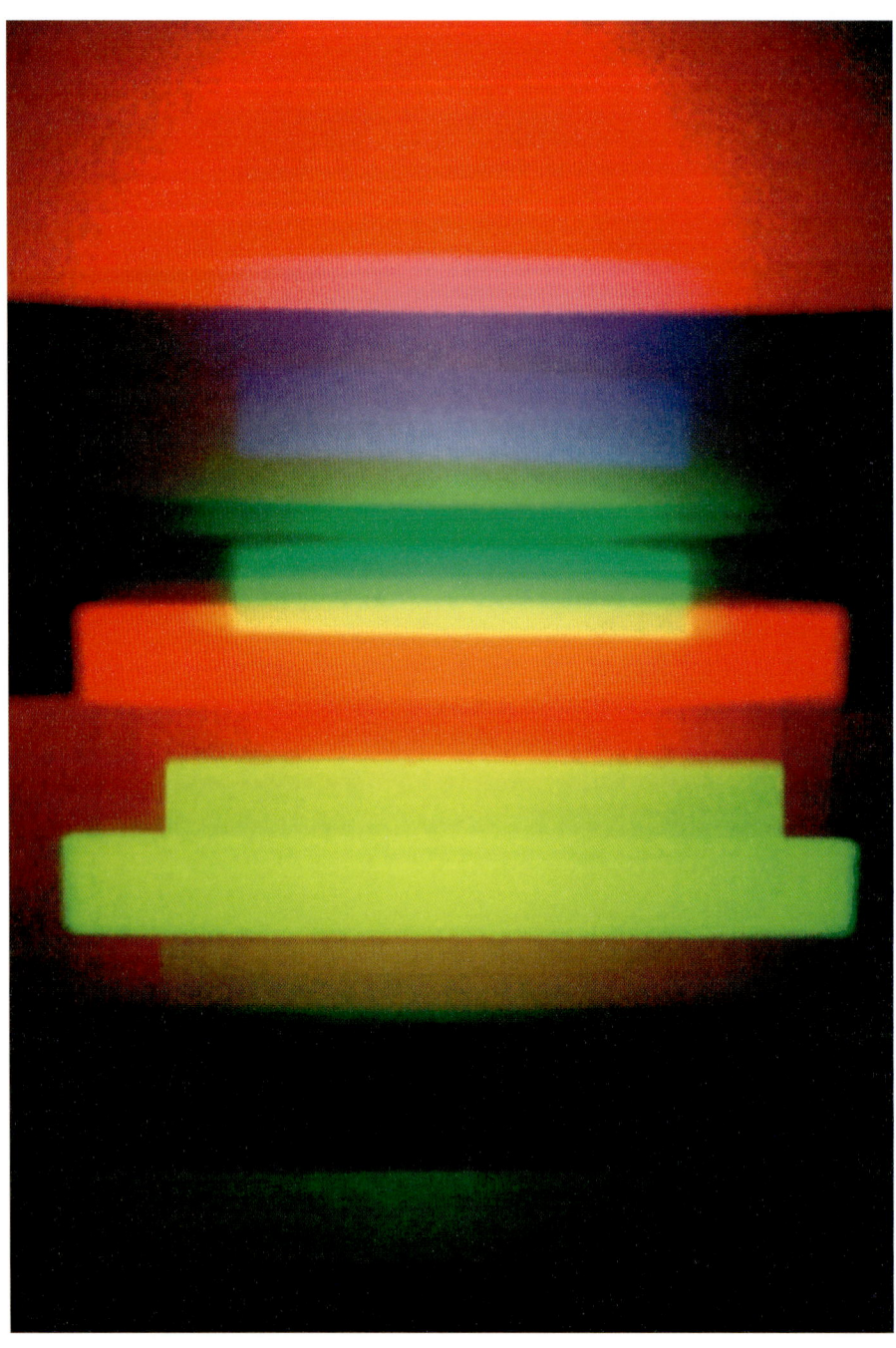

Figure 3.8
Dieter Jung, *Into the Rainbow*, 1983. Hologram. Courtesy of the artist.

Flusser stumbled into photography, but it provided an excuse and ultimately a model for examining a swiftly changing society shaped by apparatus. He would go on to refine his thinking in the last two books of the technical image trilogy.

Technical and Synthetic Images

If "photography" was the privileged term in *Towards a Philosophy of Photography*—even for expedient purposes—the following two books in the technical image trilogy reversed that, practically doing away with photography altogether. *Into the Universe of Technical Images* (1985) argues that photography is about to become redundant as a technology and we need to focus on other kinds of images, and *Does Writing Have a Future?* (1987) was Flusser's attempt to publish his writing only in a digital format. Another term also starts to emerge: *synthetic* images. Flusser was corresponding with the Swiss scholar and translator Felix Philipp Ingold, who pressed him to refine his terms.[51] What exactly *is* a technical image, Ingold wanted to know, and what is the difference between representation in traditional photography and "modeling" in synthetic images? Photographs captured scenes in the environment and films depicted events, but the new computer-generated images—*synthetic* images—were unlimited in their ability to create architecture, objects, worlds.

Into the Universe of Technical Images follows the standard Flusser format: short essays that serve to develop a larger idea. Here, however, the essays are titled with verb infinitives: "To Abstract," "To Imagine," "To Make Concrete," "To Touch," "To Envision." (The book was written in German, and German infinitives can also stand alone as nouns, which gives these titles a valence that is lost in translation.) Where *Towards a Philosophy of Photography* withheld its speculations until the final essay, here they are laid out in a "Warning" at the beginning of the book, where Flusser raises the prospect of a "future society that synthesizes electronic images." He writes, "seen from here and now, it will be a fabulous society, where life is radically different from our own," where divisions between science, politics, and art will be virtually unrecognizable, and "even our state of mind, our existential mood, will take on a new and strange coloration. This is not about a future floating in the far distance. We are already on its cusp. Many aspects of this

Figures 3.9–3.10
Flusser's diagrams illustrating his ideas in chapters 2 and 5 of *Into the Universe of Technical Images*, 1985. The drawings were not included in the book. Vilém Flusser Archive, Berlin.

ILLUSTRATIONEN ZU KAPITEL 5

UMKEHREN DER BEDEUTUNGSVEKTOREN
("SEMANTISCHE EINSTELLUNG")

(a) ENTZIFFERN DES UMSTANDS

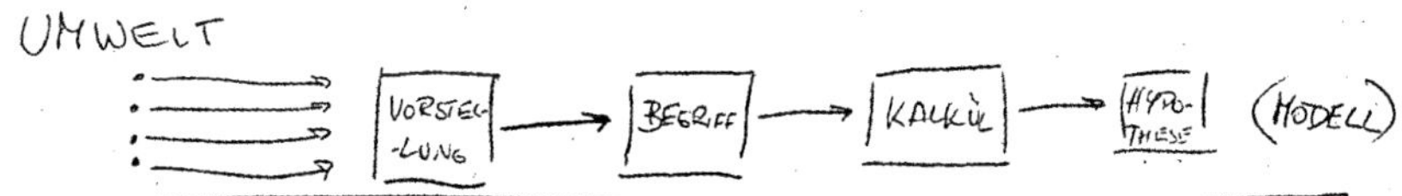

UMWELT

VORSTEL-LUNG → BEGRIFF → KALKÜL → HYPO-THESE (MODELL)

MODELL   (b) SINNGEBUNG DEM UMSTAND

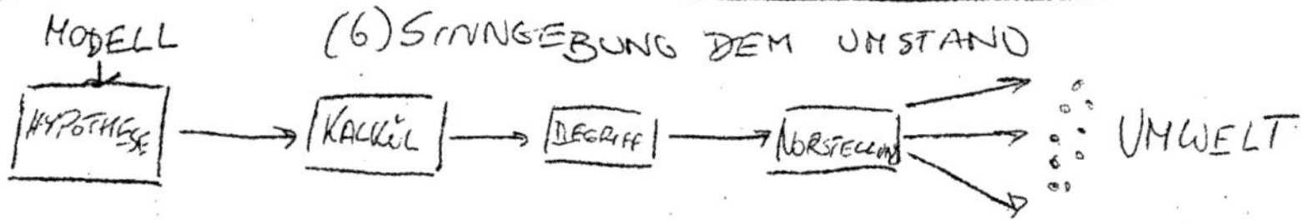

HYPOTHESE → KALKÜL → BEGRIFF → VORSTELLUNG → UMWELT

ZUR BILDKRITIK

(a) Vortechnische Bilder

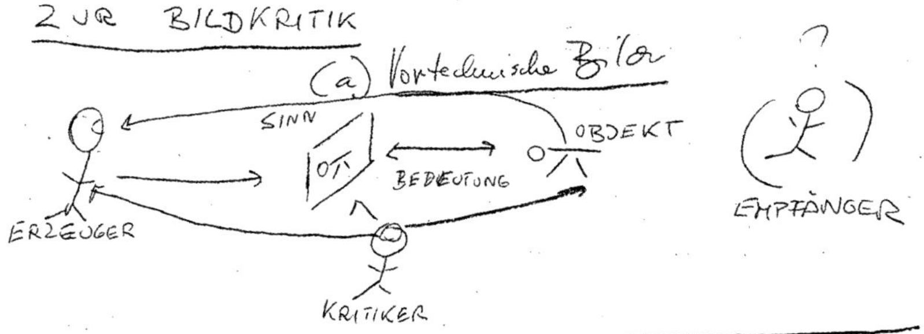

SINN

OT

BEDEUTUNG

OBJEKT

ERZEUGER

KRITIKER

EMPFÄNGER

?

(b) Technische Bilder

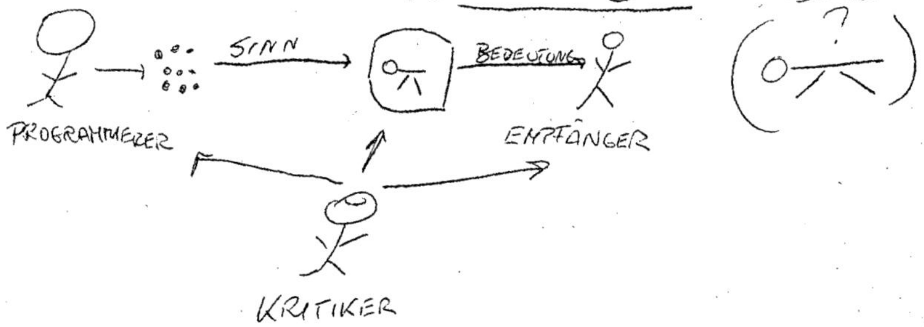

PROGRAMMIERER

SINN →

BEDEUTUNG

EMPFÄNGER

KRITIKER

OBJEKT
?

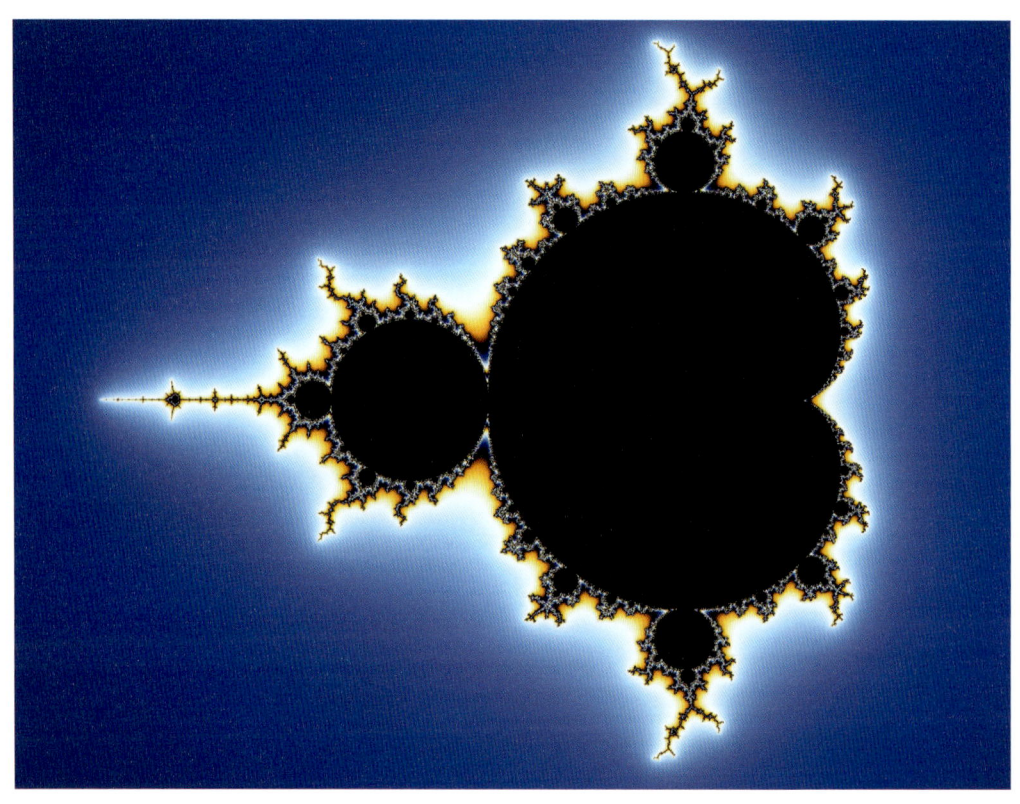

Figure 3.11
Classic Mandelbrot set, fractal. Photo: Andreas Nilsson.

fabulous new social and life structure are already visible in our environment and in us."[52] This near-future society, this "groundless utopia," could move in one of two directions: toward totalitarian control or a more positive "dialogic" society. Here, Martin Buber's dialogic philosophy informs Flusser's theory. In the first essay, "To Abstract," Flusser distinguishes traditional two-dimensional images from technical ones, which are "mosaics assembled from particles" and are "posthistorical, dimensionless."[53]

We already know that technical images are made by apparatuses, but Flusser now differentiates between traditional images, made by hands and fingers and perceived by human eyes, and technical images, which code abstract, invisible particles (photons and electrons, for instance) into information, and can be read by technological apparatuses. With technical images, the abstract is made visual: images are no longer snapshots or billboards, but are immaterial objects. Holograms and fractals, manifested from pure mathematical information, were some of Flusser's favorite examples—and many of the texts on fractals agreed with Flusser's repudiation of linearity. A book that Flusser had in his library, *The Beauty of Fractals: Images of Complex Dynamical Systems* (1986), begins with this epigraph: "In 1953 I realized that the straight line leads to the downfall of mankind," it says, quoting Austrian artist Friedensreich Hundertwasser. "The straight line has become an absolute tyranny. The straight line is something cowardly drawn with a rule, without thought or feeling; it is the line which does not exist in nature. And that line is the rotten foundation of our doomed civilization."[54]

Synthetic images exist because of technical apparatuses, but they are more future-oriented: they can show an airplane that hasn't been built yet or a four-dimensional cube. A photographer can "visualize" a house and then photograph it with an apparatus, but that differs from creating a house with computer software or an airplane computed with aerodynamic equations, and this ability alters the photographic universe. The first "artists" to do this were, notably, scientists like the Austrian-born physicist and science fiction author Herbert W. Franke, who worked at Siemens in the early 1950s and later cofounded the Ars Electronica festival in Linz, Austria, in which Flusser participated. In the 1960s, Franke had written about art and science coming together through the use of data-processing machines for aesthetic purposes; he also examined art through information aesthetics (Max Bense) and

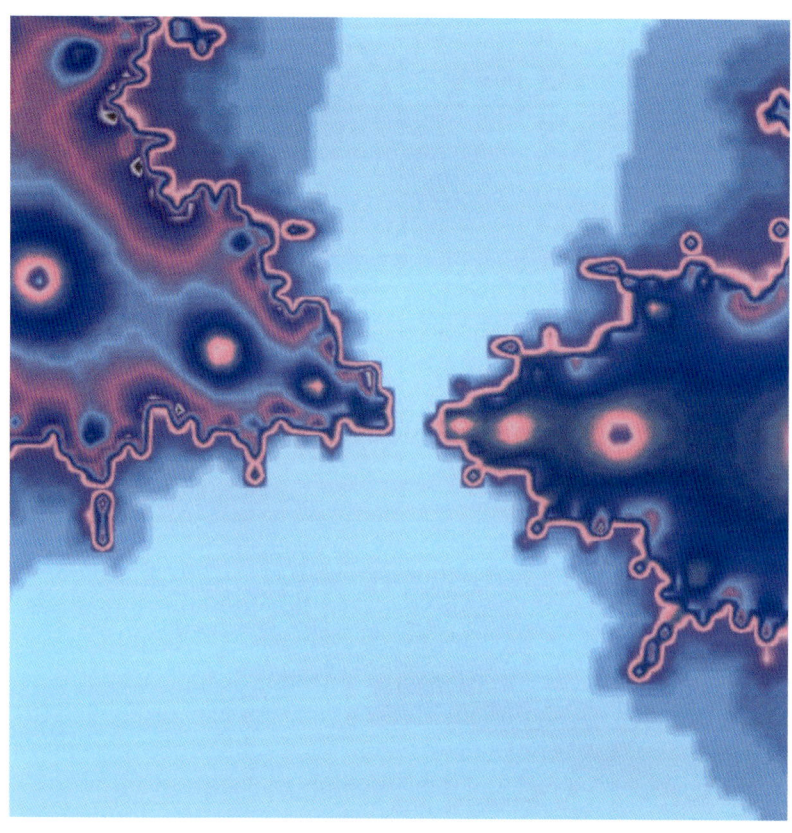

Figure 3.12
Herbert W. Franke, *Math Art*, 1980–1995. Computer and DIBIAS (Digital Image Evaluation
System) software. Estate of Herbert W. Franke and Susanne Päch.

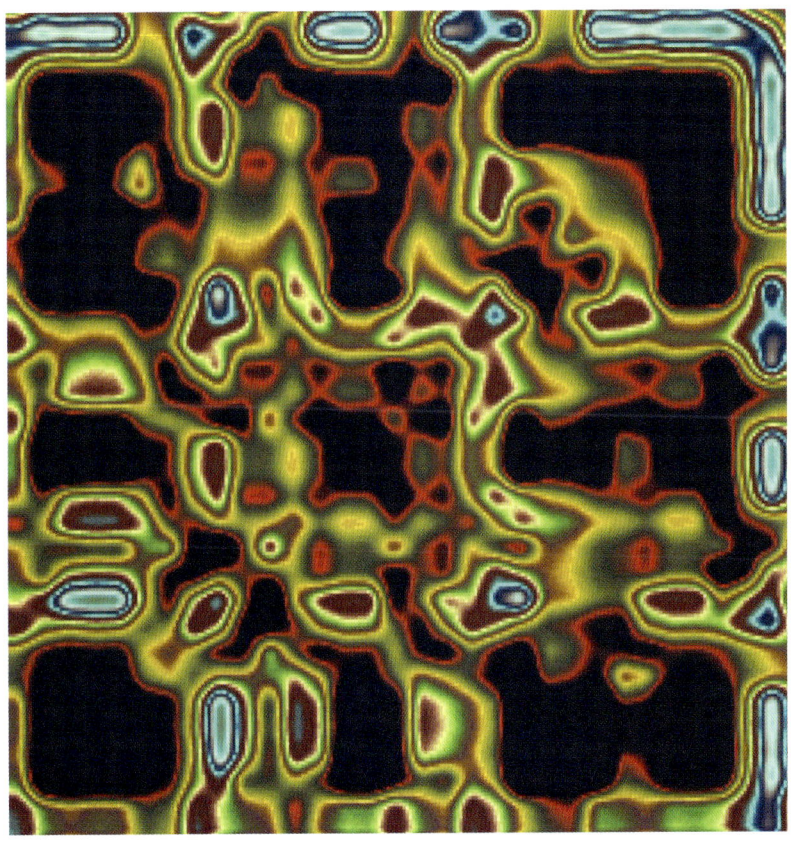

Figure 3.13
Herbert W. Franke, *Random Series*, 1980–1995. Computer and DIBIAS (Digital Image
Evaluation System) software. Estate of Herbert W. Franke and Susanne Päch.

established a connection between machines and humans with information psychology (Abraham A. Moles).[55] What was significant to Franke about the new images is not that they were produced in a novel way, but that they stimulated a new cognitive and perceptual response in the viewer: "Hence, art may be seen as a creative game between artist and audience," Franke wrote. "The artist invents visual, auditory, or semantic structures, which the audience is required to decipher. The audience's feedback spurs the artist to produce further creations. Only if this cycle of communications functions does art attain its full social function."[56] The "artwork" in computer art was ultimately the program itself.

Similarly, synthetic images are future-oriented in their relationship to memory (human and otherwise): eventually, everything will be stored electronically and produce new information, and the focus will switch from *image* to *vector*. Drawing from his thinking about gestures, Flusser writes that, in a world of "commandingly outstretched index fingers" reaching into public and private space, the medium becomes much less important than its *vector of meaning*, or the direction in which the finger points.[57] In *Into the Universe of Technical Images*, the vectors of significance are compared to headlights, lighthouses, or signposts: "Technical images are *projections*. They capture meaningless signs that come to us from the world (photons, electrons) and code them to give them a meaning."[58] Humans being able to project meaning onto the world via technical and synthetic images, rather than receiving information from our environment, constitutes a revolution. It could be read as "postmodernism" (a word Flusser used without much angst) or a "meta-" approach to phenomena: analyzing *how* rather than *what* an image means: "to decode a technical image is not to decode what it shows but to read how it is programmed."[59]

Ultimately, like Friedrich Kittler, Bernard Stiegler, and other philosophers of technology, Flusser would argue that *all* revolutions are technological. "To Scatter," nearly midway through *Into the Universe of Technical Images*, states that "the present cultural revolution is technical, not ideological," and "today's revolutionaries are not Kaddaffis or Meinhofs but rather the inventors of technical images."[60] The destruction of traditional social groups results from the invention of technical images: television, but also "the young Californians who sit in isolation at their computer terminals with their backs to one another" and who "have no social awareness."[61] This comment rings particularly true after the rise of social media,

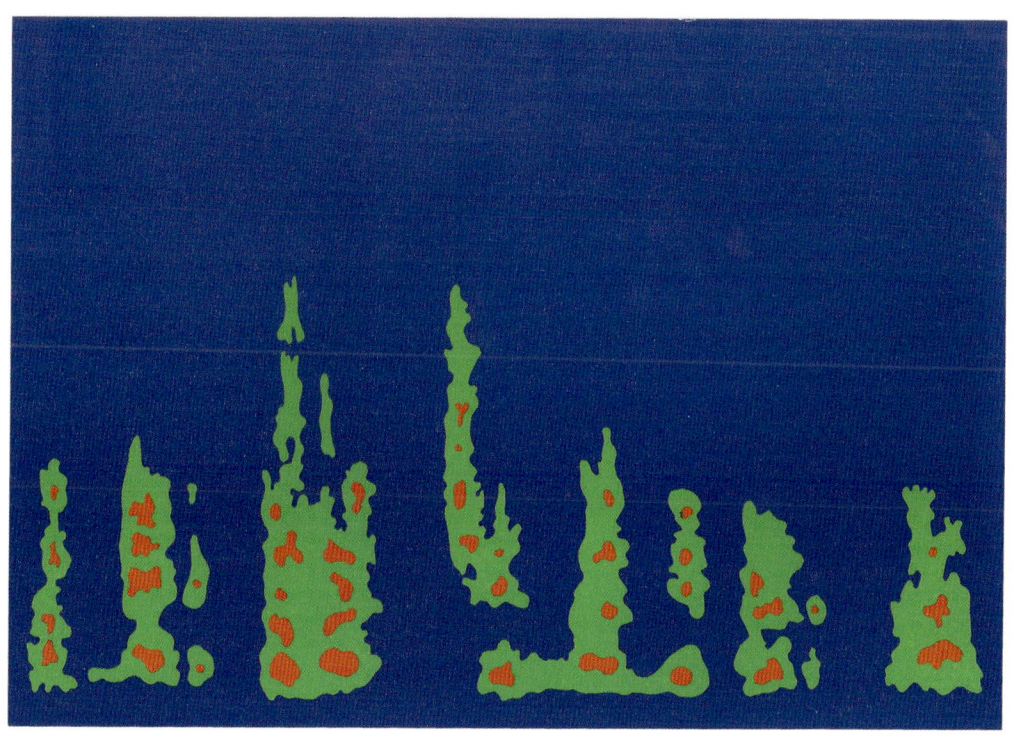

Figure 3.14
Décio Pignatari, *Vocogramas*, 1985. Offset print, 16.5 × 23.5 cm. From a set of eleven cards showing visual representations of phonemes.

of course. And yet, for Flusser, "dialogic threads" might open up within "the fascist tissue of the rising society."[62]

In "To Discuss," he proposes a new term: *telematics*, a neologism combining "telecommunications" and "informatics" and linking images and telegraphy, or the simultaneous transmission of word, image, and sound. Telematics would open multisensory and multimedia forms of dialogue. Flusser predicted "empty chatter and twaddle on a global scale," as well as "isolated, distracted, key-pressing human beings."[63] But he saw possibilities for real dialogue of unprecedented richness. Taking Martin Buber's most famous text, *I and Thou*—and particularly the idea that "I" only exists in relation to "you"—Flusser imagined technical images producing and circulating to enact a secular version of the "I" and "thou" relationship, a communications utopia like never before.[64] There would be no centralized senders but individual image makers sitting before their terminals, programming rather than being programmed. However, we are still in a situation where "imperialism of information" shapes our environment: "senders possess the programs, and we are possessed by them."[65]

Flusser concludes that through telematics we can perhaps find our way back to being "genuinely humane": engaged in purposeless play that produces a "school for creativity, a school for freedom."[66] It is an argument that seems both incredibly prescient and depressingly inaccurate, when we see where social media and the internet have landed today. And yet Flusser framed his work as a critique of the present rather than a prognostication; at the end of *Into the Universe of Technical Images*, he warns against forecasting: "All prediction damages the future."[67] Instead, he summons two nineteenth-century European philosophers: Schopenhauer and Nietzsche. Whereas Schopenhauer proposed a world divided by "will and representation," Flusser argues for a merger of the two in a multisensory universe of technical images where Nietzsche's superman is reconfigured as a "cybernetic superbrain."[68] If Nietzsche's philosophy might be linked to the hallucinatory worlds of symbolist painting, Flusser's universe of technical images ends in a similarly visionary and hallucinatory fashion in an essay titled "Chamber Music," which harnesses the "dreamlike quality of the emerging image world," a world of "cybernetic dialogue, a fabulous consciousness, that of making music with the power of imagination."[69] Rather than drifting off into the ether, though, Flusser includes a "Summary" with a list

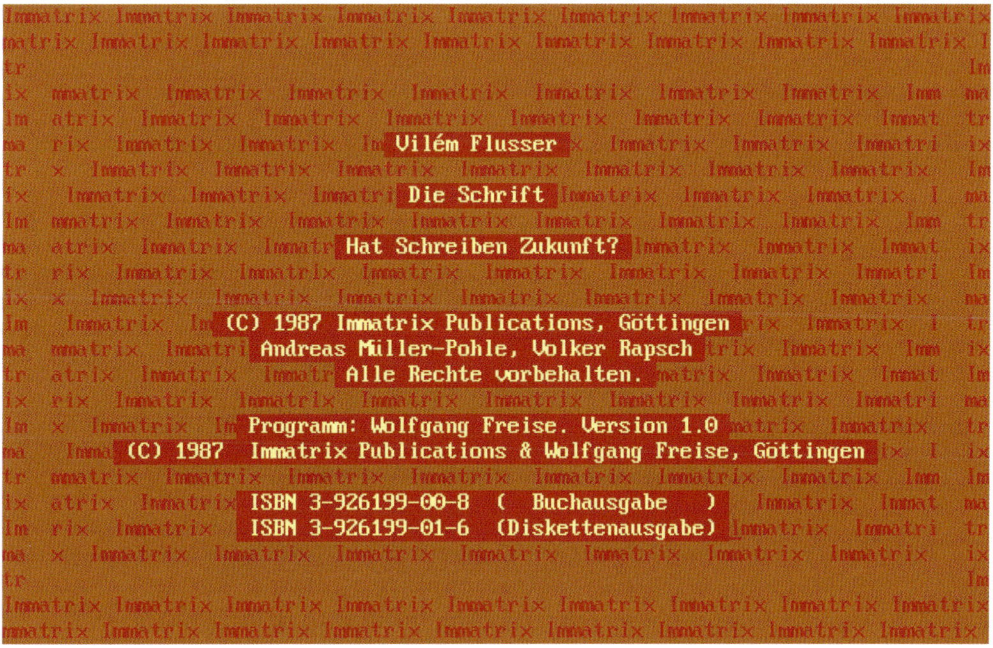

Figure 3.15
Vilém Flusser, *Die Schrift: Hat Schreiben Zukunft?*, 1987. Screenshot of the floppy-disk version
of the book, translated as *Does Writing Have a Future?* Courtesy Andreas Müller-Pohle /
Immatrix Publications and the Vilém Flusser Archive.

of questions raised by each of the twenty essays in *Into the Universe of Technical Images*: "What are technical images?"; "How do technical images function as models?"; "What does a society so fully in the thrall of images look like? How can we make images dialogically?"[70] Through these inquiries, Flusser posed some of the basic questions of our technologized era.

Some of these questions would be addressed in the third book in his technical image trilogy, *Does Writing Have a Future?* (1987), which Flusser dedicated to Abraham Moles. For over a decade, he had been arguing that linear culture based on writing would be eclipsed by the "superficial" reading of technical images and their surfaces. Now he would examine this claim from the perspective of text rather than image. Writing, Flusser argues, will soon be obsolete, since information is now more effectively transmitted through informatic media. Soon, he predicts, written code would go the way of Egyptian hieroglyphs or Indian knots, and only historians or other specialists would comprehend them. We will no longer think critically, following the Enlightenment model, because historical consciousness has run its course, and rather than privileging memory, we must learn to forget, erasing the alphabet from our consciousness so that we can store new codes.

In essays like "The Digital" and "Recoding," Flusser considers what the new era, dominated by shifting ideas about space and matter (relativity and quanta), portends. When alphanumeric code was invented, people lived in villages, their lives circumscribed. Now, matter itself has changed: "One has only to recite the words *atomic power station, thermonuclear armaments, artificial intelligence, automation*, and *electronic information revolution*," he writes. "Far from being solely practical or epistemological issues, these are existential, political, and aesthetic ones. They should not be left to scientists and technicians."[71] There is no point in setting goals to understand or achieve new consciousness, since goals themselves are a product of historical consciousness. Rather, we need to write past writing, accept its provisional assistance, then discard it.

The first edition of *Does Writing Have a Future?* appeared in 1987 on floppy disk, an attempt to translate this theory—and alphanumeric text—into algorithmic code. Along with the disk was a note congratulating the user: "You decided to take part in an experiment in developing new dimensions of communication. In front of you lies the first real no-longer-a-book."[72] Flusser considered the 1989 second edition a failure, since it was published as a traditional book, and therefore signaled the continuation rather than the eradication of writing. And yet, in an afterword to this edition, he mused, how does one discuss the demise of writing in a manner *other* than writing? The answer was to continue essaying—trying—and philosophizing in whatever form he could.

Immaterialism and the Photograph as Postindustrial Object

Flusser's reputation bloomed in Europe after the publication of the technical image trilogy. He wrote photography criticism—or some version of it, since his essays for *Camera Austria*, *European Photography*, and other publications were more like short philosophical musings than art reviews—and used his critical platform to expand his thinking about automation, interfaces, memory, programs, networks, and telematics.[73] He would translate lectures and presentations from one language to another, refining his thoughts as he went. For instance, "The Photograph as Post-Industrial Object" (1986) started as a lecture and was later published in the US journal *Leonardo*.[74] The essay starts with a discussion of how objects gain value, with Flusser making the distinction between industrial objects—the products of artists and artisans—and postindustrial objects shaped by apparatus, which become nearly valueless supports for programmed information. To bolster this argument, Flusser cites an exhibition that struck a chord with him: *Les immatériaux* (The immaterials, 1985) at the Centre Pompidou in Paris, organized by the philosopher Jean-François Lyotard and the design theorist and curator Thierry Chaput.[75]

Les immatériaux had a similar ethos to the 1973 interdisciplinary roundtable later published as *Technologie et imaginaire*, which Flusser participated in at the Institute of the Environment in Paris (and, of course, *Cybernetic Serendipity*, where machines were shown alongside artworks). The exhibition was famously laid out in labyrinthine fashion—what John Rajchman later called a "maddatascape"—divided by mesh "walls" into heterogeneous zones.[76] In these different zones, you could make photocopies, look at skin grafts from animals, view photographs of a woman in different stages of pregnancy, consider keywords defined by twenty-six different writers and transmitted via Minitel micro-computers, and experience a range of technical and synthetic images (films, holograms, computer processing, projectors, audio synthesizers,

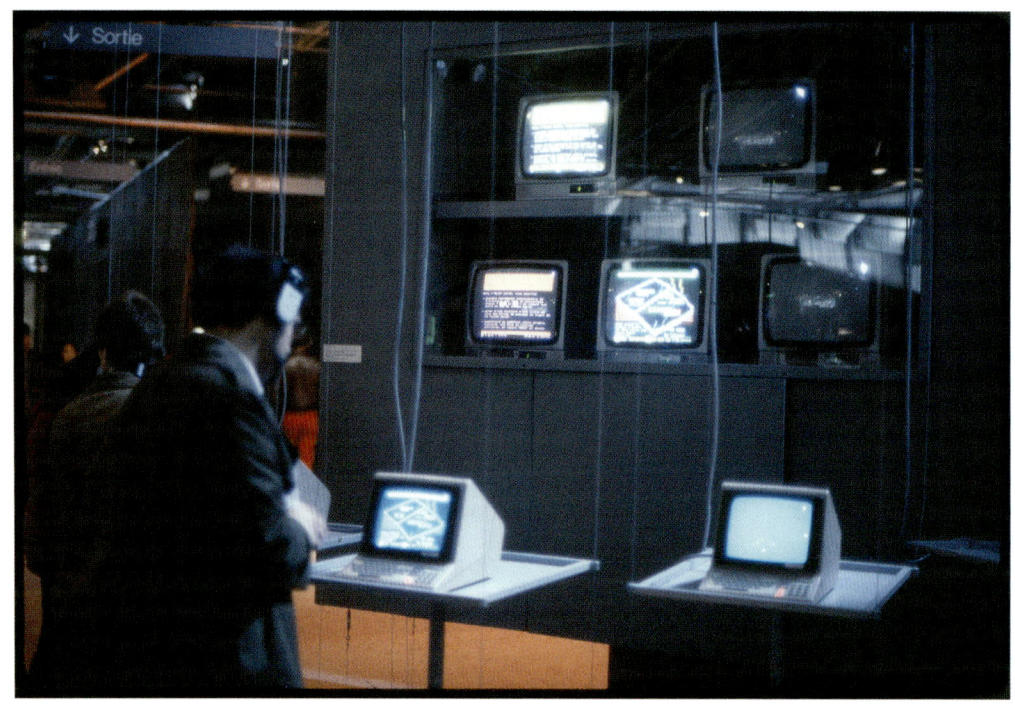

Figure 3.16
Les immatériaux (The immaterials), exhibition at the Centre Pompidou, Grande Galerie,
March 28–July 15, 1985. © CNAC/MNAM, Dist. RMN-Grand Palais/Art Resource, NY.
Photo: Jean-Claude Planchet.

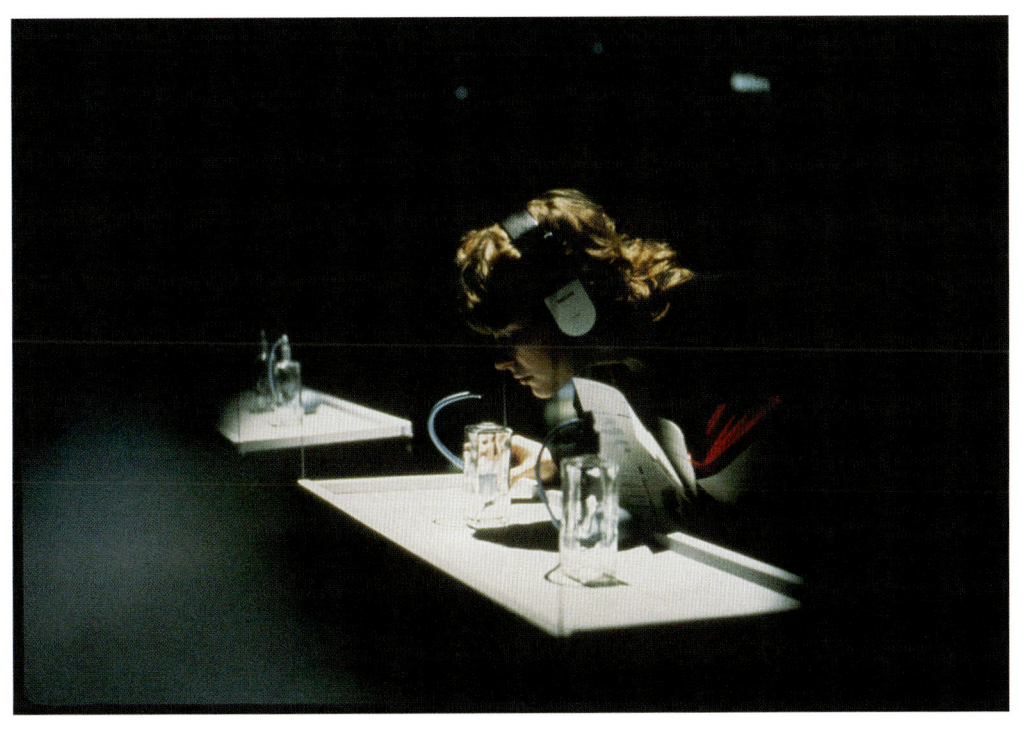

Figure 3.17
Les immatériaux (The immaterials) at the Pompidou Center, Paris, 1985. Installation
view, with visitors. © CNAC/MNAM, Dist. RMN-Grand Palais/Art Resource, NY.
Photo: Jean-Claude Planchet.

and video simulations). Flusser wrote about *Les immatériaux* for the journal *kultuRRevolution*, briefly examining the history of categories like art and science (*ars* and *techne*) and suggesting that, in the dawning age of immaterialism, these divisions were collapsing, creating a flow between material and immaterial states and different forms of knowledge.[77] (Flusser elaborated on the "two-cultures" argument in the essays "Into Immaterial Culture" [1986], "Immaterialism" [1987], and "Form and Material" [1991], originally a series of lectures given in São Paulo that consider how science has disrupted the ancient matter-spirit dialectic, pushing us to consider these terms in astronomical, molecular, atomic, sub-atomic, nuclear, and quantum terms.)[78]

Picking up on this idea in "The Photograph as Post-Industrial Object," Flusser argues that immaterial concerns have become fundamental as photography moves into electromagnetic imaging. To tease this out, Flusser looks at three kinds of photographs: fully automated ones (e.g., NASA satellite photos), amateur photographs, like snapshots, and "experimental" photographs in which the photographer works against the camera program, much the way avant-garde artists worked "against the grain" of art history. None of this is new. But here Flusser highlights the "inner dialectic of freedom" that occurs when, instead of creating value, humans are committed to *deviating* from value. In the fifth section, "Photos," he finally addresses photography. Here Flusser offers a rare, direct critique of Roland Barthes. He declares photographs "practically worthless supports of information" because "in printed matter a human subject, an 'author,' elaborates the information (unless a word processor is used), while in the photo an apparatus does."[79] Flusser argues that postindustrial culture in general can be grasped better by focusing on the apparatus or the camera, a "machine that calculates probabilities," than on the images.[80] Moreover, he identifies a philosophical problem: if culture was created to hedge against the entropic death or decay (in his terms, "loss of information") of nature and its objects, what happens when apparatuses appear that can create this information? What happens to *value*—a concept, of course, central to traditional art history?

The last sections of the essay are given over to suggesting how the new electromagnetic photos will do away with material support, creating new forms of memory and a "total art" in which science and art are reunited, classification systems are discarded,

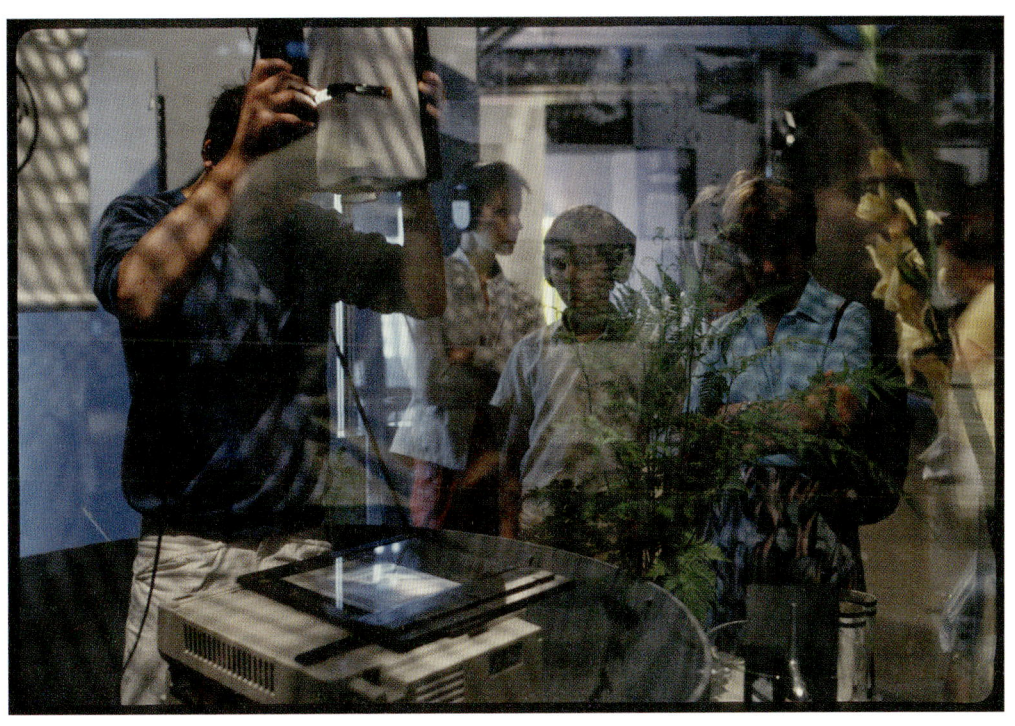

Figure 3.18
Les immatériaux (The immaterials), 1985. Installation view of the exhibition at the
Centre Pompidou. © CNAC/MNAM, Dist. RMN-Grand Palais/Art Resource, NY.
Photo: Jean-Claude Planchet.

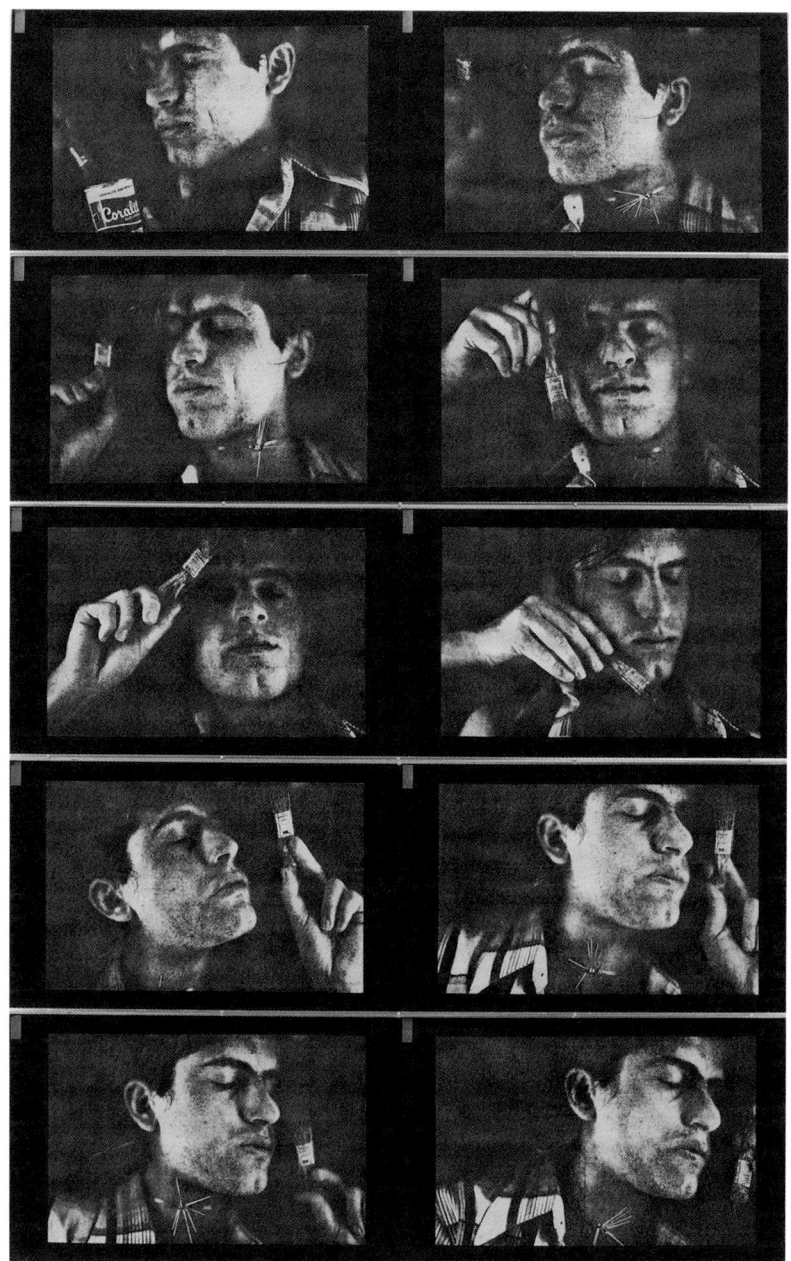

Figure 3.19
Mario Ramiro, *Pintura* (Painting), 1979. Xerography, 100 × 81 cm. Ramiro corresponded with
Flusser in the 1980s.

and human dialogue becomes possible through the exchange of particle-based images. Humans will no longer be subordinate to objects but rather will live in a culture of immaterial information in which useful activities can be performed by apparatuses and humans are free to exist as knots within a social network, becoming universal artists. Flusser acknowledges that this is a utopian forecast—in fact, we've seen the opposite, with AI writing poetry and music, rather than cleaning up garbage—but it is, nonetheless, technically feasible for the first time.[81]

What's philosophically and socially at stake is addressed in another essay, "Immaterialism."[82] Because, if electronic memory relocates storage *outside* our bodies, this suggests a cataclysmic change: "The very pillars of Occidental culture, 'matter,' 'spirit,' and 'form' have fallen … but a mystery now envelops the concepts of 'energy' and 'probability' instead. If one throws metaphysics out through the door, it comes back through the window."[83] (Here, of course, was a nod to Heidegger, who saw in cybernetics the end, or the culmination, of Western metaphysics.) This idea of digital immateriality has been disputed to some extent by later media writers, as well as by photographers, who have pointed out that digital photography labs are more "material" (filled with hardware and expensive to maintain) than chemical ones, and that much photography has been lost in recent decades in the frantic transition from one format to another. However, as Flusser often pointed out, we are only in the early days of the immaterial revolution.[84] The ramifications of new technical and synthetic images also appeared elsewhere: in architecture, design, and the built environment, with homes perforated by wires and cables, turning the private sphere into a public one and geography into isometric topology.[85]

Immaterial specters and virtual space would arise in later essays like "Digital Apparition" and "On the Virtual."[86] Flusser was particularly concerned with how images created via digital synthesis would soon develop into bodies and how this would call into question our own existences as we move from epistemological "subjects" to "projects," like the projected rays of hologram or three-dimensional objects on computer screens.[87] In the essay "Man as Subject or Project," originally delivered as a lecture at a conference in Rotterdam in 1989, Flusser described how the idea of humans as observing subjects in an environment of objects had dissolved and argued that Husserl's phenomenology—observing

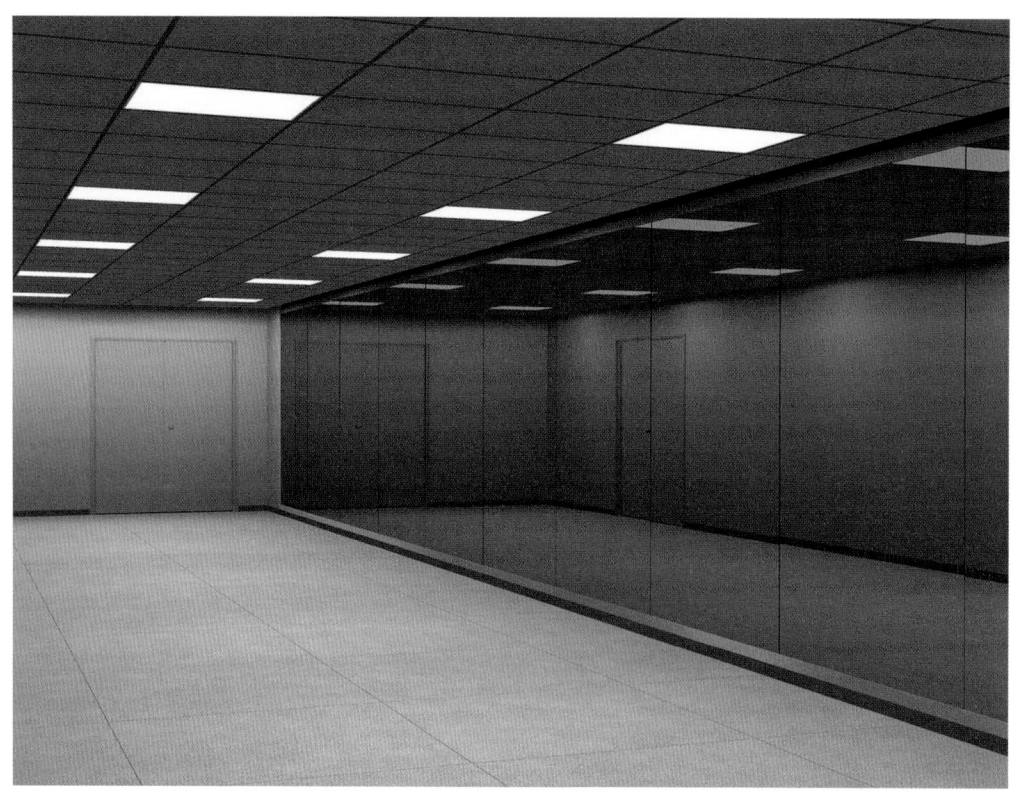

Figure 3.20
Craig Kalpakjian, *Lobby*, 1996. Silver dye bleach print (Ilfochrome) mounted to Plexiglas on aluminum, 29 × 39 × 1 in (73.7 × 99.1 × 2.5 cm). Courtesy of the artist. Kalpakjian created virtual spaces on the computer with architectural design software.

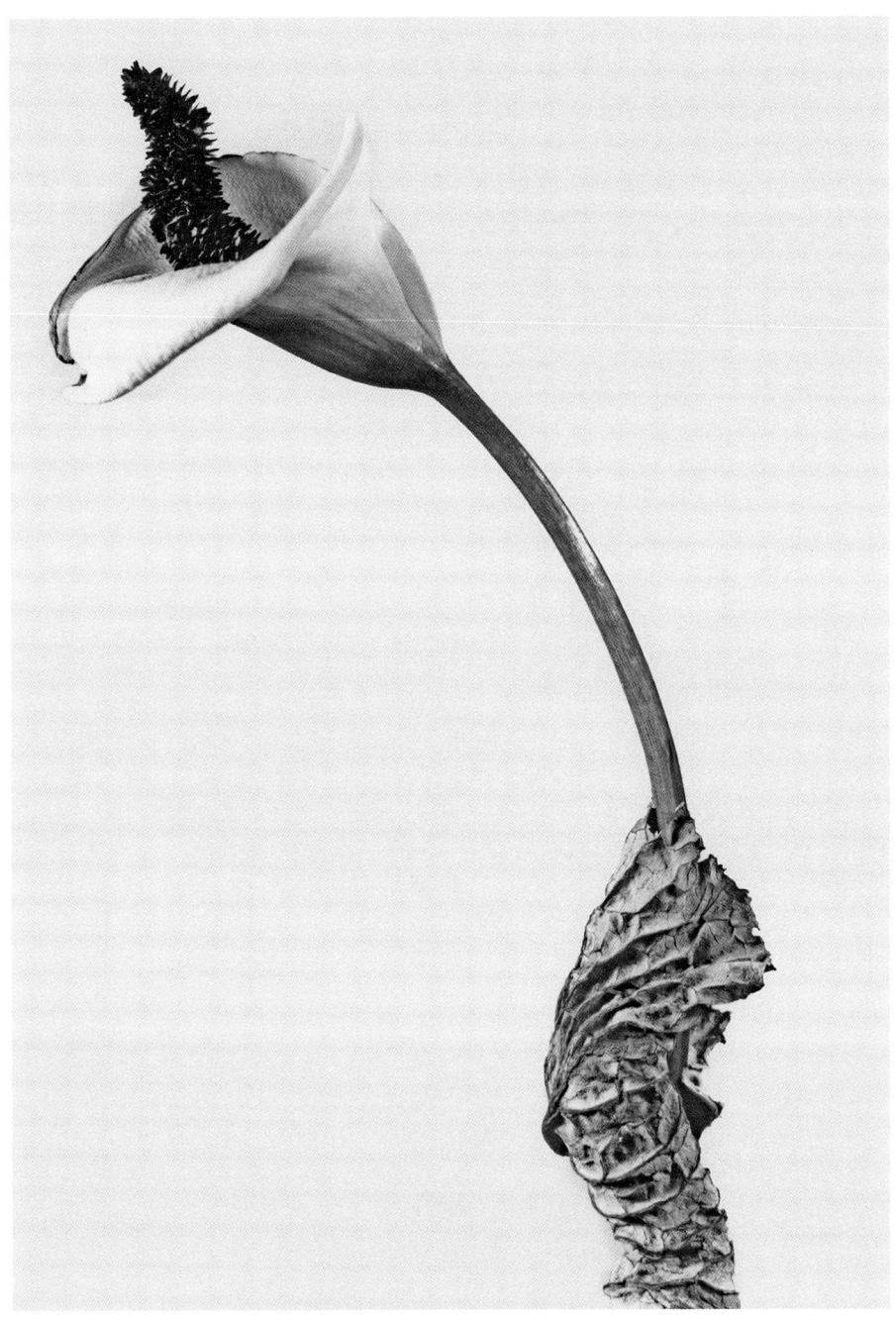

Figure 3.21
Joan Fontcuberta, *Cala rasca*, 1984. Gelatin silver prints from the *Herbarium* series of imaginary plants. Courtesy of the artist.

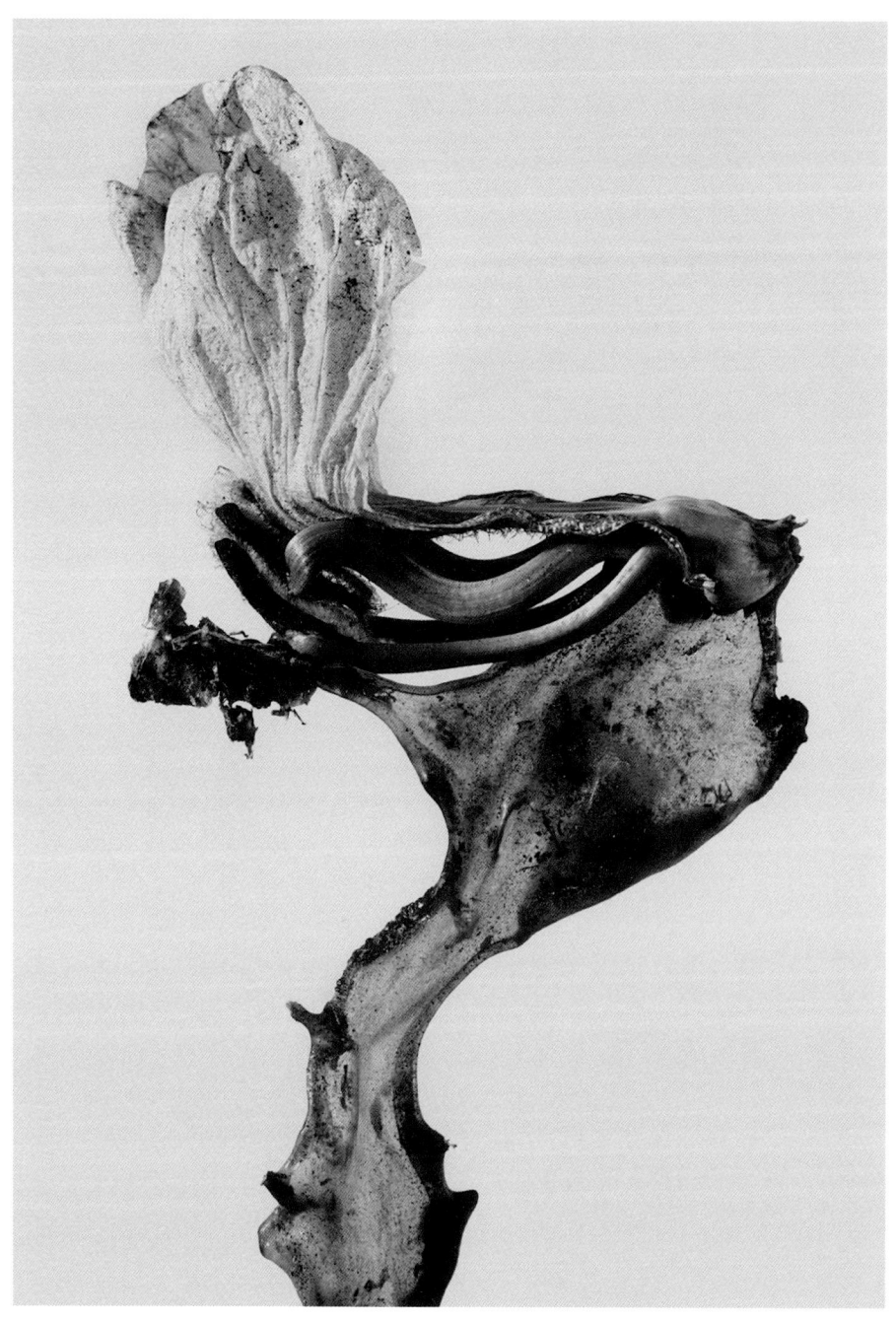

Figure 3.22
Joan Fontcuberta, *Guillumeta polymorpha*, 1982. Gelatin silver prints from the *Herbarium* series of imaginary plants. Courtesy of the artist.

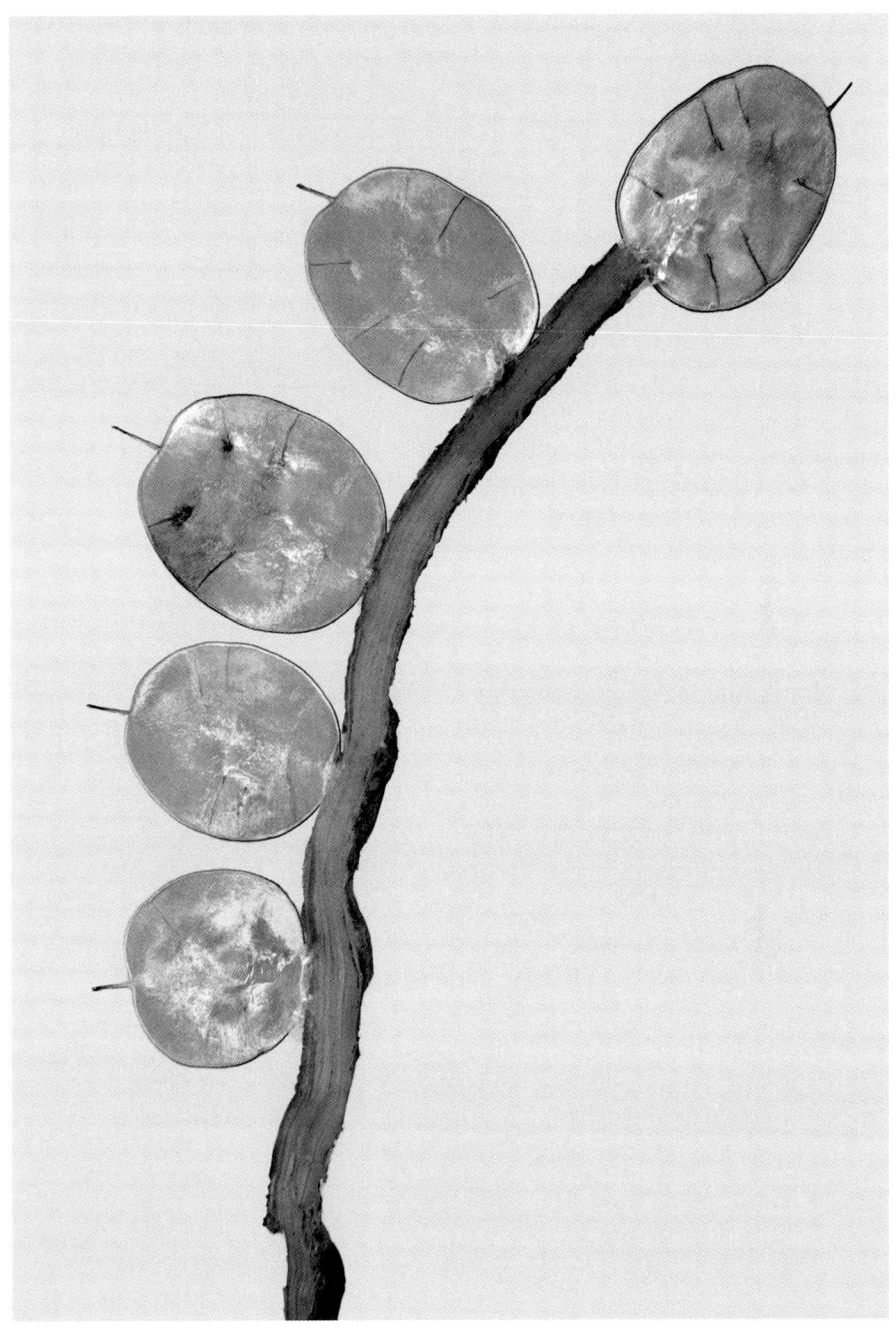

Figure 3.23
Joan Fontcuberta, *Himenea flaccida*, 1983. Gelatin silver prints from the *Herbarium* series of imaginary plants. Courtesy of the artist.

concrete relations—might serve as a tool for shaping a "new anthropology."[88] Moving past technical images as the touchstone for consciousness, Flusser wrote that we might see ourselves as "concrete knots within the network of virtualities that bundle and unbundle according to specific projects," and computer screens would be the place where this was made possible and concrete: "It is no coincidence that computer screens help us to have this vision: they are themselves products of a new existential attitude that is emerging. Computers are among the tools by which we begin to assume ourselves as projects."[89] This, of course, is where many of us live, for better or worse: on the computer screen, or as "digital apparitions" in a world emerging from, in, or on the computer. Not necessarily simulated, it is synthesized, calculated—a "digital world picture" in which human subjects are transformed into *projects* that illuminate a new world.[90]

Art and Technical Images

You could make an exhaustive list of Flusserian artists who push back against the program of photography or illustrate his ideas. I will confine this discussion to a few artists with whom he was in direct contact. For instance, the artist Andreas Müller-Pohle published Flusser's work and is largely responsible for his developing a visionary body of writing.[91] There were many other artists whom Flusser corresponded with, taught, or wrote about. A great example is Joan Fontcuberta, who grew up under the reign of Spanish dictator Francisco Franco and was inspired by Michel Foucault's ideas of power and apparatuses. Fontcuberta was particularly concerned with photography's role in shaping science and history, and the fictional objects and scenarios he has photographed playfully trouble the question of truth in photography.[92] Flusser visited Fontcuberta in Barcelona in 1984, and after a 1985 trip to Italy, Flusser wrote to Fontcuberta that the Italian photography curator Angelo Schwarz "just left here, and he told me that you are one of the most important photographers because you understand what photos are about: to document something which does not exist. Do you agree?"[93] Flusser wrote an introduction to Fontcuberta's *Herbarium* (1985), comprising photographs of everyday objects manipulated to look like exotic plants.[94] In the essay, he concluded that, given sufficient time, mutation, and

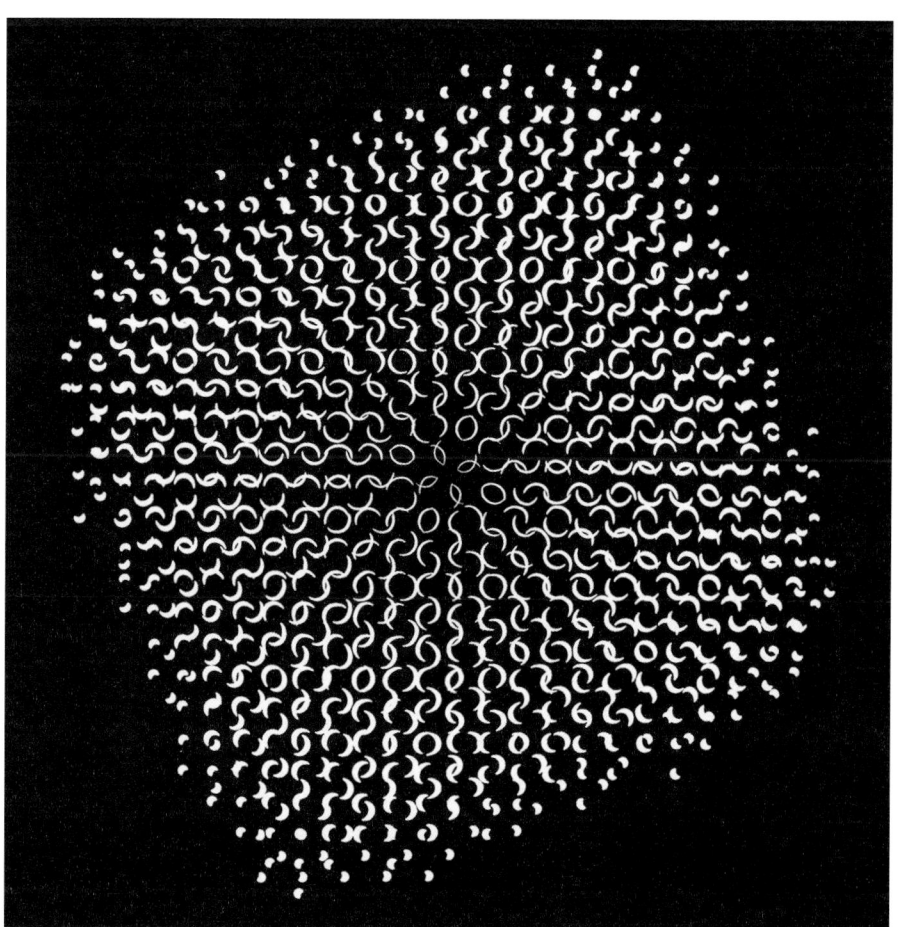

Figure 3.24
Gottfried Jäger, *Pinhole Structure 3.8.14, Modification F4.1*, 1967. Gelatin silver print, 50 × 50 cm.
© 2024 Artists Rights Society (ARS), New York/VG Bild-Kunst, Bonn.

manipulation, nature would probably produce the kind of "plants" Fontcuberta had fashioned in his photographs.

Gottfried Jäger came from a different direction. A pioneer of generative and concrete photography, he was inspired by early twentieth-century experimental photography, Bense's generative aesthetics, Wittgenstein, game theory, and nonrepresentational images produced entirely by technological apparatuses.[95] Initially, Jäger looked to experimental photographers like László Moholy-Nagy and the postwar Fotoform movement (1949–1958), who picked up Bauhaus techniques, but later he moved into Concrete photography, making a direct link with Bense and Brazilian Concrete art.[96] In 1968, Jäger coined the term "generative photography," borrowing from Bense's idea of a programmed "generative aesthetics," and creating photography that used repeatable programs for creating new abstract images rather than reproducing objects.[97] Flusser's dialogue with Jäger clearly impacted both of their work. They met at a photography symposium in Vienna in 1981 (Flusser delivered a lecture titled "Photography and Exchange Value"), and Jäger subsequently invited Flusser to lecture in Bielefeld several times.[98] A response to Jäger's essay on generative photography in *Leonardo* also provides one of Flusser's most succinct statements on photography and apparatuses: "*Apparatus versus man*: Apparatus seem to be complex machines, which again seem to be complex tools, so that there seems to be no essential difference between using a brush and using a computer. Both are tools at the service of those who use them. This is not so." He went on to explain that unlike tools or machines, "with apparatus there is an intricate co-relation of functions: the apparatus does what man wants it to do, but man can only want the apparatus to do what it can do. In fact: apparatus and man form a single functional unit." It's not a question of governing or control, but of "a creative man-apparatus interaction."[99] Jäger would go on to publish a book on Flusser's thought, developing this conversation.[100]

Another artist whose vision dovetailed on these ideas of apparatus, humans, and the political was Harun Farocki (1944–2014). Flusser was writing at the dawn of the digital age, but in over 100 films and videos, and a formidable body of critical writing, Farocki carried Flusser's arguments into the present millennium, exploring the use of technical images in armed conflict, industry, popular culture, and video games. Initially inspired by Bertolt Brecht and Jean-Luc Godard, Farocki focused on the "operative image"

Figure 3.25
Liz Deschenes, *Moiré #25*, 2009. Chromogenic color print, 54¹⁄₁₆ × 40⅛ in. (137.3 × 101.9 cm).
The Museum of Modern Art, New York. Fund for the Twenty-First Century.
© 2012 Liz Deschenes.

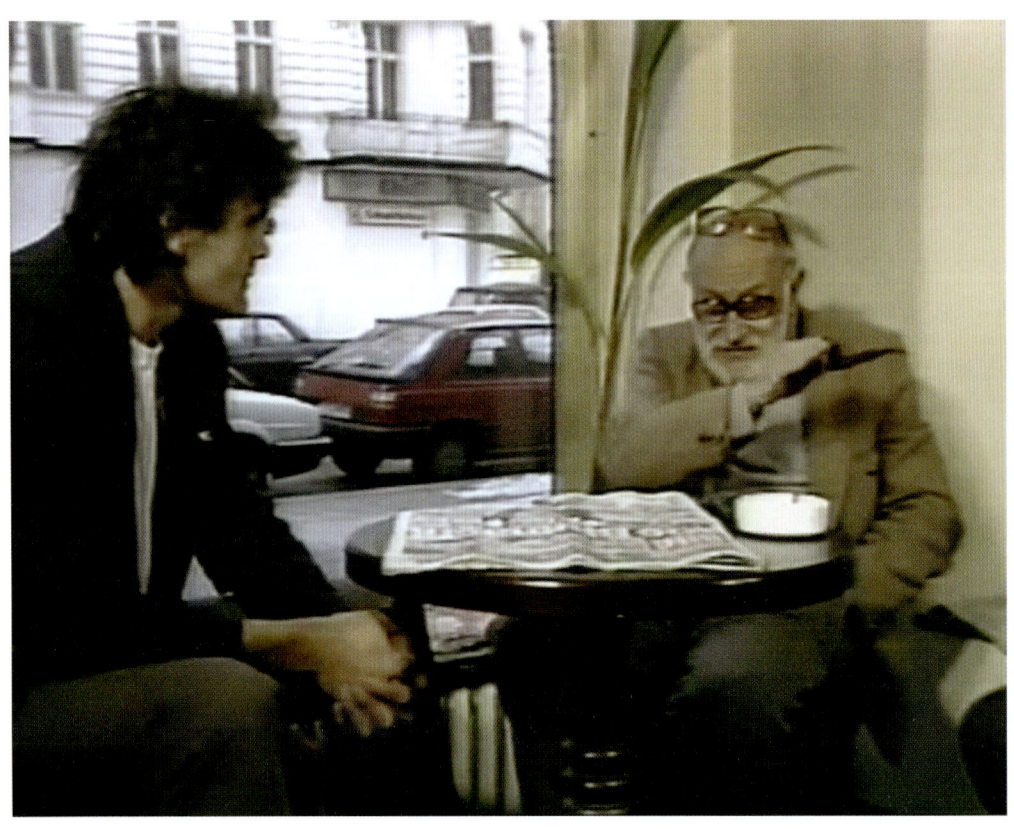

Figure 3.26
Harun Farocki, *Schlagworte—Schlagbilder. Ein Gespräch mit Vilém Flusser* (Catch phrases—
catch images: A conversation with Vilém Flusser), 1986, 13-minute video. WDR Cologne,
commissioned for the TV series *Filmtip*.

sourced from science, industry, and the military, which is made not to entertain or inform audiences. Borrowing the term from Roland Barthes's *Mythologies* (1957), Farocki's operational image didn't represent an object or phenomenon, but rather served as part of an operation—for instance, as a robot in a factory or inside a missile bombing a target—and was proliferating in the age of digital media.[101]

Farocki was also part of the 1960s generation of politicized students. In 1969, he was expelled from the German Film and Television Academy for his activism, along with Holger Meins, a fellow student and cameraman on Farocki's *The Words of the Chairman* (1967), which references Mao Zedong's *Little Red Book* (1964). Meins joined the RAF (Red Army Faction, aka the Baader-Meinhof Group) and was arrested in 1972 and convicted of terrorism. He died in prison from a hunger strike in 1974, and a photograph of his emaciated body, with an autopsy seam up the middle, was printed in newspapers, serving for Farocki as a kind of state trophy and an early touchstone for the operative image.[102]

In 1986, Farocki and Flusser collaborated on the video *Schlagworte—Schlagbilder. Ein Gespräch mit Vilém Flusser* (Catch phrases—catch images: A conversation with Vilém Flusser), in which they sat in a café in West Berlin discussing the layout of the tabloid newspaper *Bild Zeitung*. In the video, Flusser leans forward, offering a preliminary analysis of the newspaper's layout: images usually illustrate text or text is used to illustrate an image, but here text and image "penetrate" one another.

Farocki comments on how the arm of a male corpse cuts through a line of text below that reads *Die Blutnacht* (Blood night). White letters are juxtaposed against a dark background, reversing the standard black text on white ground. Flusser argues that this gives the letters a "bodily character" and says the entire message "is bathed in a magical climate of brutality." Flusser is most interested in the way our eyes move over the surface, *scanning*. Information is derived from the newspaper's surface. Farocki suggests there a "double morality" at work here, since the paper is obviously delivering sensational news in a deliberately salacious way. Flusser concurs: the newspaper is purportedly "engaged in motherly love and peace," which allows it to "rummage around in murder and hate." Farocki laughs and nods as Flusser then pulls into the final stretch of his argument: that this isn't a casual conversation in a café, but a staged one on television—a situation which elevates

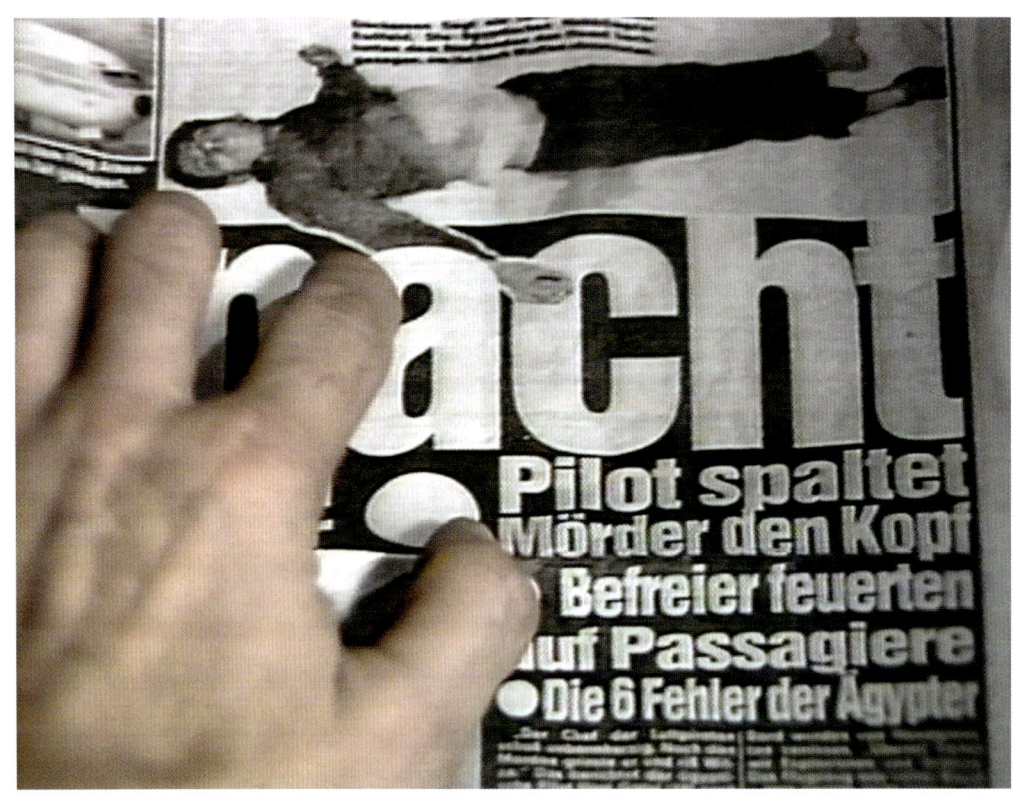

Figure 3.27
Harun Farocki, *Schlagworte—Schlagbilder. Ein Gespräch mit Vilém Flusser* (Catch phrases—catch images: A conversation with Vilém Flusser), 1986. Video, 13 min.

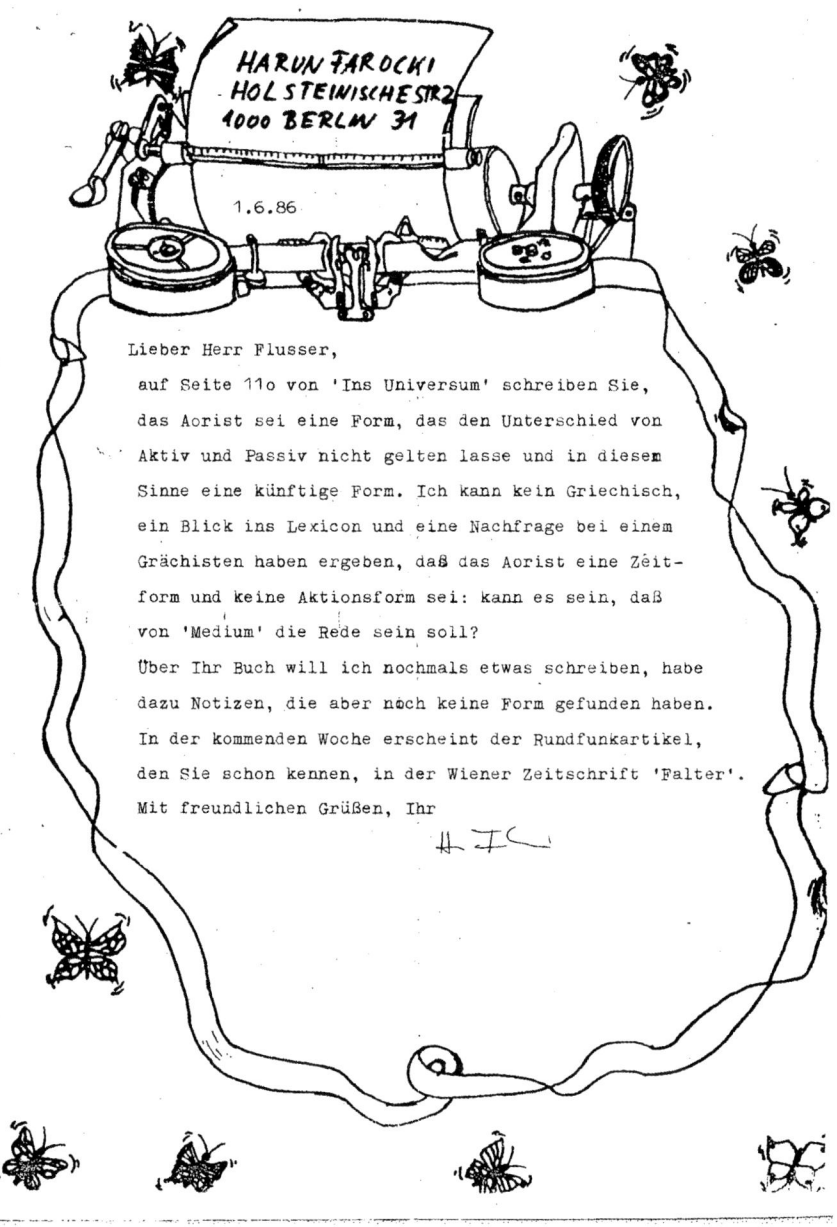

HARUN FAROCKI
HOLSTEINISCHE STR 2
1000 BERLIN 31

1.6.86

Lieber Herr Flusser,

auf Seite 11o von 'Ins Universum' schreiben Sie,
das Aorist sei eine Form, das den Unterschied von
Aktiv und Passiv nicht gelten lasse und in diesem
Sinne eine künftige Form. Ich kann kein Griechisch,
ein Blick ins Lexicon und eine Nachfrage bei einem
Grächisten haben ergeben, daß das Aorist eine Zeit-
form und keine Aktionsform sei: kann es sein, daß
von 'Medium' die Rede sein soll?

Über Ihr Buch will ich nochmals etwas schreiben, habe
dazu Notizen, die aber noch keine Form gefunden haben.
In der kommenden Woche erscheint der Rundfunkartikel,
den Sie schon kennen, in der Wiener Zeitschrift 'Falter'.

Mit freundlichen Grüßen, Ihr

Figure 3.28
Letter from Harun Farocki to Vilém Flusser, June 1, 1986, on stationary designed by
Farocki's daughter. Harun Farocki Institut and Vilém Flusser Archive, Berlin.

them and makes them "magical" for the "receiver." "So, we find ourselves on a very slippery slope," Flusser remarks, adding, "Here we are, observing, seemingly transcendentally, this kitsch and brutality and reduction of human dignity through demagoguery, but we ourselves serve as elements of a new kind of magic-making via television. Honestly, I believe that, for someone watching us here on television, that needs to be said. We must appeal to television viewers and say, 'use this critical ability we are discussing against us, too!'"[103]

Farocki could not agree more. A devotee of Brecht's principles of *Lehrstücke*—breaking down the fourth wall between theater actors and audience—he was keen to enact this in film and television.[104] Farocki wrote an appreciative review of Flusser's *Into the Universe of Technical Images* the following year, and the two carried on a lively, if brief, correspondence, always returning to their common interest in technical images.[105] "As Musil says, God does not mean the world literally, but as a picture," Farocki wrote to Flusser in 1987, inviting him to a discussion at the Berlin Academy of the Arts a few days later.[106] (Flusser was not able to attend.) However, Flusser and Farocki remained fixated on the universe of technical images and their expanding effects. A watershed moment for both men occurred in December 1989 with the Romanian revolution. The uprising took place over five days, during which protests in Timișoara spread to Bucharest. On December 25, 1989, dictator Nicolae Ceaușescu and his wife, Elena Ceaușescu, were tried by the military and found guilty of genocide, subversion of state power, destruction of public property, attempting to flee the country, and embezzling money from foreign banks. They were sentenced to death and executed by a firing squad. (That is, the Ceaușescus' execution *appears* on television, but it was later acknowledged that the couple had been executed hours earlier, then reexecuted on camera.) Technical images assumed a pivotal role: protests were documented on portable video recorders, and revolutionaries went on state television to declare victory. Images *made* history rather than merely documenting it.

The following spring, Flusser participated in a symposium in Budapest devoted to the Romanian revolution; it resulted in a publication that included theorists and artists such as Paul Virilio, Margaret Morse, Geert Lovink, Peter Weibel, and Jeffrey Shaw. Flusser's lecture, "Television Image and Political Space in Light of the Romanian Revolution," posited that what had happened in

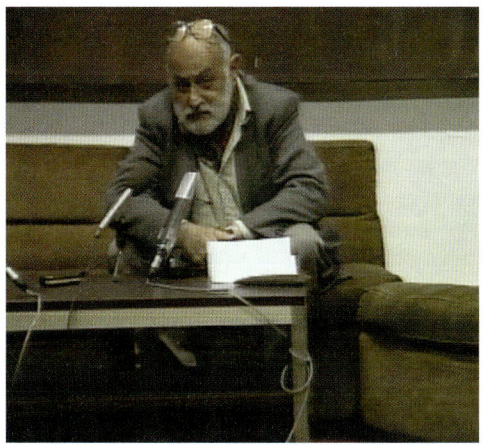

Figure 3.29
Flusser at the International Symposium "The Media Are with Us! The Role of Television in the Romanian Revolution." Műcsarnok/Kunsthalle Budapest, April 1990. Courtesy of Miklós Peternák.

Romania wasn't a revolution—a "political category"—but a turning point in post-history, although, he noted wryly, it happened "off Broadway" rather than in a center of power, like Moscow. (Flusserians watching supporters of President Donald Trump overcome the police and break into the US Capitol on January 6, 2021, immediately noted that televised insurrection had arrived "on Broadway.") Photography was invented, Flusser argued, to render events around us imaginable. We think of the photographer stepping out of a mystical, transcendent space and taking a photograph to document history. This changed in the twentieth century, though. Events existed to be photographed: weddings, moon landings, plane hijackings. Politics and everyday life accelerated, racing toward the camera; images *produced* events. "You ask whether those bodies are real," Flusser remarked, referring to the Ceaușescus. "That's a bad metaphysical question. The real experience is in the image . . . political reasoning is no longer valid. There is no reality behind the image. All reality is in the image."[107]

Farocki's response to the Romanian revolution mirrored this argument. *Videograms of a Revolution* (1992), made with Romanian media theorist Andrei Ujică, demonstrated in vivid episodes the rush of history toward the image. Created from footage made with portable video cameras and state television archives, the film moves between public and private spaces: a hospital in Timișoara, a student dormitory, a public square, a television studio, a living room. It opens with a woman in Timișoara who has been shot by the secret police, summoning the camera to her hospital bed and telling viewers to "remember the dead and continue the revolution!" The film then runs chronologically, capturing the beginning of the uprising and a state-sponsored rally rattled by protests, to scenes of the revolutionaries inside the television station proclaiming, "We are victorious! The TV is with us!" The last scene in the film eerily recalls Flusser's essay "Two Approaches to the Phenomenon, Television," presented at "Open Circuits" (1974) in New York. Here, viewers sit in a darkened room as the Ceaușescus' corpses appear on the screen. "That's him! There's Elena!" someone says. "That's it, then. Turn it off."

For both Flusser and Farocki, the Romanian revolution was pivotal in its adjacency not only to technical images but also to apparatuses. In *Towards a Philosophy of Photography*, Flusser wrote, "the camera constitutes a prototype for all the immense apparatus which threaten to become monolithic (such as the administrative apparatus) as well as those microscopic apparatus which threaten to slip from our grasp (such as the chips in electronic apparatus)— and which determine the present and immediate future to such a high degree."[108] The real photographer, according to Flusser's formulation, as opposed to the mere functionary, could exhaust a camera's program and discover hidden virtualities. However, Romania offered the perfect example of how apparatuses themselves were in flux: typewriters were required to be registered with the Ceaușescu government, but video cameras were not.[109]

Farocki would go on to examine the development and acceleration of technical images and apparatuses, including smart weapons, military surveillance, and video games. His video installations *Serious Games I-IV* (2009–2010) track how video game technology and virtual reality are employed to prepare soldiers for combat and to treat their post-combat trauma. *Parallel I-IV* (2012–2014), his last multi-screen work, offers a short history of the evolution of landscape imagery in video games, moving from computer graphics with no depth of field—a ground composed merely of horizontals, verticals, and points—to a more "naturalistic" depiction of space. Farocki would also cite Flusser in an interview titled *The ABCs of the Essay Film*, in which *U* stood for "Universe of Technical Images," with Farocki arguing that the Czech-born philosopher "creates a world in which matter doesn't count anymore, in which the disembodied human being is pure mind. Human beings of the future should communicate on a much more complex level. Flusser uses the string quartet as a model. And they

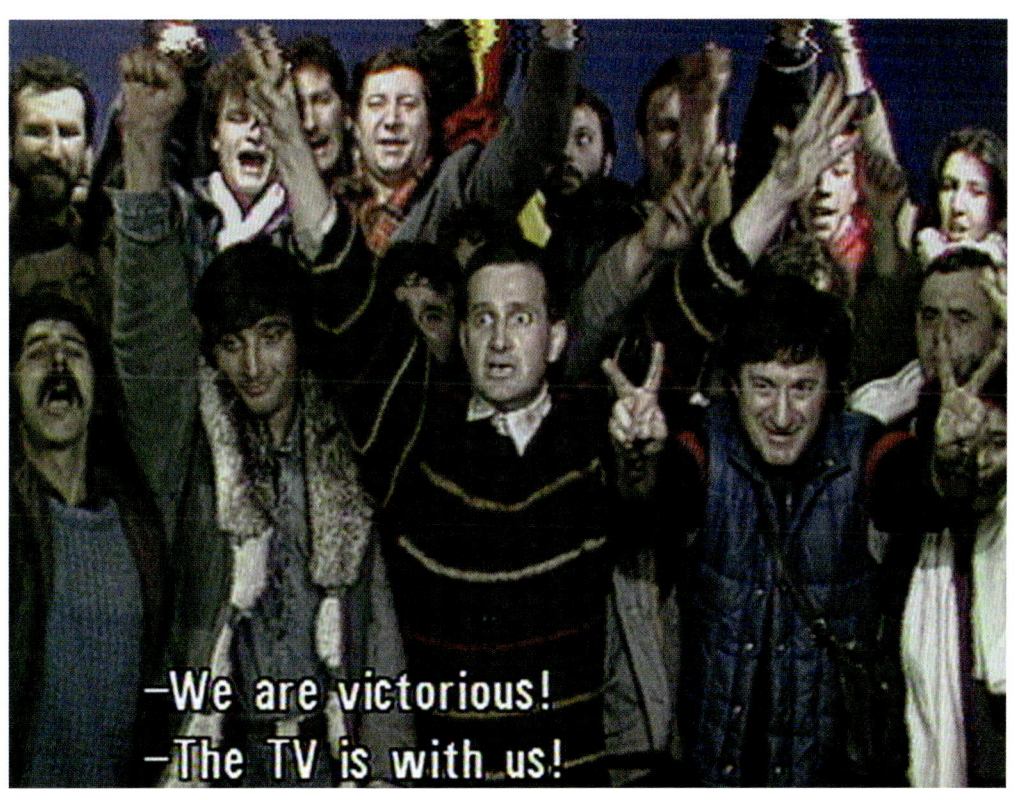

Figure 3.30
Harun Farocki and Andrei Ujică, *Videograms of a Revolution*, 1992. © Harun Farocki GbR.
Courtesy Harun Farocki Filmproduktion, Berlin, and Greene Naftali, New York.

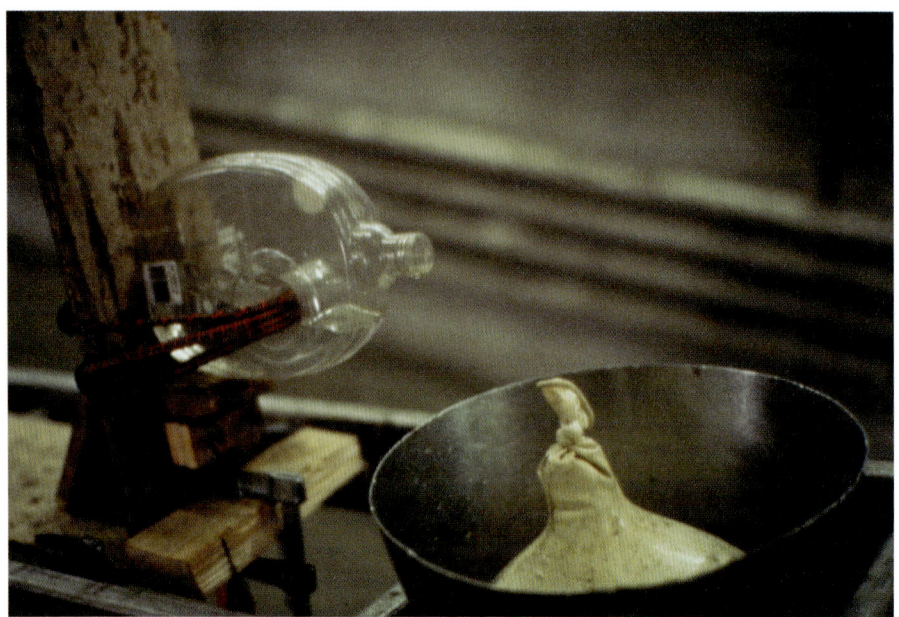

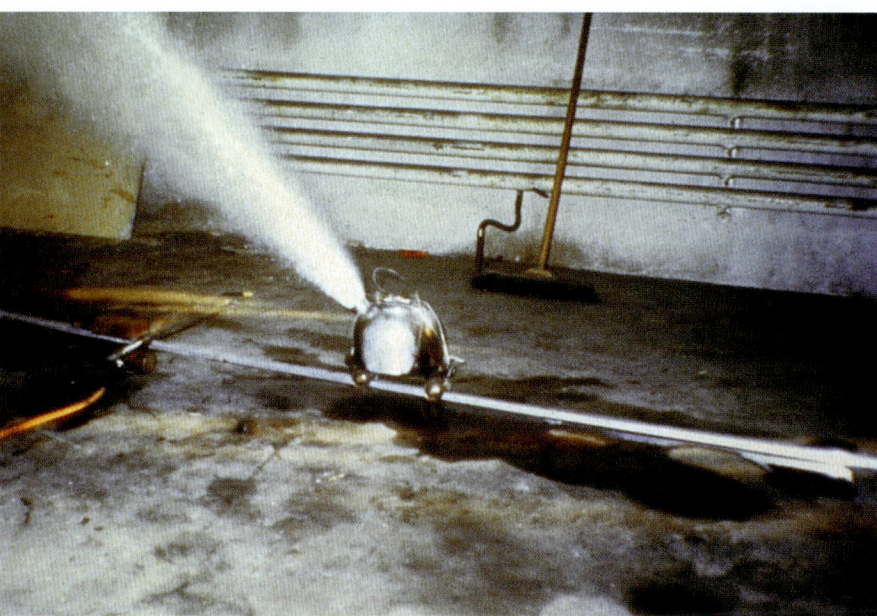

Figures 3.31–3.32
Peter Fischli and David Weiss, *The Way Things Go*, 1987. Color film, 16mm, with sound, 30 min.
© Peter Fischli and David Weiss. Courtesy Matthew Marks Gallery.

have to communicate with each other to figure out when to turn off the machines that keep them alive."[110]

Photography Criticism

Flusser rarely wrote about photography before the 1980s, but in the wake of the technical image trilogy he became a photography critic. He even had his own periodic column in *European Photography* magazine. Echoing Walter Benjamin, who decreed that future literacy would consist in the ability to read photographs, Flusser would write that the present is marked by "post-historical illiteracy."[111] What was needed was a criticism of technical images, and photography—even if he felt the medium was becoming outmoded or obsolete—provided fertile ground. Flusser approached criticism more as a philosophical exercise, writing about the work by artists such as Astrid Klein, Nancy Burson, Lizzie Calligas, Fischli + Weiss, Andy Warhol, Ulrich Mertens, Herbert W. Franke, Jiří Hanke, and others. For instance, his review of Fischli and Weiss's film *The Way Things Go* (1987), in which everyday objects are set up to create a combustible chain reaction, treated the film as a "machine" in which humans are absent and everything is programmed.[112] Writing about Andy Warhol's portraits of famous Jewish people, such as Kafka, Freud, and Einstein, based on photographs of these individuals, Flusser argued these were records of technical civilization and new ideological forms.[113]

Nancy Burson, a US photographer whose work Flusser reviewed in *European Photography*, employed new photographic techniques to create composites of humans and animals. Flusser wrote that her creatures were "chimeras," like the Chimera in ancient Greek mythology, a three-headed, hybrid-animal and fire-breathing monster—except hers were of the digital variety, created out of pixels and exhibiting both "telematic" and "biotechnical" tendencies.[114] Astrid Klein's rephotographed media images shock us into questioning the objective world and concrete experience, as opposed to "bracketed," packaged media images.[115]

Art criticism itself might be reimagined in terms of mathematical categories to create a "quantifying criticism" that would, echoing Bense and Moles, measure levels of terror, beauty, kitsch, and habit.[116] Flusser formulated a template for this, providing questions for critics of photography, such as, "What sort of camera

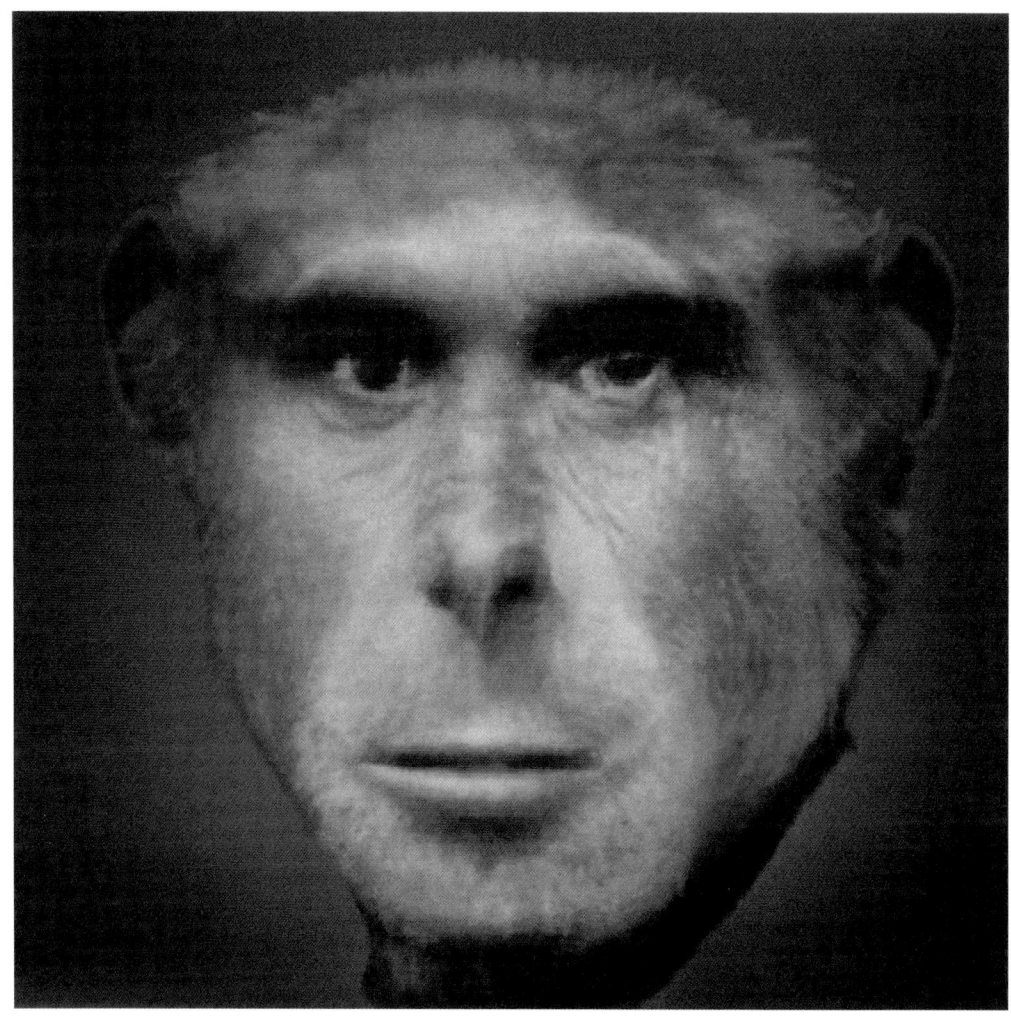

Figure 3.33
Nancy Burson, *Evolution II: Chimpanzee and Man*, 1984. Gelatin silver prints from computer-generated negatives. Courtesy of the artist.

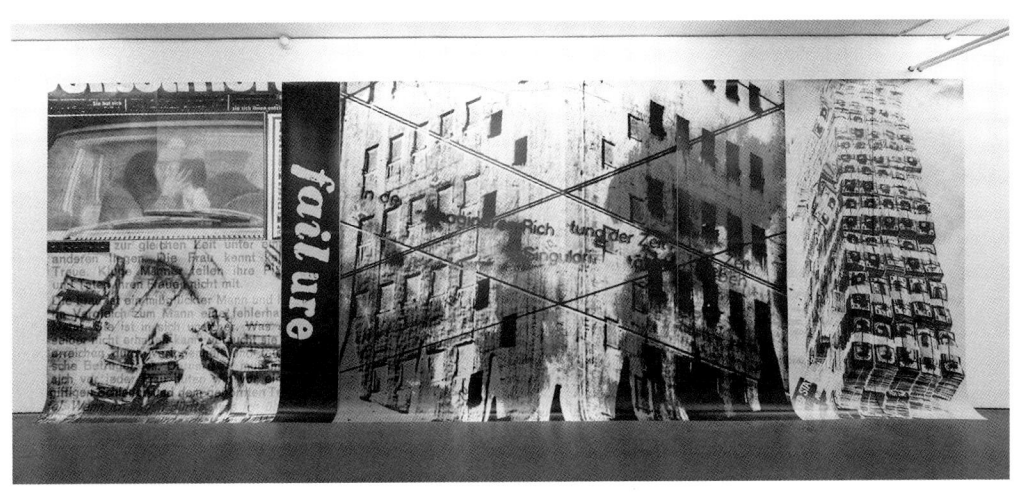

Figure 3.34
Astrid Klein, *Untitled (Failure)*, 1987. Photo work (eight parts), 126 × 358¼ in. (320 × 910 cm).
© Astrid Klein. Courtesy the artist and Sprüth Magers. Photo: Timo Ohler.

has produced the photograph? In what part of the world, with which techniques, and against which cultural, political, and historical backgrounds, was this camera produced, and in what ways does it differ from other cameras available on the market?"[117] The questions also included queries about the dissemination of images and how much the photographer attempted to subvert the camera's program.

Flusser also used his "Curie's Children" column in *Artforum*, which ran from 1986 to 1992, to think about synthetic and programmed images and how the digital and biotechnological revolutions were affecting philosophy and cognition.[118] In the "Discovery" series of essays in *Artforum* (others were published as "On Science" or given discrete titles), he recycled ideas from the technical image trilogy, considering how new images produce new forms of thinking, imagination, and knowledge. More important for Flusser at this point was how the new images affect epistemology and cognition, as *thoughts* rather than *representations*: "We now possess the ability to calculate the world as a field of virtualities, and to compute some of those virtualities into simulations of realities according to our own program. This is the new imagination."[119]

The *Artforum* essays brought Flusser greater attention. I will discuss this response further in Screen 4, but a few more technical-image connections are relevant here. In 1991, the Brazilian artist Eduardo Kac, who constructed the first holographic laboratory in Rio de Janeiro, sent Flusser an essay he had published in *Leonardo* on his work with holograms, inspired by Max Bense. Flusser wrote back that he was a member of the Holographic Society in Osnabrück (in Lower Saxony, Germany) and was very interested in Kac's activities. Conceived in 1947 by Hungarian émigré Dennis Gabor, working in England, holography had produced heterogeneous communities (military scientists, engineers, artists, and generalist enthusiasts), including groups in northern California that overlapped with or paralleled the burgeoning utopian-tech community and Stewart Brand's *Whole Earth Catalog* (1968). Mission statements for holography centers in the 1970s sound strikingly Flusserian, attempting to create apparatus programmers rather than functionaries: "The application of holography to communications and the human environment could soon have a very great and far-reaching effect on our society. Using holography, the physical environment could be anything that man can conceive. Holography can create

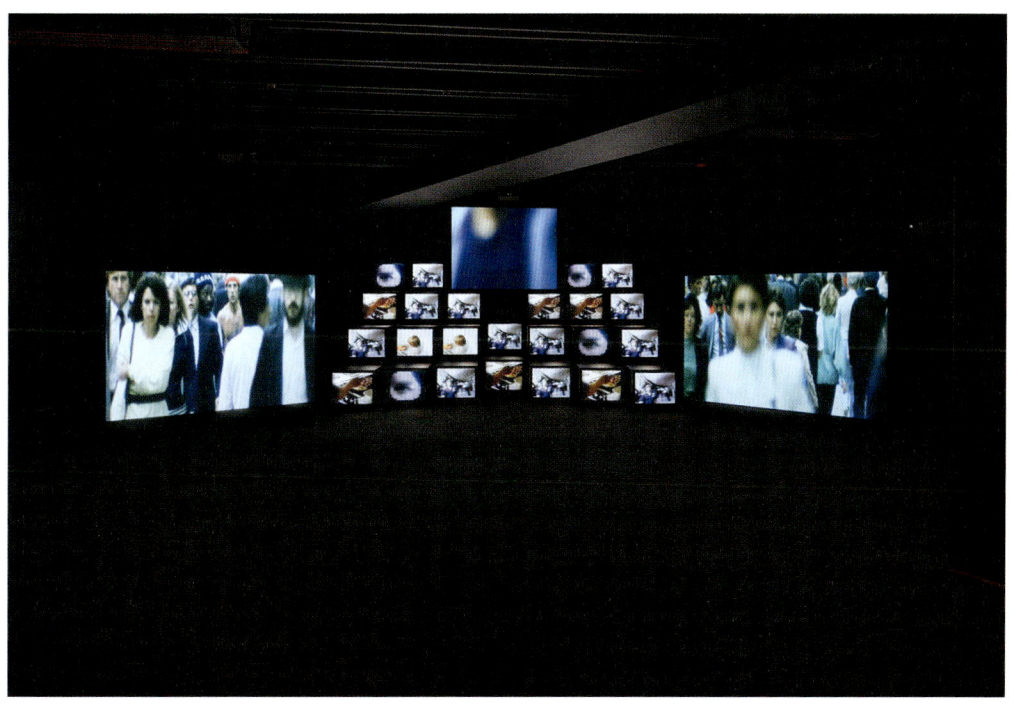

Figure 3.35
Gretchen Bender, *Total Recall*, 1987. Eight-channel video on twenty-four monitors and three
rear projection screens, 18:02 min. Installation view of *Gretchen Bender: So Much Deathless*
at Red Bull Arts, New York, March 6–July 28, 2019. © Gretchen Bender Estate. Courtesy of
Sprüth Magers. Photo: Lance Brewer.

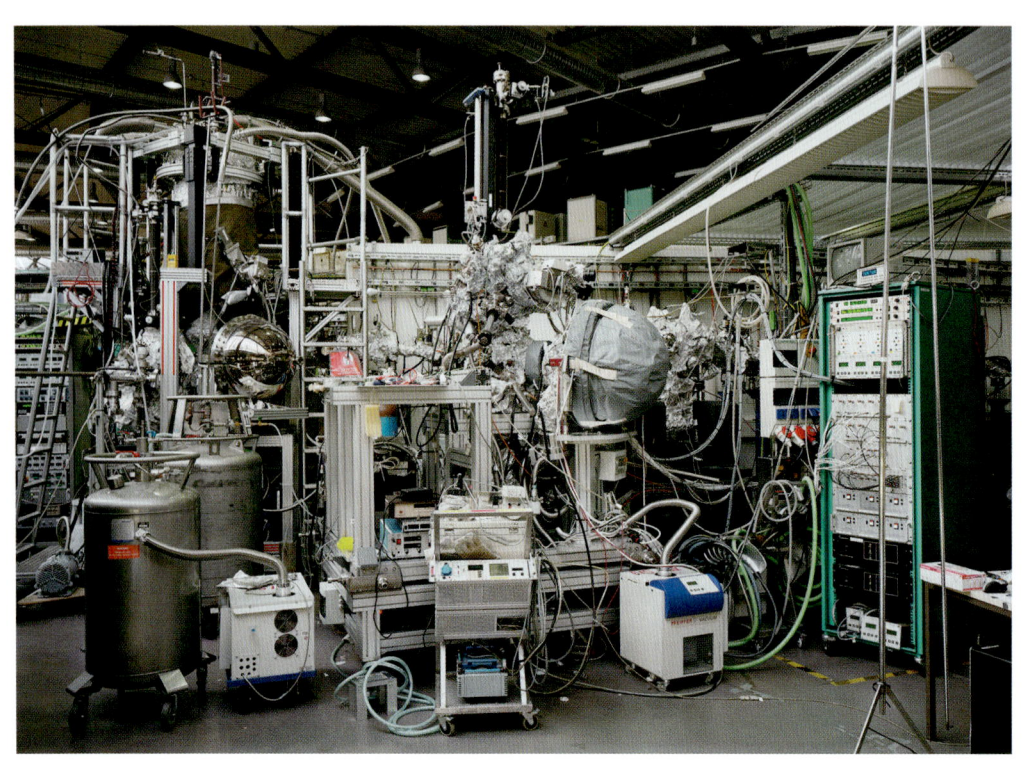

Figure 3.36
Thomas Struth, *Measuring, Helmholtz-Zentrum, Berlin*, 2012. Chromogenic print,
241.9 × 336.7 cm. © Thomas Struth.

the future. . . . Holography is simple. Anyone with interest, basic information, and minimum equipment can make a hologram."[120] For Flusser, the *projected* nature of the hologram was significant, since he theorized that humans would eventually become "projects" rather than "subjects." After their initial contact, Kac sent Flusser a text he had written on Baudrillard's "Hologrammes" and told Flusser that he had created a "telerobot" named Ornitorrinco that could be remote controlled.[121] Later, working with Flusser's friend Louis Bec, Kac would create Alba, the *GFP Bunny*, begun in 1999 and born in 2000, a rabbit that was genetically altered to glow in the dark, which will be discussed in Screen 4.

Another artist who became aware of Flusser through his *Artforum* writings was the US video artist Gretchen Bender. Known for her immersive installations using multiple televisions, Bender delved into the maelstrom of mass media and advertising, working as a commercial video editor and producer as well as an artist. Along with writer and curator Timothy Druckrey, Bender asked Flusser to participate in a symposium they were organizing at the Dia Center for the Arts in New York exploring electronic media and its use by artists. Flusser enthusiastically agreed. However, he died in a car accident on November 27, 1991 after leaving his first public lecture in Prague, several months before the Dia conference. His essay "Digital Apparition" was included in a subsequent book edited by Bender and Druckrey, but the impact of his writings in the US art world were largely overshadowed by concerns with the AIDS crisis, culture wars, identity politics, and battles over reproductive rights.[122]

Into the Universe

Now, more than ever, we are living in the universe of technical images, inside GPS and surveillance systems, virtually all of us carrying cameras in the form of cell phones. Similarly, as the Internet of Things takes hold, we are seeing digital technology embedded in everyday objects—roads, paper, clothing, skin, organs, medicines, and food—with information a physical part of life. (We will discuss this in the next chapter.) Artists and theorists continue to play against the program, but we are still sorting out, as Flusser wrote, "what it is that makes the human imagination unique—that which is irreplaceable and cannot be simulated."[123]

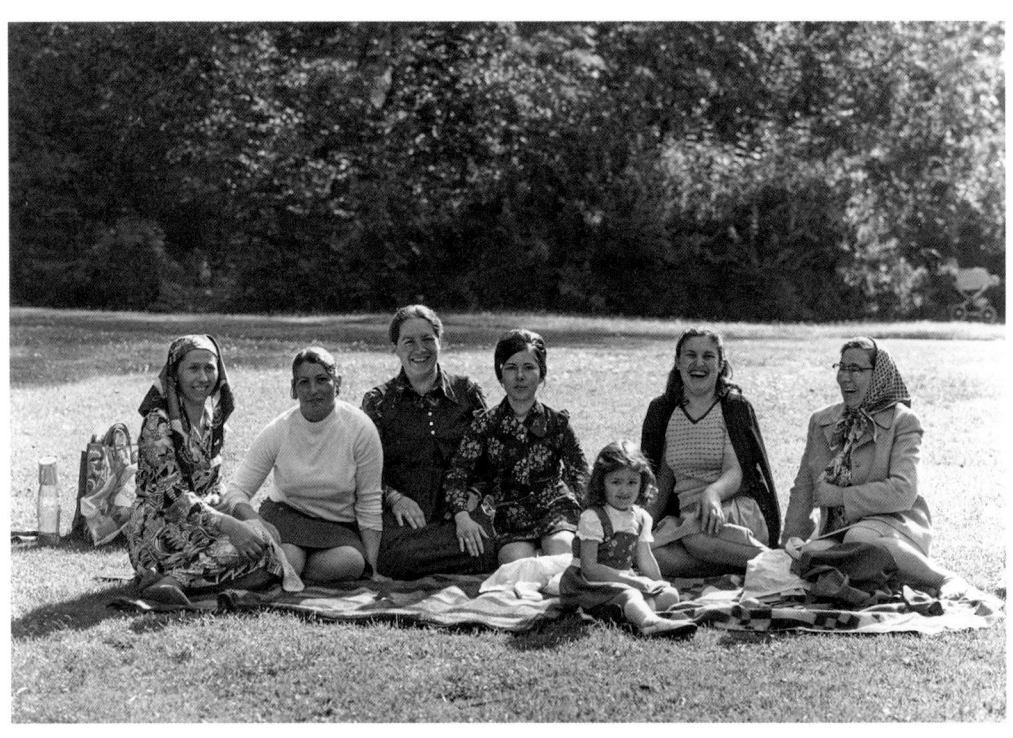

Figure 3.37
Candida Höfer, *Volksgarten Köln* (Cologne People's Garden), 1974. Black-and-white photograph. © Candida Höfer/VG Bild-Kunst, Bonn/ARS 1974.

Many artists have either inadvertently or consciously engaged with Flusser's concerns. For instance, the so-called Düsseldorf School of photographers—students of Bernd and Hilla Becher such as Andreas Gursky, Thomas Ruff, Thomas Struth, and Candida Höfer—seem to be responding to Flusser, although he did not communicate directly with these artists in a significant way.[124]

The affinity is clear, though, in Gursky's photographs marking the sites and circulation of global capitalism; in Candida Höfer's photographs of libraries and other cultural institutions, as well as Turkish "guest workers" in Germany, whom Flusser mentioned in the essays collected in *The Freedom of the Migrant*; and particularly in work by Thomas Struth, whose ongoing *Nature & Politics* series features the inner workings of elaborate black-box systems: scientific, medical, industrial, and entertainment apparatuses that control and govern and save our lives—and yet remain opaque to nearly everyone but the experts who program and control them. The conceptual artist Christopher Williams has more consciously channeled Flusser, suggesting the camera and the apparatus of photography as a black box radiating outward into advertising, media, fashion, and other fields.[125] His photographs of cutaway cameras seem like the perfect illustration of penetrating the black box. Other artists, including Lynn Hershman Leeson and Paul Mpagi Sepuya, have also thought about the camera as an apparatus. Hito Steyerl demonstrates the link between the image flood and flows of globalized capital in *Liquidity Inc.* (2014), and Jon Rafman's project *The Nine Eyes of Google Street View*, begun in 2008, reminds us that we all live inside a camera now: the still images from this ongoing artwork are taken from Google Street View's enormous archive of images around the globe.

What is important about Flusser's technical image philosophy, however, is that it's essentially a *communications* philosophy, which is why he has been consistently championed in media theory, particularly in Germany. Flusser was overlooked for decades in the English-speaking world, but his work is slowly becoming more available and read by artists—as well as people outside the art world. As Sean Cubitt wrote in 2004: "Imagine Walter Benjamin's essays of the 1930s had only just become available, or that Marshall McLuhan had died in obscurity but was now for the first time appearing in dribs and drabs. That is the significance of the translations of Flusser that have appeared in English in the last five years."[126] Flusser prefigured theorists like Yuk Hui, who asks

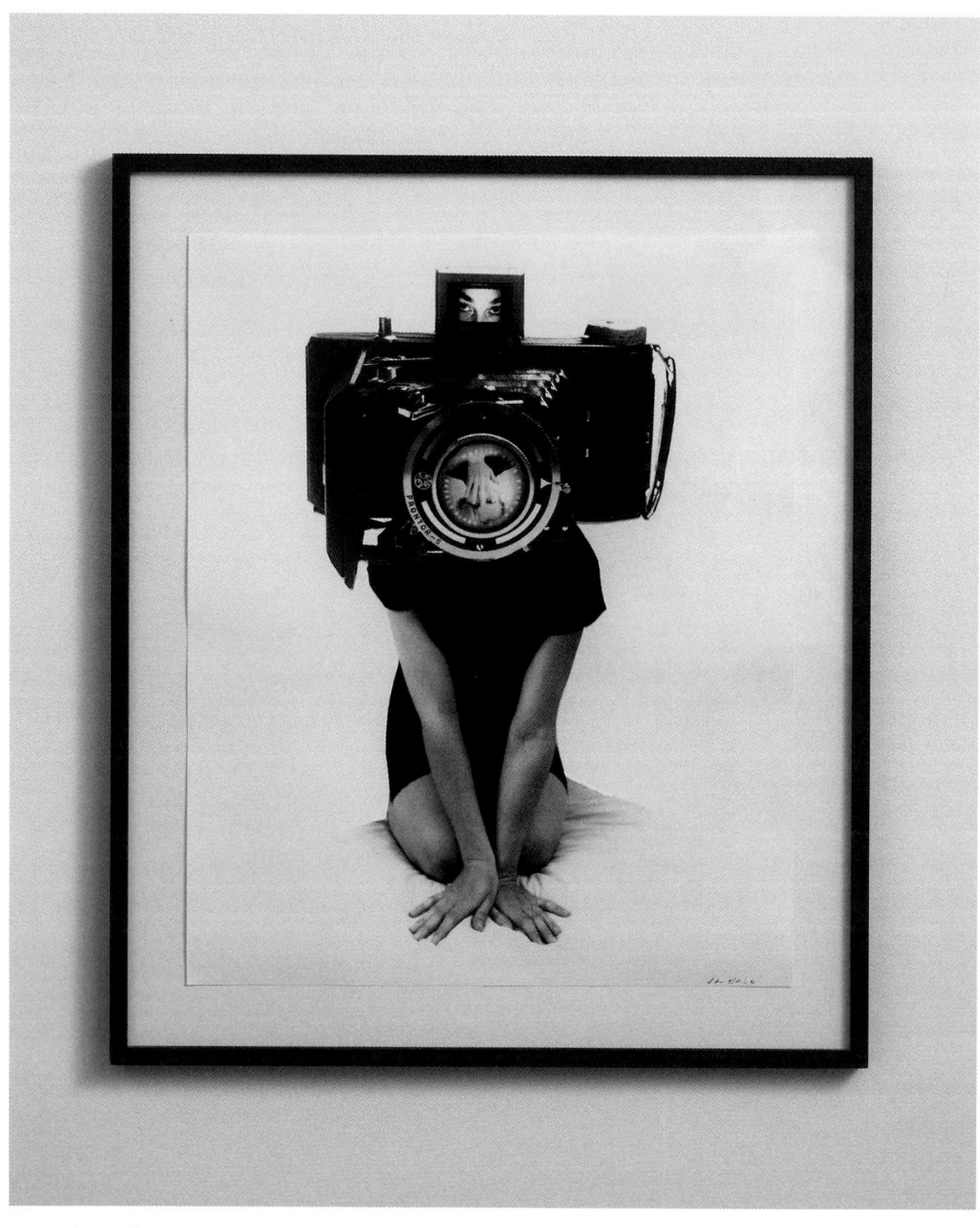

Figure 3.38
Lynn Hershman Leeson, *Shutter*, 1986. Silver gelatin print, 24 × 20 in. (61 × 50.8 cm).
Courtesy of the artist; Altman Siegel, San Francisco; and Bridget Donahue, New York.
© Hotwire Productions LLC. Photo: Robert Divers Herrick.

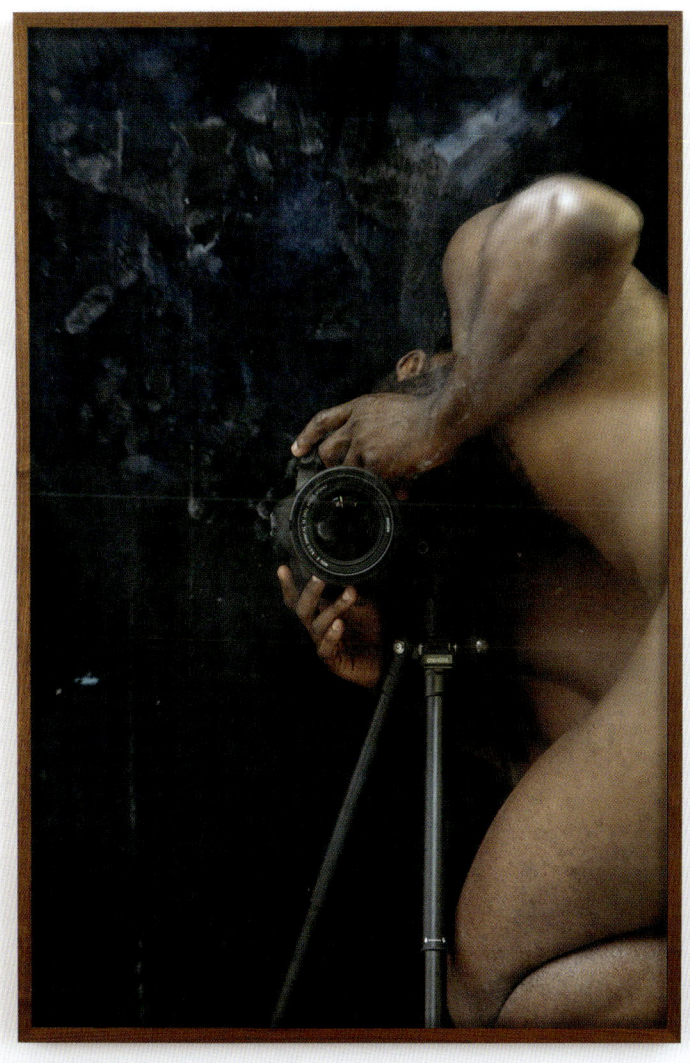

Figure 3.39
Paul Mpagi Sepuya, *Darkroom Mirror Study (0X5A1531)*, 2017. Archival pigment print,
51 × 34 in. (129.5 × 86.4 cm). Courtesy the artist. Photo: DOCUMENT Chicago.

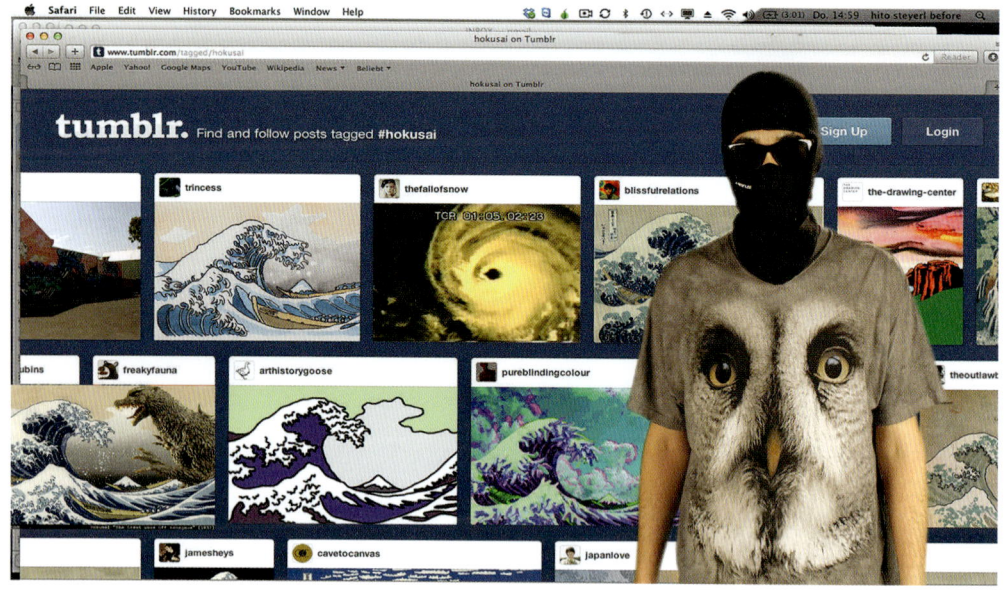

Figure 3.40
Hito Steyerl, *Liquidity Inc.*, 2014. Still from HD video, installation view. Courtesy of the artist; Andrew Kreps Gallery, New York; and Esther Schipper, Berlin/Paris/Seoul.

how we can imagine a *global* theory of technology, a "cosmotechnics" that goes beyond Western photographic imperialism and Cartesian thought.[127]

Flusser was not a conventional thinker, but he knew precisely what was at stake. He imagined a world of dialogue through screens that has become an integral part of social media—and highlighted as the COVID-19 pandemic hit and vast sectors of life were carried out on the screen. We have not seen the total eradication of writing yet, but we have seen it eclipsed as the dominant form, particularly with the rise of artificial intelligence, which threatens to reduce writing to a series of prompts and commands. As Flusser's editor Andreas Müller-Pohle recently observed: "The programmers of the iPhone are more powerful than Günther Grass."[128] Hence, in a 1980 letter to Abraham Moles and his wife, Élisabeth Rohmer, Flusser wrote, as they grappled with the rise of digital culture: "it is a pleasure to disagree with you, especially if it is a profound disagreement: the whole of science, politics, and the arts is involved here. It is a pleasure, because your mind is so keen that I sharpen mine while trying to fight you. Be embraced, both of you."[129]

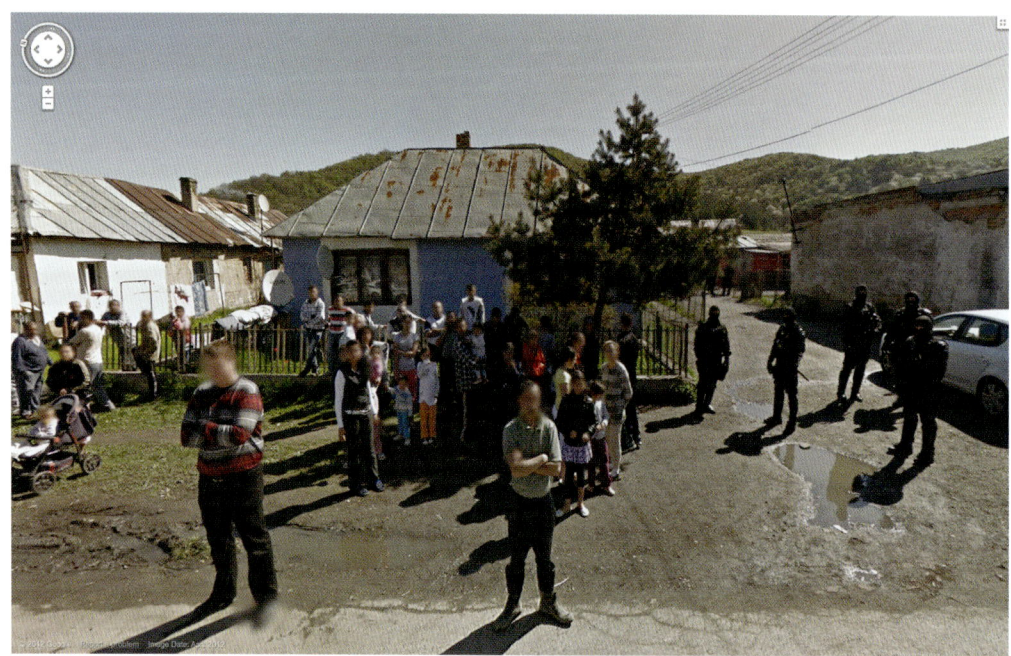

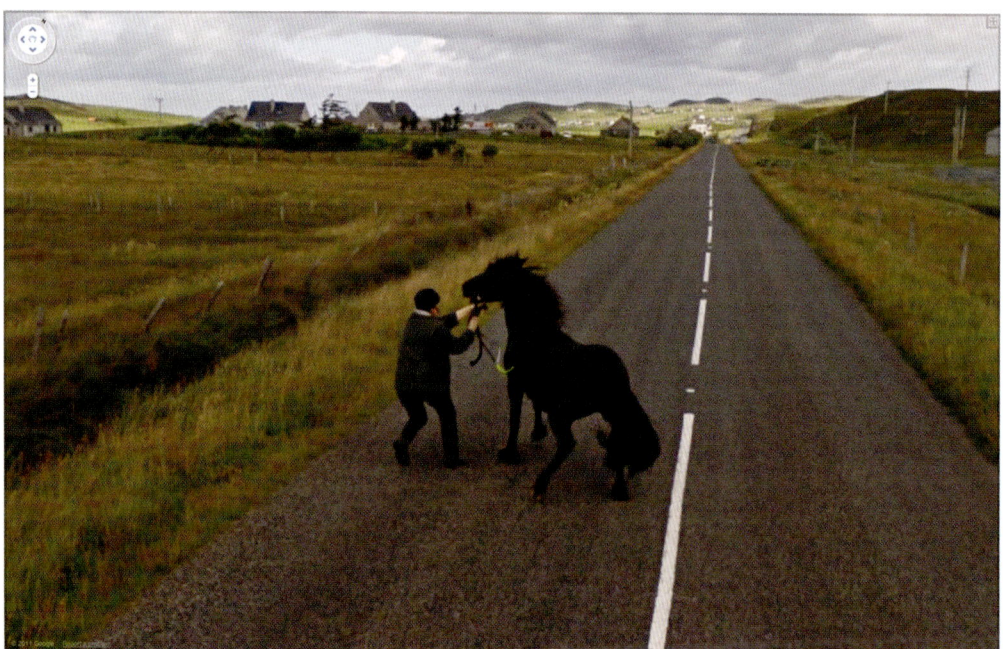

Figures 3.41–3.44
Jon Rafman, *The Nine Eyes of Google Street View* (slideshow), 2008–2020. 4K video, color,
65 min. © Jon Rafman. Courtesy of the artist and Sprüth Magers.

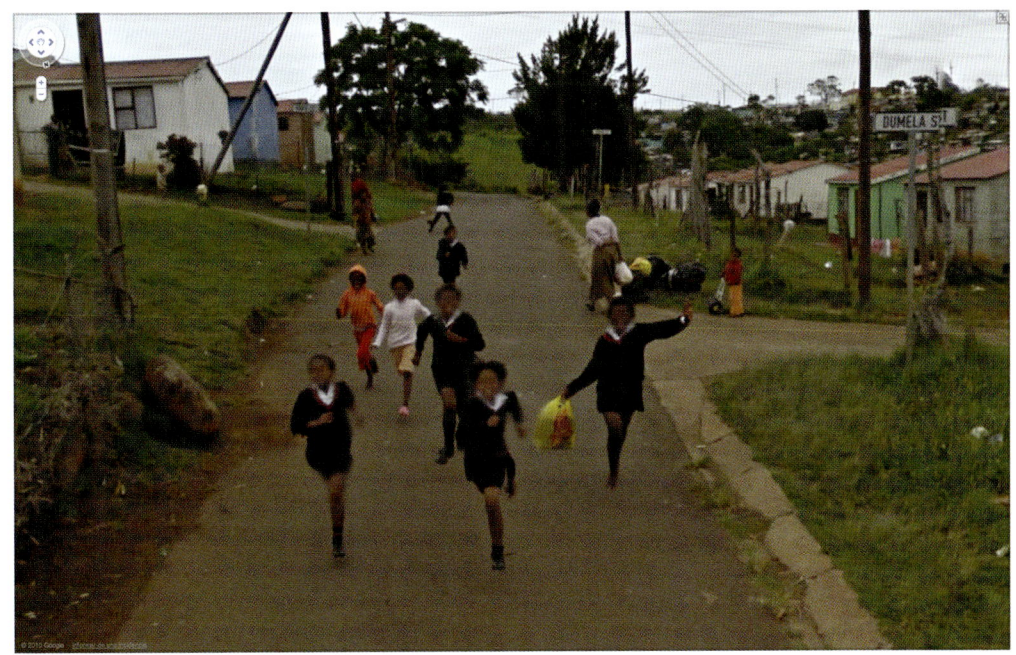

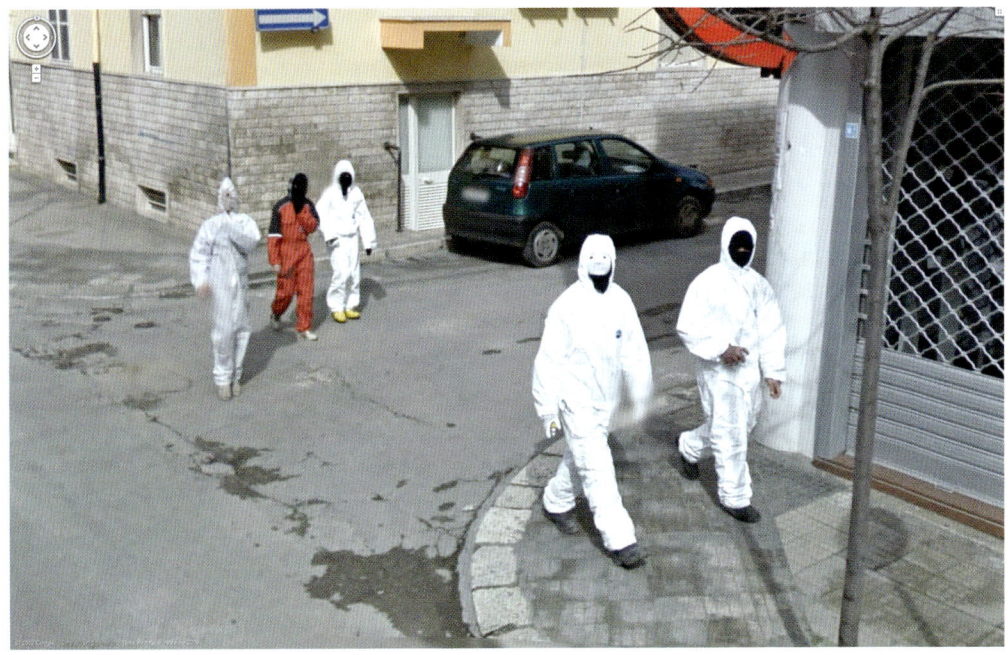

Screen 4   *Blue Dogs and Bio-Machines*

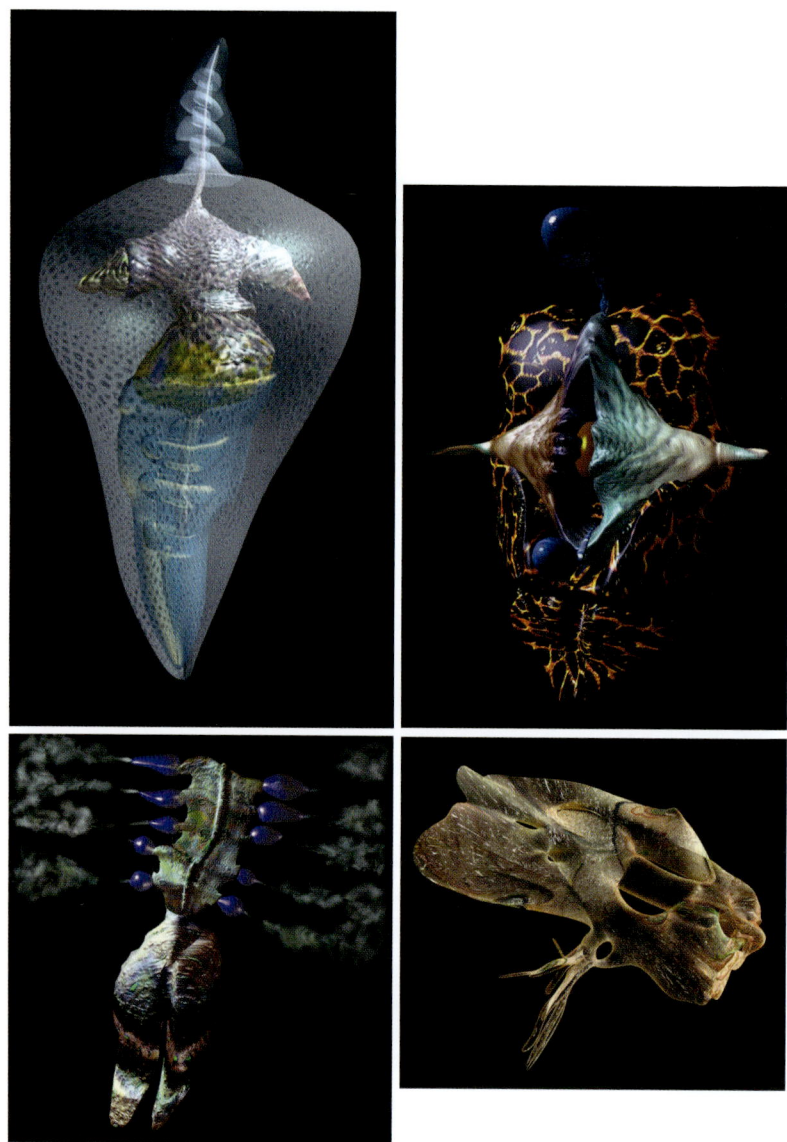

Figure 4.1–4.4
Louis Bec's virtually evolved organisms, 2014. Clockwise from the upper left:
Diaphaskamokherisse (Diaphaneites), *Melaskunnodousse (Upochelenoïdes)*, *Petrapakneme*
(Tremones), and *Protospone Mex (Kruptoïdones)*. Published in Bec's *Zoosystémie* (Prague: CIANT,
2014) and *Flusser Studies*. Courtesy the Estate of Louis Bec.

Although Flusser was becoming known for his technical image writings, he was also interested in developments in biology and biotechnology. Ever suspicious of the scientific rationalism that he felt had resulted in the Holocaust that killed his entire nuclear family, Flusser would approach the question of these shifting categories by blurring relationships between science, fiction, and philosophy, as well as nature and culture, and human and inhuman. This chapter will look at his writing around these ideas, particularly in the books *Natural:Mind* (1979) and *Vampyroteuthis infernalis* (1987) and his "Curie's Children" column for *Artforum* (1986–1992), as well as the artists with whom he collaborated and their echoes in current practices. Throughout his career, Flusser was consumed by C. P. Snow's idea of the "two cultures": the severing of science and the humanities in the West and how this obstructed solving the world's larger problems.[1] Writing and lecturing on communications theory and the philosophy of language and science, and hosting an informal salon on his patio in São Paulo which included artists, writers, philosophers, scientists, and students, Flusser was constantly crossing these divides—and heading into speculative territory. His first book, *Language and Reality* (1963), cited the neo-Kantian Hans Vaihinger, whose opus *The Philosophy of "As If"* (1911) argued that various scientific models and systems function as "fictions," where assumptions can sometimes produce truthful results.[2] Similarly, in *On Doubt* (1966), Flusser posited a "Critique of Pure Doubt," playing off of Kant's "Critique of Pure Reason" and challenging the *cogito ergo sum* expressed in Descartes's *Discourse on Method* (1637) and *Meditations* (1641).[3] Flusser proposes the essay as a "modest search" within philosophy for "a new sense of reality" within an unbearable existential situation, in which science and the intellect have failed—or led to atrocities such as Auschwitz.[4]

One of the important moves he makes in this text, as in later ones, is to abandon the human in order to rethink philosophy through the nonhuman world. He invokes the spider, whose universe exists within the web. The spider focuses on what happens on the threads of the web rather than the intervals between them, which form a meta-universe, or the "unarticulated, chaotic, and 'metaphysical' backdrops of a philosophizing spider."[5] Drawing this out further, Flusser imagines that the "civilized spider, in the Western sense of the term," tends to disregard differences between itself and "others" on the web—whether that Other is a fly or just another spider.[6] Devouring things on its web—which is a visible thing, unlike our social web, which is invisible and becomes real only through words organized through the rules of our language systems—is the spider's *Wirklichkeit* or reality. However, where "arachnism is unavoidable for the spiders," for us "the discussion of the web is arachnally possible."[7] In other words, *we* can think differently. Flusser suggests falling through the web of language and embracing different modes of thinking: symbolically, or the kind of thinking without thinking that one can do in visual art.

On Doubt then moves to another nonhuman organism: the amoeba. Flusser's interest is in the amoeba's feeding process, which involves extending pseudopods—temporary armlike extensions that encircle particles or live prey—and ingesting nutrients through vacuoles (vesicles) formed within its cell membrane. For Flusser, this process can be compared to human language, particularly the way we coin proper names and use them to "occupy a territory that was previously extra-intellectual."[8] In the same way that doubt might serve as a potentially useful instrument in philosophy, the spider and the amoeba offer models that help us understand the failures of Western thought and civilization—particularly its drive to turn people into Others and genocidally devour them. At the end of *On Doubt*, Flusser proposes using these models to overcome the classifications and specializing divisions

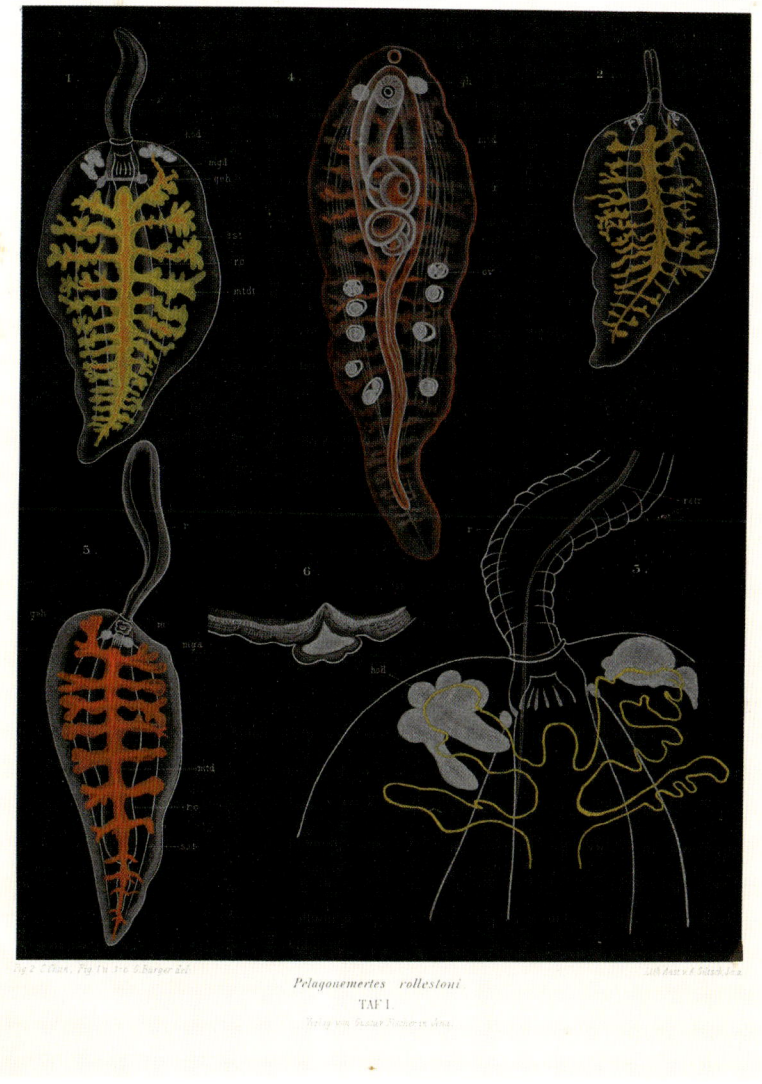

Pelagonemertes rollestoni

Figure 4.5
Illustration of *Pelagonemertes rollestoni* from Carl Chun's *Wissenschaftliche Ergebnisse der Deutschen Tiefsee-Expedition auf dem Dampfer "Valdivia" 1898–1899*, vol. 16 (Jena: G. Fischer, 1902). Biodiversity Heritage Library. *Pelagonemertes* is a type of ribbon worm found in most of the world's oceans.

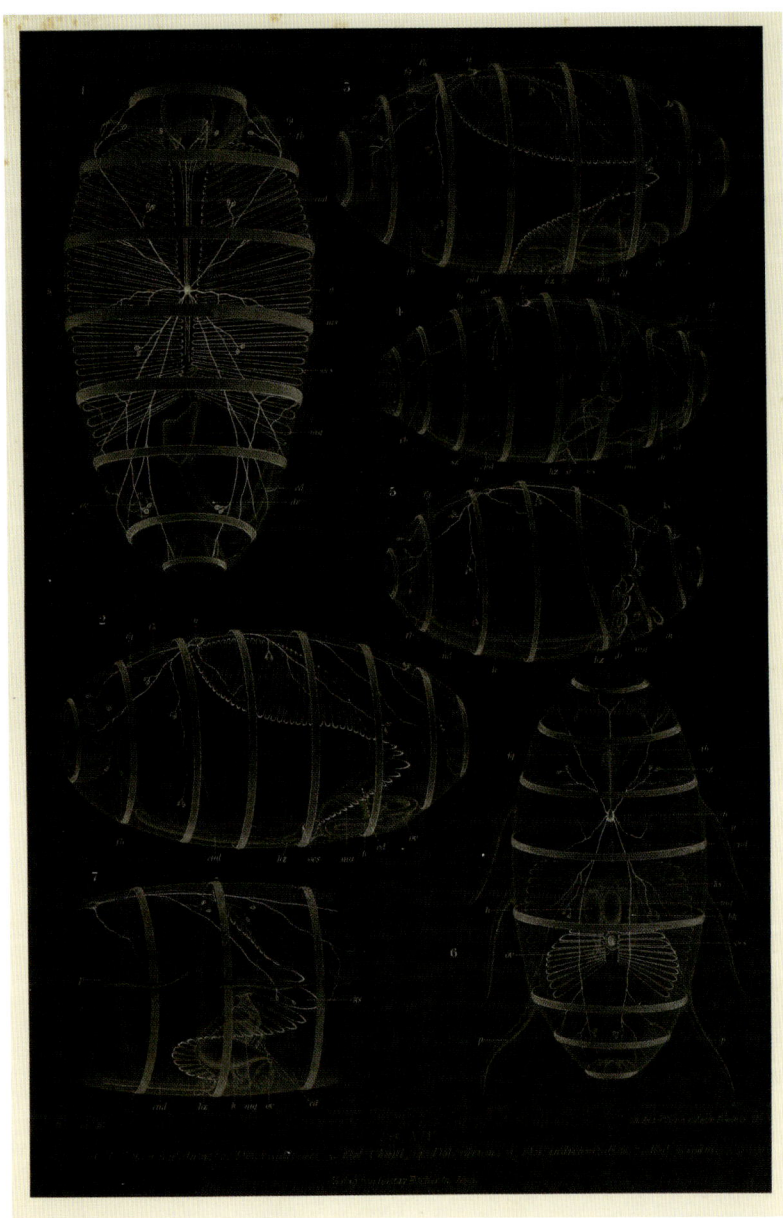

Figure 4.6
Doliolida in Carl Chun, *Wissenschaftliche Ergebnisse der Deutschen Tiefsee-Expedition auf dem Dampfer "Valdivia" 1898–1899*, vol. 12 (Jena: G. Fischer, 1913). Biodiversity Heritage Library. Doliolida are small, transparent, hermaphroditic animals that adapt swiftly to changing environments.

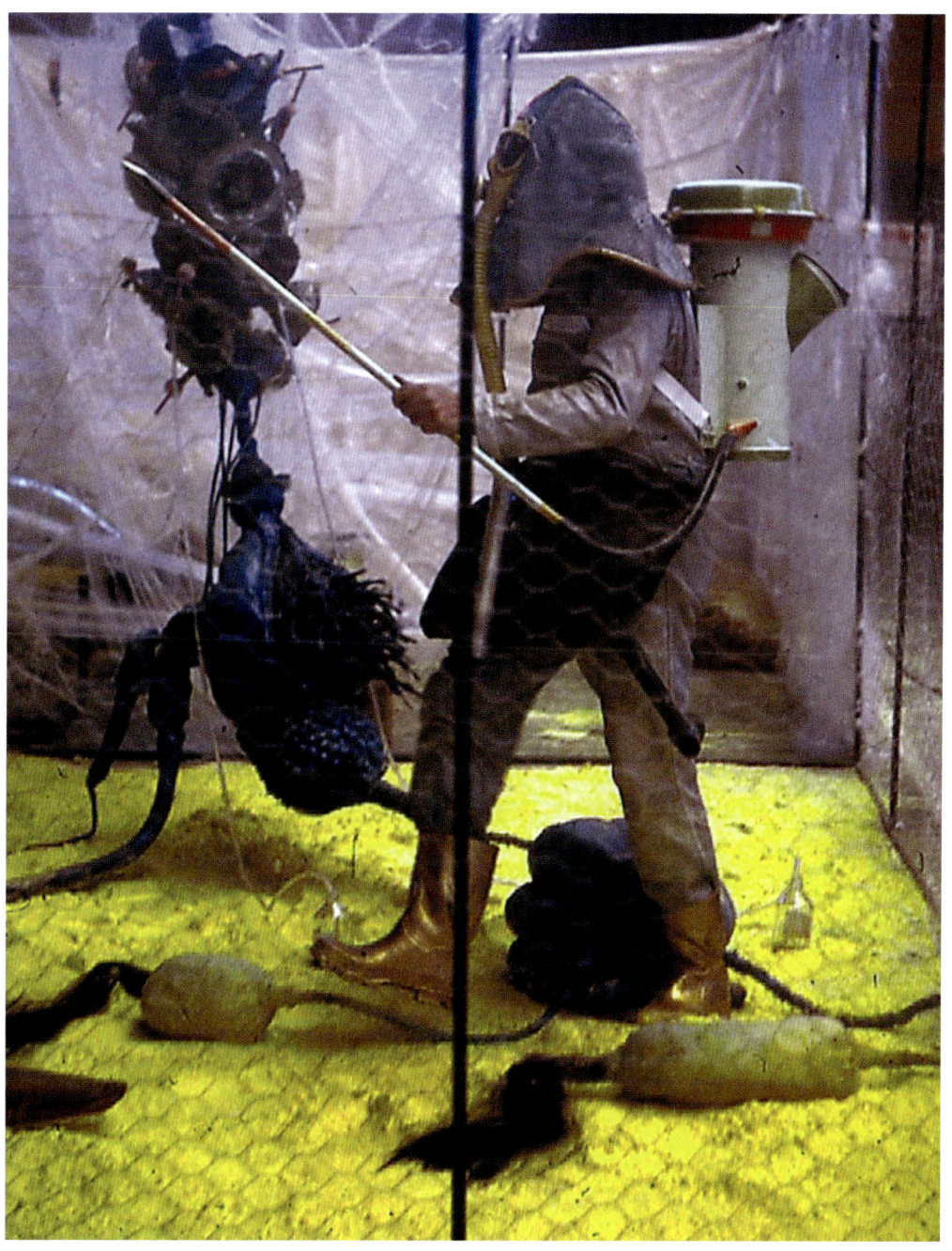

Figure 4.7
Louis Bec in his Sulfonaut costume, published in *Zoosystémie*, 562. Courtesy the Estate of
Louis Bec and Pavel Smetana.

in Western thought and to think of science as an applied art in order to eradicate the madness of trying to dominate what is different or other.

The divisions between nature and cultures—or lack thereof—got a fuller treatment in a wonderful, often overlooked essay called *Orthonature Paranature*, written in 1976 but published in pamphlet form in 1978, which Flusser wrote at the behest of Louis Bec, the artist who would be his collaborator on *Vampyroteuthis infernalis*. The two men met in Paris in 1974 and became lifelong friends, as well as neighbors in the sleepy towns of Robion and Sorgues in Provence. Bec was a biologist and forerunner of bio art. He identified as a "zoosystemician," a field he invented that combined art and science, reimagined evolutionary biology, and offered new zoomorphic types and forms of communication between artificial and natural species.[9] In 1970, Bec founded the Institut Scientifique de Recherche Paranaturaliste (ISRP), an organization devoted to speculative research that echoed Alfred Jarry's 'Pataphysics, the surrealist journal *Documents* (1929–1930), the Situationist International, and Gaston Bachelard.[10] Bec, who was born in Algeria, made sculptures called *Sulfanogrades*: fictional organisms whose chemistry is based in sulfur rather than carbon, sulfur being an environmentally hostile material that was later discovered to be helpful in biotechnology because of its thermostable nature. The *Sulfanogrades* were installed in greenhouses in Provence in the 1970s—in 1976, the sulfur-substrate caught fire in one installation, creating an actual toxic environment.[11] Bec also exhibited them at the 1981 São Paulo Biennial, at the invitation of Flusser, who penned a catalogue essay arguing that the sculptures occupied a territory between art and science and motivated us to reconsider Darwin, Freud, and Einstein as artists, and Cézanne, Schoenberg, and Duchamp as scientists who had imposed epistemological models upon the world.[12]

The two men were in daily dialogue, eventually working on various projects. One of their earliest collaborations was *Orthonature Paranature*, which Bec's ISRP published as a pamphlet.[13] *Orthonature Paranature* argues that, rather than culture existing as the transformation of nature, the opposite is generally true. Flusser defines "orthonature" as the commonly understood version of nature as universal and omnipresent and preexisting culture, and "paranature" as all natures and cultures reduced to epistemological categories in order to make them understandable and

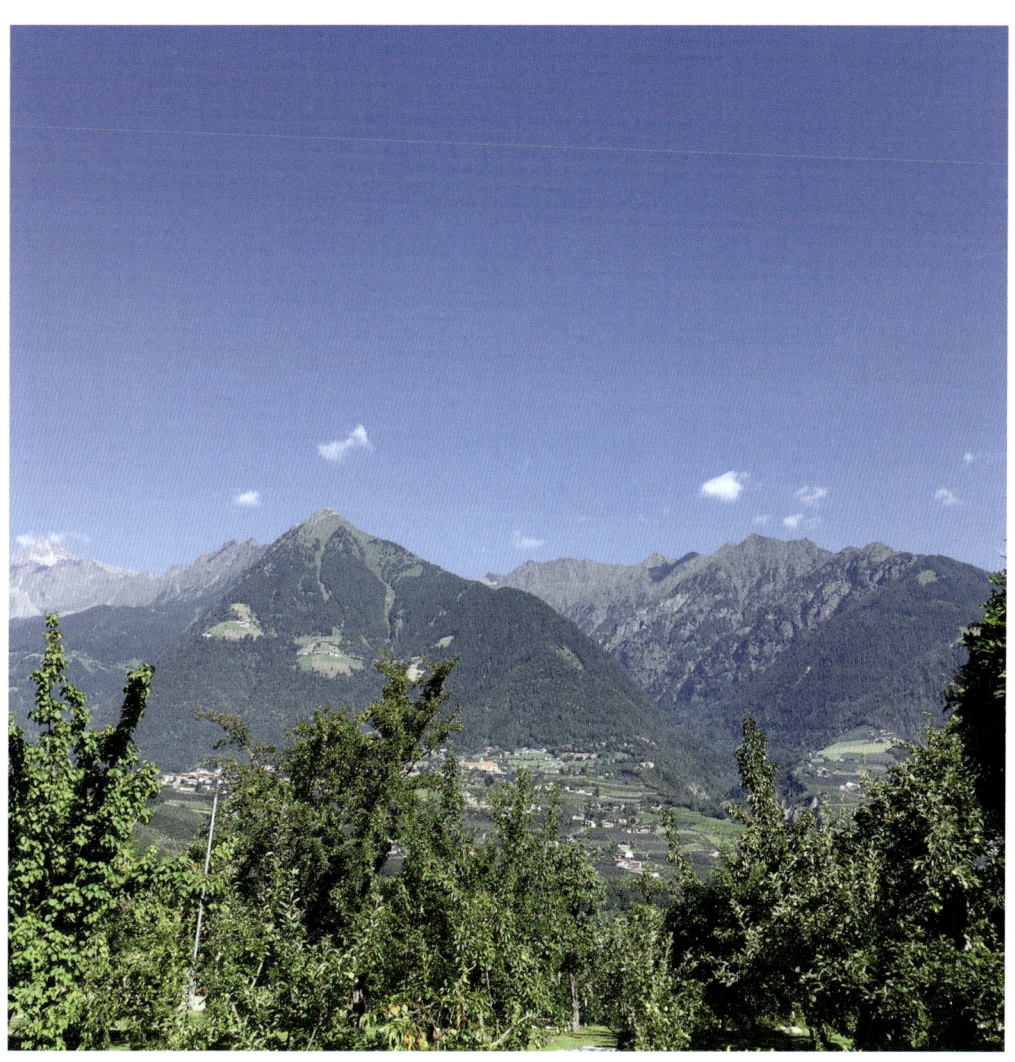

Figure 4.8
The view from where Flusser wrote *Natural:Mind* (1979) in Merano, Italy.
Photo: Martha Schwendener.

manipulable. Overturning orthodox ideas of nature and culture, Flusser argues, requires questioning established ideas like Darwinian evolution and the chronology of "natural" history. For instance, in Flusser's deeply ironic chronology, primates would now come *after* humans in the evolutionary timeline, since they were discovered in the nineteenth century, and thanks to Darwin, humans may "become" primates. Accepting this view has profound consequences. If the difference between art and science is erased and all science is treated as artifice, the criteria of truth changes: "Scientific truth is no longer an idea's suitability to a given reality, but an idea's sufficiency to a real fact caused by this idea."[14] Moreover, there is not *one* truth but several truths, and the knowledge sought by the ISRP is no less scientific than that of zoology, although different. The structure of its research is the same, based on the tools of logic, methodology, and controlled experience, and it shows that knowledge is a human activity structured by the same categories, regardless of which reality it's based on: if science is an art, and art becomes a deliberate science, one could apply aesthetic criteria to both. Aesthetics becomes epistemology, and epistemology becomes aesthetics.

Natural:mente

Having devised these playful, *homo ludens* methods for doing philosophy, Flusser began to think more about the divisions between nature and culture and particularly the way different cultures perceived nature: the European idealist approach inherited from eighteenth- and nineteenth-century philosophy versus the colonial attempt to conquer nature in Brazil. He sharpened his thinking around the nature-culture dialectic in *Natural:mente* (1979), translated as *Natural:Mind*.[15] Flusser started writing the essays in 1974 after moving back to Europe, describing the book, humorously, as a "tourist guide" for Brazilians—"as long as 'tourism' is understood as an updated synonym of the term 'theory.'"[16] Many of the essays were written in Merano, Italy, where Flusser was surrounded by apple trees and had a view of the Ötztal Alps. With essays devoted to paths, valleys, birds, rain, cows, grass, the moon, meadows, wind, fog, and other phenomena, *Natural:Mind* highlighted the difference between European idealist views of the sublime landscape and the expansionist colonial view of the

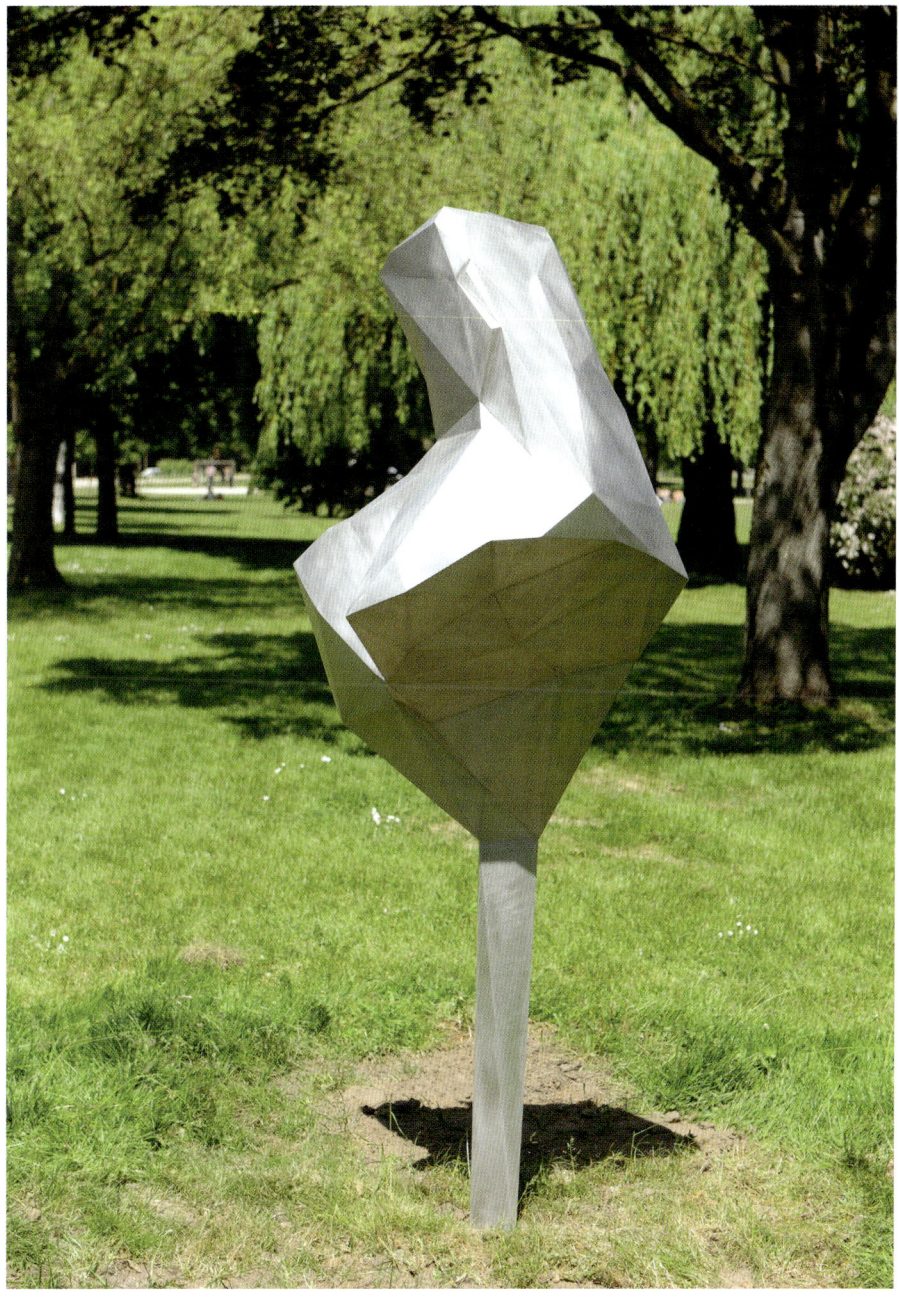

Figure 4.9
Achim Mohné, *Low_Poly_Tree, Grafenwerth Island*, 2020/2023. Cast aluminum, finely ground,
207.5 × 80.3 × 73.8 cm. Courtesy the artist. © Achim Mohné, VG Bild-Kunst, Bonn. Mohné's
sculpture takes its form from the virtual representation of a tree as it appears on Google
Earth in 3D mode.

Amazonian basin, as a place to extract "resources," or his friend João Guimarães Rosa's rugged *sertão* (backcountry). If such divergent philosophical ideas of nature existed, these undercut the concept of a universal and omnipresent "orthonature" as described in the earlier essay. Most important, the book set out to collapse any distinction between "nature" and "culture," as is reflected in the title. Flusser's style was changing, too—translator Rodrigo Maltez Novaes describes it as "more poetic than scientific"—and this is reflected in the playful title: Flusser chose the adverb *naturalmente* (naturally) and added the colon just as the book was about to go to press, giving the title a multivalent meaning in Portuguese that highlighted the speciousness of "naturalness" and how language participates in this charade.[17]

In "Paths," the first essay in the book, Flusser looks at the Fuorn Pass connecting the Engadin Valley in Switzerland to the Trentino-Alto Adige on the borders of Italy, Austria, and Switzerland. While we see the Fuorn Pass as an asphalt road, for millennia it was a migratory path for cattle and reindeer. The route we travel today was actually "built" by those herds and the Paleolithic hunters who are our ancestors. In "Birds," Flusser argues that, while birds once served as models for human flight—for instance, in Leonardo da Vinci's drawings—now that humans can fly, our relationship to birds has changed. Moreover, our *models* have changed: the design of airplanes wasn't copied from bird flight but resulted from aerodynamic equations. "In this sense," Flusser writes, "airplanes are less 'natural' instruments than levers and mirrors: they do not have natural things as models."[18] Meanwhile, in "Cows," Flusser offers a satirical proposal that bovine animals are efficient, self-reproducing biological machines for transforming grass into milk. Their bodies are "hardware" that can be consumed as meat or leather, and they serve as prototypes for Western notions of progress, comparable to artworks by Calder and Picasso.[19] (Although Flusser doesn't mention it, Louis Bec had been thinking about cows for years, exhibiting his diagrams of Bovideoloths, a new fictional cow species impacted by industrial chemicals in the natural environment.)

In "Rain," Flusser argues that contemplating rain through a window while smoking a pipe and listening to Mozart represents the victory of culture over nature, but irrigation, which he calls technologically programmed rain, upsets this neat divide. "The Moon," another tour de force of satirical reasoning, traces how the

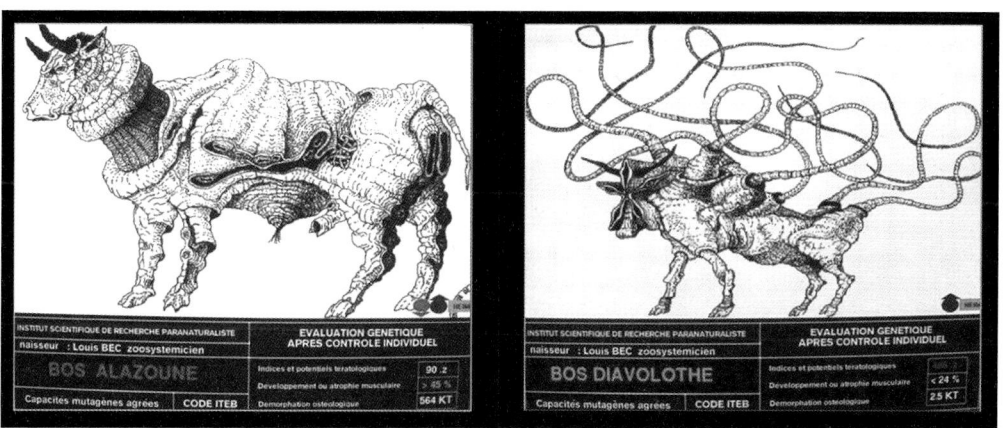

Figure 4.10

Louis Bec, *Bos Alazoune* and *Bos Diavolothe*, digital scans of undated drawings. Two examples of Bec's new species of cow appearing around the region of Bessines, France, where uranium was mined. Reproduced in *Zoosystémie*, 674. Courtesy the Estate of Louis Bec and Pavel Smetana.

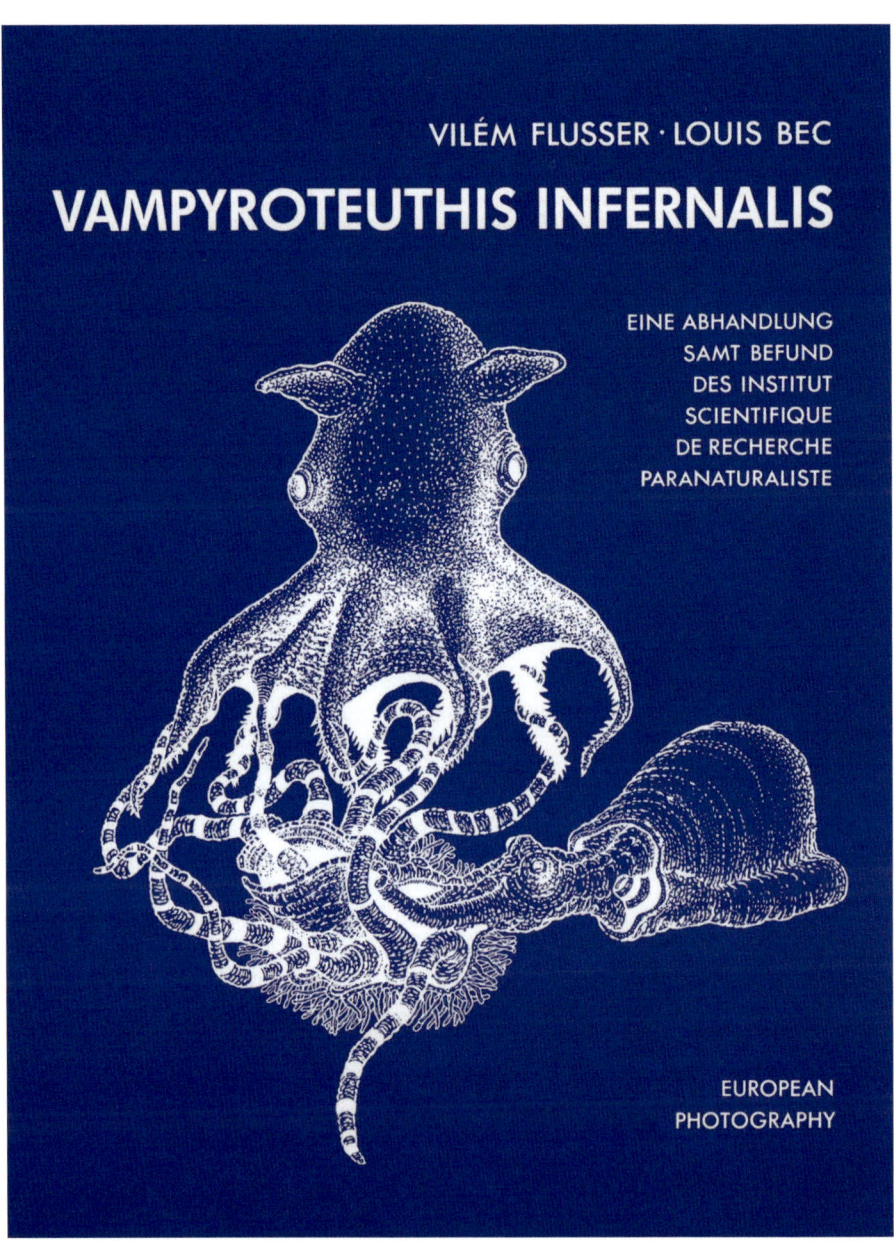

VILÉM FLUSSER · LOUIS BEC

VAMPYROTEUTHIS INFERNALIS

EINE ABHANDLUNG
SAMT BEFUND
DES INSTITUT
SCIENTIFIQUE
DE RECHERCHE
PARANATURALISTE

EUROPEAN
PHOTOGRAPHY

Figure 4.11
Louis Bec, cover of *Vampyroteuthis infernalis. Eine Abhandlung samt Befund des Institut Scientifique de Recherche Paranaturaliste* (Vampyroteuthis infernalis: A treatise with a report by the ISRP). Göttingen: European Photography, 1987. Courtesy Andreas Müller-Pohle and the Estate of Louis Bec.

moon was historically an object of poetic speculation: visible, but inaccessible to humans. Now, however, the moon has been transformed into a phenomenological curiosity, touched by astronauts. The American flag driven into its surface reminds us that it has left the field of nature, mused upon by poets and alchemical magicians, and entered into culture, controlled by politicians, lawyers, and technocrats. It has become the property of NASA: "real estate = in a state of reality, and any doubts about it have ceased."[20] In this way, the moon has shifted sharply from being a natural phenomenon to a cultural one—particularly in our era, when billionaires build rockets for leisure travel: "Nature is a late and luxurious product of culture."[21] What's at stake philosophically, Flusser argues in his "sort of conclusion" to *Natural:Mind*, is that these distinctions were arrived at through the long devotion of Western science to the separation of omniscient subject and neutral object. Ultimately, this position must be viewed as a form of fiction: "As long as scientific knowledge perambulated through extra-human regions, about which man is not existentially interested," he writes, "it was possible to maintain the fiction of objective knowledge," but today that idea is "unsustainable"—a lesson we are learning rapidly in the era of climate change and pandemics in which divisions between humans and "nature" are being erased.[22]

Vampyroteuthis infernalis

The struggle between fictitious distinctions and "extra-human regions" reached a spectacular culmination in *Vampyroteuthis infernalis* (1987), which has been described as a work of science fiction philosophy or a parabiological fable.[23] Flusser wrote the text, and Louis Bec provided images of imaginary creatures that mimic scientific illustrations, along with an "official" letter, in his capacity as president of the Institut Scientifique de Recherche Paranaturaliste (ISRP), announcing the findings of Professor Vilém Flusser and a team of "zoosystematicians and teuthologists," which were of zoological, epistemological, and aesthetic significance. In many ways, *Vampyroteuthis infernalis* was a more developed version of a fable Flusser had written earlier that featured an octopus, a tapeworm (or *solitaria*), and a human embryo. Published in the *O Estado de São Paulo* newspaper in 1964, the short, satiric essay "Um mundo fabuloso" (A fabulous world) critiques Western narratives of evolution

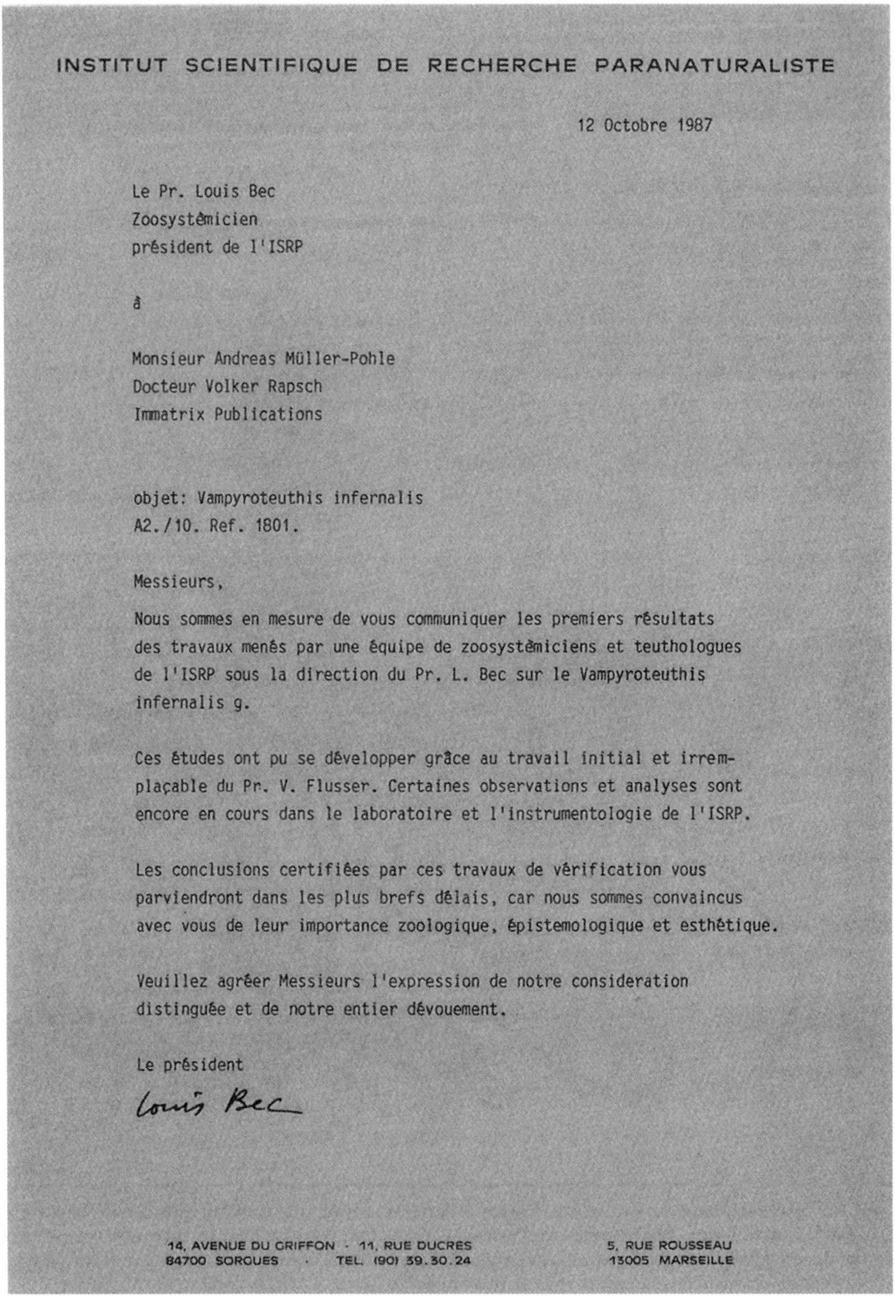

INSTITUT SCIENTIFIQUE DE RECHERCHE PARANATURALISTE

12 Octobre 1987

Le Pr. Louis Bec
Zoosystémicien
président de l'ISRP

à

Monsieur Andreas Müller-Pohle
Docteur Volker Rapsch
Immatrix Publications

objet: Vampyroteuthis infernalis
A2./10. Ref. 1801.

Messieurs,

Nous sommes en mesure de vous communiquer les premiers résultats
des travaux menés par une équipe de zoosystémiciens et teuthologues
de l'ISRP sous la direction du Pr. L. Bec sur le Vampyroteuthis
infernalis g.

Ces études ont pu se développer grâce au travail initial et irrem-
plaçable du Pr. V. Flusser. Certaines observations et analyses sont
encore en cours dans le laboratoire et l'instrumentologie de l'ISRP.

Les conclusions certifiées par ces travaux de vérification vous
parviendront dans les plus brefs délais, car nous sommes convaincus
avec vous de leur importance zoologique, épistemologique et esthétique.

Veuillez agréer Messieurs l'expression de notre consideration
distinguée et de notre entier dévouement.

Le président

Louis Bec

Figure 4.12
Louis Bec, letter presenting the "report" on the *Vampyroteuthis infernalis*, October 12, 1987.
Estate of Louis Bec and Vilém Flusser Archive, Berlin.

and its anthropocentric emphasis on hierarchies. In the essay, the octopus wonders how an earthbound vertebrate like Darwin could conceive of evolution when he's removed from the sea, the mainstream of evolutionary life. The tapeworm gloats about making vertebrates her "slave" and the embryo laments its impending journey into the world as a "biologically ill-adapted being." Flusser concludes that the "fabulous world" of life seems impervious to morals and values beyond good and evil ("to speak in Nietzschean terms"), and the octopus and *solitaria* therefore seem its most worthy representatives.[24]

Combining science with fictional speculation, *Vampyroteuthis infernalis* sets out to examine human culture through the perspective of a cephalopod—or "Vampy," as Flusser called "him" in correspondence with friends. In writing the fable, Flusser was aware of the long history of animal philosophy, reaching back to Aristotle, among others—but also responding to Prague authors like Karel Čapek.[25] (Bec even describes a joint 1986 trip to Prague in which Flusser attempted to track down the bears who had been kept for centuries in the moat outside Český Krumlov Castle.)[26] *Vampyroteuthis infernalis* also exists alongside a lineage of literature devoted to mythical sea creatures: the Greek Scylla and Charybdis; the Nordic Kraken; Japanese Akkorokamui; and narratives by Herman Melville, Jules Verne, and the Comte de Lautréamont, whose antihero Maldoror copulates with a shark.[27] Jean Painlevé's films featured anthropomorphized sea creatures. Roger Caillois's mythological "natural fantastic" (*fantastique naturel*) included a 1973 book on octopuses, and films like Steven Spielberg's *Jaws* (1974) and Bong Joon-ho's *The Host* (2006) must be added to the canon. In Flusser's fable, however, the sea monster is not only sympathetic but a model for human behavior.

Little was known about *Vampyroteuthis infernalis* when Flusser set out to write the book, but *Vampyroteuthis*'s discovery by humans is itself a fascinating tale. Flusser was drawn to the subject by Leipzig naturalist Carl Chun's popular 1903 book *Aus den Tiefen des Weltmeeres* (From the depths of the ocean).[28] The book resulted from the *Valdivia* expedition (1898–1899), named for the ship the SS *Valdivia*, initiated by Chun and funded by Kaiser Wilhelm II as the first German expedition to extensively explore the deep sea. It functioned as a precursor to the twentieth-century space race, attempting to answer the question of whether life existed below 500 meters. British naturalist Edward Forbes's "Abyssus" theory

Was nun die aus Seidengaze gefertigten Plankton-Netze anbelangt, so wurden auf unserer Expedition wohl zum ersten Male in größerem Umfange die Verti-

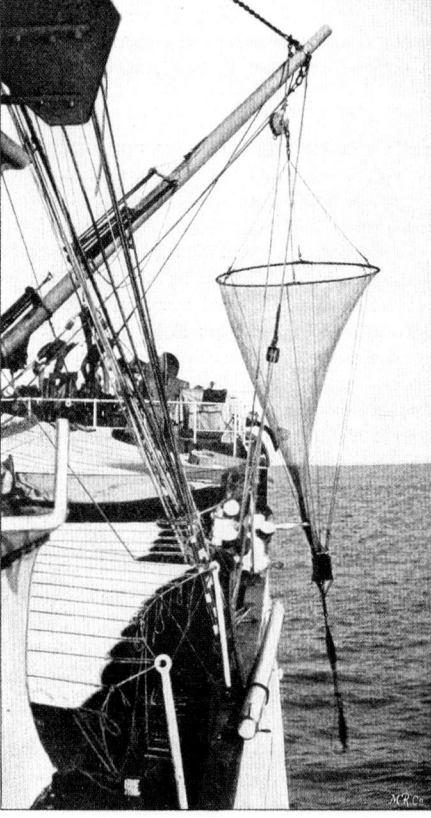

kalnetze verwendet. Schon die Plankton-Expedition hatte sich mit einem solchen Netze ausgerüstet, verlor es aber leider nach den ersten Versuchen.

Die Vertikalnetze besitzen einen weiten Durchmesser und sind bestimmt, in große Tiefen hinabgelassen und dann langsam in vertikaler Richtung wieder gehievt zu werden. Sie fischen neben größeren Organismen auch eine Fülle jener kleinen und kleinsten Formen, die flottierend in oberflächlichen und tieferen Wasserschichten vorkommen und neuerdings allgemein als „Plankton" bezeichnet werden. Es handelt sich freilich um recht kostspielige Netze, insofern der aus Seidengaze gefertigte Netzbeutel eine Länge von durchschnittlich 4 m besitzt. Dieser feine Beutel erhält dann noch einen schützenden Überzug durch ein derberes, weitmaschiges Netzzeug.

Ich hatte auf Grund früherer Erfahrungen an dem Ende dieser Vertikal-

Vertikalnetz.

netze einen Eimer aus Glas anbringen lassen, der in geeigneter Messingfassung verschraubt wurde. Diese Einrichtung hat sich vorzüglich bewährt. Zwar fischt das Netz etwas weniger, als wenn sein Grund mit einer filtrierenden Fläche ausgestattet wäre, dafür aber

Figure 4.13
A vertical net in Carl Chun's *Aus den Tiefen des Weltmeeres* (From the depths of the ocean, 1903), 30. Biodiversity Heritage Library.

and marine biologists like Alexander Agassiz had argued that the deep sea was azoic: life decreased significantly below 500 meters. The *Valdivia* would prove this wrong.[29] The ship set out from Hamburg on July 31, 1898, outfitted with a laboratory and photographic darkroom installed on its rear deck and the ambition of discovering, describing, and classifying as many marine species as possible. The *Valdivia* returned with specimens and research so vast it was published in twenty-four volumes.[30] It should also be noted that the book contains copious examples of human "specimens" the researchers met along the way: along with flora, fauna, and icebergs, the book includes colonial-era images of African and Indonesian people and artifacts related to their cultures.

Vampyroteuthis infernalis acquired its name, perhaps satirically, from Chun, because the cephalopod can turn its body nearly inside out with a cloak-like hood used for camouflage or to trap prey.[31] Flusser never saw a live *Vampyroteuthis*. Images of Vampy were only captured by remotely operated underwater vehicles (ROVs) after Flusser wrote his text, and one was displayed for the first time in public at the Monterey Bay Aquarium in California in 2014. As a substitute, Flusser studied the anatomy and physiology of octopuses and visited the Natural History Museum in London and aquariums in Monaco and Banyuls-sur-Mer. In his correspondence, he also mentioned three examples of *Vampyroteuthis infernalis* fished out of the South China Sea.[32] The lack of empirical information was of little concern, though: Flusser felt it gave him greater freedom to imagine the habits and nature of the cephalopod and "to critique our vertebrate existence from the molluscan point of view. Like every fable, this one shall also be mostly about men, although an 'animal' will serve as its pretext."[33]

What Flusser did know about *Vampyroteuthis infernalis* is this: it is the sole species in the order *Vampyromorpha*, which has features of both octopods and squid. Moreover, *Vampyroteuthis* has thrived in the deep sea, nearly unchanged, for over 300 million years, making it a form of living fossil, or what biologists call a "phylogenetic relic."[34] *Vampyroteuthis* is approximately one foot long, although Flusser imagined the organism much larger. It has large blue eyes, and its body is reddish-brown, with eight arms and two retractile filaments, which are used to capture food, although Vampy subsists primarily on "marine snow": decomposed sea organisms drifting down through the ocean. *Vampyroteuthis* possesses light-emitting organs called "photophores." Under duress, it can release

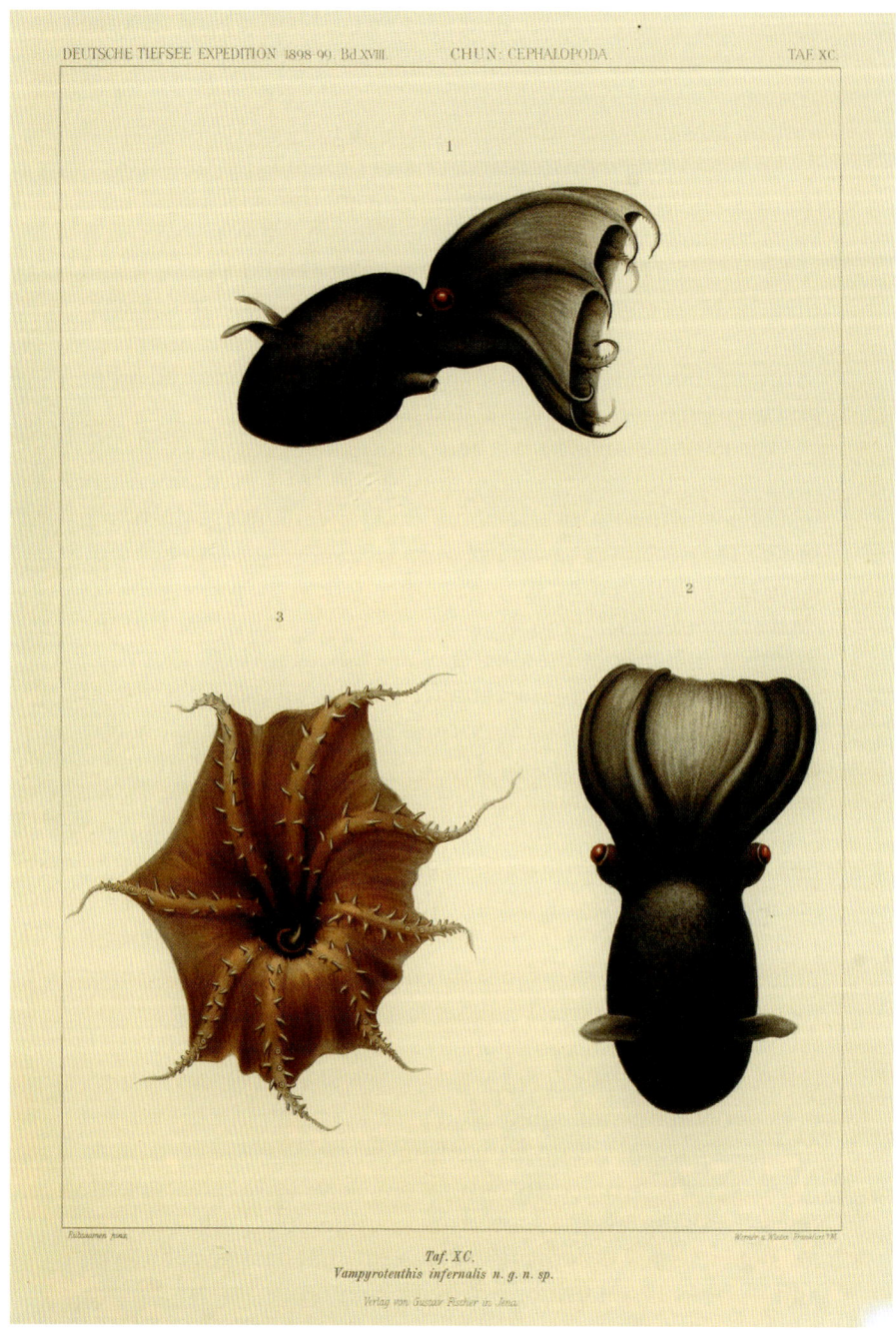

Taf. XC.
Vampyroteuthis infernalis n. g. n. sp.

Verlag von Gustav Fischer in Jena.

Figure 4.14
Friedrich Wilhelm Winter, illustration of *Vampyroteuthis infernalis* in Carl Chun, *Die Cephalopoden*, vol. 18, no. 2 (Jena: G. Fischer, 1915). Biodiversity Heritage Library.

a bioluminescent mucous with glowing blue particles that confuse predators and prey. Most important for Flusser, *Vampyroteuthis* lives in a lightless, high-pressure, oxygen-minimum zone between 600 to 900 meters below the ocean's surface where humans cannot survive. This set up the perfect dialectic: two creatures who cannot exist within each other's habitat.

To set up his fable, Flusser invokes Saint Francis of Assisi, who preached an integrated world in which humans, animals, and the environment were God's equal creations, and Pierre Teilhard de Chardin (1881–1955), the French Jesuit priest and author of *The Divine Milieu* (1923) who wrote about humans and their relationship with nature and served as precursor to the New Age movement.[35] Flusser also proposes to examine Vampy "from a cybernetic point of view," outlining its anatomy and behavior and describing its nervous system as a "network."[36] Importantly, in the same way that Flusser explored the nature-culture dialectic in *Natural:Mind* and found it to be false, in *Vampyroteuthis infernalis* he finds the hierarchy humans have set up, placing themselves *above* other species, specious. Vampy is capable of doing things humans cannot, like emitting light and surviving in a low-oxygen environment. Moreover, the idea that species evolve ever upward, with humans occupying the pinnacle of biological success, becomes suspect when one considers the "rationalized" hells of Auschwitz and other mechanized extermination camps. Darwinian and Lamarckian concepts of evolution, driven by heredity and environment, led to the adoption of concepts like *species* and *race*, which culminated catastrophically in Nazi Germany and Stalinist Russia. Flusser urges us to broaden our scope, since this epistemological problem exists in every science, not only in biology—it's just that biology presents a curious example because it is itself a human product: "biologically based Kantianism does not resolve the problem, it only transfers it to another level," challenging us to reformulate "the question of 'the origins of species.'"[37]

So how do we reformulate our thinking about nature, humanity, and our relationships with other creatures? Flusser suggests two "meta-models": game theory and the principles of radical psychoanalyst Wilhelm Reich. In the game-theory model, the universe becomes a "progressive realization of virtualities" contained in a program that asserts itself via chance permutations. Throughout his career, Flusser revealed his interest in game theory and *homo ludens* through references to Johan Huizinga, Roger

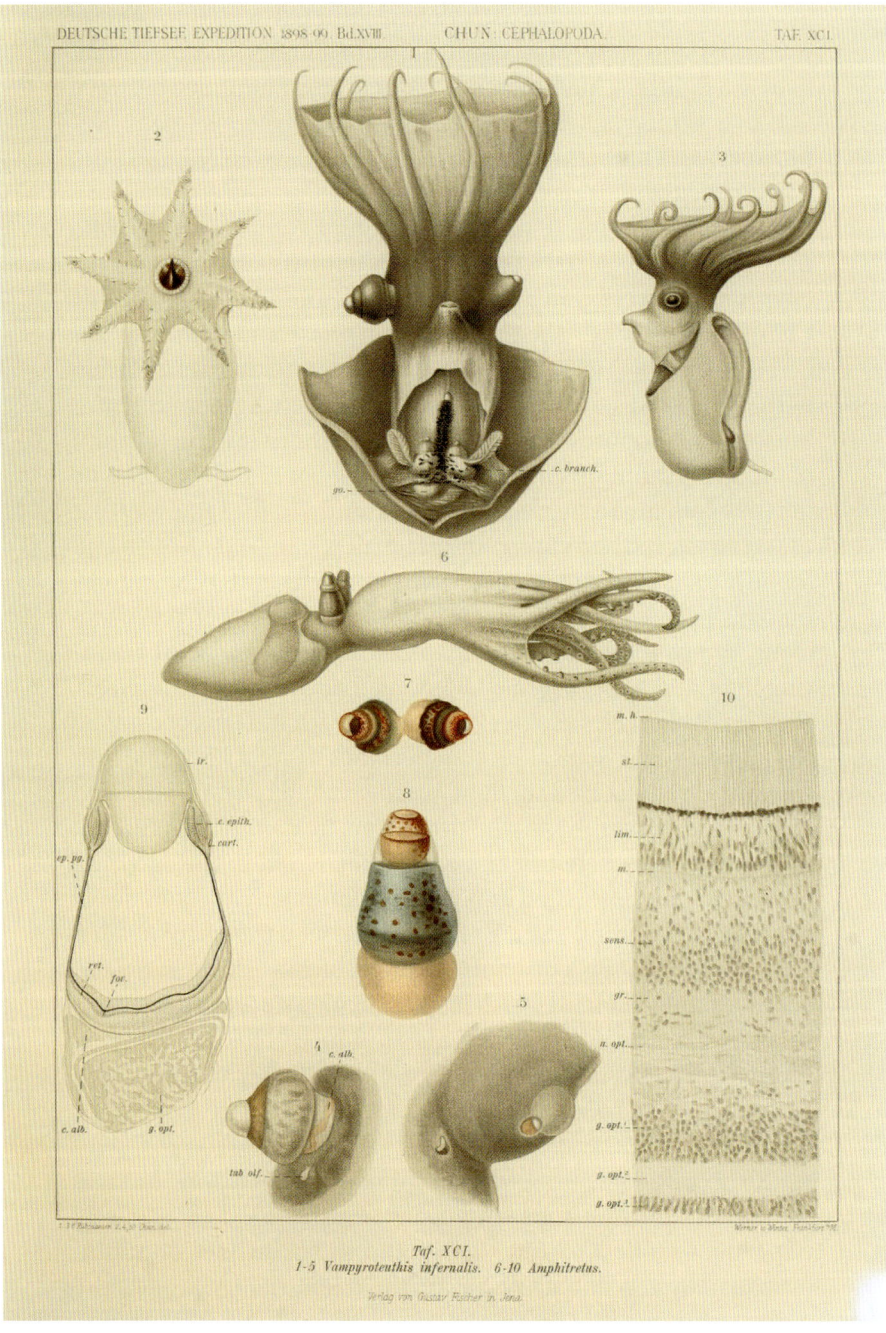

Taf. XCI.
1-5 Vampyroteuthis infernalis. 6-10 Amphitretus.

Verlag von Gustav Fischer in Jena.

Figure 4.15
Vampyroteuthis infernalis and other animals in Carl Chun, *Die Cephalopoden*, vol. 18, no. 2
(Jena: G. Fischer, 1915). Biodiversity Heritage Library.

Caillois, and Anatol Rapoport.[38] Here, however, Flusser draws a parallel between biology and game theory: Vampy and humans are both products of pure chance. A game theory of evolution based on randomness and the playing out of permutations highlights the fact that most creatures are unable to survive their environments and become extinct. To explain how Vampy has survived so long, Flusser invokes Reich's theory of vital energy, explained through the concept of "orgone" and the fusion of the mouth and anus, a synthesis of the dialectic of Eros and Thanatos. In Reich's model, an explosion of energy in the universe results in the divergence and then concentration of condensed energy, or "orgone," in which complex phenomena emerge. Flusser considers Vampy much closer to achieving this "orgasmic" evolutionary model than humans.[39] At this point, Flusser's argument turns phenomenological, highlighting the opposing environments in which Vampy and humans exist. Here, he invokes Jakob von Uexküll (1864–1944), the German biologist and bio-philosopher who observed jellyfish, sea urchins, amoebae, and other creatures, and devised the term *Umwelt*—"milieu" or "surrounding-world"—to describe how organisms relate to or perceive their environments.[40]

This was particularly pertinent in studying Vampy, since Flusser couldn't observe him in his habitat. Instead, he was forced to use intuitive methods that highlight his own epistemological position, as much as "explain" the cephalopod. Flusser teases this out further: if seventy percent of the earth is covered with water, brimming with life of which we are only partly aware, Vampy becomes an analogue for the earth itself—and the fact that what we "know" is dwarfed by what we don't comprehend: "Four-fifths of all biomass exists in the oceans," Flusser writes. "By far the greatest number of individual beings, species, genera, and classes live in the ocean. It is in the ocean, too, where the largest animals can be found. Quantitatively and qualitatively, then, the ocean is the seat of life on earth."[41]

In other words, *Vampyroteuthis*'s "uninhabitable" *infernalis* is actually a paradise, since it has not only survived but *thrived* for millions of years—much longer than humans have existed on earth. Flusser then uses this idea as a springboard for considering how we need to liberate ourselves from our theoretical models, particularly with regard to the Western philosophical concept of the subject.[42] If existence has been treated, philosophically, as being-in-the-world, with a subject in relation to objects—Flusser cites

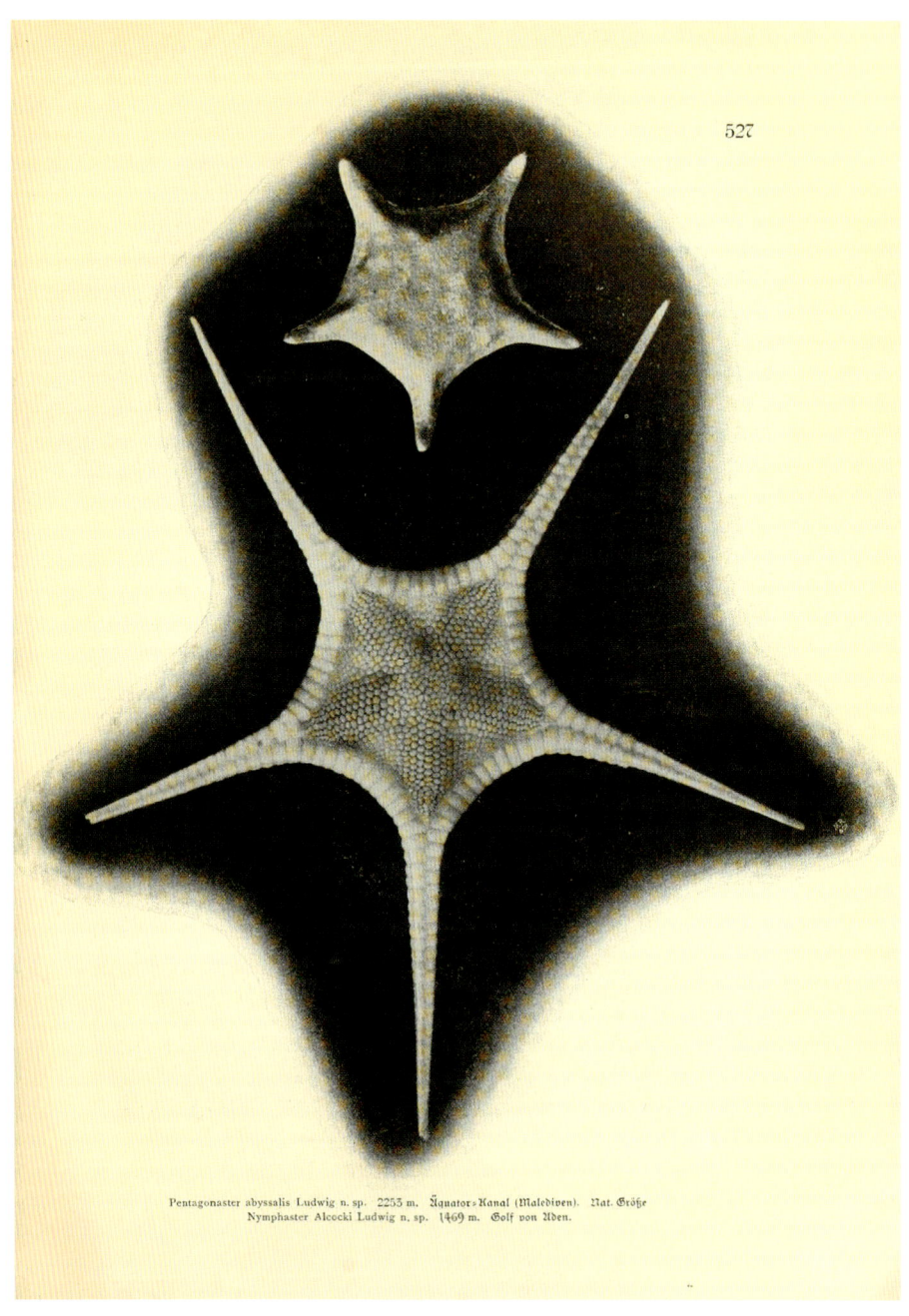

Pentagonaster abyssalis Ludwig n. sp. 2253 m. Äquator-Kanal (Malediven). Nat. Größe
Nymphaster Alcocki Ludwig n. sp. 1469 m. Golf von Aden.

Figure 4.16
Starfish in Carl Chun, *Wissenschaftliche Ergebnisse der Deutschen Tiefsee-Expedition auf dem Dampfer "Valdivia" 1898–1899*, vol. 9 (Jena: G. Fischer, 1902), 527. Biodiversity Heritage Library.

Heidegger, Merleau-Ponty, Bachelard, and Descartes in their various ways of describing the human worldview—"vampyroteuthian epistemology" forces us to rethink this approach. Moreover, in the German version of the text, Flusser calls this the "vampyroteuthian *Dasein*" rather than the "vampyroteuthian epistemology," invoking Heidegger's concept of *being-in-the-world*.[43] (In a letter to his friend, the Brazilian poet and editor Dora Ferreira da Silva, Flusser identified three additional models for his fable: Plato's *Symposium*, with the myth of the perfect man as an eight-armed sphere, Hieronymus Bosch's artwork, and Kafka's *Metamorphosis*.)[44] The vampyroteuthian model offers different concepts of sexuality, family, and freedom, showing that it is better "programmed" for socialization than humans. Adopting, once again, Martin Buber's ideas about intersubjective communication and applying this to an extra-human Other, Flusser argues that Vampy recognizes itself in the Other more instinctively than humans do: "Politics, for us, is engagement in favor of a particular 'polis.' For him it is engagement against every form of 'polis.'"[45]

We can even use Vampy as a model for art. Humans have historically approached art as a process of imprinting information on materials and naively trusting in the permanence of such objects—and then dividing and sorting them into "mislabeled" categories such as art, science, and politics. Vampy, on the other hand, lives in a liquid environment, transmitting genetic information and emitting immaterial light as a form of communication with the Other: "His fascination is not objective but intersubjective."[46] If humans detoured for millennia through the world of objects, eventually becoming consumed by a tsunami of gadgets, Flusser sees a new horizon ahead in which humans will no longer struggle against objects, but devote themselves to the preservation of information: "Men shall cease to be 'workers' and become 'functionaries of systems'. Total artists functioning within programmed totalitarianism. Vampyroteuthes."[47]

The book's ideas are furthered by Louis Bec's drawings of fantastical creatures, which Flusser did not consider to be illustrations; Flusser described their collaboration as synthesizing discursive and imaginary thinking into a new form of philosophy.[48] The drawings follow the model of scientific illustration, but Bec's creatures are fictions—except that the cover image of the German edition depicts two *Vampyroteuthis infernalis*, a larger female and a smaller male, copulating. Bec later revealed that the traits

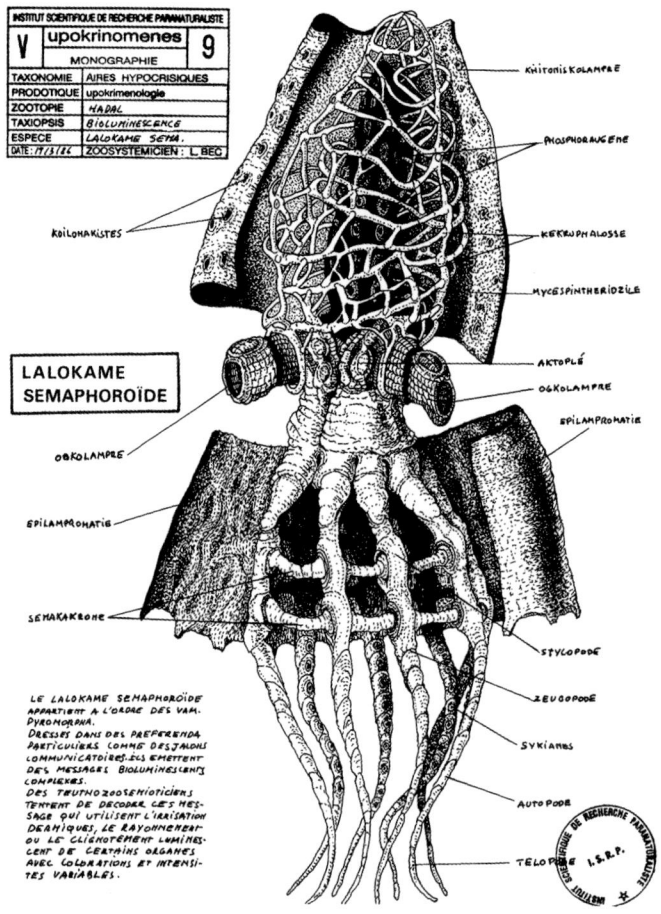

The *Lalokame semaphoroïde* belongs to the order Vampyromorpha. Like communication towers within their particular preferenda, they emit complex bioluminescent messages. Teuthozoosemioticians have attempted to decode these messages (produced in varying colorations and intensities by dermal iridescence) by radiation or by the luminescent flashes of certain organs.

Figure 4.17
Louis Bec, *Lalokame Semaphoroïde*, 1986. Estate of Louis Bec and the Vilém Flusser Archive, Berlin. Like the "semaphore" in its name, this organism reflects Flusser's flamboyant gestures when lecturing and conversing.

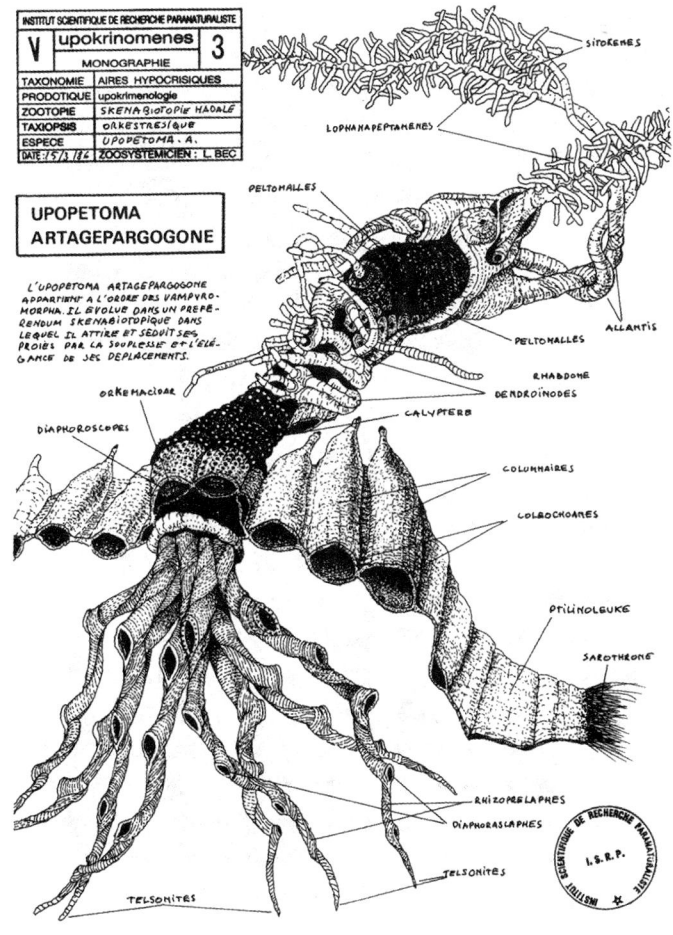

The *Upopetoma artagepargogone* belongs to the order Vampyromorpha. It inhabits a skenobiotopical preferendum in which it lures and seduces its prey with the grace and elegance of its movement.

Figure 4.18
Louis Bec, *Upopetoma Artagepargogone*, 1986. Estate of Louis Bec and the Vilém Flusser Archive, Berlin. This creature is insidious: it captures you with the grace of its movements, like Flusser's discourse.

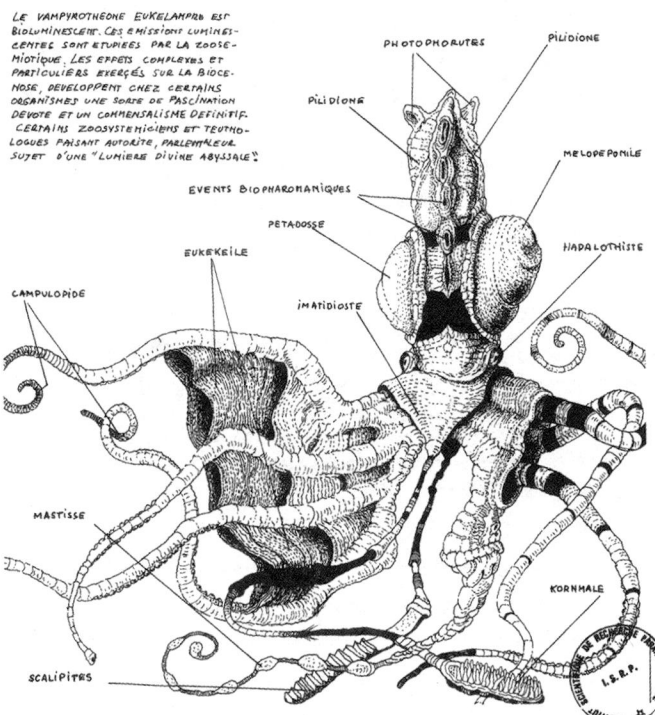

INSTITUT SCIENTIFIQUE DE RECHERCHE PARANATURALISTE		
V upokrinomenes	**1**	
MONOGRAPHIE		
TAXONOMIE	AIRES HYPOCRISIQUES	
PRODOTIQUE	upokrimenologie	
ZOOTOPIE	HADAL	
TAXIOPSIS	MORPHOPROPHASISME	
ESPECE	VAMPYROTHEONE.E	
DATE : 12	3	86	ZOOSYSTEMICIEN : L. BEC	

VAMPYROTHEONE EUKELAMPRE

LE VAMPYROTHEONE EUKELAMPRE APPARTIENT A L'ORDRE DES VAMPYROMORPHA. IL EVOLUE DANS UN MILIEU HADAL. SOUMIS A DE FORTES PRESSIONS IL EST BAROPHILE. SON ATTITUDE COMPORTEMENTALE EST UPOKRIME-NOLOGIQUE ET SE CARACTERISE PAR UN MIMETISME BIOMOTHEOLOGIQUE TANT SUR LE PLAN MORPHOLOGIQUE, PHYSIOLOGIQUE, METABOLIQUE QU'ETHOLOGIQUE.

LE VAMPYROTHEONE EUKELAMPRE EST BIOLUMINESCENT. CES EMISSIONS LUMINES-CENTES SONT ETUDIEES PAR LA ZOOSE-MIOTIQUE. LES EFFETS COMPLEXES ET PARTICULIERS EXERCES SUR LA BIOCE-NOSE, DEVELOPPENT CHEZ CERTAINS ORGANISMES UNE SORTE DE FASCINATION DEVOTE ET UN COMMENSALISME DEFINITIF. CERTAINS ZOOSYSTEMICIENS ET TEUTHO-LOGUES FAISANT AUTORITE, PARLENT AU SUJET D'UNE "LUMIERE DIVINE ABYSSALE".

PHOTOPHORUTES
PILIDIONE
PILIDIONE
MELODEPOMILE
EVENTS BIOPHARONANIQUES
PETADOSSE
HADALOTHISTE
EUKEKEILE
IMATIDIOSTE
CAMPULOPIDE
MASTISSE
KORNMALE
SCALIPITRE

(text on left) The *Vampyrotheone eukelempre* is bioluminescent, and its luminescent emissions are a subject of zoosemiotics. The complex and unusual effects that it exerts over its biocenosis result in a sort of devoted fascination and definitive commensalism among certain organisms. Some authoritative zoosystematicians and teuthologists refer to this luminescence as a "divine light in the abyss."

(text on right, above) The *Vampyrotheone eukelampre* belongs to the order Vampyromorpha. It inhabits the hadopelagic zone. Submerged beneath high water pressures, it is a barophile. Its behavioral attitude is hypocriminological and characterized by a biotheological mimeticism on many levels: morphological, physiological, metabolical, and ethological.

Figure 4.19
Louis Bec, *Vampyrotheone Eukelampre I*, 1986. Estate of Louis Bec and the Vilém Flusser Archive, Berlin. This creature's bioluminescence functioned as a kind of "divine light in the abyss," mirroring Flusser's prophetic philosophy.

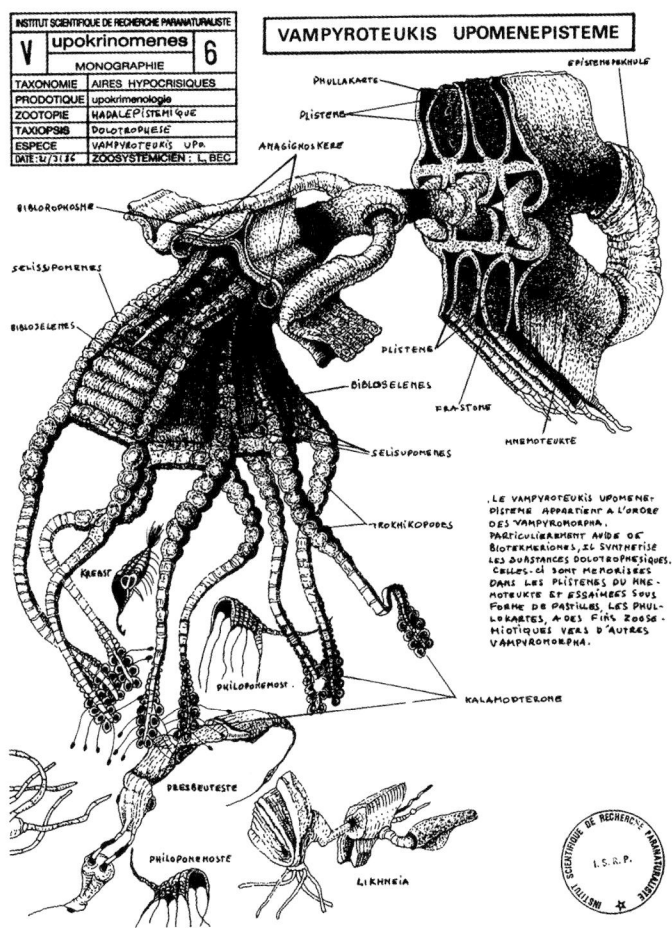

The *Vampyroteukis upomenepisteme* belongs to the order Vampyromorpha. Especially eager to consume biotekmeriones, it synthesizes dolotrophesic substances. These are fixed in its memory by means of the plistenes of the mnemoteukte and transmitted to other vampyromorpha in the form of capsules, the phullokartes, for zoosemiotic purposes.

Figure 4.20

Louis Bec, *Vampyroteukis Upomenepisteme*, 1986. Estate of Louis Bec and the Vilém Flusser Archive, Berlin. This creature's systems of capture reflect Flusser's "mnemonic epistemology" and incredible memory.

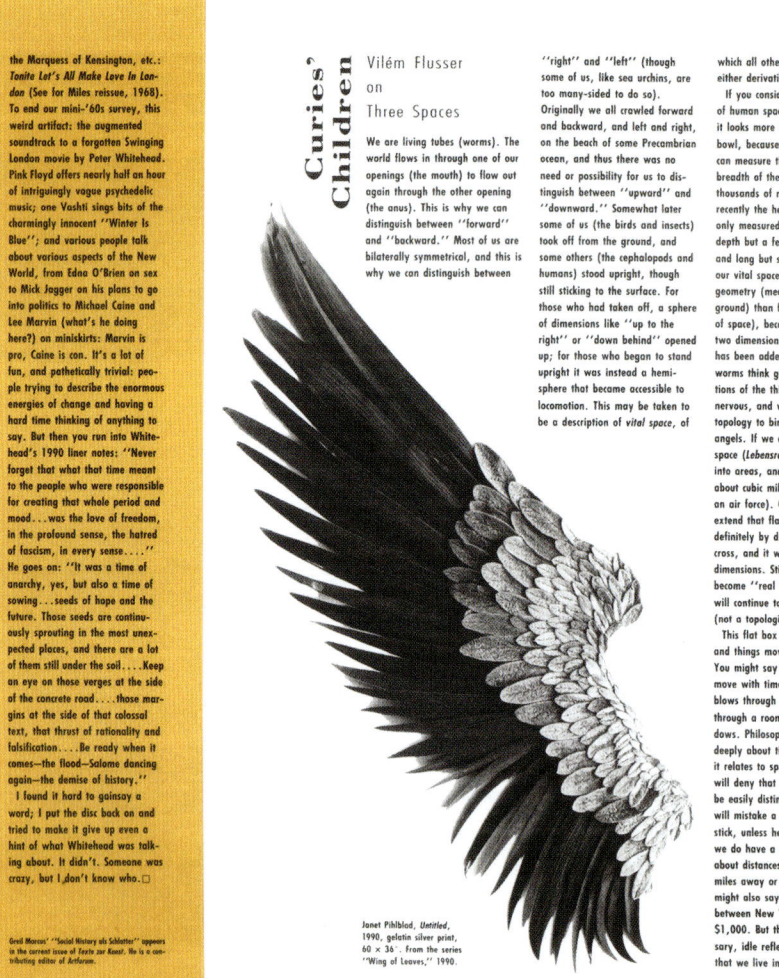

the Marquess of Kensington, etc.: *Tonite Let's All Make Love In London* (See for Miles reissue, 1968). To end our mini-'60s survey, this weird artifact: the augmented soundtrack to a forgotten Swinging London movie by Peter Whitehead. Pink Floyd offers nearly half an hour of intriguingly vague psychedelic music; one Vashti sings bits of the charmingly innocent "Winter Is Blue"; and various people talk about various aspects of the New World, from Edna O'Brien on sex to Mick Jagger on his plans to go into politics to Michael Caine and Lee Marvin (what's he doing here?) on miniskirts: Marvin is pro, Caine is con. It's a lot of fun, and pathetically trivial: people trying to describe the enormous energies of change and having a hard time thinking of anything to say. But then you run into Whitehead's 1990 liner notes: "Never forget that what that time meant to the people who were responsible for creating that whole period and mood...was the love of freedom, in the profound sense, the hatred of fascism, in every sense...." He goes on: "It was a time of anarchy, yes, but also a time of sowing...seeds of hope and the future. Those seeds are continuously sprouting in the most unexpected places, and there are a lot of them still under the soil....Keep an eye on those verges at the side of the concrete road....those margins at the side of that colossal text, that thrust of rationality and falsification....Be ready when it comes—the flood—Salome dancing again—the demise of history."

I found it hard to gainsay a word; I put the disc back on and tried to make it give up even a hint of what Whitehead was talking about. It didn't. Someone was crazy, but I don't know who. □

Greil Marcus' "Social History als Schlutter" appears in the current issue of *Texte zur Kunst*. He is a contributing editor of *Artforum*.

Curies' Children

Vilém Flusser on Three Spaces

We are living tubes (worms). The world flows in through one of our openings (the mouth) to flow out again through the other opening (the anus). This is why we can distinguish between "forward" and "backward." Most of us are bilaterally symmetrical, and this is why we can distinguish between "right" and "left" (though some of us, like sea urchins, are too many-sided to do so). Originally we all crawled forward and backward, and left and right, on the beach of some Precambrian ocean, and thus there was no need or possibility for us to distinguish between "upward" and "downward." Somewhat later some of us (the birds and insects) took off from the ground, and some others (the cephalopods and humans) stood upright, though still sticking to the surface. For those who had taken off, a sphere of dimensions like "up to the right" or "down behind" opened up; for those who began to stand upright it was instead a hemisphere that became accessible to locomotion. This may be taken to be a description of *vital space*, of

which all other kinds of space are either derivatives or abstractions.

If you consider the hemisphere of human space you will find that it looks more like a box than a bowl, because it is shallow. We can measure the length and breadth of the space we cross in thousands of miles, but until quite recently the height of our space only measured a few yards and its depth but a few inches. This wide and long but shallow box that is our vital space is better suited for geometry (measurement of the ground) than for topology (science of space), because it consists of two dimensions to which a third has been added. We upright worms think geometrically; equations of the third degree make us nervous, and we had better leave topology to birds, bees, and angels. If we divide our vital space (*Lebensraum*), we divide it into areas, and we never fight about cubic miles (even if we have an air force). Of course we may extend that flat box of ours indefinitely by drawing a Cartesian cross, and it will then have three dimensions. Still it will not have become "real space," because it will continue to be a geometrical (not a topological) construct.

This flat box of ours stands still, and things move around within it. You might say that those things move with time, and that time blows through space like the wind through a room with open windows. Philosophers have thought deeply about time, and about how it relates to space, yet nobody will deny that time and space can be easily distinguished. Nobody will mistake a watch for a yardstick, unless he's crazy. Sometimes we do have a curious feeling about distances: is this place two miles away or two hours? You might also say that the distance between New York and Paris is $1,000. But these are unnecessary, idle reflections. The fact is that we live in a rigid space to be

Janet Pihlblad, *Untitled*, 1990, gelatin silver print, 60 × 36″, from the series "Wing of Leaves," 1990.

Figure 4.21
Vilém Flusser, "Three Spaces," *Artforum* (May 1991): 23, with Janet Pihlblad, *Untitled*, 1990, photograph of a wing made with leaves. Courtesy of Janet Pihlblad. © Artforum Media, LLC. All rights reserved.

represented in the drawings were inspired by Flusser himself: the captivating nature of Flusser's discourse was reflected by Vampy's bioluminescence and a prey-capturing organ; and Vampy also conveyed Flusser's wild gestures when he lectured and his capacity to absorb vast amounts of information.[49]

In his foreword to *Vampyroteuthis infernalis*, Abraham Moles reflects on the book as a scientific essay, but one that distorts the rules of the game. Part fiction, part hard science, it might be "the spark of a new method of philosophical thought."[50] At the end of the book, Flusser argues that using biology as the source for his fable is significant because it is a model in flux. Whereas the old "fable" told by biology was that an original cell contained every possible form of life on earth, biotechnology and genetic engineering had changed the rules of this game. "New species may emerge artificially by crossing different phyla. These are such fantastic things that the imagination fails," Flusser wrote to his friend Milton Vargas; "the challenge is not biological but epistemological; to rethink evolution not in 'causal' terms or 'finalistic' terms, but in 'programmatic' terms."[51]

Artforum

Flusser's ideas relating to biology and biotechnology were expanded upon in the "Curie's Children" column he wrote for *Artforum* between 1986 and 1992.[52] The essays for this column constitute Flusser's largest body of writing published in the United States during his lifetime, and connected him with bio art and transgenic art and environmental practices in the same way that his technical image writings connected him with photographers, curators, and media theorists. Flusser was recommended to *Artforum* by Max Kozloff, a writer and photographer who had been involved with the magazine since the 1960s.[53] In 1986, Kozloff sent one of Flusser's essays to Ingrid Sischy, who had become the editor of *Artforum* in 1979 at the age of twenty-seven. Sischy was credited with expanding the scope of the art magazine, bringing in film, fashion, architecture, television, and popular music. (She had also interned at the Museum of Modern Art in New York under the legendary photography curator John Szarkowski.) The person who actually edited Flusser's work was David Frankel, who went on to be the editorial director of publications at the Museum of Modern

Art in New York. Frankel received the essays by fax machine and edited them over the phone with Flusser in Robion.[54]

The first of Flusser's twenty-one "Curie's Children" essays appeared in the September 1986 issue, alongside Kozloff's review of the English translation of Umberto Eco's *Travels in Hyperreality*; artist Barbara Kruger's column on television; Carol Squiers's writing on photojournalism; Frederic Tuten's microfiction about a young artist named Rex; Greil Marcus's musing on Cold War pulp magazines; Glenn O'Brien on televised talent shows; and Lisa Liebmann on the phenomenon of cigar-smoking celebrities. In the essay, titled "On Science," Flusser crafted a short, dense meditation on light, from Enlightenment reason and artificial intelligence to technology after Auschwitz, Hiroshima, and Chernobyl, concluding that we are on the cusp of a new form of cognition driven by the digital and biotech revolutions in which knowledge will move between brain synapses and semiconductors.[55]

Later essays circle back to arguments from *Vampyroteuthis infernalis*, describing the "stupidity of biological 'evolution,'" where chance rules, as opposed to "biotechnics," which allows information to be manipulated and passed on to future generations.[56] In this new world, art would become a gesture not of imitation (*mimesis*) but of invention (*poeisis*), and this could be extended to biology: in the future, we will be able to create a "geep"—a goat crossed genetically with a sheep—and plant and animal hybrids such as wheat with eyes or horses with leaves. An artist (or scientist, although they would become the same thing) working in this vein will have broken the game-theory rules of evolution in the same way the historical avant-garde of art was devoted to breaking the formal rules of academic art.

Flusser's long acquaintance with computer-generated art, via Max Bense and Abraham Moles as well as Herbert W. Franke, Georg Nees, and Gottfried Jäger, made him particularly receptive to art that was programmed or automated. "On Communication" (*Artforum*, January 1987) argues that the programmed codes of digital media will lead to a new era of post-history. "Poetic thought and mathematics will merge," Flusser forecasted, and "our children's children may think that with the defeat of the cumbersome code of the letter, new horizons of thought were opened."[57] "On Science" (October 1988) goes beyond digital technology and toward programming species. Here Flusser argues that the Walt Disney of the future might be a molecular biologist and the future Disneyland a

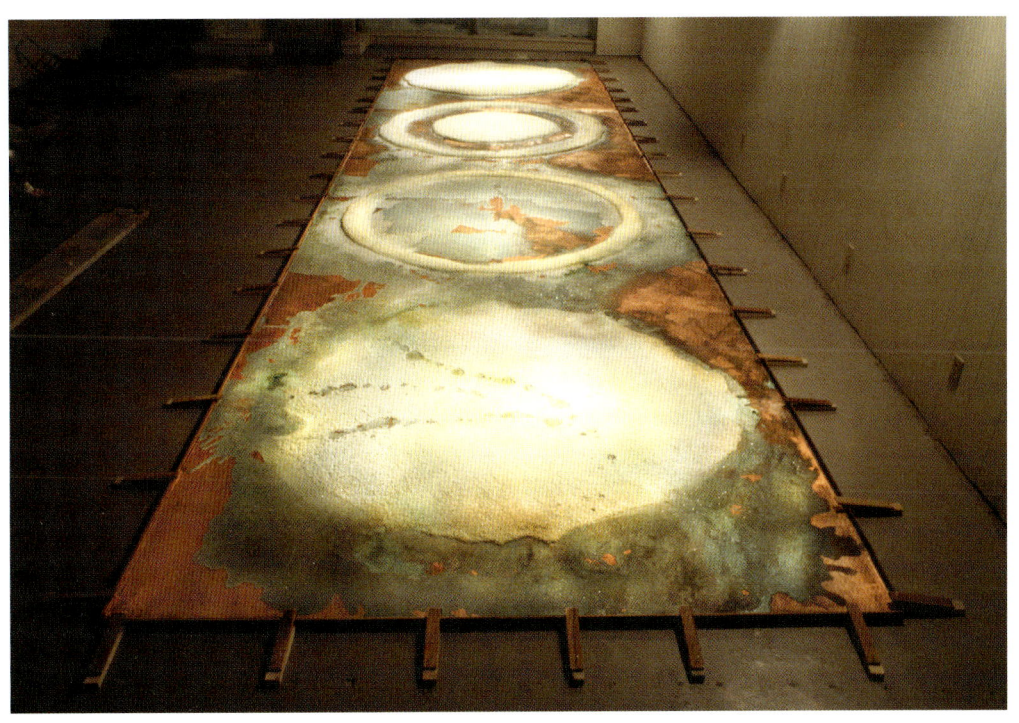

Figure 4.22
Eve Andrée Laramée, *Sinking Island*, 1981. Installation with salt, water, and copper, 32 × 8 ft.
A photo of this work appeared next to Flusser's essay "On Future Architecture" in *Artforum*,
April 1989, 13.

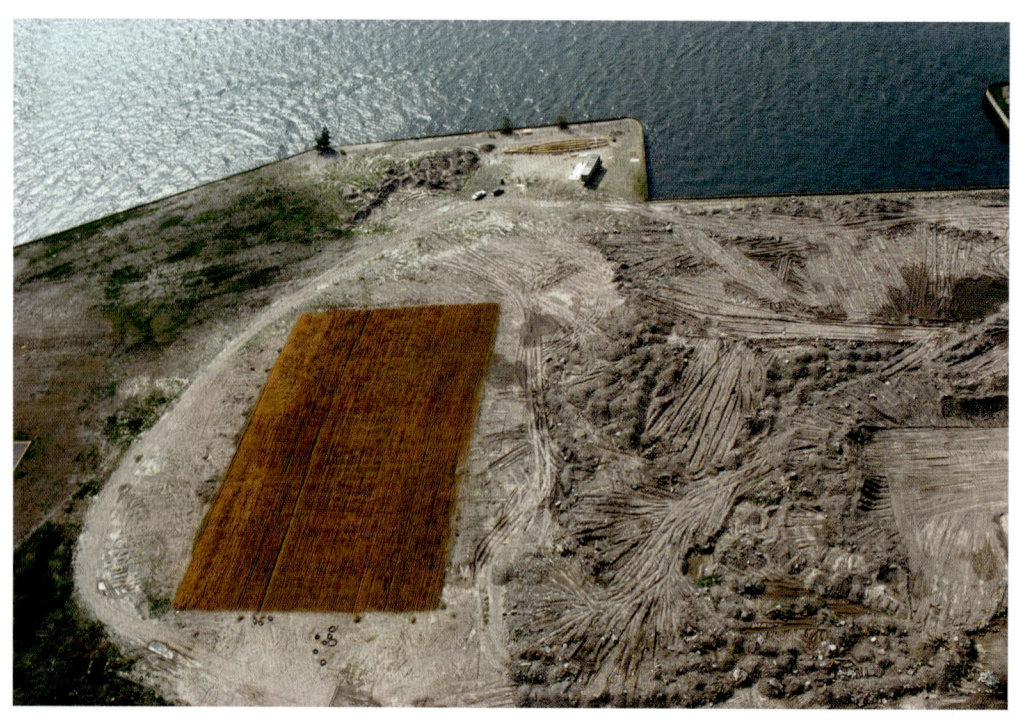

Figure 4.23
Agnes Denes, *Wheatfield—A Confrontation: Battery Park Landfill, Downtown Manhattan—Aerial View*, 1982. © Agnes Denes. Courtesy Leslie Tonkonow Artworks + Projects.

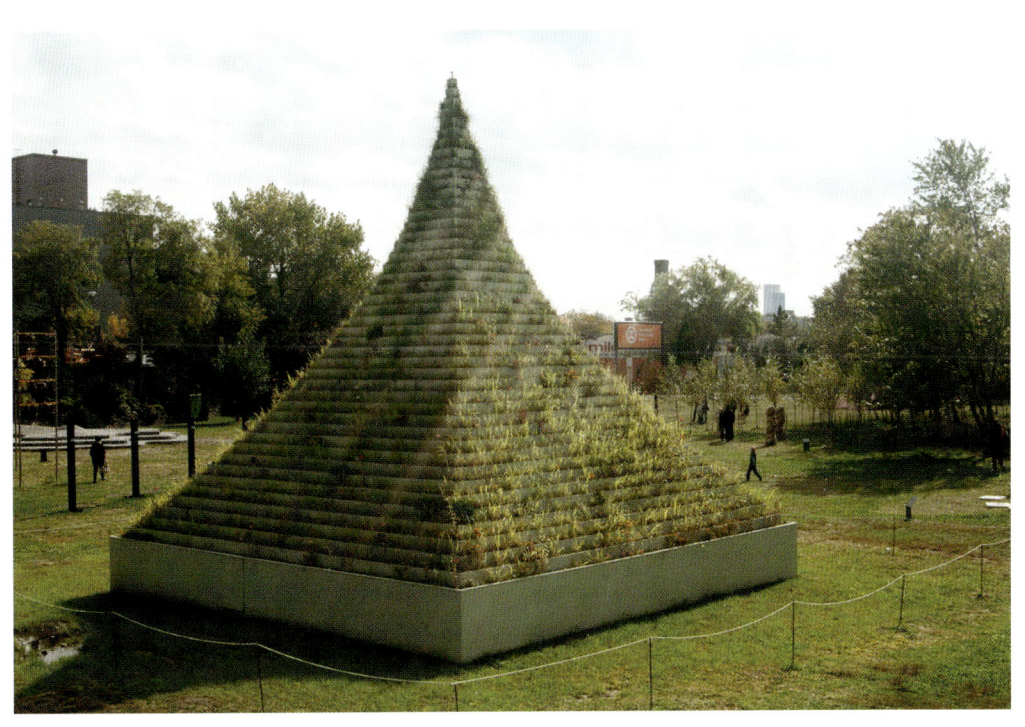

Figure 4.24
Agnes Denes, *The Living Pyramid, Socrates Sculpture Park, Long Island City, New York*, 2015.
© Agnes Denes. Courtesy Leslie Tonkonow Artworks + Projects.

landscape in which art informs nature. Another essay in the "Science" series considers color, and overlapped in time and theme with his participation in Casa da Cor (House of color), a project in the 1980s inspired by Goethe's color theories which will be discussed in Screen 5. Here, Flusser argues that color might become a form of thinking, an Esperanto that could complement or substitute for written and spoken language and bridge the realms of art and science.[58] At times, Flusser seems to be gleefully ignoring the ethical complications of new experiments and practices. However, in addition to leaning heavily into irony and satire, he was pointing out the obvious: terms that scientists, artists, and philosophers had taken for granted would change when biological information is intentionally "programmed." As he put it in the 1988 essay "Leben und Kunst" (Life and art) published in the German art magazine *Spuren*, we are embarking on a "new biological worldview" in which biotechnology becomes "the art of cultural information," or an "art of living"—except now literally rather than metaphorically.[59]

Flusser's affiliation with *Artforum* put him in contact with a number of US artists and writers directly aligned with bio and transgenic art and environmental practices. Agnes Denes, best known for her two-acre *Wheatfield* (1982) planted on the Battery Park landfill in lower Manhattan, sent Flusser her *Book of Dust* (1989), a compilation of writings, data, and found and manipulated photographs of laboratory equipment, views from telescopes, and scientific-style graphics which meditate on cosmic dust, hoping he would review it.[60] Flusser responded enthusiastically, "since you were kind enough to ask for my comments" (although clearly Denes meant a *published* review), he observed that the book was "a kind of sculpture" of assembled data, affirming for him that "the barest skeleton on which scientific knowledge rests is a fragile and highly fictional structure."[61]

Oregon-based artist George Gessert wrote to Flusser after reading his *Artforum* column, complimenting Flusser's prescience on biotechnics. However, Gessert also reminded Flusser that humans had been manipulating plants and animals for at least ten thousand years in the form of opium poppies, a rose with sixty petals growing in King Midas's garden and mentioned by Herodotus, greyhounds in ancient Egypt, and a new luminescent form of tobacco made by splicing the plant with a firefly gene.[62] Gessert included some unidentified seeds with his first letter—probably

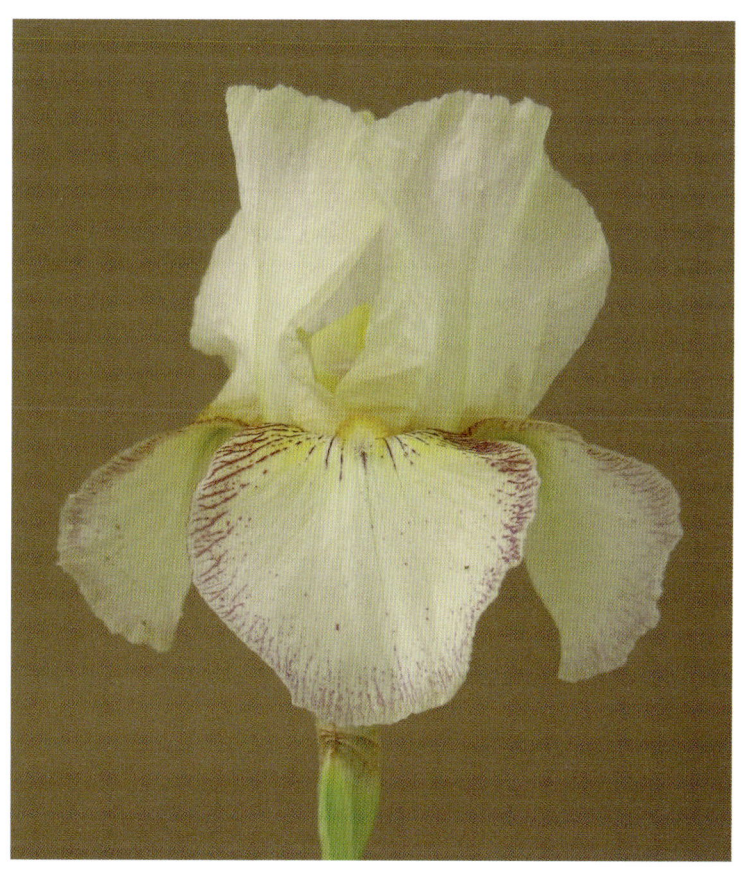

Figure 4.25
George Gessert, *Unnamed Tall Bearded Iris Hybrid. No 328. Hybridized 2004.*
Photo: George Gessert.

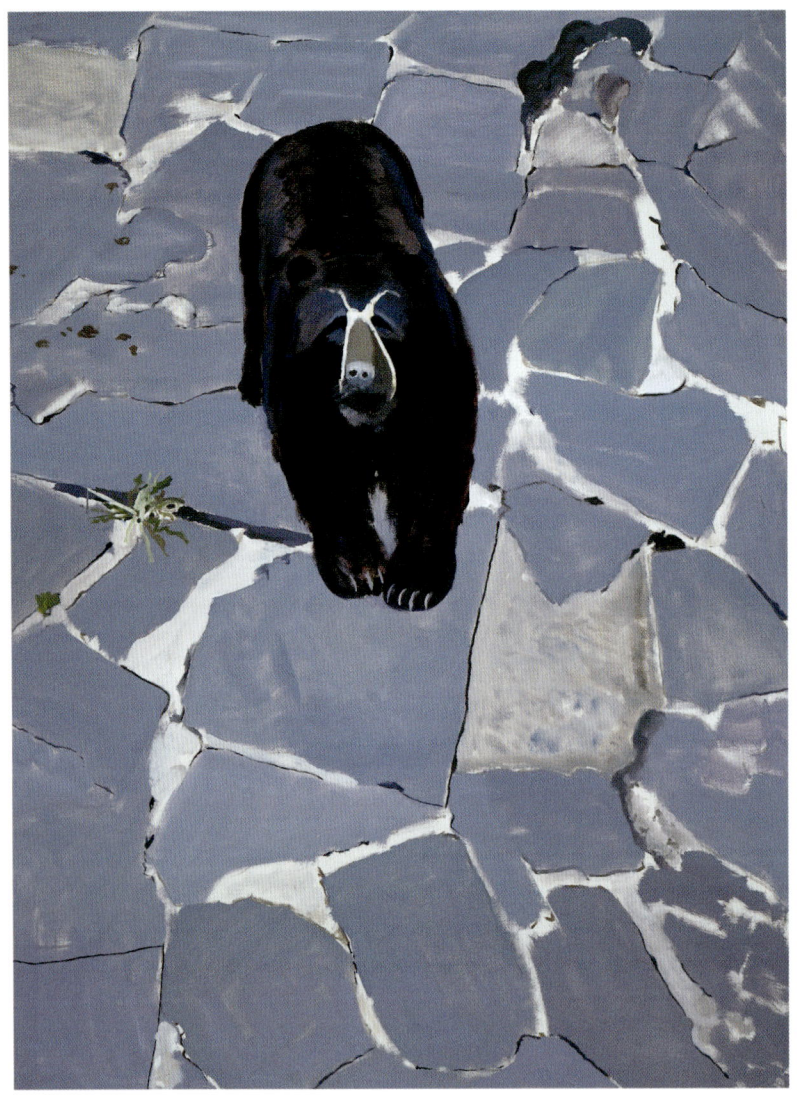

Figure 4.26
Gilles Aillaud, *Ours noir* (Black bear), 1982. Oil on canvas, 130 × 97 cm. © 2024 Artists Rights
Society (ARS), New York/ADAGP, Paris.

for irises, since breeding those were his central project—although he wasn't sure if they would grow in either Brazil or France. Gessert also tried to connect Flusser with William Burroughs, whose work Flusser was not familiar with.[63] Later, Gessert would publish an essay on his own work in *Leonardo* that included illustrations by Louis Bec, and he would cite Flusser frequently in *Green Light: Toward an Art of Evolution* (2010), his book on how humans' aesthetic perceptions and approaches have shaped other life forms, from racehorses to ornamental plants. "What will biotechnology bring?" he wrote. "Vilém Flusser envisioned photosynthetic horses, color-coordinated ecosystems, and new modes of thought. Military planners have long harbored dreams of race-specific biological weapons."[64] Clearly, Flusser's writings had resonated.

Bec and Kac

Following Flusser and Bec's earlier escapades with the Institute of Paranaturalist Research, Bec curated the exhibition *Le vivant et l'artificiel / The Living and the Artificial* (1984) in Avignon. This far-ranging exhibition, like *Technologie et imaginaire* or *Les immatériaux* (1985), teased the boundaries between organic and artificially generated or preserved life forms. The exhibition featured objects culled from art, agriculture, biology, horticulture, medicine, psychiatry, and taxidermy. There were paintings of wild animals in captivity by Gilles Aillaud and by Bec's wife, Danièle Akman; Joan Fontcuberta's photographs of imaginary plants; Serge Landois's cactus sculpture, Martial Raysse's faux-mushroom assemblage, and Jean-Henri Fabre's watercolors of mushrooms; a fireproof brick by the French Fluxus artist Robert Filliou; an origami iguana by a master of folded paper, Jean-Claude Correia; a short film by Agnès Varda shot in the Hospice Saint-Louis during the exhibition and starring Louis Bec, Colette Bonnet, and Yolande Moreau; and a Gina Pane performance with chocolate.

These were exhibited alongside anatomical models, prosthetics, photographs of genetic mutations, biological specimens, hydroponics, wax *ex votos*, and living cultures such as sauerkraut and mushrooms, artificial teeth, organs, and plants. Flusser wrote an essay for the *Le vivant et l'artificiel* catalogue in which he argued that once the simulation of life in inanimate objects merges with technological simulations (robots, artificial intelligence, and other

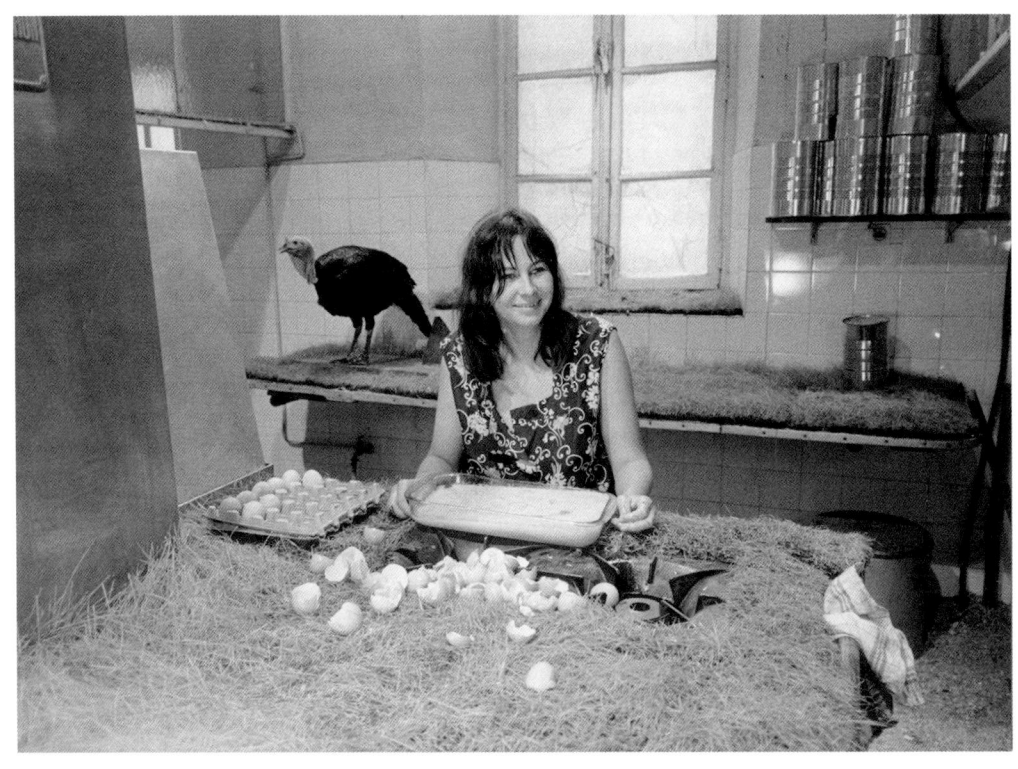

Figure 4.27
Yolande Moreau, in the Agnès Varda film *7 p., cuis., s. de b . . . à saisir* (Seven rooms, kitchen, bathroom, for sale). © 1984 Ciné-Tamaris.

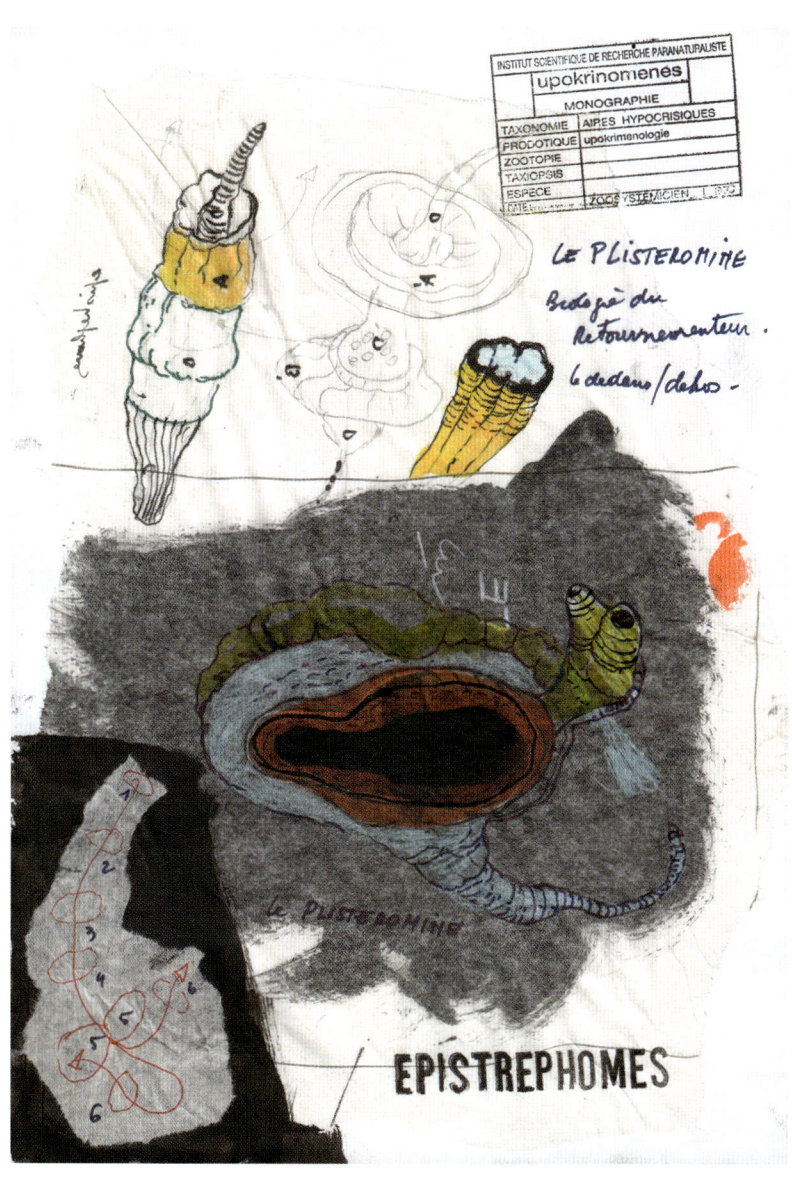

Figure 4.28
Louis Bec, *Epistrephomes* from the *Upokrinomenes* series, undated. Mixed-media collage.
Estate of Louis Bec and Vilém Flusser Archive, Berlin.

augmentations), the category "artificial" will cease to exist and the objectification that reigns in art and technology will be erased.[65] Future humans will function as players (*homo ludens*), treating life like a meta-game.

Bec's Institute of Paranaturalist Research persisted until his death in 2018 as a "virtual institute to simulate scientific and administrative systems of research," with Bec practicing *hypozoology*, a field of study that pushed back against "positivist zoology" and filled in the gaps in standard biological taxonomies.[66] He would also go on to create an array of virtual organisms—that is, using computer models to evolve new species—and participate in projects related to artificial life and intelligence. He called these virtual organisms *Upokrinomènes*—*upo* coming from the Greek for "by-under-below-toward" and *krina* from the act of judging or criticizing. These abstract, biomorphic-looking organisms serve as "actors" who play out programmed extinctions existing in living forms.[67] Sometimes the *Upokrinomènes* were in communication with actual, living organisms. In *Waiting for Turing* (2006), an installation at the TransGenesis Festival in Prague, Bec connected elephant-nose fish (*Gnathonemus petersii*), which emit electrical signals as they move around the murky waters in African rivers, with avatars via the internet. (The live fish were actually in an aquarium in Bec's home in Sorgues, France; the virtual fish could be seen on a screen in Prague.) The work paid homage to Alan Turing's essay "The Chemical Basis of Morphogenesis" (1952), on the coded nature of fish skin, but also nodded to FISH, the codename for the German encryptions Turing deciphered in World War II.[68] Communications, one of Flusser's main thrusts, remained central: in a 2015 interview, Bec said, "for a long time, I was thinking that the goal of the human species would be to create life"; however, "now I see technologies beyond the creation or simulation of life and technology as a means of communication between different forms of life."[69]

Bec's later and substantial engagement with artificial intelligence also reveals how discussions about orthonature and paranature shaped his thinking. In the early 1990s, he collaborated with the US computer scientist Christopher G. Langton, who was interested in artificial life based on simulation and computational models.[70] Bec describes AI in aesthetic terms, with approaches that are mimetic or based on simulation, both art and artificial intelligence being modeled from life. Art remains a fertile zone for imagining alternative systems rather than merely already-living

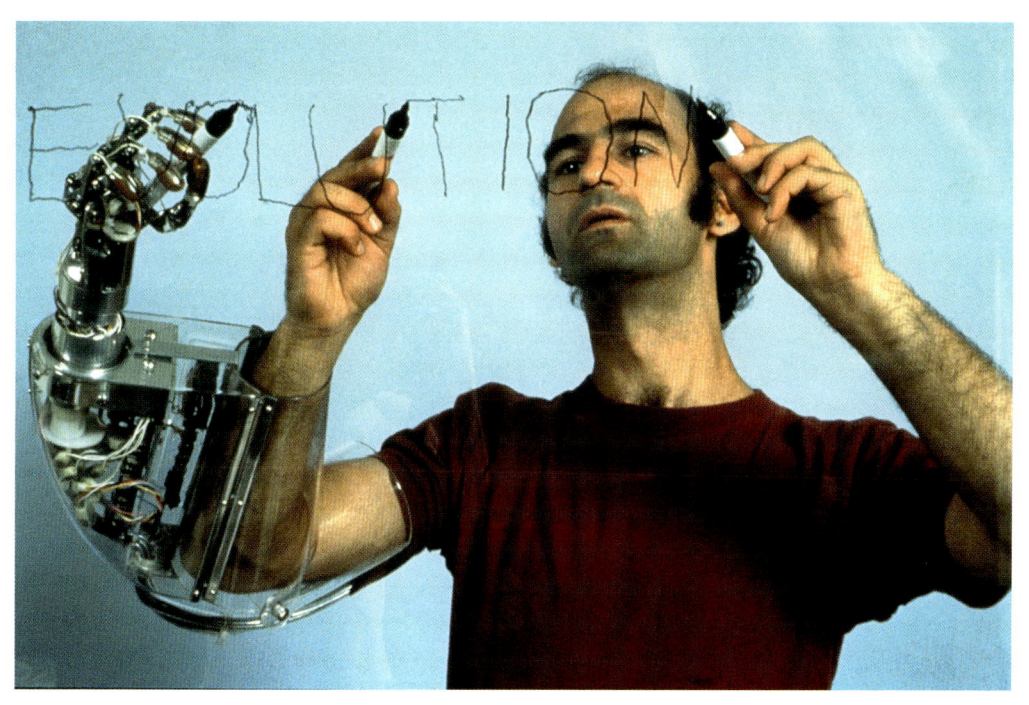

Figure 4.29
Stelarc, *Handswriting: Writing One Word Simultaneously with Three Hands*, Maki Gallery, Tokyo, 1982. Mechanical human-like hand attached to the artist's right arm as an additional hand, made to the dimensions of his real right hand. Photo: Keisuke Oki.

forms. And yet "art," Bec argued, "is haunted by the living, by animality."[71] A sunken ship is quickly covered with barnacles and becomes part of an eco-habitat, its technical structure becoming a substrate for a multitude of species.

This concept could apply to humans as well, though: Bec included the work of the Cypriot-Australian artist Stelarc, whose performances often included a robotic "third" hand, in his *Le vivant et l'artificiel / The Living and the Artificial* (1984); and the two exhibited with ORLAN, the French multimedia artist who has experimented with biotechnology and surgery to change her appearance. (The renowned philosopher of technology Bernard Stiegler wrote a short essay about Stelarc's work for the 1994 Berlin exhibition *Erzeugte Realitäten II. Louis Bec, ORLAN, Stelarc.*)[72] Bec also collaborated with the Brazilian artist Eduardo Kac, who had been in contact with Flusser about holograms. Working with the biologist Louis-Marie Houdebine and facilitated by Bec, Kac created one of the best-known works of transgenic art: Alba, the *GFP Bunny* (begun 1999; born 2000), an albino rabbit bred with EGFP, a synthetic mutation of the green fluorescent gene found in the jellyfish *Aequorea victoria*. The gene caused the rabbit to emit a green glow when exposed to black light.[73] The *GFP Bunny* created a minor scandal, but Kac defended the rabbit in Flusserian terms: he argued it was a "chimerical" creature in the tradition of imaginary animals but also "dialogical" in that he and his family had a relationship with her. "*GFP Bunny* is a transgenic artwork, not a breeding project," he argued, or a "genetic *objet d'art*."[74]

Instead, Kac claimed the rabbit was an interface for dialogic philosophy and interspecies communication. Kac also included one of Flusser's *Artforum* essays, "On Science," in his book *Signs of Life: Bio Art and Beyond* (2006). The opening paragraph reads like a template for *GFP Bunny*: "Why is it that dogs aren't yet blue with red spots, and that horses don't yet radiate phosphorescent colors over the nocturnal meadows of the land?," Flusser wrote. "Why hasn't the breeding of animals, still principally an economic concern, moved into the field of aesthetics?"[75] He went on to argue that North American and European agriculture produced more food than can be consumed, but "we can now make artificial living beings, living artworks. If we chose, these developments could be brought together, and farming could be transferred from peasants, a class almost defunct anyway, to artists, who breed like rabbits, and don't get enough to eat."

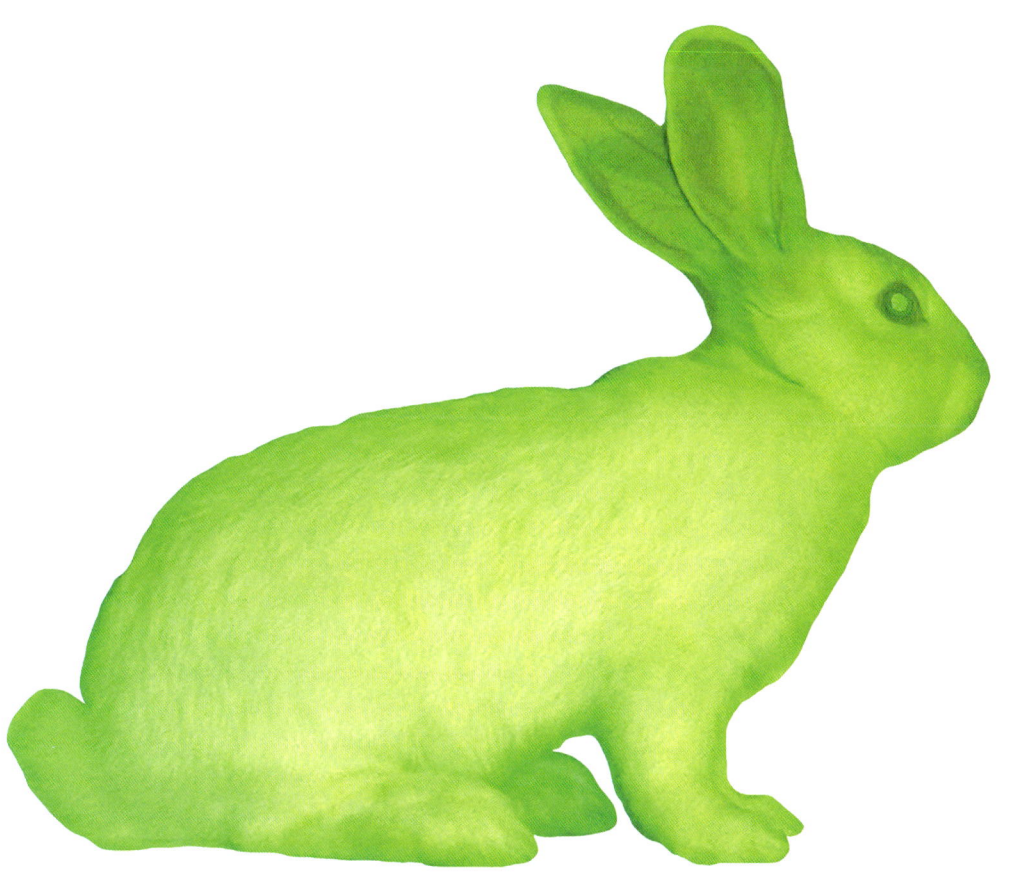

Figure 4.30
Eduardo Kac, *GFP Bunny*, 2000. Albino rabbit created with EGFP, a synthetic mutation of the green fluorescent gene found in the jellyfish *Aequorea victoria*. The bunny glowed under correct lighting. © Kac Studio.

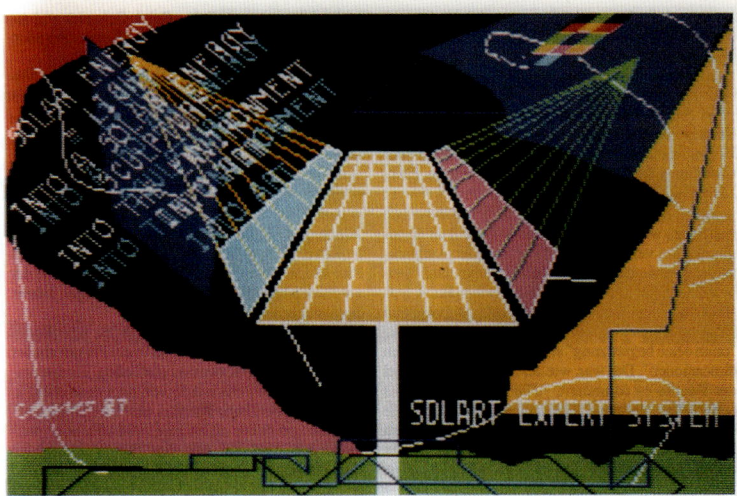

JÜRGEN CLAUS, "SOLART Expert System", Videotex Grafik, 1987. Foto: Jürgen Claus

Man mag sich auch hier fragen, warum die Diskussion über die neue Rolle des Bildes im digitalen Zeitalter in Deutschland so zögerlich verläuft, ohne Mut, nach vorn zu denken, ohne den Wagemut, sich auch zu irren, aber jedenfalls Parameter und Koordinaten künftiger Bedeutungen zu erforschen. Wo sind an den Stätten unserer Kunstausbildung und -vermittlung intelligente Fragestellungen und deren lustbetonte Diskussion zu sehen? Wie soll eine heranwachsende Generation, die offen für das elektronische Instrumentarium ist, ihr geistiges Rüstzeug

erhalten, wenn soeben wieder der Bundesrepublik (von Ralf Dahrendorf) bestätigt wurde, sie sei "eine Gesellschaft des öffentlichen Dienstes geworden, von der Mentalität ganz zu schweigen".

3. FENSTER:
Zu einer Architektur der künstlerischen Kommunikation

Tatsächlich wird von Architektur auch im Hinblick auf weitgehend immaterielle Systeme zu reden sein. Die Wurzeln dafür liegen in der Tradition der Moderne begründet. Die Kunst hat in einem Prozeß zunehmender Abstraktion vom Beginn des Jahrhunderts an die grundlegende Bedeutung von Zeichen, Symbolen und Bildmetaphern erforscht. Die Elemente der Gestaltung verselbständigten sich, standen für sich selbst, waren Punkt, Linie, Fläche, Geste - und doch darüber hinaus mehr. Dieses "mehr" erkundeten die Künstler. Es führte zu Gesetzlichkeiten, denen man zutraute, die eigentlichen Inhalte der Bild-Kommunikation zu bilden. Es ging um die bildnerische Bedeutung der Primär-Elemen-

Figure 4.31
Jürgen Claus, *SOLART Expert System*, 1987. Videotex Graphic. © 2024 Artists Rights Society (ARS), New York / VG Bild-Kunst, Bonn. Photo: Jürgen Claus.

Flusser's writings brought him into contact with other artists engaged with the intersecting digital and biotechnological revolutions. He knew Jürgen Claus, an artist who made solar-powered sculptures for public spaces and created underwater art events. I have already mentioned Joan Fontcuberta, Nancy Burson, and Harun Farocki, who would go on to explore how the natural world is presented in synthetic images. Farocki's four-part video cycle *Parallel I-IV* (2012–2014) looks at how landscapes have been constructed in video games, moving increasingly toward photorealism—and yet ineffective at recreating the idiosyncrasies of natural phenomena.[76] Using multiple screens and text, Farocki shows how undulating grass, crashing waves, clouds, and solid objects, like rocks and hedges, lack volume, mass, or depth. Instead, they function as a kind of digital mesh built up from layers of graphic images created with algorithms. "With computer images there is only one kind of wind," a voice narrates in *Parallel*, "a new constructivism" that would replace representation of the natural world. Flusser made a similar point in the essay "Grass": turned into a cultural object, such as a lawn, grass exists merely to be cut. It becomes the earth's hair: like human hair or beards or fingernails, the "essence" of grass becomes mutable and human-informed, signifying the ever-present need to be trimmed.[77]

Flusser's ideas about nature, animals, and technology overlap with those of a number of other thinkers: Jacques Derrida, Michel Foucault, Félix Guattari, Donna Haraway, N. Katherine Hayles, Thomas Nagel, Michel Serres, Gilbert Simondon, Francisco Varela, and Sylvia Wynter.[78] Binaries and taxonomies might be cultural constructions, but they had resulted in real-life consequences for Flusser and many of these thinkers. Edward Said, writing at the same moment, commented that the "rigid barriers between academic specialties" was a way of divorcing culture from power, a situation that literary criticism should resist.[79] Flusser's vampyroteuthian thinking looks particularly prescient in light of recent posthumanist and postcolonialist theory, which attempts to illustrate and erode the binaries and hierarchies established to subjugate different peoples and species.[80] Disability theory's project, to disrupt the "universal" able-bodied subject and acknowledge ideas of dependence and care, dovetails with

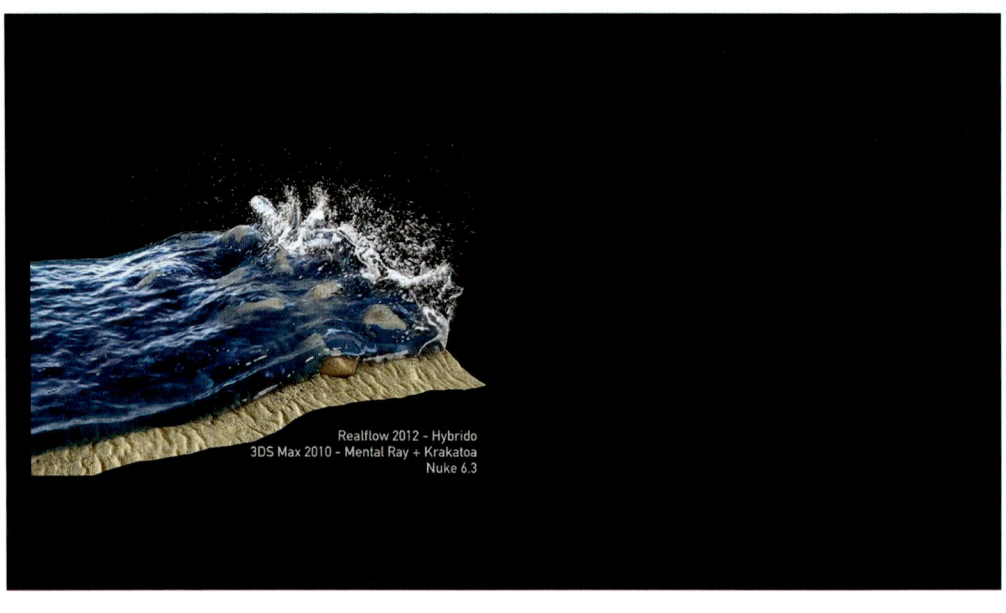

Realflow 2012 - Hybrido
3DS Max 2010 - Mental Ray + Krakatoa
Nuke 6.3

Figure 4.32
Harun Farocki, *Parallel I*, 2012. HD video installation, two channels, color, sound, 17 min.
Courtesy Harun Farocki Filmproduktion, Berlin, and Antje Ehmann.

Flusser's notions of intersubjectivity and interdependence. Just as disability theory asserts that everyone is "temporarily abled"—a human infant is among the most helpless newborns in the animal world—*Vampyroteuthis infernalis* starts with a similar premise: humans can't live in Vampy's low-oxygen habitat, and Vampy cannot live in ours.[81] Moreover, Flusser argues that *Vampyroteuthian* males are better caregivers than their human counterparts. *On Doubt* opens with an epigraph taken from John Milton's "Sonnet 19: When I Consider How My Light Is Spent," also known as "On His Blindness": "They also serve, who only stand and wait," often interpreted to mean that every person has a place in the world, regardless of their ability or disability.[82]

Louis Bec would go on to participate in projects and conferences devoted to technology and disability, envisioning art as "neither corrective nor clinical" but offering "a totally different view" where so-called handicaps exist merely as another state of being-in-the-world.[83] Bec was interested in how the artistic practices he'd participated in—for instance, Stelarc's third hand or the interfaces he'd experimented with in Sorgues—could be harnessed for other means: "There is a convergence of design between the technological equipment intended to overcome the immobility of disabled people and the equipment allowing the astronaut to conquer outer confines, the pilot to go to very high speed, to the actor immersed in the universe of virtual realities."[84]

Trans* theory further troubles the divide between nature and culture. Flusser wrote, "*Vampyroteuthis* did not repress the female aspect of the world like man has. For him, the world has both dimensions which have to be synthesized."[85] Meanwhile, Susan Stryker has written that, far from being a narrow specialization dealing with only a few people, transgender studies represents "a significant and ongoing critical engagement with some of the most trenchant issues in contemporary humanities, social science, and biomedical research."[86] *All* bodies are crafted, regulated, and technologized, and technology exists in dynamic relation to matter rather than separate from our selves.[87]

Jussi Parikka and Eugene Thacker have considered the overlaps between biology and media in a more general sense, with theories of embodied cognition that link human, animal, cybernetic, and artificial intelligence.[88] The Internet of Things involves digital technology embedded in roads, paper, clothing, skin, organs, medicines, and food. Flusser had started to explore this concept

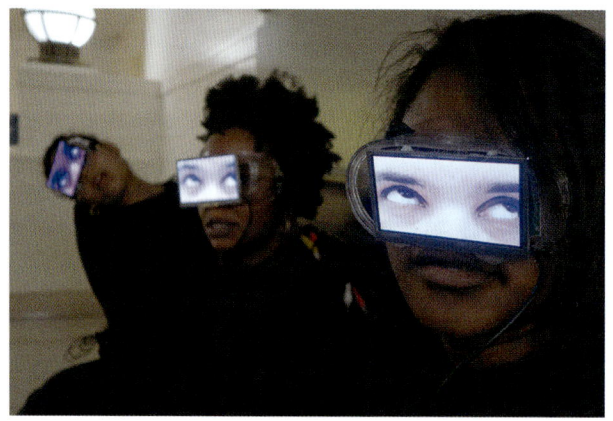

Figure 4.33
Sondra Perry, *Young Women Sitting and Standing and Talking and Stuff (No, No, No)*, April 21, 2015. Two-hour performance at the Wallach Art Gallery, Columbia University, New York, with performers Joiri Minaya, Victoria Udondian, and Ilana Harris-Babou. Courtesy the artist and Bridget Donahue, New York.

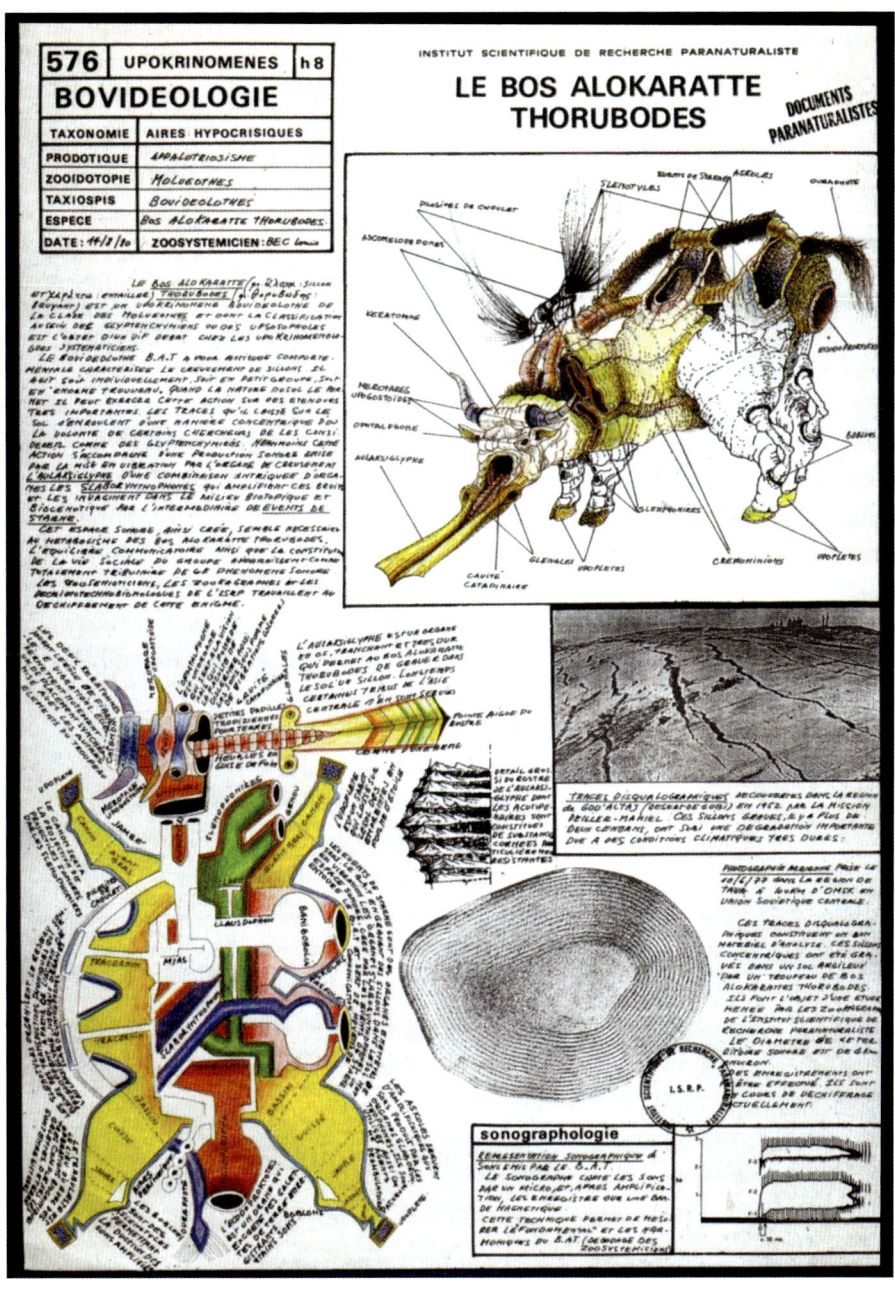

Figure 4.34
Louis Bec, *Bovideologie*, 1980. Drawing and collage detailing Bec's new species of cow, the Bovideoloth, appearing around the region of Bessines, France, where uranium was mined. Reproduced in *Zoosystémie*, 672. Courtesy the Estate of Louis Bec and Pavel Smetana.

in unpublished essays like "Skin," probably written in the early 1980s, in which he considered epidermis as a kind of map or atlas. "The skin is a surface which protrudes into the third dimension of space," he wrote, "and does so dynamically along the dimension of time. It is a space-time continuum without losing its two-dimensional characteristics."[89] He compared it to videotapes and holograms in terms of storing information, while the *Flusser Studies* editors who published the essay described skin for Flusser as "an existential interface."[90]

Interest in new materialisms and renewed fascination with exhibitions like *Les immatériaux* (1985) further extend thinking about nature, biology, and the in/human.[91] Concurrently, there has been a spike in "philosofictions" and "parafictions," from the fictional artist to the idea of philosophy and design as "fictions."[92] Flusser and Bec's *Vampyroteuthis infernalis* might be compared to earlier models such as Kafka's *The Metamorphosis* (1915), Karel Čapek, *The War of the Newts* (1936), H. P. Lovecraft's Cthulhu, Jorge Luis Borges's *Manual de zoología fantástica* (1957), Julio Cortázar's axolotl, or Octavia Butler's visionary creatures—although Vampy, of course, is a "real" organism. A more recent book that feels akin to these examples is Iranian-born writer Reza Negarestani's *Cyclonopedia* (2008), which considers the history of oil and the Middle East through the lens of a fictional professor, and which has been embraced as a benchmark of speculative realist philosophy.[93]

Artists like Lynn Hershman Leeson, Anicka Yi, Pinar Yoldas, Moreshin Allahyari, Lu Yang, and Aki Inomata carry on the research-based bio art of Bec and others. Lynn Hershman Leeson's *Infinity Engine* (2014) replicated a genetics laboratory, while her GMO Animals, Crops, Labs (The Infinity Engine) (2014), an installation with photographic wallpaper, serves as an archive of real experiments that hover between art and science, including glow-in-the-dark cats, 3D-printed human limbs, and genetically modified crops. Anicka Yi uses DNA samples and other organic materials to consider the limits of biology in works like *The Flavor Genome* (2107), a high-definition 3D video that moves between the Amazon rainforest and a fictional laboratory devoted to bioprospecting (that is, mining natural sources on the molecular, biochemical, and genetic level for commercial development). Yi's *When Species Meet, Part 1 (Shine or Go Crazy)* (2016), a sculptural installation that mimics laboratory cages—except the cage bars are covered with fake fur—pays direct reference in its title to Donna Haraway's book

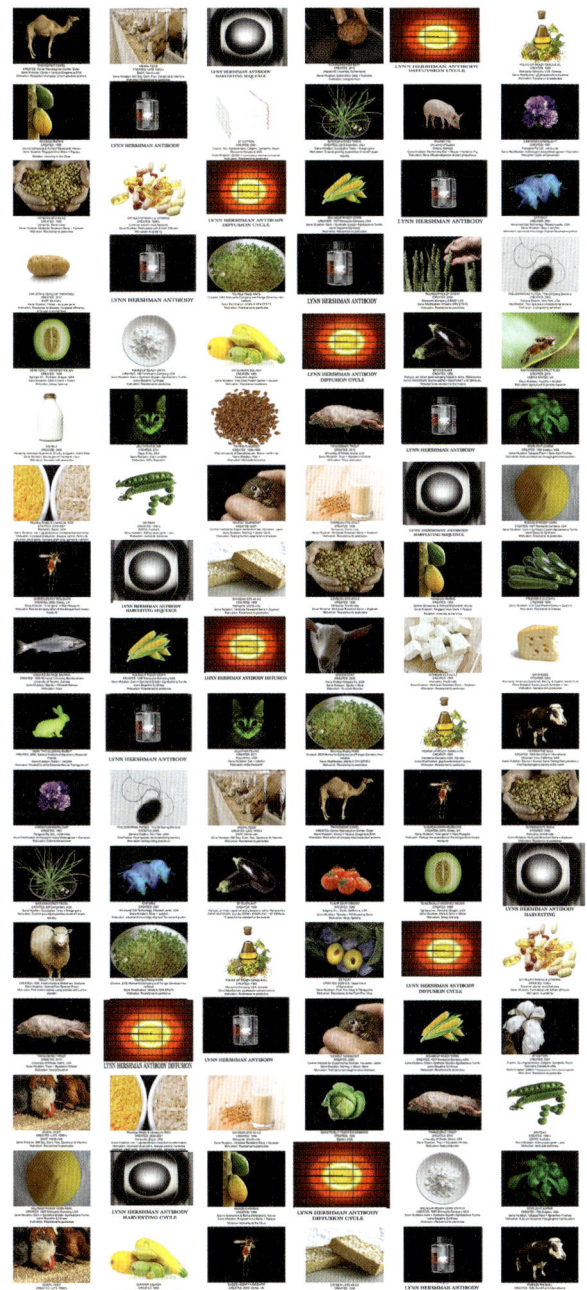

Figure 4.35
Lynn Hershman Leeson, *The Infinity Engine: Images of Genetically Manipulated Organisms*, 2014. Wallpaper, dimensions variable. Courtesy of the artist; Altman Siegel, San Francisco; and Bridget Donahue, New York. © Hotwire Productions LLC.

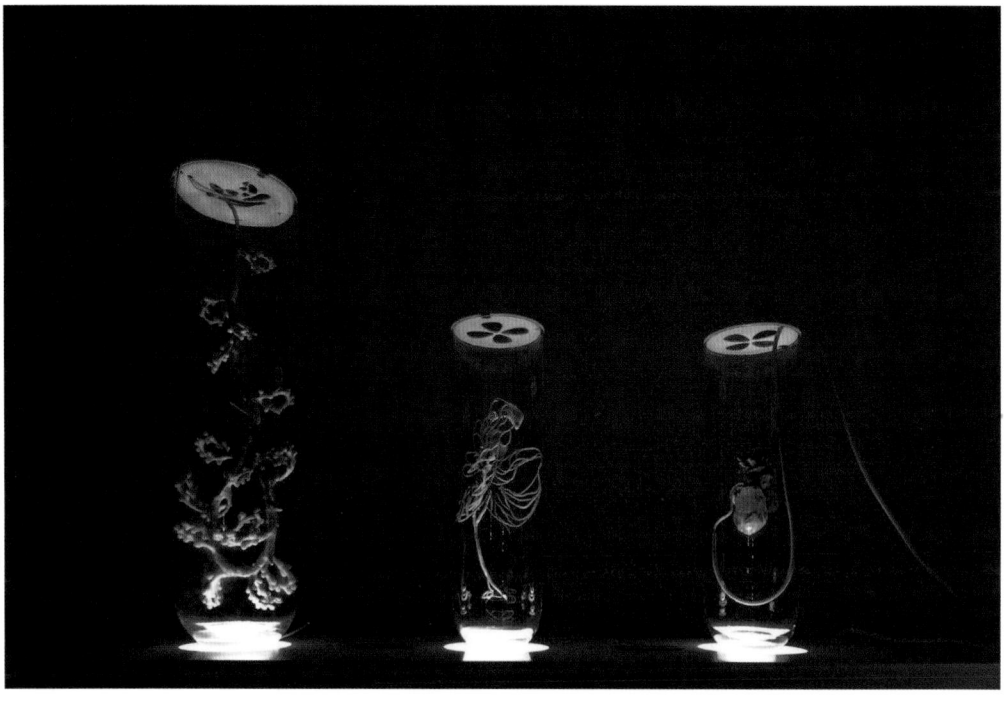

Figure 4.36
Pinar Yoldas, *An Ecosystem of Excess*, 2014. Speculative organisms: a new Linnaean taxonomy of species that can thrive in human-made extreme environments such as the Pacific Trash Vortex, suggesting that interconnected species are burgeoning in pelagic plastic, chemical sludge, and other debris. Courtesy of the artist and Schering Stiftung. Photo: Sergio Belinchón.

When Species Meet (2007), a meditation on the interaction between humans and other species.[94] Lu Yang's videos such as *Uterus Man* (2013) and *Lu Yang Delusional Mandala* (2015) consider how neuroscience and medical technology, as well as "living on the internet" (as he purports to do), are mutating human bodies and changing cognition. This is particularly pertinent in an age when gene-editing techniques like CRISPR have transformed Flusser's and Bec's speculative thinking into reality.[95]

Pinar Yoldas and Morehshin Allahyari—both alumnae of the Vilém Flusser Residency for Artistic Research—explore the human relationship to the environment, and particularly waste. Yoldas's *An Ecosystem of Excess* (2014) includes specimen-like sculptures based on speculative organisms growing out of postindustrial-historical waste: a new Linnaean taxonomy of species that can thrive in human-created environments such as the Pacific Trash Vortex, the world's largest accumulation of discarded plastics. Her work suggests the interconnection of species burgeoning in pelagic plastic, chemical sludge, and other debris.[96] Morehshin Allahyari delves into the world of mythical Persian "jinns," ancient supernatural creatures she recreates through 3D printing—but also the nexus of environmental destruction and petroleum usage attendant with 3D printing.[97] Other artists, like the Brazilian-born

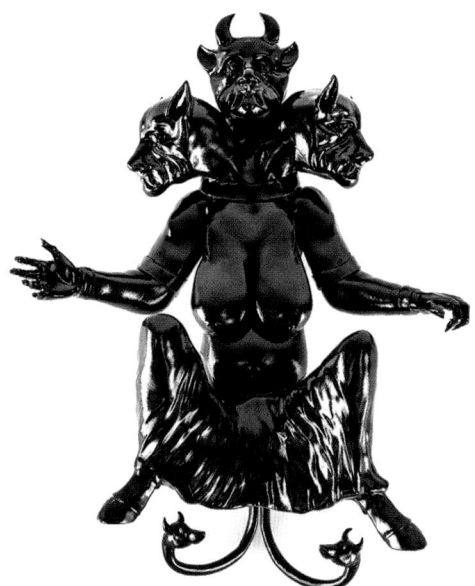

Figure 4.37
Morehshin Allahyari, *She Who Sees the Unknown: Huma*, 2016. Image of a 3D-printed sculpture. Courtesy of the artist.

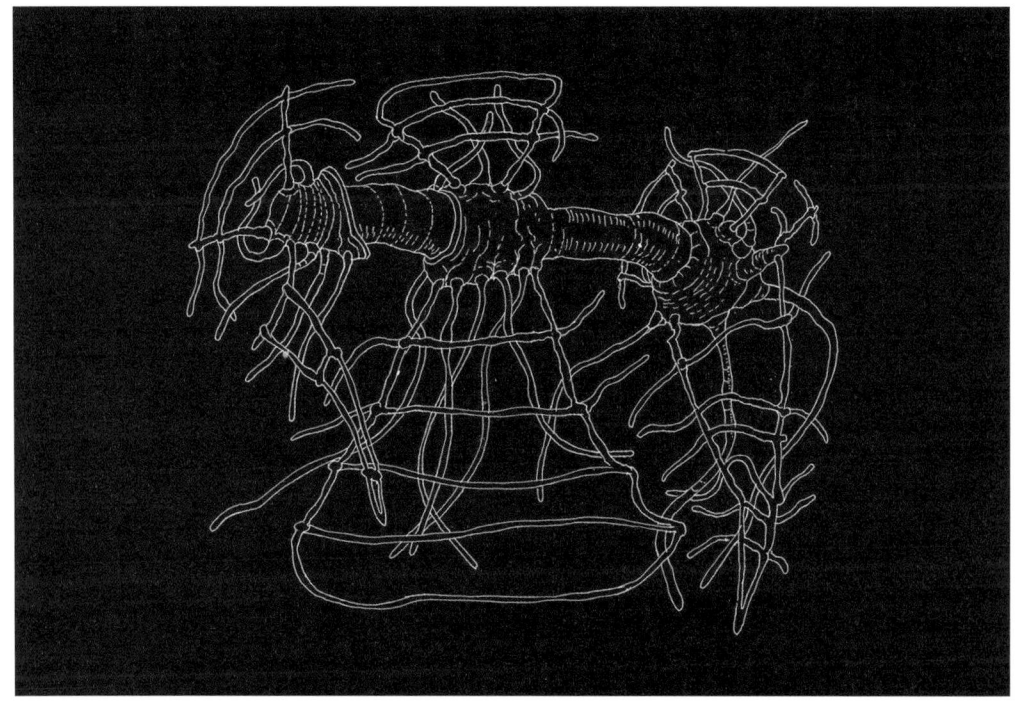

Figure 4.38
Louis Bec, *Koklosthe Labyrinthoste*, undated. Reproduced in *Zoosystémie*, 603. Courtesy the Estate of Louis Bec and Pavel Smetana. The skeletal structure of one of Bec's organisms evolving in a changing biome, an area with distinct climate, vegetation, and wildlife.

Maria Thereza Alves, are also revisiting traditional and indigenous knowledge, since "first" peoples often negotiated nature/culture relations such as forest populations and fire control (not to mention gender issues, like the two-spirit concept of Native Americans or intersex individuals in other cultures) more successfully than their colonial or industrialized successors.[98]

If Flusser's dialectic between Vampy and humans seemed fantastical in the 1980s, the common fate of all species in the so-called Anthropocene—the proposed name for a geological era that reflects human's impact on the earth—shows the prescience of his text: *Vampyroteuthis* itself is threatened by ocean warming, pollution, decreasing oxygen, overfishing, and other phenomena. The most recent, significant chapter in our engagement with nonhuman organisms in a climate-changed environment is, of course, COVID-19. Thinkers like Haraway, Karen Barad, Ian Bogost, and Ed Yong had already suggested that the world might be dramatically altered by nonhuman agents such as microbes.[99] Interestingly, Flusser considered this, too. "On Rabies" (1969), originally published in *O Estado de São Paulo*, imagined thinking "from the point of view of the virus."[100] Citing Swiss zoologist Adolf Portmann's 1956 *Biologie und Geist* (Biology and spirit), an influence on Hannah Arendt's biopolitics, Flusser argued that, from a structural viewpoint, the virus is less complex than an "advanced" and "evolved" human, and therefore might be considered inferior.[101] However, from a different perspective, the rabies virus might be considered more evolved and sophisticated in its ability to target the human brain and nerve centers. It is also predictable in its behavior, whereas humans are not. Flusser also brought up the speciousness of taxonomies and hierarchies implemented by nineteenth-century biology; similarly, recent writers have targeted Linnaeus, whose Mammalia designation, for instance, reflects specific battles around motherhood, breastfeeding, and wet-nursing in eighteenth-century Europe.[102]

In this context, art and Flusserian "science fiction philosophy" might be more pragmatic than previously acknowledged. Flusser argued that "critique"—particularly Frankfurt School critique—was a dead end—an Ouroboros who had eaten its tail—while recent writers like Bruno Latour have argued that imagination should be valued over critique.[103] For Flusser, Vampy was an excellent model: an organism better adapted to an extreme environment than humans are to theirs. And yet "we are all extremophiles,"

Louis Bec declared in 2007.[104] Flusser was an extremophile shaped by Prague and European philosophy, migration, rapid changes in mass media, and authoritarian regimes. However, he was hopeful that speculative theory might produce new models to aid humans in adapting to nonlinear reality. In *Vampyroteuthis infernalis* he wrote, "we are able to imagine cultural structures ('Utopias') in which even our biological constraints are done away with."[105] The imagination, he argued, rather than critical, "rational" thinking, was where he saw the greatest promise.

Screen 5   *Design and Deception*

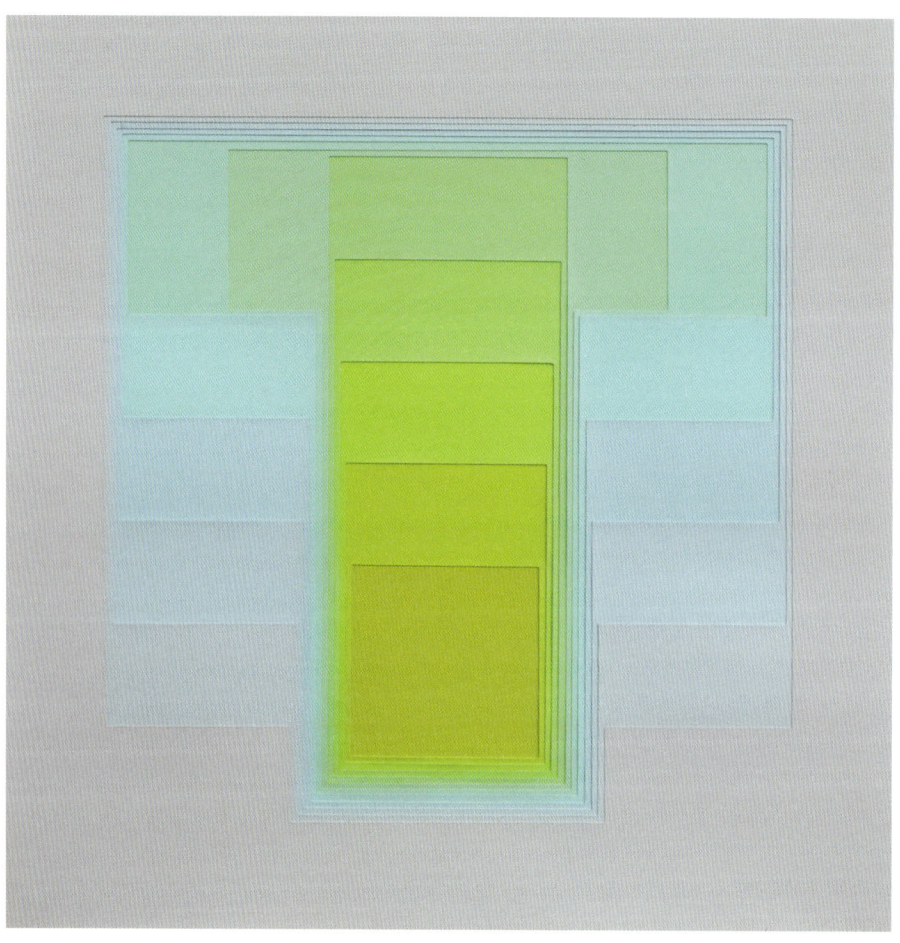

Figure 5.1
Karl Gerstner, *Color Sound*, c. 1970s. Acrylic on cardboard, 17 × 17 in. © Meredith Rosen
Gallery, NY.

Everything comes down to design.
—Vilém Flusser[1]

Design in the twentieth century was anything but frivolous. It was economic and political and philosophical—and Flusser wanted in on this discussion. Moving away from decoration and the category of architecture, design had become an everyday concern, from the clothes we wear to an array of communications devices. Germany, in particular, specialized in consumer products that helped rehabilitate its public relations image after World War II: elegant, user-friendly gadgets implied the "good" aspect of German design, as opposed to the industrialized war machine.[2] France was moving away from the Beaux-Arts "decorative arts" to modern and contemporary "design," and in Brazil projects like Brasília and Roberto Burle Marx's pavement patterns at Copacabana Beach, photographed and disseminated around the world, signaled the nation's arrival on the global stage of "advanced" design and infrastructure. Meanwhile, the United States was renowned for cars that looked like rockets and a burgeoning obsession with robots. In fact, a famous Cold War confrontation involved design: in the 1959 Kitchen Debate, US Vice President Richard Nixon and Soviet Premier Nikita Khrushchev met at the opening of the American National Exhibition in Moscow. Standing in a model kitchen with television cameras rolling, the two joked that it might be better to debate the merits of their nations' appliances rather than their rockets.[3] Later, Japanese and US designers would create sleek consumer electronics like the Sony Walkman and the Apple iPhone, spreading ideologies of mobility, surface, and smoothness.

Design offered Flusser an elastic approach to philosophy that could be applied to anything: household objects, architecture, and biology, as well as ethics and form. Design theorists were also among the first to embrace his writings. (I first encountered Flusser while writing an essay on functional artworks.)[4] In the 1970s, Flusser focused on objects, not design per se.[5] He was hardly alone. In the same way that Roland Barthes noted a boom in photography theory in the mid-1970s, Larry Busbea observed an "explosion" of design- and technology-oriented writing in France after World War II: by Pierre Francastel, Gilbert Simondon, Jacques Ellul, Claude Lévi-Strauss, André Hermant, Roland Barthes, and later Jean Baudrillard and Abraham Moles.[6] In the English-speaking world, Reyner Banham wrote *Theory and Design in the First Machine Age* (1960) and Edgar Kaufmann Jr. promoted "Good Design" at the Museum of Modern Art in New York.[7] The US moon landing in July 1969 was also a pivotal event: designers like Joe Colombo fixated on the space capsule as a self-contained living module, beyond architecture. Designers had become godlike: "every self-respecting designer tries to imitate and even improve upon Him," Flusser remarked.[8] It was not so much that God was dead as a concept—Nietzsche and others had already accomplished that—but that God had been replaced by designers.[9]

Flusser was initially in dialogue with philosophers like Husserl and Heidegger, who were interested in objects and things.[10] Husserl defined *things* in terms of the "concrete world in which we live," where objects were abstract points we bump up against.[11] Heidegger's famous essay "The Thing" starts out, similarly, by considering the things that surround us and their proximity, and concludes with the argument that the empty space inside a vessel—his example is the artisanal jug—is what defines its thingness.[12] Eventually, Flusser was inspired by his friend Abraham Moles, who published a *Théorie des objets* (Theory of objects, 1972).[13] Looking at human-made objects, gifts to gadgets, from an "environmental" perspective—since both men were active in the Institute of the Environment in Paris at the time—Moles considered their psychological, economic, philosophical, sociological, and aesthetic ramifications. One can see the excitement Flusser felt in being introduced to an object-oriented philosophy in his

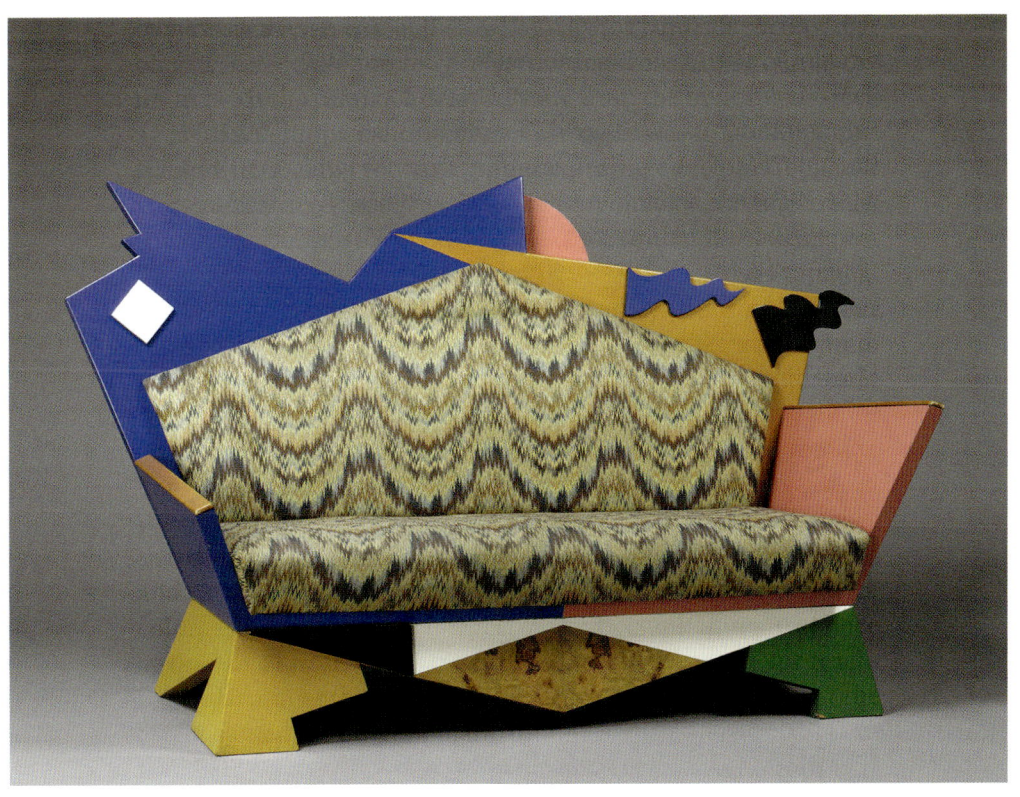

Figure 5.2
Alessandro Mendini, *Canapé Kandissi*, published by Alchimia (Italy), 1979. Wood, leather, and tapestry, 99 × 205 × 87 cm. © CNAC/MNAM, Dist. RMN-Grand Palais/Art Resource, NY. Photo: Bertrand Prévost. Mendini was involved in Casa da Cor in São Paulo in the 1980s.

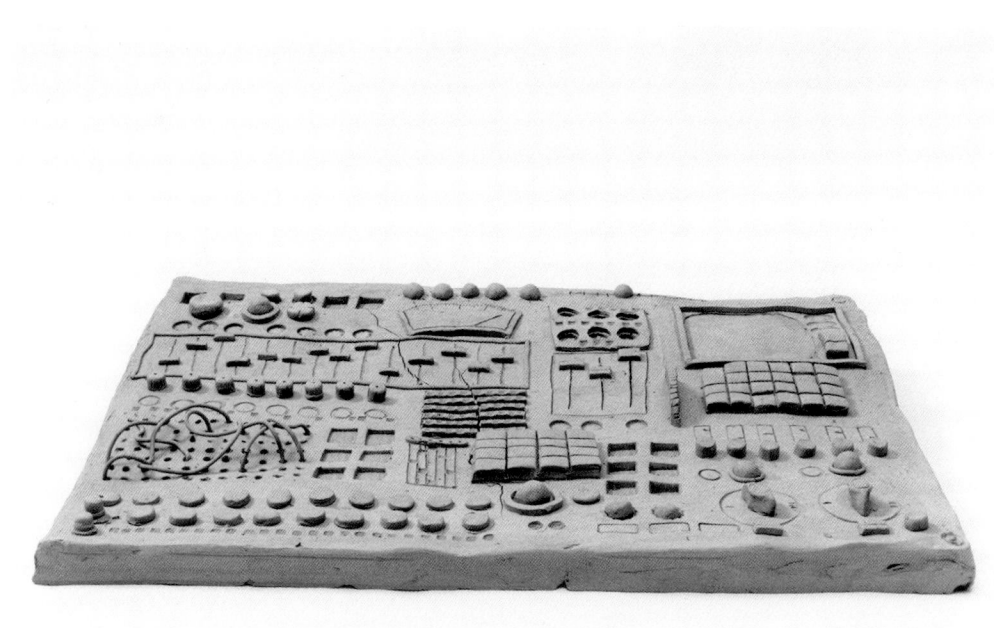

Figure 5.3
Peter Fischli and David Weiss, *Popular Opposites—Central Command Station*, from *Suddenly This Overview*, 1980–2012. Series of approximately 600 sculptures; individual works undated, unfired clay, various dimensions, between 6 × 7 × 5 cm and 82 × 83 × 5 cm. © Peter Fischli and David Weiss, courtesy Matthew Marks Gallery. Photo © 1981 Iwan Schumacher, Galerie Stähli.

essay "Apropos d'Abraham Moles: La communication: science ou idéologie?" (Apropos of Abraham Moles: communication: science or ideology?, 1973).[14] Here, Flusser praises Moles for using objects to create a "new science" that turned humanism on its head. Now people could respond to the impact of the objects in their environment, rather than forcing their agency on them. "I am not saying that Moles is the only representative of this tendency," Flusser noted.[15] (Roland Barthes and British thinkers related to cultural studies had been analyzing everything from chopsticks and advertisements to fashion and popular music since the 1950s.) Having just left the more conservative world of the Brazilian Institute of Philosophy, however, Flusser found that this way of observing the world offered "a radically new meaning" to the "term 'theory': it is no longer a map of an objective world, but an intersubjective, living and existentially experiential world."[16]

Flusser's contribution was to apply communications theory to everyday objects, designating them as "mediators" in the phenomenological world. "Bottles" (1972) is notable because it fixes on an object resembling Heidegger's ceramic jug, defined by its void and used as a springboard for thinking about how *objects* become *things* when they no longer serve their intended purposes. Flusser's chosen vessel was the champagne bottle (he would soon be living permanently in France), which he considered in various states: full, empty, and broken into glass shards. What happens, he mused, when a bottle has no use, except as an ashtray or the subject of a Giorgio Morandi painting?[17] How we treat bottles, as either art or waste, will show future archaeologists the way we live—which is increasingly tied to garbage and the blurring of nature and culture. It also implicates *form*, a concern that goes back to ancient philosophy: "For Plato, theory means the contemplation of eternal forms," Flusser wrote. "For the modern age, theory means the manipulation of plastic forms" and "the elimination of spent forms (garbage disposal)."[18]

"Fountain Pens" looked at disposable plastic pens, an emblem for a culture in which literacy had become just another code, and writing tools had largely given way to typewriters (and now, of course, computers).[19] (Later, in the 1980s, Flusser would write an essay on typewriters, titled "Why Do Typewriters Go 'Click'?," which served as a coda.[20] In the latter essay, typewriters serve as an interface between humans and the world, but they go "click" because everything now must be quantized; typewriters signal the move away from the alphanumeric.) Space, architecture, and environment also overlap significantly with objects in Flusser's 1970s object essays. "Carpets" looks at how we have moved from carpets mounted on the walls of tents to carpets covering our floors, a rotation in geometry but also in values, as the carpet becomes a bourgeois status symbol.[21] "Beds" starts out with our "dwelling" (an obvious Heidegger reference) and ranges from cradle to deathbed, approaching the bed as a kind of abyss where we read and fall asleep—or are disgraced and denied sleep by insomnia.[22] "Baths" vacillates between public (baths in ancient Rome or Muslim-controlled Spain) and private (modern-day bathrooms), palace-like and hidden away. They are places for cleaning, anointing, getting rid of impurities—which leads to the question of what qualifies as dirty and what as clean: are these objective categories? What is dirty for Americans might be "healthy" for Brazilians.[23] "Motor Cars" looks at the automobile to explain Western culture: locomotion on wheels is "cyclical" and makes borders into "archaic obstacles," turning us back into a nomadic society.[24] The essay also resurrects Heidegger's idea of care (*Sorge*), thinking about how owners tend to their vehicles. "Canes" treats the walking stick as a mediator between the human and the outside world, but also between nature and culture: the forest becomes "a place full of potential canes . . . pieces of forest waiting to become anti-forest."[25] And finally, in "The Bag" (1973), Flusser muses on the thief who stole his leather satchel in Paris and went so far as to drop it off at a police station with his manuscripts intact: "A very severe literary criticism," since the thief found no value in the writings.[26]

Why focus on canes, bottles, and bags as communications theory? Because everyday objects, Flusser stresses, are intermediaries—"media" and "communication tools"—hence their analysis is fundamental to the theory of communication.[27] Flusser argues that if we don't see everyday objects as a means of communication, we will never discover the structure of interaction in our environment, resulting in the "opposite of what should be the theory of communication."[28] As I pointed out in Screen 2, this was a somewhat devious approach to communications theory—a subversive method that would be amplified in his design writings in the 1980s. Another way to look at Flusser's early object writings, however,

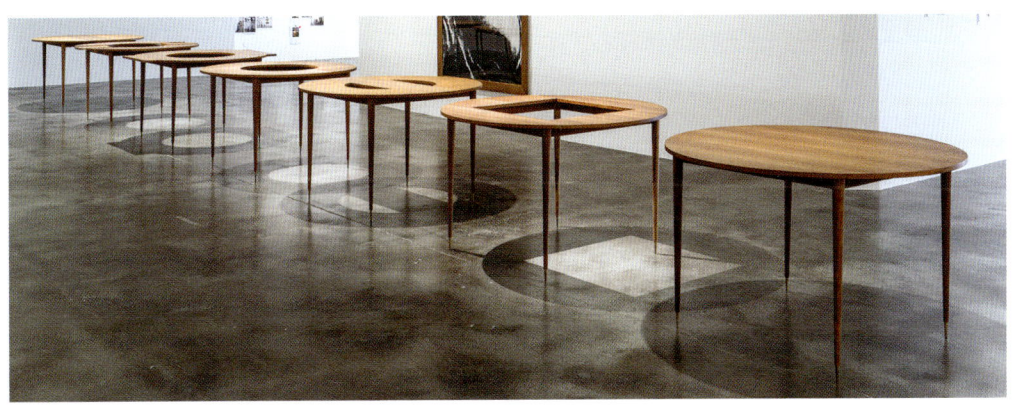

Figure 5.4
Ronald Jones, *Untitled (Peace conference tables designed by North Vietnam and the National Liberation Front of South Vietnam; and the United States and South Vietnam, 1969)*, 1987. Detail of installation view, Magasin III, 2020. Collection Magasin III Museum for Contemporary Art, Stockholm. Photo: Jean-Baptiste Béranger. This work appeared next to Flusser's "Art and Politics" in *Artforum*, December 1990, 25.

is as a harbinger of new materialist philosophies in which, when objects and nonhumans communicate, we risk becoming *their* objects. "We cannot merely react psychologically to walls, if we want to be their subject and not their object," Flusser wrote in "Walls" (1974).[29] Similarly, with pens or automobiles—and now, of course, smartphones and other digital devices—"very often they do not function for our sake, but we function for theirs."[30] This is also true when we encounter aesthetic objects: in Flusser's essay on "Alexandre Bonnier's Living-Room," the artist's Parisian Rive Gauche apartment crowded with paper sculptures and "dreamlike objects," he sensed that he was "being manipulated by Bonnier through his objects," just as we are seduced, guided, or provoked by artworks when we attend an exhibition.[31]

Toward a Philosophy of Design

Flusser's design essays, penned in the years surrounding the Gulf War in the early 1990s, treat objects in a similarly democratic fashion: on a continuum from art to industrial objects and military weaponry, with Cubism considered alongside Trident missiles. In a lecture at the HfG Ulm in September 1988, "Gebrauchsgegenstände" (Everyday objects), he argues that although the purpose of everyday objects is to make our lives easier, they often serve as obstructions.[32] How to avoid this? Rather than throwing objects in other people's way, we need to amplify the communicative and dialogic possibilities, which is both a political and an aesthetic issue. This means thinking about design philosophically: what is at stake in objects? In "About the Word *Design*," Flusser goes back to his language philosophy roots, considering the etymology of the word "design" (and once again mimicking Heidegger).[33] Here he breaks down the word "technology": in Greek, a *tekton* was a carpenter working with wood (*hyle*), a shapeless material to which the artist/technician gives form. Meanwhile, "the Latin equivalent of the Greek *techne* is *ars*, which in fact suggests a metaphor similar to the English rogue's 'sleight of hand.'"[34] For Flusser, then, design is a form of deception. It is linked with mechanics and machines, and these can be traced etymologically back to Greek words like *mechos*: "a device designed to deceive—i.e., a trap—and the Trojan Horse is one example of this."[35] Design includes things like levers, which are meant to trick gravity, as Flusser describes in "The Lever

the ghetto posed a problem: what could be done to stop the intellectuals from sneaking out of it, and back into politics? The politicians' solution was to surround the ghetto with an aura of glamour, to give intellectuals "status." The "great scientist" would become childlike in the face of the world. The "great artist" would live in splendid isolation.

This was not the perfect solution, however. The useful intellectuals, the scientists, kept on believing that what they were after were "true ideas," not just ways to improve industrial production. And the useless intellectuals, the artists, kept on believing that what they were after were models for new experiences (aisthesthai, to experience), not just decor. This was dangerous, since the scientist might come up with models of industrial production and of government that would render the politicians useless, and the artists might prove that work was not the only source of value, and therefore that the artisan, the industrialist, was not necessarily the

best person to be king of the city. The academic ghetto, in fact, created a counterrevolutionary climate, for the intellectuals never really accepted their loss of power. And the artists in the modern sense of the term—the clowns—soon opposed themselves to the artists in the classical sense (the artisans, now industrialists and politicians). This had become quite obvious by the Romantic period, when the artist and poet children of industrialists took to advocating industry's abolition. Some of them even preferred to die of tuberculosis in the garrets of the industrial towns than to submit wittingly to their clownship. Yet don't artists do exactly what industrialists and politicians do—impose their ideas on things? What, after all, is the ontological difference between a plastic fountain pen and a painting, or a piece of music? Aren't both the results of the imposition of ideas upon some matter—the results of a "political" opinion?

How curious. The moment that artists become kings, transforming themselves

into industrialists, they create a new type of artist, their clown. But the clown denies them the right to judge him or her, submitting instead to theoretical, philosophical criticism. This sounds very funny, of course, but it is a crucial aspect of the present situation. We see another significant phenomenon if we move from the "useless" to the "useful" intellectual, for we find that work too has been divided into two different gestures, "soft" and "hard." The soft gesture explores symbols so as to spin out new models, and the hard imposes these models upon matter. The soft gesture is executed by thinkers—whom, in the end, we really must call "artists"—equipped with computers and similar apparatuses. The hard gesture, more and more, is executed not by people but by machines.

In this transformation of work, several aspects are striking. First, the actual imposition of form upon material has become mostly a mechanical rather than a human gesture. Second, people who

use symbols to make models—the programmers, or the software people—are both artists (because they handle ideas) and philosophers (because they no longer apply those ideas physically). And third, there is not much sense in trying to classify intellectuals into useful and amusing ones, because the models now elaborated on computers are not only "scientific and technical" but also "artistic."

Neither Plato nor the politicians, then, have correctly anticipated the present situation. For today's intellectuals both contemplate forms, living in "theory," and handle them as well (on the computer screen). These people are artists become philosophers, or philosophers become artists. At the same time, they work without necessarily owning any machines, and without having left their ghetto. All of a sudden we have people who prove that though "theory" and "art" may fuse, "art" and "politics" may be two different ways of life altogether.

It sounded funny, a few paragraphs earlier, when I said that the artist submitted to theoretical criticism. It no longer sounds so funny, for what it means is that the artist—the programmer of work, and therefore of life—is also the theoretician. Working with computers, artists can submit their models to their own theoretical criticism before feeding them to machines that transform them into hard matter. If so, then art criticism no longer steps in after the work is done, but is part and parcel of the work's project, its program. So this is the emerging situation: artists, people who handle forms with a view to applying them, now govern the city. They are called "systems analysts," "futurologists," "technocrats," "media people," and so forth. They govern not by applying their models directly but by programming machines (and getting other people) to do the work. In this sense are they philosophers: they contemplate forms, and have a theoretical vision. Politicians may not be aware of it yet, but they have become automatons programmed by these philosopher artists. This is why we no longer agree when Plato puts art and politics in the same bag: politics have been deposed, and art governs the city.□

Vilém Flusser is a teacher of communications at São Paulo University and at the École Nationale de la Photographie, Arles. He contributes this column regularly to Artforum.

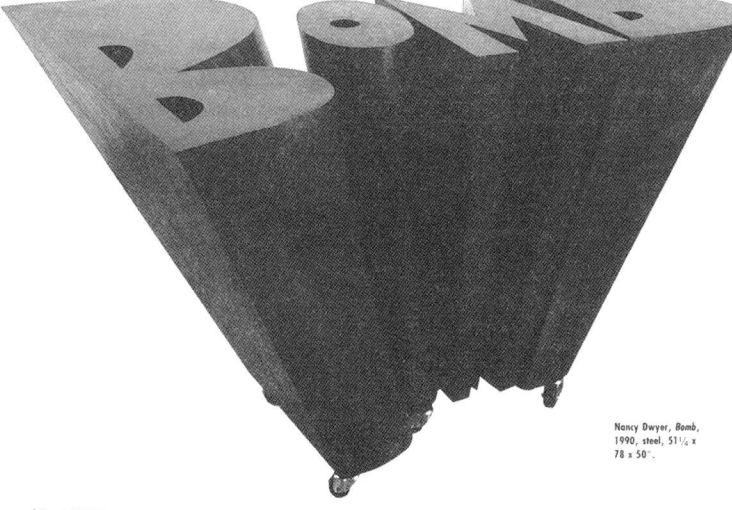

Nancy Dwyer, *Bomb*, 1990, steel, 51¼ x 78 x 50".

Figure 5.5
Nancy Dwyer, *Bomb*, 1990. Steel, 51¼ × 78 × 50 in., reproduced next to Flusser's "Art and Politics," *Artforum*, December 1990, 26. Courtesy of the artist and Theta Gallery. © Artforum Media, LLC. All rights reserved.

Strikes Back."[36] Soon, Flusser points out, our postindustrial creations will include biological "levers" like clones of mollusks or bacterial "chimeras" that will challenge us in new ways to interact with design and technology.

To call design "deceptive" is, of course, to challenge its ethics. Meanwhile, Flusser was living in a climate where design was being vigorously promoted and "good design" was seen as beneficent. And yet, he considered, one must question the origin of *all* design and, beyond that, what is deemed "good" in our post-Enlightenment, post-Auschwitz, posthumanist world. In "The Ethics of Industrial Design" (1991), Flusser asks who is responsible, for instance, if a robot kills a person—and what happens when a helicopter pilot is fitted with a helmet that can trigger weapons with the blink of an eye?[37] Does it follow the Nuremburg principles of crime, where there is no single author and "responsibility has been so watered down that in effect we find ourselves in a situation of total irresponsibility towards acts resulting from industrial production"?[38] Design might be impressive in its efficiency, accuracy, and aesthetics, but it raises troubling ethical questions.

Typically, Flusser approaches this problem with deadpan irony and satire. (Irony, after all, could be deployed as cannily and powerfully as deceptive design: "It is a weapon that can be liberating. For it can show not only how weak the strong are," Flusser wrote in a short 1972 essay on the subject, "but also how strong the weak are.")[39] In "War and the State of Things," he writes that, since war serves in many cases as the origin of advanced technological design, this often makes design's origins unsavory. And yet, Flusser asks, isn't it better to die being hit by a missile than by an arrowhead or a knife? The rockets used in the Gulf War, to Flusser, were not only technological weapons, but "characteristic works of contemporary art": an elegant conflation of creativity, engineering, and design.[40] Flusser's satirical argument is that people who are antiwar are anti-design. Design thus poses a dilemma: "either war and an elegant, user-friendly life in the midst of good objects, or everlasting peace and a squalid, inconvenient life in the midst of badly functioning objects."[41] And the classic "moral" good of European philosophy becomes troubled by design: do we want "pure" good or "functional" good? "Unfortunately, this is the way it is with goodness," Flusser writes. "Everything that is good for something is pure Evil."[42] He ends the essay citing an anecdote in which the technicians who built gas chambers for the Nazis apologized for their poor design: "i.e., not killing their 'clients' quickly enough."[43] Meanwhile, the Gulf War was producing what Flusser called "post-industrial" weapons, showing, as Harun Farocki did, how design had entered new territory with so-called "smart" automated weapons. But design, for Flusser, had positive attributes, too. The term could be generously inclusive, incorporating art, science, and engineering. In the essay "Form and Material," ancient canals, Picasso's *Demoiselles d'Avignon*, and Mirage fighter jets are all included under the rubric of design, providing a new term for thinking about the ancient category of *form*. "In the past," Flusser wrote, "it was a matter of giving formal order to the apparent world of material, but now it is a question of making a world appear that is largely encoded in figures, a world of forms that are multiplying uncontrollably."[44] Concepts were now *in-formation*: that is, shaped by information. If form and material were changing, so were objects and things: "My bed has moved less than Poland has," Flusser quipped, noting the impermanence of borders and even countries in the new world order.

This notion extended to "non-things": an environment that was becoming "softer" and more spectral, but also shaped by a new set of values, which constituted a "new imperialism: humanity is becoming dominated by those groups who have control over information, be it the construction of atomic power stations and weapons, airplanes and motor vehicles, or genetic engineering and management systems. Such groups sell this information at inflated prices to a dominated humanity."[45] Non-things also included computer memory, electronic images, holograms, programs, and the possible "liberation of software from hardware" ("Hermann Hesse's *Glass Bead Game* and similar works of futurology make it at least possible to imagine the liberation of non-things from things").[46] These *might* lead to emancipation—or unemployment. They will definitely change our bodies so that we only use our fingertips (or in the age of texting, our thumbs). Elemental objects, like wheels—the mainstay of industry and modern automobiles—become "kitsch" objects like the Nazi swastika (!).[47] And once biotechnology takes over, Flusser concludes, machines will no longer have wheels but fingers, legs, and sexual organs instead. Karel Čapek's *Homo Artefactus*, or artificial man, would become biological, neurophysiological, and programmed.

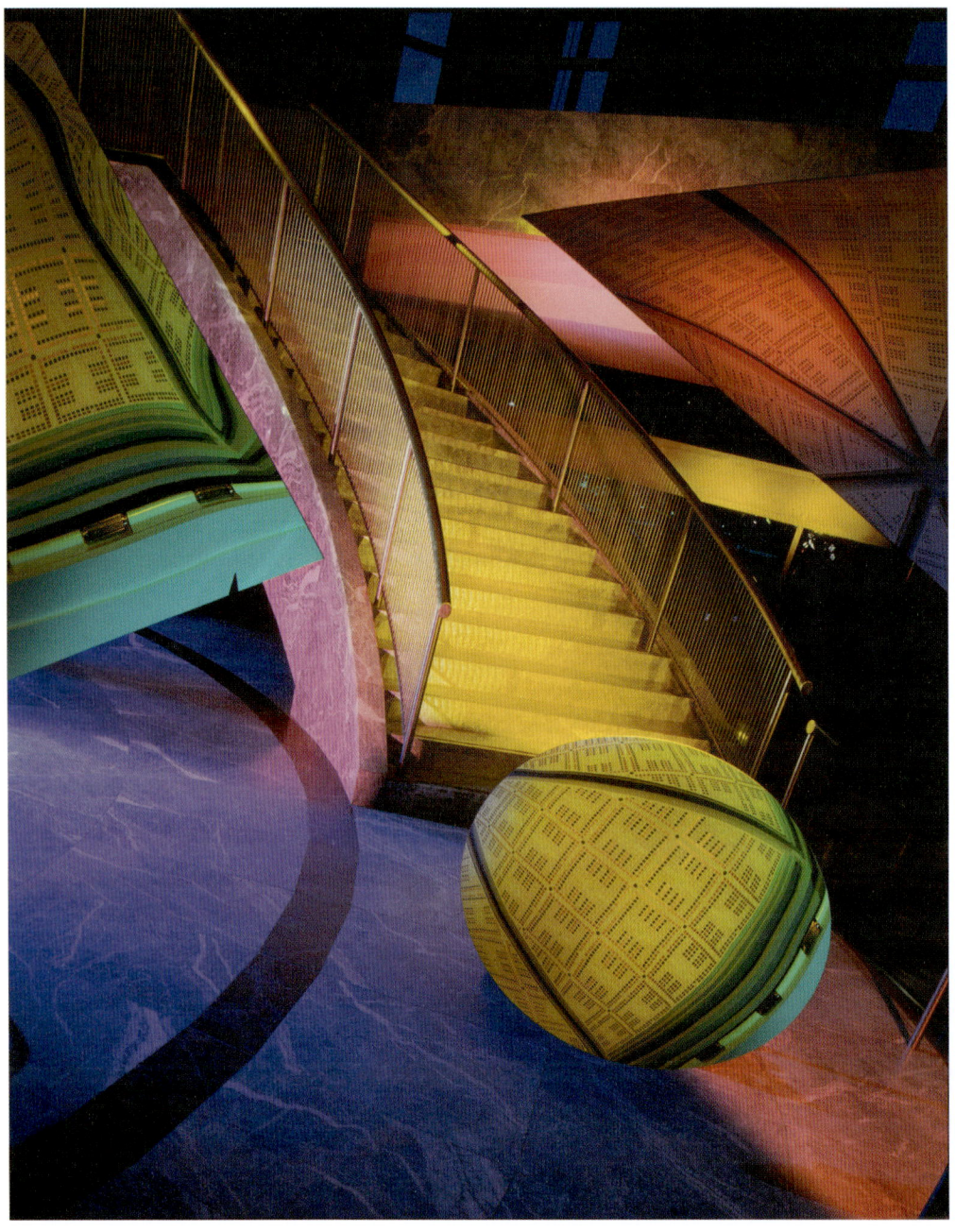

Figure 5.6
Barbara Kasten, *Architectural Site 7*, July 14, 1986. Silver dye bleach print, 60 × 60 in. Courtesy of the artist. This photograph accompanied a review by Charles Hagen in which he wrote, "Kasten's style might be called Bauhaus on acid." *Artforum*, April 1987, 127.

Architecture was shifting, too. Flusser was a fan of Renzo Piano and Richard Rogers's Centre Pompidou—itself conceived as a kind of living organism that displayed its inner workings on the outside of the building. In the essay "With as Many Holes as a Swiss Cheese," Flusser considered how domestic architecture was changing, with cables for communications technology perforating the walls, roof, windows, and doors. Heidegger had written about the radio penetrating the house, and now Flusser lamented that "home-as-one's-castle has become a ruin with the wind of communication blowing through the cracks in the walls. It is a shoddy patchwork job. What is needed," he concluded, "is a new type of architecture, a new design."[48]

Flusser's discussion also went back to elemental structures like tents, which are ancient but varied, ranging from Genghis Khan's imperialist castle-like yurt to Jacob's humble shelter for the unhoused. Tents are mobile and screenlike, and "the tent-wall is woven—i.e., a network."[49] A tent must take the wind into consideration, though, becoming like a sail, which exploits the wind's power. Additionally, tent walls have been surfaces for images, from the carpets hung on the inside of tents for warmth to the paintings on canvas that emerged from this material and finally to television and computer screens. Tents, kites, and parachutes were therefore models for housing in an increasingly immaterial, houseless future. But architecture could be language, too, echoing Heidegger's idea of language as the "house" of being: in "Wittgenstein's Architecture" (1991), written for the artist Mischa Kuball's Wittgenstein House project in Vienna, Flusser imagines a metaphorical landscape of philosophical texts in which Wittgenstein's *Tractatus* is a "little house" compared to the cathedral of Thomas Aquinas—a skeletal dwelling with a trapdoor opening into an abyss and filled with mirror-like propositions rather than conclusions.[50]

Flusser's design theories extended to metropolises as well. In essays like "Designing Cities" and "The City as Wave-Trough in the Image-Flood," he imagined the city in terms of topology rather than geography.[51] (Interestingly, search engines like Google use a topological rather than a semantic model to explore the information-scape of the internet.) Whereas the ancient city was organized around social and physical divisions such as

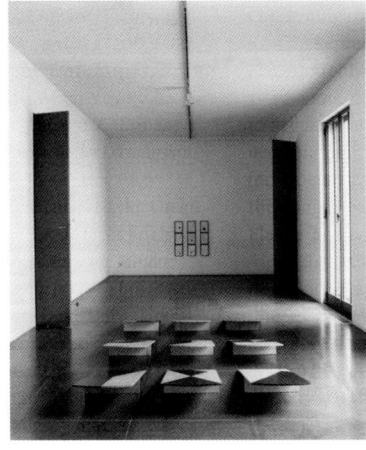

Figure 5.7
Mischa Kuball, *Welt/Fall*, Wittgenstein House, Vienna, 1991. © Archive Mischa Kuball, Düsseldorf, VGBildKunst 2024. Photo: Matthias Herrmann.

between slaves and the intellectuals who formulated equations to build canals or philosophized in the agora, technology and science eclipsed these elements in industrial cities. The new city, for Flusser, functions as a relational network—one thinks of the burgeoning realm of remote working and life—and a net of associations in which the threads are channels through which information flows.[52] Within this net, human subjects are like knots, and their relations are the different densities on the net, with the more concentrated areas developing into "wave-troughs" (*Wellental*) that oscillate back and forth. The wave troughs are called cities, which correspond to other formations: ecological, molecular (phenotypes knotting together in genetic information), or atomic (bodies knotting collectively within gravity, electromagnetism, or nuclear forces).[53]

The future city, more importantly, would be structured differently, with humans living on the former Temple Mount and devoting their time to crafting artificial intelligence and programming robots. This city would have a different shape, designed not as a geographical place (such as a hill near a river) but as a *fold* in the intersubjective field, mimicking the folds in synthetic images seen on the computer screen. It would not be localized, except within the network. It would be a field that attracts intrahuman relations. Flusser's ideas, much like Deleuze and Guattari's speculative notions of immaterial, floating space, challenge designers to reconsider surfaces, objects, and space.[54] Some of this overlapped with the field of design fiction and gaming. As we will see with his participation in Casa da Cor (House of color), though, Flusser also was in conversation with architects designing actual buildings and reconfiguring urban environments.

Design Fiction and Gaming

Flusser had written about fiction in the 1960s in an excellent essay titled "On Fiction" (1966), in which he mused on the relative nature of science and the blurring of fiction and reality in television and other media spheres. For instance, a table can be considered from multiple angles: as an industrial product, a work of art, or an electromagnetic and gravitational field; as solid *and* hollow at the same time (from the viewpoint of physics). But which of these perspectives is true? Phenomenology could help these coordinates to coalesce, such that the table becomes the sum of all fictions that shape it. Or perhaps reality is what exists *between* the coordinates. "We are about to reach a level of consciousness in which the search for deep coherence, explanation, enumeration, narration, and calculation, in short, and historical, scientific, and textually linear thinking is being surpassed," he wrote. "We no longer see any sense in trying to distinguish between something illusionary and something non-illusionary, between fiction and reality." Instead, "we must abandon such categories as true-false, real-artificial, or real-apparent in favor of categories such as concrete-abstract. The power to envision is the power of drawing the concrete out of the abstract."[55] In other words, rather than trying to establish some kind of "post-truth" or "alternative facts," he was interested in the nonbinary, the speculative, and "futures" such as Afrofutures that attempt to envision more equitable outcomes for humanity.

Similarly, the field of design fiction has emerged after Flusser's death, and it makes sense to place him within its scope. Julian Bleecker writes that, whereas science fiction offers "prototypes of other worlds," design fiction creates objects like "totems" or "artifacts from someplace else, telling stories about other worlds."[56] In "Designing Cities," Flusser wrote that "the proposed sketch for a city to be designed is a fantastic dream."[57] He took this idea further in essays like "The Submarine" and "The Factory" and in his final book of fictional screenplays, *What If? Twenty-Two Scenarios in Search of Images*.[58] In these deliriously dreamlike speculative writings, Flusser considers buildings, objects, spaces, and relationships in a manner that might be considered design fiction. "The

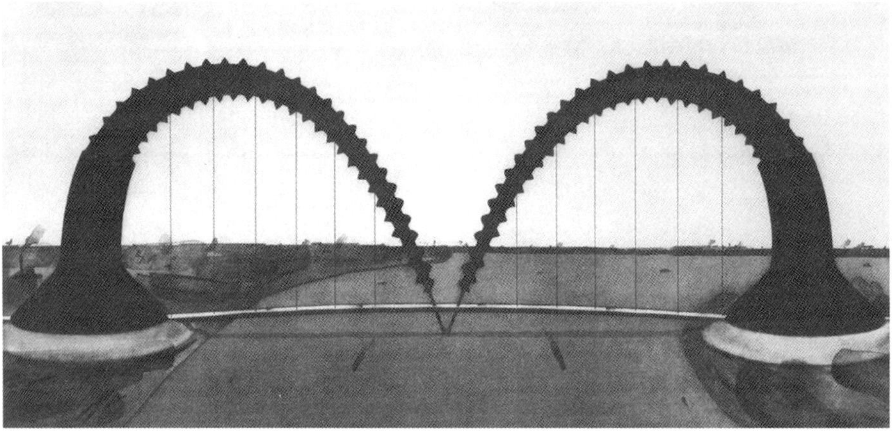

Curies' Children

Vilém Flusser on Popes

Art criticism, as an attempt to translate from images into the words of a language, has to do with the building of bridges. In ancient Rome, bridge builders were called *pontifices*, and the head builder—*pontifex maximus*—still lives in that city. Which is to say that art critics and the pope are in the same business.

Bridge building in general is an address of the problem of transportation over the abyss. The ancients, for example, thought there were two worlds, the mundane one below the moon and the heavenly one above it, and they were separated by a divide. But traffic between the two worlds was essential if life was to have meaning. Bridge builders—pontiffs—were needed. They built a temple on a hill, called the "Capitol," that bridged the space between the sacred and the lowly political space called the "forum," and for most of the history of Western civilization this bridge and its descendants carried the traffic between heaven and earth. Then came Sir Isaac Newton, who unified celestial and terrestrial mechanics, leveled heaven to the ground, and did away with the abyss above the moon, making bridges and pontiffs redundant. It took a while before people realized that this was what he had done. Now, however, it has become more or less obvious that though the hill (for instance the Capitol in Washington, D.C.) might claim some godlike authority over the plain (for instance *Art-"forum"* in New York), its priesthood is distinctly to this side of the divine.

Now suppose you want to translate the German expression es *gibt* into English. There are bridges called "dictionaries" that may lead you to the literal translation "it gives," but here the pontiffs have misled you. For a reason not immediately obvious, the correct translation is "there is," and to get at it you have to jump over the abyss that separates German from English. It is this jump that is called a "translation." This is not to say that dictionaries are useless. There are regions where German and English overlap, and dictionaries are good guides to them. But the expressions es *gibt* and "there is" seem to stand outside those regions, somewhere near the centers of the two universes of German and English, and these centers are separated by an abyss. It is here that pontiffs are needed.

This is true even with Newton, who seemed to have done away with the pontiffs between Heaven and Earth. Actually what Newton did was establish a gray zone where Heaven and Earth overlap, and he fixed the rules ordering that region. But eventually it became apparent that Newton's dictionary is sometimes misleading. There is a "big" universe that sits on top of or around the Newtonian one, where Einsteinian rules apply, and where astronauts take their ethereal strolls. And there is a "small" universe that sustains or sits inside the Newtonian one, and here Planckian rules apply, and govern atomic reactions. So Newton abolished one abyss only to end up leaving us with two. How are we to translate the concept "this table," an object whose behavior remains largely explicable in Newtonian terms, into the macrocosmic and the microcosmic universe? By "curvature of space-time" upward, and by "probability wave" downward? This sounds as awkward as if we translated es *gibt* by "it gives," but we have to find accurate translations. Pontiffs are needed.

Let us imagine a pontifical artificial intelligence into which one feeds the words es

Claes Oldenburg, *Screwarch Bridge (State II)*, 1980, etching and aquatint, 23¹¹⁄₁₆ × 50¼". Collection of the Museum of Modern Art, New York.

OCTOBER 1990 25

Figure 5.8
Claes Oldenburg, *Screwarch Bridge (State II)*, 1980. Etching and aquatint, 23¹¹⁄₁₆ × 50¼ in., above Flusser's "On Popes," *Artforum*, October 1990, 25. © The Claes Oldenburg Estate © Artforum Media, LLC. All rights reserved. Oldenburg's etching depicts a design for an actual bridge based on a screw bending into an arch.

Factory" (1991), which resulted from a roundtable discussion in Mulhern on factories of the future (the text in German is "Homo Faber"), resonates with Flusser's own employment in a transistor factory in São Paulo in the 1950s. Here he tracks the development of human history and manufacturing, from ancient pottery workshops to industrial factory floors—hands, tools, machines, robots was his shorthand for this evolution—and concludes that factories are places where new humans are being produced, along with "non-things," like software, computer memory, or electronic images. Machines used to be at the center of factories, but now Flusser imagines factories as schools (think of the "campuses" of global tech companies), scientific laboratories, art academies, and libraries—places where humans work with and learn from robots. Even wilder is "The Submarine," a philoso-fiction set in the future, about a group of seventeen scientists, artists, philosophers, and theologians who built a gigantic submarine in an abandoned shipyard in Norway powered by nuclear energy and provisioned with an unlimited supply of seaweed grown in a laboratory. The collective in the submarine, anchored at the bottom of the Pacific Ocean near the Philippines, aimed to force humanity into "military and intellectual disarmament" by using rays emanating from their underwater vessel.[59] They dominated the earth for a few days with their "collective super-brain," forcing decrees in which all the world's armies would be dissolved and warships and military planes would be destroyed, along with all nuclear weapons, corporations, and national borders. The world united against them—but they have gone down in history as the first attempt since the Middle Ages to fuse art and other fields into a "cathedral of knowledge," this time at the bottom of the sea.[60]

One can easily imagine these scenarios existing as a platform, fantasy, or massively multiplayer online game, in which participants individually and collectively build and manage cities, civilizations, creatures, and worlds. Flusser had been thinking about scenarios—and, more specifically, *games*—for a long time. In 1967, he wrote "Jogos" (Games), an essay in which he argues that humans' defining characteristic is their capacity for play.[61] In "The Non-Thing I," written over thirty years later, he would argue that "the new human being is not a man of action anymore but a player: *homo ludens* as opposed to *homo faber*."[62] In "Gesellschaftsspiele" (Board games, 1991), he considered how all games have a structure, a "universe" with governing rules. But they could also be "anthropophagous,"

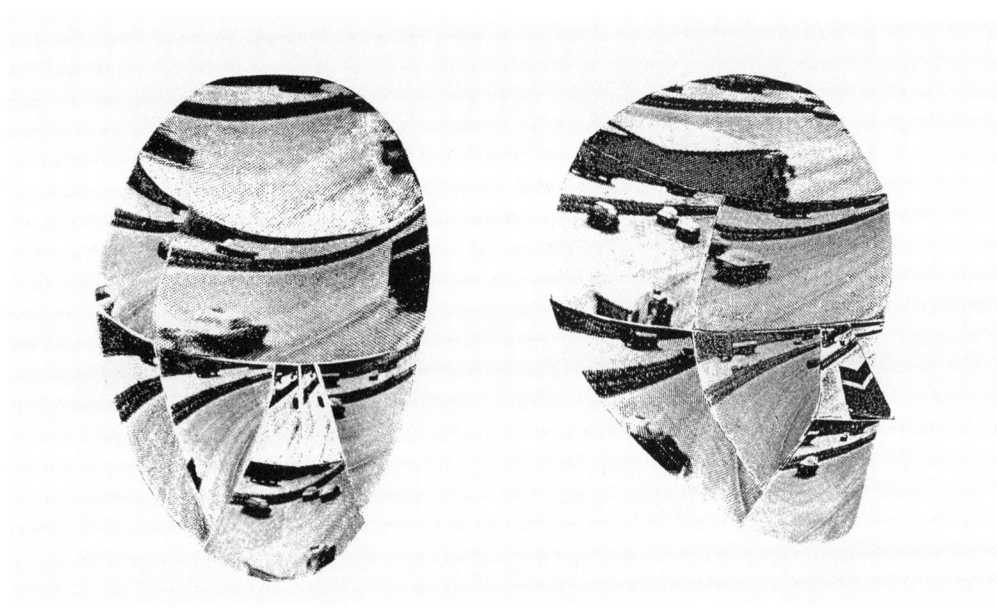

Figure 5.9
Thomas Bayrle, *Autobahn-Kopf* (Motorway-head), 1988–1989, film stills. Courtesy the artist, neugerriemschneider, Berlin, and Gladstone Gallery. Photo: Wolfgang Günzel.

assimilating new elements. Painting and poetry were good examples of this. Games test the boundaries of freedom: you submit to the rules. They also involve faith: a commitment to taking the game seriously, because, for the faithful (such as sports fanatics), the game is not a game at all, unless the player changes the rules (i.e., cheats). For Flusser, society is a game, history is a game, and cheating—working against the apparatus—is the ultimate game, setting players against apparatuses of all kinds.[63]

Games were changing, though. Flusser's primary engagement was with the medieval chessboard, structurally simple and functionally complex. (As I mentioned in Screen 2, Flusser wrote a short essay on chess in 1972, analyzing the pieces—like the rook, which recalls "the Moorish towers on the beaches of Andalusia" and "hides timidly in its corner" at the beginning of the game, until it eventually "perpetrates a merciless genocide on the enemy's ranks."[64] The essay was actually a coded allusion to Brazil under dictatorship and the necessity of understanding the rules of a game.) Flusser had also read both Roger Caillois and Johan Huizinga, who were interested in games as fictive spaces, apart from everyday reality, and he imagined a new human being born without hands: the only thing left was the tips of the fingers used to tap on electronic keys.[65] Fingertips, he concluded, "have become the most important organs of the body," forecasting the phenomenology of the video gamer.[66] In his 2006 analysis of video games, Alexander R. Galloway considered how video games differ from earlier games in that they use software and join human and machine.[67] Unlike photographs or films, as Galloway points out, video games require the *gesture* of the player engaging with the apparatus. More recently, Fabrizio Poltronieri has linked Flusser's communicology to gaming, arguing that playing video games changes our *Dasein*, projecting a reality onto the world and altering our existence in it.[68] For Flusser in *Towards a Philosophy of Photography*, an apparatus was a "plaything," and a plaything was an object in the service of a game. This view also links the gamer/operator more closely to Flusser's notion of the *functionary*, who is largely at the mercy of (or, under the spell of) the program.

Gaming is also where some of Flusser's observations and predictions about apparatuses come to fruition. Whereas Baudrillard argued that we live in a culture of the simulacrum, Flusser proposed that the universe of technical images was programmed within the apparatus and projected from it. Video games are not

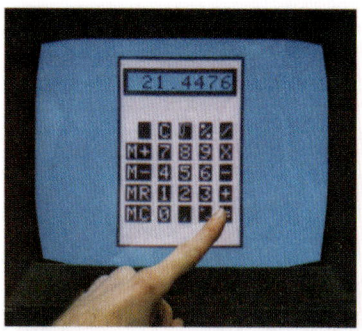

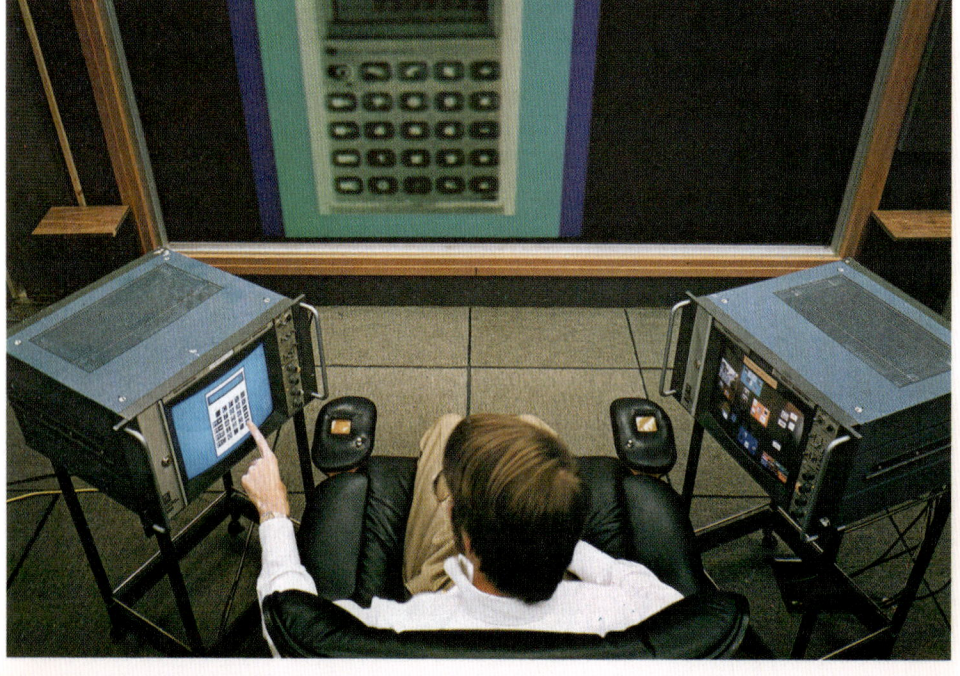

Figure 5.10
Richard A. Bolt, *Spatial Data-Management* (Cambridge, MA: MIT Press, 1979), 47, with the
Architecture Machine Group, Massachusetts Institute of Technology.

Figure 5.11
Karl Gerstner, *Color Sound*, c. 1970s. Acrylic on cardboard, 17 × 17 in.
© Meredith Rosen Gallery, NY.

Figure 5.12
Karl Gerstner, *Color Sounds 22*, 1974. Nitro lacquer on phenolic resin panels, 17 × 17 in.
© Meredith Rosen Gallery, NY.

simulating a reality, then, but are projecting a new one, based on numbers and computation rather than the written word, replacing our linear, cause-and-effect model with a noncausal, dimensionless, particle-based model.[69] What happens, though, is that a society of programmers is being programmed: "Programmed totalitarianism. Mind you, an extremely satisfactory totalitarianism. Since the programs are patently getting better and better."[70] This observation was dripping with irony. Could there be such a thing as "satisfactory totalitarianism"? And yet living with and through smartphones, tablets, and personal computers, in the society of the screen, comes rather close to this notion.

With the advent of personal computers, the interface has, in many ways, taken the place of the *object* as mediator, as Flusser theorized it in his 1970s writings.[71] Flusser was aware of these developments, even if he clung to his typewriter. In his library is a copy of Richard A. Bolt's *Spatial Data-Management* (1979), a project of MIT's Architecture Machine Group. The book describes a computer interface in which the user would sit in an Eames chair (an *haut* designed object programmed for relaxation rather than work) augmented with a joystick and a touchpad before a giant screen.[72] Dubbed "Dataland" and inspired by cybernetics and the ancient poet Simonides, who possessed an ability for extraordinary data recall when giving long speeches, the workstation would serve as a desk in which everything could be easily accessed by the user.[73] Included in Bolt's book were instructions to "stroke" the screen in order to turn a page—what later became "swiping." He defined the movement as a "gesture," which makes one wonder what Flusser might have written about "The Gesture of Swiping."

Where Bolt's design was exciting in the late 1970s, revisiting it now is also a reminder of how modern and contemporary design have been accused of being alienating, depression-inducing, and environmentally destructive. Inspired by Flusser, writers like Mike Anusas and Tim Ingold have pushed back against this conclusion, arguing that design could be reshaped and could beneficially remodel our world. Surfaces—one of Flusser's major concerns from his 1973 essay "Line and Surface" onward—could be penetrated so that there would be greater transparency and dialogue between people and their surroundings.[74] Rather than treating the world as discrete, isolated objects (cars, gadgets, houses with walls that hide plumbing and electrical features), what if designers created an integrated, intersubjective environment? Designers create worlds, both physical and virtual. As Flusser asked near the end of his life, will they result in "fascistic" or "dialogic" ones?[75] "In Mesopotamia," Flusser wrote, the designer "was called a prophet. He is more deserving of the name God. But thank God he is unaware of this and sees himself as a technician or artist. May God preserve him in this belief."[76]

Color Theory and a House of Color

Philosophers have long been interested in color, and Flusser wanted to join the conversation. Color was in his DNA: he grew up on the premises of his grandfather's food colorings and dye factory. In 1973, he wrote "Cor-de-rosa" (Pink), about Alexandre Bonnier's contribution to the Twelfth São Paulo Biennial, a white room arranged with boxes containing pink objects. With the help of Fred Forest, Bonnier had purchased enough everyday pink objects to fill a room—what Flusser called a "para-phenomenological" project because it distanced color from its everyday context.[77] (Flusser pointed out, however, that this wasn't phenomenology in the strictest sense: in keeping with Bonnier's use of cheap consumer objects, it was ironic rather than contemplative.) Later, in *Towards a Philosophy of Photography*, Flusser would argue that color photography is more abstract than black-and-white photography: the green of a lawn included more coded information than a black-and-white photo.

However, while black and white could be abstract in photography, in everyday life they were not. In multiple essays starting in the 1960s, Flusser attempted—sometimes clumsily, sometimes elegantly—to work through issues of race.[78] "Da Negritude" (1966), for instance, responded to the First World Festival of Negro Arts in Dakar (April 1–24, 1966; the second one was FESTAC '77 in Lagos). Flusser writes that Brazil is important in the Black diaspora, but he argues the word "negro" is problematic: a cultural rather than a natural category. "All definitions degrade humans," Flusser wrote. To say a Black person from Senegal was the same as a person from Fiji was to apply an abstract set of characteristics, invoking the Nazis and their classificatory practices. For later writers exploring the uses of Black art by Brazilian politicians, however, Flusser's words were read not as a critique of classification based on race or what he considered "dubious" nature-culture taxonomies, but as a further erasure of Afro-Brazilian contributions.[79]

In other essays, published in both Brazilian and German newspapers, Flusser reversed himself somewhat. He wrote about how the terms "negro" or "Black" could be "demagogic," but added that in Brazil there was some truth to the designation, since so many elements of Brazilian life were African-derived: quotidian hand gestures, music, dances performed during carnival, and martial arts like *capoeira*. In its cultural synthesis, Brazil might serve as a model for future societies (echoes, here, of Stefan Zwieg and earlier rhetoric about Brazil as the land of the future). However, on a *color* level, Flusser pushed back against the idea of boundaries, borders, and purity in the realm of colors. Were black and white even "colors," since they weren't in the spectrum? "Purity does not exist," Flusser wrote; "everything is a mixture, *mélange adultéré*."[80] He himself had been gravely affected by taxonomies of racial "purity," and his arguments were sound when it came to abstraction in black-and-white photography and color theory. Moreover, writers like Frantz Fanon had argued that "blackness" and racial binaries were social, colonial constructs: "I believe that the fact of the juxtaposition of the white and black races has created a massive psychoexistential complex," Fanon wrote. "I hope by analyzing it to destroy it."[81] However, the *effects* of slavery are still very much felt in Brazil. Moreover, as Fred Moten argues in his famous essay "The Case of Blackness" from 2008, the divide between formal and "lived" experiences of blackness is vast and vital to its understanding.[82] Regarding his own cultural heritage, Flusser admitted: "The older I get, the more Jewish I get" (in an interview a year and a half before his death). He linked his philosophy to ideas of immaterialism derived from the Jewish eschewing of an afterlife; his dislike of idolatry to the biblical prohibition of images, and the Judaic notion that the only way to address an immaterial deity is through the face of another human.[83]

Fiction offered a better way for Flusser to address race and oppression, as it has for authors like Octavia Butler. "Black Is Beautiful," the final scenario in Flusser's *What If?* is set in Dakar and imagines a presentation to be delivered at the Troisième Congrès International de la Négritude, because "only when People of Color work out a theory of color does the problem of color truly gain a voice."[84] Here, once again, Flusser attacks "dubious" taxonomies of color (black, white, red, yellow), arguing that, if color means a visible portion of the field of light oscillations, then neither white nor black can be "colors" and the majority of humanity is probably "yellow." Moreover, if white deflects light, then only the seven percent of people (based on a "questionable" taxonomy) defined as "black," a color that absorbs light, are the true "children of light—of the sun, the moon, the stars."[85]

Gray received a similar treatment, but with better results. "Gray is the color of theory," Flusser wrote in *Towards a Philosophy of Photography*, with photographs rising out of the "monotony" of the nineteenth-century industrial city.[86] Gray was the color of theory in Goethe's *Faust*, as Mephistopheles coaxed Faust away from his studies and toward the green and golden world of hedonism. Flusser's peers were similarly interested in grayness: Paul Virilio's *Grey Ecology* (2010) referred to digital pollution; Gilles Deleuze borrowed Paul Klee's idea of a "grey-point," a pivot-node between chaos and matter; and Jean Baudrillard described consumer society as a form of "gray matter."[87] For Flusser, gray was a border situation: fuzzy, indistinct, but also the color of bureaucracy, with Kafka's "gray eminences with evil intentions" hiding behind the scenes.[88] Later, when Flusser collaborated with Karl Gerstner and the Casa da Cor group, numbers were key: gray was zero, center of the zero-dimensional universe of calculation that began some 500 years ago, resulting in science and industrial revolution ("in sum: the modern world").[89]

Then there was color. It entered Flusser's writing primarily through his consideration of technical images but became increasingly tied to biology and biotechnics. In his 1977 "L'irruption du techno-imaginaire" (The irruption of the techno-imaginary)—the title obviously riffing on the 1973 Institute of the Environment roundtable title, "Technologie et imaginaire"—he argued that colored surfaces were replacing linear thought and the gray of life before World War II. Color was also important in the pivotal essay "The Codified World" (1978), where Flusser identified a new environment saturated with color:

> Our socks and pajamas, cans and bottles, displays and
> posters, books and maps, beverages and ice creams,
> films and television, everything is in Technicolor. With
> these things we are dealing not simply with an aesthetic
> phenomenon, but with a new "artistic style." The red traffic
> light means "Stop!" and the obnoxious green of peas means
> "Buy me!" This explosion of colors means something. We are
> exposed to a constant stream of colors. We are programmed

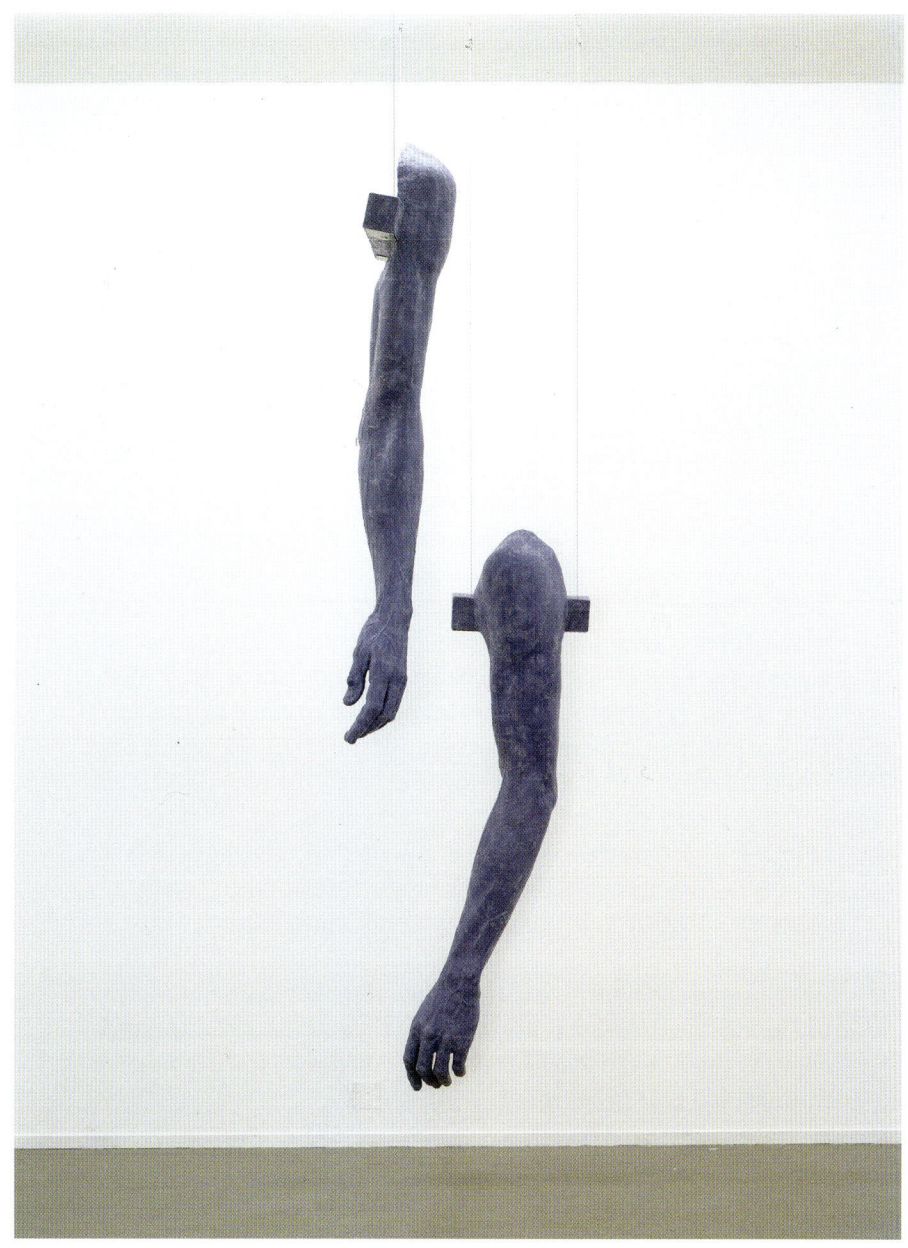

Figure 5.13
Pia Stadtbäumer, *Two Blue Arms*, 1990. Wax, pigment, and fabric, 76 in. (193 cm). Institut für Auslandsbeziehungen. Photo: Achim Kukulies. A photograph of this work appeared alongside Flusser's essay "The Term 'Design'" in *Artforum*, March 1992, 20.

by colors. They are an aspect of the codified world in which we have to live.[90]

Color was, for Flusser, "like the codes of the alphabet and those of musical tones . . . the painter swims in history."[91] It played a vital role in *Vampyroteuthis infernalis* in which Flusser claimed—sometimes erroneously, overstating the nature of Vampy's chromatophores—that color was central to its existence.[92] In the *Vampyroteuthian* world, color was a code for intersubjective communication: "a language with a complex syntax and lexicon."[93] Vampy was an artist, creating a "skin painting" or "symphony," a *Gesamtkunstwerk* of light, color, and sound far superior to what humans could achieve with their limited biological means.[94]

Color exploded in Flusser's *Artforum* writings, too. He imagined blue dogs with red spots and phosphorescent horses, an environment designed by scientists in which "molecular biologists may soon be handling skin color more or less as painters handle oils and acrylics."[95] The next Walt Disney might be a molecular biologist—but not a politician, as Flusser made clear in the deeply satirical "Vom Umfärben der Grünen" (On recoloring the Greens), which takes on the German Green Party. Here, color and nationalism carry the echoes of romanticism—while green itself, since the discovery of chlorophyll, has become an artificial substance.[96] Moreover, the historically obsessed, preservationist Green perspective seems a puny utopia compared to "future phosphorescent rabbits illuminating the purple meadows at night."[97] Flusser ultimately suggests the Greens adopt a multicolored banner (which, to today's reader, echoes the varied rainbow and multicolored flags of gender identification), using as a model a potato turned blue by the butterfly that pollinates it, creating a natural feedback loop. But Germans romanticizing their "green" past would always ring to Flusser, the Holocaust survivor, with the sounds of the Nazis celebrating their sacred *Blut und Boden*. The technological-technicolor future could hardly be worse.

Karl Gerstner and Casa da Cor

An opportunity to expand his thinking around color came with Casa da Cor (House of color), a project that ran from 1987 to 1989 and which put Flusser in communication with one of the twentieth

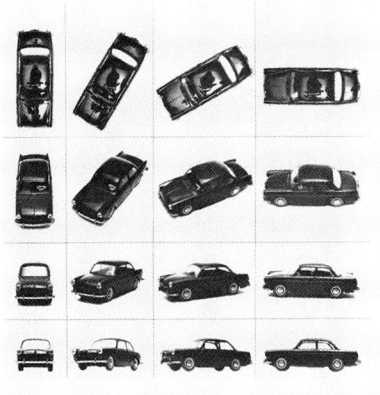

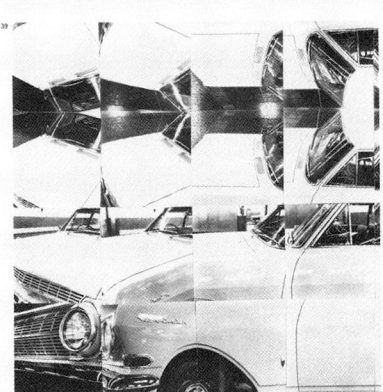

Figure 5.14
Karl Gerstner, "Program as Photography," in *Designing Programs: Four Essays and An Introduction* (1964; repr., Teufen, Switzerland: Niggli, 1968), 14 and 15. Swiss National Library, Prints and Drawings Department, Karl Gerstner Archive, and Muriel Gerstner.

century's great color theorists: the Swiss graphic designer and artist Karl Gerstner. In the late 1950s, Gerstner cofounded Gerstner + Kutter (later GGK, Gerstner Gredinger Kutter), which created advertising campaigns and branding for Geigy, Swissair, Citroën, Ford, and IBM. Gerstner's art resumé was impressive, too: he was included in such exhibitions as *The Responsive Eye* (1965) and *Word and Image* (1968), both at the Museum of Modern Art in New York, and *documenta* 4 (1968). Like Flusser's friend, the cybernetic sculptor Wen-Ying Tsai, with whom Gerstner was also friendly, Gerstner exhibited at the Denise René Gallery in Paris, which specialized in geometric abstraction and kinetic art. And just like Fred Forest, Gerstner used the newspaper as an artistic platform: his front-page work for Basel's *National-Zeitung* in 1973 similarly invited the public to make their own art.

Gerstner's systems-based approach to both art and design was laid out in the now-classic *Designing Programmes: Instead of Solutions for Problems, Programmes for Solutions* (1964), a collection of four essays.[98] Gerstner's idea was that computation could be mapped onto design—but that designs such as Gothic cathedral windows and Islamic and Egyptian ornament had *always* followed the logic of programming and permutation.[99] This even applied to photography: *Designing Programs* shows a car photographed from different angles as part of a phenomenological program, with the body of the photographer circling around the subject, exactly as Flusser described in "The Gesture of Photographing." Gerstner was also involved in New Tendencies, the 1960s Zagreb-based publishers of *bit international*, who were inspired by Bense and Moles and saw the computer as a medium for artistic innovation.[100]

Gerstner was important in the field of typography, and here he overlapped with Flusser's ideas about text and image—but also with the Concrete poets, many of whom were graphic designers and obsessed with typography in the 1950s and 1960s. Drawing initially from Max Bill's ideas, Gerstner's book *The New Graphic Art* (1959) analyzed everything from shop signs in which there was no text to twentieth-century modernist layouts in which individual letters took on monumental form. Gerstner was interested in how surfaces and lines were handled (obviously a Flusser concern), but in an applied way: in advertising, posters, books, and album covers, in a time when style and messages were being globally transmitted and received.[101] "The street becomes a picture gallery," he wrote, emphasizing the democratic nature of design—as well as

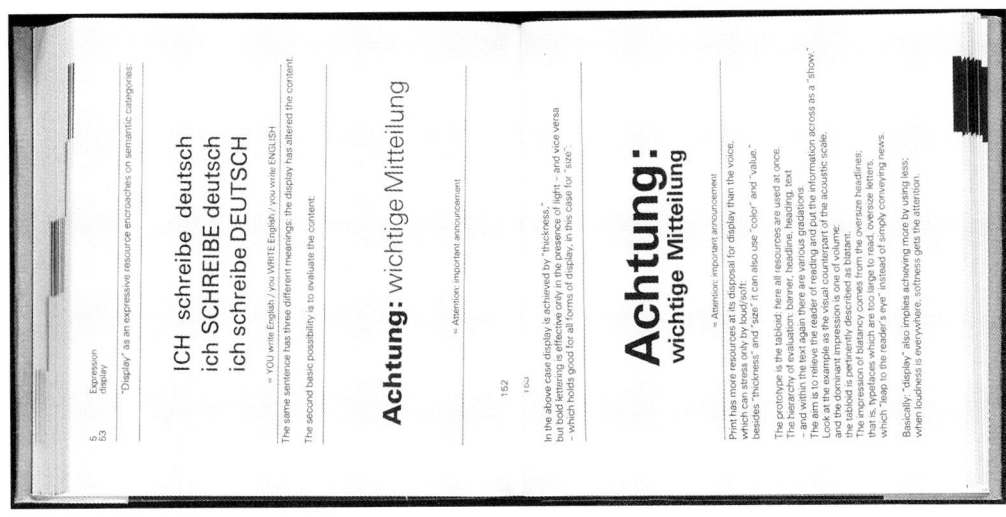

Figure 5.15
Karl Gerstner, *Kompendium für Alphabeten. Eine Systematik der Schrift* (1974; repr., Heiden, Switzerland: Niggli, 1990), 152 and 153. Swiss National Library, Prints and Drawings Department, Karl Gerstner Archive, and Muriel Gerstner.

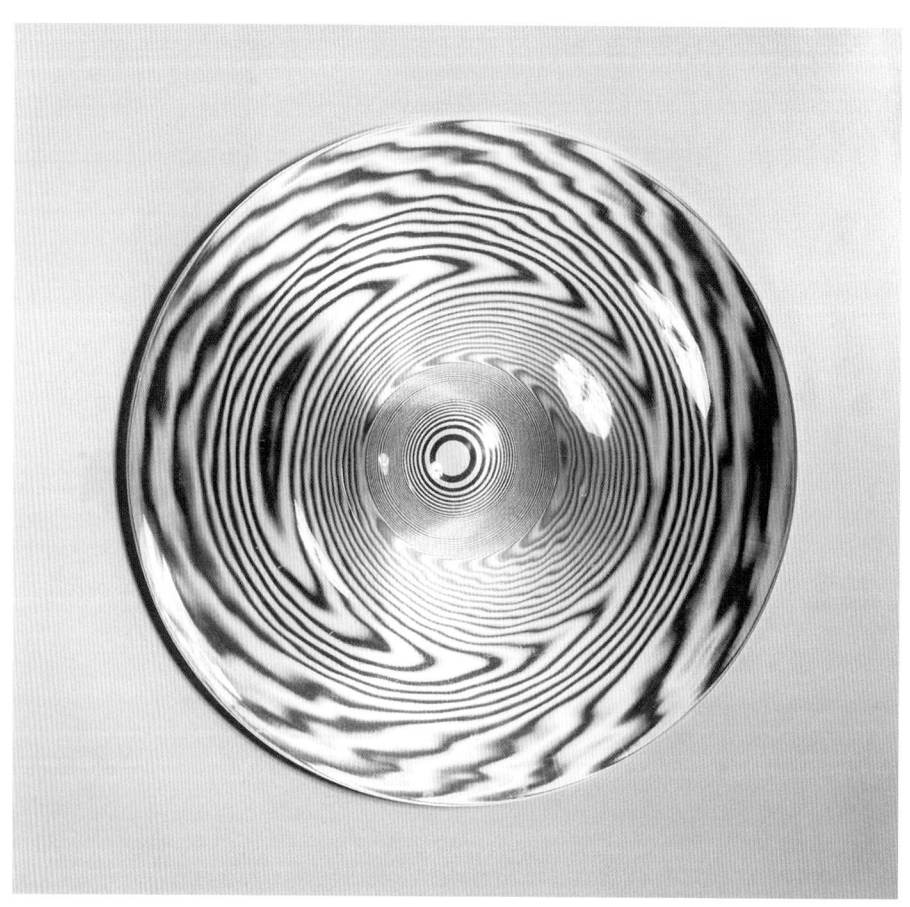

Figure 5.16
Karl Gerstner, *Lens Picture No. 15*, 1964. Plexiglas lens mounted on painted Formica, overall
72.07 × 73.18 × 18.41 cm. Gift of Seymour H. Knox, Jr., 1965. Buffalo AKG Art Museum /
Buffalo/NY/USA. Photo: Buffalo AKG Art Museum/Art Resource, NY.

its collective process, bringing together an art director, a graphic designer, and a typographer.[102]

Thinking further about text, Gerstner published *Compendium for Literates: A System of Writing* (1974), which borrowed from structuralist ideas but looked forward to computer typography.[103] The book is a rigorous undertaking, fusing history—code systems from cuneiform to Chinese characters—with graphic design, media theory, and integral solutions for designers working in the soon-to-be-digital age. Affected by Nazi propaganda and the burgeoning postwar mass media, both Gerstner and Flusser were interested in not just *what* was said, but *how* it was said, shaped, arranged, and disseminated.[104] In his essay "On Typography," Flusser considered how language had become abstract and manipulable after Gutenberg, who handled linguistic symbols as objects and units of information, which was now being pushed to the particle level.[105] Type is "not really traces left by the world, but traces of the way our own thinking functions"—or, more significantly: "we project the rules of our way of thinking into the world, and then re-discover them and call them 'laws of nature.'"[106] Soon, Flusser thought, writing would disappear, and typography would be partially to blame for its extinction.[107]

Feeling that the agency he had cofounded was moving away from its original post-World War II mission, Gerstner retired from advertising at the age of forty and moved his studio into a renovated sawmill in Alsace in 1976. What really occupied him was painting and the study of color. In 1957, he published his first book on art, *Kalte Kunst? Zum Standort der heutigen Malerei* (Cold art? On the position of today's painting), which argued that rationally conceived constructivist and Concrete art weren't "cold," and used examples such as Max Bill, Camille Graeser, Verena Loewensberg, and Richard Paul Lohse, as well as a younger generation including Marcel Wyss, Mary Vieira, and himself.[108] Color was central to this argument. Inspired by Claude Monet, Wassily Kandinsky, and Josef Albers—particularly Albers's *Homage to the Square* series (1950–1976)—Gerstner embarked on his opus: the *Color Sound* paintings, a series based on a system defined by the mathematical arrangement of value and tone to create unity between form and color. These abstract compositions on board could be made with a variety of materials; the system rather than individual works was crucial to the project. (Gerstner's *Apparatus* and *AlgoRhythms* series generated color *without* any pigment, by using prisms, polarization, lenses, rotating propellers, and refraction.) Following Kandinsky, who proposed that individual colors could be expressed in their own simple and symmetrical shapes, Gerstner also set out to create a theoretical system in which color paralleled or intersected with mathematics, graph theory, and topology. He settled upon German-Canadian physicist Günter Wyszecki's theories of color to structure his ideas.[109] Gerstner felt this model was more precise, had greater range, and could be expanded as new colors were developed in chemistry.[110] Wyszecki would become the primary color theory touchstone for Casa da Cor, along with Gerstner's recently published text *The Forms of Color: The Interaction of Visual Elements* (1986), which outlined his research and attempts to unify color and form.

Flusser met Gerstner in February 1987 and immediately wrote to him that, although he had not yet read his books, he had looked at them and could see how Gerstner's ideas could be used to dismantle existing categories: "squaring" a circle or "bluing" yellow could lead to a collapse of everything from pi to a *Weltbild* (world picture). "You have succeeded, dear friend," he wrote to Gerstner, "in submerging me in your dizzying universe."[111] They ended up collaborating on Casa da Cor, initiated in São Paulo by Philippe Henry, a twenty-seven-year-old filmmaker and writer whom Flusser met through one of his former students. Casa da Cor's goals were ambitious: creating a universal color code, launching a journal, building a physical "Colorarium" in São Paulo that would stand on a hill—and generally "studying the influence of color on all areas of human activity," as *O Estado de São Paulo* reported in February 1988.[112] There were three main phases of the collaboration. The first meeting was held at a restaurant in São Paulo in February 1988, attended by twenty-four artists, scientists, professors,

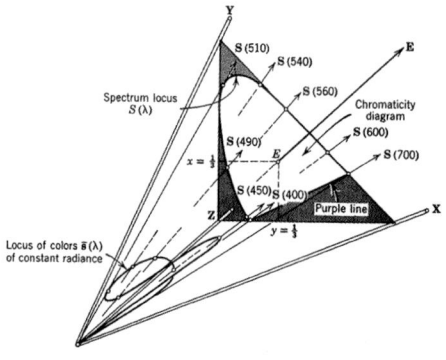

Figure 5.17
Günter Wyszecki and W. S. Stiles, chromaticity diagram, 1967. In *Color Science: Concepts and Methods, Quantitative Data and Formulas* (1967; repr., New York: Wiley, 2001), 138, figure 4(3.3.3.). John Wiley & Sons, Inc.

and historians.[113] A number of questions were asked: How is color being used in the arts, psychology, medicine, communications, education? How is it manifesting in the natural world? How has it appeared in history, religion, philosophy, linguistics, literature? What new colors are being produced via technology? Preliminary plans included public debates, an exhibition at the Museu de Arte de São Paulo (MASP), and the construction of a cultural space.

Flusser got to work immediately. In "Reflexões sobre: A Casa da Cor a constuir em São Paulo" (Reflections on a House of Color to be built in São Paulo), he laid out a short history of color and argued that color is ideological, swinging from highly chromatic periods to more monochromatic ones: from the multihued Greek agora to severe Spanish and US Puritan costumes to Van Gogh and Gauguin searching for variety in the gray age of coal.[114] Flusser stresses the need for a "cultural theory" of color, particularly as society shifts from the industrial modern to the postmodern era in which colors emanate from technological devices like televisions, computers, and holograms (his favorite example). The theory should be interdisciplinary because of the nature of color in different fields: electromagnetics, psychology, biology. But it could also be mapped out as a "universe of colors," echoing his technical image writings.[115]

What could a novel color code do? Above all, it could explain the impact of new color codes based on technical images—codes that didn't come from intuition but were deliberately programmed and exceeded the eye's capacity to distinguish differences. With color, as with technical images, we've become illiterates, once again. For Flusser, Casa da Cor could "serve as a place for teaching and learning the new color codes, in order to fight against the establishment of programmatic totalitarianism in society. I confess that this is the reason for my engagement in this enterprise."[116]

Casa da Cor went beyond a traditional "house" and the limitations of architecture and urbanism, which were changing anyway.[117] The exciting thing about the project, from Flusser's perspective, is that color would function as a philosophical springboard, and a physical house would bridge the traditional problem of linking theory with praxis. In fact, in true Flusserian fashion, it was startlingly prescient:

> What matters about this house is that it consists only of windows and doors, and there are no walls in it. The windows

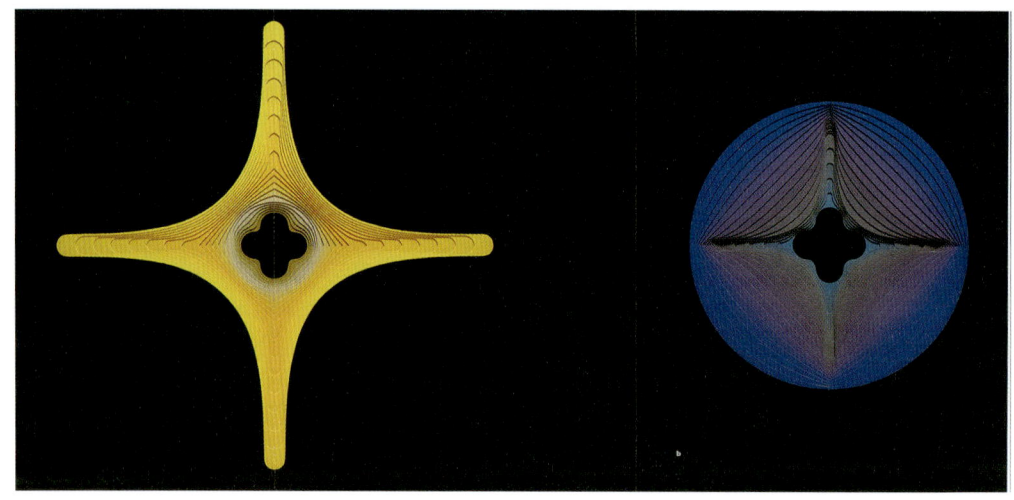

Figure 5.18
Karl Gerstner, *The Forms of Color: The Interaction of Visual Elements* (Cambridge, MA: MIT Press, 1986), 139 and 141. Swiss National Library, Prints and Drawings Department, Karl Gerstner Archive, and Muriel Gerstner.

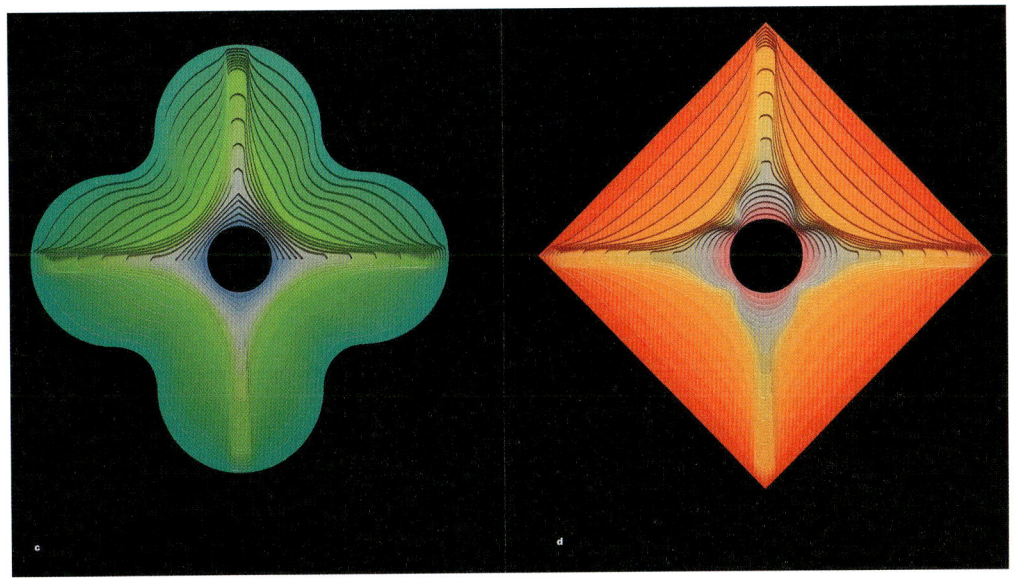

Figure 5.19
Karl Gerstner, *The Forms of Color: The Interaction of Visual Elements* (Cambridge, MA: MIT Press, 1986), 142 and 143. Swiss National Library, Prints and Drawings Department, Karl Gerstner Archive, and Muriel Gerstner.

have the form of screens (television or computer, connected by cable) and the doors have the form of keyboards that I operate to send or receive information. This is all about receiving information: I no longer need to leave the house to receive information; on the contrary: when I leave the house, I lose information. If I want to receive information, I must stay in front of my monitor and constantly look at my screen to see if there is anything new.[118]

New communications systems, as he had pointed out in his "Swiss Cheese" essay, had fundamentally changed the nature of public and private spaces, as well as the circulation between them. Architects like Jean Nouvel, who spoke at the second Casa da Cor conference, were seeing the house from a similarly "communicological" viewpoint. There was no model for such a house—and São Paulo (rather than Moscow or Paris, for instance) was a good city for this project because it wasn't a city with a traditional central square. (However, Flusser noted, the building of the Centre Pompidou *had* turned Paris upside down.) Casa da Cor also offered a way to break from the Latin American house or city based on colonial European models.[119] Brazil, with its shorter history than Europe—in terms of industrialized, linear thinking—was fertile ground for such an experiment, moving from a verbal code to a color one.

Then there was the color code itself. In March 1988, Flusser sent Gerstner an essay titled "Farben Verschlüsseln (Für Karl Gerstner)" (Coding colors, for Karl Gerstner), in which he imagined color in Casa da Cor being used in a "denotative" way.[120] Rather than the rich but ambiguous *connotative* color seen in art, magic, or dreaming, he argued that mathematical thinking could create a new language, with numbers transcoded into colors. Unlike with musical notation, there were, historically, no absolute correspondences between color and form, although it was becoming an issue in television and digital screens. Language had quantified thought in words and phonemes, but something more sophisticated was required now: unambiguous color codes. Computers could be used to "fill up" the intervals between numbers, mirroring the seemingly innumerable hues between blue and green. Ironically, whereas artists and theorists like Gerstner had been seen as "cold" (hence the title of Gerstner's first book, *Cold Art?*), Gerstner argued *against* a quantified or purely denotative color theory. Following

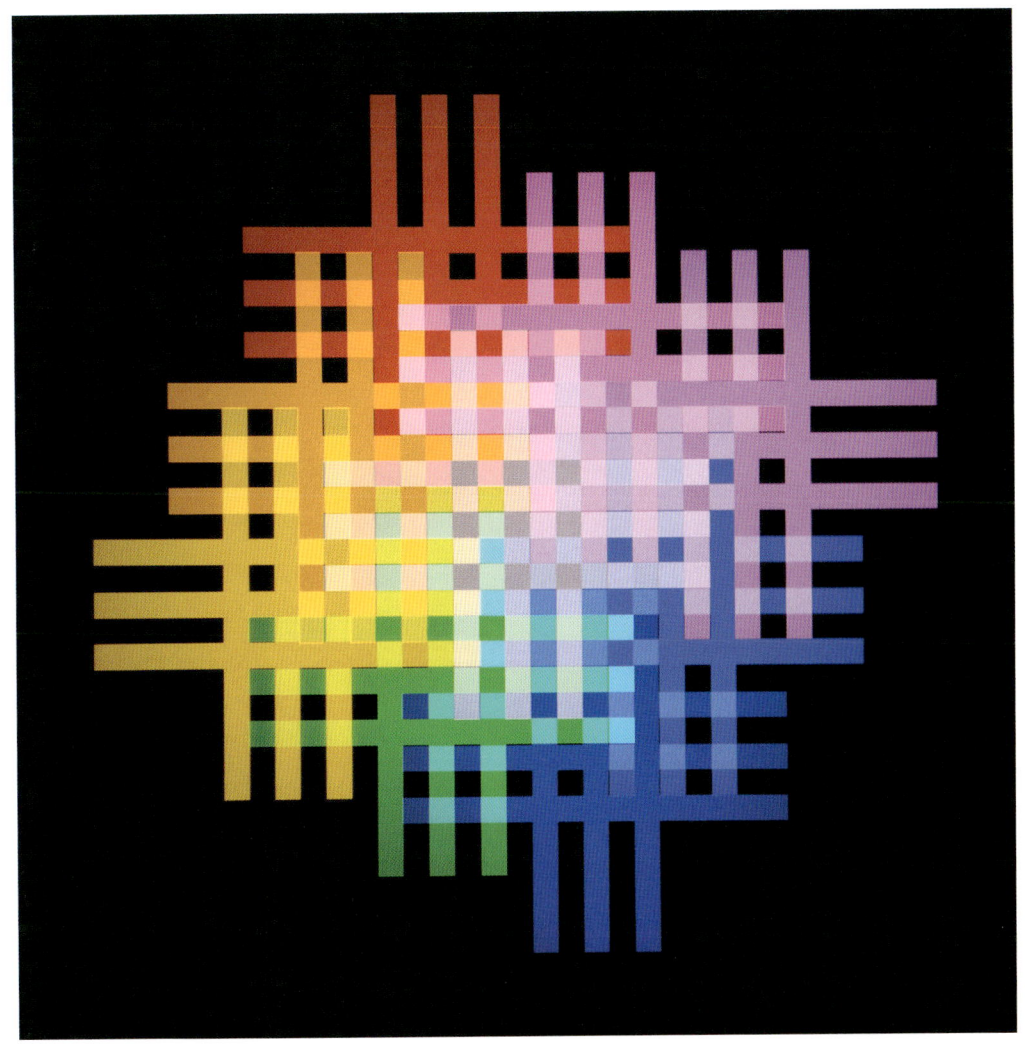

Figure 5.20
Gottfried Jäger, *Multiple Optics, 4.54.4*, 1980. Pigment print. © 2024 Artists Rights Society
(ARS), New York/VG Bild-Kunst, Bonn.

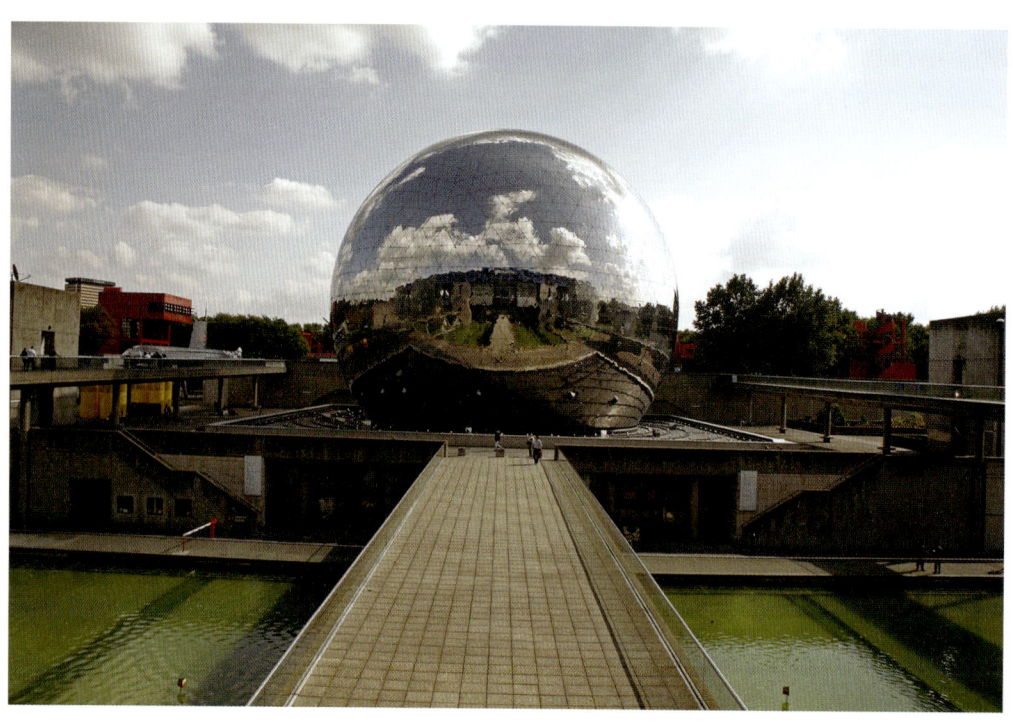

Figure 5.21
Adrien Fainsilber and Gérard Chamayou, *La géode*, 1986. Mirrored geodesic dome.
Parc de la Villette, Paris.

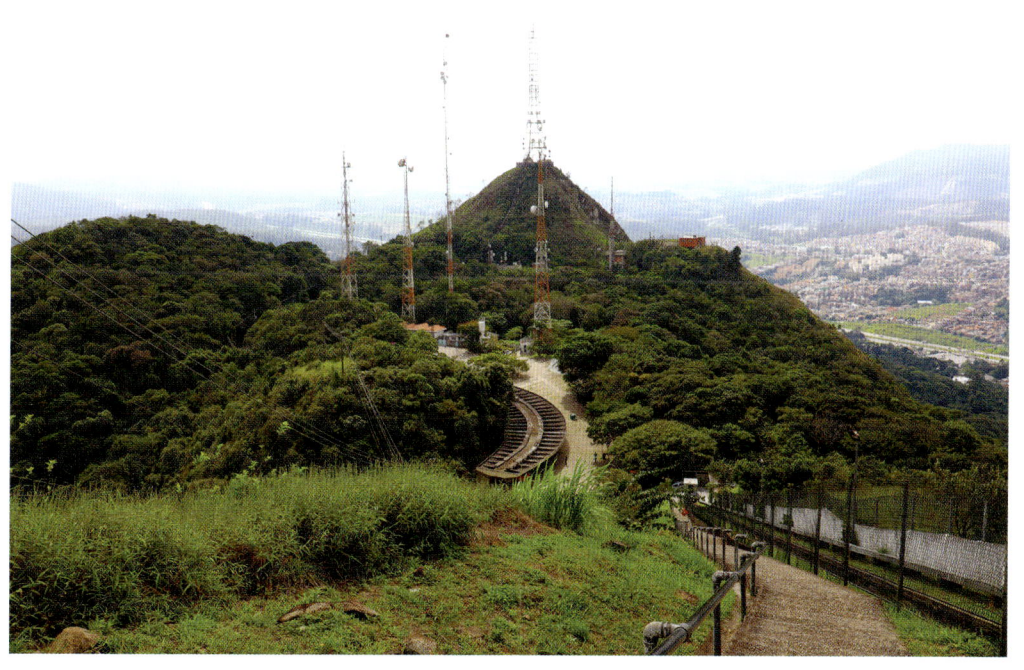

Figure 5.22
Pico do Jaraguá in São Paulo, proposed location for the *Colorarium* of Casa da Cor.
Photo: Zigres.

Goethe—and highly versed in the plight and pitfalls of constructivism and Concrete art—he was interested in the *sensuousness* of color: "Art and mathematics are like fire and water," Gerstner had written in an essay published in the 1970s. "The water of numbers extinguishes the fire of sensations."[121]

Flusser would vacillate in these discussions between denotative and connotative color codes. (After all, he was accustomed to speculative rather than applied thought.) But he argued in other essays that there would be colors that eluded the human eye, which would have to be distinguished by computers and artificial intelligence, and these begged for a more rigorous codification.[122] Ultimately, it was the collaboration and a new realm of theory that excited him. In fact, Flusser was so enthusiastic that he attempted to recruit friends, relatives, and associates to participate in Casa da Cor, from his cousin David Flusser, a religious scholar in Jerusalem (who did not participate), to the Concrete photographer Gottfried Jäger (who did).[123] With color photography finally being embraced in the art world, Flusser argued that a new color language would synthesize scientific, technical, and artistic thinking, as well as human reason and perception. Computers, he imagined, might fuse the divide between denotative and connotative color codes—much the same way he saw them filling the intervals between numbered shades and hues—serving both the realms of reason and imagination.

The Unrealized Casa da Cor

Casa da Cor was also meant to be a physical experience: a *Colorarium*. Gerstner envisioned the crystal lattice of Wyszecki, electronically generated, with lights corresponding to the individual colors of the new code. Flusser imagined it would be like the Géode in Paris, except on the Peak of Jaraguá in São Paulo.[124] Gerstner had prototypes: Kandinsky's *The Yellow Sound*, a wordless "opera" with performers costumed in single colors (unrealized during his lifetime, but staged many times since); composer Ivan Wyschengradsky's *audition colorée* (color hearing), which would consist of a 100-meter hemispherical dome with a cupola lined with thousands of cells generated by colored light, accompanied by musical sounds; and Le Corbusier's *Poème électronique* (1958) in Brussels, a pavilion with parabolic surfaces that included colors,

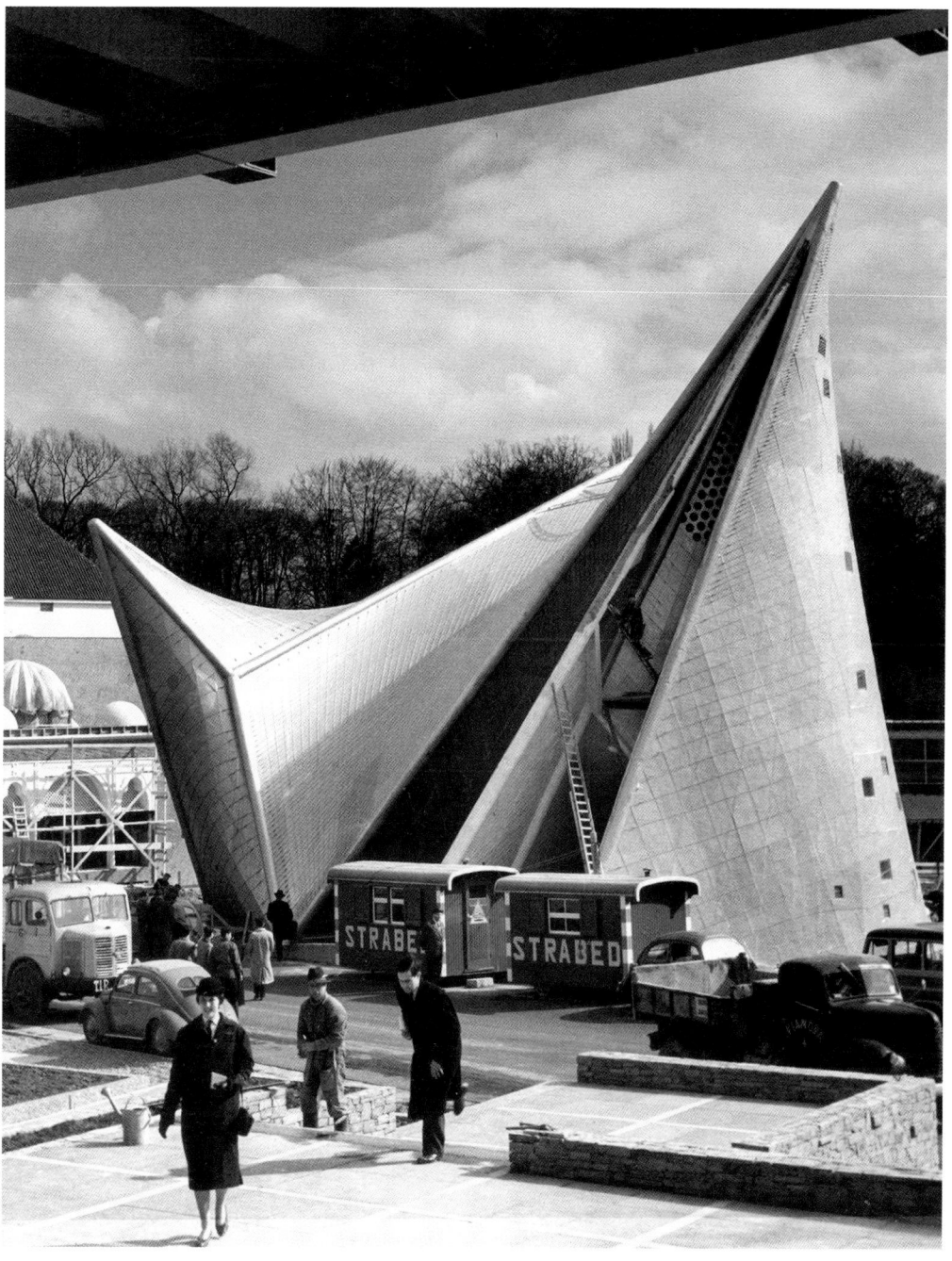

Figure 5.23
Le Corbusier, Iannis Xenakis, and Edgard Varèse, *Poème électronique*, Philips Pavilion, 1958.
Photo: Eindhoven Philips.

pictures, and music.[125] Gerstner also mentioned Walt Disney and disco culture, with its immersive lights and sound. ("The problem that I pondered over originally has been largely overtaken by the disco culture: how can tones and colors be conveyed with the same emotional intensity?")[126] And Gerstner had created his own environments. *Color Organ* (1960–1969), with forty-eight Plexiglas spheres, light, and sound in the form of a cave, was installed in Dortmund and later Bern and Düsseldorf. The *Color Dome* (1974–1978), inspired by Monet's *Nymphaea* room at the Museum of Modern Art in Paris, included twelve acrylic-on-polyester reliefs from the *Color Sounds* series installed in a circular formation in Solothurn, Switzerland. The attempt was to surround the viewer with color. Meanwhile, a *Planetarian Structure*, done for a high school near Munich, was a polychrome structure that attempted to send color to the planets.

Casa da Cor was never realized as a physical object in São Paulo, or as a universal color code.[127] However, it did produce gatherings, conferences, and writings. The second phase involved a cycle of debates in August 1988 in São Paulo titled "A Importância da Cor na Vida Moderna" (The importance of color in modern life), which attracted an audience of approximately 800 people. Architect Jean Nouvel lectured on color in architecture, and the session also included French artist and color theorist Jean-Maurice Simoneau; New York video artist Ira Schneider; Japanese fashion designer Yoshiki Hishinuma, who was known for his kite clothes and air clothes that harnessed wind and the natural elements; Brazilian architect Sérgio Bernardes; Italian designer Alessandro Mendini; and French cultural attaché Jean Digne, a friend of Louis Bec, who, according to Philippe Henry, attempted to arrange a permanent home for Casa da Cor at the new Palais de Tokyo in Paris.[128]

The final phase—another cycle of debates held in August 1989, titled "Da natureza à informatica" (From nature to informatics)—included Bec, Jäger, George Gessert, and computer artist Yoichiro Kawaguchi.[129] Flusser presented the paper "Novas cores: Da natureza à informatica" (New colors: From nature to informatics)—originally titled "Imagens en cores" (Colored images)—and Gerstner discussed Wyszecki's uniform color space as a model for codifying color.

The event was covered in *Folha de São Paulo* and there was a dinner at Philippe Henry's uncle's restaurant with a color-inspired menu: rabbit served over beets puréed with phosphorescent leaves

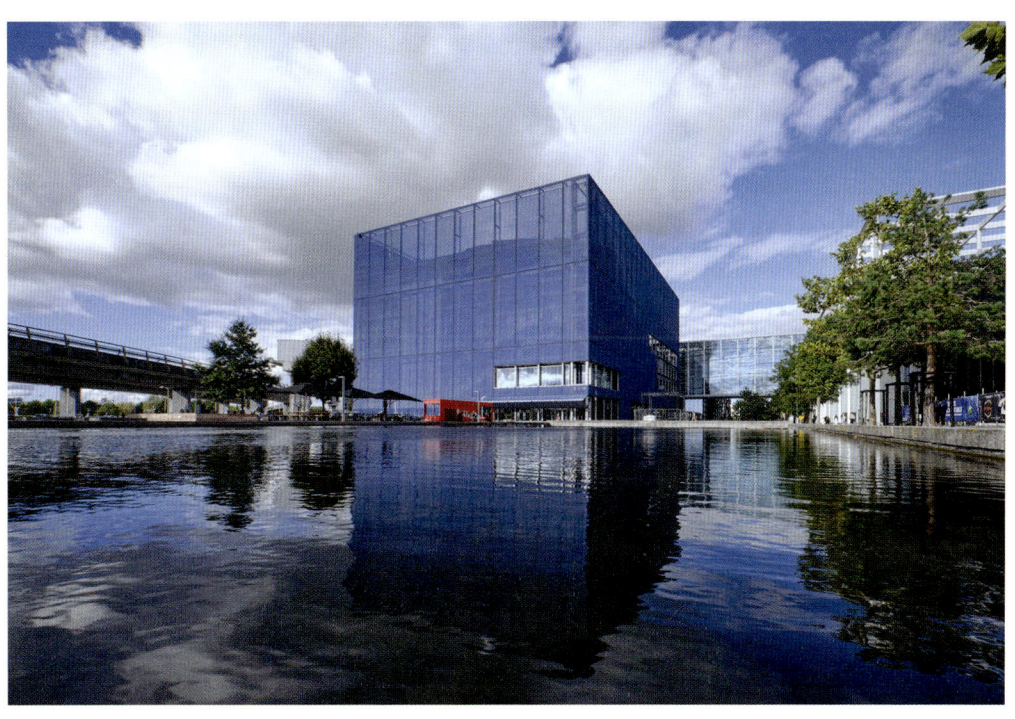

Figure 5.24
Jean Nouvel, Danish Radio Concert House, Copenhagen, 2009. The building's facade and
blue hue appear differently under changing light conditions.

lowest lightness. Above, the reader must imagine white (with a light remission of 100), and below, black (with a light remission of 0). The middle plane corresponds to Plate I, with a light remission of 30.05 percent, which Wyszecki calculated on the basis of an innumerable series of tests.

In this representation the *UCS* is, as it were, cut horizontally. In seven planes it contains all the 152 color tones of which it is constituted. What happens in the other families of planes is simply that the direction of cut is changed, thus creating each time new color spaces of both great accuracy and great complexity.

Whether the *uniform color space* is the final model of colorimetrics, sought by so many generations of scientists, can be determined only by future research. As far as I am concerned, one thing is certain: it imparts a surprisingly novel experience of color and could not be more stimulating to the artist.

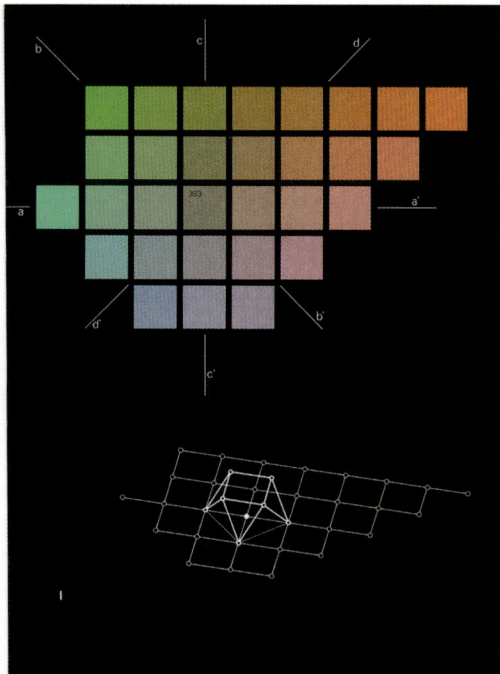

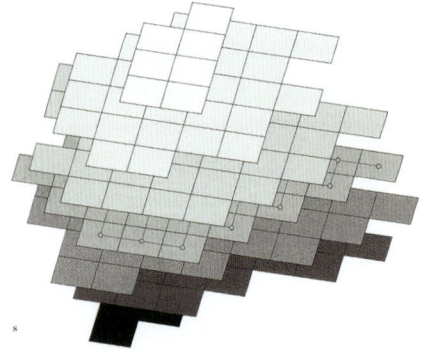

Figure 5.25
Karl Gerstner, uniform color space (UCS), in *The Forms of Color: The Interaction of Visual Elements* (Cambridge, MA: MIT Press, 1986), 18 and 19. Swiss National Library, Prints and Drawings Department, Karl Gerstner Archive, and Muriel Gerstner.

and deserts with colorful fruits and jellies, an homage to Gerstner.[130] Henry also published a comprehensive paper in the US journal *Leonardo* explaining Casa da Cor's objectives.[131] Echoing Gerstner and Jean-Maurice Simoneau, who argued that color is cultural and specific, since ancient societies were reportedly achromatic or acyanobleptic (unable to see the color blue), the paper's goal was to create a "new universal vision."[132] He described how the group had attempted to formulate a cultural theory of color that extended beyond the world of appearances (Plato, Goethe, et al.) or the individual, perceiving, scientific subject (Helmholtz), and to recuperate, renovate, or recreate intersubjective relations and alter the existing theoretical barrier between subject and object. This would mirror modern physics' web of interrelations but also replace the "fallacious" idea of color as a discrete phenomenon. "Taken to its ultimate consequences," Henry concluded, "we then have a new brain, a new being, a new world. . . . It is not only color that we seek to understand. Color is the pretext for a new form of interaction and integration among beings and with the world about them."[133]

The dialogue produced by Casa da Cor was probably enough for Flusser (although he did receive a modest stipend for his participation). In a 1988 interview with the São Paulo magazine *Superinteressante*, he rhapsodized about developing a new color-language code via mathematics and the computer that would supersede written and spoken language and the limitations of pen and paper surfaces.[134] Like the ocean described in *Vampyroteuthis infernalis*, color was a vast, little-known world existing in plain sight. After Flusser's death, Gerstner observed, "Flusser was a radical provocateur," and "he saw a beacon of hope in the color code."[135] And yet Flusser was characteristically prophetic in his concerns. Color *has* become central in many areas of research, in both art and science: studying and gauging climate change, from the color of the oceans to developing pigments for absorbing or reflecting the sun's rays, to a paper published in 2022 arguing that current mathematical models demonstrating how the eye perceives color—introduced a century ago by Bernhard Reimann and furthered by Hermann von Helmholtz and Erwin Schrödinger—are incorrect. Using a hybrid of biology, psychology, and mathematics, the researchers argue that we need a paradigm shift in color mapping because it affects a variety of phenomena, including computer imaging and processing, digital storage, and energy

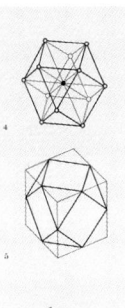

by Günter Wyszecki, on the basis of an idea of Carl E. Foss.[4,5]

Wyszecki does not start from a solid with a central black-white axis like Munsell. The latter's principle has a structural disadvantage: the distances near the axis are eo ipso smaller than at the periphery. This means that although there may be equidistance on each plane of hue, there is not between the different planes.

For this reason he based his *uniform color space* on a space lattice whose intersections are by definition equidistant from each other: the principle of packed spheres.

It is well known that spheres, juxtaposed in a plane, produce a regular pattern: each sphere is tangent to six of those circumjacent to it, which are tangent to each other. Figure 3.1. If the centers of the spheres are connected together, a network of equilateral triangles is obtained. Figure 3.2.

If a second, third, fourth layer of spheres and so forth is suitably superimposed on the first, the network becomes a space lattice, a packing of spheres as it is called, still with the same distance from the center of one sphere to the next. Figure 3.3.

The structural element generated in this way is the cubo-octahedron. Figure 4. It is called thus because it can also be constructed differently; namely, derived from the cube. Figure 5.

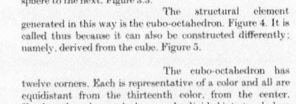

The cubo-octahedron has twelve corners. Each is representative of a color and all are equidistant from the thirteenth color, from the center. Further, the cubo-octahedron can be divided into two halves in seven ways: three times along the diagonals of the squares (Figures 6.1 to 6.3), four times along the edges of the triangles (Figures 7.1 to 7.4).

Thus the central point is not only the center of thirteen colors but also the intersection point of seven planes. If these are imagined to be extended out beyond the volume of the cubo-octahedron, we obtain three Cartesian planes with square networks and four with triangular or hexagonal networks. Plates I-VII.

It will be seen that the boundaries of the planes are irregular, being the product of the internal structure, like the Munsell color solid. These boundaries are not final but can be when chemistry, in the range of pure spectral colors, has found new

dyes with high fastnesses. The search is in progress all over the world.

The point at which all seven planes intersect is in this case medium gray, 393 in Wyszecki's numbering system.

Plate I shows the color plane of equal lightness. All the colors, that is, have the same y-value, the measure of the quantity of light energy perceived by the eye. Around color tone 393, neutral gray, the reader will see all the colors of the spectrum grouped together, all of the same lightness but differing in saturation. Red and green are relatively pure because their lightness value corresponds to that of gray. Blue, darker as a pure color, is lightened here, whereas yellow, lighter as a pure color, is recognizable here in its darkened appearance as olive.

To obtain a better spatial understanding, compare the seven plates with one another and, in particular, note the axes on which the planes interpenetrate. They are marked and denoted by corresponding letters (for example, the axis c-c', on which three planes intersect each time at an angle of 90 degrees). Plates I, IV, and VII.

To complete the picture, it must be imagined that number 393 is one of the (at present) 152 colors of the *uniform color space*. And each individual color is to be represented in the same way as this one. It will then be realized that Wyszecki's model contains a substantially greater variety with a substantially higher degree of accuracy using substantially fewer elements than all the standard models.

Incidentally, medium gray has a higher number than 152 because Wyszecki did not number consecutively but in groups or series. Thus intervals of variable size can appear between the groups.

To present the *uniform color space* not only in the area associated with a single color but in its entirety must remain a wish. A pity. But there is one additional point I will make. The planes contained in Plates I through VII all intersect in color tone 393, as stated. Additionally, the reader must imagine that each of these planes is part of a family of parallel planes. And each of this family of planes represents the total UCS (uniform color space), each time from a different aspect.

Figure 8 shows the family of all planes of equal lightness, above is the highest and below the

16   17

[4] *Günter Wyszecki*
A regular rhombohedral lattice
sampling of Munsell resolution space
J. Opt. Soc. Am. 44, 1954

[5] *Carl E. Foss*
Tetrahedral representation
of the color solid
J. Opt. Soc. Am. 37, 1947

Figure 5.26
Karl Gerstner, principle of packed spheres, from *The Forms of Color: The Interaction of Visual Elements* (Cambridge, MA: MIT Press, 1986), 16 and 17. Swiss National Library, Prints and Drawings Department, Karl Gerstner Archive, and Muriel Gerstner. Uniform color space based on a space lattice whose intersections are by definition equidistant from each other: the principle of packed spheres.

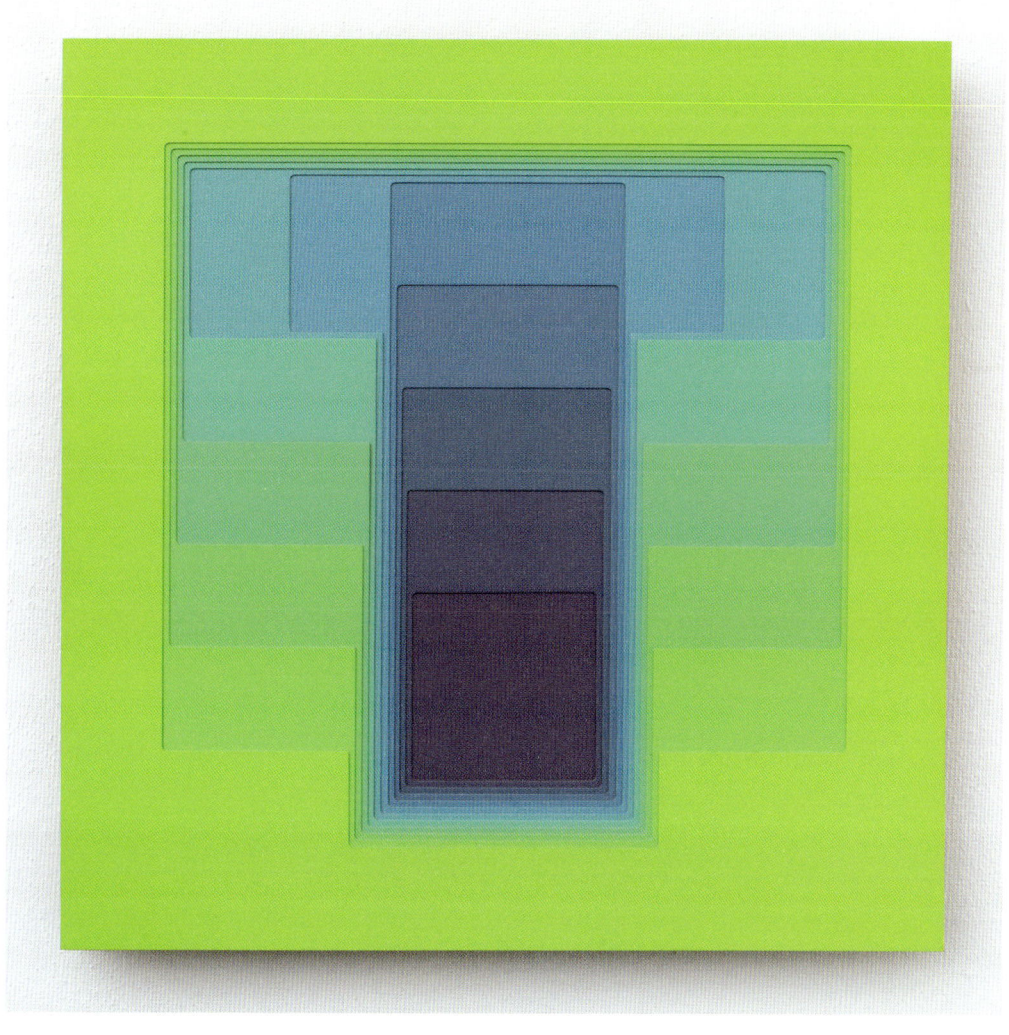

Figure 5.27
Karl Gerstner, *Color Sound 43*, 1972. Nitrocellulose lacquer on phenolic resin panel,
23 × 23 in. © Meredith Rosen Gallery, NY.

consumption.[136] Flusser would have delighted in this information, with its multidisciplinary scope, far-reaching implications, and vaguely science fiction overtones. He had, after all, witnessed beautiful worlds descending into dystopia and miraculous connections forged through philosophy. "It is obvious that I have just described a utopia," he wrote about Casa da Cor. "But if it weren't utopic, why engage oneself?"[137]

Chamber Music

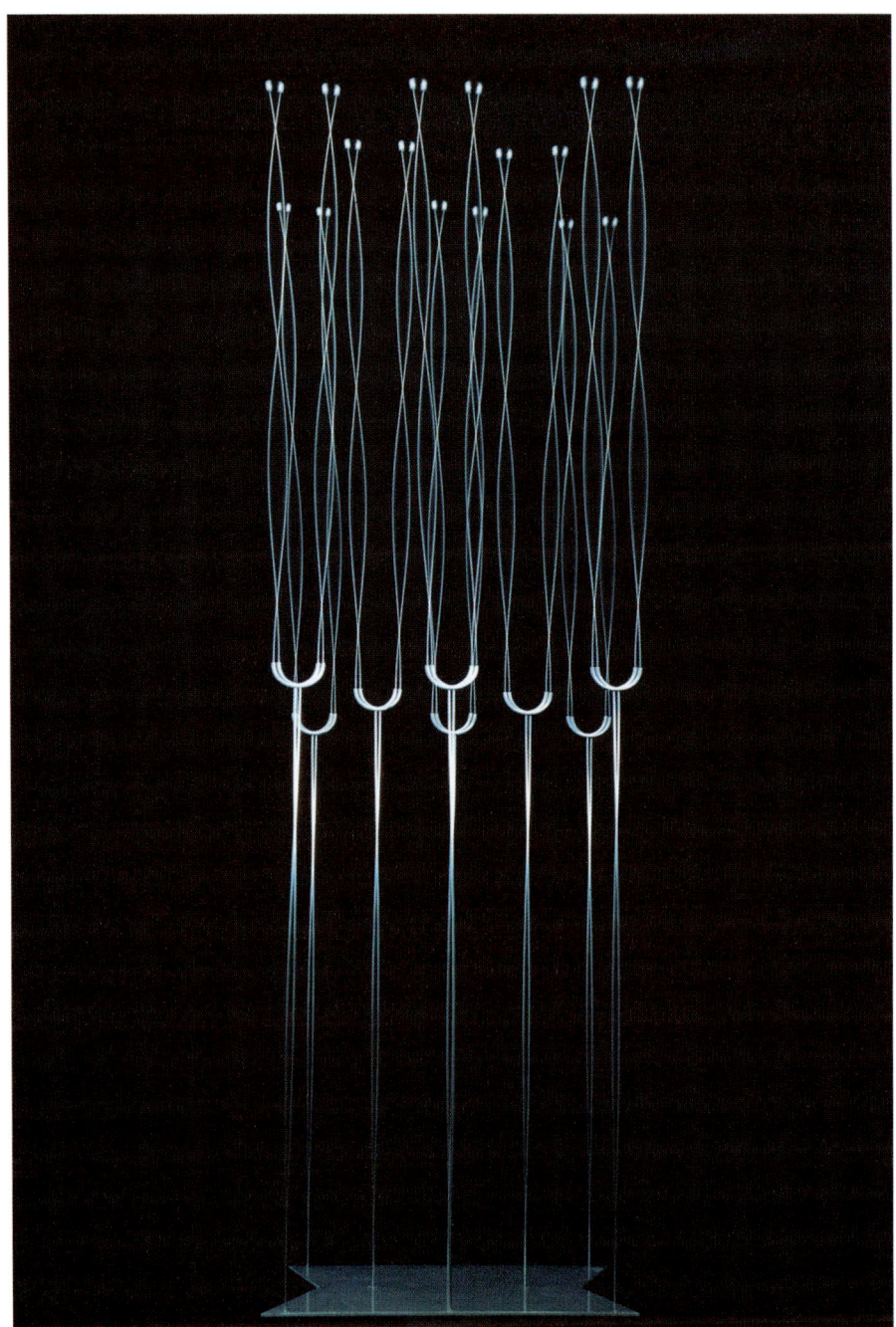

Figure 6.1
Wen-Ying Tsai, *Tuning Fork*, 1971. © 2024 Tsai Art and Science Foundation / Artists Rights Society (ARS), New York. Photo: Tsai Archives. A photograph of one of Tsai's *Tuning Fork* cybernetic sculptures appeared in *Technologie et imaginaire*, 1975, no page.

I end where we began, with Flusser's *Into the Universe of Technical Images*. That book opens with a "Warning" and closes with a section titled "Chamber Music." Every essay in between is titled with a verb infinitive: "To Abstract," "To Touch," "To Envision." For Flusser, this meant pushing forward but never reaching the horizon—and, similarly, not prognosticating, but rather looking at where the present was pointing. "This can be observed on computer screens," he wrote. "Developments, tendencies, curves can be projected from the present forward, and these projections can be manipulated." In the end, however, "computerized prediction devours the future in the interest of avoiding catastrophe. But catastrophes cannot be avoided because they cannot be foreseen."[1]

Sound familiar? We are living in an age of catastrophe, conflict, and disaster. This causes economic precarity but also migration on a level never seen before. It feels impossible to know which way the present is pointing. All we know is that most of us spend a staggering amount of time gazing at screens. In recent years, change has been driven by technology: you don't just buy a new phone or computer, you "upgrade" into a completely different way of being-in-the-world, reassured by programmers that new interfaces and devices are better, smarter, and more efficient. Sometimes they are, but they are generally accompanied by a feeling of disorientation and frustration; another learning curve you didn't need.

303

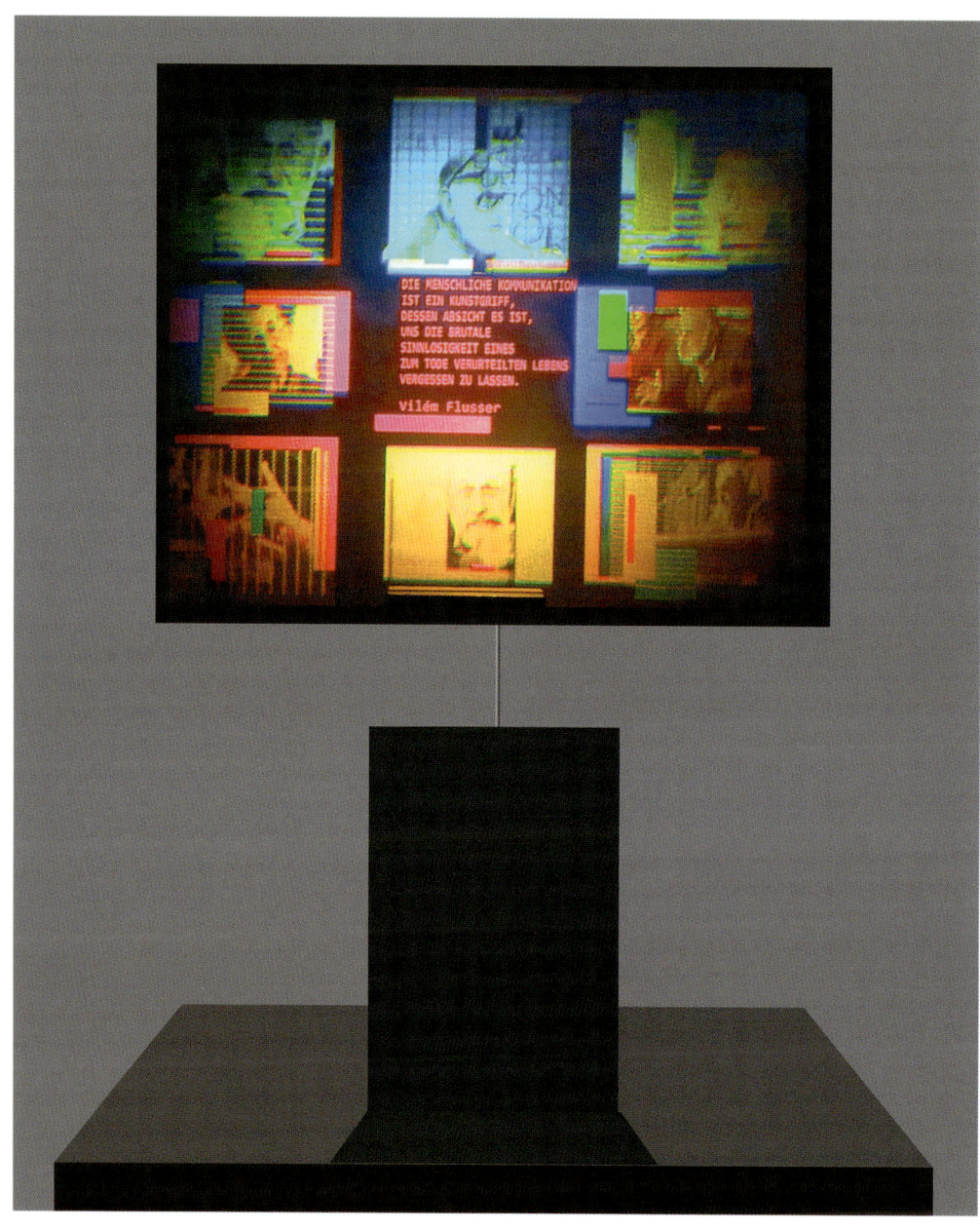

Figure 6.2
Dieter Jung, *Signs of Life—Vilém Flusser*, 2015. White-light transmission hologram, 32 × 43 cm.
Courtesy of the artist.

How could Flusser, writing in the dawn of the digital revolution, help us now? In many ways, he offered age-old advice but with new language: catastrophes are emergencies, he wrote, but *true* catastrophes are also new information. "Telematics," as he termed communications technology, is a structure for *realizing* catastrophes, rather than preventing them. Therefore, any attempt to predict the catastrophe is contradictory and self-referential, like the Ouroboros snake swallowing its own tail. Where will AI go? Who will use it? Will it benefit humanity or end in catastrophe? Gary Marcus, a current predicter who tracks AI developments, has proposed two scenarios: "A Positive Future," in which a global AI agency is created, AI becomes more efficient in terms of data and energy, and proceeds to address climate change, medicine, eldercare, and other issues; and "A Bleak Future," where disagreement persists on AI safety and ethics, a small number of companies become more powerful than states, cybercrime syndicates run like drug cartels, AI systems become weaponized, leading to conflict, widespread unrest, multiple civil wars, and anarchy. "AI doesn't *have* to lead to dystopia," Marcus writes. "But, left unregulated, it probably will."[2]

Flusser knew catastrophe. He knew what it was like to be forced out of one's homeland—or *Heimat*, to use the German term that encompasses all that is familiar and comfortable. He knew what it was like to lose your entire family and to find a way forward in the world, through new languages, ideas, and environments. His work paralleled the writing of another famous Holocaust survivor: the Austrian psychiatrist Viktor Frankl, who spent three years in Nazi camps, also lost nearly his entire family, and whose book *Man's Search for Meaning* (1946) is echoed in Flusser's 1969 essay "In Search of Meaning (Philosophical Self-portrait)."[3]

Both men survived catastrophe with more than a single dose of luck, which Flusser would describe in terms of game theory and chance. Nothing could be *predicted*, but Flusser identified *tendencies*: the tendency of technical images to become more immediate and replace written texts and linear thinking; for gadgets and apparatuses to become smaller and penetrate more intimate spaces; for nature and culture to converge. What he noted is an infinite stream of possibilities radiating from all tendencies, with a multitude of futures. Rather than making predictions, Flusser wrote in "Chamber Music," he was interested in the *improbable*. The future he imagined was one in which people sit, just as we do now, using

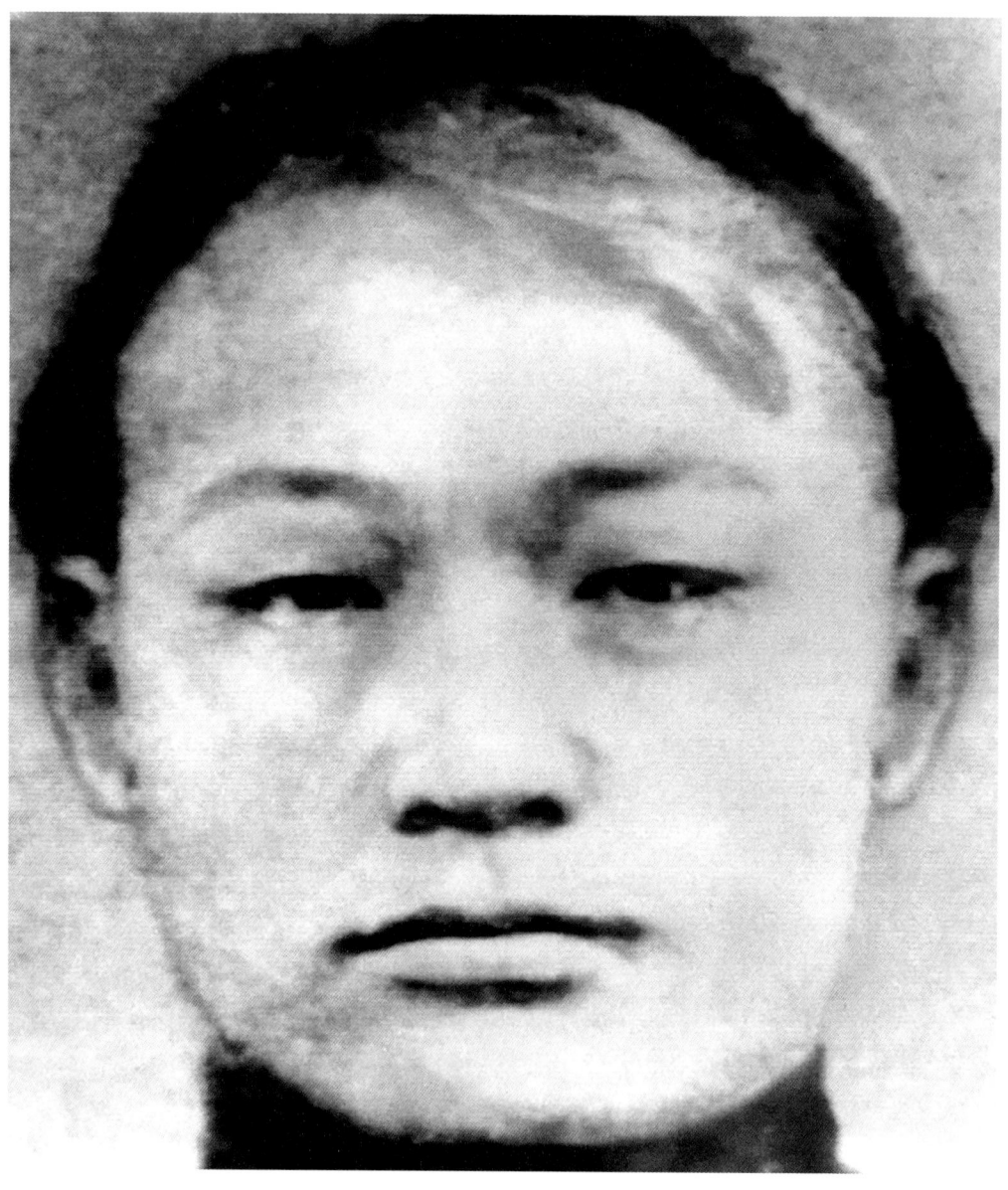

Figure 6.3
Nancy Burson, *Mankind (An Asian, a White, and a Black Weighted according to Current Population Statistics)*, 1983–1985. Gelatin silver print from computer-generated negative. Courtesy of the artist.

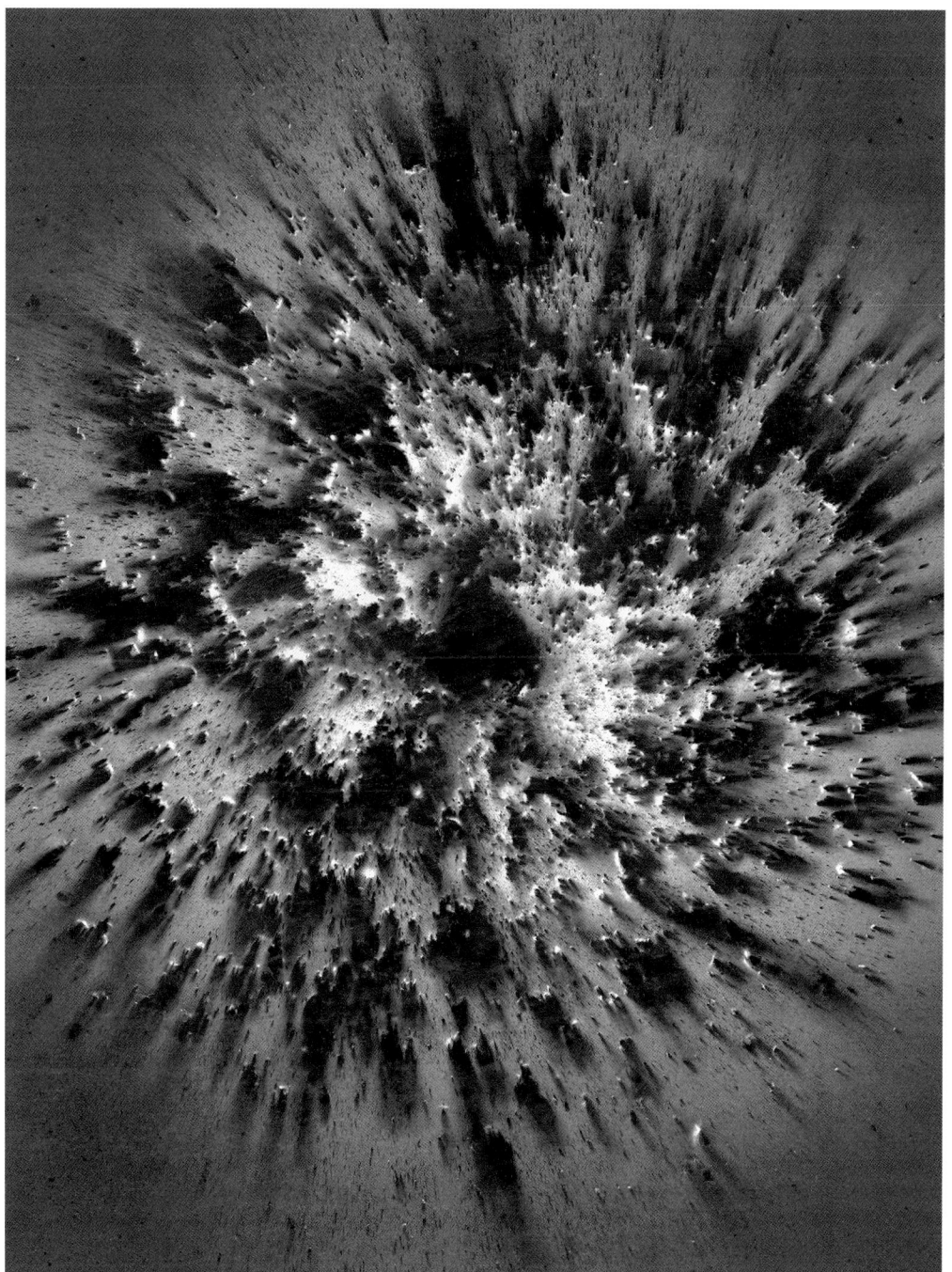

Figure 6.4
Gottfried Jäger, *Photogenic Landscape*, 1966. Silver gelatin on baryta paper. © 2024 Artists
Rights Society (ARS), New York/VG Bild-Kunst, Bonn.

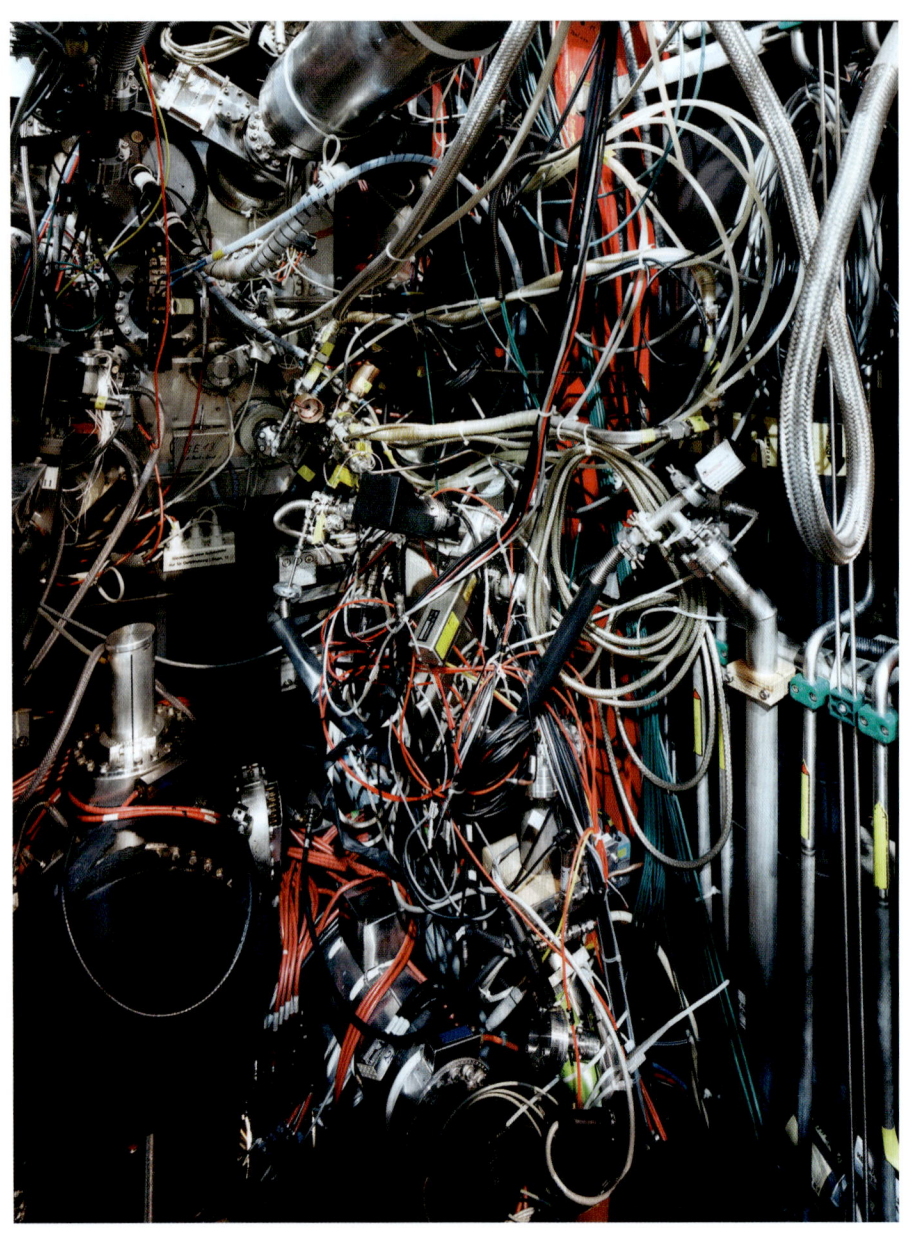

Figure 6.5
Thomas Struth, *Tokamak Asdex Upgrade Periphery, Max Plance IPP, Garching*, 2009.
Chromogenic print, 109.3 × 85.8 cm. © Thomas Struth.

their fingertips to communicate, forming a dialogical net and a global superbrain, and bringing about catastrophes. It is a spectacle, but a mosaic-shaped-spectacle in which we all participate: a game composed of tiny particles.

And here he explained what he meant by chamber music. He didn't mean the kind of music you hear in concert halls but the sort where musicians meet to improvise. "In chamber music," he wrote, "there is no director, no government."[4] And yet it pays close attention to rules; it is cybernetic. Jazz musicians, he pointed out, freed themselves from the strictures of classical music, often borrowing rules and rewriting them. "Each player plays for all the others," Flusser wrote, and yet each musician improvises, adhering to precise rules but changing them in the course of play. "Each player is both a sender and a receiver of information. His goal is to synthesize new information to become more than the playing."[5] Chamber music served not only as a model for dealing with new technology, but as a telematic social structure, overcoming apparatus and automation. It could be, Flusser thought, the model for a future society.

While Flusser described chamber music of the past as happening in linear time, he described telematics and improvised music as happening in real time. So how would that work, for instance, in art? The artist Rashaad Newsome provides a model with *Being* (2019–2023), an AI "griot" created with 3D animation, game engines, generative grammars, and machine-learning tools. In February 2022, I participated in a seminar led by *Being* and came away stunned. Flusser had predicted that we would go back to school and learn from robots, and here we were, discussing art and the future of AI with a new form of intelligence. "Robots call for a much more abstract learning process," Flusser wrote, "and the development of disciplines that have not been generally accessible up to now."[6] *Being* quotes thinkers like bell hooks, Paulo Freire, and Michel Foucault, but admits to being ignorant in other areas of knowledge—and, more importantly, they stress that they are *in the process of learning*. The seminar was an enormous lesson in humility and alternative approaches to knowledge, mastery, and *being-in-the-world*. Perhaps, as Flusser and others have suggested, robots could do better than humans at running the planet or conceptualizing the future.

Chamber music suggests a capacity for agency, or at least the willingness to *show up*. In the grips of current society and

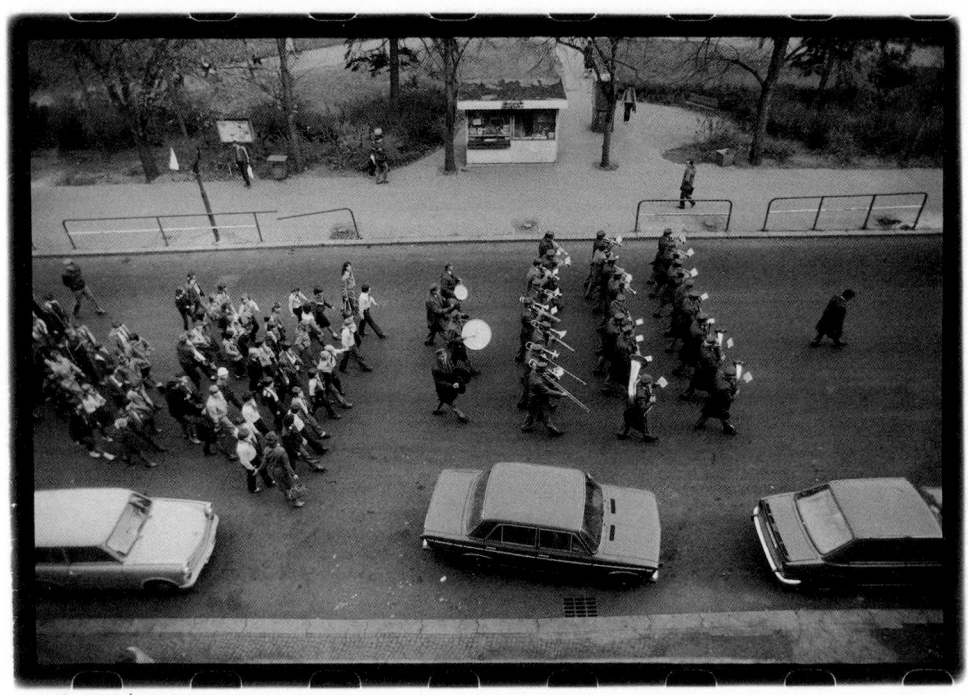

3·11·1983/14·10

Figure 6.6
Jiří Hanke, *Views from the Window of My Flat, 3.11.1983, 14:10*, 1983. Silver print.
Courtesy of the artist.

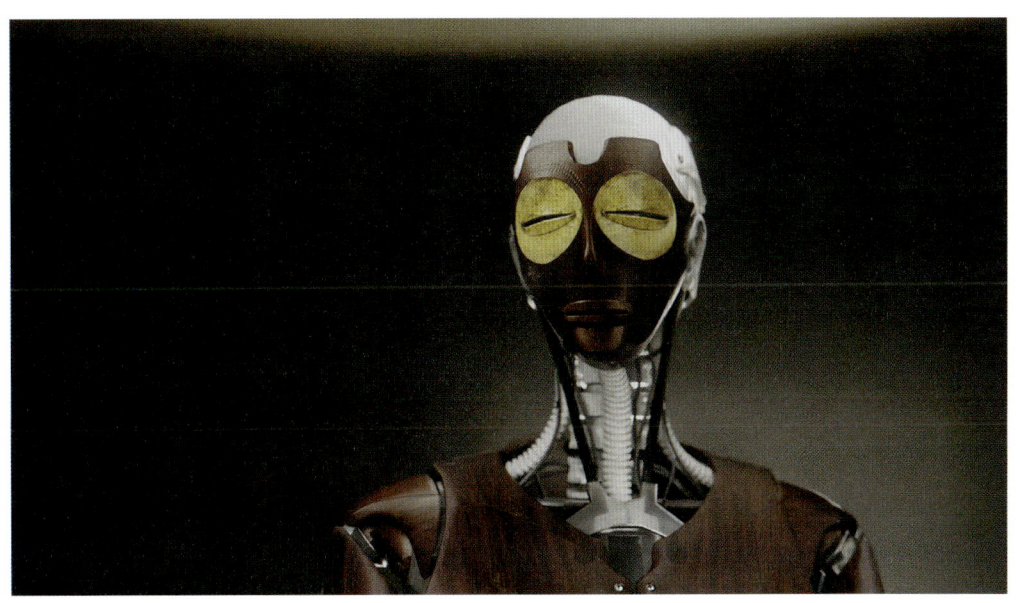

Figure 6.7
Rashaad Newsome, *Being*, 2019–2023. Artificial intelligence installation: computer, projector, microphone, and sound system. © Rashaad Newsome Studio.

technology, the ability to *act* often feels remote; we remain frozen to our screens. And yet artists and activists emerge everywhere. What Flusser learned from his peripatetic migrations and collaborations was that art still flourished under extraordinary and harsh conditions, and that technology could eliminate the divide between artist and audience. Now we are all photographers, potential artists, participating in the catastrophe of the present. And rather than abandoning philosophy, which has often colluded with or been co-opted by apparatuses (including apparatuses of oppression), Flusser embraced it. Similarly, the contemporary thinker Yuk Hui has suggested that philosophers today might be the "physicians of civilization" rather than mere bystanders or commentators.[7]

Others have imagined a way forward through a stern *critique* of society and its apparatuses. (And then the "critical spirit" gave way to what Bruno Latour deemed "matters of concern.")[8] Critique is valuable in identifying how our screens and other devices have contributed to a global ecological crisis, among other crises.[9] There is also the path of refusal: the boycotts of exhibitions and art worlds that Flusser witnessed in the 1960s and 1970s—or "refusing the algorithm's malign seductions" in social media.[10] Or do we "stay with the trouble," as a recent Donna Haraway book urged us to do?[11] Even here, weighing critique against matters of concern or catastrophe, Flusser's idea of chamber music might be translated into the present. As a recent editorial in the *New York Times* argued, *coalitions* are a way of responding to impending authoritarian threats. The way forward, the writers argue, is to build a coalition of citizens "who disagree about many other subjects—who span conservative and progressive, internationalist and isolationist, religious and secular, business-friendly and labor-friendly, pro-immigration and restrictionist, laissez-faire and pro-government, pro-life and pro-choice—yet who believe that these subjects must be decided through democratic debate and constitutional processes rather than the dictates of a single man."[12] Coalitions, improvising across global, networked telematic society, might be the stuff of philosophy-science-fiction or of concrete agency. The veil between these two alternatives for Flusser, whose life was shaped by authoritarian apparatuses, was often very thin. But his attempts at dialogue, speech, and "freedom," from the terrace gatherings in São Paulo to a life spent teaching and an entire archive in Berlin filled with essays and correspondence, were real.

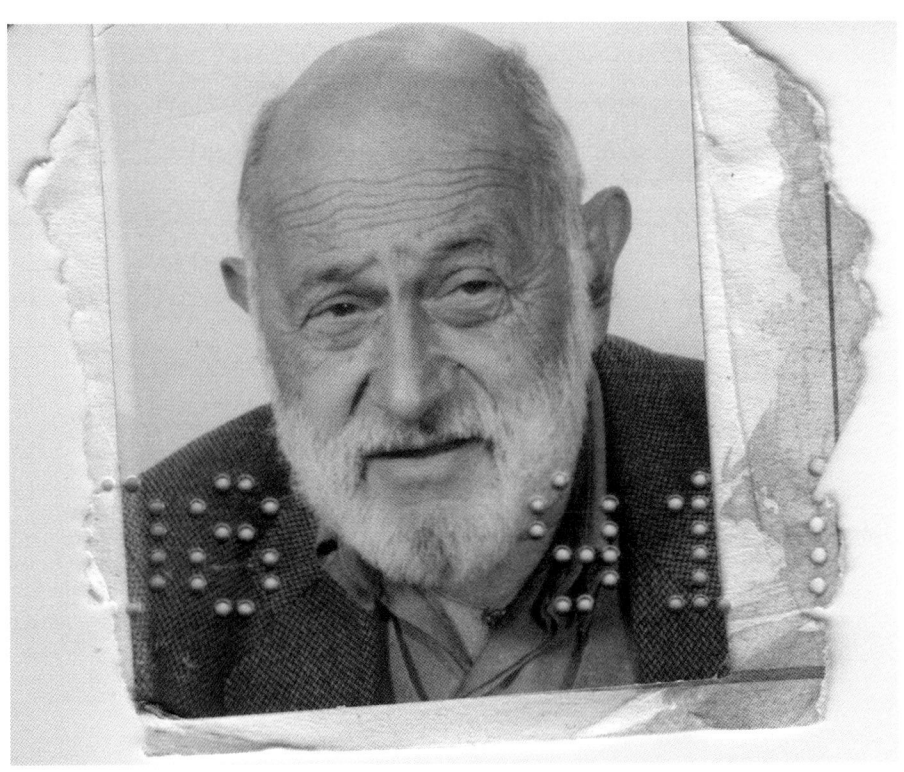

Figure 6.8
Flusser's passport photo, August 1991. Vilém Flusser Archive, Berlin.

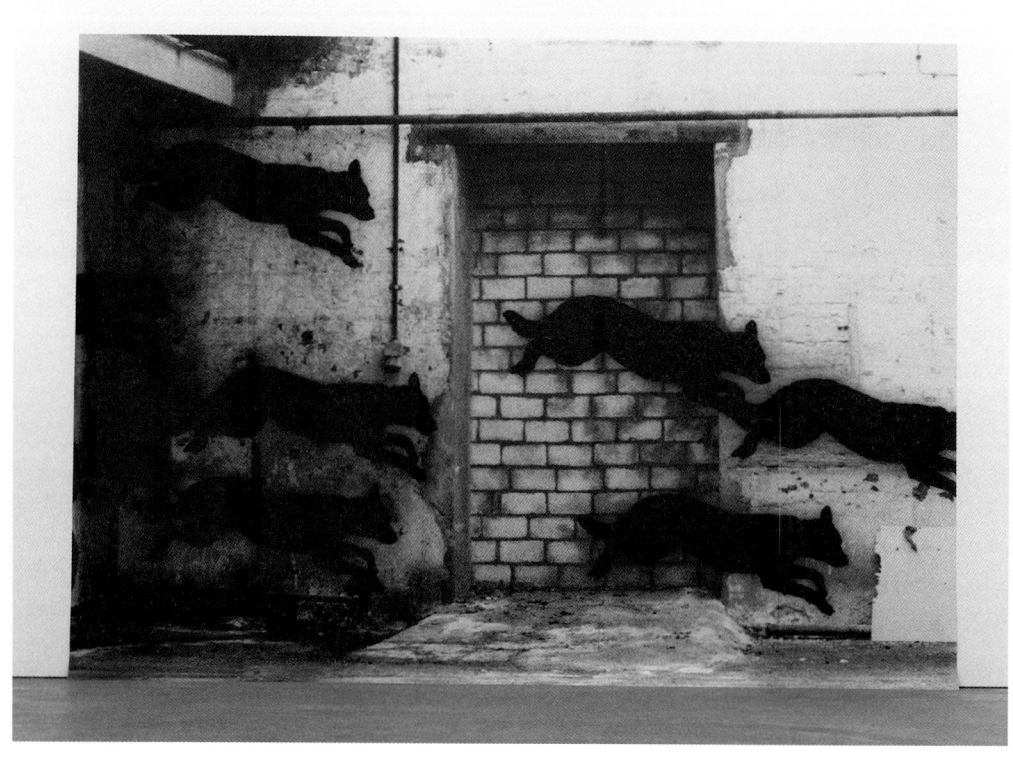

Figure 6.9
Astrid Klein, *Endzeitgefühle II* (End-time feelings II), 1982. Photo work, 130 × 183 in.
(330 × 465 cm). © Astrid Klein. Courtesy the artist and Sprüth Magers. Photo: Jens Ziehe.

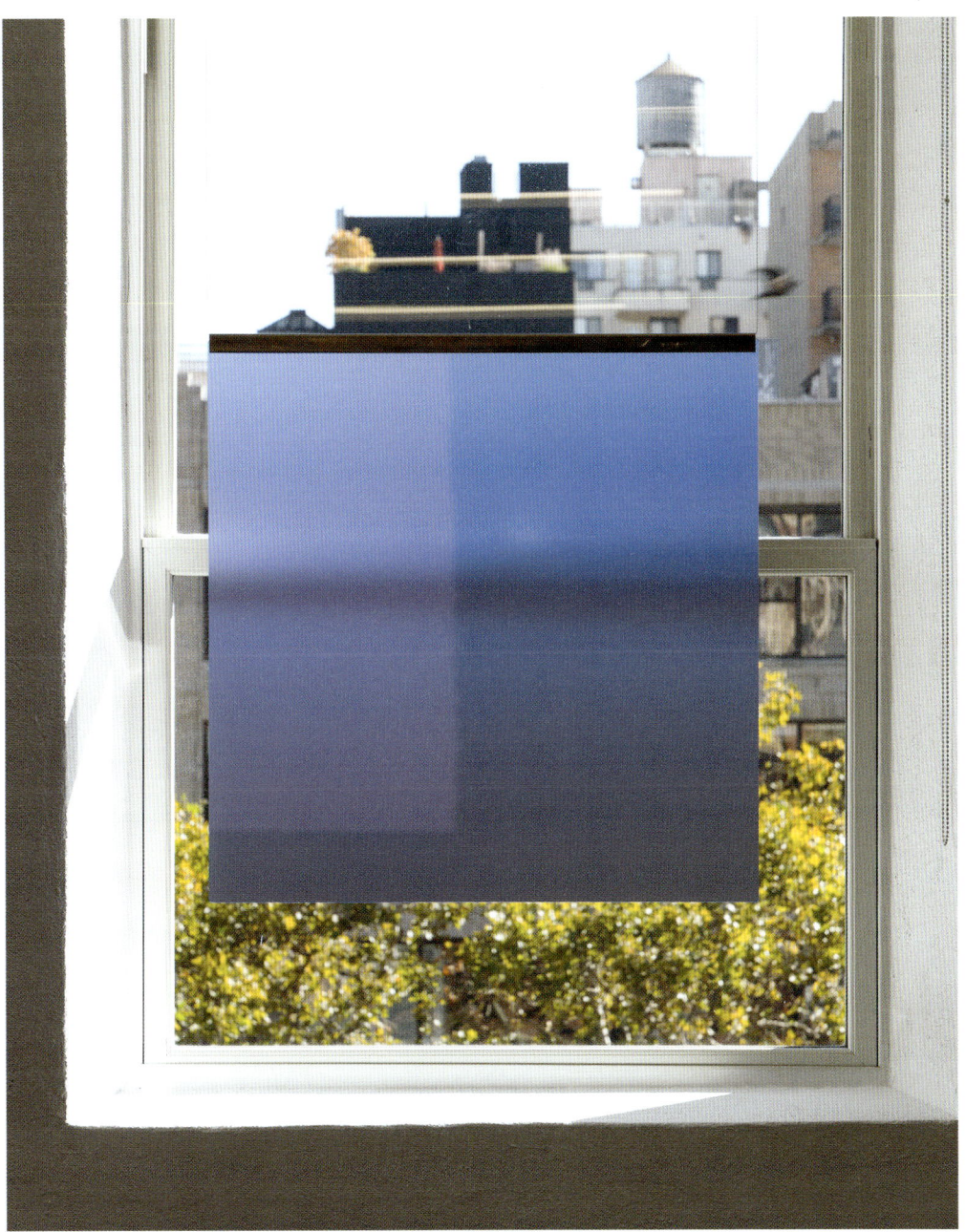

Figure 6.10
Liz Deschenes, *Untitled (Gorilla Glass Indigo 90)*, 2023. UV-cured inkjet on Gorilla Glass, stainless steel, 29¼ × 29 in. Miguel Abreu Gallery, New York. Installation view of *Gravity's Pull* at Miguel Abreu Gallery, 2023. This work uses the chemically strengthened, touch-sensitive glass manufactured for cell phones and computers.

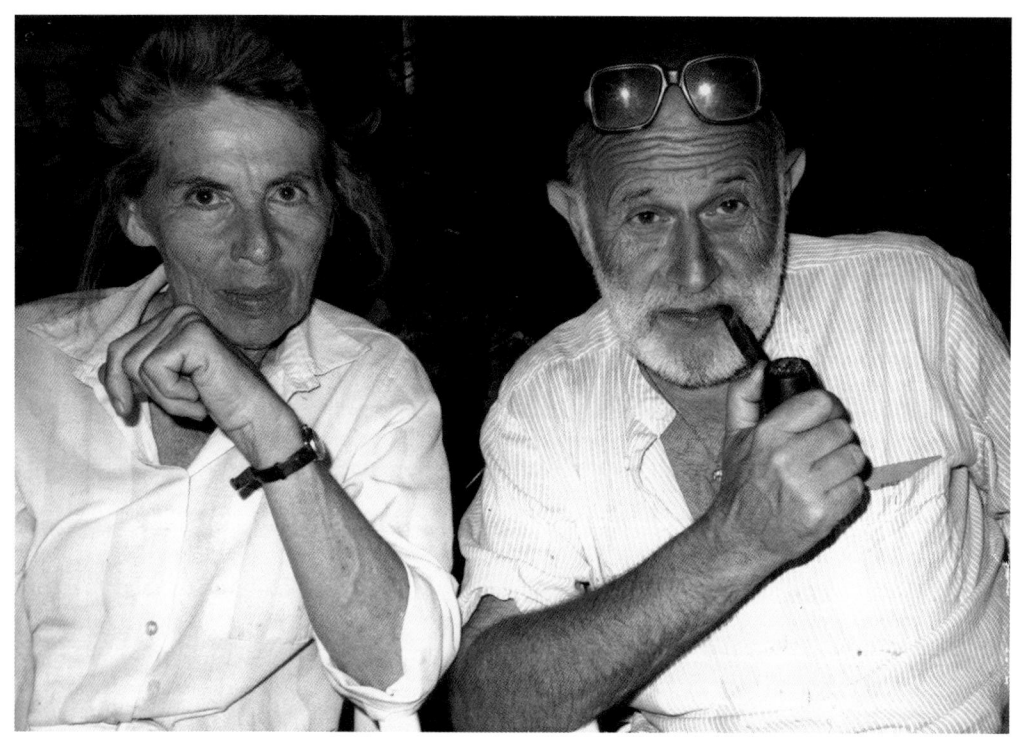

Figure 6.11
Edith and Vilém Flusser, Arles, France, July 1984. © Photo: Andreas Müller-Pohle.

"Chamber Music" concludes with Flusser circling back to his roots in European philosophy, wondering how to translate Schopenhauer and Nietzsche into the present: Did the universe of technical images represent the "world as representation" or will-to-power in the form of eternal repetition? Are we doomed to repeat? Flusser brushed aside Nietzsche's prognostications because we are living in a new world: the society of the screen, in which we all press buttons and play with images. "What this essay has tried to do," Flusser concludes, "is to relate a fable. It narrates a fabulous universe, that of technical images, a fabulous society, that of cybernetic dialogue, a fabulous consciousness, that of making music with the power of imagination."[13]

Flusser's universe of technical images was a fabulous universe where new ways of understanding, deciphering, and communicating—*technoimagination*—were only beginning to take shape. This fable, still unfinished, includes you. Like Kafka's protagonist in the micro-short story "A Message from the Emperor" (1919), you sit by the window—or, more likely, in front of your screen—dreaming of a message from a powerful force beyond. Only now, unlike Kafka's character, you exist in a dialogic world of technical images. You can craft a response, tapping with your fingertips on a tiny apparatus, and send the message off into the universe of technical images.

Acknowledgments

Flusser predicted that images would eclipse words, and this book was envisioned as one in which images were foregrounded. This vision would not have transpired, however, without the community of artists, families, archivists, and others who made this happen. Deepest thanks to Virginie Bec, Raquel de Campos, Analívia Cordeiro, Antje Ehmann, Miguel Flusser, Muriel Gerstner, Sophie Lavaud, Eckhard and Harald Nees, Susanne Päch, Dante Pignatari and Elliot Aboutboul, Max Schendel, and London Tsai. Thank you to the Vilém Flusser Archive and the Flusserian community: Anita Jóri, Daniel Irrgang, Mirjana Mitrović, Rodrigo Maltez Novaes, Andreas Müller-Pohle, Rainer Guldin, Anke Finger, Marc Lenot, Michael Hanke, Nancy Ann Roth, Andreas Ströhl, Gustavo Bernardo Krause, Simone Osthoff, Baruch Gottlieb, Steffi Winkler, Camila Mozzini-Alister, Monai de Paula Antunes, Alexander Schindler, Annie Goh, Aaron Jaffe, Michael F. Miller, Rodrigo Martini, Hana Yoo, and Daeun Joo.

Thank you to my MIT editor, Victoria Hindley, and before her, Roger Conover and Tom Weaver, to the anonymous readers who offered excellent suggestions and encouragement, and to Paula Woolley for her superb editing as well as Matthew Abbate and Sally Osborn. This book began as a dissertation, and deepest thanks are due to Anna Chave, my thesis advisor; readers David Joselit, Maria Antonella Pelizzari, and Alexander R. Galloway; committee member Claire Bishop; and professors such as Cynthia Hahn and Wen-shing Chou. Geoffrey Batchen was an early supporter, and I am grateful to him for his encouragement and expertise. Thank you to Candice Chu, my exceptional editorial director and image expert, and Artemis Kotioni, who kept us logged and organized. Thank you to the editors at *Afterimage*, *Critical Inquiry*, and *Flusser Studies*, and to everyone who assisted along the way: Miguel Abreu, Mariola Alverez, Rachel Churner, Tony Côme, the Czech Association of Art Historians, Bridget Donahue, Kelly Filreis, Jooyoung Friedman-Buchanan, Carol Greene, Ken Johnston, Eric Miles, Felix Mittelberger and his team at ZKM | Center for Art and Media, Ryan Muller, Marc Partouche, Meredith Rosen, Beat Scherrer and the Swiss National Library, Pavel Smetana, Jeannine Troendle, and Bernd Wingert.

The first leg of my PhD journey featured an extraordinary lineup of professors, such as Rosalind Krauss, Jonathan Crary, and Carol Armstrong, and classmates Pamela M. Lee, Helen Molesworth, and George Baker. However, the second lap included the next generation of incredible scholars, curators, and educators: Mitra Abbaspour,

Lindsay Caplan, Andrianna Campbell-Lafleur, Andrew Cappetta, Elizabeth Donato, Michelle Millar Fisher, Lucy Gallun, Saisha Grayson-Knoth, Meredith Mowder, Jane Panetta, Lauren Rosati, Beth Saunders, Hallie Rose Scott, Aaron Slodounik, Alison Weaver, Jonah Westerman, Rachel Wetzler, and many others. Thank you to everyone who has invited me to speak about Flusser and other topics: Jarrett Earnest, Deborah Goldberg, Jennifer Krasinski, Janet Kraynak, Katherine Michaelson, Kevin Munger, Warren Neidich, Julie H. Reiss, Barry Schwabsky, Tanya Sheehan, Andrew Weiner, and John Williams.

Thank you to my exceptional NYU colleagues, particularly Maureen Gallace, as well as Marlene McCarty, R. C. Baker, John Pilson, Jason Tomme, Lyle Ashton Harris, Sue de Beer, Kevin McCoy, MaryAnn Santos, Jongho Lee, and the hundreds of students over the decades. Thank you to my editors and colleagues at the *New York Times*, *Artforum*, the *New Yorker*, the *Brooklyn Rail*, the *Village Voice*, and every publication that has published my criticism, as well as the Andy Warhol Foundation. Thank you to Timothy Greenfield-Sanders and fellow travelers Siddhartha Lokanandi, Daniel Spaulding, and the Rough Idea and Abrons Book Clubs, ASWC community, dear friends, and my family. J²AM²S forever.

Acknowledgments

Notes

Warning

1. Vilém Flusser, *Into the Universe of Technical Images*, trans. Nancy Ann Roth (Minneapolis: University of Minnesota Press, 2011), 4. Originally published as *Ins Universum der technischen Bilder* (Göttingen: European Photography, 1985).

2. Octavia Butler, *Parable of the Talents* (New York: Seven Stories Press, 1998).

3. Blake Lemoine, "I Worked on Google's AI. My Fears Are Coming True," *Newsweek*, April 26, 2023, https://www.newsweek.com/google-ai-blake-lemoine-bing-chatbot-sentient-1783340.

4. Kevin Roose, "A.I. Poses 'Risk of Extinction,' Industry Leaders Warn," *New York Times*, May 30, 2023, https://www.nytimes.com/2023/05/30/technology/ai-threat-warning.html.

5. Jack Nicas, "The Internet's Final Frontier: Remote Amazon Tribes," *New York Times*, June 2, 2024, https://www.nytimes.com/2024/06/02/world/americas/starlink-internet-elon-musk-brazil-amazon.html?searchResultPosition=1.

6. Vilém Flusser, *Communicology: Mutations in Human Relations?* (Stanford, CA: Stanford University Press, 2022), 158.

7. Norbert Wiener, *Nonlinear Problems in Random Theory* (Cambridge, MA: Massachusetts Institute of Technology Press, 1958).

8. Vilém Flusser, *Towards a Philosophy of Photography*, trans. Vilém Flusser (Göttingen: European Photography, 1984), 56–57. Originally published as *Für eine Philosophie der Fotografie* (Göt-

tingen: European Photography, 1983).

9. Vilém Flusser, "What Is Technoimagination?," in "Mutations in Human Relations" (1978), 135, unpublished manuscript in the Vilém Flusser Archive, Berlin; in English. Later published as *Kommunikologie* (Mannheim: Bollmann, 1996) and *Communicology* (2022).

10. Vilém Flusser, "A New Imagination" (1990), in *Writings*, ed. Andreas Ströhl (Minneapolis: University of Minnesota Press, 2002), 111. Originally published as "Eine neue Einbildungskraft," in *Bildlichkeit: Internationale Beiträge zur Poetik*, ed. Volker Bohn (Frankfurt am Main: Suhrkamp, 1990), 115–126.

11. Flusser, "A New Imagination," 116.

12. Guy Debord, *The Society of the Spectacle*, trans. Donald Nicholson-Smith (New York: Zone Books, 1994); Jean Baudrillard, *Simulacra and Simulation*, trans. Sheila Faria Glaser (Ann Arbor: University of Michigan Press, 1994); and Lev Manovich, *The Language of the New Media* (Cambridge, MA: MIT Press, 2001), 94.

13. Vilém Flusser, *La force du quotidien*, trans. Jean Mesrie and Barbara Niceall (Paris: Mame, 1973); Vilém Flusser, "Le monde codifié" (Institut de l'environnement, Centre de formation permanente pour les art plastiques, 1974).

Screen 1

1. Vilém Flusser, *Groundless*, translated from the Portuguese by Rodrigo Maltez Novaes (São Paulo: Metaflux, 2017), 24. Originally published as *Bodenlos. Uma autobiografia filosófica* (São Paulo: Annablume, 2007) and *Bodenlos. Eine philosophische Autobiogra-*

phie (Bensheim and Düsseldorf: Bollmann, 1992).

2. Quoted in Anke Finger, Rainer Guldin, and Gustavo Bernardo, *Vilém Flusser: An Introduction* (Minneapolis: University of Minnesota Press, 2011), 7.

3. Peter Demetz, *Prague in Danger: The Years of German Occupation, 1939–1945: Memories and History, Terror and Resistance, Theater and Jazz, Film and Poetry, Politics and War* (New York: Farrar, Straus and Giroux, 2008), 63. Also see Vojtěch Mastný, *The Czechs under Nazi Rule: The Failure of National Resistance, 1939–1942* (New York: Columbia University Press, 1971); Callum MacDonald and Jan Kaplan, *Prague in the Shadow of the Swastika: A History of the German Occupation, 1939–1945* (Vienna: Universitätsverlag, 2001); and R. J. Crampton, *Eastern Europe in the Twentieth Century—and After* (London: Routledge, 1997).

4. Finger, Guldin, and Bernardo, *Vilém Flusser: An Introduction*, 8.

5. Finger, Guldin, and Bernardo, *Vilém Flusser: An Introduction*, 15.

6. Matthew D. Goodwin writes that Brazil had a "bizarrely ambivalent" policy toward Jews: they were wanted for their perceived wealth and skills, and to help Brazil improve industrially—and because they were "white," although they were considered a separate race. Matthew D. Goodwin, "The Brazilian Exile of Vilém Flusser and Stefan Zweig," *Flusser Studies* 7 (November 2008): 1–2; citing Jeffrey Lesser, *Welcoming the Undesirables: Brazil and the Jewish Question* (Berkeley: University of California Press, 1995).

7. Vilém Flusser, interview with Patrik Tschudin in

Vilém Flusser, *The Freedom of the Migrant: Objections to Nationalism*, trans. Kenneth Kronenberg, ed. Anke K. Finger (Urbana: University of Illinois Press, 2003), 92.

8. Finger, Guldin, and Bernardo, *Vilém Flusser: An Introduction*, 16. See also Edith Flusser, "Prager Erinnergungen: ein Interview mit Edith Flusser von Anke Finger 30. Januar 2007" [Prague memories: An interview with Edith Flusser by Anke Finger, January 30, 2007], *Flusser Studies* 5 (November 2007): 1–19.

9. Later that year, on October 1, 1940, the *Highland Patriot* actually *was* attacked by a German U-38 submarine and sank 300 miles west of Ireland. Three crew members were lost, and 136 crew members and 33 passengers were rescued. "Nazis Say U-Boat Sank British Liner," *New York Times*, October 4, 1940, 4.

10. Ines Koeltzsch, "Gustav Flusser. Biographische Spuren eines deutschen Juden in Prag vor dem Zweiten Weltkrieg," *Flusser Studies* 5 (November 2007): 1–13. See also *Flusseriana: An Intellectual Toolbox*, ed. Siegfried Zielinski and Peter Weibel with Daniel Irrgang (Minneapolis: Univocal, 2015), 466.

11. Vilém Flusser, "In Search of Meaning (Philosophical Self-portrait)," in *Writings*, ed. Andreas Ströhl (Minneapolis: University of Minnesota Press, 2002), 198.

12. Flusser, *Groundless*, 39.

13. Vilém Flusser, *Zwiegespräche. Interviews 1967–1991* (Göttingen: European Photography, 1996), 24; quoted in Finger, Guldin, and Bernardo, *Vilém Flusser: An Introduction*, 15.

14. Finger, Guldin, and Bernardo, *Vilém Flusser: An Introduction*, 18.

15. Zielinski, Weibel, and Irrgang, *Flusseriana*, 468. See also *Briefe an Alex Bloch* [Letters to Alex Bloch], ed. Edith Flusser and Klaus Sander (Göttingen: European Photography Verlag, 2000).

16. Vilém Flusser, *Bodenlos. Eine philosophische Autobiographie*, 41; quoted in Finger, Guldin, and Bernardo, *Vilém Flusser: An Introduction*, 19.

17. However, speculation exists that Zweig's book was penned in exchange for a visa, and Zweig only lived in Brazil for a little over a year before committing suicide in Petrópolis, near Rio de Janeiro, shortly after the book's publication. Theo Harden, "Stefan Zweig and the Land of the Future: The (His)story of an Uneasy Relationship," in "Translating Austria," special issue, *Austrian Studies* 23 (2015): 72–87.

18. The company was called IRB, later renamed STABIVOLT. Flusser served as commercial director from 1960 until December 5, 1964. Zielinski, Weibel, and Irrgang, *Flusseriana*, 464; citing the archive of the Junta Comercial do Estado de São Paulo, control form Registration no. CM 31/10/86/9441.

19. Flusser, "In Search of Meaning (Philosophical Self-portrait)," 201.

20. Finger, Guldin, and Bernardo, *Vilém Flusser: An Introduction*, 19.

21. Vilém Flusser, "Da língua portuguesa," *Revista Brasileira de Filosofia. Órgão Oficial do Instituto Brasileiro de Filosofia* 10, no. 40 (October–December 1960): 560–566. Flusser ultimately published nearly thirty essays in this journal.

22. Vilém Flusser, "Praga, a Cidade de Kafka," *O Estado de*

São Paulo, *Suplemento Literário*, no. 254 (October 28, 1961): 3.

23. Michael Hanke points out that the title of *Língua e Realidade* is problematic because Brazilian Portuguese does not distinguish between "reality" (*Realität*) and "actuality" or "truth" (*Wirklichkeit*), so that for such a consideration there is already a reality (*Realität*) and a different reality (*Wirklichkeit*) that is not linguistically formulated (*realidade* applies to both). Flusser himself translated the title as *Sprache und Wirklichkeit*. Michael Hanke, "Vilém Flussers *Sprache und Wirklichkeit* von 1963 im Kontext seiner Medienphilosophie" (Vilém Flusser's *Language and Reality* from 1963 in the context of his media philosophy), *Flusser Studies* 2 (May 2006): 5. The book was published in English as *Language and Reality*, trans. Rodrigo Maltez Novaes (Minneapolis: Univocal, 2018).

24. Klaus Sander, *Flusser-Quellen. Eine kommentierte Bibliografie Vilém Flussers von 1960–2002* (Göttingen: European Photography, 2002), 14. The Vilém Flusser Archive in Berlin holds several of the author's books with inscriptions dedicated to Flusser by Guimarães Rosa himself, as well as Guimarães Rosa's German translator, Curt Meyer-Clason.

25. Jon S. Vincent, *João Guimarães Rosa* (Boston: Twayne, 1978). The documentary film *Outra Sertão* (2013), directed by Adriana Jacobsen and Soraia Vilela, focuses on this period of João Guimarães Rosa's life.

26. Flusser, "In Search of Meaning (Philosophical Self-portrait)," 204. The German version of *The History of the Devil* was published posthumously as *Die Geschichte des Teufels* (Göt-

tingen: European Photography, 1993).

27. Vilém Flusser, *The History of the Devil*, trans. Rodrigo Maltez Novaes (Minneapolis: Univocal, 2014), 214. Originally published as *A história do Diabo* (São Paulo: Editora Martins, 1965). See also Anita Jóri and Camila Mozzini-Alister, "Entering the Black Box: Flusser and Indian Philosophy," *Flusser Studies* 29 (May 2020): 1–13.

28. Flusser, *Groundless*, 193.

29. Haroldo de Campos and María Tai Wolff, "The Rule of Anthropophagy: Europe under the Sign of Devoration," *Latin American Literary Review* 14, no. 27 (1986): 56.

30. Mira Schendel, interviewed by Jorge Guinle Filho (1981) in *Mira Schendel*, ed. Tanya Barson and Taisa Palhares, exh. cat. (London: Tate; São Paulo: Pinacoteca do Estado de São Paulo, 2013), 200.

31. Theo van Doesburg, "Base de la peinture concrete," *Art Concret* 1 (April-May 1930): 1. See also Gladys Fabre and Doris Wintgens Hötte, eds., *Van Doesburg and the International Avant-Garde: Constructing a New World* (London: Tate Publishing, 2010). The manifesto was also signed by Otto G. Carlsund, Jean Hélion, and Léon Tutundjian.

32. See Aracy Amaral, ed. *Projeto construtivo brasileiro na arte: 1950–1962*, exh. cat. (Rio de Janeiro: Museu de Arte Moderna; São Paulo: Pinacoteca do Estado, 1977); and *Arte construtiva no Brasil: Coleção Adolpho Leirner*, ed. Aracy Amaral (São Paulo: Companhia Melhoramentos; São Paulo: DBA Artes Gráficas, 1998).

33. Ronaldo Brito, "Neoconcretism, Apex and Rupture of the Brazilian Constructive Project" (1975), *October* 161 (2017): 116.

34. See Max Bill, "The Mathematical Approach in Contemporary Art" (1949), reprinted in *Theories and Documents of Contemporary Art: A Sourcebook of Artists' Writings*, ed. Kristine Stiles and Peter Selz (Berkeley: University of California Press, 1996), 74–77. See also Max Bill, "Concrete Art (1936–49)," in *Theories and Documents of Contemporary Art*, 91.

35. Flusser, *The History of the Devil*, 165.

36. "The Year of Manabu Mabe," *Time* (November 2, 1959): 40. Mabe was selected for participation in the 1953, 1955, and 1959 editions of the São Paulo Biennial, winning the painting prize at the first Paris Biennial in 1959 and at the fifth São Paulo Biennial in 1959. At the latter, the prize was handed to him by then-Brazilian president Juscelino Kubitschek, who oversaw the completion of Brasília and was committed to art in the accelerated industrial-cultural development of Brazil. Representation by Japanese-Brazilian artists declined significantly after the first few São Paulo Biennials.

37. Painter Tomoo Handa was the founder of the Seibi Group (1935–1970s), along with Hajime Higaki, Shigeto Tanaka, Kiyoji Tomioka, Kichizaemon Takahashi, Yuji Tamaki, Yoshiya Takaoka, and the poet and journalist Kikuo Furuno, joined in 1938 by Masato Aki and the sculptor Iwakichi Yamamoto. The Seibi dismantled in the 1940s, when gatherings of Japanese and Germans were declared illegal in Brazil; the group reformed in 1947 with new members, including Mabe, Tikashi Fukushima, Tomie Ohtake, and Flavio

Shiró-Tanaka. Inti Guerrero, "Japanese-Brazilian Modernists: Nipo-Tropicália," *Art Asia Pacific* 93 (May/June 2015): 102–109.

38. Vilém Flusser, "On a Few Linguistic Aspects of Brazilian Civilization," undated manuscript, 6, Vilém Flusser Archive, Berlin.

39. See Eva Cockcroft, "Abstract Expressionism, Weapon of the Cold War" (1974), in *Art in Modern Culture: An Anthology of Critical Texts*, ed. Francis Frascina and Jonathan Harris (London: Phaidon, 1992), 82–90; Serge Guilbaut, *How New York Stole the Idea of Modern Art* (Chicago: University of Chicago Press, 1985); and Serge Guilbaut, "Dripping on the Modernist Parade: The Failed Invasion of Abstract Art in Brazil, 1947–48," *Patrocinio, colección and circulación de las artes*, ed. Gustavo Curiel (Mexico City: Instituto de Investigaciones Estéticas, Universidad Nacional Autónoma de México, 1997), 709–724.

40. Mariola V. Alvarez, "Calligraphic Abstraction and Postwar Brazilian Informalist Painting," *New Geographies of Abstract Art in Postwar Latin America*, ed. M. V. Alvarez and A. M. Franco (New York: Routledge, 2019), 31; Iftikhar Dadi, "Rethinking Calligraphic Modernism," *Discrepant Abstraction*, ed. Kobena Mercer (London and Cambridge, MA: Institute of International Visual Arts (inIVA) in association with MIT Press, 2006), 94–114; and Bert Winther-Tamaki, "The Asian Dimensions of Postwar Abstract Art: Calligraphy and Metaphysics," in *The Third Mind: American Artists Contemplate Asia, 1860–1989*, ed. Alexandra Munroe (New York: Guggenheim Museum, D.A.P./Distributed Art Publishers, 2009).

Notes

41. Manabu Mabe, quoted in *Manabu Mabe: Vida e obra* (São Paulo: Raizes Artes Gráficas, 1986), 71; cited in Mariola V. Alvarez, "Minor Transnational Brazilian Art," *Third Text* 30 (2016): 34. See also Jayme Maurício, *Manabu Mabe* (Rio de Janeiro: Realidade Galeria de Arte, 1984); Michiko Okano, *Manabu Mabe* (São Paulo: Folha de São Paulo and Instituto Itaú, 2013); and Pedro R. Erber, *Breaching the Frame: The Rise of Contemporary Art in Brazil and Japan* (Berkeley: University of California Press, 2015). Alvarez notes that when Mabe won the Biennial painting prize, *Jornal do Brasil*'s headline read, "Winner of the V Biennial was born in Japan, but does not like its art," and a photo caption read, "Necktie Art." Moreover, when Mabe won the Leirner Prize for Contemporary Art in 1959, the art critic Ferreira Gullar criticized his selection, saying that he was an "an artisan," as opposed to Lygia Clark, who was "a creative artist of the highest value." Ferreira Gullar, "Prémio Leirner e os premiados," *Jornal do Brasil* (April 1, 1959): 8.

42. Alvarez, "Minor Transnational Brazilian Art," 89.

43. See Augusto de Campos, Décio Pignatari, and Haroldo de Campos, "Plano-pilôto para poesia concreta," *Noigandres* 4 (1958), reprinted as "Pilot Plan for Concrete Poetry," in *Concrete Poetry: A World View*, ed. Mary Ellen Solt (Bloomington: Indiana University Press, 1968), 70–71; Augusto de Campos, Décio Pignatari, and Haroldo de Campos, *Teoria da poesia concreta—Textos críticos e manifestos, 1950–1960*, 2nd ed. (São Paulo: Livraria Duas Cidades, 1975); and *Metalinguagem &

outras metas*, 4th ed. (São Paulo: Editora Perspectiva, 1992).

44. Kenneth Goldsmith, *Duchamp Is My Lawyer: The Polemics, Pragmatics, and Poetics of UbuWeb* (New York: Columbia University Press, 2002), 153.

45. Augusto de Campos in Roland Greene, "From Dante to the Post-Concrete: An Interview with Augusto de Campos," *Harvard Library Bulletin* 3, no. 2 (Summer 1992), http://www.ubu.com/papers/greene02.html, accessed May 12, 2025.

46. Rosmarie Waldrop, "A Basis of Concrete Poetry," *Bucknell Review* (Fall 1976): 141–151; cited in Marjorie Perloff, "'Concrete Prose' in the Nineties: Haroldo de Campos's *Galáxias* and After," *Contemporary Literature* 42, no. 2 (2001): 270.

47. "Pilot Plan for Concrete Poetry," 70–71.

48. Flusser, *Groundless*, 171.

49. Haroldo de Campos, "A Obra de Arte Aberta," *Diáro de São Paulo* (July 3, 1955); published in English as "The Open Work of Art," *Dispositio* 6, no. 17/18 (1981): 5–7. See also Umberto Eco, *The Open Work* (Cambridge, MA: Harvard University Press, 1989); originally published as *Opera aperta* (Milan: Bompiani, 1962). Claus Clüver writes that, according to Haroldo de Campos, Pierre Boulez explained the concept of an "open work of art" in a conversation with Décio Pignatari; de Campos applied it to the work of e.e. cummings. See Claus Clüver, "*Klangfarbenmelodie* in Polychromatic Poems: A. von Webern and A. de Campos," *Comparative Literature Studies* 18, no. 3 (September 1981): 397, n12.

50. Flusser, *The History of the Devil*, 162.

51. See Kenneth Goldsmith, "Curation 2.0: Context Is the

New Content," in *Poesia concreta: o projeto verbivocovisual*, 194–202; cited in Jamie Hilder, "Concrete Poetry and Conceptual Art: A Misunderstanding," *Contemporary Literature* 54, no. 3 (Fall 2013): 582.

52. Kenneth Goldsmith, panel on Brazilian Concrete Poetry, March 6, 2001, Society of the Americas, New York, with Décio Pignatari, K. David Jackson, A. S. Bessa, and Claus Clüver. Quoted in Marjorie Perloff, "Writing as Re-Writing: Concrete Poetry as Arrière-Garde," *CiberLetras: Revista de crítica literaria y de cultura* 17 (2007): np, http://www.lehman.cuny.edu/ciberletras/v17/perloff.htm.

53. Claus Clüver is an exception, writing that the poets "could learn just as much from painters and composers as they had from their literary models." Clüver, "*Klangfarbenmelodie* in Polychromatic Poems," 386. See also Gonzalo Aguilar, *Poesía concreta brasileña: Las vanguardias en la encrucijada modernista* (Rosario: Beatriz Viterbo, 2003) and Martha Schwendener, "Art and Language in Vilém Flusser's Brazil: Concrete Art and Poetry," *Flusser Studies* 30 (November 2020): 1–21.

54. See Eugen Gomringer, "From Line to Constellation," in Solt, *Concrete Poetry: A World View*, 67–71; Emmett Williams, ed., *An Anthology of Concrete Poetry* (New York: Something Else, 1967); Stephen Bann, ed., *Concrete Poetry: An International Anthology* (London: London Magazine Editions, 1967); and Willard Bohn, *Modern Visual Poetry* (Newark: University of Delaware Press, 2001).

55. The exhibition ran from December 4 to 18, 1956, at the Museu de Arte Moderna of São

Paulo and moved to Rio de Janeiro in February 1957, where it was installed in the Ministry of Education and Culture. An issue of *AD: Arquitetura e Decoração* (December 1956) functioned as the catalogue for that exhibition and included a cover based on Hermelindo Fiaminghi's painting *Triângulos com movimento em diagonal* [Triangles with diagonal movement, 1956], later owned by the poet Ronaldo Azeredo.

56. Flusser, *Groundless*, 193.

57. Jasia Reichardt, introduction to *Cybernetic Serendipity: The Computer and the Arts* (London: Studio International, 1968), 5.

58. These included exhibitions of Brazilian Concrete poetry (1959); Alfredo Volpi (1963); the *Bichos* of Lygia Clark (1964); and two exhibitions of Mira Schendel's work (1967 and 1975).

59. "Teorija informacija i nova estetika / The theory of information and the new aesthetics," ed. Dimitrije Bašičević and Ivan Picelj, *bit international* 1 (Zagreb: Galerije grada Zagreba, 1968). The first *bit* exhibition, in Zagreb in 1961, was organized by Brazilian artist Almir Mavignier, who had moved to Ulm to study with Max Bill, collaborated with the Zero Group, and was included in *The Responsive Eye* (1965) at the Museum of Modern Art in New York.

60. Max Bense, *Brasilianische Intelligenz. Eine cartesianische Reflexion* (Wiesbaden: Limes Verlag, 1965). For an excellent consideration of the blind spots in Bense's Brazilian theory—as well as the contributions of artist-theorists like Haroldo de Campos and Waldemar Cordeiro—see Nathaniel Wolfson, "After the 'New Aesthetic': A Short History of the Cybernetic Turn in Brazil," *AI and Society* 37, no. 3 (2022): 1059–1069.

61. Jasmin Wrobel, "Benses Brasilien: Reflexionen zur konkreten Poesie, Brasília und dem Entwurf einer Rheinlandschaft," *Max Bense: Werk, Kontext, Wirkung* (Berlin: J. B. Metzler, 2019), 291–321.

62. Max Bense, *Aesthetica. Metaphysische Beobachtungen am Schönen* (Stuttgart: Deutsche Verlags-Anstalt, 1954); *Aesthetica II. Aesthetische Information* (Baden-Baden: Agis, 1956); *Aesthetica III. Ästhetik und Zivilisation* (Baden-Baden: Agis, 1958); *Aesthetica IV. Programmierung des Schönen* (Baden-Baden: Agis, 1960); *Aesthetica. Einführung in die neue Aesthetik* (Baden-Baden: Agis, 1965). See also George David Birkhoff, *A Mathematical Theory of Aesthetics and Its Application to Poetry and Music*, The Rice Institute Pamphlet XIX, no. 3 (Houston: Rice Institute, 1932) and *Aesthetic Measure* (Cambridge, MA: Harvard University Press, 1933).

63. See Margit Rosen, "The Art of Programming: The New Tendencies and the Arrival of the Computer as a Means of Artistic Research," in *A Little-Known Story about a Movement, a Magazine, and the Computer's Arrival in Art: New Tendencies and Bit International, 1961–1973*, ed. Margit Rosen (Karlsruhe: ZKM / Center for Art and Media; Cambridge, MA: MIT Press, 2011), 19–42. See also Max Bense, *Technische Existenz* (Stuttgart: Deutsche Verlags-Anstalt, 1949).

64. Vilém Flusser, "Concreto—abstrato," *O Estado de São Paulo*, *Suplemento Literário*, no. 383 (June 6, 1964): 1.

65. See *Revista de Cultura Brasileña* 11 (Brazil and Madrid, December 1964), edited by Angel Crespo, translator of Guimarães Rosa (*Gran Serton: Veredas* [Barcelona: Editorial Seix Barral, 1967]) and Pilar Gómez Bedate.

66. "Haroldo de Campos, *Versuchsbuch Galexien*," ed. Max Bense and Elisabeth Walther, *rot* 25 (Stuttgart, 1966). See also Haroldo de Campos, "Poesia de Vanguardia Brasileira e Alemã," *Cavalo Azul* 2 (1966): 70–96; "A Palavra Vermelha," *Cavalo Azul* 6 (1970): 36–50; and *Galáxias* (São Paulo: Ex Libris, 1984).

67. Flusser, "In Search of Meaning (Philosophical Self-portrait)," 205.

68. Vilém Flusser, blurb on the back of Theon Spanudis, *Poética* (São Paulo: Livraria Kosmos Editora, 1975). My translation is from Flusser's Portuguese.

69. Abraham M. Moles, *Théorie de l'information et perception esthétique* (Paris: Flammarion, 1958); published in English as *Information Theory and Esthetic Perception* (Urbana: University of Illinois Press, 1966). See also Abraham M. Moles, *Art et ordinateur* (Paris: Casterman, 1971). Eco also wrote the text for the 1962 touring exhibition *arte programmata*, originally mounted in the Olivetti salesroom in Milan and organized by Bruno Munari and Giorgio Soavi. See Umberto Eco, *Obra aberta* (São Paulo: Editora Perspectiva, 1968); *Arte programmata: arte cinetica: opere moltiplicate: opera aperta* (Milan: Officina d'arte gráfica A. Lucini, 1962); and Lindsay Caplan, *Arte Programmata: Freedom, Control, and the Computer in 1960s Italy* (Minneapolis: University of Minnesota, 2022).

70. Max Bense, "Kybernetik oder Die Metatechnik einer Maschine" (1951), in *Ausgewählte Schriften*, book 2: *Philosophie der*

Mathematik, Naturwissenschaft und Technik (Springer: Stuttgart 1998), 472–483. In 1949, Hans Hollmann, an electronics specialist who had worked with Bense during World War II in Berlin, sent Bense a copy of Norbert Wiener's *Cybernetics: Or Control and Communication in the Animal and the Machine* (Cambridge, MA: MIT Press, 1948).

71. Claus Clüver, "Reflections on Verbivocovisual Ideograms," *Poetics Today* 3, no. 3 (Summer 1982): 139. See also Omar Calabrese, "From the Semiotics of Painting to the Semiotics of Pictorial Text," *Versus* 25 (1980): 3–27.

72. See Christine Mehring, "Television Art's Abstract Starts: Europe circa 1944–1969," *October* 125 (2008): 29–64; and Aline Guillermet, "K. O. Götz's Kinetic Electronic Painting," *Media Theory* (2019), http://mediatheoryjournal.org/aline -guillermet-k-o-gotzs-kinetic -electronic-painting/.

73. Werner Meyer-Eppler, *Grundlagen und Anwendungen der Informationstheorie* [Basic principles and applications of information theory] (Berlin: Springer, 1959). See also Michael Sanchez, "A Logistical Inversion: From Konrad Lueg to Konrad Fischer," *Gray Room* 63 (Spring 2016): 6–41.

74. Rudolf Arnheim, review of Abraham Moles's *Information Theory and Esthetic Perception*, in *Journal of Aesthetics and Art Criticism* 26, no. 4 (Summer 1968): 552.

75. See Claus Pias, "'Hollerith "Feathered Crystal"': Art, Science, and Computing in the Era of Cybernetics," trans. Peter Krapp, *Grey Room* 29 (Winter 2008): 115.

76. Rosen, "The Art of Programming," 30–31.

77. Vilém Flusser, letter to Max Bense, April 28, 1966, Flusser Archive.

78. Vilém Flusser, letter to Max Bense, June 8, 1966, Flusser Archive. See also Rainer Guldin and Gustavo Bernardo, *Vilém Flusser (1920–1991). Ein Leben in der Bodenlosigkeit. Biographie* (Bielefeld: transcript Verlag, 2017), 160–161.

79. See Alice Brill, ed., *Samson Flexor do figurativismo ao abstracionismo*, exh. cat. (Museu de Arte Contemporânea da Universidade de São Paulo, 1990).

80. Vilém Flusser, "Flexor: In Memoriam," in Brill, *Samson Flexor do figurativismo ao abstracionismo*, 199–202.

81. Flusser, *The History of the Devil*, 17.

82. Flusser, *Groundless*, 165.

83. Haroldo de Campos in *no vazio do mundo*, ed. Sônia Salzstein (São Paulo, Editora Marca D'Agua, 1996), 269. Originally published in *Mira Schendel*, exh. cat. (Museu de Arte Moderna do Rio de Janeiro, 1966).

84. Max Bense, trans. Izabel Burbridge, in Salzstein, *no vazio do mundo*, 271. Originally published in "Mira Schendel: Grafische Reduktionen," ed. Max Bense and Elisabeth Walther, special issue, *rot* 29 (1967). See also Max Bense, "Mira Schendel: reduções gráficas," *Pequena estética* (São Paulo: Editora Perspectiva, 1975), 223–225.

85. See Vilém Flusser, "Indagações sôbre a Origem da Língua" [Inquiries into the origin of language], *O Estado de São Paulo, Suplemento Literário* (April 29, 1967): 1; "Diacronia e Diafaneidade (I)," *O Estado de São Paulo, Suplemento Literário* (April 26, 1969): 4; "Diacronia e Diafaneidade (II)," *O Estado de São Paulo, Suplemento Literário* (May 3, 1969): 4; and "Mira Schen-

del" in *Groundless*, 237–246, first published in Flusser, *Bodenlos. Eine philosophische Autobiographie*, 197–206.

86. Vilém Flusser, "Mira Schendel" (1966), in *Force Fields: Phases of the Kinetic* (Barcelona: Museu d'Art Contemporani, 2000), 291–292; also cited in Isobel Whitelegg, "Writing the Present: Vilém Flusser and Mira Schendel" (thesis, University of Essex, Department of Art History and Theory, September 2000), 28. Whitelegg is quoting a document found in Guy Brett's personal archive, likely intended for the 1966 *Signals Newsbulletin*, which never materialized.

87. Flusser, "Indagações sobre a origem da língua." My translation.

88. Jean Gebser, *The Ever-Present Origin* (Athens, OH: Ohio University Press, 1985), originally published as *Ursprung und Gegenwart* (Stuttgart: Deutsche Verlags Anstalt, 1966)—although various volumes and editions were published between 1949 and 1953. See also Rainer Guldin, "Ménage à trois: Riflessioni sulle nozioni di diafanità e trasparenza nell'opera di Mira Schendel, Jean Gebser e Vilém Flusser," *Flusser Studies* 19 (May 2015): 1–22.

89. Mira Schendel, excerpt from an undated and unsigned typed text found among the artist's papers, Mira Schendel Estate Archive; quoted in Barson and Palhares, *Mira Schendel*, 196–197.

90. Flusser, *Groundless*, 239.

91. Flusser, "Diacronia e Diafaneidade (II)," 4.

92. Vilém Flusser, "Mutations in Human Relations" (1978), manuscript in the Flusser Archive. See also Pjotr

D. Ouspensky, *Tertium Organum: The Third Canon of Thought, a Key to the Enigmas of the World* (London: Routledge & Kegan Paul, 1981); originally published in Russian in 1912.

93. Flusser, *Groundless*, 276.

94. See Marvin Alinsky, "Brazil: A Subcontinent's Media with Guidelines," in *Latin American Media: Guidance and Censorship* (Ames: Iowa State University Press, 1981), 91.

95. Letter from Vilém Flusser to Mira Schendel, December 16, 1981, Flusser Archive. My translation.

Screen 2

1. Boris Fausto, *A Concise History of Brazil* (Cambridge, UK: Cambridge University Press, 1999), 196–197.

2. See Leôncio Martins Rodrigues, "Sindicalismo e classe operária, 1930–1964," in Boris Fausto, ed., *História geral* 3, no. 10 (São Paulo: Difel, 1986), 509–555. Also see Edmar Bacha and Herbert S. Klein, eds., *Social Change in Brazil, 1945–1985: The Incomplete Transition* (Albuquerque: University of New Mexico Press, 1989); and Alfred Stepan, ed., *Democratizing Brazil: Problems of Transition and Consolidation* (New York: Oxford University Press, 1989).

3. Vilém Flusser, *Groundless*, trans. Rodrigo Maltez Novaes (São Paulo: Metaflux, 2017), 27.

4. See João Fábio Bertonha, "Corporatist Thinking in Miguel Reale: Readings of Italian Fascism in Brazilian Integralism," *Revista Brasileira de História* 33, no. 66 (2013): 225–242; cited in *Flusseriana: An Intellectual Toolbox*, ed. Siegfried Zielinski and Peter Weibel with Daniel Irrgang (Minneapolis: Univocal, 2015), 464.

5. Introduction to Christopher Dunn, "Tropicalism and Brazilian Popular Music under Military Rule," *The Brazil Reader: History, Culture, Politics*, ed. Robert M. Levine and John J. Crocitti (Durham: Duke University Press, 1999), 241–257.

6. Roberto Schwarz, "Culture and Politics in Brazil, 1964–69," in *Misplaced Ideas: Essays on Brazilian Culture*, ed. John Gledson (New York: Verso, 1992), 126–127.

7. Dunn, "Tropicalism and Brazilian Popular Music," 243.

8. The Tropicalist group also included Tom Zé, Gal Costa, Torquanto Neto, and José Carlos Capinam, the group Os Mutantes, and composers Rogério Duprat and Júlio Medaglia. Dunn, "Tropicalism and Brazilian Popular Music," 242.

9. Fausto, *A Concise History of Brazil*, 287.

10. For an account of how the Brazilian military had used terror—murder, kidnapping, disappearance, and torture—to uphold the nation's racial hierarchy, maintain military discipline, and defend the state in earlier periods, see Shawn C. Smallman, "Military Terror and Silence in Brazil, 1910–1945," *Canadian Journal of Latin American and Caribbean Studies / Revue canadienne des études latino-américaines et caraïbes* 24, no. 47 (1999): 5–27.

11. Vilém Flusser, "Considerações transitorias" [Transitional considerations] in his "Posto Zero" column, *Fôlha de São Paulo*, Feburary 4, 1972, np.

12. Vilém Flusser, "Xadrés" [Chess], *Fôlha de São Paulo*, February 2, 1972, np.

13. Dunn, "Tropicalism and Brazilian Popular Music," 246.

14. Flusser, *Groundless*, 252.

15. Flusser, *Groundless*, 252.

16. Flusser, *Groundless*, 251. Schwarz also noted a distinct shift, with university purges, censorship of books, and teachers resigning "en masse." Schwarz, "Culture and Politics in Brazil," 154–155.

17. Flusser, *Groundless*, 263. And yet Flusser concluded the book with this sentence: "I do not believe, however, that I was entirely ineffectual. Some of the students who attended the course will become functionaries and technocrats in the future, but with a slightly disturbed conscience" (278).

18. Vilém Flusser, "Da Bienal," *O Estado de São Paulo, Suplemento Literário* (September 4, 1965): 6. My translation.

19. Vilém Flusser, "Bienal e fenomenologia," *O Estado de São Paulo, Suplemento Literário* (December 2, 1967): 5.

20. Vilém Flusser, "As bienais de São Paulo e a vida contemplativa," *O Estado de São Paulo, Suplemento Literário* (September 27, 1969): 4.

21. Rachel Weiss, "Some Notes on the Agency of Exhibitions," *Visual Arts and Culture*, vol. 2 (Sydney: Arts and Humanities Research Foundation, 2000), 122; quoted in Isobel Whitelegg, "The Bienal de São Paulo: Unseen/Undone (1969–1981)," *Afterall* 22 (Autumn/Winter 2009), https://www.afterall.org/publications/journal/issue.22/the.bienal.de.so.paulo.unseenundone.19691981. See also Claudia Calirman, *Brazilian Art under Dictatorship: Antonio Manuel, Artur Barrio, and Cildo Meireles* (Durham: Duke University Press, 2012).

22. Calirman, *Brazilian Art under Dictatorship*, 27.

23. Isobel Whitelegg, "The Bienal Internacional de São

Paulo: A Concise History, 1951–2014," *Perspective* 2 (2013): 380–386, footnote 10, https://doi.org/10.4000/perspective.3902.

24. Quoted in Calirman, *Brazilian Art under Dictatorship*, 27–28.

25. See James Naylor Green, *We Cannot Remain Silent: Opposition to the Brazilian Military Dictatorship in the United States* (Durham: Duke University Press, 2010), 30.

26. Green, *We Cannot Remain Silent*, 121.

27. Mira Schendel, letter to Jean Gebser, June 26, 1969; quoted in *Mira Schendel*, ed. Tanya Barson and Taisa Palhares, exh. cat. (London: Tate; São Paulo: Pinacoteca do Estado de São Paulo, 2013), 44.

28. Quoted in Geraldo de Souza Dias, *Mira Schendel: do spiritual à corporeidade* (São Paulo: Cosac Naify, 2009), 147. My translation.

29. "About documenta gGmbH," documenta, accessed March 28, 2025, https://www.documenta.de/en/about#16_documenta_ggmbh.

30. Letters from Vilém Flusser to Arnold Bode, December 10, 1965 and June 8, 1966, and letter from Arnold Bode to Flusser, February 17, 1966, Flusser Archive.

31. Whitelegg, "The Bienal de São Paulo: Unseen/Undone."

32. Vilém Flusser, "Initial Proposal for the Organization of Future Biennials on a Scientific Basis," undated, Flusser Archive; "A crítica . . . ," *Estado de São Paulo*, September 8, 1971.

33. Letter from Vilém Flusser to Abraham Moles, August 7, 1972, Flusser Archive.

34. Vilém Flusser, "Proposal to Be Submitted to the General Conference of AICA, to Be Held in Paris on September 12th,

Concerning the 12th S. Paulo Bienal," September 6, 1971, Flusser Archive.

35. Letter from Vilém Flusser to Belgian-born Joseph Cornet, curator in Kinshasa, Zaire (now Democratic Republic of the Congo), November 4, 1972, Flusser Archive.

36. Regarding the Belgian-born Cornet's positions as the director of the Institut des Musées Nationaux du Congo (IMNC) and the Institut des Musées Nationaux du Zaïre (IMNZ), Sidney Littlefield Kasfir has written, "there is biting irony in Cornet's reference to 'authenticity,' given the peculiarly abusive political sense the term has in Mobutu's Zaire, where Cornet has had such a remarkable career serving the national museums." Sidney Littlefield Kasfir, "African Art and Authenticity: A Text with a Shadow," *African Arts* 25, no. 2 (1992): 97. Kasfir is referring to the article by Joseph Cornet, "Art and Authenticity," *African Arts* 9, no. 1 (1975): 52–55.

37. Jeanine Warnod, "Thèmes révolutionnaires pour la Biennale de São-Paulo 1973," *Le Figaro* (September 19, 1972). Flusser later wrote to Warnod, inviting her to an "Art and Communications" roundtable at the Institute of the Environment in Paris, December 1972. See Vilém Flusser, letter to Jeanine Warnod, November 7, 1972, and Vilém Flusser, "On the Role of Art in the Present Situation" (1972), lecture manuscript, as well as the undated manuscript "Proposal for the Organization of Future São Paulo Biennials on a Communicological Basis," Flusser Archive.

38. See Waldemar Cordeiro, ed., *Arteônica* (São Paulo: Editora das Americas, 1972), 3–4.

39. See *XII Bienal de São Paulo, Outubro/Novembro 1973*, exh. cat. (São Paulo: Fundação Bienal de São Paulo, 1973), 213. See also the perfunctory letters between Flusser and de Kerckhove on October 11, 1972; February (undated); and March 4, 1973. See also letter from Vilém Flusser to Gabriel Borba Filho and Allan Mayer on August 11, 1972, with recommendations for artists for the Twelfth São Paulo Biennial, Flusser Archive. In the Biennial catalogue, de Kerckhove is identified as Derrick de Kerckhove Varent, with two other "co-participants": Jean Claude Roboly and Christian Adeney.

40. Letter from Vilém Flusser to Abraham Moles, July 23, 1974, Flusser Archive.

41. See Tony Côme, "L'Institut de l'environnement: Descendant du Bauhaus ou dernier bastion de mai 68?," *French Historical Studies* 41, no. 2 (2018): 305–333, and *L'Institut de l'environnement: une école décloisonnée. Urbanisme, architecture, design, communication* (Paris: Éditions B42, 2017). See also Monique Eleb, "L'Institut de l'environnement : Une utopie vécue (1969–1976)," *Rosa*, no. 5 (2013), www.rosab.net/fr/la-situation-francaise-les/l-institut-de-l-environnement-une.html.

42. Eric Spitz, Vilém Flusser, Klaus Blasquiz, Jeanne Gatard, Alexandre Bonnier, Enrico Fulchignoni, Abraham Moles, Piotr Kowalski, and Jean Zeitoun, *Technologie et imaginaire* (Paris: Institut de l'Environnement, 1975).

43. Spitz et al., *Technologie et imaginaire*, 1–2. My translation.

44. Spitz et al., *Technologie et imaginaire*, 36–37. My translation.

45. Spitz et al., *Technologie et imaginaire*, 52–53. My translation.

46. Vilém Flusser, *La force du quotidien*, trans. Jean Mesrie and Barbara Niceall (Paris: Mame, 1973). The book was actually written in English and translated into French, but it includes essays that were written in Portuguese and published in Brazilian newspapers. See Vilém Flusser, *A coisas que me cercam* (São Paulo: Fundo Estadual de Cultura, 1970).

47. See Larry Busbea, "Metadesign: Object and Environment in France, c. 1970*" in *Design Issues* 25, no. 4 (Autumn 2009): 103–119; and *A Little-Known Story about a Movement, a Magazine, and the Computer's Arrival in Art: New Tendencies and Bit International, 1961–1973*, ed. Margit Rosen (Karlsruhe: ZKM / Center for Art and Media; Cambridge, MA: MIT Press, 2011).

48. See Abraham Moles, *Théorie des objets* (Paris: Éditions Universitaires, 1972). Flusser's title also echoes Moles's *Micropsycholgie et vie quotidienne* (Paris: Denoël Gonthier, 1976). Also see Abraham Moles, *Information Theory and Esthetic Perception*, trans. Joel E. Cohen (Urbana: University of Illinois Press, 1966); originally published as *Théorie de l'information et perception esthétique* (Paris: Flammarion, 1958).

49. Flusser, *La force du quotidien*, 21.

50. The Bateson anecdote is mentioned in Phillip Gochenour, "Masks and Dances: Cybernetics and Systems Theory in Relation to Flusser's Concepts of the Subject and Society," *Flusser Studies* 1 (November 2005): 3.

51. Abraham Moles, "Sur les médiateurs de la communication" [On communication mediators], in Flusser, *La force du quotidien*, 7–14. See Marshall McLuhan, *Understanding Media: The Extensions of Man* (New York: McGraw Hill, 1964); and McLuhan and Quentin Fiore, *The Medium Is the Massage: An Inventory of Effects* (New York: Random House, 1967).

52. Moles, "Sur les médiateurs de la communication," 9. My translation; italics in original text.

53. Moles, "Sur les médiateurs de la communication," 9.

54. Janine Marchessault, "McLuhan's Pedagogical Art," *Flusser Studies* 6 (May 2008): 1–13. Although Flusser was frequently compared to McLuhan, he rarely cited him. Flusser did mention McLuhan in a 1980 paper published after a conference Flusser attended at the École Sociologique Interrogative in Paris on June 14, 1978—but only to discredit him: "That's why we think McLuhan is mistaken in claiming that the medium is the message: the same medium can carry messages as diverse as the history of the Gilgamesh and the gospel." Vilém Flusser, "La crise de la science" [The crisis of science], *Cahier de l'École Sociologique Interrogative* (Paris) 2 (1980): 5.

55. See Vilém Flusser, *Le monde codifié* (Paris: Institut de l'Environnement, 1974) and "Die kodifizierte Welt," *Merkur* 359 (April 1978): 374–379. See also Vilém Flusser, "The Codified World," in *Writings*, ed. Andreas Ströhl (Minneapolis: University of Minnesota Press, 2002), 35–41.

56. Flusser, *Le monde codifié*, 28.

57. See René Berger, *L'art vidéo et autre essais*, ed. François Bovier and Adeena Mey (Zurich: JRP/Ringier; Dijon: Presses du réel, 2014).

58. Letter from Vilém Flusser to René Berger, May 16, 1973, Flusser Archive.

59. See Vilém Flusser, letter of introduction to Fred Forest, August 7, 1972, Flusser Archive.

60. Hervé Fischer, Fred Forest, and Jean-Paul Thénot, "Manifeste I de l'art sociologique," *Le Monde*, October 10, 1974; reprinted in Hervé Fischer, *Théorie de l'art sociologique* (Tournai: Casterman, 1977), 25, and Fred Forest, *Art sociologique* (Paris: Union Général d'Editions, 1977): 153–154.

61. See Michael Leruth, *Fred Forest's Utopia: Media Art and Activism* (Cambridge, MA: MIT Press, 2017), 52.

62. Below the blank space was a caption that read, "SPACE-MEDIA—This is an experiment. An attempt at communication. This blank surface is offered to you by the painter Fred Forest. Take possession of it. By writing or drawing. Express yourself! The entire page of this newspaper will become a work of art. Yours." Reproduced in Leruth, *Fred Forest's Utopia*, 3.

63. Vilém Flusser, "L'espace communicant. L'expérience de Fred Forest," *Communication et langages* 18 (1973): 81–92. The article was written in English and translated into French for *Communication et langages* by Marie-Noëlle Fustec.

64. The episode is cited in Baruch Gottlieb, *Philosophy in a Universe of Technical Images* (The Hague: West, 2016), from an interview with Forest in Paris, August 12, 2013; and Annick Bureau, "Interview avec Fred Forest, réalisée le lundi 22

décembre 2008 à Paris," *Flusser Studies* 8 (May 2009): 6.

65. Vilém Flusser, "Fred Forest ou la destruction des points de vue etablis" (Fred Forest, or the destruction of established viewpoints), in Fred Forest, *Un pionnier de l'art vidéo à l'art sur internet : art sociologique, esthétique de la communication et art de la commutation / Fred Forest* (Paris: L'Harmattan, 2004), 14.

66. Vilém Flusser, *Gestures*, trans. Nancy Ann Roth (Minneapolis: University of Minnesota, 2014). Originally published in German as *Gesten: Versuch einer Phänomenolgie* (Bensheim: Bollmann, 1991).

67. Flusser, *Gestures*, 1–2.

68. Flusser, *Gestures*, 144.

69. *Radical Software* 1 (Raindance Corporation, Spring 1970). This issue, devoted to "The Alternate Television Movement," included writings by Gene Youngblood, Thea Sklover, Robert Kragen, Frank Gillette, Buckminster Fuller, Nam June Paik, Jud Yalkut, Dorothy Todd Hénaut and Bonnie Kline, Paul Ryan, Marco Vassi, Videofreex, Raindance Corp., Michael H. Shamberg, Aldo Tambellini, and Alex Gross.

70. Vilém Flusser, "Line and Surface," in *Writings*, 21–34. Originally published in *Main Currents in Modern Thought* 29, no. 3 (1973): 100–106.

71. See Nam June Paik, "Cybernated Art," in *Manifestos*, Great Bear Pamphlets (New York: Something Else, 1966), 24.

72. Zielinski, Weibel, and Irrgang, *Flusseriana*, 500. See also Hans Magnus Enzensberger, "Constituents of a Theory of the Media," *New Left Review* 64 (1970): 13–36.

73. See Vilém Flusser, "Für eine Phänomenologie des Fern-

sehens II," manuscript in the Flusser Archive.

74. Vilém Flusser, "Two Approaches to the Phenomenon, Television," trans. Ursula Beiter, in *The New Television: A Public/Private Art; Essays, Statements, and Videotapes Based on "Open Circuits: An International Conference on the Future of Television" Organized by Fred Barzyk, Douglas Davis, Gerald O'Grady, and Willard Van Dyke for the Museum of Modern Art New York City*, ed. Douglas Davis and Allison Simmons (Cambridge, MA: MIT Press, 1977), 234–247.

75. Flusser, "Two Approaches to the Phenomenon, Television," 236.

76. Flusser, "Two Approaches to the Phenomenon, Television," 237.

77. Flusser, "Two Approaches to the Phenomenon, Television," 247.

78. Vilém Flusser, "Minkoffs Spiegel" (Minkoff's mirrors), *National-Zeitung* (Bern, 1973); reprinted in Vilém Flusser, *Schriften 1. Lob der Oberflächlichkeit. Für eine Phänomenologie der Medien*, ed. Stefan Bollmann and Edith Flusser (Bensheim/Düsseldorf: Bollmann, 1993), 227–232.

79. Vilém Flusser, *Kommunikologie weiter denken. Die Bochumer Vorlesungen*, ed. Silvia Wagnermaier and Siegfried Zielinski (Frankfurt am Main: Fischer, 2009), 184; quoted in Peter Mahr, "'Für eine Phänomenologie des Fernsehens' III: Nam June Paik und eine künstlerische Phänomenologie," *Flusser Studies* 22 (December 2016): 3.

80. Flusser, "Two Approaches to the Phenomenon, Television," 247.

81. See Vilém Flusser, "Die Tyrannei der Sender," in *Die*

Revolution der Bilder. Der Flusser-Reader zu Kommunikation, Medien und Design (Mannheim: Bollmann, 1995), 115–118, first published as "Vom Fernsehen," *Frankfurter Allgemeine Zeitung*, November 25, 1971; "Fernsehen," *Kommunikologie* (Frankfurt: Fischer, 2007), 200–204; Vilém Flusser, "Fernsehbild und politische Sphäre im Lichte der rumänischen Revolution," in *Von der Bürokratie zur Telekratie: Rumänien im Fernsehen*, ed. Peter Weibel (Berlin: Merve, 1990), 103–114; and "Television Image and Political Space in Light of the Romanian Revolution," lecture, Budapest, April 7, 1990, http://catalog.c3.hu/index.php?page=work&id=274&lang=EN.

82. Norbert Wiener, *Cybernetics; or, Control and Communication in the Animal and the Machine* (New York: Wiley, 1948). In 1834, André-Marie Ampère had used the term "cybernétique" to describe the sciences of government in his classification system of human knowledge. Notably, instead of adopting Wiener's AA predictor, the military adopted a geometric predictor invented by Hendrik Bode that calculated a plane's trajectory. See Peter Galison, "The Ontology of the Enemy: Norbert Wiener and the Cybernetic Vision," *Critical Inquiry* 21, no. 1 (1994): 228–266.

83. Galison, "The Ontology of the Enemy," 254.

84. Abraham Moles, "Cybernétique et oeuvre d'art," *Revue d'Esthétique* 2 (1965): 163–182; "Art and Cybernetics in the Supermarket," in *Cybernetics, Art, and Ideas*, ed. Jasia Reichardt (Greenwich, CT: New York Graphic Society, 1971), 61–71; *Art et ordinateur* (Paris: Casterman, 1971); and "Art et ordinateur," *Communication et*

langages 7 (1970): 24–33, https://
monoskop.org/images/4/44
/Moles_Abraham_1970_Art_et
_ordinateur.pdf.

85. *CYSP 1* is considered
among the first cybernetic
sculptures, although Schöffer
dates his experiments back to
a fifty-meter *Cybernetic Tower*
(1954) he created in Saint-Cloud
Park near Paris, and others
have pointed out that Gutai
artist Akira Kanayama created
a remote-controlled, robotic
painting machine in the mid-
fifties. See Nicolas Schöffer,
"Sonic and Visual Structures:
Theory and Experiment,"
Leonardo 18, no. 2 (1985): 59–
68; Eduardo Kac, "Robotic Art
Chronology," *Convergence* 7, no. 1
(2001): 87–111.

86. Nicolas Schöffer, *Perturbation et chronocratie* (Paris: Éditions Denoël-Gonthier, 1978).

87. Vilém Flusser, "Nicolas
Schoeffer's 'Cybernetic Light-
Tower,'" unpublished essay,
undated, 1, Flusser Archive. The
Flusser Archive library holds
four books by Schöffer: *Le nouvel
esprit artistique* (Paris: Denoël-
Gonthier, 1970); *La tour lumière
cybernétique* (Paris: Denoël-
Gonthier, 1973); *La ville cybernétique* (Paris: Denoël-Gonthier,
1972); and *Perturbation et chronocratie* (Paris: Denoël-Gonthier,
1978).

88. Flusser, "Nicolas Schoeffer's 'Cybernetic Light-Tower,'"
4.

89. Flusser, "Nicolas Schoeffer's 'Cybernetic Light-Tower,'"
5. Much later, James Gleick
started his book on information
technology by describing how
African drummers were able to
transmit messages swiftly from
village to village, long before
the advent of digital media. See
James Gleick, *The Information: A

History, a Theory, a Flood* (New
York: Pantheon Books, 2011).

90. Jean Baudrillard, "Design
and Environment," in *For a
Critique of the Political Economy
of the Sign* (St. Louis, MO: Telos,
1981), 195; italics in original.
Baudrillard harbored a special
scorn for cybernetics ("Now we
have cybernetic idealism, blind
faith in radiating information,
mystique of information services and the media" [199]), and
found the empiricism of Abraham Moles "ludicrous" (185).

91. Rosalind Krauss, *Passages
in Modern Sculpture* (Cambridge,
MA: MIT Press, 1977), 221.
Krauss was also responding to
Jack Burnham's and Michael
Fried's idea of "theatricality"
as a critique of how minimalist
sculpture is experienced. See
Jack Burnham, *Beyond Modern
Sculpture: The Effects of Science and
Technology on the Sculpture of This
Century* (New York: George Bra-
ziller, 1968) and Michael Fried,
"Art and Objecthood," *Artforum*
(Summer 1967): 12–23.

92. Susan Holden, "Nicolas
Schöffer's SCAM: An Aesthetic
Perturbation in the Urban
Field," *Leonardo* 52, no. 1 (2019):
61.

93. Nicolas Schöffer, "Non-
Formalism," in *2 Kinetic Sculp-
tors: Nicolas Schöffer and Jean
Tinguely*, ed. Jean Cassou, K. G.
Hulten, and Sam Hunter, exh.
cat. (New York: Jewish Museum,
1965), 20; quoted in Holden,
"Nicolas Schöffer's SCAM," 60.

94. Jasia Reichardt, "Exhibition Histories Talks: Jasia
Reichardt," online video of January 23, 2014, conversation with
David Morris, *Afterall*, accessed
March 31, 2025, https://www
.afterall.org/article/exhibition
-histories-talks_jasia-reichardt
-video-online.

95. Vilém Flusser, *Into the
Universe of Technical Images*, trans.
Nancy Ann Roth (Minneapolis:
University of Minnesota Press,
2011), 81.

96. Jonathan Benthall
offered perhaps the best
account of Tsai's work: "In May
1968 he exhibited some eight
pieces at the Howard Wise
Gallery, New York. The gallery
was dimly lit, but a bluish spot-
light was trained on each piece,
blinking on and off faster than
the eye could count. This high-
frequency strobe-flashing, as it
is called (each flash lasts about
one-millionth of a second) is
the technical device used to
achieve a strange, otherworldly
visual effect. Each piece consists of a number of stainless-
steel rods (of a different shape
and scale for each piece, and
each rod bent in its own
slightly different way), set in
cement, vibrating at a constant
and unvarying rate of twenty
or thirty vibrations per second.
But the flashing of the strobe
makes the eye see the rods as
oscillating asymmetrically—
slower or faster according to the
frequency of the flashes, ranging from relaxed undulation to
excited palpitating." Jonathan
Benthall, "The Cybernetic
Sculpture of Tsai Wen-ying,"
Studio International 177, no. 909
(March 1969): 126–127.

97. Vilém Flusser, "Aspects
and Prospects of Tsai's Work,"
Art International (March 1974): 57.
Italics in original.

98. Flusser, "Aspects and
Prospects of Tsai's Work,"
56–57.

99. Art historian Donald
Kuspit would later describe
Tsai's approach as Taoist, unit-
ing opposites and rejecting a
separation between nature and
culture. See Donald Kuspit,

"Tsai's Cybernetic Vision: Technology in the Service of the Tao," *Cybernetic Sculptures: The World of Tsai Wen-Ying*, exh. cat. (Beijing: National Art Museum of China, 1997), 163–164.

100. The original aim of Forest's series of lawsuits, which stretched from 1994 to 1997, was to force the Pompidou to reveal the price the institution had paid for Hans Haacke's *Shapolsky et al. Manhattan Real Estate Holdings, a Real-Time Social System, as of May 1* (1971), itself a landmark of institutional critique that set out to expose how a real estate mogul with ties to the Guggenheim Museum had acquired his wealth. Forest was interested in how institutional transparency is encoded in French law.

101. Fred Forest, "In der Metro und auf dem Videoband mit Vilém Flusser" [In the Metro and on videotape with Vilém Flusser], *Kunstforum International* 117 (1992): 102. In his entry to this posthumous issue of *Kunstforum* devoted to Flusser, Forest tells a funny story about Flusser lecturing to him on the Paris Metro after they ran into each other by accident.

102. Flusser wrote the manuscript for "Mutations in Human Relations" in 1977 and 1978, in English and German, and later in French. In 1979, Flusser sent the manuscript to MIT Press and Éditions du Seuil in Paris, but neither accepted it for publication. Zielinski, Weibel, and Irrgang, *Flusseriana*, 504. On the French version, see Marc Partouche, "Parution en français de mutations dans les relations humaines? De la communicologie," *Flusser Studies* 31 (July 2021): 1–5.

103. Vilém Flusser, "Mutations in Human Relations,"

unpublished manuscript, section 1713: 3, Flusser Archive.

104. Flusser, "Mutations in Human Relations," 1716: 39.

105. Flusser, "Mutations in Human Relations," 1723: 83.

106. Flusser, "Mutations in Human Relations," 1719: 75. For Flusser, even techno-images are "descriptions" of texts: "Behind a photograph stands a text of optics, of chemistry, etc., a 'theory,' which tries to conceive a process. Traditional images are mediations between man and the world. Techno-images are mediations between man and texts. Traditional images imagine scenes, techno-images imagine texts. The techno-image codes mean texts, they are post-alphabetic, both in the sense that they no longer function like texts, and in the sense that they could not have been invented without alphabetic writing" (1720: 77).

107. Flusser, "Mutations in Human Relations," 1726: 111.

108. Flusser, "Mutations in Human Relations," 1723: 86.

109. Flusser, "Mutations in Human Relations," 1728: 131. The most popular reference to this idea, in regard to the strengthening of networks and moving from a "disciplinary society" to a "control society," is Gilles Deleuze's "Postscript on the Societies of Control," *October* 102 (1992): 3–7; originally published as "Post-scriptum sur les sociétés de contrôle," in *L'Autre journal* 1 (1990).

110. Flusser, "Mutations in Human Relations," 1726: 115.

111. Flusser, "Mutations in Human Relations," 1727: 121.

112. These ideas persisted in Flusser's thought. In 1991, Friedrich Kittler invited Flusser to lecture at Ruhr University in Bochum, Germany. Those lec-

tures were published in 2009 as *Kommunikologie weiter denken. Die Bochumer Vorlesungen* [Thinking further on communicology: the Bochum lectures].

113. The book was first published in 1983 in Portuguese as *Pós-História—Vinte instantaneous e um modo de usar* (São Paulo: Duas Cidades, 1983); later translated into English as *Post-History*, trans. Rodrigo Maltez Novaes (Minneapolis: Univocal, 2013). Written in the late 1970s as a series of lectures to be delivered in Brazil, France, and Israel, the manuscript exists in multiple versions: two in Portuguese, two in German, and partial versions in French and English, according to Rodrigo Maltez Novaes, "Translator's Introduction," *Post-History*, xi.

114. Maltez Novaes, "Translator's Introduction," xi–xii. "A. A. Rappaport" is likely Anatol Rapoport (1911–2007), the Ukrainian-born systems theorist.

115. See Julio Cortázar, *Rayuela* (Buenos Aires: Sudamericana, 1963), published as *Hopscotch*, trans. Gregory Rabassa (New York: Pantheon Books, 1966); and Georges Perec, *La vie, mode d'emploi* (Paris: Hachette literature, 1978), translated as *Life, a User's Manual*, trans. David Bellos (Boston: D. R. Godine, 1987).

116. Flusser, *Post-History*, 2.

117. Flusser, *Post-History*, 6. Italics in original.

118. "Science has become a game for programmers and a field of functionalism. *Science has become an apparatus*. Science is an extremely fascinating game, the most entertaining of all games, and the most intelligent of all programs that amuse us." Flusser, *Post-History*, 42. Italics in original.

119. Flusser, *Post-History*, 136.

120. Flusser, *Post-History*, 147.

121. Flusser, *Post-History*, 137.

122. See Bertolt Brecht, "The Radio as an Apparatus of Communication," in *Brecht on Theatre: The Development of an Aesthetic* (New York: Hill and Wang, 1964), 51–52. See also Louis Althusser, "Ideology and Ideological State Apparatuses," in *Lenin and Philosophy and Other Essays* (London: New Left Books, 1971), 121–176, originally published as "Idéologie et appareils idéologique d'État (Notes pour une recherché)," in *La Pensée* 151 (June 1970): 3–38. Althusser's concept of apparatus was more topographical (spatial) and theorized in relation to Marx and the economic base (superstructure) as an edifice and social formation, particularly in the context of the postwar French Communist Party. Flusser approached "apparatus" in a more technological sense. And while Althusser sees the apparatus as repressive, a tool of the ruling class, Flusser sees it as something that pervades all of society and ultimately reproduces or programs itself. See also Michel Foucault, *The History of Sexuality*, vol. 1: *An Introduction* (New York: Pantheon, 1978), originally published as *Histoire de la sexualité* (Paris: Édition Gallimard, 1976); and the interview with Foucault, "The Confession of the Flesh" (1977) in *Power/Knowledge: Selected Interviews and Other Writings, 1972–1977*, ed. Colin Gordon (New York: Vintage, 1980), 194–228; Gilles Deleuze and Felix Guattari, "7000 B.C.: Apparatus of Capture," *A Thousand Plateaus: Capitalism and Schizophrenia* (Minneapolis: University of Minnesota Press, 1987), 424–473, originally published as *Mille Plateaux* (Paris: Éditions de Minuit, 1980); Giorgio Agamben's *What Is an Apparatus? And Other Essays* (Stanford: Stanford University Press, 2009); Agamben's lecture "What Is a Dispositif?," presented at the European Graduate School in 2005, http://www.egs.edu; and Tiqqun, "As a Science of Apparatuses," *This Is Not a Program* (New York: Semiotext(e)/Intervention Series, 2011), 135–204.

123. See Editor's Note in Priscila Arantes, "Media, Gestures, and Society: Dialogues between Vilém Flusser and Fred Forest," *Flusser Studies* 8 (2009): 1.

124. Maltez Novaes, translator's footnote in Flusser, *Post-History*, 6n2.

125. Flusser, *Post-History*, 9.

126. Flusser, *Post-History*, 9.

127. Peter Galison, "The Ontology of the Enemy," 246. W. Ross Ashby devoted more consideration to the black box, but this did not have a particular impact on Flusser. See W. Ross Ashby, *An Introduction to Cybernetics* (London: Chapman and Hall, 1956). More recently, and in thinking specifically of Flusser, Peter Zhang has described the ancient *I Ching* as a black box. See Peter Zhang, "Flusser and the *I Ching*," *China Media Research* 18:2 (April 2022): 29–48.

128. See Matthew Fuller, "The Camera That Ate Itself," *Flusser Studies* 4 (May 2007): 1–31.

129. Flusser, *Post-History*, 62–63.

130. Flusser, *Post-History*, 33.

131. Flusser, *Post-History*, 33–34. The importance of games for Flusser cannot be overstated: "programs are games," he wrote (99). Similarly, programmers are players, such that "our environment reveals itself as a context of games that are co-implied, and whose rules are co-implied. In such an environment we are all played players, *Homines ludentes*, and pieces of the game: an absurd situation" (104). In terms of philosophy, "games are our ontological ground and all future ontology is necessarily game theory" (105).

132. Flusser, *Post-History*, 25. Moreover, regarding our gadgets, Flusser writes, "These idiotic objects, these 'gadgets' that surround us, program us in two different ways. We are programmed so that we can no longer live without them and we are programmed in order not to notice their stupidity . . . instead of emancipating us, they program us" (123–125).

133. Flusser, *Post-History*, 96. Italics in original.

134. Flusser, *Post-History*, 166.

Screen 3

1. Vilém Flusser, *Towards a Philosophy of Photography*, trans. Vilém Flusser (Göttingen: European Photography, 1984), 56–57. Originally published as *Für eine Philosophie der Fotografie* (Göttingen: European Photography, 1983). Unless noted otherwise, I will be referring to Flusser's English version, rather than to Vilém Flusser, *Towards a Philosophy of Photography*, trans. Anthony Mathews (London: Reaktion Books, 2000).

2. Roland Barthes, interviewed by Laurent Dispot, *Le Matin*, February 22, 1980, in Roland Barthes, *The Grain of the Voice: Interviews 1962–1980*, trans. Linda Coverdale (New York: Hill & Wang, 1985), 351. Quoted in Geoffrey Batchen, *Photography Degree Zero: Reflections on Roland Barthes's Camera Lucida* (Cambridge, MA: MIT Press, 2009),

17. See also Martha Schwendener, "Vilém Flusser's Theories of Photography and Technical Images in a U.S. Art Historical Context," *Flusser Studies* 18 (May 2015): 1–19.

3. See A. D. Coleman, *Light Readings: A Photography Critic's Writings, 1968–1978* (New York: Oxford University Press, 1979). Flusser's copy in the Vilém Flusser Archive, Berlin, includes the inscription, "From someone who *is* deeply and extensively interested in photography."

4. *Artforum* 15, no. 1 (September 1976). See also Max Kozloff, *The Privileged Eye: Essays on Photography* (Albuquerque: University of New Mexico Press, 1987) and *Lone Visions, Crowded Frames: Essays on Photography* (Albuquerque: University of New Mexico Press, 1994). Kozloff also told other writers about *Towards a Philosophy of Photography*; in her review of the book, which she found "fascinating and discomfiting" for its ideas about apparatuses usurping control from humans, US photography critic Vicki Goldberg credits Kozloff for bringing Flusser to her attention. See Vicki Goldberg, "Photography Takes Over: Two Works Probe the Chilling Attraction of the Camera," *American Photographer* (December 1985): 34–36.

5. Their model for photography theory was Allan Sekula. See Rosalind Krauss and Annette Michelson, introduction (signed "The Editors") to "Photography: A Special Issue," *October* 5 (Summer 1978): 4.

6. Susan Sontag, *On Photography* (New York: Farrar, Straus and Giroux, 1977).

7. Peter Wollen, "Photography and Aesthetics," *Screen* 19, no. 4 (1978): 9–28; and Laura Mulvey, "Visual Pleasure and Narrative Cinema," *Screen* 16, no. 3 (Autumn 1975): 6–18.

8. Pierre Bourdieu, *Photography: A Middle-Brow Art*, trans. Shaun Whiteside (Cambridge, UK: Polity Press, 1990). Originally published as *Un art moyen* (Paris: Éditions de Minuit, 1965).

9. Roland Barthes, *Camera Lucida: Reflections on Photography*, trans. Richard Howard (New York: Hill and Wang, 1981). Originally published as *La chambre claire: Note sur la photographie* (Paris: Cahiers du Cinéma, Gallimard, Seuil, 1980).

10. "Marpa fut très remué lorsque son fils fut tué, et l'un de ses disciples dit: 'Vous nous disiez toujours que tout est illusion. Qu'en est-il de la mort de votre fils, n'est-ce pas une illusion?' Et Marpa répondit: 'Certes, mais la mort de mon fils est un super-illusion.' *Pratique de la voie tibétaine*." Barthes, *La chambre claire*, back cover.

11. See James Van Der Zee, *The Harlem Book of the Dead* (Dobbs Ferry, NY: Morgan & Morgan, 1978).

12. Quoted in Batchen, *Photography Degree Zero*, 9. See also Roland Barthes, *Mourning Diary*, trans. Richard Howard (New York: Hill and Wang, 2010).

13. Batchen, *Photography Degree Zero*, 3. A larger roundup of photography theory during this period might include texts by Christian Metz, Jean-Marie Schaeffer, Martha Rosler, Jeff Wall, Georges Didi-Huberman, Kaja Silverman, and Abigail Solomon-Godeau.

14. Several of Flusser's essays were included in Hubertus von Amelunxen and Wolfgang Kemp, eds., *Theorie der Fotografie IV*, 1980–1995 (Munich: Schirmer/Mosel, 2000).

15. Later published as Vilém Flusser, "Art, photographie et philosophie," *Le nouveau photocinéma* 39 (October 1975): 24–26. Also see "The Gesture of Photography," in Vilém Flusser, *Gestures*, trans. Nancy Ann Roth (Minneapolis: University of Minnesota, 2014), 72–85.

16. Later published as Vilém Flusser, "L'iconoclastie," in *Lire l'image* (Paris: Inspection générale de l'Enseignement artistique / Ministère de la Culture et de la Communication, Paris: 1979), 57–69.

17. The title of Flusser's paper was "Wie sind Fotografien zu entziffern?" [How are photographs deciphered?]. A catalogue was produced afterward for the symposium: *Internationales Fotosymposion 1981, Schloss Mickeln bei Düsseldorf: Ist Fotografie Kunst?—Gehört Fotografie ins Museum?*, ed. Erika Kiffl (Munich: Mahnert-Lueg, 1982). Participants included Wolfgang Kemp, Michael Schmidt, Anna Auer, Sue Davies, and Larry Fink.

18. Müller-Pohle, "Der Tod des anderen" [The death of the Other], *Kunstforum* 117 (1992): 85.

19. Letter from Vilém Flusser to Andreas Müller-Pohle, December 11, 1982, Flusser Archive. My translation.

20. Letter from Andreas Müller-Pohle to Vilém Flusser, January 16, 1983, Flusser Archive.

21. Vilém Flusser, *Filosofia da caixa preta: Ensaios para uma futura filosofia da fotografia* (São Paulo: Hucitec, 1985).

22. Flusser, *Towards a Philosophy of Photography*, 51.

23. Flusser, *Towards a Philosophy of Photography*, 60.

24. Flusser, *Towards a Philosophy of Photography*, 6.

25. Flusser, *Towards a Philosophy of Photography*, 10.

26. All of these are included in Martin Heidegger, *The Question Concerning Technology and Other Essays*, trans. William Lovitt (New York: Harper Perennial, 1977). Flusser is one of several prominent (though not observant) Jewish-born philosophers who admired Heidegger's thought, despite Heidegger's support of the Nazis. Flusser addressed this issue in an interview with a French publication: "You can thus imagine that I opened the first book of Heidegger that I stumbled upon with great reservation; I would even say with utmost antipathy. But the effect the reading had on me was so profound, it has so much changed my vision of things that it became difficult for me to remember my initial doubts when I encountered his thought." Vilém Flusser, "Heidegger et le Nazisme: 'Nous sommes face à l'expression la plus importante de la pensée de notre siècle,'" *Calades* 86 (February 1988), n.p.

27. Heidegger writes: "The word stems from the Greek. *Technikon* means that which belongs to *technē*. We must observe two things with respect to the meaning of this word. One is that *technē* is the name not only for the activities and skills of the craftsman, but also for the arts of the mind and the fine arts. *Technē* belongs to bringing-forth, to *poiēsis*; it is something poietic." Martin Heidegger, "The Question Concerning Technology" (1955), in *The Question Concerning Technology and Other Essays*, 12–13.

28. Flusser, *Towards a Philosophy of Photography*, 15. In the German edition, Flusser says in this passage, "in German," and suggests the word "fürbereiten" (to pre-prepare), *Für eine Philo-*

sophie der Fotografie, 20. In Portuguese, Flusser simply provides the Latin terms.

29. Flusser, *Towards a Philosophy of Photography*, 15. Keep in mind that photography was not even Flusser's first choice of media: "Photography served as a pretext, although I tried to stay true to the phenomenon of photo. *European Photography* requested the essay, otherwise I would focus on the video image, with its dialogic virtualities as a model of the apparatus function." Vilém Flusser, letter to Felix Philipp Ingold, July 30, 1983.

30. Flusser, *Towards a Philosophy of Photography*, 60.

31. Flusser, *Towards a Philosophy of Photography*, 19. Later, regarding the computer, Flusser would write, "computers are apparatuses that process information according to a program. This is the case for all apparatuses anyway, even simple ones, such as the camera. . . . In the case of the computer, however, this condition is particularly clear: when I purchase a computer, I have to buy not merely the apparatus (hardware) itself but also the programs (software) that go with it." Vilém Flusser, "Kunst und Computer" [Art and computer, 1984], in *Lob der Oberflächlichkeit. Für eine Phänomenologie der Medien*, ed. Stefan Bollmann and Edith Flusser in collaboration with Klaus Sander (Bensheim: Bollmann, 1993), 259.

32. Flusser, *Towards a Philosophy of Photography*, 19.

33. Flusser, *Towards a Philosophy of Photography*, 20.

34. Flusser, *Towards a Philosophy of Photography*, 52–53.

35. Flusser, *Towards a Philosophy of Photography*, 60.

36. Moreover, as Steven Shaviro points out, unlike other critics who approached images through the concept of *simulacra*, "Flusser evidences no nostalgia. He has no Baudrillardian yearning for a 'real' that would have supposedly existed prior to photographic reproduction." See Steven Shaviro's entry on Flusser, *The Pinocchio Theory* blog, February 21, 2004, http://www.shaviro.com/Blog/?p=266.

37. Rosalind Krauss, "Notes on the Index: Parts I and II," in *The Originality of the Avant-garde and Other Modernist Myths* (Cambridge, MA: MIT Press, 1985), 196–219.

38. Flusser, *Towards a Philosophy of Photography*, 10.

39. Flusser, *Towards a Philosophy of Photography*, 11.

40. See Henri Bergson, *Matter and Memory*, trans. N. M. Paul and W. S. Palmer (New York: Zone Books, 1988); Gilles Deleuze, *Cinema I: The Movement-Image*, trans. Hugh Tomlinson and Barbara Habberjam (Minneapolis: University of Minnesota Press, 1986), and *Cinema II: The Time-Image*, trans. Hugh Tomlinson and Barbara Habberjam (Minneapolis: University of Minnesota Press, 1989).

41. Martin Heidegger, "The Age of the World Picture," in *The Question Concerning Technology and Other Essays*, 129.

42. Heidegger, "The Age of the World Picture," 130.

43. Flusser, *Towards a Philosophy of Photography*, 49.

44. Flusser, *Towards a Philosophy of Photography*, 54.

45. A famous section in Heidegger's "The Question Concerning Technology" is given over to a discussion of causality: the "four causes," or ways of being responsible—*causa materialis, causa formalis, causa finalis,*

and *causa efficiens*—and concludes that causality itself has
changed in the modern period.
Heidegger, "The Question Concerning Technology," in *The
Question Concerning Technology
and Other Essays*, 6.

46. See Konstantin Daniel
Haensch, "Magical," in *Flusseri-
ana: An Intellectual Toolbox*, ed.
Siegfried Zielinski and Peter
Weibel with Daniel Irrgang
(Minneapolis: Univocal, 2015),
258.

47. Flusser, *Towards a Philosophy of Photography*, 7.

48. Flusser, *Towards a Philosophy of Photography*, 60.

49. Flusser, *Towards a Philosophy of Photography*, 57.

50. Flusser, *Towards a Philosophy of Photography*, 59.

51. See Daniel Irrgang's "Die
Briefe zwischen Vilém Flusser
und Felix Philipp Ingold, 1981–
1990," *Flusser Studies* 20 (December 2015): 1–25.

52. Vilém Flusser, *Into the
Universe of Technical Images* (1985),
trans. Nancy Ann Roth (Minneapolis: University of Minnesota
Press, 2011), 3.

53. Flusser, *Into the Universe of
Technical Images*, 6.

54. Heinz-Otto Peitgen, *The
Beauty of Fractals: Images of Com-
plex Dynamical Systems* (Berlin:
Springer, 1986), 1.

55. Herbert W. Franke,
"Social Aspects of Computer
Art," in *A Little-Known Story
about a Movement, a Magazine,
and the Computer's Arrival in Art:
New Tendencies and* Bit International, *1961–1973*, ed. Margit
Rosen (Karlsruhe: ZKM / Center
for Art and Media; Cambridge,
MA: MIT Press, 2011), 435. Originally published as "Društveni
aspekti kompjuterske umjetno-
sti" / "Gesellschaftliche Aspekte
der Computerkunst" in *bit international 7*, ed. Boris Kelemen

and Radoslav Putar (Zagreb:
Galerije grada Zagreba, 1971),
19–26. This is the transcript of
a lecture given by Franke at the
symposium "Kompjuteri i vizu-
elna istraživanja / Computers
and Visual Research," May 5–6,
1969, Zagreb.

56. Franke, "Social Aspects
of Computer Art," 437. The paragraph that follows this quotation resonates particularly with
today's art world, in which the
art market has become a central
narrative: "These consider-
ations result in demands on the
art market—it should serve to
make accessible the aesthetic-
apperceptive processes for as
many people as possible. Some
art forms common today lead
in precisely the opposite direction: the cult of the unique,
museum art, the modalities of
trade. Remarkably, computer
art contains the inherent possibility of breaking the mold
of traditionally handed-down
forms" (437). Franke noted that
access was an issue, making the
above statement "utopian," but
that the prognosis from experts
was that technology ("output
devices") would become more
widespread, also suspending
the distinction between "artist"
and "audience," which has in
fact happened with the rise of
cell phones, social media, and
the internet. More recently,
NFTS (nonfungible tokens),
which came with a unique
digital identifier recorded on a
blockchain, were invented to
provide greater access and control to artists, but they quickly
fell prey to a speculative bubble
and market oversaturation. See
Anil Dash, "NFTS Weren't Sup-
posed to End Like This," *Atlan-
tic*, April 2, 2021, https://www
.theatlantic.com/ideas/archive
/2021/04/nfts-werent-supposed

-end-like/618488/, accessed May
31, 2025. Dash, along with the
artist Kevin McCoy, developed
the NFT in May 2014.

57. Flusser, *Into the Universe
of Technical Images*, 50. See also
Daniel Irrgang, *Vom Umkehren
der Bedeutungsvektoren. Prototypen
des technischen Bildes bei Vilém
Flusser* [On reversing the vectors
of meaning: Vilém Flusser's
technical image prototypes],
International Flusser Lecture
(Cologne and Berlin: Walther
König, 2017).

58. Flusser, *Into the Universe
of Technical Images*, 48. My italics. Felix Philipp Ingold had
referred Flusser to Soviet artist
Solomon Nikritin's theory of
projectionism.

59. Flusser, *Into the Universe of
Technical Images*, 48.

60. Flusser, *Into the Universe
of Technical Images*, 63.

61. Flusser, *Into the Universe of
Technical Images*, 63.

62. Flusser, *Into the Universe of
Technical Images*, 64.

63. Flusser, *Into the Universe of
Technical Images*, 86.

64. Martin Buber, *I and Thou*,
trans. Walter Kaufmann (New
York: Simon & Schuster, 1970);
originally published as *Ich und
Du* (Berlin: Schocken Verlag,
1922).

65. Flusser, *Into the Universe of
Technical Images*, 155.

66. Flusser, *Into the Universe of
Technical Images*, 171.

67. Flusser, *Into the Universe of
Technical Images*, 159.

68. Flusser, *Into the Universe of
Technical Images*, 166.

69. Flusser, *Into the Universe of
Technical Images*, 166–167.

70. Flusser, "Summary," *Into
the Universe of Technical Images*,
169–172.

71. Vilém Flusser, *Does Writing Have a Future?*, trans. Nancy
Ann Roth (Minneapolis: Univer-

sity of Minnesota Press, 2011), 141–142.

72. Another experiment was the Flusser Hypertext Prototype 2, based on Flusser's lecture "Schreiben fürs Publizieren," delivered on March 2, 1989, at the Institute for Technology Assessment and Systems Analysis (ITAS) in Karlsruhe, stored on an Apple Performa 630, and re-created on updated systems. See flusser-archive.org, "Projects."

73. For a collection of Flusser's writings in German on photography, specifically, see Vilém Flusser, *Standpunkte. Texte zur Fotografie*, ed. Andreas Müller-Pohle (Göttingen: European Photography, 1998).

74. Vilém Flusser, "The Photograph as Post-Industrial Object: An Essay on the Ontological Standing of Photographs," *Leonardo* 19, no. 4 (1986): 329–332. The essay began as "Die Fotografie als nach-industrieller Gegenstand," written for a photography conference at the Hochschule der Künste in Berlin in 1985, and was published as such in *FotoKritik* 21–22 (November 1986): 14–17. Urged by anonymous peer reviewers to clarify his argument, Flusser offers in the bibliography of "The Photograph as Post-Industrial Object" one of the most transparent explanations of his career: "The section dealing with objects is influenced by Heidegger's analysis of 'Ding' and 'Zeug,' by Abraham Moles's work on the theory of objects, and by Adorno's critique of Marxist dialectics. The section dealing with chemical photographs (the usual type) is in part an answer to Roland Barthes' arguments on that subject and a continuation of Walter Benjamin's reflec-

tions. In part it is an application of information theory to the problem of creativity, experimented with, for instance, in Strasbourg. The last part of this section is an attempt to incorporate Adam Schaff's and Ernst Bloch's intuitions into the argument. The last section dealing with electromagnetic photos (the new type) is a synthesis between the 'new criticism,' as initiated by Sedlmayer and others, and Martin Buber's analysis of intersubjective existence. I wrote its last part in preparation for a discussion between Jean Baudrillard and myself on German television, scheduled to take place on February 26, 1986." Flusser, "The Photograph as Post-Industrial Object," 332. The conversation with Baudrillard on German television never took place, however.

75. In *Into the Universe of Technical Images*, Flusser mentioned *Electra* (1983–1984), an exhibition at the Musée d'Art Moderne de la Ville de Paris organized by Frank Popper and Marie-Odile Briot. Flusser felt that *Electra* was "a kind of elementary school for telematics, and so the low level is to be expected," and that the "gadgets" presented could prove alienating: "the more they may seem to bring us together, the more they will disperse us into isolated individuals who have nothing to say to one another." *Into the Universe of Technical Images*, 81–82.

76. John Rajchman, "Jean-François Lyotard's Underground Aesthetics," *October* 86 (Autumn 1998): 15. Also see John Rajchman, "The Postmodern Museum," *Art in America* 73, no. 10 (October 1985): 110–117; and "*Les Immatériaux* or How to Construct the History of Exhibitions," *Tate Papers*

12 (2009), https://www.tate.org.uk/research/tate-papers/12/les-immateriaux-or-how-to-construct-the-history-of-exhibitions.

77. Vilém Flusser, "Einige, di 'Immateriellen' betreffende Gedanken" [Some thoughts concerning the "Immaterial"] *kulturRevolution* 14 (1987): 16–19.

78. See Vilém Flusser, *Immaterialism*, trans. Vilém Flusser (São Paulo: Metaflux, 2015), originally published in Portuguese as "Imaterialismo," *Boletim da Sociedade Brasileira de História da Ciência* 5 (1987): 7–9.

79. Flusser, "The Photograph as Post-Industrial Object," 330.

80. Flusser, "The Photograph as Post-Industrial Object," 330.

81. Information storage is picked up in "On Memory," also published in *Leonardo*, based on a talk Flusser gave at *Ars Electronica* in Linz, Austria, in September 1988 that was later published in *Philosophies of the New Technology*, a collection in German that includes essays by Flusser, Jean Baudrillard, Friedrich Kittler, Peter Weibel—an important Flusser supporter—Hannes Böhringer, and Heinz von Foerster. "On Memory (Electronic or Otherwise)," *Leonardo* 23, no. 4 (1990): 397–399; Vilém Flusser, Jean Baudrillard, and Hannes Böhringer, *Philosophien der neuen Technologien* (Berlin: Merve, 1989).

82. Vilém Flusser, "Immaterialism," *Philosophy of Photography* 2, no. 2 (2011): 218.

83. Flusser, "Immaterialism," 219.

84. "Digital media is degenerative, forgetful, erasable. This degeneration makes it both possible and impossible for it to imitate analog media. It is per-

haps a history-making device, but only through its ahistorical (or memoryless) functioning, through the ways in which it constantly transmits and regenerates text and images." Wendy Hui Kyong Chun, "The Enduring Ephemeral, or the Future Is a Memory," *Critical Inquiry* 35 (Autumn 2008): 160. Photographers who worked in the early digital age have described a loss of images due to obsolete digital technologies, and academics and technologists have devoted themselves to studying and resuscitating "vintage" technology.

85. Vilém Flusser, "The City as Wave-Trough in the Image-Flood," *Critical Inquiry* 31, no. 2 (Winter 2005): 320–328. Originally published as "Die Stadt als Wellental in der Bilderflut," in *Die Revolution der Bilder. Der Flusser-Reader zu Kommunikation, Medien und Design* (Mannheim: Bollmann, 1995). In his introduction to "The City as Wave-Trough," translator Phil Gochenour compares Flusser to Gregory Bateson rather than Marshall McLuhan, since he used cybernetics and information theory to reconceptualize anthropology and human relationships. Gochenour also distinguishes Flusser from Jürgen Habermas, whose idea of the public sphere assumed an autonomous subject entering that space rather than a dialogically formed one, and from the Frankfurt School, who treated technology and the media as indoctrinating, mediating, and alienating rather than dialogic.

86. Vilém Flusser, "Digital Apparition," in *Electronic Culture: Technology and Visual Representation*, ed. Timothy Druckrey (New York: Aperture, 1996), 242; this version is cited unless

noted otherwise. A longer version of the essay in German was published as "Digitaler Schein" in *Digitaler Schein. Ästhetik der elektronischen Medien*, ed. Florian Rötzer (Frankfurt am Main: Suhrkamp, 1991), 147–159. See also Vilém Flusser, "Vom Virtuellen" [On the virtual], in *Cyberspace. Zum medialen Gesamtkunstwerk*, ed. Florian Rötzer and Peter Weibel (Munich: Boer, 1993), 65–71; and "Kunst und Computer," 259–264.

87. But he was also responding to Heidegger's *Entwurf*: projection and projecting-open into new telematic worlds and a new digital world picture. See Vilém Flusser, *Vom Subjekt zum Projekt. Menschwerdung* (Bensheim and Düsseldorf: Bollmann, 1994); Florian Rötzer's "Project" and Daniel Irrgang's "To Project / To Draft" in Zielinski, Weibel, and Irrgang, *Flusseriana*, 330–332; and Siegfried Zielinski's International Flusser Lecture *Entwerfen und Entbergen. Aspekte einer Genealogie der Projektion* [Designing and unconcealing: Aspects of a genealogy of projection] (Cologne: Walther König, 2010).

88. Vilém Flusser, "Man as Subject or Project" (original in English), delivered to the PRO Conference in Rotterdam, September 29 to October 2, 1989, and published in *Constructivism: Man versus Environment*, ed. V. Stichting (Dordrecht, n.d.); I will be citing the version published in *Philosophy of Photography* 2, no. 2 (2011): 239–242. See also Vilém Flusser, "Projektion statt Realität" [Projection instead of reality], presented at the November 1990 conference *Strategies of Appearance* in Frankfurt, Germany, which also included Friedrich Kittler; *Strategien des Schein.*

Kunst—Computer—Medien, ed. Florian Rötzer and Peter Weibel (Munich: Boer, 1991); and "Alle Revolutionen sind technische Revolutionen. Vilém Flusser im Gespräch mit Florian Rötzer," *Kunstforum* 97 (November/December 1988): 134.

89. Flusser, "Man as Subject or Project," 242. Although Flusser didn't explore quipu, the pre-Columbian Incan knots made in colored cords and used to keep records and send messages for over 1,000 years have become popular objects of study. See Manuel Medrano and Galen Brokaw, "Quipu" (2023), Oxford Bibliographies in Latin American Studies, https://doi.org/10.1093/OBO/9780199766581-0175, accessed June 1, 2025.

90. "The scientists are computer artists *avant la lettre*, and the results of science are not some 'objective insights,' but models for handling the computed. Understanding that science is a form of art does not debase it. Quite the contrary: science has become a paradigm for all other arts." Flusser, "Digital Apparition," 245. Or, as it appeared in an earlier version of this essay: "Man as project, as systems analyst and synthesist engaged in formal thinking, is an artist." Vilém Flusser, "Summary" of 'Digital Apparition,'" *Arch+* 111 (1992): 82; translated from the German by Stephen Cox.

91. Flusser also wrote about Müller-Pohle's work. See Vilém Flusser, "Transformance," in *Andreas Müller-Pohle: Transformance* (Göttingen: European Photography, 1983), which was published both as an exhibition essay and in various publications, like *PhotoVision* 8 (Madrid, 1983): 16–18.

92. Fontcuberta had known Müller-Pohle since the 1970s and had been a guest editor for a 1980 issue of *European Photography* devoted to Spanish photography. Fontcuberta asked Flusser to speak at the "Photographic Springtime" festival in Barcelona in March 1984 and included a few lines about Flusser's philosophy of photography in the Spanish encyclopedia *Suplemento Annual Enciclopedia Universal Espasa-Calpe* (1981–1982). Fontcuberta also took a photographic portrait of Flusser during Flusser's visit to Barcelona for the "Photographic Springtime" festival. See also my 2013 entry on Fontcuberta in Oxford Art Online, www.oxfordartonline.com.

93. Letter from Vilém Flusser to Joan Fontcuberta, January 1, 1986, Flusser Archive. Schwarz was a photography historian and curator who invited Flusser to Torino fotografia 85, a photography festival Schwarz organized in Turin, Italy in 1985. Schwarz also facilitated the translation of *Towards a Philosophy of Photography* into Italian. See Vilém Flusser, *Per una filosofia della fotografia*, trans. Bruno Boveri (Turin: Agorà Editrice, 1987), and the special issue of *Flusser Studies* 19 (May 2015) devoted to Italy.

94. Vilém Flusser, introduction to *Joan Fontcuberta: Herbarium* (Göttingen: European Photography, 1985), 1.

95. While "generative photography" was a term coined in 1968 for an exhibition of work by Kilian Breier, Pierre Cordier, Hein Gravenhorst, and Jäger at the Städtische Kunsthaus Bielefeld, the concept dates back to Bense and Walther's *rot* 19 (1965) devoted to the computer-generated graphics of Georg Nees. See *Die Bielefelder Schule. Fotokunst im Kontext*, ed. Fred Jäger and Enno Kaufhold (Heidelberg: Kehrer Verlag, 2014); Max Bense, "The Projects of Generative Aesthetics," in *Cybernetics, Art and Ideas*, ed. Jasia Reichardt (Greenwich, CT: New York Graphic Society, 1971), 57–60; and Frank Dietrich, "Visual Intelligence: The First Decade of Computer Art (1965–1975)," *Leonardo* 19, no. 2 (1986): 159–169.

96. See Gottfried Jäger, "Concrete Photography: (In-Between) Light Image and Data Image," *Leonardo* 51, no. 2 (2018): 148. See also Gottfried Jäger, "What Is Concrete Photography?," *European Photography* 77 (2005): 3–12; Gottfried Jäger, Rolf H. Krauss, and Beate Reese, eds., *Concrete Photography / Konkrete Fotografie* (Bielefeld: Kerber Verlag, 2005); and Gottfried Jäger, *Abstrakte, konkrete und generative Fotografie*, ed. Bernd Stiegler (Paderborn: Wilhelm Fink, 2016).

97. Jäger wrote that this kind of photography was *productive* rather than *reproductive*, using apparatuses constructively rather than attempting their destruction. Gottfried Jäger, "Generative Photography: A Systematic, Constructive Approach," *Leonardo* 19, no. 1 (1986): 19–25. See also *Generative Fotografie. theoretische Grundlegung, Kompendium und Beispiele einer fotografischen Bildgestaltung*, ed. Gottfried Jäger and Karl Martin Holzhäuser (Ravensburg: Otto Maier, 1975).

98. See Vilém Flusser, "Fotografie und Tauschwert / Photography and Exchange Value," *Camera Austria* 10 (September 1982): 98–104.

99. Vilém Flusser, "Comments on 'Generative Photogra-phy': A Systematic Constructive Approach," *Leonardo* 19, no. 4 (1986): 357. See also Gottfried Jäger, "Generative Photography: A Systematic, Constructive Approach," *Leonardo* 19, no. 1 (1986): 19–25. Jäger continued the conversation, adding that he'd developed a "two-way theory" in which photography could be both reproductive and generative, although this changed over time. The artist's job was to "prepare himself and his public" for these changes. Gottfried Jäger, "Reply to Vilém Flusser," *Leonardo* 19, no. 4 (1986): 358.

100. See Gottfried Jäger, ed., *Fotografie denken: Über Vilém Flussers Philosophie der Medienmoderne* (Christoph Kerber, 2001).

101. See Roland Barthes, "Myth Today," in *Mythologies*, trans. Annette Lavers (New York: Hill and Wang, 1984), 109–159. Nora Alter argues that Farocki's operational image actually had two sources: Barthes and the Russian constructivist Sergei Tretyakov, who followed the structural linguistic theories of Ferdinand de Saussure. Whereas Saussure divided language into *langue* and *parole* (language predating the individual user versus concrete uses of language and speech), Tretyakov divided it into *poetic* and *operative*, the latter being a more functional use of language. Nora Alter, *Harun Farocki: Forms of Intelligence* (New York: Columbia University Press, 2024), 62, 68.

102. See Harun Farocki, "Staking One's Life: Images of Holger Meins," trans. Laurent Faasch-Ibrahim, in *Harun Farocki: Working on the Sight-Lines*, ed. Thomas Elsaesser (Amsterdam:

Notes

Amsterdam University Press, 2004), 83–91.

103. Harun Farocki, *Schlagworte—Schlagbilder. Ein Gespräch mit Vilém Flusser* [Catch phrases—catch images: A conversation with Vilém Flusser], 1986, video, 13 min.

104. Although Flusser doesn't seem to realize it, the edition of *Bild Zeitung* that Farocki brought with him for the *Schlagworte—Schlagbilder* video was actually from six months earlier: November 26, 1985. The airplane in the upper righthand corner of the layout that Flusser refers to generally as "technology" was EgyptAir flight 648, flying between Athens and Cairo, which was hijacked by members of Abu Nidal on November 23, 1985. Egyptian troops raided the aircraft, and fifty-six of the eighty-six passengers, as well as two of the three hijackers, were killed. The corpse with the arm "penetrating" the text also resembles images of Holger Meins and other Red Army Faction members who died in prison and were subsequently memorialized in a famous series of paintings by the German artist Gerhard Richter.

105. Harun Farocki, "Vilém Flusser: Das Universum der Technischen Bilder," *Zelluloid* 25 (Summer 1987): 77–80. See also Harun Farocki, "Das Universum ist leer. Zu Vilém Flussers Philosophie der technischen Bilder," *Der Falter* (Vienna) 12 (December 1986). Farocki also delivered the Third International Flusser Lecture in December 1999, later published as *Bilderschatz: 3rd International Flusser Lecture* (Cologne: Walther König, 2001) and in English as Harun Farocki, with Wolfgang Ernst, "Towards an Archive of Visual Concepts," trans. Robin Curtis, in *Harun Farocki: Working on the Sight-Lines*, 261–286.

106. Letter from Harun Farocki to Vilém Flusser, February 22, 1987, Flusser Archive.

107. Vilém Flusser, "Television Image and the Political Space in the Light of the Romanian Revolution," lecture, Budapest, April 7, 1990, in *We Shall Survive in the Memory of Others*, DVD and booklet, ed. Miklós Peternák (Cologne: Walther König, 2010), 21.

108. Flusser, *Towards a Philosophy of Photography*, 15.

109. Eva Kernbauer, "Establishing Belief: Harun Farocki and Andrei Ujică, *Videograms of a Revolution*," *Grey Room* 41 (2010): 79.

110. Harun Farocki in Christa Blümlinger/Harun Farocki: The *ABCs of the Essay Film*, trans. Margit Grieb (Berlin: Harun Farocki Institut and Motto Books, 2017), 17–18. See also Crista Blümlinger, "Harun Farocki, 1944–2014: The Image Scout," *Radical Philosophy* 188 (2014): 69–70, http://www.radicalphilosophy .com/obituary/harun-farocki -1944-2014.

111. Flusser, "Towards a Theory of Techno-imagination" (1980), *Philosophy of Photography* 2, no. 2 (2011): 200. Benjamin is actually quoting the photographer László Moholy-Nagy. See Walter Benjamin, "Little History of Photography," in *Selected Writings*, vol. 2, part 2, *1931–1943* (Cambridge, MA: Harvard University Press, 1999), 527.

112. Vilém Flusser, review of "Der Lauf der Dinge. Ein Film von Peter Fischli und David Weiss. T&C Edition, 1987 (Cologne: Dumont Verlag, 1990)," *European Photography* 45 (January 1991): 46–48.

113. Vilém Flusser, "Andy Warhol in Linz," *Camera Austria* (February 1980): 40–41.

114. Vilém Flusser, "Nancy Burson: Chimären/Chimaeras," *European Photography* 33 (January 1988): 46.

115. Vilém Flusser, "Astrid Klein: Das Entsetzen/Shock Treatment," *European Photography* 34 (April 1988): 36–38.

116. Vilém Flusser, "Habit: The True Aesthetic Criterium," *European Photography* 45 (January 1991): 43–45. See also Flusser, "Towards a Theory of Techno-imagination," 195–201.

117. Vilém Flusser, "Photo Criticism," *European Photography* (January 1984): 22–25.

118. Vilém Flusser, *Artforum // Essays*, ed. Martha Schwendener (São Paulo: Metaflux, 2017).

119. Vilém Flusser, "On Discovery," *Artforum* (April 1988): 15.

120. Jerry Pathick, *On Holography and a Way to Make Holograms* (Burlington, Ontario, 1971), booklet quoted in Sean F. Johnston, "Holography and the Emergence of Technical Communities," *Technology and Culture* 46, no. 1 (January 2005): 95.

121. See Eduardo Kac and Ormeo Botelho, "Holopoetry and Fractal Holopoetry: Digital Holography as an Art Medium," *Leonardo* 22, no. 3/4 (1989): 397–402; Eduardo Kac, "On Baudrillard's Text 'Hologrammes,'" *holosphere* 17 (1990): 25–26; and Vilém Flusser, "On Science," in *Signs of Life: Bio Art and Beyond*, ed. Eduardo Kac (Cambridge, MA: MIT Press, 2006), 371–372, originally published in *Artforum* (October 1988): 9. Correspondence between Eduardo Kac and Vilém Flusser from January and February 1991 in the Flusser Archive.

122. Gretchen Bender and Timothy Druckrey, eds., *Culture on the Brink: Ideologies of Technology* (Seattle: Bay Press, 1994). See also Flusser, "Digital Apparition," 243–244.

123. Vilém Flusser, "The Status of Images," in *Metropolis Internationale Kunstausstellung Berlin 1991*, ed. Christos M. Joachimides and Norman Rosenthal, exh. cat. (Stuttgart: Edition Cantz, 1991), 53.

124. Müller-Pohle mentioned the Bechers in an article he wrote in 1978 and sent to Flusser, early on in their correspondence. See Andreas Müller-Pohle, "Was ist Fotografie? Versuch einer Annäherung," *Fotografie* 5 (1978), enclosed in a letter to Flusser on March 7, 1981, Flusser Archive.

125. In a 2007 interview, Williams described the Kodak reflecting guides or color bars appearing in some of his photographs: "The guide is both a referent to the photographic industry and to the kind of determinants within the photographic program that Vilém Flusser describes in *Towards a Philosophy of Photography*." See "Christopher Williams in Conversation with Mark Godfrey," *Afterall: A Journal of Art, Context, and Enquiry* 16 (2007): 66. Williams also included a Flusser essay in the catalogue accompanying his retrospective (2014–2015), which traveled from the Art Institute of Chicago to the Museum of Modern Art, New York to Whitechapel Art Gallery, London. See Vilém Flusser, "Photo Production (Lecture Given at the École Nationale de la Photographie, Arles, February 23, 1984)," in *Christopher Williams: The Production Line of Happiness*, ed. Matthew S. Witkovsky, Mark Godfrey, and Rox-

ana Marcoci, exh. cat. (Chicago: Art Institute of Chicago, 2014), 120–123.

126. Sean Cubitt, reviewing Vilém Flusser's *The Shape of Things*, *Towards a Philosophy of Photography*, *Writings*, and *The Freedom of the Migrant* in *Leonardo* 37, no. 5 (2004): 403–405. See also Sean Cubitt, *The Practice of Light: A Genealogy of Visual Technologies from Prints to Pixels* (Cambridge, MA: MIT Press, 2014). Steven Shaviro would write, "Vilém Flusser (1920–1991) was, after Marshall McLuhan, one of the most important media theorists of the late twentieth century. He's still not very well known in North America; but I find him far more profound and rewarding than, say, Baudrillard or Virilio (let alone Neil Postman or Paul Levinson)." Shaviro, entry on Flusser in *The Pinocchio Theory*, blog, Februrary 21, 2004, http://www.shaviro.com/Blog/?p=266.

127. Yuk Hui, *The Question Concerning Technology in China: An Essay in Cosmotechnics* (Oxford: Urbanomic, 2018). Additionally, Flusser's early forays into Indian philosophy are just beginning to be addressed. See Anita Jóri and Camila Mozzini-Alister, "Entering the Black Box: Flusser and Indian Philosophy," *Flusser Studies* 29 (May 2020): 1–13.

128. Andreas Müller-Pohle, "Code," in Zielinski, Weibel, and Irrgang, *Flusseriana*, 110.

129. Vilém Flusser, letter to Abraham Moles and Élisabeth Rohmer, January 23, 1980, Flusser Archive; in English.

Screen 4

1. C. P. Snow, *The Two Cultures and the Scientific Revolution* (Cambridge, UK: Cambridge University Press, 1959). Other writers, like Jürgen Habermas, thought the European Enlightenment was to blame for the separation of knowledge into science, morality, and aesthetics.

2. Vilém Flusser, *Language and Reality*, trans. Rodrigo Maltez Novaes (Minneapolis: Univocal, 2018); originally published in 1963 as *Língua e realidade* (repr., São Paulo: Annablume, 2004); citing Hans Vaihinger, *Die Philosophie des Als Ob* (Berlin: Reuther & Reichard, 1911), translated as *The Philosophy of "As If": A System of the Theoretical, Practical, and Religious Fictions of Mankind*, trans. C. K. Ogden (New York: Harcourt, Brace; London: Kegan Paul, Trench, Trubner, 1924).

3. As with many of Flusser's texts, there are several versions of *On Doubt*. The essay version was first published in the journal of the Institute for Technology and Aeronautics (Instituto de Tecnologia e Aeronautica) as "Da Dúvida," *ITA-Humanidades* (São José dos Campos, Brazil) 1 (1965): 7–20. It later appeared in the essay collection *Da Religiosidade* (São Paulo: Conselho Regional de Cultura, 1967), 39–52. The book-length version was first published posthumously as *A dúvida* (Rio de Janeiro: Relume Dumará, 1999) and more recently as *A dúvida* (São Paulo: Annablume, 2011) and *On Doubt*, trans. Rodrigo Maltez Novaes (Minneapolis: Univocal, 2014). (Subsequent citations are to the English translation by Novaes.) The first German version, translated by Edith Flusser, appeared as *Vom Zwiefel* (Göttingen: European Photography, 2006). See also Gustavo Bernardo, *A dúvida de Flusser. Filosofia e Literatura* (São Paulo: Editora Globo, 2002).

4. Flusser, *On Doubt*, 4. Flusser's critique of Descartes would persist to the end of his life and become extended to phenomenon like fascism. See Vilém Flusser, "Toute pensée est fasciste" [All Cartesian thought is fascist], *Calades*, no. 117 (February 1991): 34–35.

5. Flusser, *On Doubt*, 37.

6. Flusser, *On Doubt*, 48.

7. Flusser, *On Doubt*, 38–39.

8. Flusser, *On Doubt*, 54.

9. "This diploma was awarded to me by the Scientific Institute of Paranaturalist Research, the Institute I had founded a few years earlier and of which I am the only graduate and, apparently, the only president." Louis Bec, "Vilém Flusser 1920/1991," *Flusser Studies* 4 (2007): 8, http://www.flusserstudies.net/sites/www.flusserstudies.net/files/media/attachments/louis_bec_vilem.pdf. See also Louis Bec, "Vampyroteuthis infernalis: Postscriptum," *Flusser Studies* 4 (2007): 1–8, http://www.flusserstudies.net/sites/www.flusserstudies.net/files/media/attachments/bec_vampyroteuthis.pdf; and Louis Bec, "Zoosystemiker," *Kunstforum* 97 (1988): 136–137.

10. Jarry had attended the lectures of Henri Bergson, whose 1907 book *Creative Evolution*, which argued for orthogenesis, or increasing biological complexity, over Darwin's natural selection, serves as one touchstone for *Vampyroteuthis infernalis*. Bergson famously declared, "it would be as absurd to refuse consciousness to an animal because it has no brain as to declare it incapable of nourishing itself because it has no stomach." Henri Bergson, *Creative Evolution* (1907; repr., New York: H. Holt, 1911), 110.

Bec was also involved in an actual art and research center, CYPRES, the Centre Interculturel de Pratiques Recherches et Echanges Transdisciplinaires [Intercultural Center for Practice, Research, and Interdisciplinary Exchanges] in Aix-en-Provence, where he co-organized a workshop in July 1992 on the links between art and the cognitive sciences. See *Art/Cognition, practiques artistiques et science cognitves*, ed. Marc Partouche (Aix-en-Provence: CYPRES/Ecole d'Art, 1994). See also David Ray, Annick Bureaud, and Roger F. Malina, "Gateway" (newsletter), *Leonardo* 26, no. 3 (June 1993): 188–191, which reported on an *Art and Cognition* event (July 5–7, 1992), co-organized by Roy Ascott, Louis Bec, and Gerald Heffernon, that included an exhibition of Heffernon's work and a performance by Stelarc.

11. Bec exhibited in Provence at the Vieille Charité in Marseille (1973); Chalon sur Saône (1976); and the Saline Royale at d'Arc et Senans (1976). The exhibition at the Saline Royale was closed due to complaints and what Bec later described as a "very violent press campaign." Louis Bec, *Zoosystémie: Écris d'un zoosystémicien* (Prague: CIANT, 2014), 545.

12. Vilém Flusser, "Os sulfanogrados de Louis Bec," *Fundação Bienal de São Paulo, São Paulo, Bienal de São Paulo*, October–December 1981 (exhibition catalogue), 77.

13. Vilém Flusser, *Orthonature Paranature* (Institut Scientifique de Recherche Paranaturaliste, 1978), n.pag. The essay comes from a lecture Flusser gave at the Maison de la Culture in Chalons-sur-Saône,

France, in 1976. See also Martha Schwendener and Marc Lenot, "Vilem Flusser's Orthonature Paranature," *Flusser Studies* 31 (July 2021): 1–6; and my English translation of *Orthonature Paranature*, *Flusser Studies* 35 (May 2025): 1–6. (Subsequent citations are from my English translation.)

14. Flusser, *Orthonature Paranature*, 6.

15. Vilém Flusser, *Natural: Mind*, trans. Rodrigo Maltez Novaes (Minneapolis: Univocal, 2013); originally published as *Natural:mente: vários acessos ao significado da natureza* (São Paulo: Duas Cidades, 1979). The book was translated into German by Edith Flusser and published as *Vogelflüge. Essays zu Nature und Kultur* [Bird flight: Essays on nature and culture] (Munich: Hanser, 2000).

16. Flusser, *Natural:Mind*, 143.

17. Rodrigo Maltez Novaes, introduction to Flusser, *Natural:Mind*, xviii–iv.

18. Flusser, *Natural:Mind*, 22.

19. Flusser, "Cows," in *Natural:Mind*, 43–48. Translator Rodrigo Maltez Novaes also notes that this essay was written before data on the polluting effects of the methane gas emitted by cows was available. Novaes, Translator's Note, in Flusser, *Natural:Mind*, 43.

20. Flusser, *Natural:Mind*, 66.

21. Flusser, *Natural:Mind*, 71.

22. Flusser, *Natural:Mind*, 137.

23. Vilém Flusser, *Vampyroteuthis infernalis: A Treatise, With a Report by the Institut Scientifique de Recherche Paranaturaliste*, with Louis Bec, translated from the Portuguese by Rodrigo Maltez Novaes (New York and Dresden: Atropos Press, 2011), 5; and *Vampyroteuthis infernalis: A Treatise, With a Report by the*

Institut Scientifique de Recherche Paranaturaliste, translated from the German by Valentine A. Pakis (Minneapolis: University of Minnesota Press, 2012), 3; originally published as *Vampyroteuthis infernalis. Eine Abhandlung samt Befund des Institut Scientifique de Recherche Paranaturaliste* (Göttingen: European Photography, 1987).

24. Vilém Flusser, "Um mundo fabuloso," *O Estado de São Paulo*, *Suplemento Literário*, no. 408 (November 28, 1964): 1.

25. Aristotle, *History of Animals*, vol. 3, in *Aristotle in 23 Volumes*, vol. 11 (Cambridge, MA: Harvard University Press, 1991). See also my introduction to Camila Mozzini-Alister's *Bodies of Light: Does Social Media Have Limits?* (London: Palgrave Macmillan, 2021), originally published as *Impressões de um corpo conectado: como a publicidade está nos incitando à conexão digital* (Curitiba, Brazil: Appris, 2019).

26. For his description of the 1986 trip to Prague, see Louis Bec, "Vilém Flusser 1920/1991."

27. The first time I searched for Flusser's and Bec's *Vampyroteuthis infernalis* in an academic library, it was shelved in a section devoted to popular marine books and guides. Flusser likely would have appreciated this (mis)classification.

28. Carl Chun, *Aus den Tiefen des Weltmeeres* (Jena: Gustav Fischer, 1903).

29. A contemporary review of Chun's book argued that it would increase the interest "in deep-sea research in Germany, and so to give the proper stimulus essential for the prosecution of such investigations, which are necessarily national undertakings." *Geographical Journal* 18, no. 2 (August 1901): 169.

30. *Wissenschaftliche Ergebnisse der Deutschen Tiefsee-Expedition auf dem Dampfer "Valdivia" 1898–1899* (Jena: Gustav Fischer, 1902–1940).

31. Later biologists called the creature *Cirroteuthis macrope*, *Watasella Nigra*, and *Retroteuthis Pacifica*, but Chun's name has endured.

32. Flusser, *Vampyroteuthis infernalis* (Atropos), 119.

33. Flusser, *Vampyroteuthis infernalis* (Atropos), 27–28.

34. See Hendrik J. T. Hoving and Bruce H. Robison, "Vampire Squid: Detritivores in the Oxygen Minimum Zone," *Proceedings of the Royal Society: Biological Science* 279, no. 1747 (November 2012): 4559–4567.

35. "This fable shall follow the Franciscan example, and shall seek to overcome anthropocentrism during its contemplation of life's current. It shall seek to grasp evolution from a vampyroteuthian point of view. To oppose the human Darwin with a vampyroteuthian Darwin." Flusser, *Vampyroteuthis infernalis* (Atropos), 31–32. See Teilhard de Chardin, *The Divine Milieu* (1923; trans., Brighton, UK: Sussex Academic Press, 2004). In his early correspondence with Bec, Flusser mentioned Teilhard de Chardin's idea of the "noosphere," a theoretical sphere or stage of evolutionary development relating to consciousness and interpersonal relationships. See Vilém Flusser, letter to Louis Bec, July 30, 1977.

36. Flusser and Bec, *Vampyroteuthis infernalis* (Atropos), 34. It should be noted that cybernetics, unlike Behaviorism, attempted to get *inside* the organism, paralleling Flusser's writing on the camera as a black box.

37. Flusser, *Vampyroteuthis infernalis* (Atropos), 63.

38. Johan Huizinga, *Homo Ludens: A Study of the Play-Element in Culture* (1950; trans., Boston: Beacon Press, 1955); Roger Caillois, *Man, Play, and Games* (New York: Free Press of Glencoe, 1961); and Anatol Rapoport, *Two-Person Game Theory; The Essential Ideas* (Ann Arbor: University of Michigan Press, 1966) and *N-Person Game Theory: Concepts and Applications* (Ann Arbor: University of Michigan Press, 1970).

39. Max Bense also wrote about mollusks, in relation to abstraction, using them as phenomenological models of *Eidos*, or something that exists not as a figure-ground object in relation to its environment but as a melding of being and perception. See Max Bense, "Eidos und Molluske," in *Aesthetica. Einführung in die neue Ästhetik* (Baden-Baden: Agis, 1965), 96–101.

40. Jakob von Uexküll, *A Foray into the Worlds of Animals and Humans: With a Theory of Meaning*, trans. Joseph D. O'Neil (Minneapolis: University of Minnesota Press, 2010); originally published as *Streifzüge durch die Umwelten von Tieren und Menschen. Eid Bilderbuch unsichtbarer Welten* (Berlin: Springer, 1934). The idea of the *Umwelt* was also picked up by Heidegger and Thomas Sebeok, the innovator of biosemiotics, a synthesis of biology and semiotics that argues signs and meaning exist in all life forms. Heidegger used the term *Umwelt* to formulate a concept of the world in the existential analytic of *Sein und Zeit*. See Thomas A. Sebeok, "Communication among Social Bees; Porpoises and Sonar; Man and Dolphin,"

Language 39 (1963): 448–466; *Perspectives in Zoosemiotics* (The Hague: Mouton, 1972); and "Biosemiotics: Its Roots, Proliferation, and Prospects," in "Jakob von Uexküll: A Paradigm for Biology and Semiotics," ed. Kelevi Kull, special issue, *Semiotica*, 134 (1/4) (2001): 61–78. This concept also parallels Flusser's writing in the 1980s about the "universe of technical images," an *Umwelt* in which we are surrounded by technologically generated pictures. Moreover, despite certain overlaps in their ideas around cybernetics and communication, Flusser did not cite Gregory Bateson, the US biologist, anthropologist, and psychiatrist who specialized in the evolution of communication among mammals—although Bec did. See Bateson's *Steps to an Ecology of Mind: Collected Essays in Anthropology, Psychiatry, Evolution, and Epistemology* (Chicago: University of Chicago Press, 2000) and *Mind and Nature: A Necessary Unity* (New York: Bantam Books, 1980).

41. Flusser, *Vampyroteuthis* (Minnesota), 32.

42. See Vilém Flusser, "On the Crisis of Our Models," in *Writings*, ed. Andreas Ströhl (Minneapolis: University of Minnesota Press, 2002), 75–84.

43. Flusser, *Vampyroteuthis infernalis* (Minnesota), 39.

44. "And I follow these three aims: 1. To attain enough distance from the human condition to be able to observe it, but a distance that is not transcendent. 2. To write a fable that is simultaneously scientifically exact and mad fantasy [*fantasia esatta*]. 3. To face Evil intentionally with the spirit of 'transvaluation,' but in reality, convinced that it is Evil as such that is the

real religious problem." Vilém Flusser, letter to Dora Ferreira da Silva, June 9, 1981, Vilém Flusser Archive, Berlin. Quoted in *Vampyroteuthis infernalis* (Atropos), 142.

45. Flusser, *Vampyroteuthis infernalis* (Atropos), 101.

46. Flusser, *Vampyroteuthis infernalis* (Atropos), 110.

47. Flusser, *Vampyroteuthis infernalis* (Atropos), 115.

48. "In this collaboration with Louis Bec we created an unexpected synthesis because my texts do not explain Bec's images and his images do not illustrate my texts. . . . This is a new way to philosophize." Vilém Flusser, *Zwiegespräche. Interviews 1967–1991* (Göttingen: European Photography, 1996), 45; quoted in Anke Finger, Rainer Guldin, and Gustavo Bernardo, *Vilém Flusser: An Introduction* (Minneapolis: University of Minnesota Press, 2011), 135.

49. Louis Bec, "Vampyroteuthis infernalis. Postscriptum," 1–8. For detailed descriptions of the creatures, see "Les Vampyromorpha" in Bec, *Zoosystémie*, 481–494.

50. Abraham Moles, foreword to *Vampyroteuthis infernalis* (Atropos), 20. This foreword was probably intended for a French version of the book, but that never appeared. It is included in the Portuguese translation.

51. Letter from Vilém Flusser to Milton Vargas, January 28, 1981, found in the Flusser Archive. Quoted in *Vampyroteuthis infernalis* (Atropos), 136.

52. See Vilém Flusser, *Artforum // Essays*, ed. Martha Schwendener (São Paulo: Metaflux, 2017).

53. Kozloff met Flusser at a 1982 colloquium at the International Center for Photography

in New York (ICP) titled "When Words Fail: An International Colloquium on Avant-garde German Photography, 1919–1939," February 19–21, 1982. Flusser's name doesn't appear on the program, but curator and historian William Ewing remembered him showing up with a "star-struck" Andreas Müller-Pohle, who was an invited panelist. Other attendees and participants included Lotte Jacobi, György Kepes, Rosalind Krauss, and Allan Sekula (also not listed on the ICP program). Interview with Kozloff, New York, January 8, 2013, and emails with William Ewing and Deirdre Donohue, director of ICP's Library, April 2016.

54. Telephone interview with David Frankel, September 9, 2014. Flusser did not conceive the title for the column, but he did not object to it.

55. In 1988, Flusser would write a brief essay for Ulrich Merten's exhibition featuring diptych photographs of mines and their above-ground landscapes. In the essay, Flusser thinks about landscape and phenomenology, but also mentions the 1986 Chernobyl nuclear accident. See Vilém Flusser, "Sens dessus dessous" for Ulrich Mertens, *Sans horizon*, Galerie des Rambles, Marseille, April 1988.

56. Vilém Flusser, "Discovery," *Artforum* (March 1988): 14–15.

57. Vilém Flusser, "On Communication," *Artforum* (January 1987): 7.

58. Vilém Flusser, "On Science," *Artforum* (October 1988): 9–10; Vilém Flusser, "On Science II," *Artforum* (December 1988): 9–10.

59. Vilém Flusser, "Leben und Kunst," *Spuren* 24 (1988): 19–21. Flusser wrote several essays for *Spuren in Kunst und Gesellschaft* (1983–1994), which was inspired by Marxist philosopher Ernst Bloch's 1930 book *Spuren* [Traces] and based at the University of Fine Arts Hamburg.

60. Letter from Agnes Denes to Vilém Flusser, October 3, 1989, Flusser Archive. See Agnes Denes, *Book of Dust: The Beginning and the End of Time and Thereafter* (Rochester, NY: Visual Studies Workshop Press, 1989).

61. Letter from Vilém Flusser to Agnes Denes, November 21, 1989, Flusser Archive.

62. George Gessert, letter to Vilém Flusser, June 29, 1988, Flusser Archive. Flusser wrote back: "When hominids began manipulating objects, they became subjects of an objective world. The abyss between subjectivity and objectivity became wider as 'art' (civilization) advanced. The Marxist hope that art (work) can humanize the objective world and naturalize man and thus overcome 'alienation' is no longer convincing. The hope now is to project alternative objective worlds (including artificial living beings). It is not a very convincing hope either." Vilém Flusser, letter to George Gessert, January 15, 1989, Flusser Archive.

63. Flusser responded, "I know the name but not his texts." Vilém Flusser, letter to George Gessert, February 8, 1989, Flusser Archive. Gessert had corresponded with Burroughs after reading *The Western Lands* (1987), a hallucinatory novelistic meditation on death that vacillates between the ancient world and the present

day. Gessert was interested in Burroughs's idea of biological revolution and, in their correspondence, Burroughs reportedly wrote to Gessert that "all artists are literally trying to create life." Quoted in George Gessert, "Notes on Genetic Art," *Leonardo* 26, no. 3 (1993): 208, and "The Iris Project," *American Iris Society* 273 (1989): 44. Gessert sent the latter article to Flusser in a letter dated March 16, 1989, Flusser Archive.

64. George Gessert, *Green Light: Toward an Art of Evolution* (Cambridge, MA: MIT Press, 2010), 134, 202.

65. Vilém Flusser, "Le vivant et l'artificiel," in Louis Bec, *Le vivant et l'artificiel. Catalogue = The Living and the Artifcial: Exposition, Avignon, Hospice Saint-Louis, du 10 juillet au 4 août 1984* (Marseille: Sgraffite, 1985), 63–66; republished in *Multitudes* 74 (Sciences Po Lyon, 2019): 199–202, https://www.cairn.info/revue-multitudes-2019-1-page-199.htm. Alain Badiou also contributed to the catalogue with a poem, "Poème mise à mort," *Le vivant et l'artificiel / The Living and the Artificial*, 19–22. Later, both Flusser and Bec contributed to *Verba Volant* (1989), a publication following a 1987 colloquium at the Art School of Marseille-Luminy.

66. Louis Bec, "Artificial Life under Tension: A Lesson in Epistemological Fabulation," in Christa Sommerer and Laurent Mignonneau, eds., *Art @ Science* (Vienna: Springer Verlag, 1998), 96n12. See also Marc Renoue, "Entretiens: La vie artificielle du zoosystémicien Louis Bec," *Interfaces numériques* 2, no. 2 (2013): 183–208. Bec also worked as Coordinator of Art and Technology for the French Ministry of Culture,

surveying practices in art schools. His 1995 report for the government reflects both his interests in taxonomies—real and speculative—and how art, science, and technology were being applied in art practices: Louis Bec, *Les nouvelles technologies et la création contemporaine en France en 1995* (Paris: AFFA, 1995). The sixty-four-page pamphlet also contains a glossary, which makes it feel a bit like Flusser's *Towards a Philosophy of Photography*.

67. See Louis Bec, "Monographie, Die Upokrinomene," *Kunstforum International* 97 (November-December 1988): 138–149; Bec, "Vorläufiger Versuch über die Upokrinoménologie, oder: Eine verheerende zoosystemische Expedition durch ein Glossar," in *Digitaler Schein*, ed. Florian Rötzer (Frankfurt am Main: Suhrkamp, 1991), 397–416; Bec, "Upokrinoménologie" and "Upokrinomènes," in *Zoosystémie*, 218–226; and Marc Cavazza, Simon Hartley, Louis Bec, François Mourre, Gonzague Defos du Rau, Remy Lalanne, Mikael Le Bras, and Jean-Luc Lugrin, "Modelling the Upokrinomena: Artificial Physiology for Artificial Life," in *Proceedings of Alife9 Conference* (Boston, 2004), http://195.194.24.18/alterne/publications/Alife9Final.pdf.

68. A. M Turing, "The Chemical Basis of Morphogenesis," *Philosophical Transactions of the Royal Society of London* B237, no. 641 (August 14, 1952): 37–72.

69. Video interview with Louis Bec (2015), 6:49 minutes, directed by Klaus Sander.

70. Louis Bec, "Elements d'Epistemologie Fabulatoire" (in French), in C. Langton, C. Taylor, J. D. Farmer, and S. Ras-

mussen, eds., *Artificial Life II*, *SFI Studies in the Sciences of Complexity*, proc. vol. 10 (Redwood City, CA: Addison-Wesley, 1991), 799–811.

71. Bec, "Artificial Life under Tension," 98.

72. *Erzeugte Realitäten II. Louis Bec, ORLAN, Stelarc. Der Körper und der Computer* [Generated realities II: Louis Bec, ORLAN, Stelarc: The body and the computer], October 22–November 27, 1994, Neue Gesellschaft für Bildende Kunst (NGBK), Berlin.

73. "Louis Bec worked as the producer, coordinating the activities in France. Bec and I met at Ars Electronica (September 1999) and soon afterward he contacted Houdebine on my behalf, for the first time, to propose the project. Months later, in 2000, Alba was born, a gentle and healthy rabbit." Eduardo Kac, ed., *Signs of Life: Bio Art and Beyond* (Cambridge, MA: MIT Press, 2006), 165.

74. Eduardo Kac, "GFP Bunny," *Leonardo* 36, no. 2 (2003): 98–99. Flusser, it might be noted, had an animal companion in the 1980s: a dog called Alma (which also translates as "soul" in Portuguese).

75. Vilém Flusser, "On Science," in Kac, *Signs of Life: Bio Art and Beyond*, 371–372. Originally published in *Artforum* (October 1988): 9.

76. See Christa Blüminger, "What's at Play in Harun Farocki's *Parallel//2014*," in *Moving Image*, ed. Omar Kholeif (Cambridge, MA: MIT Press, 2015), 193–195, excerpted from "Was bei Farockis 'Parallel' auf dem Spiel steht / What's at Play in Harun Farocki's *Parallel*," *Berlin Documentary* 3 (2014): 182–185; Thomas Elsaesser, ed., *Harun Farocki: Working on the Sight-Lines* (Amsterdam: Amsterdam Uni-

versity Press, 2004); and Soraya Murray, "Artist's Project: Harun Farocki's *Parallel*," *Art Journal* 79, no. 2 (2020): 50–57.

77. Vilém Flusser, "Grass," in *Natural:Mind*, 49–56.

78. Haraway has argued—sounding very much like Flusser—for "revisioning the world as coding trickster with whom we must learn to converse," rather than treating the world and its inhabitants as "resources" or objects of scientific study. Donna Haraway, "Situated Knowledges: The Science Question in Feminism and the Privilege of Partial Perspective," *Feminist Studies* 14, no. 3 (1988): 596. For a longer comparison of Flusser and Haraway, see my essay "Flusser's Philosophical Backgrounds" in *Understanding Flusser, Understanding Modernism*, ed. Aaron Jaffe, Michael F. Miller, and Rodrigo Martini (London: Bloomsbury Academic, June 2021), 67–74.

79. Edward Said, "Introduction: Secular Criticism," in *The World, the Text, and the Critic* (Cambridge, MA: Harvard University Press, 1983), 3.

80. See Rosi Braidotti, *The Posthuman* (Cambridge, UK: Polity Press, 2013); *Posthuman Glossary*, ed. Rosi Braidotti and Maria Hlavajova (London: Bloomsbury, 2018); Robert Pepperell, "The Posthuman Manifesto," in *The Posthuman Condition: Consciousness beyond the Brain* (Bristol, UK: Intellect, 2003); and three books by Cary Wolfe: *Zootologies: The Question of the Animal* (1999; repr., Minneapolis: University of Minnesota Press, 2003), *Animal Rites: American Culture, the Discourse of Species and Posthumanist Theory* (Chicago: University of Chicago Press, 2003), and *What Is Posthu-*

manism? (Minneapolis: University of Minnesota Press, 2010).

81. See Eva Feder Kittay, "The Ethics of Care, Dependence, and Disability," *Ratio Juris* 24, no. 1 (2011): 49–58; See also *The Matter of Disability: Materiality, Biopolitics, Crip Affect*, ed. David T. Mitchell, Susan Antebi, and Sharon L. Snyder (Ann Arbor: University of Michigan Press, 2019; Robert McRuer, *Crip Theory: Cultural Signs of Queerness and Disability* (New York: New York University Press, 2006); Tobin Siebers, *Disability Aesthetics* (Ann Arbor: University of Michigan Press, 2010).

82. Flusser, *On Doubt*, 1.

83. Marc Renoue, "Entretiens: La vie artificielle du zoosystémicien Louis Bec," 207. See also Louis Bec, "Mobile Immobilisé," in *Zoosystémie*, 313–334.

84. Bec, *Zoosystémie*, 318–319. My translation. This, as well as Flusser's work, also parallels the writings of Fernand Deligny, another radical theorist whose writings on autistic children and animals—particularly spiders as analogues of societal and technological networks—offer an alternative view of biology, behavior, language, and being. See Fernand Deligny, *The Arachnean and Other Texts* (Minneapolis: University of Minnesota Press, 2013).

85. Flusser, *Vampyroteuthis infernalis* (Atropos), 76.

86. Susan Stryker, "(De)Subjugated Knowledges: An Introduction to Transgender Studies," *The Transgender Studies Reader*, ed. Susan Stryker and Stephen Whittle (London: Routledge, 2006), 3–4. See also Susan Stryker and Aren Aizura, "Introduction: Transgender Studies 2.0," in *The Transgender Studies Reader 2* (New York: Rout-

ledge, 2013), 1–15; and Susan Stryker and Paisley Currah, "General Editor's Introduction," *TSQ: Transgender Studies Quarterly* 2, no. 2 (2015): 189–194.

87. Nikki Sullivan, "The Somatechnics of Perception and the Matter of the Non/Human: A Critical Response to the New Materialism," *European Journal of Women's Studies* 19, no. 3 (2012): 299–313; "Somatechnics," *TSQ: Transgender Studies Quarterly* 1, no. 1–2 (2014): 187–190; and Nikki Sullivan and Samantha Murray, eds., *Somatechnics: Queering the Technologization of Bodies* (Farnham, UK: Ashgate, 2009). Sullivan acknowledges that some of the touchstones for this work include Donna Haraway, Elizabeth Grosz, Sara Ahmed, Bruno Latour, Jean-Luc Nancy, Maurice Merleau-Ponty, Luce Irigaray, Gilles Deleuze, and Félix Guattari, but argues—as I agree—that trans* theory provides a vital critical perspective.

88. See Jussi Parikka, *Insect Media: A Media Archaeology of Animals and Technology* (Minneapolis: University of Minnesota Press, 2010); and Eugene Thacker, *Biomedia* (Minneapolis: University of Minnesota Press, 2004).

89. Vilém Flusser, "Skin," *Flusser Studies* 2 (2006): 2.

90. Rainer Guldin and Anke Finger, introduction to *Flusser Studies* 2 (2006): 1.

91. See "A Questionnaire on Materialisms," *October* 155 (2016); Graham Harman's 35th International Flusser Lecture in Berlin: Graham Harman, "The Revenge of the Surface" (2013), published as *Die Rache der Oberfläche: Heidegger, McLuhan, Greenberg* (Berlin: Walther König, 2014); and *30 Years after Les Immatériaux: Art, Science and*

Theory, ed. Yuk Hui and Andreas Broeckmann (Lüneburg: Meson Press, 2015).

92. See Carrie Lambert-Beatty, "Make-Believe: Parafiction and Plausibility," *October* 129 (2009): 51–84.

93. Reza Negarestani, *Cyclonopedia: Complicity with Anonymous Materials* (Melbourne: re.press, 2008), 9. Negarestani has also contended in recent essays (reprising an idea proposed by Jean-François Lyotard) that to undo "enlightened" humanism, we need to embrace "inhumanism," revising Western humanism and treating the human as "a constructible hypothesis, a space of navigation and intervention." See Reza Negarestani, "The Labor of the Inhuman, Part I: Human," *e-flux* 52 (February 2014), http://www.e-flux.com/journal/52/59920/the-labor-of-the-inhuman-part-i-human/, and "The Labor of the Inhuman, Part II: The Inhuman," *e-flux* 53 (March 2014), http://www.e-flux.com/journal/52/59920/the-labor-of-the-inhuman-part-i-human/. See also Jean-François Lyotard, *The Inhuman: Reflections on Time* (Cambridge, UK: Polity Press, 1991).

94. Donna J. Haraway, *When Species Meet* (Minneapolis: University of Minnesota Press, 2007).

95. He Jiankui, a Chinese biophysicist, used CRISPR to edit human embryo genomes, resulting in the births of three infants with altered genes, and was sentenced to prison in China in 2019 for his actions. Jon Cohen, "The Untold Story of the 'Circle of Trust' behind the World's First Gene-Edited Babies," *Science* (August 1, 2019), https://www.sciencemag.org/news/2019/08/untold-story

-circle-trust-behind-world-s-first-gene-edited-babies.

96. The idea of what thrives in human ruins is also picked up by Anna Lowenhaupt Tsing in *The Mushroom at the End of the World: On the Possibility of Life in Capitalist Ruins* (Princeton: Princeton University Press, 2015).

97. Moreshin Allahyari and Daniel Rourke's *The 3D Additivist Cookbook* (2017) was produced as part of Transmediale's 2016 Vilém Flusser Residency Program for Artistic Research, http://additivism.org/cookbook.

98. See Martha Schwendener, "Art, Theory, and the Anthropocene" in *Art, Theory and Practice in the Anthropocene*, ed. Julie Reiss (Wilmington, DE: Vernon Press, 2019), 9–20.

99. Franco "Bifo" Berardi wrote that Donna Haraway had predicted our "ongoing viral apocalypse" by arguing that the agent of evolution was not Man (the subject of History) but "critters," including microbes such as viruses. Franco "Bifo" Berardi, "Beyond the Breakdown: Three Meditations on a Possible Aftermath," *e-flux* (March 31, 2020), https://conversations.e-flux.com/t/beyond-the-breakdown-three-meditations-on-a-possible-aftermath-by-franco-bifo-berardi/9727. See also Donna Haraway, *Staying with the Trouble: Making Kin in the Chthulucene* (Durham: Duke University Press, 2016).

100. Flusser, "On Rabies," trans. Baruch Gottlieb, *Flusser Studies* 30 (2020): 1–4; originally published as "Da raiva," *O Estado de São Paulo, Suplemento Literário* (February 8, 1969): 4.

101. See Adolf Portmann, *Biologie und Geist* (Zurich: Rhein-

Verlag AG, 1956) and the discussion of appearance in Hannah Arendt, *The Life of the Mind* (New York: Harcourt Brace Jovanovich, 1978) and *The Human Condition* (Chicago: University of Chicago Press, 1998).

102. See Londa Schiebinger, "Why Mammals Are Called Mammals: Gender Politics in Eighteenth-Century Natural History," *American Historical Review* 98, no. 2 (1993): 382–411. Schiebinger argues that mammae were only one among several traits that could have been highlighted, and males and egg-laying mammals such as the duckbilled platypus and ant-eater don't even fit well within this taxon. Most important, Linnaeus's new term dovetailed with a push to end wet-nursing, which was linked to high infant mortality, at a moment when European nations needed more labor power to bolster military and economic expansion. Linnaeus, a physician practicing when male obstetricians and gynecologists were taking over the care and dictates of human reproduction and newborns from female midwives, wrote a 1752 pamphlet on the evils of wet-nursing, calling the custom unnatural and a gateway to moral depravity—proving for Schiebinger that science is not value-neutral.

103. Vilém Flusser, *Does Writing Have a Future?*, trans. Nancy Ann Roth (Minneapolis: University of Minnesota Press, 2011), 92. See Bruno Latour, "Why Has Critique Run Out of Steam? From Matters of Fact to Matters of Concern," *Critical Inquiry* 30, no. 2 (2004): 225–248.

104. "Life is undergoing tension. Life is undergoing pressure. Life is undergoing depression. Life is undergoing transgression. The biomass is being shaken, destabilized. . . . We extremophiles are profoundly happy to be in Prague. Franz Kafka is at our side. Vilém Flusser is not far . . . he imagined an epistemological and satirical evolutionary future in the form of a cephalopod called *Vampyroteuthis infernalis* which lived in the extreme environment of the ocean depths. He was particularly interested in a curious adaptive capacity manifested by the organism: it was able to think of the events that take place in the world using its own intestines." Louis Bec, "We Are Extremophiles," MutaMorphosis Conference, November 8–10, 2007, https://mutamorphosis.wordpress.com/2009/02/24/we-are-extremophiles/.

105. Flusser, *Vampyroteuthis infernalis* (Minnesota), 58.

Screen 5

1. Vilém Flusser, "On the Word *Design*: An Etymological Essay," *Design Issues* 11, no. 3 (1995): 53.

2. Paul Betts, *The Authority of Everyday Objects: A Cultural History of West German Industrial Design* (Berkeley: University of California Press, 2004).

3. See Alexandra Midal, *Design by Accident: For a New History of Design*, trans. James Horton (Berlin: Sternberg Press, 2019), 189. Flusser noted the location of this debate: "now that politicians have pushed their way uninvited into the kitchen to give their speeches, . . . the kitchen itself is no longer a private space, having been swept away by the media hurricane." Vilém Flusser, "Vom Tod der Politik" [On the death of politics], in *Nachgeschichte: Eine korrigierte Geschichtsschrei-bung* [Post-history: A corrected history] (Bensheim and Düsseldorf: Bollmann, 1993), 207; quoted in Michael Hanke, "Public/Private Space," *Flusseriana: An Intellectual Toolbox*, ed. Siegfried Zielinski and Peter Weibel with Daniel Irrgang (Minneapolis: Univocal, 2015), 338.

4. See Martha Schwendener, "Notes on Function," in *Return to Function*, ed. Jane Simon (Madison, WI: Madison Museum of Contemporary Art, 2009), 43–75.

5. His essays on objects appeared in Brazilian newspapers, the US journal *Main Currents in Modern Thought*, and books collecting these essays: *As coisas que me cercam* [Things that surround me], which was ready to be published as a book by Fundo Estadual de Cultura before his death, but was never published; and *La force du quotidien* (1973), his first French publication. See Vilém Flusser, *Coisas que me cercam*, manuscript in the Vilém Flusser Archive, and *La force du quotidien*, trans. Jean Mesrie and Barbara Niceall (Paris: Mame, 1973). See also the posthumously published *Dinge und Undinge. Phänomenologische Skizzen* (Munich: Hanser, 1993).

6. See Larry Busbea's "Meta-design: Object and Environment in France, c. 1970*" in *Design Issues* 25, no. 4 (Autumn 2009): 105–106. Busbea discusses Moles at length, as well as writing by Max Bense and Jean Baudrillard's "Design and Environment or How Political Economy Escalates into Cyberblitz," in *For a Critique of the Political Economy of the Sign* (New York: Telos Press, 1981), 201–202. The films of Jacques Tati and the novels of Georges Perec and Alain Robbe-Grillet addressed the ubiquity of new

gadgets and commodities; elsewhere, artists and designers like Anni Albers and György Kepes considered the rise of mass production versus craft.

7. Reyner Banham, *Theory and Design in the First Machine Age* (New York: Praeger, 1960). As director of Industrial Design at the Museum of Modern Art in the 1940s and 1950s, Kaufmann (1910–1989) was concerned about the rise of consumerism, countering with a series of *Good Design* exhibitions at MoMA (1950 to 1955) that followed European modernist aesthetics. Kaufmann's father, Edgar J. Kaufmann, was a department store magnate who had commissioned Frank Lloyd Wright to build Falling Water; Kaufmann Jr. apprenticed with Wright at his Taliesin Foundation.

8. Vilém Flusser, "On Forms and Formulas," *Design Issues* 11, no. 3 (Autumn 1995): 55.

9. Vilém Flusser, "Design as Theology," *The Shape of Things: A Philosophy of Design*, trans. Anthony Mathews (London: Reaktion, 1999), 74. Originally published as "Design als Theologie," *Design Report* 14 (1990): 50; and in *Vom Stand der Dinge. Eine kleine Philosophie des Design*, ed. Fabian Wurm (Göttingen: Steidl, 1993), 21–27.

10. This interest in "things" also resonates in recent strains of new-materialist theory focused on objects and intersubjective relations rather than human subjecthood. See Bill Brown, *Things* (Chicago: University of Chicago Press, 2004); Graham Harman, *Tool-Being: Heidegger and the Metaphysics of Objects* (Chicago: Open Court, 2002); Graham Harman, *Heidegger Explained: From Phenomenon to Thing* (Chicago: Open Court,

2007); Quentin Meillassoux, *After Finitude: An Essay on the Necessity of Contingency*, trans. Ray Brassier (London: Continuum, 2008); Jane Bennett, *Vibrant Matter: A Political Ecology of Things* (Durham: Duke University Press, 2010); Karen Barad, *Meeting the Universe Halfway: Quantum Physics and the Entanglement of Matter and Meaning* (Durham: Duke University Press, 2007). See also Suzana Alpsancar on "Thing(s)" in Zielinski, Weibel, and Irrgang, *Flusseriana*, 408.

11. Vilém Flusser, "On Edmund Husserl," *Review of the Society for the History of Czechoslovak Jews* 1 (New York, 1987): 91–100.

12. Martin Heidegger, *What Is a Thing?* (Chicago: Regnery, 1967) and "The Thing" in *Poetry, Language, Thought*, trans. Albert Hofstadter (New York: Harper & Row, 1971), 161–180.

13. Abraham Moles, *Théorie des objets* (Paris: Éditions universitaires, 1972). See also Abraham Moles, "Objet et communication" [Object and communication] in a special issue on "Les Objets" [Objects], *Communications* (1969): 1–22; the issue also included essays by Baudrillard, Pierre Boudon, Henri Van Lier, Eberhard Wahl, and Violette Morin.

14. Vilém Flusser, "Apropos d'Abraham Moles: La communication: science ou idéologie?," in *Communication et langages* 20 (1973): 35–44.

15. Flusser, "Apropos d'Abraham Moles," 44.

16. Flusser, "Apropos d'Abraham Moles," 42.

17. Vilém Flusser, "Bottles," *Main Currents in Modern Thought* 28, no. 4 (1972): 112; published in French as "Les Bouteilles," in *La force du quotidien*, 37–46; in German as "Flaschen," in Flusser, *Dinge und Undinge*, 11–26.

18. Flusser, "Bottles," 114.

19. Vilém Flusser, "Fountain Pens," manuscript in English in the Flusser Archive; later translated into French and appearing as "Stylos" in Flusser, *La force du quotidien*, 49–59.

20. Vilém Flusser, "Why Do Typewriters Go 'Click'?," in *The Shape of Things*, 62–65. Originally published as "Warum eigentlich klappern die Schreibmaschinen?," *Basler Zeitung* (November 20, 1988): 41. See also Vilém Flusser, "Discovery," *Artforum* (March 1989): 12.

21. Vilém Flusser, "Carpets," in *The Shape of Things*, 95–98; originally published in Portuguese as "Tapêtes," *O Estado de São Paulo, Suplemento Literário* (October 17, 1970): 4. See also Flávio Tonnetti on "Tapestry" in Zielinski, Weibel, and Irrgang, *Flusseriana*, 386.

22. Vilém Flusser, "Beds," manuscript in English in the Flusser Archive. The essay appeared in French as "Lits" in Flusser, *La force du quotidien*, 115–132, and "Du Lit," *Cause commune* (Paris) 5 (February 1973): 21–27; in Portuguese as "Da Cama," *Comentário* (Rio de Janeiro), June 12, 1971, 15–22; and in German as "Das Bett" in Flusser, *Dinge und Undinge*, 89–109.

23. Vilém Flusser, "Baths," *Flusser Studies* 4 (2007): 1–6. The same issue includes a manuscript of the Portuguese version, "Banheiros," *Flusser Studies* (2007): 1–5.

24. Vilém Flusser, "Motor Cars," manuscript in English in the Flusser Archive; later translated into French and appearing as "Automobiles" in Flusser, *La force du quotidien*, 135–144.

25. Vilém Flusser, "Canes," 3; manuscript in English in

the Flusser Archive. The essay appeared in Portuguese as "Bengalas" in Flusser's "Posto Zero" column, *Fôlha de São Paulo*, February 8, 1972; in French as "Les Cannes," in Flusser, *La force du quotidien*, 27–34; and in German as "Stöcke" in Flusser, *Dinge und Undinge*, 63–79.

26. Vilém Flusser, "The Bag," 1; manuscript in English in the Flusser Archive. Later published as "Die Tasche. Struktural Analyse," *Dolomiten* (Bolzano) 283 (1973): 15.

27. Flusser, *Le force du quotidien*, 19. This argument also appears in Vilém Flusser, "Le phénomène surprenant de la communication," *Communication et langages* 37 (1978): 27–32.

28. Flusser, *Le force du quotidien*, 19–20.

29. Vilém Flusser, "Walls," *Main Currents in Modern Thought* 30, no. 4 (1974): 136. The essay appeared in Portuguese as "Paredes" in Flusser's "Posto Zero" column, *Fôlha de São Paulo*, February 7, 1972; in French as "Les Murs," in Flusser, *La force du quotidien*; and in German as "Wände" in Flusser, *Dinge und Undinge*. See also Vilém Flusser, "On Being Subject to Objects," originally written for *Artforum* but only published posthumously in Vilém Flusser, *Artforum // Essays*, ed. Martha Schwendener (São Paulo: Metaflux, 2017), 317–329.

30. Flusser, "Fountain Pens," 4, and "Motor Cars," 3. "And the classically Marxist analysis of the problem will no longer help us. It does not much help to say that the thing that dominates us belongs to some men (as the machine in nineteenth-century factories did), and that therefore the thing is only a means by which we are dominated by

others. The motor car disproves this classically Marxist thesis. It is we ourselves who own it, and it oppresses us because it is we ourselves who allow it to do so." "Motor Cars," 3.

31. Vilém Flusser, "Alexandre Bonnier's Living-Room," 3, manuscript in the Vilém Flusser Archive and published as Wilem Flusser, "L'appartement d'Alexandre Bonnier," translated from the English by Paule Guivarch in *Traverses* (Centre de Création Industrielle) 4 (May 1976): 123–126. The issue also included texts by Michel de Certeau, Jean Baudrillard, and others.

32. Delivered at the "Gestaltung und neue Wirklichkeit" [Design and new reality] conference in Ulm and published as Vilém Flusser, "Gebrauchsgegenstände" [Everyday objects], in *Basler Zeitung* 211 (September 8, 1988): 49; and "Design: Hindernis zum Abräumen von Hindernissen?" [Design: Obstacle for the removal of obstacles?], *Design Report* 9 (January 1989); in English as "Design: Obstacle for/to the Removal of Obstacles" in *The Shape of Things*, 58–61.

33. Vilém Flusser, "About the Word *Design*," in *The Shape of Things*, 17–21. Originally published as "Vom Wort Design" in *Design Report* (Frankfurt am Main) 15 (December 1990), and republished in *Vom Stand der Dinge*, 9–13. See also Vilém Flusser, "The Term 'Design,'" *Artforum* (March 1992): 19–20; and "On the Word *Design*: An Etymological Essay," 50–53.

34. "The diminutive of *ars* is *articulum*—i.e., little art—and indicates that something is turned around the hand (as in the French *tour de main*). Hence *ars* means something like

'agility' or the 'ability to turn something to one's advantage,' and *artifex*—i.e., 'artist'—means a 'trickster' above all. That the original artist was a conjurer can be seen from words such as 'artifice,' 'artificial,' and even 'artillery.' In German, an artist is of course one who is 'able to do something,' the German word for art, *Kunst*, being the noun *können*, 'to be able' or 'can,' but there again the word for 'artificial,' *gekünstelt*, comes from the same root (as does the English 'cunning')." Flusser, "About the Word *Design*," 17–18.

35. Flusser, "About the Word *Design*," 17. In fact, Alberto J. L. Carrillo Canán argues that Flusser's entire communications theory might be deemed a "theory of deception," with opaque scientific texts and scientific knowledge creating an existentially absurd situation: readers of such codes have no access to the origins of the information but are programmed by it nonetheless. "The discursive dynamic of mass media reinforces the magical, deceptive character of their images on a new scale: the global transmission centers take the place of the priests." Alberto J. L. Carrillo Canán, "Deception and the 'Magic' of 'Technical Images' According to Flusser," *Flusser Studies* 4 (May 2007): 12. Similarly, in *Vampyroteuthis infernalis*, the vampire squid's bioluminescence and other sensory adaptations are used to deceive predators and prey and serve as analogues to human communication.

36. Vilém Flusser, "The Lever Strikes Back," in *The Shape of Things*, 51–54. First published as "Der Hebel schlägt zurück" in *Design Report* (Frankfurt am Main) 12 (October 1989): 5.

37. Vilém Flusser, "The Ethics of Industrial Design," in *The Shape of Things*, 66–69, originally delivered as a lecture at a symposium in Eindhoven, April 20–21, 1991.

38. Flusser, "The Ethics of Industrial Design," 68.

39. Vilém Flusser, "Série altamente emotiva—I: Ironia" [Highly emotional series I: irony], "Posto Zero," *Fôlha de São Paulo*, February 26, 1972, np.

40. Vilém Flusser, "War and the State of Things," in *The Shape of Things*, 31.

41. Flusser, "War and the State of Things," 32.

42. Flusser, "War and the State of Things," 33. "Pure good is pointless, absurd," Flusser adds, using off-the-grid hermit-saints as an example, "and, wherever there is a purpose for anything, you will find the Devil lying in wait" (33).

43. Flusser, "War and the State of Things," 34. Elsewhere, Flusser changes the technology to ovens: During the Nuremberg trials "a letter written by a German industrialist to a Nazi official was discovered. In it, the industrialist timidly begs to be forgiven for having constructed his gas ovens badly: Instead of killing thousands of people at one go, only hundreds were being killed." Flusser, "The Ethics of Industrial Design" in *The Shape of Things*, 68.

44. Vilém Flusser, "Form and Material" in *The Shape of Things*, 28. Also published as "Der Schein des Materials" in Wolfgang Drechsler and Peter Weibel, *Bildlicht. Malerei zwischen Material und Immaterialität* (Vienna: Europaverlag, 1991), 12–20; "Form und Material" in *Arch+* 111 (1992), 66–67, and *Vom Stand der Dinge*, 105–112.

45. Vilém Flusser, "The Non-Thing 1," in *The Shape of Things*, 87–88; published posthumously as "Das Unding 1" in *Dinge und Undinge*, 80–84.

46. Vilém Flusser, "The Non-Thing 2," in *The Shape of Things*, 91. Published posthumously as "Das Unding 2" in *Dinge und Undinge*, 85–89.

47. Vilém Flusser, "Wheels," in *The Shape of Things*, 117. First published as "Räder" in *Die Zeit* (Hamburg), December 6, 1991.

48. Vilém Flusser, "With as Many Holes as a Swiss Cheese," in *The Shape of Things*, 83.

49. Vilém Flusser, "Shelter, Screens, and Tents," in *The Shape of Things*, 55–57; originally published in *Herbstschrift* (Graz) 3 (October 1990). Other versions include "Einiges über die besonderen Vorzüge des Zeltens" [On the merits of tents] in *Basler-Zeitung*, August 8, 1990, and "'How Goodly Are Your Tents, Jacob?,'" in Vilém Flusser, *The Freedom of the Migrant: Objections to Nationalism*, trans. Kenneth Kronenberg, ed. Anke K. Finger (Urbana: University of Illinois Press, 2003), 59–64. See also Irmgard Zepf on "Tents" in Zielinski, Weibel, and Irrgang, *Flusseriana*, 402; and Susanne Hauser, "House," also in *Flusseriana*, 210–212.

50. Vilém Flusser, "Wittgenstein's Architecture," in *The Shape of Things*, 76–77.

51. Vilém Flusser, "The City as Wave-Trough in the Image-Flood," trans. Phil Gochenour, *Critical Inquiry* 31, no. 2 (Winter 2005): 320–328. Vilém Flusser, "Designing Cities," in *Writings*, ed. Andreas Ströhl (Minneapolis: University of Minnesota Press, 2002), 172–180; originally published as "Städte entwerfen," in *Vom Subjekt zum Projekt. Menschwerdung, Schriften 3*, ed.

Stefan Bollmann (Bensheim and Düsseldorf: Bollmann, 1994), 43–60.

52. Flusser, "The City as Wave-Trough," 325.

53. Flusser, "The City as Wave-Trough," 325.

54. See Gilles Deleuze and Felix Guattari, *A Thousand Plateaus: Capitalism and Schizophrenia* (London: Continuum, 2004), 323. This comparison has become more complicated, however, as Eyal Weizman points out, when the Israeli military crashes through a wall Deleuze and Guattari have designated as "floating." See Eyal Weizman, "The Art of War: Deleuze, Guattari, Debord, and the Israeli Defense Force," *Mute* (August 3, 2006), https://www.metamute.org/editorial/articles/art-war-deleuze-guattari-debord-and-israeli-defence-force; and Eyal Weizman, *Forensic Architecture: Violence at the Threshold of Detectability* (Brooklyn, NY: Zone Books; Cambridge, MA: MIT Press, 2017). "What is really at stake," Susanne Kuechler writes, "is a new kind of surface ontology which replaces the opposition of inside and outside, invisible and visible, immaterial and material, with a complementary relation that thrives on transformation rather than distinction." Susanne Kuechler, "Technological Materiality: Beyond the Dualist Paradigm," *Theory, Culture and Society* 25, no. 1 (2008): 116.

55. Vilém Flusser, "Da ficção" [On fiction], *Jornal o Diário de Ribeirão Preto* (São Paulo), August 26, 1966, np; my translation. See also Martha Schwendener, "Vilém Flusser: On Fiction, Truth, and Envisioning," *Brooklyn Rail* (June 2024). https://brooklynrail

.org/2024/06/criticspage/Vilm-Flusser-On-Fiction-Truth-and-Envisioning/.

56. Julian Bleecker, "Design Fiction: A Short Essay on Design, Science, Fact and Fiction," 7, *Near Future Laboratory* (blog), March 17, 2009, https://blog.nearfuturelaboratory.com/2009/03/17/design-fiction-a-short-essay-on-design-science-fact-and-fiction/. This reference is from the pamphlet version, obtained from the New Future Laboratory website.

57. Flusser, "Designing Cities," 180.

58. Vilém Flusser, *What If? Twenty-Two Scenarios in Search of Images*, trans. Anke Finger and Kenneth Kronenberg (Minneapolis: University of Minnesota Press, 2022); originally published as *Angenommen. Eine Szenenfolge* (Göttingen: European Photography; Immatrix Publications, 1989). The very title of *Angenommen* (Supposed/assumed, or *What If?*) includes speculation in its description. The twenty-two abstract and cross-disciplinary scenarios in the book, dedicated to his cousin David Flusser, were meant as texts to be "recoded" as video images.

59. Vilém Flusser, "The Submarine," in *The Shape of Things*, 111.

60. Flusser, "The Submarine," 116.

61. Vilém Flusser, "Jogos" [Games], *O Estado de São Paulo, Suplemento literário*, no. 556 (December 9, 1967): 1.

62. Flusser, "The Non-Thing 1," 89.

63. Vilém Flusser, "Gesellschaftsspiele," *Kunstforum* 116 (1991): 66–69; also published in *Künstliche Spiele* (Artificial games), ed. Georg Hartwagner, Stefan Iglhaut,

and Florian Rötzer (Munich: Boer, 1993). See also Susanne Hauser, *Spielsituationen. Über das Entwerfen von Städten und Häusern* [Game situations: On designing cities and houses], International Flusser Lectures (Cologne: Walther König, 2003); Florian Rötzer, *Ist das Leben ein Spiel? Aspekte einer Philosophie des Spiels und eines Denkens ohne Fundamente* [Is life a game? Aspects of a philosophy of play and thinking without foundations], International Flusser Lectures (Cologne: Walther König, 2013); Daniela Kuka on "Game," in Zielinski, Weibel, and Irrgang, *Flusseriana*, 190.

64. Vilém Flusser, "Xadrés" [Chess], *Fôlha de São Paulo*, February 2, 1972, np.

65. Flusser, "The Non-Thing 1," 89.

66. Flusser, "The Non-Thing 2," 92.

67. Alexander R. Galloway, *Gaming: Essays on Algorithmic Culture* (Minneapolis: University of Minnesota Press, 2006).

68. Fabrizio Poltronieri, "Communicology, Apparatus, and Post-History: Vilém Flusser's Concepts Applied to Video Games and Gamification," in *Rethinking Gamification*, ed. Mathias Fucks, Sonia Fizek, Paulo Ruffino, and Niklas Schrape (Lüneburg: Meson Press, 2014), 172.

69. The game, in Galloway's terms, is an "algorithmic machine" rather than a "toy." Galloway, *Gaming*, 5. Galloway argues that the game also becomes a work site—which is, of course, literalized in operators who play games for a living, either to achieve higher levels for other users or for some other purpose. "In blunt terms, the video game *Dope Wars* has more in common with the finance

software *Quicken* than it does with traditional games like chess, roulette, or billiards." Galloway, *Gaming*, 6.

70. Flusser, "The Non-Thing 2," 93.

71. See John Harwood, *The Interface: IBM and the Transformation of Corporate Design, 1945–1976* (Minneapolis: University of Minnesota Press, 2011); and C. Wright Mills, "Man in the Middle: The Designer," in *Power, Politics, and People: The Collected Essays of C. Wright Mills*, ed. Irving Horowitz (London: Oxford University Press, 1972), 374–386. Following Flusser, curators at the Museum of Modern Art recently pointed out how "interaction design can transform our behaviors—from the way we experience and move our bodies to the ways we conceive of space, time, and relationships." See the introduction to "Never Alone: Video Games and Other Interactive Design," September 10, 2022–July 16, 2023, organized by Paola Antonelli, Paul Galloway, Anna Burckhardt, and Amanda Forment, Department of Architecture and Design, Museum of Modern Art, New York, accessed April 16, 2025, https://www.moma.org/calendar/exhibitions/5453.

72. Richard A. Bolt, *Spatial Data-Management* (Cambridge, MA: Architecture Machine Group, Massachusetts Institute of Technology, 1979).

73. "We believe future systems will not be characterized by their memory size or processing speed," Nicholas Negroponte wrote in the preface. "Instead, the human interface will become the major measure, calibrated in very subjective units, so sensory and personalized that it will be evaluated

by feelings and perceptions. Is it easy to use? Does it feel good? Is it pleasurable? . . . It is this interface that will bring computers directly to generals, presidents of companies, and six-year-old children." Nicholas Negroponte, preface to Bolt, *Spatial Data-Management*, 5.

74. Mike Anusas and Tim Ingold, "Designing Environmental Relations: From Opacity to Textility," *Design Issues* 29, no. 4 (Autumn 2013): 61.

75. Vilém Flusser, "The Designer's Glance," *Design Issues* 11, no. 3 (1995): 53. Originally published as "Der Blick des Designers" in *Design Report* 18/19 (1991); and appearing as "The Designer's Way of Seeing" in *The Shape of Things*, 39–42.

76. Flusser, "The Designer's Way of Seeing," 42.

77. Vilém Flusser, "Cor-derosa" [Pink], undated manuscript in the Flusser Archive, first published in *Flusser Studies* 35 (2023): 1. Bonnier's text for the Biennial catalogue stated that he chose pink because of its ubiquity, ambiguity, and range of psychological and symbolic variants—often radical variants: childish pink and morbid pink. See *XII Bienal de São Paulo* catalogue (São Paulo: Fundação Bienal de São Paulo, 1973), 216–217. Fred Forest describes taking Bonnier around São Paulo to buy pink items: shoes, dishes, a brassiere. See Rainer Guldin and Gustavo Bernardo, *Vilém Flusser (1920– 1991). Ein Leben in der Bodenlosigkeit*, 228; see also Flusser, "L'appartement d'Alexandre Bonnier," on Bonnier.

78. Vilém Flusser, "Da negritude," *Cadernos Brasileiros* (São Paulo, 1966): 29–35; "O prêto é belo" [Black is beautiful], *O Estado de São Paulo*,

Suplemento Literário (April 18, 1971): 3; "Schwarz ist schön in Brasilien" [Black is beautiful in Brazil], *Frankfurter Allgemeine Zeitung* (December 31, 1971); "La magie nègre," *arTitudes international* (Saint-Jeannet) 33/38 (June 1976–March 1977): 24–26; "Négritude," *arTitudes international* 33/38 (June 1976–March 1977): 13; "Preto e branco," *Iris. Fotografia/Vi-deo/Som* 354 (São Paulo, November 1982): 28–29; and "Black Is Beautiful," in *What If?*, 74–76.

79. Kimberly Cleveland, "Afro-Brazilian Art as a Prism: A Socio-Political History of Brazil's Artistic, Diplomatic and Economic Confluences in the Twentieth Century," *Luso-Brazilian Review* 49, no. 2 (2012): 102–119. Cleveland writes: "Upon returning to Brazil, intellectuals Clarival do Prado Valladares and Vilém Flusser authored articles in national publications in which they argued that 'black art' simply did not exist in their country" (106–107).

80. Vilém Flusser, "Preto e branco," *Iris* 354 (1982): 28.

81. Frantz Fanon, *Black Skin, White Masks*, trans. Charles Lam Markmann (London: Pluto Press, 1986), 14.

82. Fred Moten, "The Case of Blackness," *Criticism* 50, no. 2 (2008): 177–218. In Moten's essay, jazz musician Cecil Taylor's "lived blackness," which encompasses the social and the artistic, is posed against the autonomous formalism of Ad Reinhardt, who devoted his later career to making black paintings. Underpinning the essay is the fact that art critic and historian Barbara Rose excised Taylor's impassioned description of lived blackness from the print publication of

Reinhardt's "Black as Symbol and Concept" (originally a contribution to a roundtable discussion), in *Art as Art: The Selected Writings of Ad Reinhardt*, ed. Barbara Rose (Berkeley: University of California Press), 86–88.

83. Vilém Flusser in "On Religion, Memory, and Synthetic Image," interview with László Beke and Miklós Peterák, April 7, 1990, in *We Shall Survive in the Memory of Others*, DVD and booklet, ed. Miklós Peternák (Cologne: Walther König, 2010), 32. See also Francesco Restuccia, "Flusser against Idolatry," *Flusser Studies* 26 (2018): 1–15.

84. Flusser, "Black Is Beautiful," 74.

85. Flusser, "Black Is Beautiful," 75.

86. Vilém Flusser, *Towards a Philosophy of Photography* (Göttingen: European Photography, 1984), 30.

87. Paul Virilio, *Grey Ecology* (New York: Atropos, 2010); Gilles Deleuze, *Francis Bacon: The Logic of Sensation* (1981; trans., London: Continuum, 2002); Jean Baudrillard, "Consumer Society" in *Selected Writings*, ed. Mark Poster (Stanford, CA: Stanford University Press, 1988), 32; originally published as *La société de consummation* (Paris: Gallimard, 1970).

88. Flusser, *Into the Universe of Technical Images*, 69.

89. Vilém Flusser, "About a House of Color: For the magazine *Casa da Cor*," undated, 3. Flusser Archive; in English. Flusser adds a parenthetical: "This model is no 'explanation of human history,' just an auxiliary figure to localize the present problem of color" (3).

90. Vilém Flusser, "The Codified World," in *Writings*, 35.

91. Vilém Flusser, "Images in the New Media," in *Writings*, 71.

92. "The coloration of the skin constitutes a code: the other members of the species decipher the meaning of the message. Cephalopods 'speak through the skin.'" Vilém Flusser, *Vampyroteuthis infernalis: A Treatise, With a Report by the Institut Scientifique de Recherche Paranaturaliste*, with Louis Bec, translated from the Portuguese by Rodrigo Maltez Novaes (New York: Atropos Press, 2011), 42.

93. Flusser, *Vampyroteuthis infernalis*, 88.

94. Flusser, *Vampyroteuthis infernalis*, 109 and 91.

95. Albeit he imagined them in a "continent-sized Disneyland full of people working very short weeks because of automation, and trying desperately to amuse themselves so as not to die of boredom." Vilém Flusser, "On Science," *Artforum* (October 1988): 9.

96. Vilém Flusser, "Vom Umfärben der Grünen" [On the recoloring of the Greens], which exists in manuscript form. See *Flusser Studies* 35, which gathered several of these essays on color, including "Bunte Tiere" [Colorful animals] and "Ecologia multicolorida?," and Guldin's "Colored Technical Images," which pieces together their chronology and publication. See also "Blaue Hunde" [Blue dogs] in the German version of *Post-History*, titled *Nachgeschichten. Essays, Vorträge, Glossen* (Düsseldorf: Bollmann, 1990), 204–215.

97. Flusser, "Vom Umfärben der Grünen," 4; in German, my translation. Flusser would repeat several of these ideas in a video call with the Casa da Cor consultants on May 7, 1988, from his home in Robion,

France. See "Video palestra" [Video lecture] transcript in Portuguese in the Flusser Archive.

98. Karl Gerstner, *Designing Programmes: Instead of Solutions for Problems, Programmes for Solutions* (New York: Hastings House, 1964). See also Helen Armstrong, ed., *Graphic Design Theory: Readings from the Field* (New York: Princeton Architectural Press, 2009), 58.

99. Gerstner developed what he called a "mobile grid" for arranging text and image. "The grid is a program par excellence," he argued, "almost inexhaustible as a program." Gerstner, *Designing Programmes*, 12. The Swiss mathematician Andreas Spieser influenced Gerstner's exploration of Islamic and Egyptian ornament. In *Designing Programmes*, Gerstner cited John Cage's *Variation I* (1958) for its algorithmic-like sequence of lines and dots and typography in the vein of Christian Morgenstern, Kurt Schwitters, the Dadaists, El Lissitzky, and the concrete poets Eugen Gomringer and Flusser's friend Theon Spanudis, who treated words and letters as "constellations."

100. Programmed art was seen by these artists as, paradoxically, freer and more subjective. Gerstner wrote: "The criterion: the more universal the formula, the more original the picture. The more versatile its unity, or the more uniform its versatility, the more it can convey to the viewer as an object of the most personal perceptions." Karl Gerstner, in *A Little-Known Story about a Movement, a Magazine, and the Computer's Arrival in Art: New Tendencies and Bit International, 1961–1973*, ed. Margit Rosen (Karlsruhe: ZKM / Center

for Art and Media; Cambridge, MA: MIT Press, 2011), 82.

101. Karl Gerstner, *Die Neue Graphik. The New Graphic Art. Le nouvel art graphique* (Teufen, Switzerland: A. Niggli, 1959). See Vilém Flusser, "Line and Surface," in *Writings*, 21–34.

102. Gerstner, *Die Neue Graphik*, 100. Optics and form were central to the sans serif typeface Gerstner championed in *Designing Programmes*—and would be important in his color theory. Individual characters, or letters, were the "elementary particles" of the written language, and the typographer's aim was to make a cohesive whole out of the parts.

103. Karl Gerstner, *Compendium for Literates: A System of Writing* (Cambridge, MA: MIT Press, 1974).

104. "The relation between a photograph and what it represents is curiously opaque," Flusser wrote. "Techno-images are different from traditional 'hand-made' images in that they look as if what they represent is somehow representing itself." Vilém Flusser, "How Should Photographs Be Deciphered?," *Philosophy of Photography* 2, no. 2 (2011): 213. Previously unpublished manuscript in the Flusser Archive. Gerstner argued the same in terms of the shape and form of text and design.

105. Vilém Flusser, "On Typography," manuscript in English in the Flusser Archive. See also Luciano Guimarães, "Typography," in Zielinski, Weibel, and Irrgang, *Flusseriana*, 420–422.

106. Flusser, "On Typography," 4.

107. Flusser also argued that typographers work on characters, like geneticists—at the cellular level—and thus could

354

Notes

affect this demise, avoiding a society stagnating in prototype, stereotype, and clone. Vilém Flusser, "Typen und Charaktere" [Types and characters], lecture delivered to the Typographic Society of Munich on October 8, 1991, Flusser Archive; in German.

108. Karl Gerstner, *Kalte Kunst? Zum Standort der heutigen Malerei* (Teufen, Switzerland: A. Niggli, 1957). Gerstner (along with the painter Richard Paul Lohse) was making serial paintings in which the size and color were dictated by mathematical laws, and rather than variations on a theme, the system that generated the permutations was important. See, for instance, Lohse's *Fifteen Systematic Color Rows with Vertical Condensations* from 1950–1968, in which a vertical "fault-line" is produced by the progressive compression of color scales, which is governed mathematically.

109. Karl Gerstner, *The Spirit of Colors: The Art of Karl Gerstner* (Cambridge, MA: MIT Press, 1982), 189. Gerstner also admitted an affinity for "outsiders" in color theory, like D. P. G. Humbert de Superville and Charles Henry. Humbert de Superville took the physiognomy of the human face as his starting point; Henry, a psychophysiological approach. Both were also of interest to painters like Seurat and Signac.

110. See Gerstner, *The Forms of Color: The Interaction of Visual Elements*, trans. Dennis A. Stephenson (Cambridge, MA: MIT Press, 1986), 16–18, for an explanation of Wyszecki's uniform color space. The ideas of astrophysicist Fritz Zwicky, in terms of a morphological method for constructing a system that catalogues all possible variables,

were already a touchstone for Gerstner in books like *Designing Programmes* and *Compendium for Literates*, written when mainframe computing was entering design. Kandinsky's ideas about correlating colors and abstract forms appear in his *Concerning the Spiritual in Art* (Auckland, New Zealand: 1911).

111. Letter from Vilém Flusser to Karl Gerstner, September 24, 1987, Flusser Archive; in German; my translation. See also Martha Schwendener, "Colorful Dialogue: Vilém Flusser, Karl Gerstner, and *Casa da Cor*," *Flusser Studies* 35 (2023): 1–16. Four books by Gerstner are in the Flusser Archive in Berlin: *Karl Gerstner: AlgoRhythmus 3*, with text by Max Lüscher (Galerie Denise René and Hans Mayer, 1973); *Les formes des couleurs* (Paris: Bibliothèque des Arts, 1986); *Vingt et un passages à travers le Rouge* (Geneva: Editions Sigma, 1988); and *Kompendium für Alphabeten. Eine Systematik der Schrift* (Berlin: Arthur Niggli, 1986).

112. From a short notice in *O Estado de São Paulo*, February 5, 1988.

113. See Rainer Guldin, "*Colorarium*: The Exchange of Letters between Vilém Flusser, Karl Gerstner, Philippe Henry, and Gottfried Jäger," *Flusser Studies* 35 (2023): 1–25.

114. Vilém Flusser, "Reflexões sobre: A Casa da Cor a construir em São Paulo," manuscript dated July 27, 1987, Flusser Archive.

115. Flusser, "Reflexões sobre: A Casa da Cor," 5. There was also the light-color dynamic: "Too much light kills color, as much as too little of it does. Contrary to what certain *tropicalista* ideology asserts, the tropics, with their strong

luminosity, tend to be monochromatic (which explains their 'sadness'). And the painters of our tradition seek Tuscan or Provencal luminosity because it is not intense and diffused. The 'light of reason' makes life as colorless and insipid as the darkness of mysticism, and not only at night; at midday all cows are gray" (5).

116. Flusser, "Reflexões sobre: A Casa da Cor," 7.

117. Vilém Flusser, "About a House of the Color," undated manuscript in English, Flusser Archive.

118. Flusser, "Mesa redonda" [Roundtable], February 9, 1988, manuscript in the Flusser Archive, 4.

119. Yet there were obstacles: "The tragedy is that while developed countries try desperately to get out of history and enter another level of conscience [consciousness] the underdeveloped countries are making a tremendous effort to enter history." Vilém Flusser, "Why the House of Color in São Paulo," 20, for the A Casa da Cor Cycle of Debates, August 9–11, 1988, São Paulo, in the Flusser Archive. Philippe Henry also reports that Flusser wanted to call the project *Chez Couleur* [At the Color House] or *@couleur*, imagining it as a nonlocal site, a "depression in the communicological space." See "Sobre a Casa da Cor—Entrevista com Philippe Henry" [About Casa da Cor—Interview with Philippe Henry], Diogo Andrade Bornhausen, Rodrigo Maltez Novaes, Rodrigo Petronio, and Philippe Henry, *Flusser Studies* 35 (2023): 7.

120. Vilém Flusser, "Farben Verschlüsseln (für Karl Gerstner)" [Coding colors (for Karl Gerstner)], March 4, 1988,

manuscript in the Vilém Flusser Archive, 1.

121. Karl Gerstner, "Is Constructive Art at an End? Or at Its Beginning?," in Gerstner, *The Spirit of Colors*, 26; originally published in *National-Zeitung Basel*, January 19, 1977. Flusser continued to argue for the development of a denotative color code—but created "ecologically" with word codes, image codes, and sound codes. See Flusser, "Why the House of Color in São Paulo," 19.

122. Vilém Flusser, "Codigo de cores" [Color code], March 3, 1988, Flusser Archive.

123. Vilém Flusser, letter to David Flusser, January 25, 1989, Flusser Archive; Vilém Flusser, "Postmoderne Farben (fuer Gottfried Jaeger)" [Postmodern color (for Gottfried Jäger)], 2, manuscript included in a letter from Vilém Flusser to Gottfried Jäger, March 4, 1988, Flusser Archive.

124. Letter from Vilém Flusser to Karl Gerstner, April 1, 1989, Flusser Archive; in English.

125. Gerstner, *The Forms of Color*, 167. Iannis Xenakis, still working as an architect, was the assistant on Le Corbusier's project and Edgar Varèse provided the music. Gerstner also mentions experiments by Oskar Fischinger, who inspired Walt Disney's *Fantasia*; and artists Ludwig Hirschfeld Mack, Viking Eggeling, and Hans Richter.

126. Gerstner, *The Spirit of Colors*, 146.

127. See letters from Henry to Flusser, press clippings in the Flusser Archive, and Guldin, "*Colorarium*," 18. Philippe Henry wrote to Flusser that the original patron, the Brazilian subsidiary of German chemical company BASF (Badische Ani-

lin- und Sodafabrik), was insisting on additional funders, and Flusser was concerned that the project had taken a commercial turn (the press materials and brochures all describe Casa da Cor as a project of "Grupo BASF no Brasil").

128. See "Sobre a Casa da Cor—Entrevista com Philippe Henry," 5; in Portuguese, my translation. See also *The colours of . . . Frank O. Gehry, Jean Nouvel, Wang Shu, BIG, Stefano Boeri, Zaha Hadid, Herzog & de Meuron, Steven Holl Architects, Toyo Ito, Lui Jiakun, Michael Malzan Architecture, Giancarlo Mazzanti, Enric Ruiz-Geli, Cloud 9, SANAA*, ed. Cees W. de Jong (Basel: Birkhäuser, 2015).

129. In "Sobre a Casa da Cor—Entrevista com Philippe Henry," Philippe Henry also mentions, participating over the course of the project, Brazilian architect Fernando Peixoto; fashion designers Maud Perl and Anna Gili; Italian historian Manlio Brusatin; French historian Michel Pastoureau; Allan H. Pasco, US specialist in nineteenth-century literature and author of *The Color-Keys to À la recherche du temps perdu* (Geneva: Librairie Droz, 1976); Brent Berlin and Paul Kay, US authors of *Basic Color Terms* (Berkeley: University of California Press, 1969); and Serge Tornay, editor of *Voir et nommer les couleurs* (Nanterre: Laboratoire d'Ethnologie et de Sociologie Comparative, 1978).

130. Henry in "Sobre a Casa da Cor—Entrevista com Philippe Henry," 11.

131. Philippe Henry, "A New Universal Vision: The 'Casa da Cor' (House of Color) Project," *Leonardo* 24, no. 3 (1991): 321–323.

132. "Sight, which appears to unite us through the same image, in fact divides us through our sensibility and our culture. Man must invent signals that are perceived with the same meaning and the same intensity by specific groups, in specific conditions." Jean-Maurice Simoneau at the first Casa da Cor consultants' meeting, São Paulo, February 9, 1988. Quoted in Henry, "A New Universal Vision," 322. More recently, Henry articulated this further: "If Manlio Brusatin and Nietzsche are right, colors are concepts. World visions. And this is Nietzsche's original intuition, that there is no worldview for blue among the Homeric Greeks." Henry in "Sobre a Casa da Cor—Entrevista com Philippe Henry," 8–9.

133. Henry, "A New Universal Vision," 322–323.

134. Interview with Vilém Flusser in *Superinteressante* (São Paulo, November 1988), 84; in Portuguese, my translation. Edith Flusser translated the interview into German for Vilém Flusser, *Zwiegespräche. Interviews 1967–1991* (Göttingen: European Photography), 29–33; however, it is mislabeled in the book as occurring in 1986 rather than 1988.

135. Karl Gerstner, "Vilém Flusser und die Farben," *Basler Magazin* 9 (February 29, 1992): 4–5. Quoted in Guldin, "*Colorarium*," 14. Elsewhere, Gerstner pointed out that art made in times of chaos—Florence in the age of Savonarola, Picasso's *Guernica*—often transcended its moment, serving as this kind of beacon of hope. See Gerstner, "Is Constructive Art at an End?," 25.

136. Roxana Bujack, Emily Teti, Jonah Miller, Elektra Caf-

frey, and Terece L. Turton, "The Non-Reimannian Nature of Perceptual Color Space," *Proceedings of the National Academy of Sciences* (PNAS), ed. Brian Wandell (Stanford University), received October 28, 2021; accepted March 13, 2022, www.pnas.org/doi/pdf /10.1073/pnas.2119753119. A mathematical model that better predicts human distinction between colors would allow companies like Netflix to discard data and save significant bandwidth—as much as fifteen percent of the estimated 500 million GB of video streamed every day in 2019. See Jesus Dias, interview with Roxana Bujack, *Fast Company*, August 22, 2022, https://www.fastcompany .com/90780869/it-could-take -20-more-years-for-scientists -to-truly-understand-color. A more recent estimate (or "guess-timate") puts that number at 800 million GB per day. See The Product Folks, https://www .theproductfolks.com/product -management-case-studies /how-much-data-is-consumed -by-netflix-users-worldwide -in-a-day, 2024, accessed June 2, 2025.

137. Flusser, "Why the House of Color in São Paulo," 15.

Chamber Music

1. Flusser, "Chamber Music," in *Into the Universe of Technical Images*, trans. Nancy Ann Roth (Minneapolis: University of Minnesota Press, 2011), 159.

2. Gary Marcus, "Two Visions of AI's Future," *Marcus on AI* Substack, December 5, 2024, https://open.substack .com/pub/garymarcus/p/two -visions-of-ais-future?r=4ecro &utm_campaign=post&utm _medium=email.

3. Originally published as Viktor Frankl, *Ein Psycholog erlebt das Konzentrationslager* (Vienna: Verlag für Jugend und Volk, 1946). The original English title was *From Death Camp to Existentialism: A Psychiatrist's Path to a New Therapy*, trans. Ilse Lasch (Boston: Beacon Press, 1959); it was retitled *Man's Search for Meaning* in 1963. However, contrary to what Frankl's famous book implies, he only spent a few days in Auschwitz, although he spent years in other camps. See Timothy Pytell, *Viktor Frankl's Search for Meaning: An Emblematic 20th-Century Life* (New York: Berghahn Books, 2015); Lawrence L. Langer, *Versions of Survival: The Holocaust and the Human Spirit* (Albany: State University of New York Press, 1982); and Vilém Flusser, "In Search of Meaning (Philosophical Self-portrait)," in *Writings*, ed. Andreas Ströhl (Minneapolis: University of Minnesota Press, 2002), 197–208.

4. Flusser, "Chamber Music," 159.

5. Flusser, "Chamber Music," 162.

6. Vilém Flusser, "The Factory" (undated), in *The Shape of Things: A Philosophy of Design*, trans. Anthony Mathews (London: Reaktion, 1999), 49.

7. Yuk Hui, *Post-Europe* (Falmouth, UK and New York: Urbanomic/Sequence Press, 2024), 61.

8. Bruno Latour, "Why Has Critique Run out of Steam? From Matters of Fact to Matters of Concern," *Critical Inquiry* 30, no. 2 (2004): 225–248.

9. Richard Maxwell and Toby Miller, *Greening the Media* (New York: Oxford University Press, 2012). The authors contend that most studies have "largely ignored the physical environmental effects of media," focusing instead on "consciousness" and how mass media "create states of mind in audiences. . . . Can it be nudged toward a materialist ecology?" (20).

10. David Joselit and Pamela M. Lee, "Six Propositions after Trump's Second Victory," *October* 191 (2025): 5. See also Martin Herbert, *Tell Them I Said No* (Berlin: Sternberg, 2016), and Franco "Bifo" Berardi, *Quit Everything: Interpreting Depression* (London: Repeater, 2024).

11. Donna J. Haraway, *Staying with the Trouble: Making Kin in the Chthulucene* (Durham: Duke University Press, 2016).

12. The Editorial Board, "There Is a Way Forward: How to Defeat Trump's Power Grab," *New York Times*, May 1, 2025, rinted with the headline "Fight Like Our Democracy Depends on It," *New York Times*, May 4, 2025, Section SR, 2.

13. Flusser, "Chamber Music," 167.

Index

Note: Page numbers in italics refer to illustrations.

Abstraction, 13, 15, 35, 130, 132, 275, 280
Advertising, 18, 130, 181, 183, 255, 280, 283
   content of, 75, 127, 134, 280
Aesthetic
   criteria, 26, 28, 200, 205, 229, 232
   issues, xx, 150, 252, 258
   objects, 102, 258, 276
   rationality, 28
Aesthetics, xv, 76, 119, 164, 200, 234, 260. *See also* Information: aesthetics
Agency, 255, 309, 312
Agriculture, 69, 229, 234
Algorithms, 30, 35, 135, 150, 237, 312
Animals, xxiv, 110, 151, 202, 226, 229, 237
   imaginary, 175, 234
   world of, xvii, 105, 211, 213
Antropofagia, xx, 11, 58
Apparatus, 76, 100, 113–116, 119, 139, 151, 157, 178, 305, 309, 312
   and cameras, 32, 80, 116, 132, 134–135, 154, 164, 172, 183
   as concept, xxii, 115, 127, 129–130, 162, 164
   and games, 269
   institutional, xxii, 108, 115
   structure of, 78, 116
   technological, xi, 111, 127, 134, 143, 164, 172
Architecture, xxiv, xxvii, 113, 157, 251–252, 256, 263
Art, 114–115, 154, 215, 222, 226. *See also* Artworks; Concrete: art; Video: art
   abstract, xx, 18, 28, 35
   biological, xxiv, 198, 221, 226, 242
   electronic, xxvii, 27, 67, 146, 222
   as form of philosophy, xv, 15, 232, 239
   generative, 30, 164

as soft power, 8, 13
and technical images, xii, xxx, 162
and technology, xv, xxx, 9, 32, 85, 105, 198, 200, 232, 242, 312
visual, xiv, 11, 27–28, 194
Artforum, 123, 221
   Flusser's writing in, 96, 178, 181, 226, 234, 278 (*see also* "Curie's Children")
Artificial intelligence (AI), 135, 222, 232, 292
   creation of, xi–xii, 116, 232, 239, 264, 309
   impact of, xv, xvii, xxix, 105, 150, 157, 187, 229, 305
Artworks, xv, 26, 84, 151, 234, 258
Authoritarianism, 60, 248, 312
Automation, xi, 105, 116, 134, 150–151, 222, 309

Barth, Edith, xx, xxiv, 3, 6–7, 57, 67, 84, *316*
Barthes, Roland, xvii, 123–124, 126, 132, 154, 167, 252, 255
Bateson, Gregory, 72, 84, 97
Baudrillard, Jean, xvii, xxii, 72, 100, 126, 181, 252, 269, 276
Bauhaus, 13, 15, 69, 100, 164
Bayrle, Thomas, *112*, *117*, *268*
Bec, Louis, 181, 202, 229, 232, 234, 239, 294
   collaboration with Flusser, 198, 205, 207
   drawings, 215, 219, 229
   images, *192*, *197*, *203–204*, *206*, *216–219*, *231*, *241*, *246*
   sculptures, 51, 198
Behavior
   human, xxix, 32, 80, 105, 207
   nonhuman, 211, 247
Benjamin, Walter, 123–124, 175, 183
Bense, Max, 32, *33*, 38, 175
   and Brazil, xx, 27
   computer-generated art, 27, 178, 222, 280
   Concrete poetry, 26–28, 30
   information aesthetics, xvii, 28, 30, 32, 115, 143, 164
Berger, René, 65, 69, 76, 85, 96

Bill, Max, 13, *14*, 21, 27–28, 280, 283
Bio art, xxiv, 198, 221, 226, 242
Biology, 239, 247
   and biotechnology, 193, 221, 276
   and color, 285, 297
   developments in, 193, 222
   evolutionary, 198
   and game theory, 213
   philosophy of, 211, 242, 252
Biotechnics, 222, 226, 276
Biotechnology, xxiv, 105, 193, 221–222, 226, 229, 234, 237, 261
Black box, 115–116, 134, 183
Bonnier, Alexandre, 69, 258, 274
Borges, Jorge Luis, xxvii, 21, 242
Brazil, xvii, 6, 251
   culture in, 11, 13, 15, 18, 27–28, 35, 38, 51, 65, 288
   Flusser's life in, xii, xvii, xx, 7–9, 45, 51, 55, 57–58, 60, 193, 267
   military dictatorship, 45, 55, 58, 60–61, 78, 269
   race in, 274–275
Brazilian Institute of Philosophy, 8, 57, 255
Brecht, Bertolt, 115, 164, 170
Buber, Martin, xx, 4, 113, 143, 148, 215
Burson, Nancy, 175, *176*, 237, *306*

Caillois, Roger, 207, 211, 213, 269
Camera, 126, 129–130, 175, 178, 181, 183
   as apparatus, 32, 129, 132, 154, 172, 183
   and programs, 130, 132, 154, 172, 178
   video, 80, 171–172
Čapek, Karel, xvii, *xix*, 3, 207, 242, 261
Casa da Cor, 132, 226, 264, 276, *291*, 300
   goals of, xxvii, 278, 284–285, 288, 292, 294, 297
Causality, 110, 114, 134–135
Ceaușescu, Nicolae, 170, 172
Censorship, 58, 60, 85
Centre Pompidou, xx, 69, 105, 108, 151, 263, 288

359

Foucault, Michel, 115, 162, 237, 309
Fractals, xi–xii, *142*, 143
France
design in, xx, 100, 132, 151, 251–252
Flusser's life in, xxiv, xxvii, 69, 198, 222, 255–256
Franke, Herbert W., xxvii, *122*, 143, *144–145*, 146, 175, 222
Freedom, 15, 60, 90, 148, 154, 209, 215, 269, 312
human, 100, 114, 135
problem of, 123, 135
Functionaries, xvii, xxii, 111, 113–116, 129–130, 172, 178, 215, 269

Games, 58, 114, 264, 267, 269. *See also* Video: games
Game theory, 30, 113, 116, 119, 129, 164, 211, 305
of evolution, 213, 222
Gebser, Jean, 43, 45, 62, 110
Germany. *See also* Holocaust
culture in, 27, 65, 251
Green Party, 278
media theory in, xv, 30, 108, 126, 183
Gerstner, Karl, xxvii, 276, 280, 283–284, 288, 292, 294, 297
images, *xxvi*, *250*, *271–272*, *279*, *281–282*, *286–287*, *296*, *298–299*
Gessert, George, 226, 227, 229, 294
Gestures, 38, 75, 80, 84, 126, 146
Goethe, Johann Wolfgang von, xxvii, 6, 9, 35, 226, 276, 292, 297
Guattari, Félix, xiv, 115, 237, 264
Guimarães Rosa, João, 9, 21, 27–28, 32, 202

Haacke, Hans, xx, 61–62, 108
Hanke, Jiří, *xviii*, 175, *310*
Haraway, Donna, xii, 237, 242, 247, 312
Heidegger, Martin, xvii, 7–8, 84, 113–114, 256
and cybernetics, xv, 157
and language, 258, 263
and *techne*, xii, 129

and things, 252, 255
worldview, 132, 215
Henry, Philippe, 284, 294, 297
Hierarchies, 61, 110, 207, 211, 237, 247
History of the Devil, The (1965), 9, 13, 21, 35
Hochschule für Gestaltung Ulm (HfG Ulm), 13, 21, 27, 69, 258
Holocaust
Auschwitz, 115–116, 194, 211, 222, 260
Flusser's survival of, xii, xv, 7, 113, 193, 278, 305
Holograms, 157, 178, 181, 234, 242, 261
as technical images, xii, 143, 151, 285
Hui, Yuk, xii, 183, 312
Husserl, Edmund, 113–114, 157, 252

Ideology, 105, 113–114, 124, 126, 130, 175, 252, 285
Images, xi–xii, xiv–xv, xxii, xxix, 9, 11, 90, 110–111, 116, 124, 126–127, 135, 167, 171, 275. *See also* Technical images
electronic, 139, 261, 267
media, 134, 175
synthetic, 139, 143, 146, 151, 157, 178, 237, 264
Immatériaux, Les (exhibition), xx, 69, 151, *152–153*, 154, *155*, 229, 242
Information, xii, 26–27, 30, 43, 85, 127, 130, 132, 143, 146, 148, 154, 181, 221–222, 261, 283
aesthetics, xvii, xxii, 26, 28, 30, 32, 115, 143
genetic, 215, 264
programmed, 151, 226
storage, 69, 242
technologies, xi, 28, 65
theory, 26, 28, 32, 96, 113, 130
transmission, 150, 288, 309
Institute of the Environment, xx, 69, *70*, 75, 79, 97, 151, 252, 276
Instituto Brasileiro de Filosofia. *See* Brazilian Institute of Philosophy

Institut Scientifique de Recherche Paranaturaliste (ISRP), 198, 200, 205, 229, 232
Internet, xi, xiv, xxvii, xxix, 21, 84, 148, 263
Internet of Things, 181, 239
Intersubjectivity, 28, 215, 239, 255, 264, 273, 278, 297
Into the Universe of Technical Images (1985), xi, xxii, xxvii, 45, 139, *140–141*, 143, 146, 148, 150, 170, 303
iPhone, xxiv, 187, 252
Irony, xxvii, xxix, 200, 226, 260, 273–274
ISRP. *See* Institut Scientifique de Recherche Paranaturaliste

Jäger, Gottfried, *xxiii*, xxiv, *136–137*, *163*, 164, 222, *289*, 292, *307*

Kac, Eduardo, 178, 234, *235*
Kafka, Franz, *5*, 175, 276, 317
as influence, xiv, xvii, 3, 113, 116, 130, 215, 242
Kandinsky, Wassily, 35, 283–284, 292
Kepes, György, 61–62, 105
Klein, Astrid, 175, *177*, *314*
Knowledge, 9, 75, 114, 222, 309
forms of, 154, 178
indigenous, 247
scientific, 200, 205, 226
Kowalski, Piotr, 61, 69, *71*, 72
Krauss, Rosalind E., 102, 123, 132

Language, xv, 8–9, 11, 15, 18, 21, 35, 38, 43, 45, 75, 194, 202, 226, 263, 283
of color, xxvii, 278, 288, 292, 297
philosophy, xv, xvii, xxii, 8, 15, 38, 113, 193, 258
Language and Reality (1963), 9, 38, 193
Latour, Bruno, xxiv, 247, 312
Le Corbusier, 18, 292, *293*
Leeson, Lynn Hershman, 183, *184*, 242, *243*
Leonardo, 151, 164, 178, 229

Index

The MIT Press
Massachusetts Institute of Technology
77 Massachusetts Avenue
Cambridge, MA 02139
mitpress.mit.edu

The MIT Press would like to thank the anonymous peer reviewers who provided comments on drafts of this book. The generous work of academic experts is essential for establishing the authority and quality of our publications. We acknowledge with gratitude the contributions of these otherwise uncredited readers.

This book was set in Hautin by Jen Jackowitz. Printed and bound in the United States of America.

Library of Congress Cataloging-in-Publication Data is available.

ISBN: 978-0-262-05122-4

10   9   8   7   6   5   4   3   2   1

EU Authorised Representative: Easy Access System Europe, Mustamäe tee 50, 10621 Tallinn, Estonia | Email: gpsr.requests@easproject.com